LAW AND POPULAR CULTURE: TEXT, NOTES, AND QUESTIONS

LAW AND POPULAR CULTURE: TEXT, NOTES, AND QUESTIONS

David Ray Papke
Professor of Law
Marquette University

Melissa Cole Essig
Attorney at Law
Los Angeles, California

Christine Alice Corcos
Associate Professor of Law
Louisiana State University Law
Center

Peter Henry Huang
Professor of Law
Harold E. Kohn Chair
Temple University School
of Law

Lenora P. Ledwon
Professor of Law
St. Thomas University School
of Law

Diane H. Mazur
Professor of Law
University of Florida College
of Law

Carrie Menkel-Meadow
Professor of Law & A. B.
Chettle Jr. Chair in Dispute
Resolution
and Civil Procedure
Georgetown University Law
Center

Philip N. Meyer
Professor of Law & Director,
Legal Writing Program
Vermont Law School

Binny Miller
Professor of Law & Director,
Criminal Justice Clinic
American University College
of Law

ISBN#: 1-4224-1166-4

NOTE TO USERS
To ensure that you are using the latest materials available in this area, please be sure to periodically check the LexisNexis Law School web site for downloadable updates and supplements at www.lexisnexis.com/ lawschool

---

Editorial Offices
744 Broad Street, Newark, NJ 07102 (973) 820-2000
201 Mission St., San Francisco, CA 94105-1831 (415) 908-3200
701 East Water Street, Charlottesville, VA 22902-7587 (434) 972-7600
www.lexis.com

(Pub.3190)

DEDICATION

For those willing to find law in not only their law books but also their culture.

PREFACE

The United States is the world's most legalistic nation due to not only its laws, lawyers, and courts, but also its abundant law-related popular culture. This large body of films, television shows, radio programs, and inexpensive fiction has an immense impact on what Americans expect from their legal institutions and government. Indeed, American law-related popular culture even affects what citizens in other countries think of the United States.

Law and Popular Culture is the first classroom text to examine the full range of American law-related popular culture. The text resembles a traditional casebook, but it contains relatively few cases or appellate opinions. Instead, the text's fourteen chapters include discussions of various contemporary topics, numerous notes and questions, and well over one hundred excerpts from articles by leading law and popular culture scholars. The excerpts appear in edited form without footnotes, but readers might refer to the provided citations if they wish to consult the complete articles from which the excerpts are taken.

After an introductory chapter addressing the study of popular culture and outlining the text's goals, the text's remaining chapters fall into two categories. Six chapters concern pop cultural portrayals of important legal actors and institutions — law students, lawyers, clients, witnesses, judges, and juries. The other seven concern assorted areas of law — Constitutional Law, Criminal Law, and Torts from the first-year law school curriculum and Business Law, Family Law, International Law, and Military Law from among familiar upper-level electives. Each of the chapters begins with a list of five readily available feature films that are relevant to the particular chapter, and instructors might screen or assign selections from the lists in conjunction with their use of the text.

The authors of *Law and Popular Culture* wish to thank Jennifer A. Beszley, our editor at LexisNexis, for her support and guidance and Robert M. Jarvis, Professor of Law at the Nova Southeastern University Law Center, for his work recruiting the book's authors and launching the book project. In addition, the authors thank readers and users of this text for scrutinizing the role popular culture plays in shaping the American legal consciousness. We hope teachers and students alike can profitably use *Law and Popular Culture* to explore what Americans expect from their law and legal institutions while in the process honing their own understanding of law and the meaning of justice under law.

SUMMARY TABLE OF CONTENTS

TABLE OF CONTENTS

PART II: LEGAL ACTORS AND INSTITUTIONS

PART III: LEGAL SUBJECT AREAS

ACKNOWLEDGMENTS

Chapter 1

Bergman, Paul, *Teaching Evidence the "Reel" Way*, 21 Quinnipiac L. Rev. 973 (2003). Copyright © 2003. Reprinted with permission.

Denvir, John, *What Movies Teach Law Students*, Picturing Justice; http://www.usfca.edu/pj. Copyright © 2003. Reprinted with permission.

Freedman, Monroe H., *Atticus Finch — Right and Wrong*, 45 Ala. L. Rev. 404 (1994). Copyright © 1994. Reprinted with permission.

Friedman, Lawrence M., *Law, Lawyers, and Popular Culture*, 98 Yale L.J. 1579 (1989). Copyright © 1989. Reprinted with permission.

Papke, David Ray, *The American Courtroom Trial: Pop Culture, Courthouse Realitites, and the Dream World of Justice*, 40 S. Tex. L. Rev. 919 (1999). Copyright © 1999. Reprinted with permission.

Salzman, Victoria S. & Dunwoody, Philip T., *Prime-Time Lies: Do Portrayals of Lawyers Influence How People Think About the Legal Profession?*, 58 SMU L. Rev. 411 (2005). Copyright © 2005. Reprinted with permission.

Shapiro, Carole, *Do or Die: Does Dead Man Walking Run?*, 30 U.S.F. L. Rev. 1143 (1996). Copyright © 1996. Reprinted with permission of the *University of San Francisco Law Review*.

Wagner, Kenneth, A Man for All Seasons, Picturing Justice, http://www.usfca.edu/pj. Copyright © 2005. Reprinted with permission.

Chapter 2

Corcos, Christine Alice, *"We Don't Want Advantages": The Woman Lawyer Hero and Her Quest for Power in Popular Culture*, 53 Syracuse L. Rev. 1225 (2003). Copyright © 2003. Originally published in the *Syracuse Law Review*. Reprinted with permission.

Engler, Russell, *The MacCrate Report Turns 10: Assessing Its Impact and Identifying Gaps We Should Seek to Narrow*, 8 Clinical L. Rev. 109 (2001). Copyright © 2001. Reprinted with permission of the author and the *Clinical Law Review*.

Louisiana State University, Code of Student Professional Responsibility (2006). Reprinted with permission.

Rosato, Jennifer, *The Socratic Method and Women Law Students: Humanize, Don't Feminize*, 7 S. Cal. Rev. L. & Women's Stud. 37 (1997). Copyright © 1997. Reprinted with permission.

Torrey, Morrison, *You Call That Education?*, 19 Wis. Women's L.J. 93 (2004). Copyright © 2004 Wisconsin Women's Law Journal. Reprinted with permission.

Vitiello, Michael, *Professor Kingsfield: The Most Misunderstood Character in Literature*, 33 Hofstra L. Rev. 955 (2005). Copyright © 2005. Reprinted with permission of the *Hofstra Law Review Association*.

Chapter 3

Asimow, Michael, *Bad Lawyers in the Movies*, 24 Nova L. Rev. 531 (2000). Copyright © 2000. Reprinted with permission.

Asimow, Michael, *Embodiment of Evil: Law Firms in the Movies*, 48 UCLA L. Rev. 1339 (2001). Copyright © 2001. Reprinted with permission.

Bergman, Paul, *The Movie Lawyers' Guide to Redemptive Legal Practice*, 48 UCLA L. Rev. 1393 (2001). Copyright © 2001. Reprinted with permission.

Menkel-Meadow, Carrie, *Can They Do That? Legal Ethics in Popular Culture: Of Character and Acts*, 48 UCLA L. Rev. 1305 (2001). Copyright © 2001. Reprinted with permission.

Simon, William H., *Moral Pluck: Legal Ethics in Popular Culture*, 101 Colum. L. Rev. 421 (2001). Copyright © 2001. Reprinted with permission.

Chapter 4

Cook, Nancy, *Legal Fictions: Clinical Experiences, Lace Collars, and Boundless Stories*, 1 Clinical L. Rev. 41 (1994). Copyright © 1994. Reprinted with permission.

Dinerstein, Robert D., *Client-Centered Counseling: Reappraisal and Refinement*, 32 Ariz. L. Rev. 501 (1990). Copyright © 1990. Reprinted with permission.

Kruse, Katherine R., *Fortress in the Sand: The Plural Values of Client-Centered Representation*, 12 Clinical L. Rev. 369 (2006). Copyright © 2006. Reprinted with permission.

Margulies, Peter, *Representation of Domestic Violence Survivors as a New Paradigm of Poverty Law: In Search of Access, Connection, and Voice*, 63 Geo. Wash. L. Rev. 1071 (1995). Copyright © 1995. Reprinted with permission.

Miller, Binny, *Teaching Case Theory*, 9 Clinical L. Rev. 293 (2002). Copyright © 2002. Reprinted with permission.

Ogletree, Charles, *Beyond Jusifications: Seeking Motivations to Sustain Public Defenders*, 106 Harv. L. Rev. 1239 (1992). Copyright © 1992. Reprinted with permission.

Polikoff, Nancy D., *Am I My Client? The Role Confusion of a Lawyer Activist*, 31 Harv. C.R.-C.L. L. Rev. 443 (1996). Copyright © 1996. Reprinted with permission.

Smith, Abbe, *The Difference in Criminal Defense and the Difference It Makes*, 11 Wash. U. J.L. & Pol'y 83 (2003). Copyright © 2003. Reprinted with permission.

Spinak, Jane, *Reflections on a Case (of Motherhood)*, 95 Colum. L. Rev. 1990 (1995). Copyright © 1995. Reprinted with permission.

White, Lucie E., *Seeking ". . . The Faces of Otherness . . . ": A Response to Professors Sarat, Felstiner, and Cahn*, 77 Cornell L. Rev. 1499 (1992). Copyright © 1992. Reprinted with permission.

White, Lucie E., *To Learn and Teach: Lessons from Driefontein on Lawyering and Power*, 1988 Wis. L Rev. 699. Copyright © 1988. Reprinted with permission.

Chapter 5

Carey, James, *Charles Laughton, Marlene Dietrich, and the Prior Inconsistent Statement*, 36 Loy. U. Chi. L.J. 433 (2005). Copyright © 2005. Reprinted with permission.

Corcos, Christine Alice, *Legal Fictions: Irony, Storytelling, Truth, and Justice in the Modern Courtroom Drama*, 25 U. Ark. Little Rock L. Rev. 503 (2003). Copyright © 2003. Reprinted with permission.

Covey, Russell Dean, *Beating the Prisoner at Prisoner's Dilemma: The Evidentiary Value of a Witness's Refusal to Testify*, 47 Am. U. L. Rev. 105 (1997). Copyright © 1997. Reprinted with permission.

Hallisey, Robert, *Experts on Eyewitness Testimony in Court — A Short Historical Perspective*, 39 How. L.J. 237 (1995). Copyright © 1995. Reprinted with permission.

Moriarty, Jane Campbell, *Wonders of the Invisible World: Prosecutorial Syndrome and Profile Evidence in the Salem Witchcraft Trials*, 26 Vt. L. Rev. 43 (2001). Copyright © 2001. Reprinted with permission.

Chapter 6

Burton, Adam, *Pay No Attention to the Men Behind the Curtain: The Supreme Court, Popular Culture, and the Countermajoritarian Problem*, 73 UMKC L. Rev. 53 (2004). Copyright © 2004. Reprinted with permission.

Goldman, Sheldon, *Judicial Confirmation Wars: Ideology and the Battle for the Federal Courts*, 39 U. Rich. L. Rev. 871 (2005). Copyright © 2005. Reprinted with permission.

Podlas, Kimberlianne, *Blame Judge Judy: The Effects of Syndicated Television Courtrooms on Jurors*, 25 Am. J. Trial Advoc. 557 (2002). Copyright © 2002. Reprinted with permission.

Posner, Richard A., *What Do Judges and Justices Maximize? (The Same Thing Everybody Else Does)*, 3 Sup. Ct. Econ. Rev. 1 (1993). Copyright © 1993. Reprinted with permission.

Ray, Laura Krugman, *Judicial Fictions: Images of Supreme Court Justices in the Novel, Drama, and Film*, 39 Ariz. L. Rev. 151 (1997). Copyright © 1997. Reprinted with permission.

Chapter 7

Marks, Hon. Patricia D., *Magic in the Movies — Do Courtroom Scenes Have Real-Life Parallels?*, N.Y. St. B.J., Vol. 73, No. 5, 40 (June 2001). Copyright © 2001. Reprinted with permission from the New York State Bar Association Journal, published by the New York State Bar Association, One Elk Street, Albany, NY 12207.

Meyer, Philip N., *"Desperate for Love II": Further Reflections on the Interpenetration of Legal and Popular Storytelling in Closing Arguments to a Jury in a Complex Criminal Case*, 30 U.S.F. L. Rev. 931 (1996). Copyright © 1996. Reprinted with permission.

Nichols, Bill, *The Unseen Jury*, 30 U.S.F. L. Rev. 1055 (1996). Copyright © 1996. Reprinted with permission.

Chapter 8

Abramson, Jeffrey, *The Jury and Popular Culture*, 50 DePaul L. Rev. 497 (2000). Copyright © 2000. Reprinted with permission.

Asimow, Michael, *Embodiment of Evil: Law Firms in the Movies*, 48 UCLA L. Rev. 1339 (2001). Copyright © 2001. Reprinted with permission.

Bender, Leslie, *Feminist (Re)torts: Thoughts on the Liability Crisis, Mass Torts, Power, and Responsibilities*, 1990 Duke L.J. 848. Copyright © 1990. Reprinted with permission.

Finley, Lucinda M., *Guarding the Gate to the Courthouse: How Trial Judges Are Using Their Evidentiary Screening Role to Remake Tort Causation Rules*, 49 DePaul L. Rev. 335 (1999). Copyright © 1999. Reprinted with permission.

Hans, Valerie P. & Dee, Juliet, *Whiplash: Whose to Blame?*, 68 Brook. L. Rev. 1093 (2003). Copyright © 2003. Reprinted with permission.

Keefe, Patrick, *Reversals of Fortune: How Hollywood Makes Heroes Out of Lawyers*, 2003 Legal Affairs 48. Copyright © 2003 Legal Affairs. Reprinted with permission.

Rodent, The, *The Real King of Torts: Famed San Francisco Lawyer Was More Entertaining Than Fiction*, ABA J. e-Report, Feb. 8, 2003. Copyright © 2006. Reprinted by permission. ABA Journal and ABA Journal e-Report are published by the American Bar Association.

Shapiro, Carole, *Women Lawyers in Celluloid: Why Hollywood Skirts the Truth*, 25 U. Tol. L. Rev. 955 (1995). Copyright © 1995. Reprinted with permission.

Shuman, Daniel W., *The Role of Apology in Tort Law*, 83 Judicature 180 (2000). Copyright © 2000. Reprinted with permission.

Vidmar, Neil, *The American Civil Jury for Ausländer (Foreigners)*, 13 Duke J. Comp. & Int'l L. 95 (2003). Copyright © 2003. Reprinted with permission.

Chapter 9

Corcos, Christine Alice, *Legal Fictions: Irony, Storytelling, Truth, and Justice in the Modern Courtroom Drama*, 25 U. Ark. Little Rock L. Rev. 503 (2003). Copyright © 2003. Reprinted with permission.

Corcos, Christine Alice, *Prosecutors, Prejudices, and Justice: Observations on Presuming Innocence in Popular Culture and Law*, 34 U. Tol. L. Rev. 793 (2003). Copyright © 2003. Reprinted with permission.

Donovan, Jeremiah, *Some Off-the-Cuff Remarks About Lawyers as Storytellers*, 18 Vt. L. Rev. 751 (1994). Copyright © 1994. Reprinted with permission.

Dow, David R., *Fictional Documentaries and Truthful Fictions: The Death Penalty in Recent American Film*, 17 Const. Comment. 511 (2000). Copyright © 2000. Reprinted with permission.

Elkins, James R., *Profane Lawyering*, http://www.wvu.edu/~lawfac/jelkins/mythweb99/profane.html. Copyright © 1999-2007 James R. Elkins. Reprinted with permission.

Foster, Teree E., I Want to Live! *Federal Judicial Values in Death Penalty Cases: Preservation of Rights or Punctuality of Execution?*, 22 Okla. City U. L. Rev. 63 (1997). Copyright © 1997. Reprinted with permission.

Meade, Christopher J., *Reading Death Sentences: The Narrative Construction of Capital Punishment*, 71 N.Y.U. L. Rev. 732 (1996). Copyright © 1996. Reprinted with permission.

Meyer, Philip N., *Convicts, Criminals, Prisoners, and Outlaws: A Course in Popular Storytelling*, 42 J. Leg. Educ. 129 (1992). Copyright © 1992. Reprinted with permission.

Meyer, Philip N., *Visual Literacy and the Legal Culture: Reading Film as Text in the Law School Setting*, 17 Leg. Stud. Forum 73 (1993). Copyright © 1993. Reprinted with permission.

Meyer, Philip N., *Why a Jury Trial Is More Like a Movie Than a Novel*, 28 J.L. & Soc'y 133 (2001). Copyright © 2001. Reprinted with permission.

Sarat, Austin, *The Cultural Life of Capital Punishment: Responsibility and Representation in* Dead Man Walking *and* Last Dance, 11 Yale J.L. & Human. 153 (1999). Copyright © 1999. Reprinted with permission.

Sherwin, Richard K., *Law Frames: Historical Truth and Narrative Necessity in a Criminal Case*, 47 Stan. L. Rev. 39 (1994). Copyright © 1994. Reprinted with permission.

Smith, Abbe, *Defending the Innocent*, 32 Conn. L. Rev. 485 (2000). Copyright © 2000. Reprinted with permission.

Yankah, Ekow N., *Good Guys and Bad Guys: Punishing Character, Equality, and the Irrelevance of Moral Character to Criminal Punishment*, 25 Cardozo L. Rev. 1019 (2004). Copyright © 2004. Reprinted with permission.

Chapter 10

Akram, Susan M. & Johnson, Kevin R., *Race, Civil Rights, and Immigration Law After September 11, 2001: The Targeting of Arabs and Muslims*, 59 N.Y.U. Ann. Surv. Am. L. 295 (2002). Copyright © 2002. Reprinted with permission.

Allison, Gary D., *Sanctioning Sodomy: The Supreme Court Liberates Gay Sex and Limits State Power to Vindicate the Moral Sentiments of the People*, 39 Tulsa L. Rev. 95 (2003). Copyright © 2003. Reprinted with permission.

Fiss, Owen M., *A Tribute to Justice Thurgood Marshall*, 105 Harv. L. Rev. 549 (1991). Copyright © 1991. Reprinted with permission.

Jones, D. Marvin, *"We Must Be Hunters of Meaning": Race, Metaphor, and the Models of Steven Winter*, 67 Brook. L. Rev. 1071 (2002). Copyright © 2002. Reprinted with permission.

Post, Robert C., *The Constitutional Concept of Public Discourse: Outrageous Opinion, Democratic Deliberation, and* Hustler Magazine v. Falwell, 103 Harv. L. Rev. 601 (1990). Copyright © 1990. Reprinted with permission.

Redish, Martin H. & Mathews, Andrew L., *Why Punitive Damages Are Unconstitutional*, 53 Emory L.J. 1 (2004). Copyright © 2004. Reprinted with permission.

Sippel, Richard L., *The Warren Court and American Politics*, 48 Fed. Law. 55 (2001). Copyright © 2001. Reprinted with permission.

Chapter 11

Asimow, Michael, *Divorce in the Movies: From the Hays Code to* Kramer vs. Kramer, 24 Leg. Stud. Forum 221 (2000). Copyright © 2000. Reprinted with permission.

Dolgin, Janet L., *Why Has the Best-Interest Standard Survived? The Historic and Social Context*, 16 Child. Leg. Rts. J. 2 (1996). Copyright © 1996 Children's Legal Rights Journal. Reprinted with permission. The article appears here as it was originally printed in Volume 16, Number 2, in compliance with the copyright holder's policy on Copyright and Terms of Use. The CLRJ is edited by students at the Loyola University Chicago School of Law, the ABA Center on Children and the Law, and the National Association of Counsel for Children. The CLRJ is published by William S. Hein & Co., Inc.

Field, Martha A., *Surrogacy Contracts — Gestational and Traditional: The Argument for Nonenforcement*, 31 Washburn L.J. 1 (1991). Copyright © 1991. Reprinted with permission.

Gillers, Stephen, *Taking* L.A. Law *More Seriously*, 98 Yale L.J. 1606 (1989). Copyright © 1989. Reprinted with permission.

Lurvy, Ira & Eiseman, Selise E., *Divorce Goes to the Movies*, 30 U.S.F. L. Rev. 1209 (1996). Copyright © 1996. Reprinted with permission.

Chapter 12

Chapter 13

Chapter 14

PART I:

INTRODUCTION

Chapter 1

STUDYING LAW AND POPULAR CULTURE

A. FILMOGRAPHY

Inherit the Wind (1960)

Anatomy of a Murder (1959)

Dead Man Walking (1996)

A Man for All Seasons (1966)

To Kill a Mockingbird (1962)

B. LAW-RELATED AMERICAN POPULAR CULTURE

Since the founding of the Republic, law, lawyers, and legal institutions have had special importance in America. In the early decades of the nineteenth century the citizenry not only rejected demands to throw off the English common law but also began developing what would become a huge statutory law. The legal profession grew rapidly, and lawyers became the leading figures in civic and political affairs. The Constitution, the nation's highest law, became an icon of the civil religion, and courtroom trials, either watched in person in county courthouses or followed in the urban penny press, were familiar rituals affording specific verdicts and judgments as well as larger lessons and meanings. When the French aristocrat Alexis de Tocqueville toured the United States at the request of his government in the 1830s, he was struck by the large roles played by lawyers and courts in Americans' daily lives and also by the way Americans, unlike his fellow Frenchmen, looked at the law with something resembling parental affection. "The spirit of the law, which is produced in the schools and courts of justice," de Tocqueville wrote, "gradually penetrates beyond their walls into the bosom of society, where it descends to the lowest classes, so that the whole people contracts the habits and tastes of the magistrate." Alexis de Tocqueville, *Democracy in America* 207–08 (1835; reprint, 1946).

Given the legalistic nature of American life, it is hardly surprising that law and legal themes became a part of cultural expression as well. The poet William Cullen Bryant, the essayist Richard Henry Dana, and the popular storyteller Washington Irving had early in their lives been lawyers before turning to literary pursuits. Legal themes found a place in selected pieces of their work, as did a bit of resentment regarding the authors' abandoned profession. *The Pioneers* (1923), the first of James Fenimore Cooper's Leatherstocking novels, includes a book-long debate between champions of what we would today call natural law and legal positivism. In the decades immediately before the Civil War novels featuring heroic lawyers as well as conniving pettifoggers were common. The former tended to be hardworking Protestants who moved to the city to study and practice law and to fall in love and do good. The pettifoggers, meanwhile, stirred up litigation and duped even their own clients, but at least in most cases they received their just deserts.

Toward the end of the nineteenth century, law-related pop cultural products became staples of the rapidly developing modern culture industry. Committed to selling cultural works and experiences to mass audiences, the culture industry was vertically integrated and employed literally thousands of professional workers. Some have argued that the large number of cultural products made and distributed by the culture industry prefigured the even larger production and distribution of general consumer goods in the 1920s.

At first, the production and distribution of law-related popular culture was most likely to involve works in print and, in particular, law-related cheap fiction. The West Virginia lawyer Melville Davisson Post could have claimed to be the developer of the first law-related pop cultural product line. He was successful but unhappy practicing law in the 1890s in Wheeling and Grafton, and while trying to figure out what to do with his life, began writing stories about a fictional lawyer named Randolph Mason. G.P. Putman's, a major publishing house, published one collection of the stories and then another as the public rose like fish to the bait.

Post's successes were far surpassed by two other early twentieth century writers of law-related fiction — Arthur Train and Erle Stanley Gardner. Train, a Harvard Law School graduate and former New York City practitioner, published 87 stories about the fictional lawyer Ephraim Tutt in *The Saturday Evening Post,* the nation's most popular magazine. Beloved by middlebrow readers, the Tutt stories were also collected in volumes such as *Tut, Tut, Mr. Tutt* (1923), and Train even published a mock autobiography of Tutt, which was reviewed in the *Harvard Law Review*. Gardner was a disgruntled California practitioner who published his first two novels about the fictional Perry Mason in 1933. The public never seemed to tire of a lawyer who could dramatically free his innocent client and also identify the true perpetrator, and working on a ranch he called the "fiction factory," Gardner wrote a total of 82 Perry Mason novels.

In later decades, pop fiction about law and lawyers continued to appear, but law-related radio shows, movies, and television series joined published fiction in the pop cultural marketplace. The first national radio networks emerged in the 1920s, and during the so-called "Golden Age of Radio" in the 1930s and early 1940s, as much as forty percent of network radio programming was drama. Radio detectives of the era included not only the venerable Sherlock Holmes but also Nick Carter, Hercule Poirot, Ellery Queen, Sam Spade, and Nero Wolfe. Each episode of *Gangbusters*, a police procedural, started with an especially noisy salvo that spawned the expression "Coming on like Gangbusters." The most popular lawyer program was *Mr. District Attorney*, which aired weekly in thirty-minute episodes on NBC radio from 1939–51.

Law-related films were also immensely successful, especially after the technology for "talkies," which appeared in the late 1920s, enabled filmmakers to show lawyers doing what they sometimes do best — talking. The courtroom setting, meanwhile, was ideal for film. Producers could choose a courtroom for shooting or even build one on the set, and filming could take place with relatively fixed points of sound and light.

However, this does not mean one particular legal genre dominated the 1930s and '40s. Screenwriters adapted several of the Perry Mason novels for the silver screen, and even more popular were films featuring energetic, crime-stopping prosecutors. These films included *State's Attorney* (1932), in which a character played by John Barrymore overcame his reform school youth and prosecuted a leading mobster, and *Manhattan Melodrama* (1934), in which a district attorney played by William Powell is elected governor after successfully prosecuting a boyhood friend played by Clark Gable. John Barrymore won an Oscar for his portrayal of an alcoholic lawyer who defended his daughter's suitor in a murder trial in *A Free Soul* (1931). Barrymore also starred in *Counsellor At Law* (1933), the story of a man who rose from the Lower East Side to a palatial law office in the Empire State Building, only to find his world crashing down around him. The period even concluded with the delightful legal comedy *Adam's Rib* (1949), in which Spencer Tracy and Katharine Hepburn appear as husband-and-wife lawyers representing opposite sides in a trial for attempted murder.

While law-related Hollywood cinema of the 1930s and '40s was fascinating in a scrambled way, it was during the 1950s and early '60s that law-related Hollywood cinema reached its greatest heights. Films from the period included *12 Angry Men* (1957), *Witness for the Prosecution* (1957), *I Want to Live* (1958), *Anatomy of a Murder* (1959), *The Young Philadelphians* (1959), *Compulsion* (1959), *Inherit the Wind* (1960), *Judgment at Nuremberg* (1961), and *To Kill a Mockingbird* (1962). Enriched by superb writing, directing, and acting, most of these films were critical and popular successes, earning a raft of Oscar nominations and qualifying as some of the very best films of their period.

When network television programming began at the end of the 1940s, producers drew more heavily on radio than on the Hollywood movie studios for their stars and types of shows. Also, as was the case with radio, much of the earliest law-related television programming was performed live before a studio audience. The set was customarily a courtroom, and the drama took the form of a trial, usually with actors playing some, but not necessarily all, of the roles. In *They Stand Accused* (1949–52, 1954), for example, actors played defendants and witnesses but Chicago attorney Charles Johnson was the judge. At the end of each trial, "jurors" chosen from the studio audience were asked to render a verdict. *Famous Jury Trials* (1949–52) reenacted actual trials and then used a jury verdict to reveal to viewers which version of the events suggested at trial was really accurate. These shows and a dozen like them reinforced the courtroom trial as a central ritual of American life and also, of course, buoyed the belief that truth and justice were achievable through legal institutions.

This particular type of live programming largely disappeared from prime-time television in the 1950s, as the networks settled instead on a weekly series featuring the exploits of an attractive fictional lawyer practicing on his own or perhaps with a partner. Erle Stanley Gardner, who had guided Perry Mason onto the printed page and disapprovingly watched the production of the Perry Mason films, now brought his hero to television. Portrayed by Raymond Burr, Perry Mason not only became television's first superstar lawyer but also could count dozens of colleagues in the fictional television bar. *The Defenders* (1961–65), starring E.G. Marshall and Robert Reid as father-and-son lawyers, was the most respected series, but lawyer dramas also included *The Law and Mr. Jones, Sam Benedict, The Trials of O'Brien, Judd for the Defense, Harrigan and Son, The Bold Ones, Owen Marshall,* and *Petrocelli,* to name only a handful. Americans found primetime shows with lawyers tending to innocent clients and a justice system that worked to be soothing, escapist television fare.

In the present, law-related popular culture is a sprawling cultural smorgasbord. New types of stories about law, lawyers, and legal institutions have emerged, but many of the older types have also lived on, compounding into the present in updated formats. The long-running *Law & Order,* for example, lionizes the work of prosecutors in ways reminiscent of radio shows and films in the 1930s.

The publication of fiction in cheap paperbacks and popular magazines such as *The Saturday Evening Post* ended in the post-Vietnam era, but starting in the 1980s lawyers-turned-writers such as John Grisham, Scott Turow, and Lisa Scottolini published dozens of best-selling novels about fictional lawyers and their cases. The covers and publicity for these novels emphasize the authors themselves more than the plots or even titles of individual works. Often lawyers are not so much heroic as they are flawed and complex human beings — everymen with law degrees.

With the exception of networks of small Christian stations, radio has for the most part stopped broadcasting fictional narratives, but Hollywood continues to produce large numbers of legal films. This body of popular culture is not as stirring as the law-related films of the late 1950s and early 1960s, but the current law-related cinema is nevertheless engaging and delightful. Relatively recent films such as *A Few Good Men* (1992) and *Philadelphia* (1993) tell familiar tales of heroic defense counsel who win their cases and in the process heal themselves. Hollywood has included a significant number of women in the pop cultural bar in films such as *The Big Easy* (1987), *Suspect* (1987), *The Client* (1994), *I Am Sam* (2001), *High Crimes* (2002), and *Two Weeks Notice* (2003). Hollywood has also brought fictionalized versions of actual cases to the local cineplex, as in *The Accused* (1988), *A Civil Action* (1999), and *Erin Brockovich* (2000), and legal comedies have included *My Cousin Vinny* (1992), *Jury Duty* (1995), and *Legally Blonde* (2001). Sometimes these comedies ridicule lawyers, as in *Liar Liar* (1997), an extended joke about how difficult it is for lawyers to tell the truth.

Legal shows also continue to roll off television's assembly lines. A show such as *Matlock* (1986–95) was a throwback, albeit a popular one, to the heroic independent lawyer shows of the 1950s, but new types of shows have also appeared. The exemplar for modern-day primetime evening programming is *L.A. Law* (1986–94). Each episode included courtroom scenes, but the heroic trial work of a single lawyer was not crucial to the show's success. Instead, a group of lawyers working in a bureaucratic and hierarchical setting were our protagonists, and their personal dilemmas and relationships with one another were as important as their legal cases. *The Practice* (1997–2004) struck some as a grimier, east-coast version of the show. Other embodiments of the type such as *Ally McBeal* (1997–2002) and the current *Boston Legal* (2004–present) strive for comedic effect and sometimes display large amounts of cynicism. On daytime television of the present viewers can watch syndicated shows featuring resourceful jurists resolving disputes in something resembling small claims courts. *The People's Court* with the grandfatherly Judge Joseph Wapner launched the modern genre in the 1980s, but the biggest star of the present is Judge Judith Sheindlin of *Judge Judy*. Her caustic, insulting manner appeals to millions of viewers and is also the model to which a dozen other ersatz daytime television judges aspire.

For Americans in all walks of life, popular works of fiction, film, and television revolving around law, lawyers, and legal themes have for decades been sources of delight and edification. Those who characterize the United States as the most legalistic nation in the world should to some extent be prepared to base that claim on not only the number of American laws and importance of American legal institutions but also the amount, variety, and popularity of law-related popular culture. This popular culture is not simply a "picture" of American life, but has become a powerful force in the shaping of Americans' understanding of and attitudes about law. It seeps into our consciousnesses. It affects what Americans and even foreign consumers expect from their legal institutions and governments. For law students, lawyers, and judges, law-related American popular culture holds special potential for education and provides a huge and continuing opportunity for critical reflection.

NOTES & QUESTIONS

1. Innumerable stories about law, lawyers, and legal institutions appear in several of our most important varieties of popular culture — fiction, film, and television. To what extent does the medium dictate the type of law-related story that can be told and the manner in which it is told? What is the potential for law-related narrative in such other forms of popular culture as the comics, recorded music, and video games?

2. Almost from the beginning, the various branches of the culture industry have been interconnected. As the industry's adaptations of the famous Scopes trial from 1925 suggest, a pop cultural narrative that catches the public's eye in one medium is likely to be reproduced in a second and a third. In the original trial John Scopes, a science teacher from Dayton, Tennessee, was prosecuted for violating the state's ban on teaching evolutionary theory in the public schools. The American Civil Liberties Union took up Scopes' cause, and the famed litigator Clarence Darrow became his defense counsel. Protestant fundamentalists supported Tennessee's statute, and famous politician and former Secretary of State William Jennings Bryan joined the prosecution. The media cast the trial as the ultimate battle between science and religion, and hundreds of reporters descended on the small Tennessee courtroom. The trial was the first to be broadcast nationally on radio. Later, in fictionalized form, the trial became *Inherit the Wind,* a highly successful Broadway play by Jerome Lawrence and Robert E. Lee. The play, in turn, was adapted in 1960 for the equally successful United Artists film of the same name starring Spencer Tracy, Fredric Marsh, and Gene Kelly.

What explains the way the culture industry routinely reproduces a law-related pop cultural work successful in one medium in other media? What does this process underscore about the nature of popular culture?

3. The contemporary United States is a polyglot, postmodern nation. It lacks the socio-cultural coherence of a traditional society. To what extent must the existence of different American ethnic, racial, and regional subcultures be taken into consideration in gauging the meaning, reception, and popularity of law-related pop cultural works? Can we speak of one American popular culture or should we recognize a family of popular cultures?

C. GOALS IN THE STUDY OF LAW AND POPULAR CULTURE

As an emerging area of inquiry, the formal study of law and popular culture does not insist or rely on a particular approach. Quite the contrary, law and popular culture is eclectic in the best sense of that term. Those who teach, write, and study in the area have a wide range of styles, methods, and disciplines. Subsequent chapters will exemplify this academic eclecticism, but some of the most common goals in the study of law and popular culture can be underscored at the outset.

1. Points of Law and Practice Skills

The most venerable use of law-related popular culture in legal education is as an illustration of a legal rule or of a practice skill. The obscure rhythms of the Rule against Perpetuities, for example, might be illustrated by screening selected scenes from *Body Heat* (1981), a film in which William Hurt plays a neglectful lawyer overcome by his passions. Or one could use the scene in *The Verdict* (1982), in which a defense attorney played by James Mason prepares an anesthesiologist for testimony as an illustration for pretrial witness preparation. Illustrations from films can be especially effective in an era in which all students and almost all instructors are as comfortable with and engaged by visual presentations as they are with written texts.

In the following excerpt Professor Paul Bergman discusses why he likes to use film clips while teaching Evidence. He also goes on to highlight three scenes from the classic *Anatomy of a Murder* (1959) and points to the ways the scenes may be used to illustrate points of evidence law.

TEACHING EVIDENCE THE "REEL" WAY
Paul Bergman
21 Quinnipiac Law Review 973 (2003)

Rather than analyzing the social meaning of law in film, the discussion below considers the effective classroom use of scenes from law-related films in an Evidence course. Lawyers and courtroom trials have been fodder for countless films, and scenes from such films can serve as excellent texts for illustrating evidentiary doctrine and presenting problems for classroom analysis. Of course, films almost always dramatize or even parody actual legal relationships and proceedings. However, this increases students' engagement with the texts without detracting from the clips' usefulness as teaching devices. . . .

Perhaps the strongest rationale for using film clips is that they are an efficient and involving method of providing context for the application of evidence rules. Teaching Evidence to students who lack understanding of the trial process is like teaching "the crawl" to someone who has no idea what a swimming pool or other body of water look like. Film clips depict problems and process simultaneously and thus provide a level of understanding that the reading of appellate case opinions does not. Moreover, film clips help train students' ears, as well as their eyes, and thereby promote students' abilities to recognize evidentiary issues as they arrive in the oral courtroom process . . .

Character Evidence: Impeachment with Prior Acts and Convictions

Background: Character evidence is potentially admissible to attack a witness' credibility. Subject to judicial discretion, a cross-examiner can ask questions about misdeeds that bear on truthfulness but did not result in a conviction, but cannot offer extrinsic evidence of the misdeeds if the witness denies their occurrence. Prior convictions can be admissible to impeach a witness' credibility, and if they involve crimes of dishonesty they are automatically admissible.

Clip: Anatomy of a Murder — Lt. Manion is charged with murdering Barney Quill. Manion admits killing Quill but claims that he was temporarily insane (acted under an uncontrollable "irresistible impulse") after learning that Quill had raped and beaten Manion's wife. The prosecutor calls a jailhouse snitch, who testifies that Manion had told him that he (Manion) had deceived the lawyer and the jury and intended to beat up his wife after being acquitted of murder. On cross, the defense attorney attacks the snitch's testimony with a variety of misdeeds, including the snitch's having served three prison terms for larceny. The witness had also been in jail on charges of indecent exposure, window peeping, perjury, and disorderly conduct.

Analysis: The prison sentences presumably followed felony convictions. Larceny is a crime involving dishonesty and thus is automatically admissible. Questioning and evidence regarding the other felony convictions is admissible subject to judicial discretion. The snitch's jail time could have been the result either of simple arrest or of conviction of misdemeanors. If the snitch had been convicted of perjury, that too is automatically admissible regardless of whether it constituted a felony or a misdemeanor. The questions referring to arrests or convictions for indecent exposure, window peeping, and disorderly conduct are improper. Arrests may not be inquired into at all, and most of the acts themselves, or even convictions, would be improper because the acts do not involve dishonesty. Subject to judicial discretion, however, the defense attorney could cross-examine about the perjury incident even if it did not result in a conviction, since perjury involves dishonesty.

Defense Psychiatrists and the Ultimate Opinion Rule

Background: The Federal Rules of Evidence abolished the common law rule that forbade expert opinion testimony concerning a dispute's "ultimate issue." However, Congress resurrected the limitation with respect to expert witnesses testifying to criminal defendants' mental states. Expert testimony as to a criminal defendant's mental condition that constitutes an element of a crime or a defense is inadmissible.

Clip: Anatomy of a Murder — To support Lt. Manion's claim that he was temporarily insane when he shot and killed Barney Quill, the defense presents an army psychiatrist who examined Manion after the shooting. The psychiatrist testifies that Manion was "temporarily insane" at the time of the shooting. He also testifies that Manion suffered from "dissociative reaction" at the time of the shooting, a popular term for which is "irresistible impulse."

Analysis: Despite the limitation in FRE 704(b), criminal defendants are often able to offer a significant amount of expert testimony concerning their mental states. To some extent, what the rule forbids is crassness, meaning that a defendant cannot offer expert testimony that parrots the exact legal language that constitutes a charge or a defense. Under this interpretation, the rule would probably render improper the psychiatrist's testimony that Manion was temporarily insane. A broader interpretation of the rule might also prevent the doctor from testifying that "Manion was under the influence of dissociative reaction at the moment of the shooting." However, the doctor could testify that Manion suffered from dissociative reaction, because that is a medical diagnosis and not a legal judgment. The doctor could also testify that irresistible impulse is a popular name for dissociative reaction.

The Rape Shield Law

Background: Reversing many years of common law practice, the rape shield rule bars character evidence concerning the prior sexual behavior of a sexual assault victim. The topic obviously must be dealt with sensitively in the classroom. Appellate court opinions, problems, and film clips should be selected with regard to the potential feelings and past experiences of students, and classroom discussions should be thorough but respectful.

Clip: Anatomy of a Murder — The prosecution's factual theory is that the victim, Barney Quill, did not rape Mrs. Manion; rather, they were lovers. Manion found out about the affair and killed Quill in a jealous rage. Testifying on direct examination, Mrs. Manion denies that she had an affair with Quill and insists that Quill raped her. The scene for analysis depicts part of the prosecutor's cross-examination. He elicits evidence from Mrs. Manion that she had previously been married, that she married Manion three days after her divorce was final (defense counsel volunteers this information) and suggests, therefore, that she must have known Manion before her divorce.

Analysis: The scene offers students an opportunity to consider a number of less-than-obvious rape shield issues. The prosecutor does not refer to any overt sexual behavior by Mrs. Manion; rather, he asks about her divorce and when she began dating Lt. Manion. However, FRE 412 refers broadly to "other sexual behavior," and the context in which the questions are asked suggests that the prosecutor is attacking Mrs. Manion's sexual character. The subtle suggestion is that she cheated on her first husband, and therefore may have been cheating on Manion. Nevertheless, the questions would probably not be barred by FRE 412. By its terms, FRE 412 applies only in proceedings "involving alleged sexual misconduct. As this is a murder trial, it seemingly does not involve sexual misconduct. If it did, however, Mrs. Manion would be protected even though she is not the complaining witness because the rape shield rule protects "any alleged victim." . . .

NOTES & QUESTIONS

1. Bergman acknowledges that law-related films "almost always dramatize or even parody actual legal relationships and proceedings," but he argues that this does not detract from the usefulness of the films as teaching devices. Do you agree? What are the pitfalls in using scenes from dramatic Hollywood films to illustrate either points of law or practice skills?

2. While teaching law and film courses at the University of Connecticut School of Law and at Vermont Law School, Professor Philip N. Meyer was delighted with his students' visual literacy. In an article excerpted in chapter 9 of this text concerning criminal law and popular culture, Meyer reported, "Participants revealed a heightened and stunning visual sophistication and acuity that I had not anticipated." Philip N. Meyer, *Visual Literacy and the Legal Culture: Reading Film in the Law School Setting*, 17 Legal Studies Forum 73, 92 (1993). However, he also found that detachment, cynicism, and even anger were part of his students' visual literacy. He speculated that this attitude was a product of the students' immersion in a law school culture that devalued narrative and also their leeriness of the visual and aural stories bombarding them in advertising, television, radio, politics, and sound-byte news. "Although extremely thoughtful and perceptive, they were sensitive to manipulation and tended to disbelieve their eyes and ears." *Id.*, 83.

2.   Inaccuracies and Misrepresentations of Law and Legal Institutions

In the late 1980s a small group of scholars began to call for more sustained and systematic considerations of the relationships between law and popular culture. In a groundbreaking essay, law professor Anthony Chase provided what he called "a primitive accumulation" of law-related works in fiction television, nonfiction television, advertising, soap operas, and pop music. *Toward a Legal Theory of Popular Culture*, 1986 Wisconsin Law Review 527. In another important article Chase argued forcefully that a contemplation of popular culture could help us develop "a sharper focus on what Americans really think about law and how the system within which they operate really works." *Lawyers and Popular Culture*, 1986 American Bar Foundation Research Journal 281, 300.

For Chase and other early contributors to the study of law and popular culture, the question of popular culture's reliability and accuracy vis-à-vis the law surfaced. Popular culture, of course, does not hold a mirror up to actual law, lawyers, and legal institutions. Those who write novels, direct films, and produce television shows have more on their minds than being precisely faithful to the technicalities of the law and the requirements of legal proceedings. In general, the goal is engaging drama that will attract and hold readers and viewers. But still, if popular culture is as influential in shaping popular attitudes as many think, one should at least be mindful of the differences between law, legal proceedings, and legal institutions in popular culture and in real life.

In the following excerpt Professor David Ray Papke discusses the ways pop cultural courtroom trials differ from actual ones. Papke's observations rely heavily on interviews with a half dozen Indiana trial court judges.

THE AMERICAN COURTROOM TRIAL: POP CULTURE, COURTHOUSE REALITIES, AND THE DREAM WORLD OF JUSTICE
David Ray Papke
40 South Texas Law Review 919 (1999)

Some judges and trial lawyers find it virtually impossible to enjoy pop cultural trials because of their lack of correspondence to what the judges and lawyers experience in actual courtrooms. Their complaints are well taken, and the differences between pop cultural and real-life trials merit underscoring.

For starters, we of course have to acknowledge what most movies, television series, and novels do not mention: the great majority of cases never get to trial. Charges are dropped, sentences are threatened, and pleas are bargained. Defendants, after all, are not necessarily well-heeled or resourceful. In most urban areas, over seventy-five percent of the defendants are indigent.

In the small minority of cases that actually get to trial, we do not encounter the punchy, provocative opening statements so typical of pop culture. On television or in the movies, the opening statement is a powerful prologue or an extended first act, but in the real world lawyers are quite economical. They disdain large civic messages in favor of simply setting out a fact or two and identifying the legal issues.

As for the presentation of evidence and both examination and cross-examination, things are much less dramatic than in the pop cultural courtroom. Real-world attorneys do like visuals when it comes to evidence, and autopsy photos are a favorite in murder trials. But frequently physical evidence is minimal. Defense counsel, most of whom are public defenders, are particularly strapped when it comes to finding or presenting useful evidence. Their caseloads and budgets rarely allow for the large-scale utilization of investigators.

Side-bar conferences among the judge and attorneys are also rare. Usually important evidentiary questions are settled through motions in limine or through pre-trial compromise, and judges in general do not like to slow down their proceedings to sort out evidentiary or procedural matters. Little tete-a-tetes immediately before the bench are difficult because lawyers seem congenitally unable to speak in a soft voice. Excusing the jurors and adjourning to chambers, meanwhile, is risky business. The lawyers can make their way to chambers, but jurors have the distressing habit of disappearing into restrooms, wandering off, and even on occasion going home.

When people take the stand in actual trials, attorneys rarely grill them, and the attorneys also do not pepper the air with objections. Experienced practitioners appreciate that they have only a "limited good will account" with the jury. Jurors do not want lots of interruptions, and if the lawyer keeps objecting, they begin to wonder what he or she is hiding.

While in pop culture almost every witness has a critical piece of the story, real witnesses are often forgetful, boring, or unprepared. People on the stand might cry, but they do not break down, offer dramatic revelations, or confess. The most effective testimony probably comes from police officers, and this is another reason that prosecutors generally have an advantage over defense counsel. Police arrest with an eye to conviction, and in some districts their formal training includes lessons on how to testify.

The majority of defendants do not take the stand. Jurors would like to hear from the defendant, and some defendants would like to get on the stand because they are cocky enough to think they can put one over on people. But defense counsel are justifiably leery. If a defendant takes the stand, a prior record can be revealed, and in addition, defendants tend not to make good witnesses. As noted, most are poor. They also tend to be poorly educated and relatively inarticulate. These factors in turn create "believability" problems.

The roughly contemporaneous rape trials of William Kennedy Smith and Mike Tyson illustrate the point. The former — an atypical defendant — was well groomed and articulate. He took the stand and convinced the jury that he could not possibly rape anyone. Tyson is a different package and, alas, more similar to the typical defendant. When his attorneys made the mistake of putting him on the stand, Tyson's crude, sexist, uneducated world view convinced the jury that he had in fact raped someone.

Closing arguments are important in actual trials, and jurors listen intently to them. Why? It is not because the case is still undecided, as it almost always is at the time of a pop cultural closing. One theory is that even though most jurors have already made up their minds as to guilt or innocence, they are starting to collect their thoughts for the deliberations right around the corner. They are culling the closings for what they think they will need in the jury deliberation room.

In many cases the jurors hear only limited closing arguments. In Indiana, for example, closing arguments have time limits. A lawyer may request more time if he or she wishes, but the maximum time available is presumed to be twenty minutes unless the trial has gone into a second day. The closings, regardless of length, are rarely as stirring as they are on television or in the movies. A surprising number of trial lawyers are at best average speakers, and many cling desperately to their notepads during closing arguments.

As for what happens in the jury room, this is a bit of a mystery. It appears that despite the jadedness and cynicism of contemporary life, Americans still take jury duty very seriously. They may not welcome jury duty, but when they serve on a jury, they are earnest and do their best. In criminal trials the jury's "best" usually takes the form of a conviction. In most urban areas the conviction rate is between eighty-five and ninety percent. One would never guess it from prime-time television, Hollywood movies, or popular novels. Not even a couple of popular prosecutor series on prime time have led to an overall pop cultural conviction rate of any magnitude.

How do the judges perceive the real-life courtroom trial as a whole? While expressing amazement at what they see in their courtrooms, real-life judges also acknowledge that they often have significant managerial responsibilities. Trials do not necessarily have fully shaped story lines. Inconsequential matters surface. We see mistakes in procedure, displays of pettiness, and frequent delays. Sometimes observers feel as if they have walked through the bureaucratic looking glass, hardly the reaction of someone who has just enjoyed a gripping pop cultural courtroom drama. . . .

NOTES

1. Courtroom trials are so ubiquitous in law-related pop culture that the unreflective reader or viewer might erroneously assume that virtually all lawyers are litigators. In fact, less than ten percent of all lawyers routinely litigate.

2. The distinguished cultural studies scholar Fredric Jameson has said of pop songs that you never really hear them for the first time. Instead, you hear them as echoes and variations of countless other similar songs. *See* Fredric Jameson, *Signatures of the Visible* 20 (1990). Viewers of films and television shows with courtroom trials may in a sense never really see the pop cultural courtroom trial for the first time. Viewers may not know the verdict in advance, but they are familiar with the prototypical setting, participants, and process.

3. Ethics and Morality

Many men and women go to law school hoping that a law degree will help them build a better world, but a smaller number graduate with those same dreams. Family obligations begin to develop. Loan indebtedness mounts. And, some would say, simple maturity weans the law student from naïve and idealistic aspirations.

As the second chapter of this text concerning law students and popular culture indicates, legal education itself may play a role in this transformation. While one might expect questions of what is ethical and moral would surface frequently in law school, this tends not to be the pattern. Individual lessons and even whole courses and seminars focus on ethical and moral concerns, but legal education in general stresses rules posited by courts and legislatures, considers corollaries and exceptions to those rules, and sometimes addresses relevant policy concerns.

Popular culture and especially film afford an opportunity to make the study of ethics and morality a larger part of legal education. Law-related films, after all, are rarely about the laws themselves. More commonly, these films concern individual struggles for justice through, in proximity to, or despite law and legal institutions. These are the narratives that engage consumers of law-related film and law-related popular culture. In the following essay posted on the "Picturing Justice" website, University of San Francisco law professor John Denvir discusses using film to counter legal education's procedural bias, emphasis on craft skills, and general amoral relativism.

WHAT MOVIES TEACH LAW STUDENTS
John Denvir
Picturing Justice (http://www.usfca.edu/pj)

Perhaps it's time to ask exactly what the study of film adds to the student's educational experience that the traditional curriculum lacks. First, I think we have to admit that films about lawyers do not give a very accurate picture of how lawyers spend their days. . . . Movies and television take a great deal of artistic license with procedural rules, thereby diluting any claim that these fictions show students how law actually plays out in a courtroom.

But even if we can't claim verisimilitude for lawyer films and have to confess that lawyer films tend to oversimplify messy reality in their pursuit of a clear battle between good and evil, I think we can still persuasively argue that the study of movies provides an important antidote to the excessively amoral "professional" model of lawyering that infects the rest of the curriculum.

If the typical lawyer movie highlights the human desire for a "just" result with little interest in procedural niceties, the professional model concerns itself primarily with procedures. It assumes that procedural justice will yield substantive justice, but this assumption ignores the fact that when the legal resources needed to work the system are not allocated on a basis even approaching equality, injustice is often the result. Procedural justice might yield justice in a society in which all citizens had equal access to the top-flight lawyers, but this necessary condition is clearly not present in even our most wealthy societies. For instance, in *A Civil Action*, the plaintiffs fail in their suit against two large companies who allegedly have dumped toxins into the town's drinking water not because they had the lesser case in law and fact, but because the defendants had the larger bankroll.

A second element of the professional model is related to this procedural bias; it holds that we must put our faith in the procedures because there are simply no substantively "right" answers in difficult cases, only answers which favor plaintiff or defendant.

Convincing law students of the truth of the "no truth" thesis seems to be one of the major goals of the first year law school curriculum. Students must abandon "fuzzy" thinking and accept that truth and justice are chimeras. Here's how one law student put it: "I made certain naïve emotional and political arguments before law school that I no longer buy into. Part of me feels, well, there are certain things that are just right and wrong and then there's another part of me that says, well, wait a minute, things aren't that simple in the real world and you really can't go around making silly emotional arguments about what's right and wrong."

But the fact that truth is sometimes difficult to determine does not mean that there is no truth. Nor does it mean that all resolutions of a dispute have an equal claim to the adjective "just." The primary goal of a legal system should be to design systems that allow the true facts to emerge in complicated situations.

Worse yet, students are led to believe that their earlier faith in "emotional arguments" is a sign of intellectual immaturity and that adoption of the value-free professional model is a form of personal progress. I would suggest that (again to use the facts in *A Civil Action* as an example) whether or not the defendant corporations polluted the water that the plaintiffs drank is a factual question to which a true answer can be found. And if true, the related question of whether and how much compensation the plaintiffs should receive from the defendant corporations is a question of justice as well as law. And finally, acknowledging an emotional dimension to the assignment of proper legal responsibility to the defendants for their actions is not a sign of intellectual immaturity; instead it is evidence of a richer humanity.

A third element of the professional model is its definition of "good" and "bad" lawyering solely in terms of craft skills. Since law is a series of preset procedures in which plaintiff and defendant wage a form of warfare, and since there is no right answer to the issues they contest, a good lawyer is not a hero who obtains justice, but rather an expert who works the procedures to yield a result favorable to his client. The professional model pictures lawyers operating in a morally flattened universe in which craft values dominate. Once again using *A Civil Action* as an example, the professional model would argue that Jerome Facher (Robert Duvall), who keeps relevant evidence hurtful to his client away from the jury, is the "good" lawyer. Perhaps we need to broaden our definition of the "good."

I don't want to be seen as merely trashing the professional model; it has its virtues. Law students need to learn how to think through problems methodically, not just rushing to embrace emotionally appealing conclusions. But I do think it gives an unduly amoral view of the lawyer's role, one which unnecessarily subverts the idealism that brings many students to choose law as a career in the first place.

The study of lawyer films, even unrealistic lawyer films, therefore can provide an important supplement to the curriculum by teaching some important lessons. The most important lesson is that justice counts. The very quantity of "law" films demonstrates that the human appetite for justice is just as strong as our appetites for power and sex.

Good lawyer films, like *To Kill a Mockingbird* and *A Civil Action*, also teach a second important lesson: the practice of law is fraught with ethical consequence. We can still debate today whether Atticus Finch failed his client in submitting his fate to a racist state court jury instead of seeking the aid of the federal court. So too the ethical dilemmas facing Jan Schlictman, the lawyer who represents the families harmed by toxic water, are worthy of our deepest consideration. Schlictman comes in with a simple goal — to get as large a fee as possible with as little risk as possible. Yet slowly he discovers he wants more; he wants to see justice done even thought it's not exactly clear what that concept means in this context. He finds himself in a quandary. If he "takes the money and runs" as he originally planned, he is no more than the "ambulance chaser" the defense lawyers think him. But if he proceeds with the case, he puts his clients, his partners, and himself at financial risk. It's not easy for Schlictman or the viewer to balance these conflicting considerations, especially since they don't calibrate on the same measure, but I think discussion of a movie like *A Civil Action* can teach students that some of the most challenging parts of being a lawyer start just where the professional model leaves off.

NOTES & QUESTIONS

1. How might a defender of traditional legal education argue in favor of the emphasis on procedure and craft that Denvir criticizes? What are the dangers of bringing ethics and morality into legal education?

2. Films can be used in various ways to bring considerations of ethics and morality into the law school discussion. Most obviously, dozens of films raise controversial issues and go on to explore in dramatic form the legal system's response. *Erin Brockovich* (2000), for example, might be used to raise questions of environmental destruction and corporate greed. *Philadelphia* (1993) is a moving critique of homophobia and discrimination because of sexual orientation.

3. One should be aware that with sophisticated films viewers often take away different meanings. Film, like literature, might not proffer a fully achieved structure of meaning but rather an opportunity for reflective engagement. Different viewers come to that engagement with different biases, personal histories, and expectations, and may as a result find a given film to stand for variable propositions and lessons. In the following excerpt Carole Shapiro shares the manner in which her anti-capital punishment views influenced her initial reaction to *Dead Man Walking* (1996). Later, after garnering others' reactions to the film, Shapiro changed her mind and concluded it was not a powerful indictment of capital punishment. The actual film had not changed, but the viewer's response to it had.

DO OR DIE: DOES *DEAD MAN WALKING* RUN?
Carole Shapiro
30 University of San Francisco Law Review 1143 (1996)

When I first saw *Dead Man Walking*, I was moved by the strong anti-capital punishment statement I thought the film made. Discussing it with friends and strangers, however, I was surprised to hear the range of opinion about the film's point of view on this issue. Later, when I committed myself to write about *Dead Man Walking* for this law review, I decided to pursue my earlier informal inquiry and focus on what the movie, when analyzed objectively, said about the death penalty.

To help with this project, I decided to speak with death penalty lawyers and other experts in the field. While they were not all cinema mavens, I thought these people would have something intriguing to say about the movie's perspective. And they did, although their comments on the death penalty itself were equally stimulating. Also interesting to note was the group's full spectrum of responses to the film, which echoed what I had earlier observed.

I am delighted that I was able to speak to the thoughtful and busy people whose voices ended up in the pages of this article. Each of the phone interviews was important in the development of my analysis of *Dead Man Walking*, and [I] am deeply appreciative to my subjects for their time. . . .

In the course of this project, my ideas about the movie, which I ultimately saw several more times, changed. As I learned more about what the film had omitted and thought more about what had been included, I saw its limitations both as a work of art and as a statement about the death penalty. In the end, I decided that my original understanding of the film as an anti-death penalty work reflected my own feelings at least as much as the filmmaker's.

In writing this critical piece, I do not mean to downplay the film's emotional effect on many of its viewers, including one of Robert Lee Willie's victims. I just wish the film was more than I have come to understand it to be. . . .

Sister Helen Prejean's book *Dead Man Walking* is passionately anti-capital punishment. When she began spiritually ministering to Louisiana Death Row inmates, she knew little about the issue. But her immersion in the efforts to save their lives made her an anti-death penalty activist. The book details Sister Prejean's work with survivors of murder victims and also makes both a religious and political case against executions. Although readers may ultimately disagree with the author, they can have no doubt about her stance on the death penalty or her reasons for opposing it.

The movie *Dead Man Walking*, however, which has been both a critical and box office success, fails to deliver the same unequivocal abolitionist punch as the book. Indeed, despite the author's statements that she "collaborated very closely with director/screenplay writer Tim Robbins in every line, every scene" of it, viewers are torn about whether or not this is even a film with an anti-capital punishment point of view. While many experience the movie as a strongly affecting statement against executions, others see it differently. One critic, for example, provoking a flurry of letters in the *Los Angeles Times*, went so far as to assert that Robbins tries "to manipulate audiences into a revenge mode." Another, Professor Hugo Bedau, celebrated for his books and articles on capital punishment, wrote in a letter to Sister Prejean that "if [*Dead Man Walking*] is a movie in opposition to the death penalty, I shudder at the thought of a movie intended to support [it]."

Some consider the disagreement over *Dead Man Walking*'s message as virtue, as proof of its "balance" and "evenhandedness." Although Wendy Lesser, author of *Pictures at an Execution*, criticized the film for other reasons, she asserted that Tim Robbins was "under no obligation to create a piece of anti-death penalty propaganda." Moreover, she said, his film should not be judged on his success in accomplishing that. While I agree with Lesser on this point, *Dead Man Walking* would have benefited, without becoming mere agitprop, from adopting the book's more comprehensive take on the subject. Instead, Robbins' primary focus on the religious aspect of capital punishment leaves the audience clueless about the systemic inequities and arbitrariness that led Sister Prejean to abolitionist activism. And because the movie nun never gives direct voice to her death penalty opposition as a matter of principle, viewers are not sure exactly were she stands on the issue.

Given the high volume of today's law and order zeitgeist, the "balanced" *Dead Man Walking* is a lost opportunity to make an unambiguous statement against the death penalty. While several other capital punishment films are in the offing, including Sharon Stone's *Last Dance*, none will offer the confluence of art, politics, and talent that could have made *Dead Man Walking* a uniquely anti-death penalty movie. Whatever the movie's other achievements, its failure to translate the depth and breadth of the book's anti-execution position to the screen is disappointing.

While the film has considerable power and has provoked discussion, one wonders why Robbins settled for such a limited exploration of the truth — political and otherwise — about the death penalty. Rather than detracting from his cinematic artistry, a fuller, more nuanced picture of the issue would have enhanced his creation overall. . . .

NOTES & QUESTIONS

1. To what extent is it valid film criticism to argue, as Shapiro does, that a film fails because it does not take a strong enough position on a given issue? Do we expect popular films to take detectable positions on issues?

2. Professor Roberta M. Harding suggests that a simpler made-for-television movie such as *Last Light* (1992) might speak more effectively to capital punishment issues than the more self-consciously arty *Dead Man Walking. See* Roberta M. Harding, *Celluloid Death: Cinematic Depictions of Capital Punishment*, 30 University of San Francisco Law Review 1167 (1996).

3. The ethical and moral alignment of a work of law-related popular culture might emerge primarily from the actions and statements of a major character, often a lawyer. Chapter 3 of this text is devoted to lawyers and popular culture, and the chapter explores the ways in which popular culture portrays the conduct and character of lawyers. One common theme in lawyer films involves the ethical or moral redemption of a lawyer as he or she represents someone in an important case. Why might lawyer characters — more so than victims, litigants, activists, and others — be best suited for exploring ethical and moral questions? Are there drawbacks to relying on lawyer characters for these purposes?

4. Respect for the Rule of Law

Legal education not only exposes students to laws and legal procedures but also encourages them to develop a respect for the rule of law. Neutral laws, the argument goes, can and should be applied fairly to individual controversies in order to achieve justice. Surely such an approach to social ordering is better than any rule by individuals or groups.

Popular culture includes stirring, heroic figures who live by this credo, sometimes with great cost to themselves. *A Man for All Seasons* (1966) cinematically tells the story of Sir Thomas More. Paul Scofield, the film's star, won the Oscar for Best Actor, and the film also won Oscars for Best Picture, Screenplay Director, and Cinematography.

Proud to be both "a lawyer and a lawyer's son," More was the most prominent legal figure of early sixteenth-century England. While presiding in the chancery courts, he succeeded in clearing the docket and also distinguished himself by refusing to accept bribes. Early in the film More's son-in-law argues that the Devil should not be protected by due process, but More's response underscores his belief in a rule of law. "The country's planted thick with laws from coast to coast," More says, and "and if you cut them down . . . d'you really think you could stand upright in the winds that would blow then?" Surely, More concludes, we would serve our own interests by giving even the Devil due process.

The later portions of the film portray More's conflict with King Henry VIII. The latter renounced papal authority and declared himself head of the Church of England in part because he wanted to divorce his barren wife and marry Anne Boleyn. More refused to take an oath to the King's authority or to endorse his actions. After a trial for high treason, More was convicted and beheaded. Sham trials, the film invites us to conclude, violate our treasured heritage of achieving justice through a rule of law.

In the following excerpt Professor Kenneth Wagner discusses the way the film explores important jurisprudential issues.

A MAN FOR ALL SEASONS
Kenneth Wagner
Picturing Justice (http://www.usfca.edu/pj)

More's refusal to sign the oath brings up the difference between civil disobedience and conscientious objection as drawn by John Rawls. Civil disobedience for Rawls is a form of debate, a non-violent action aimed at the public and guided by political principles. Change is the central point. Rawls differentiates this from conscientious objection, which is the non-compliance with laws one sees as immoral. Conscientious objection is not meant to change the political sphere; it is just a decision to risk punishment rather than violate one's moral principles. The character of More certainly falls into the category of conscientious objector. He does not use his position to rail against the King's oath; he does not counsel others on the immorality of the oath itself (though certainly this is in part to defend himself through silence). Instead, he refers to himself as a loyal subject to the King who simply will not swear to the oath (he does not even say that by not swearing we should read into his silence disapproval of the oath).

Rawls defends civil disobedience by stating that it acts as a vigilant police on the laws of society, constantly forcing us to examine our laws and measure them by the yardstick of justice. Conscientious objection on the other hand is a personal issue; it is only morally permissible if the harm caused by non-compliance is outweighed by the correctness of the personal principle invoked in conscientious objection. What is the harm that More's refusal could possibly cause? The movie actually hints at such harm when at the beginning Cardinal Woolsey defends his "flexibility" on Church law in granting the King a divorce by pointing to the possible civil strife that could follow an heir-less sovereign. In this context, More's refusal could be a morally impermissible act.

This actually brings up two other issues of legal philosophy thrust upon us by the film. More's refusal to take the oath despite the consequences to himself, his family, and his realm constitute a form of deontological ethics. According to deontology, some acts are inherently immoral despite the consequences that follow. Thus, the philosopher Immanuel Kant in his famed categorical imperative stated that it was wrong to tell a lie, even in the case of whether one should lie to a murderer who was stalking his victim hidden in a nearby closet. Cardinal Woolsey represents another view, that of the consequentialist. He admonished More to "come down to earth" when More refused to change his position even when warned of the strife that could follow his defiance. In a similar vein, Karl Marx admonished those who clung to an abstract and "neutral" rule of law that had negative consequences on the poor and oppressed.

More's refusal also invokes the debate between positive and natural law. When his soon to be son-in-law, a political radical, argues that law must be made malleable to the interests of justice, More launches into a long defense of the importance of "man's laws." . . . More's speech invokes the theorists of positive law such as John Austin who maintained that man-made law, the order of the sovereign, is all the law there is. Ironically, it is More who is later caught up in the very positive law he defended, and in response he speaks of his duty to his soul. This appeal to God's laws invokes the perpetual counter-arguments of natural law theorists who hold that positive law can and should be measured by a "higher" Law of Nature. The King's law has the power to execute More, but does it have the authority?

One of the last striking things about this film may be a much-overlooked feature. Many viewers of the film will likely pessimistically comment on the trumped up [sic] nature of the prosecution of More played out brilliantly at the end of the film. However, such pessimism may be unwarranted. More's knowledge of law enables him to conduct a legal strategy based on the precedent that silence on an issue does not necessarily imply disapproval of the King's position (which would then warrant high treason). In his trial More is given a jury (though one surely bullied by the Crown, as in the scene where the prosecutor declares that surely no break for jury deliberations is necessary and so the verdict is immediately rendered), an account of the charges against him, and the right to defend himself (including cross-examination of witnesses). It is only because of the distortion of evidence (the implication that More took a bribe that he clearly did not) and the testimony of a false witness that More is ultimately convicted. The question of course remains, does this show the advanced state of English rights of the accused at this ancient state, or does it point to the more unsettling conclusion that even abstract legal safeguards cannot protect one when prosecutorial dishonesty rears its ugly head?

NOTES & QUESTIONS

1. *A Man for All Seasons* implies that proceedings more faithful to the rule of law would have been desirable in More's case. To what extent is it ever possible to insulate the rule of law from dishonesty and political bias?

2. An American cinematic hero who embodies a deep respect for the rule of law is Atticus Finch. The novelist Harper Lee modeled the character on A.C. Lee, her father and a lawyer in Monroeville, Alabama. *To Kill a Mockingbird*, her novel featuring Atticus Finch, won the Pulitzer Prize for fiction in 1961, and in the next year Hollywood's adaptation of the novel was honored at Oscar time. Horton Foote won the Academy Award for Best Screenplay, and Gregory Peck won the Academy Award for Best Actor for his portrayal of Atticus Finch. Few scenes in cinematic history are as much praised as those featuring Peck's Atticus Finch defending the unjustly charged African American Tom Robinson in the midst of a racist southern community. Many who came of age in the late 1950s and early 1960s point to Atticus Finch as an inspiration and as a reason they decided to become lawyers.

Does Atticus Finch have any flaws? Might his moral code, professional ethics, and understanding of the rule of law be critiqued? In the following excerpt Professor Monroe H. Freedman refers to both the original novel and film adaptation. He characterizes Finch's words of wisdom for his children after they face down a lynch mob as fatuous.

ATTICUS FINCH — RIGHT AND WRONG
Monroe H. Freedman
45 Alabama Law Review 404 (1994)

Consider, then, the moral truth that he tells to the children when they experience the lynch mob outside the jail. Walter Cunningham, a leader of the mob, is "basically a good man," he teaches them, "he just has his blind spots along with the rest of us." It just happens that Cunningham's blind spot (along with the rest of us?) is a homicidal hatred of black people. And when Jem replies, with the innocent wisdom of a child, that attempted murder is not just a "blind spot," Finch condescendingly explains to him: "[S]on, you'll understand folks a little better when you're older. A mob's always made of people, no matter what. Mr. Cunningham was part of a mob last night, but he was still a man."

What are we to make of this fatuousness? That a lynch mob is not a lynch mob because it's "made up of people"? That because Cunningham is "still a man," he has no moral responsibility for attempted murder? Who does have moral (and legal) responsibility for a wrongful action if not the person who commits the wrong?

One of the charges I have faced for past criticisms of Atticus Finch is "presentism." This clumsy neologism is meant to express the idea that it is unfair to hold someone in an earlier time to moral standards that we recognize today. Lest anyone miss the point, this contention is derived from cultural relativism. This is a philosophy that rejects the idea that there are any moral values that are absolute (or, at least, prima facie) and eternal. Instead, morality is equated with the notions of right and wrong that are recognized in the culture of a particular time and place. Slavery? Apartheid? Lynching? Sacrificing babies? Well, the cultural relativist says, we might not approve, but who are we to judge the moral standards of people in another time or place?

So let me declare myself. I do believe that there are prima facie principles of right and wrong (which can be called Natural Law), which each of us is capable of recognizing by the use of experience, intellect, and conscience. There may not be many such principles of right and wrong, but . . . the attempted lynching of Tom Robinson, and the apartheid that Atticus Finch practiced every day of his life — those things are wrong today, and they were wrong in Maycomb, Alabama, in the 1930s.

Again, let's take Finch's advice. Let's get inside the skin of the black people in Maycomb and walk around in an ordinary day of their lives. They endure, and their children grow up experiencing minute-by-minute reminders of separateness premised upon their innate inferiority. They are compelled to live in a ghetto near the town garbage dump. They cannot use the white only rest rooms, the white only water fountains, the white only lunch counters, or the white only parks. If their children go to school, their segregated schools, like their churches, have few if any books. They are even segregated in the courtroom in which Finch practices law. The jobs allowed to them are most menial. And they face the everyday threat of lawless but condoned violence for any real or imagined stepping out of line.

Tom Robinson knows this, and he knows that it will cost him his life. The last thing he says to Atticus before they take him to prison camp is: "Good-bye, Mr. Finch, there ain't nothin' you can do now, so there ain't no use tryin'." That day, "he just gave up hope." And, of course, Tom Robinson is right. He is shot to death — with seventeen bullets — on the claim that a gentle man with a useless arm, in a prison yard the size of a football field, in plain view of guards with guns, broke into a blind, raving charge in a hopeless attempt to climb over the fence and escape.

You can believe this improbable story, as Finch purports to do. But I believe (and Harper Lee appears to believe) that Tom Robinson was goaded into a desperate, futile run for the fence on the threat of being shot where he stood. Underwood's editorial in *The Maycomb Tribune* calls it a "senseless" killing — not what one would call a killing, with fair warning, of a raving man about to surmount a prison fence and escape. And if Finch averts his eyes from the truth, Scout faces it straight on. "Tom was a dead man," she realizes, "the minute Mayella Ewell opened her mouth and screamed." . . .

The charge of presentism fails also when we consider that other Whites of the time — born, raised, and living in Finch's South — are able to see that the oppression of Blacks is morally wrong. Dill, nine years old, runs out of

Robinson's trial, physically sickened by the prosecutor's racist baiting of Robinson . . . .

Maudie Anderson is another who recognizes the injustice against Blacks and, she tells the children, they'd be surprised how many others think the same way. They include prominent and respected members of the community: Judge John Taylor and Sheriff Heck Tate, the landowner Link Deas, and the editor Braxton Underwood . . . . And Jem, in response to Finch's explanation about the "ugly facts of life" and of southern justice, also recognizes right and wrong. "Doesn't make it right," he says, beating his fist softly on his knee.

What, then, do I expect of Atticus Finch *as a lawyer*? First, because there has been some misunderstanding in the past, let's be clear about what I don't expect. I have never suggested that Finch should have dedicated his life to "working on the front lines of the N.A.A.C.P." On the contrary, in rejecting the notion that Atticus Finch is a role model for today's lawyers, here is what I said: "Don't misunderstand. I'm not saying that I would present as role models those truly admirable lawyers who, at great personal sacrifice, have dedicated their entire professional lives to fighting for social justice. That's too easy to preach and too hard to practice."

In fact, part of my commentary is that Finch's adulators inaccurately represent him as a paragon of social activism. . . . Also, it is Finch's adulators who insist on rewriting the book to create a mythologized hero. Typical is a recent piece stating that Finch "decides" to represent an indigent defendant even though he hereby "incurs the obloquy of his friends." This is wrong on two counts. First, Finch does not choose to represent Tom Robinson. He accepts a court appointment, but candidly says, "You know, I'd hoped to get through life without a case of this kind, but John Taylor pointed at me and said, 'You're It.'"

Second, it is inaccurate to say that Finch's friends subject him to obloquy. It is true that many of the townspeople do, but not Finch's friends, not the people whose opinions he values. In fact, those people admire Finch for taking the case and for giving Robinson zealous representation. . . .

I don't say this to disparage Finch, but for the sake of accuracy regarding presentism. Disparagement comes with my next point, which considers what it means that Finch "hoped to get through life without a case of this kind." It means that Atticus Finch never in his professional life voluntarily takes a pro bono case in an effort to ameliorate the evil — which he himself and others recognize — in the apartheid of Maycomb, Alabama. Forget about "working on the front lines for the N.A.A.C.P." Here is a man who does not voluntarily use his legal training and skills — not once, ever — to make the slightest change in the pervasive social injustice of his own town. . . .

But let's assume, for the sake of discussion, that I am guilty of presentism. Assume too that anything Finch tried to do would be futile (which is a familiar justification for being a bystander to evil). Even if those contentions have merit, does that make Finch a role model for today's lawyer? . . .

Finch has an enviable array of admirable qualities and, in one instance, he is truly courageous. He is a loving, patient, and understanding father, successfully coping with the burden of being a single parent. In his personal relations with other people, black and white, he unfailingly treats everyone with respect. Professionally, he is a superb advocate, a wise counselor, and a conscientious legislator. A crack shot, he never touches a gun, except to protect the community from a rabid dog. Even when he heroically waits for and faces down the lynch mob, he arms himself only with a newspaper.

In short, Atticus Finch is both more and less than the mythical figure that has been made of him. He is human — sometimes right and sometimes wrong. And one criticizes Atticus Finch not from a position of superiority, but with respect, like a sports columnist reporting the imperfection in an athlete whose prowess he himself could never match.

NOTES & QUESTIONS

1. Freedman's pointed criticisms notwithstanding, most viewers of *To Kill a Mockingbird* consider Atticus Finch heroic. Indeed, in 2001 the American Film Institute ranked Gregory Peck's Atticus Finch the number-one movie hero of all time.

2. According to Paul Bergman and Michael Asimow, "Atticus Finch sets a standard to which all lawyers should aspire." *Reel Justice: The Courtroom Goes to the Movies* 139 (1996). How does Atticus Finch see the law, and what role does he think the law should play in social life?

D.   A CULTURAL JURISPRUDENCE

Law-related popular culture can play a large role in a cultural jurisprudence. The central premise of this way of thinking about law is that law inevitably lives within culture, that is, within a people's values and attitudes, their norms and behaviors. Law draws its content, tones, and aspirations from the culture in which it resides, and law in turn shapes and directs the culture. Legal scholars Austin Sarat and Thomas R. Kearns argue that "legal meaning is found and invented in the variety of locations and practices that comprise the domains of culture and that those locations and practices are themselves encapsulated, though always incompletely, in legal forms, legal regulations, and legal symbols." Austin Sarat & Thomas R. Kearns, eds., *Law in the Domains of Culture* 10 (1998).

Law-related popular culture — the commodities and experiences with legal characters and themes produced by the culture industry — is one of the "locations and practices" Sarat and Kearns have in mind. For many Americans, nothing has a greater impact on their understanding of and attitudes about the law than law-related popular culture.

The best examples of popular culture affecting law involve trials and courtroom proceedings. In the 1950s defense counsel in criminal prosecutions complained that they could never live up to the remarkable exploits of the fictional Perry Mason, America's best-known lawyer of the era. Juries, it was claimed, expected defense counsel not only to demonstrate that a reasonable doubt existed regarding the defendant's conduct but also to actually prove the defendant was innocent. Often, Perry Mason went so far as to identify the true perpetrator, who coincidentally was located in the rear of the courtroom. How could actual defense counsel be expected to do the same? In more recent years, *C.S.I.*, an extremely popular primetime television series set, has arguably made the work of prosecutors more difficult. Jurors, it seems, expect prosecutors to produce the kind of fingerprints on bullet casings and DNA test results that the crime scene investigators in *C.S.I.* shows are always able to turn over to their prosecutors. If this evidence is not available — and it rarely is — the defendant must surely be innocent.

A significant number of lawyers, judges, and law professors have written about popular culture's interrelationships with law, legal institutions, and common attitudes about law. In the following excerpt Victoria A. Salzmann and Philip T. Dunwoody cast the writers and scholars in this area as the "pop-culture legal-realist movement." The sobriquet seems too large a label to stick, but Salzmann and Dunwoody are correct that scholars have asserted that much of what contemporary Americans know of the law has been learned from popular culture.

PRIME-TIME LIES:
DO PORTRAYALS OF LAWYERS INFLUENCE HOW PEOPLE THINK ABOUT THE LEGAL PROFESSION?
Victoria S. Salzmann & Philip T. Dunwoody
58 Southern Methodist Law Review 411 (2005)

Most law students learn early that the law has no more power than society gives it. . . . Individuals create the law as something of a "collective agreement." Society at large determines the bounds of behavior; the law is recorded as a memorialization of those bounds and individuals abide by them. Thus, the law remains a fluid circular process, constantly changing as its content is created, challenged, and abandoned. It conforms to current attitudes and societal norms. In essence, the law is a living thing that both shapes our lives and reacts to our desires. It is simply what we believe it should be. But, because the law is essentially just our understanding of it, the source of the collective knowledge has particular importance.

Under the pop-culture legal realists' theory, the perception of what lawyers really do is understood via television, film, and literature. This perception builds primarily because "the law operates in places and spaces that are partially hidden from public view." John Brigham, *Representing Lawyers: From Courtrooms to Boardrooms to TV Studios*, 53 Syracuse Law Review 1165, 1169 (2003). Lawyers operate under a cloud of mystery. Aside from attorneys, very few people have the opportunity to view all the aspects of lawyering in a given conflict from beginning to end. For example, even a client who retains a lawyer to pursue his claim will see only small snapshots of the litigation process. He may meet with the attorney, attend depositions, and be present at mediations and court proceedings, but he will not see the research hours, document drafting, phone conversations, attorney conferences, and discussions in chambers that accompany such litigation. And, even when the client does participate in various stages of the litigation, he often cannot understand how his participation or that particular proceeding contributes to the overall legal process — much like a movie trailer cannot reveal the totality of emotion created by an Oscar-winning film. "The lay person enters by stepping into a metaphorical stream of legal activity. There is a specific place where the encounter occurs but much has come before and much takes place beyond." Robin Paul Malloy, *Introduction to the Law and Humanities: Symposium on the Image of Law(yers) in Popular Culture*, 53 Syracuse Law Review 1161, 1161 (2003).

There is a medium, however, that "fills in the gaps." Pop-culture legal realists believe that television, film, and literature translate the mysterious world of the lawyer into a concrete process by revealing what lawyers do and where they do it. Through popular culture, the layperson seems to view the hidden world of the lawyer, presumably understanding how discrete events shape the legal process as a whole. The layperson can see that a document drafted or a deposition taken today will have very real consequences down the road. Television and movies appear to provide the viewer with a map of the whole rather than a glimpse of selected parts. Given the impact of television, the power to perform this function makes perfect sense.

It is almost impossible to guess the magnitude of television's impact on modern society: With the single exception of the workplace, television is the dominant force in American life today. It is our marketplace, our political forum, our playground, and our school; it is our theater, our recreation, our link to reality, and our escape from it. It is the device through which our assumptions are reflected and a means of assaulting those assumptions.

Television has replaced newspapers, radio, churches, and even family as the primary force in our lives. More importantly, it has become the information source for many of its viewers. Where knowledge was once acquired through experience, it is now transmitted by passively watching the actions of others. In 1990, the A.C. Nielsen Company reported that the average American adult watched more than thirty hours of television per week. Today, with cable choices in the hundreds, the number has increased. On a webpage created by Fox television to target advertisers, Fox estimates that 100,800,000, or 98.2%, of American households own televisions. Fox further estimates that the average household now watches seven hours and twenty-six minutes of television a day, or more than thirty-nine hours a week. By the time a person has reached the age of seventy, he would have spent between seven and ten years in front of a television.

And more importantly, television has become far more than an entertainment source. It is a diversion, a companion, and a source for our perception of reality. Psychologists have noted that many people use television as a substitute for human companionship. Individuals feel uncomfortable when faced with idle time and, in response, turn on the television to fill the void. The unexpected side-effect of such viewing is a constant stream of information being "downloaded and recorded by" the viewer's psyche. What the individual views as entertainment today becomes the reality to which she compares the events of tomorrow.

Social sciences recognize this information-gathering side effect as a necessity. Individuals watch television because they have "media system dependencies" including understanding dependency, orientation dependency, and play dependency. Understanding dependency is the root of all social interaction. Individuals strive to understand how to appropriately interact in unfamiliar situations. We seek to "understand the social environments within which we must act or anticipate acting, because meaningful social action cannot occur in the absence of a definition of a situation." To meet these goals, people depend on the media to provide information about unfamiliar situations. We view how others interact and conform our behavior to those depictions, thus conquering the unknown. Our own personal experiences become secondary to those we see on television. We depend on the media for our understanding of important social contexts that we may not encounter on our own. This need for contextual information forms the root of the understanding dependency.

The second dependency, orientation dependency, involves learning how to interact with others. Even if an individual understands a particular social context, she might not understand how she is supposed to interact with others in that context. Take an agnostic who has never attended church. She may understand the purpose and content of the ceremony but may have no idea of what to do if she actually attends. Likewise, a layperson may understand what a deposition is but would have no idea how to act if deposed. The media, however, bridges this information gap. . . . Like the orientation need noted above, individuals use popular culture to shape their understanding of unfamiliar social situations and how they should interact in these otherwise unfamiliar circumstances. In essence, society depends upon television to tell it what to expect and how to act.

The effects of television on children are even greater than the effect on adults. A 1993 study indicated that while outside of school, most American children spend more time watching television than doing any other activity. The television world becomes the real world because it is often a child's only source of information during the years he creates his social foundation. If a child sees excessive violence on television, he may come to believe that violence is an acceptable way to deal with conflict. Similarly, children's perceptions of the law may be formed early through popular culture depictions.

And this phenomenon is not all buried in our subconscious moral foundations. The media overtly shapes our perception of an entire host of topics. This phenomenon is especially true for disciplines such as the law, history, or politics where the viewer has no personal framework on which to draw. . . . Over 100 million Americans watch the news every day and necessarily begin to form value-judgments based on how the media presents public issues. Likewise, television has become the foundation for most popular perceptions of the law. However, unlike some social issues presented in the news, most people do not get their information about the law from critical media such as CNN, Fox News, C-Span, or Court TV; rather, legal information is gleaned from fictionalized portrayals of lawyers. The authority of the law comes less from legal scholars and decision-makers and more from what the average person watches each night on television.

Some attorneys have already recognized this problem and complained that television creates unrealistic expectations in their clients, particularly in criminal-defense clients. Likewise, false perceptions are so far removed from the truth of lawyering that the profession itself is affected. Even lawyers have become disenchanted with their chosen career paths when they are faced with boring daily activities instead of exciting trials and client interactions. One scholar hypothesized that these dramatic portrayals are responsible both for "professional melancholy" caused when the daily life of a lawyer turns out to be much duller that that portrayed on screen, and for "public hostility toward lawyers" when real-life attorneys do not measure up to the heroic lawyers the public has come to expect. In short, pop-culture legal realists believe that popular culture has a very real impact on public perceptions of the law. . . .

Pop-culture legal realists also believe that the synergism between law and popular culture works in the opposite direction. They believe that popular culture not only creates society's perception of the legal process, but that it shapes the law itself. . . . Popular culture and public perception of the law are "two stars, locked together by their own gravity and orbiting forever around each other;" popular culture creates perception and society uses that perception to create law. Paul R. Joseph, *Saying Goodbye to Ally McBeal*, 25 University of Arkansas at Little Rock Law Review 459, 463 (2003). First, popular culture mirrors existing public perceptions of lawyers and the legal process. Second, popular culture teaches the public about the law by integrating new ideas into the viewer's preconceived framework of the law. Then, when the viewers influence or change the law, they do so using the perceptions popular culture has given them.

Viewers "expect some fundamental resonance with their understanding" of the law, and television writers oblige by giving the audience "a diet of what the audience already believes to be true."(*Id.* at 462–63) When the show presents new information or a new premise, the audience accepts it as true because it conforms to the already accepted version of the legal process. Access to celluloid law and its processes essentially creates a "benchmark trial" in our collective conscious through which all actual legal issues will be filtered. The benchmark of what viewers see on television and in movies becomes the legal process because it is the image that viewers understand. Each new portrayal is a brick in the foundation of the layperson's understanding of how the law works. The "portrayed reality" created by the depiction works in its own self-fulfilling loop; we see what we believe to be true because it is what we already believe to be true. . . . Once a film or television show is viewed, its message becomes ingrained in our collective psyche, which, in turn, becomes our basis for reality — even if the message itself was inaccurate.

The legal-realist theory applies equally to the actual creators of law, both legislators and judges. Legal realists believe these individuals are influenced by their social backgrounds (including media-created perceptions) as much, if not more, than by the black-letter law itself. These social backgrounds may also be the basis for drafting laws. According to commonly accepted principles of statutory construction, legislative history can be an acceptable means of ascertaining the legislative intent behind an ambiguous statute. In some instances, such as Establishment Clause cases, legislative purpose or motivation is the deciding factor in determining whether a law is constitutional. If a law is passed to endorse or proselytize individual legislators' religious views, that law may be deemed unconstitutional. Thus, the law itself recognizes that legislative decisions can be and are influenced by individual legislators' backgrounds, personal experiences, and moral or religious beliefs. Both the formation of the black-letter law and its constitutionality hinge on the legislator's preconceived beliefs — beliefs pop-culture realists believe are formed in no small part by media influences.

Similarly, judges formulate or interpret the law, in part, based on external forces. Since the 1920s, the legal-realist movement has taught that judicial opinion is composed of more than mere interpretations of what judges find in statues and codes. Instead, judges assimilate the same information from newspapers, books, television, and movies that the rest of society sees. And in turn, they use that information, coupled with their own personal beliefs, to make decisions. Often this "external" influence is obvious. For example, judges today turn to secondary sources such as accounting, social science, foreign affairs, psychology, and other disciplines as support for their opinions. These sources provide firm ground in the absence of established legal precedents. As a result, the law itself consists of "variant principles shaped by social needs and not of hard rules applicable through purely formal logic." And necessarily so, for the law cannot be a living, ever-changing reflection of society's ideals if its crafters cannot reinterpret legal principles to serve justice today. Pop-culture legal realists believe that, because television shapes and influences personal ideologies, and that those personal beliefs, in turn, influence legal decision-making, popular culture references have a significant affect on the law. Judges and legislators are influenced just as other television viewers are because they are simply people bringing their own personal perspective to the bar.

Legal realists believe that the analysis of popular culture can actually influence legal theory. For example, celluloid images can shed light on constitutional theory, despite the constitutional scholars' pride that the field is "the most rigorous of intellectual pursuits." Both are intellectual analyses into various social issues, though one focuses on appealing to viewers while the other seeks legal solutions to concrete problems. Movies are often designed to tell stories for entertainment, but these stories are derived from reality. Much like an ancient fable still provides a basis for moral lessons, modern movies and television provide examples of social issues that otherwise might not have any impact. . . .

There is support for this theory in actual court opinions. Popular culture references are starting to appear in case opinions just as literary references once abounded. For example, John Grisham's novels have become integrated into the actual courtroom. Not only is Grisham's work referenced in legal opinions, but some cases have actually hinged on the use of Grisham's works at trial. In *State v. Saez*, the court held that references to Grisham during closing argument did not constitute reversible error. And, in *United States v. Sabbagh*, the defendants used Grisham's novel *The Firm* to argue that trial counsel had a conflict of interest. Even more interesting are the instances when courts have actually adopted Grisham's language to explain a legal concept. For example, in *Herring v. Bocquet*, a Texas Court of Appeals quoted an entire paragraph from *The Rainmaker* to explain the art of over-billing. Several other cases have referenced to *The Rainmaker*'s plot "when discussing the distasteful reimbursement policies of certain insurance companies," or to *The Runaway Jury* when describing the particularities of tobacco litigation.

In a similar vein, media influence the way lawyers themselves behave within the system. Lawyers have recognized the shift in communication toward visual representations and have begun to employ related techniques as persuasive tools. Also, lawyers are becoming more savvy about the way the media portrays their clients. For example, during the notorious Menendez brothers' trial, defense attorney Leslie Abramson fought CBS and Fox Television over their portrayals of her clients. Prior to the brothers' re-trial, the two stations intended to show fictitious dramas of the brothers' story. The portrayals, however, did not correspond to the defense theory. Understanding the impact that these portrayals could have on jurors unable to separate fact from fiction, Abramson threatened to have Erik Menendez give a live inter-view on a rival network during the same programming slot. Her application of pressure to CBS and Fox Television was simply an attempt to put the lid on the overwhelmingly persuasive visual image that cut against the defense strategy. Unfortunately for the Menendez brothers and for other notorious criminals, their sensational trials are exactly the sort of pulp-legal fodder that television producers use. Pop-culture legal realists believe these examples show that popular culture can and does have real effects on the law and its processes. . . .

NOTES & QUESTIONS

1. Professors Salzmann and Dunwoody do not place themselves within the "pop-culture legal-realist movement." In other sections of the article from which the preceding excerpt is taken, they test the accuracy of popular cul-ture's portrayals of lawyers against the ways lawyers actually do spend their time. Salzmann and Dunwoody also surveyed first-year law students at Baylor University School of Law and South Texas College of Law to see if popular-culture portrayals of law have affected the students' expectations and under-standing of legal practice. The authors conclude that false perceptions of lawyering have for the most part not been created. But is Salzmann and Dunwoody's study of law students of much help in gauging general lay percep-tions?

2. A cultural jurisprudence clearly conflicts with any assumption that law exists unto itself and operates exclusively with reference to its own techniques, rules, and premises. In the following excerpt senior Stanford University law professor Lawrence M. Friedman discusses both popular culture about law and lawyers *and* what he calls "popular legal culture," namely, the thinking of average citizens about law and lawyers. Friedman suggests both popular cul-ture and popular legal culture are important in social theories of law, and these social theories, in his opinion, are especially valuable in explaining why law is as it is.

LAW, LAWYERS, AND POPULAR CULTURE
Lawrence M. Friedman
98 Yale Law Journal 1579 (1989)

[Popular culture and popular legal culture] are of fundamental importance in constructing *social* theories of law. By social theories, I mean theories of law whose premises deny, altogether or in large part, any notion of legal "autonomy." That is, these theories try to explain legal phenomena by searching for causes and causal factors "outside" the legal system. They treat law as a dependent variable, and assign a leading role in molding the shape of legal institutions and legal arrangements to systems or subsystems that society defines as "non-legal," that is, as economic, social, cultural, or political. Social theories assume some sort of meaningful boundary — conceptual or analytical — between law and not-law; between the legal and the social; but these theories also conceive of this boundary as wholly or largely porous, a kind of network or meshwork through which energy easily flows, rather that as a tough, tight skin.

This cluster of theories firmly rejects the idea that legal systems are sealed and inward-looking; that they respond entirely or primarily to their own logic, traditions, and demands; that they are "self-reproducing," or "self-referential," or the like. A living organism, for example, *is* "autonomous" in an important sense. A horse and a cow have clear boundaries that separate them from each other and from the world. Their skins and shapes are not purely conceptual; rather, they are the real limits of subworlds, each of which develops according to its own internal rules. Both a horse and a cow eat grass, but the digested grass turns into more horse in one case, more cow in the other; never the other way around. The internal program determines exactly how food will be processed; and the organism grows and functions by these "autonomous" rules.

Some theories of law in fact treat legal systems as organisms in the sense discussed in the previous paragraph. Theories that stress the "relative autonomy of law" seem to be enjoying some vogue among legal scholars. The old-fashioned "conceptual jurisprudence" of the nineteenth century, of course, treated law as autonomous with a vengeance. Modern autonomists claim to be different, and are surely more sophisticated. But they do share some points in common with nineteenth-century conceptualists. And they certainly insist that it makes sense to look at legal systems as if they were indeed tight, impermeable, and closed to the outside world; an insular realm controlled by the "mandarins" to a very high degree.

A social theory of law, in contrast, is "social" to the extent that it denies or downgrades the autonomy of law, and insists instead that an analysis of social forces best explains why the legal system is as it is, what shapes and molds it, what makes it ebb and flow, contract and expand; what determines its general structure, and the products that it grinds out day by day. There are, of course, many different social theories of law, real or potential — classical Marxism embodies a social theory of law, for example; so too do some versions of the law and economics movement. But social theories are neither inherently right nor left; they span the spectrum of political views. They may isolate some particular "social force," and assign it the lion's share of responsibility for law and legal institutions; or they may credit some mixture of factors in the outside world. They may focus on politics, on economic organization, or on tradition or culture. It is also perfectly possible to have a "social theory" that explains legal phenomena in terms of more implausible factors — the movements of the tides, or the signs of the zodiac. "New age" social theory may be just around the corner.

Probably no serious scholar clings absolutely to either one of the two polar positions; nobody thinks that the legal system is totally and absolutely autonomous; and nobody (perhaps) seriously puts forward the opposite idea, that every last jot and tittle, every crumb of law, even in the short, short run, can be and must be explained "externally." But most lawyers, and a good many legal scholars and theorists, tend to cluster somewhere toward the autonomous end of the scale. Social scientists interested in law, and legal scholars with a taste for social science, tend to cluster somewhere toward the other end; they prefer external to internal explanations, and are deeply suspicious of the case for autonomy. It is probably true that neither basic view can be "proved" one way or the other. Rather, they are starting points, assumptions, frameworks.

It is precisely in the sense of a methodology, a strategy, that the case for (some version of) a social theory of law is strongest. It seems to me that there is more explanatory power, more richness, more bite, in exploring the manifold connections between the legal system and its surrounding society, than in treating law as an isolated domain. . . .

Social theories, in other words, are mighty tools for grappling with problems of explanation. They are not, as some critics fantasize, infected irremediably with a disease called "behaviorism," which I assume means either a concept of human beings as crude economic robots, or a methodological stance that takes overt, physical "behavior" as the sole social reality (or, in any event, as the only reality we are able to study). Social theories can be, and usually are, deeply aware of emotion, opinion, and in fact of consciousness; and some social theories — the more anthropological ones, for example — are fixated to a fault on culture and consciousness. Nor are social theories necessarily vulnerable to the charge that they (unrealistically) assume a radical distinction between "law" and "society," instead of recognizing that the two are really inseparable, intertwined, faces of the same coin. No doubt the two *are* inseparable. However, it is possible to separate them analytically, and it may also be sociologically useful to do so since in many societies the two are undoubtedly separated in the minds of their consumers. If anything, it is the believers in the autonomous system who are open to this particular criticism; after all, they and not social theorists are the ones who insist most loudly on the radical separation of law from the social matrix.

But the *idea* of a social theory is a far cry from an actual theory, fully developed, and strong enough to carry on its back a heavy load of explanation. Most attempts at social theory of law are crude and inadequate because they ignore or gloss over what I will call the issue of the *mechanism* or channel. This is nothing more or less than the question of *how* "social forces" actually do their number on the legal system. In what way and through what paths, tubes, hollows, and conduits do the "forces" set up by concrete events, persons, situations, and structures in "society" move, as they deliver their punch to legal institutions, manufacturing or "causing" legal phenomena — statutes, rules, institutions, and cases? A social theory that does not try to answer this question is a blind and almost meaningless abstraction. . . .

NOTES & QUESTIONS

1. Professor Friedman, not surprisingly, goes on to suggest that law-related popular culture and popular legal culture are important mechanisms or channels for social forces to affect legal phenomena. In his interpretation, law as it appears in stories, in movies, and on television derives at least in part from what average citizens think law is. Law-related popular culture in turn affects what people think about law, and people's thoughts on law influence what law actually is. "To me at least," Friedman concludes in the article excerpted above, "it seems patent that explorations of legal and popular culture, and the way they interact, should be high on the list of scholarly pursuits." Lawrence M. Friedman, *Law, Lawyers, and Popular Culture*, 98 Yale Law Journal 1578, 1606 (1989).

2. Why might legal educators, lawyers, and judges be hesitant to acknowledge the power of popular culture to affect our attitudes and aspirations regarding law? How does a cultural jurisprudence challenge the traditional American ideological premise that our nation lives by a rule of law?

PART II:

LEGAL ACTORS AND INSTITUTIONS

Chapter 2

LAW STUDENTS

A. FILMOGRAPHY

Legally Blonde (2001)

The Paper Chase (1973)

Rounders (1998)

The Socratic Method (2001)

Soul Man (1986)

B. TRAINING FUTURE LAWYERS

1. The Call for Clinical Education

As law students yourselves you must wonder — in between rushing to class, trying to avoid being called on, studying for your next class, questioning why you ever decided to attend law school, cramming for exams, and taking exams — why law schools train lawyers the way that they do. Periodically, law school administrators, faculty, and accreditation boards have examined that question as well. The most recent major evaluation of law school education is the MacCrate Report. It suggested that law schools had lost touch with legal practice and had become too "academic." In an excerpt below, clinical law professor Russell Engler discusses the Report's impact.

THE MACCRATE REPORT TURNS 10: ASSESSING ITS IMPACT AND IDENTIFYING GAPS WE SHOULD SEEK TO NARROW
Russell Engler
8 Clinical Law Review 109 (2001)

The MacCrate Report was published in 1992. Officially titled *Legal Education and Professional Development — An Educational Continuum*, and issued by the American Bar Association's Section of Legal Education and Admissions to the Bar, the 414-page document constituted "The Report of The Task Force on Law Schools and the Profession: Narrowing the Gap." The blue ribbon Task Force was chaired by Robert MacCrate, whose name became synonymous with the Report.

The Report's core sets forth "The Statement of Fundamental Lawyering Skills and Professional Values": ten fundamental lawyering skills and four professional values "which new lawyers should seek to acquire." Anticipating its critics, the Report acknowledged that the purpose of developing a Statement of Skills and Values (SSV) was not to identify a definitive set of skills and values, but to provide a vehicle for beginning a process through which "discussion in all sectors of the profession could be focused on questions about the nature of the skills and values that are central to the role and functioning of lawyers in practice." The Report explained the focus and formulation of the statement and set forth possible uses of the SSV, by a range of possible users. Anticipating its critics, the Report identified "Abuses of the Statement to Be Avoided," including that the SSV should not be used "as a standard for law school curriculum," "as a measure of performance in the accrediting process," as "an enumeration of ingredients that are either necessary or sufficient to avoid malpractice," or as a "source for bar examinations."

The Report begins with over one hundred pages describing "The Profession for Which Lawyers Must Prepare," before formulating, organizing and analyzing the SSV. The Report follows the SSV with a chapter on "The Educational Continuum Through Which Lawyers Acquire Their Skills and Values" and concludes with "Recommendations of the Task Force." Consistent with its theme of the Educational Continuum, the recommendations include not only twenty-five specific recommendations directed at the law schools, but also recommendations directed to the stages of development both before and after law school, as well as the transition to practice from law school and the licensing process.

The Report emphasizes the importance of clinical legal education in the teaching of skills and values:

> Clinics have made, and continue to make, an invaluable contribution to the entire legal education enterprise. They are a key component in the development and advancement of skills and values throughout the profession. Their role in the curricular mix of courses is vital.

The Report's laudatory treatment of clinical legal education is hardly surprising, given the central role played by clinicians in shaping the document. Clinicians served as Members of the Task Force and Task Force Consultants. One of the four public hearings held by the Task Force was dedicated to hearing the views of clinical teachers, and clinicians appeared or submitted written comments at other public hearings as well. One clinical teacher, Randy Hertz of the New York University Law School, served as consultant to the subcommittee that developed the core of the Report, the SSV.

The MacCrate Report was not the first comprehensive effort to address the lack of competence among graduating lawyers. Robert MacCrate was among the many who placed the Report in the context of previous efforts including the Reed Report (1921), the writings of Jerome Frank in the 1930s and 1940s, and the Crampton Report (1979). The growth of clinical legal education beginning in the 1970s was spurred in part by "student demands for relevance in the law school curriculum." Yet, by the mid-1980s, Gary Bellow spoke for many by observing that "contrary to the view of many law faculties, our present modes of education do not properly prepare students to practice law." Outside the law schools, critics loudly decried "disjunctions . . . between legal education and the needs of lawyers and judges."

Justice Rosalie Wahl laid the predicate for the Task Force in 1987, when she chaired the ABA Section on Legal Education. The Task Force itself was comprised of members both inside and outside the field of legal education, and included liaisons both to the Association of American Law Schools and American Bar Foundations. The Task Force held seven plenary sessions between 1989 and 1992, and four public hearings, held in 1990 and 1991, at which the Task Force received both oral and written comments. A Tentative Draft of the SSV "was circulated nationally to members of the Bar and law school faculties," triggering comments from an array of groups; the comments in turn led to numerous changes to the SSV, and the Report was published in 1992.

The MacCrate Report became a lightning rod for discussion, strategizing, and critique both inside the world of legal education and in the profession as a whole. Following the Report's publication, a steady stream of conferences focused on the Report, as well as on the teaching of skills and values in general. Both the American Bar Association (ABA) and the Association of American Law Schools (AALS) dedicated considerable energy to the Report, its recommendations, and the reaction triggered by the report.

The discussions around the country were soon accompanied by scholarly articles involving descriptions, analyses, and critiques of the Report and its recommendations. The trickle of law review articles that began to appear in 1993 became a flood by 1994. Law reviews published individual articles and symposia dedicated to issues raised by the MacCrate Report. One textbook, designed to explain "the fundamental lawyering skills, values, and relationships in the practice of law," was dedicated to Rosalie Wahl and Robert MacCrate.

The earliest scholarly responses included a scathing critique from Dean John J. Costonis. Dean Costonis excoriated the Report for "essentially ignoring the most visible impediment to its implementation: the costs of its recommendations and the trade-offs that must be struck." Although Dean Costonis asserted that his primary differences with the Report were "economic, not pedagogical," the structure and language of his article suggested more substantial differences. He criticized the SSV, the vision of the law school's role in the educational continuum, and the use of ABA oversight and rulemaking to further the Report's goals. The critique was packaged in the historical context of the previous efforts to reform legal education that had failed — implying that a similar fate awaited the MacCrate Report.

Other law school Deans joined Dean Costonis in his critique, most notably through a "Dean's letter" co-signed by fourteen law school Deans. The Deans' letter explicitly opposed use of the accreditation process in its implementation. As part of their critique, the Deans fought back directly at clinicians, citing the costs of clinical legal education, the dangers of using the accreditation process to push skills training and clinical legal education, and the flaw in any strategy that might use the MacCrate Report to enhance the status of clinical teachers.

Supporters of the Report responded swiftly and directly to the critique articulated by Dean Costonis. Robert MacCrate found it

> difficult to understand, how a law school, such as Dean Costonis describes, can derive 86 percent of its income from student tuition, send its graduates as a result out into practice with huge personal debt, and not be willing to assign equal priority in the law school, along with developing the law, to preparing its students to participate effectively in the legal profession.

A different author responded that, contrary to Dean Costonis' assertions, the real problems were not financial: they were "the beliefs of law school deans, as illustrated by Dean Costonis's critique, that our current legal education is perfectly acceptable."

Law School Deans were not the only group that produced critics of the MacCrate Report. Inside the law school, non-skills teachers also worried about the restrictions on academic freedom and re-allocation of resources that would result were the Report implemented. Legal writing and research teachers criticized the Report for failing to elevate the status and role of their field, and teachers of Alternative Dispute Resolution (ADR) critiqued the Report's emphasis on litigation. Outside the academy, bar administration leaders criticized the advocacy of performance testing, and bar association leaders criticized the lack of implementation of the report's recommendations.

Clinical teachers joined in the critique as well, questioning the Report's efforts to set forth a taxonomy of fundamental lawyering skills and values in the first place, but also lamenting "the poor prospects for effective implementation of the MacCrate Report's pro-clinical recommendations. . . ." Proponents of in-house clinics worried that the effect of the Report would be to lead to an expansion of simulation courses or externship programs at the expense of in-house clinics. Externship proponents argued that the Report had undervalued the learning that occurs in field placements and exalted a particular form of clinical pedagogy that relied too heavily on top-down, supervisory structures.

Clinical teachers also cautioned that implementation of the Report's recommendations might lead to an increase in skills training without the values articulated in the Report. As Gary Bellow and Randy Hertz later explained, skills training alone would be inadequate, and needed to be "informed by a moral vision — a normative concern for the fairness, accessibility, and justness of the legal system and its influence on the social order of which it is a part." Consistent with that view, clinical teachers both criticized the Report for "giving inadequate attention to the ways in which the law and legal institutions negatively affect the poor and other disenfranchised groups," but also underscored the importance of teaching the MacCrate Report values relating to justice, fairness, and morality.

While some clinical teachers expressed concern regarding certain aspects of the MacCrate Report, the Report galvanized broader groups of clinical teachers. At least four clinical conferences were dedicated in whole or in part to discussion of the MacCrate Report in the first few years following 1992.

Newsletters from the AALS Section on Clinical Legal Education and newly-formed Clinical Legal Education Association (CLEA) were replete with references to the MacCrate Report, reactions to the Report, and efforts to implement it. Clinical teachers were central to the efforts to create committees at the state bar level in each of the fifty states for the implementation of the MacCrate Report. The AALS Section on Clinical Legal Education and CLEA appointed a joint task force on implementation, before the AALS backed off from formalizing the collaboration with the use of the AALS name.

Renamed "The Clinicians' Working Group on MacCrate Implementation," the clinicians identified six "Implementation Goals":

1. Law schools shall provide every student with appropriate instruction in the values and skills reflected in the SSV through a combination of direct client representation clinical programs, simulation courses and classroom instruction.

2. Law schools shall provide every student with a faculty supervised, direct client representation clinical experience designed to provide instruction in those values and skills reflected in the SSV which are best taught through such an experience.

3. Law schools shall make available to those students who want this experience an in-house, faculty supervised, direct client representation clinical program designed to provide instruction in the values and skills reflected in the SSV which are best taught through such an experience.

4. Law schools shall provide applicants with a copy of the SSV and advise them of the nature and availability of clinical programs and other programs for instructing students in the values and skills reflected in the SSV.

5. Law schools shall devote adequate resources toward ensuring that students fulfill their obligation to work towards enhancing the capacity of law and legal institutions to do justice.

6. Law schools shall provide every student with instruction in the skills and values necessary for the student to fulfill her obligation to provide legal services to those who cannot afford to pay for them.

The importance of the MacCrate Report to clinicians, as reflected in the meetings, newsletters and strategies, resonated through the clinical scholarship. Most of the law review articles discussing the MacCrate Report were written by clinical teachers. Issue after issue of the *Clinical Law Review* included articles in which the MacCrate Report figured prominently. Some articles articulated and defended the case for using the accreditation standards as a tool for reform, thereby responding to the attacks by Dean Costonis and others. Others used the contention that the MacCrate Report would meet a fate similar to its predecessors, such as the Crampton Report, as a rallying cry to insure that such a similar fate be avoided.

Even the rallying cries contained a note of realism. Clinicians acknowledged that sweeping change was unlikely given the realities of legal education and the forces that would oppose change. They used more tempered language, observing that "the MacCrate Report simply suggests that the current balance within law schools should be changed modestly." Some supporters urged that the Report be used to strengthen in-house clinics. Others focused on the "integration of skills education into the law school as a whole" and using the Report as a tool in "negotiation within the law school and with the larger legal community."

As the debate over the MacCrate Report swirled around the national stage, awareness of the Report and its recommendations began to grow at many individual law schools around the country. By the spring of 1993, most Deans responding to a AALS survey "reported that their faculties had already discussed the report or were planning to do so in connection with a review of their curricula." An informal survey of clinical teachers attending the Midwest Clinical Teachers Conference in October, 1993, indicated that at roughly half the schools, discussions regarding the Report already had occurred or been planned. Published articles over the next few years revealed that at least some schools moved quickly to make curricular changes either consistent with the Report's recommendations, or directly as a result of them.

NOTES & QUESTIONS

1. Do you feel the MacCrate Report has had an impact at your law school? Is there adequate skills-training? Are there abundant clinical opportunities? Does your law school adequately prepare you to practice law? Most importantly, should preparation for practice be legal education's primary mission?

2. Several of the featured films for this chapter depict law students in search of practical training. For example, Charles Johnson in *The Socratic Method* is so desperate to get a clerkship during law school that he falsifies letters of recommendation. Elle Woods in *Legally Blonde* eagerly seeks work with a practicing attorney (her criminal law professor). Do the films suggest any tensions between "on the job" and classroom learning?

3. Charles Johnson and Elle Woods seek clinical work during their first years of law school. Most law schools discourage law students from working in their first years, for what the law schools consider good reasons. What might those reasons be? Knowing what you know now about the stresses of the first year, do you agree?

4. Is experience in a law school clinic the approximate equivalent of experience one would get as a law clerk? Consider that law clerks get paid, and law students in a clinic do not — they get law school credit. What other differences can you name?

5. In *The Socratic Method*, when Charles Johnson gets a job with Mr. Meffastaffalo, he engages in what can only be described as really underhanded tactics to bring in clients. What do you make of Mr. Meffastaffalo's secretary/paralegal's explanation that Charles, and not her boss, is responsible for the tactics? Is she correct? What image does Charles' subsequent behavior in bringing in clients present to the general public about law students and their training? Does it reinforce stereotypes about lawyers in general, or does Charles' decision to quit (and his stated reasons for quitting) actually bring out heroic images of lawyers in popular culture? (Think about what he does to Kenneth Stafford). Do you think that law clinic training is designed to lessen the risk that law students might meet up with a "Mr. Meffastaffalo"? How many "Mr. Meffastaffalos" do you think are really out there?

2.   The Socratic Method

Even Harvard Law School, the bastion of the Socratic method, has started to abandon it. *See* Orin S. Kerr, *The Decline of Socratic Method at Harvard*, 78 Nebraska Law Review 113 (1999). The Socratic method no longer holds sway at most law schools to the extent that it once did. Many law school professors instead combine the Socratic method with other teaching styles, having recognized that a more diverse student body learns in many different ways. However, not all law professors agree; thus law students may still encounter a professor who uses the Socratic method with Kingsfieldian overtones. Consider the reasons for the move away from the Socratic method or its continued use in the following selections.

YOU CALL THAT EDUCATION?
Morrison Torrey
19 Wisconsin Women's Law Journal 93 (2004)

According to Plato, the essential aspects to Socrates' dialogues were: (1) elenchus, the step in which Socrates leads the responder to understand that he does not know what he thought he knew; (2) aporia, the acknowledgment of ignorance and perplexity; and (3) psychagogia, the construction of a new understanding. Typically, this occurred in small groups and voluntarily. This has been transported to large classrooms where students not only cannot walk away, but will also be graded by their questioner. To a high degree, "legal education has incorporated elements of hostility, competitiveness, and humiliation into what is, essentially, an abuse of the system." The law teacher is in a position of complete authority which can be abused or not.

In reviewing the literature about the Socratic Method, one thing became immediately clear: not only is there no agreement on the value of this pedagogical tool, but there also is no agreement on exactly what it is! I suppose it is not surprising that law professors want to define their own rules for the game; after all, that is what they do in the classroom, including "hiding the ball."

Exactly what is the Socratic Method as embraced by legal education? One professor, Paul Brest, believes that "the terrorist version of the Socratic Method has almost disappeared, and it has been replaced by a mixture of lecture, asking questions of volunteers, and responding to questions from the class at large." Another professor, Steven Childress, characterizes the Socratic Method as "a rigid relationship between teacher and student, immersion of the student in the subject and its analysis, a focus on technical distinctions and massive facts, and large class size," with the negative attributes of potential teacher abuse and covert indoctrination. Professor Gerald Lopez argues that the Socratic Method is currently practiced as "a set of mini-lectures by the teacher interrupted by questions that by now no one really expects to precipitate the kind of critical conversation among students and teacher that many imagine to be the defining strength of legal education." Professor John Cole defines the Method by what it is not; in his view, the Method is neither lecture with occasional questions designed to keep students alert and check their preparation and understanding, nor sharp questions designed to reveal the substance of the law. Rather, he believes Socratic questioning "illuminates the various competing values that inhere in the problem and forces the student to see that it is his [or her] responsibility to order those values in a coherent and defensible way." According to Professor Thomas Eisele, legal education's use of the Socratic Method is premised upon a belief that students have both carefully read assigned materials and have thought about them prior to class. Through Socratic questioning, law teachers "are demonstrating for the edification of our students — and, thus, we are training them in — techniques of thinking, ways of applying (or developing) the thinking skills they already possess." But, in order to accomplish this, the students must first learn that they don't know what they think they know. This process (demonstrating they don't know what they think they know) can be humiliating for students; despair and humiliation "are both natural and necessary" to the process.

Professor Martin Louis defines the Socratic Method as "a dialogue about the subject matter of the class going on almost continuously between the professor and the students." Professor Jennifer Rosato reduces the method to "a dialogue between teacher and student — an 'education by interrogation.'" To her, components of the Socratic Method can include the following: a teacher who knows the answers and challenges the students to win the game by providing the answer the professor wants; students who feel personal humiliation when they cannot find the right answer; competition, not communication, as the dominant classroom atmosphere; mystification and dehumanization of the law; and an atmosphere that thwarts student creativity and silences different perspectives. Professor Pierre Schlag believes that, in the true law school Socratic Method, it does not matter what resolution the student offers: In the true law school Socratic Method, the student is always wrong. The resolution always founders on a new fact scenario, or some previously unnoticed implication, or some unforeseen consequence. And there is always another question, one that is carefully tailored to expose the inadequacy of the student's previous answer. In a perfect display of the Socratic Method the questions would never stop; the class would never end.

Extending Professor Schlag's proposition, Cheryl Herden, writing as a second-year law student, sees the Socratic Method as "socializing students by teaching them the hierarchical notion that the professor knows all but he [or she] need not share his [or her] knowledge."

Professor Ruta Stropus carefully distinguishes Socratic Method from Langdellian Method: "law students read cases and then engage in a question and answer dialogue regarding those cases," learning "how courts reasoned and analyzed," developing "analytical skills to defend a 'position from attack by both faculty and fellow students.'" In sum, this teaching method will "foster analytical skills, encourage independent learning and provide students with the opportunity to practice and refine verbal and rhetorical skills." For Professor Cynthia Hawkins-Leon, the Socratic Method helps students to: (1) develop analytical skills; (2) think on their feet; (3) engage in intellectual rigor; (4) learn about the legal process; and (5) learn about the lawyer's role. Thus, the Socratic Method appears to be many things to many teachers. And, although a strict and exclusive use of this pedagogy seems to be waning in many law schools, it remains the traditional and most honored legal teaching methodology.

NOTES & QUESTIONS

1. How close are Professor Torrey's descriptions of the various Socratic methods to the teaching methods you have experienced in law school?

2. How do the Socratic methods utilized by Professor Kingsfield in *The Paper Chase*, Professor Banks in *Soul Man*, and Professor Stromwell in *Legally Blonde* differ from one another? Which version of the Socratic method is best suited for a Hollywood film set in a contemporary law school? Why?

3. Hollywood films rarely prioritize precise accuracy with regard to social settings and practices. As noted in the introductory chapter of this text, film-makers want instead to touch popular attitudes and to attract admission-paying viewers. How might the portrayal of the Socratic method as the standard law school form of teaching correspond to popular assumptions about legal education and about the legal profession in general?

4. The following excerpt discusses how Professor Kingsfield came to symbolize the Socratic method and helped fuel opposition to its use. However, Professor Michael Vitiello, the author of the article from which the excerpt is taken, nonetheless vigorously defends the Socratic method.

PROFESSOR KINGSFIELD: THE MOST MISUNDERSTOOD CHARACTER IN LITERATURE
Michael Vitiello
33 Hofstra Law Review 955 (2005)

Over thirty years have passed since Professor Kingsfield first appeared as a character in *The Paper Chase*. He instantly became a powerful symbol of what many thought was wrong with legal education. For many years, he remained synonymous with a particular form of the Socratic method, so demanding and unkind that it rendered students bitter, unhappy, and cynical. Lest he fade from memory, both the novel and film have been reissued. As a result, Kingsfield is likely to continue to haunt prospective law students and to remain a foil for critics of traditional legal education.

Criticism of the Socratic method and legal education did not begin with the publication of *The Paper Chase*. But beginning in the 1970s, attacks on the Socratic method became more frequent, were often intemperate, and treated

Kingsfield as synonymous with the Socratic method and its ills. Among the criticisms leveled at the Socratic method in the hands of Professors like Kingsfield are that it results in poorly trained lawyers; it causes incivility between attorneys; it discriminates against women; and it causes law students to lose their ideals.

Partially in response to such attacks, law schools have become gentler places in a misguided attempt to become kinder to their students. In fact, critics have questioned whether the method ought to be banned or discouraged as a teaching tool. As the cost of legal education has risen, and as law schools are increasingly dependent on alumni giving, institutional pressures have increased to make law schools more student-friendly. As a result, demanding professors like Kingsfield, where they remain in legal education, are on the defensive. While a majority of law professors continue to use some form of Socratic questioning, increasing numbers of professors engage in far less aggressive questioning of their students and adopt an array of techniques to lessen the stress, including allowing students to pass when they are called on or giving advance notice when they will be called on in class. . . .

As a law student, I certainly shared much of the distaste for the Socratic method. I began to rethink my position on my first day as a lawyer. I now believe that the Socratic method needs a vigorous defense. . . . No careful study has determined whether law schools have become gentler places over the past thirty years. One study, acknowledging that it was not statistically valid, concluded that the overwhelming majority of law professors still use the Socratic method. The study did not attempt to define the Socratic method. Beyond that, though, the study made no effort to determine whether law professors use the method in ways that are likely to increase stress. For example, the questionnaire sent to law professors did not ask what sanctions are imposed if students are unprepared or whether they allow students to pass if they do not want to be called on or whether the professor simply accepts volunteers.

Anecdotal evidence seems to cut both ways. Many articles criticizing the Socratic method assert that the method in all of its glory is still in place. But other writers have observed that the atmosphere in law schools has become gentler in recent years. Often, in comments about a retiring colleague, professors state that the honoree is no Kingsfield but instead was a master of a kinder form of the Socratic method. My own observations at four different law schools where I have taught support the latter conclusion.

Institutional pressures dampen enthusiasm for the highly demanding use of the Socratic method. As law schools become more expensive to run and more dependent on alumni giving, deans and others responsible for fundraising may have little enthusiasm for professors who are seen as "infantilizing, demeaning, dehumanizing, sadistic," and "destructive of positive ideological values." Combine institutional pressure with student evaluations that became routine around the time of *The Paper Chase*: in light of the importance that some schools place on student opinion, one doubts that an untenured professor is going to emulate Kingsfield. A quick survey of ads for law schools supports the conclusion that some law schools are no longer hospitable to Kingsfield-style professors. Southern Methodist University, for example, advertises that it has adopted a "kinder, gentler" approach to the first year of law school. Within the recent past, Vermont Law School advertised that "the days of Professor Kingsfield . . . infamy are over." Other schools make similar claims. Concord, the online law school, made much of the fact that it has no "looming" law professors or "quaking" students, while another states that it espouses a culture of civility and respect, "avoiding 'paper chase' or 'cutthroat' law school stereotypes."

At a minimum, the probable decline in the use of the highly demanding Socratic method over the past thirty years in favor of a gentler form of the method should raise doubts about empirical claims that it is a major cause of students' ills. Law schools should hesitate to make sweeping changes in legal instruction without better evidence that the Socratic method is the cause of students' woes. If the Socratic method is a major cause of students' problems, their problems should have diminished over time as the method is employed less vigorously. But the literature lacks careful longitudinal studies of students' problems. . . .

Often ignored by critics of Kingsfield and the Socratic method is that the gentle professor, sensitized not to hurt students' feelings, may create an atmosphere that is not conducive to learning. A student who is poorly prepared will not learn as well as one for whom expectations are high. By comparison, demanding professors set the standard high, forcing students to aim high to meet the professor's expectations.

If this is a problem, it is because such high expectations create a fearful environment that impairs students' learning. Whether Kingsfield-style professors still roam the halls of American law schools is difficult to determine empirically. Above, I argued that is unlikely. And while professors should aim for a classroom in which students experience enough stress to be motivated to do well, but not too much to paralyze students, the literature today suggests that many law professors are more worried about setting the bar too high, rather than too low. Many well-meaning professors, writing about their teaching, emphasize the need to reach Generation X students, students who have been raised on the media, with shorter attention spans, with less motivation than earlier generations. Those professors often write about making the classroom exchange fun, rather than challenging. . . .

Another question that needs to be explored is whether the goals advanced by advocates of a gentler law school environment necessarily ready students for the practice of law. . . . [A]re we giving our students adequate training to deal with the stress that they will face in practice? In a gentler law school, students who bruise easily will not have training in how to deal with the inevitable frustrations of practice, including the reality that they will face judges and opponents who care little about their feelings and whose conduct will be confrontational.

My point is simply that law schools today run a far greater risk of creating too gentle an environment rather than creating too rigorous an environment. For those legal educators who doubt this assertion, I pose this question: in most American law schools today, are deans more likely to be concerned about professors considered too demanding or not demanding enough? Again, I have no empirical proof. But, based on my own experiences at various law schools, deans give far more attention to trying to soften professors considered demanding than they do trying to get undemanding teachers to increase intensity in the classroom. Indeed, were a not especially demanding teacher confronted by a dean today, the professor might simply rely on the numerous articles attacking the demanding Socratic method as proof that the professor's gentler methods are more effective. . . .

A number of prominent legal educators have based their critique of the Socratic method on learning theory. Some learning theorists recognize that the Socratic method may be effective for many students and may not argue that it should be abandoned. Instead, they contend that law professors should be aware of students' different learning styles and use different methods to reach those students. Their insights are important and influential.

One cannot lightly dismiss their message. Surely, a professor ought to attempt to reach all of her students. In this section, after reviewing the arguments of the learning theorists, I do raise questions about learning theorists' arguments. My concern focuses on a practical question: how will students need to ingest material and to communicate material when they practice law? That is, learning theorists must show that lawyers who lack the ability to learn through reading, listening, and debating their points can be fully effective as practicing lawyers. Learning theorists have not effectively addressed that question.

Educators have argued that students absorb material differently from one another. They identify five kinds of learners. First, verbal learners absorb information through written texts. Second, visual learners absorb information in its entirety. Visual learners may be able to memorize well, but not solve problems well. Third, oral learners absorb information by speaking. Such students need to speak in class to maximize their learning. Fourth, aural learners absorb information by listening. Presumably, like verbal learners, they are well suited for law school because many of the traditional teaching techniques play to their strength. Hence, they benefit from class lectures and discussions. Finally, tactile or kinesthetic learners learn best by doing, e.g., by role-playing or simulation.

Learning theorists have argued that law professors spend too much time using only one or two teaching methods. For example, because so much time in law school is devoted to learning through written materials, verbal learners are more successful than their peers. By comparison, visual learners tend to end up at the bottom of their class. Some critics of current teaching strategies argue that professors can enhance learning of visual learners by using charts and diagrams. Other scholars have suggested a host of strategies to engage more of their students than are able to learn effectively through the use of the Socratic method.

Not all writers agree on the role of the Socratic method in an ideal teaching environment. Some writers have argued that law professors can maintain the academic rigor of the Socratic method and nonetheless help students who are in the bottom half of the class (or who will end up there at the end of the first year). Others have argued explicitly or implicitly that the Socratic method is not a good educational tool. For example, in arguing that their method is superior to the Socratic method, three authors developed an exercise called a Contract Activity Package ("CAP") that allows students to work at their own pace. It also permits learning through different learning styles, unlike the Socratic method.

One can only sound callous if he questions whether we ought to be addressing the learning needs of all of our students. But we must ask whether students need to have a particular learning style in order to succeed in the practice of law. I offer a simple analogy: in my sophomore year in college, I took a basic Art History course. I ended up doing well in the course because I was able to read enough about art to know what I ought to be able to see in the work. Although I did not identify the problem in these terms in 1965, my problem was that I am not a visual learner. I adapted.

Imagine that instead of taking an art course, I was deciding whether to become an art historian or art appraiser. Surely, I chose wisely when I decided not to concentrate in Art History. Had I chosen Art History and sought employment in the field, I would not have been able to compensate for my lack of visual, spatial intelligence. What, for example, if I had been employed as an art critic, to write about modern art? I lacked a skill necessary to work in that field.

Similar examples abound. Social scientists now identify several different kinds of intelligence. But most commentators do not argue that teachers in a given field should compensate for their students' lack of a particularly relevant kind of intelligence by use of different learning styles. Instead, they recognize that individuals should make career choices that call up that individual's strengths.

That point is missed in much of the discussion of learning theory in the law school context. Although learning theorists contend that law students must develop both practical and analytical skills in order to learn how to think like a lawyer, learning theorists do not focus on the particular skills that lawyers need to have. Given the wide variety of kinds of law practice, one might argue that people with different learning styles should find a niche in practice. But the practice of law does have some common denominators.

No doubt, some lawyers are rainmakers, whose interpersonal skills are more important than their analytical skills. Some lawyers have strong oral advocacy skills and weak writing skills. But the overwhelming majority of lawyers must be able to read and analyze statutes, rules, and cases. They must be able to take complex facts and figure out how the various rules and cases apply to those facts. They must be able to draft coherent legal documents whether they are litigators, transactional lawyers, or administrative advocates. They must be able to digest and synthesize large amounts of material.

The literature advocating better accommodation of students with different learning styles misses the latter point. Learning theorists writing about law school fail to ask whether students who are not verbal learners may have difficulty practicing law. Instead, they advocate more diverse teaching techniques to reach those students. Whether that is a sound strategy is debatable.

Not surprisingly, students who lack certain kinds of learning ability end up in the bottom half of the class. Implicit in the literature is that teaching and testing should change to give students without, say, verbal intelligence a better chance of academic success. That makes sense only if I am wrong in my description of what it takes to excel in the practice of law: visual learners may be better architects than lawyers but almost certainly verbal learners are better suited to practicing law than are visual learners.

Given that law schools admit students who may be visual or tactile or aural learners, one might argue that law professors must accommodate them. A similar argument has surfaced in literature that emphasizes the generational gap between law professors, sometimes derisively called "talking heads," and their students, raised on visual stimuli. That is, some commentators argue that law professors must use display technology to accommodate students raised on television.

Here, again, the discussion should begin with the essential skills needed to practice law and the way in which information will be available to practicing lawyers. Yes, lawyers can attend lectures and get some material on tape or CD. But the primary medium of communication remains the printed word. The flood of written material has increased as legislatures pile on new laws, courts publish hundreds of new opinions, and agencies promulgate new regulations. Training law students to read and analyze complex material must remain the primary focus of law school, even though some learners may have more difficulty than their peers. . . .

Law schools today are gentler places than they were when John Osborn [the author of the novel *The Paper Chase*] went to Harvard. Unlike Osborn, I am not confident that his daughter will encounter any, or at least many, Professor Kingsfields at Harvard or anywhere else in the legal academy today. Where they still teach, I suspect they are on the defensive, subject to hostile student evaluations, pressure from their deans to lighten up on their students, and criticism from their younger colleagues, who are armed with "evidence" that the Socratic method, at least the Kingsfield variety, is disabling and discriminatory.

If we listen to the current mythology, the Kingsfields of the academy are responsible for their students' incompetence, incivility, anxiety, alcohol abuse, and cynicism. In addition, Kingsfield's brand of verbal questioning is outmoded in light of a new generation of visual learners raised on television and videogames.

Law schools are heading in the wrong direction. Convinced that Kingsfield's methods lead to unfairness and incompetence, numerous law professors have urged a gentler law school environment. Often a gentler atmosphere de-emphasizes the need for thorough class preparation and places students' personal views ahead of understanding the analysis that has moved the courts. Students often mistake the nature of the enterprise: they believe that their views matter, when as practicing lawyers, their views have little relevance to the resolution of legal issues.

Empirically, "gentler" is not necessarily kinder than the methods of Professor Kingsfield. Despite widespread reliance on empirical research, many of the empirical claims do not withstand critical scrutiny. Intuitively, "gentler" may not be kinder. If the goal is comfortable classroom experience, no doubt "gentler" teaching makes sense. But if the goal of a professor is to teach students the skills that they will need to practice law, "gentler" makes little sense. Instead, law professors owe their students a tough intellectual experience; they need to expose them to the pressure of answering hard questions that force them to examine and defend their premises.

Before law schools abandon universally, or water down, the demanding form of the Socratic method, we ought to determine whether the Socratic method is responsible for the parade of ills that its critics claim. We ought to demand far more compelling empirical evidence before we abandon a teaching method that has so many virtues. Further, we ought to explore alternative ways to deal with any negative effects that it may produce. For example, we ought to ask whether more careful psychological screening prior to law school or counseling in law school might help students to adjust. If, instead, we allow students to complete law school without exposure to the demanding form of the Socratic method, we are simply shifting the time when our students come face to face with those demands, in the form of a judge or senior partner or opposing attorney. Surely, our unwillingness to use the demanding Socratic method shifts to others the responsibility of teaching our students.

NOTES & QUESTIONS

1. Professor Charles W. Kingsfield has a solid claim to being the most prominent law professor in American popular culture. He first appeared in *The Paper Chase* (1971), a novel regarding life at the Harvard Law School by John Jay Osborn, Jr. The novel seemed to some a critique of traditional legal education. For a review of the novel and other works of law school fiction, see Arthur D. Austin, *The Waste Land of Law School Fiction,* 1986 Duke Law Journal 495.

2. Twentieth Century Fox acquired the rights to adapt Osborne's novel for the cinema and used the film to showcase young actors Timothy Bottoms and Lindsay Wagner, casting the former as law student James Hart from Minnesota and the latter as his lover. Veteran actor John Houseman played Professor Kingsfield, and, to the surprise of some, became the film's most memorable character. Bottoms and Wagner failed to receive Oscar nominations, but Houseman won the Oscar for Best Supporting Actor. What made Houseman's performance so noteworthy?

3. Pop-cultural works that are successful in one medium are often remade for other media. Novels become films. Films become television series. *The Paper Chase* itself was developed into a television series. It appeared on CBS for one season, and Showtime continued to produce the series for cable for three additional seasons. Few of the actors from the film appeared in the television series, but John Houseman was once again featured as the crusty Professor Kingsfield. What might have been the challenges in converting *The Paper Chase* into a weekly dramatic series on television? For a discussion of the television series, see Walter A. Effross, *Paper Chase*, in *Prime Time*

Law: Fictional Television as Legal Narrative 105-13 (Robert M. Jarvis & Paul R. Joseph, eds., 1998).

4. Other less famous television series have featured law professors and law students. These series include *The Nancy Drew Mysteries* (Ned Nickerson was a law student and assistant to Nancy's father); *The Young Lawyers* (law students defend the accused); and *Moon Over Miami* (a law student becomes a private eye). Sometimes law students appear in television series that do not really emphasize law-related themes. In *Spin City* the character played by Michael J. Fox had a girlfriend who was a law student, and in *How I Met Your Mother* one of the recurring characters is a law student. In the *Cosby Show*, the character of Hilton Lucas, played by Bill Cosby, has a daughter who is a law student and then a lawyer, although she leaves the law to become a chef.

5. While the public probably first imagines a stern, demanding disciplinarian when it pictures a law professor, Hollywood over the years has experimented with other ways to portray the law professor. *See* David Ray Papke, *Crusading Hero, Devoted Teacher, and Sympathetic Failure: The Self-Image of the Law Professor in Hollywood Cinema and in Real Life, Too*, 28 Vermont Law Review 957 (2004).

6. In the next excerpt Professor Jennifer Rosato explores and ultimately rejects the argument that the Socratic method is especially deleterious for women. She suggests ways legal education can be humanized without being feminized.

THE SOCRATIC METHOD AND WOMEN LAW STUDENTS: HUMANIZE, DON'T FEMINIZE
Jennifer Rosato
7 Southern California Review of Law and Women's
Studies 37 (1997)

Complaints have been leveled against the Socratic Method of law teaching for many years. Notwithstanding these complaints, the Socratic Method continues to be the primary pedagogy used by law school teachers. Renewed concerns about the continued use of this teaching method have been raised by recent studies that address its effect on women law students. The results of these studies are overwhelmingly negative: they conclude that the Socratic Method alienates, oppresses, traumatizes and silences women. The study conducted at the University of Pennsylvania Law School (the "Guinier Study") reported that women students perform less well in law school, in large measure because of the teaching methodology employed during their first year. . . .

The studies also have shown that this alienation is exacerbated by the inherent maleness of the law school classroom. The women students complain that they are forced to think in a male-oriented manner: competitively, logically, unemotionally. This type of thinking differs from what has been described as a woman's way of thinking, which includes evincing more concern for the rights of others, and being more sensitive to context. Commenting on the type of analysis required of a law student in the classroom, one author noted that a woman's mind "just does not work that way."

Even more significantly, these studies document how the characteristics of the law school classroom negatively affect women's law school performance. The studies consistently show that women are silenced in the classroom: they volunteer less and ask fewer questions than their male counterparts. They feel isolated and have lost confidence in themselves. A number of women students also report that, even when "playing the game" as effectively as their male counterparts, they feel like they have unwillingly acquired a different (and less desirable) identity. Several women described it as having their voices "stolen." Overall, these studies reflect the women's alienation from the law school experience.

Furthermore, the Guinier study concluded that a significant number of female students do not play the game effectively because they fail to win its coveted prizes with the same frequency as men. The study found that men are three times more likely than women to be in the top ten percent of the first-year class, and that men gain most of the honors in law school such as membership on law reviews and moot court societies. Without extensive follow-up studies, it is unclear whether these results are representative of other law schools or unique to the University of Pennsylvania. The recent Law School Admission Council (LSAC) study, which compared results at ninety law schools, suggests similar disparities in academic performance. Although women performed overall as well as men during the first year, they performed less well than men when matched against the grade distribution, and performed less well than their undergraduate grade point averages would suggest.

Even if women students perform academically as well as their male counterparts, their performance is impaired through silencing, isolation and loss of self-esteem. This disparate impact should concern teachers and students alike. So how should we address this concern effectively? The Guinier Study strongly suggested that the law school classroom should be changed to accommodate women's different learning styles. Such a change would include limiting the use of the Socratic Method and replacing it with more "feminine" teaching methods. Although unintended, this suggestion seems to imply that methods less rigorous than the Socratic Method should be used.

As a legal educator and feminist who regularly uses the Socratic Method, I think that radically changing its use at this time would be a mistake. It would ignore other more important causes of these problems, and would fail to recognize the virtues of this method for all students — even women. Therefore, I urge retention of the Socratic Method as the principal form of pedagogy, particularly in the first year of law school when the foundations of legal analysis are being developed.

One of the primary complaints voiced by the women in these studies is of harassing and inappropriate conduct by certain male professors and fellow students. The professors make sexist jokes or ignore the valuable contributions of women students. More generally, these professors engage in "negative emotional techniques" that have the effect of intimidating women more than men, such as acting aggressively or actively insulting students.

This conduct is unacceptable to men and women students and should cease. But getting rid of the Socratic Method will not necessarily make it happen. Humiliation and harassment are not inherent to the Socratic Method. The true Socratic teacher encourages students to think critically and does not disparage them if they fail to fulfill the teacher's expectations. The true Socratic teacher also assures the students, in one way or another, that they are not expected to "win" the "contest" because it is stacked against them. . . .

The second complaint, that of requiring a woman to think in a male-oriented manner — competitively, logically, and unemotionally — is not so much a complaint about the Socratic Method itself as it is about the adversarial nature of our current adjudicatory system. A number of feminist scholars have made the case for a less male-dominated, less adversarial system of justice, and I agree that this is a long-term goal that we should seek to attain. I also agree that law school teachers have some responsibility for reducing hierarchy in the classroom to the extent necessary to create an atmosphere of openness and to encourage students to present a variety of perspectives.

On the other hand, the primary obligation that I have to my students is to prepare them with the skills and values necessary to enter the practice of law in the 1990s — where jobs are scarce and mentoring is limited. For the most part, I am not preparing my students for jobs in academia and I am not teaching them to be graduate students in the humanities. They have entered law school with the expectation that they would be prepared to become effective practicing lawyers. Therefore, I must assist them in understanding the adversarial system and in playing the role of lawyers within that system. This means that all of my students must learn the fundamentals of legal analysis, which include articulating "neutral" principles of law to decisionmakers who may not agree with them, and determining how these principles apply to problems that clients might present to them. The Socratic Method is an excellent way to help them do that. If we abandon the Socratic Method, it probably will have little impact on the adversarial system as a whole, but will result in students being ill-prepared to work within it because they will not have gained the foundational knowledge they need. Our long-term goal of a less adversarial system should not be achieved at the expense of our students' ability to become competent lawyers. . . .

The third complaint that I hear emanating from the women law students in these studies is a general lack of support in the law school, not just in the law school classroom. The traditional teaching methods would be less threatening to women if they were made to feel as if they belonged in law school. Institutional support for women law students could take various forms: for example, providing women law students with more role models by hiring more women law professors and by placing greater value in the reappointment and tenure process on a professor's contributions to women students; creating and implementing effective sexual harassment policies; providing support (financial and otherwise) for women's groups within the law school and for educational programs that are of particular interest to women students; and making more counselors available that are sensitive to the problems of women law students. None of these changes would require abandonment of the Socratic Method and they would go a long way toward making women feel as though they are an integral part of the institution. . . .

Recognizing the danger of indulging in the gender stereotypes that I eschew, I posit a few reasons why the Socratic Method might affect some women more negatively than men. First, the Socratic Method may discourage women students more easily because the method, by its nature, requires the students to recognize the limits of their knowledge. Although women and men both may feel badly when these limits are revealed publicly, women may be more likely to censor their future participation as a result. Similarly, the requirement of testing out newly formed ideas in front of a hundred peers may be considered a more significant imposition on women students because they may feel more self-conscious "sharing their thoughts" in the classroom discussion, particularly if they are not sure what they are talking about. The inherent competitiveness in attempting to garner the professor's attention may be a game that women students are less willing to play. Finally, women may not be accustomed to the male-oriented thinking required by the Socratic dialogue in the modern law school classroom.

Even if it could be shown that women are more negatively affected by the Socratic Method in these ways or others, it does not mean that the use of the Socratic Method should be circumscribed for their benefit. The Socratic Method provides valuable benefits to women students. It ensures that women students are as comfortable and experienced as men in "thinking like a lawyer." In addition, adapting the law school classroom to fit a woman's learning style (whatever that means) would send the dangerous message that women students cannot withstand the rigors of the Socratic Method or, worse yet, law school in general. . . .

Instead of feminizing the Socratic Method, we should focus on humanizing it to make it an effective teaching method for all law students, not just women. Some male students feel just as anxious about and alienated by the Socratic Method as women. Although I am not the first author to suggest that the Socratic Method be humanized, my suggestions are designed to address directly some of the complaints voiced by women law students in recent studies. Three suggestions can be implemented easily: fostering an ethic of care in the classroom, using the Socratic Method meaningfully, and demystifying the learning process. These are all lessons taken from educational psychology and are used effectively in classrooms outside of the law school.

A. Fostering an Ethic of Care

Fostering an ethic of care in the classroom is necessary to counter the unnecessary competition and alienation that may take place in the law school classroom. This ethic can be fostered by the law school teacher in a variety of ways. Most importantly, the teacher should provide positive reinforcement to students whenever possible. There are various ways to do this during class without digressing from the dialogue. First and foremost, the effective law teacher always should strive to treat students and their ideas with respect. The way in which the teacher poses questions and answers should demonstrate that disagreement about ideas is possible without disrespect for the person. Ideally, modeling that behavior will encourage students to treat each other in a more respectful manner and enable them to engage in critical dialogue with one another.

Specifically, teachers should tell students they have good answers and questions (when they actually do) and refer to their insightful answers and questions in later discussions. Students enjoy having their thoughts recognized by the large group, especially if the teacher is able to credit the student by name.

Students who are struggling with the material or who become nervous when called on also need to be assured that they are valued in the classroom. If the student is initially less than responsive to questions, try to remember to come back to the student later in the discussion: by then the student may have regained composure or focused on the relevant material. The student also may be called into the teacher's office so that the teacher can discuss her approach to class participation and can encourage the student to become more involved in class discussion.

In addition, cooperation among students should be encouraged in the Socratic dialogue by asking them to assist each other with responses — just as they might do in the "real world" of lawyering. When a student has exhausted his ability to participate in the inquiry, or even when alternative views are sought, other students may be asked to assist as "colleagues" or "co-counsel." It is difficult to alleviate the inherently competitive aspects of the dialogue, so efforts to enhance cooperation should be made wherever possible.

B. Using the Socratic Method Meaningfully

Sometimes it seems that law teachers use the Socratic Method because it is the teaching method they are most comfortable with or — worse yet — because it is the only method that they know. As with any teaching method, this one should be used to accomplish educational objectives carefully developed by the teacher. I have made the case for the continued use of the Socratic Method, but I do not advocate its exclusive use. If the teacher cannot articulate why the Socratic Method is being used, it may not be the appropriate pedagogy or the teacher's educational objectives may not be sufficiently defined. The teacher then should consider using other teaching methods such as lecture, problems, role plays, games, or a less structured discussion. Because many fundamental analytical skills are learned during the first year of law school, the Socratic Method probably should be used less frequently in the second and third years of law school. However, it should not be abandoned for other techniques that seem less rigorous and appear the easiest way to contend with the apathy and boredom upper-class students often possess.

C. Demystifying the Learning Process

There are a number of legitimate reasons why a teacher utilizing the Socratic Method might choose to withhold the answers to the questions posed in class. The teacher, like Socrates, may not know the answer. Or perhaps the educational objective is for the students to learn how to derive the answer for themselves, with the teacher providing feedback on the student's proficiency. Once the inquiry is completed, however, the teacher should feel free to discuss the objectives of the questioning with the students and how the objectives were (or were not) achieved during the dialogue. For example, tell the students why you asked particular questions and explain what types of answers you sought and why. As law teachers, we seem to think that debriefing would expose us as impostors, like the Wizard of Oz!

Debriefing has been used effectively in other educational contexts. It can be used in the law school classroom after an exercise or a dialogue without sacrificing the rigors of the Socratic Method. If debriefing is not appropriate or time does not permit it, a teacher can debrief individually with student participants after class to talk to them about the classroom dialogue that the student just experienced. I have talked to numerous students in my office about my goals for our dialogue, and have provided them with supportive and critical comments about their individual participation.

At a minimum, debriefing benefits students by reducing anxiety and isolation. Maybe this tool will help students learn to understand that the Socratic Method does not exist simply to humiliate them unnecessarily. Eventually, students may understand that there is a method to the teacher's madness. It actually may be the way students learn best, regardless of gender. . . .

NOTES & QUESTIONS

1. Do you agree with Professor Rosato that criticisms of the Socratic method should not be understood as a woman's issue? Does a female law student such as Elle Woods in *Legally Blonde* experience the Socratic method differently than a male law student such as James Hart in *The Paper Chase*? What, generally, are the relationships of gender and Socratic teaching?

2. A professor who rejects the distancing inherent in the Socratic method might encounter different kinds of problems. In *Rounders,* Mike McDermott develops a close relationship with his professor, Abe Petrovsky — so close, in fact, that the good professor offers to loan him some money. Is this a good idea?

3. Instead of taking the loan, McDermott returns to gambling, his former life and what he knows best — to raise the cash that he and his friend need to get out of trouble. Money is a dominant theme in many law school films. It is a driving force for many of the characters in the films suggested for this chapter. The desire for it pushes them to study law. The lack of it forces them to do things they would not otherwise do in order to go to or stay in school. Once again, law and money seem to be intertwined. Consider that in the real world, whether a client can pay for an attorney may well determine whether the attorney will take the case. How realistic therefore is the constant link between law school and money in these films? Or do most movies about people in school necessarily discuss financing?

C. THE NONTRADITIONAL LAW STUDENT: FEMALES, MINORITIES, GAYS, AND OTHERWISE DISADVANTAGED

Law schools were at one time filled exclusively (or almost exclusively) with students who were male, white, and (usually) well-to-do. This demographic has changed dramatically in the past 30 years, but certain kinds of students still face extra hurdles in law school. Thus, this part of the chapter examines the particular pressures faced by law students who are women, members of minority groups, or forced to cope with financial problems. Of course, in *Legally Blonde* the most prominent of the law students is one who has all the money in the world; still, Elle Woods encounters other problems as a woman, proving that money does not buy law school happiness. Use the featured films for this chapter to reflect on how law schools may fail to help some students clear the special hurdles in their lives.

"WE DON'T WANT ADVANTAGES": THE WOMAN LAWYER HERO AND HER QUEST FOR POWER IN POPULAR CULTURE
Christine Alice Corcos
53 Syracuse Law Review 1125 (2003)

Legally Blonde presents us with a comic view of the law but makes some important points about the nature of success and the nature of integrity. Elle Woods, a pretty, popular "Valley girl," a more grown up Cher, the protagonist of *Clueless*, is expecting a marriage proposal from her longtime boyfriend Warner, a wealthy East Coast preppy with political ambitions. But Warner tells her that his future does not include her. He needs to marry "Jacqueline Kennedy, not Marilyn Monroe." Elle is crushed. Her initial reaction is to try to compete with the woman he is likely to meet in law school. Only later does she begin to see herself as a real law student, and eventually as a real lawyer. At the beginning of the film, she sees herself not as the heroine of her own life, but as Snow White, or at least Cinderella. At the end, no fairy tale character corresponds to her new persona.

Elle decides to apply to Harvard Law School to maintain contact with Warner. As she tells the career services officer, she has no "back up school." "I'm going to Harvard," she says brightly. The counselor points out that she has a 4.0, but her major in fashion merchandising is not exactly the traditional pre-law curriculum. Elle, like Amanda Bonner and Kathryn Murphy, decides to re-write the rules of the game by emphasizing the transferable skills that her major and her sorority experience have given her. Her application video, professionally prepared, is a model of persuasion. The Harvard Law School admissions committee members are awed (though it must be admitted, they all seem to be men. Still, we must give Elle credit. She knows how to talk to men).

Elle's arrival at Harvard indicates the extent to which she is not willing to give up what makes her an individual. She brings along her Chihuahua, her wardrobe, and her "Valley girl" approach to life, finding solace in getting her hair and nails done. She refuses to compromise by adopting the feminist, anti-male stance of some of the other women students, nor does she abandon her mode of dress, even when faced with Warner's fiancee, a woman who dresses in tweeds, wears her hair in a Hillary Clinton-like page boy [style] and makes her disdain for Elle very clear.

Elle's first few weeks at Harvard are rocky. She shows up unprepared for her first class, is verbally skewered by the female professor, and leaves in embarrassment and anger, planning to quit. Then she takes up the challenge, takes the advice of a young man she meets on campus, whom she mistakes for another student, but who is actually Emmett, a practicing attorney assisting her criminal law professor. She begins to compete successfully with Warner and more particularly with his fiancée Vivian.

Elle makes friends with a local manicurist, who is depressed because her abusive ex-lover has kept her beloved dog Rufus. Elle confronts the man, spouting legalese and figuratively pushing him aside in order to take possession of Rufus. It is her first legal success. She obtains a coveted internship with her criminal law professor and begins work on a murder case. Her particularized knowledge of the client's history and profession, based on her "Valley girl" background, allows her to bond with the client in a way that escapes the other members of the defense team. At the same time, she faces a crisis of conscience when she discovers that the professor who offered her the internship is interested only in an affair with her. She decides to resign her internship, but the female professor who had humiliated her on her first day, and who has changed her mind about Elle's abilities, dissuades her by pointing out that if Elle resigns, she is allowing the man to set both the agenda and the tone of her future career. At the same time, the client's trust in Elle allows her (unbelievably) to take over the lead in the defense case. The client fires the evil male professor, and hires Elle instead (under Emmett's supervision). Elle wins the case, based again on her particularized knowledge of fashion and of the kinds of people who are likely to understand and appreciate fashion and design. She demonstrates that the primary witness against the client is lying about his affair with her, and that the victim's daughter is the real culprit. The daughter has testified that she did not hear the gunshot that killed the victim because she was in the shower washing her hair. As Elle points out, this is unlikely because the girl has just gotten an expensive permanent. No one with a new permanent washes her hair for at least a day; it deactivates the chemicals that curl the hair. Elle's triumph is complete when she graduates first in the class, giving a suitably "Valley girl" address. She and Vivian become best friends. Vivian abandons Warner, who finds himself without a job offer, without a girlfriend, and without honors. Emmett decides to propose to Elle. While *Legally Blonde* is a fantasy, it presents us with the image of a woman who refuses to abandon her interests, her beliefs, her friends, or her dreams, especially the dream she has recently acquired. She imagines herself as a lawyer, then becomes a lawyer. Unlike Alex Owens, the protagonist of *Flashdance*, she actually does the work necessary to achieve her goals. Yet she maintains her interest in makeup, hair styles, clothes, and good design. She calls a sexual harasser by his name, but finds the courage (aided by the female professor who terrorized her in her first year) to continue toward her goal. She finds ways to express her personality within the confines of the law school while still producing the kind of work that legal academia expects. She integrates all of these into the practice of law. Within the limits of this cinematic fantasy, Elle is heroic.

NOTES & QUESTIONS

1. To what extent do Elle Woods' problems in law school derive from the fact she is a woman? What messages does *Legally Blonde* send about female law students and their ability to compete in a male-dominated world?

2. Is Elle Woods' main problem not her gender but rather her feminine style of womanhood? Does *Legally Blonde* suggest there are right and wrong ways to be a woman?

3. Compare Elle Woods with other female law students in the films suggested for this chapter, e.g., Sarah Walker in *Soul Man,* who is a single parent, a member of a minority group, and a young woman who has to work during her first year of law school because someone else has deprived her of the scholarship she should have had. Susan Walsh in *The Socratic Method* is a fairly typical contemporary example of the female law student — she goes straight from college to law school. Her father is a successful lawyer, her fiancé is an attorney at her father's law firm, and, as her law school friends point out, she does not have to worry about getting a job offer. One is waiting for her once she passes the bar.

4. Attractive, feminine women may encounter difficulties in legal roles other than that of the law student. Contemplate the obstacles faced by the paralegal Erin Brockovich (played by Julia Roberts) in the film *Erin Brockovich* (2000).

5. In the film *Soul Man,* Mark Watson "passes" as a black man, even though he knows nothing about African Americans or African American culture (as he demonstrates by showing up at a Black Law Students Association study meeting dressed as a Black Panther). "Passing is a deception that enables a person to adopt certain roles or identities from which he would be barred by prevailing social standards in the absence of his misleading conduct. The classic racial passer in the United States has been the 'white Negro': the individual whose physical appearance allows him to present himself as 'white' but whose 'black' lineage (typically only a very partial black lineage) makes him a Negro according to dominant racial rules. A passer is distinguishable from the person who is merely mistaken — the person who, having been told that he is white, thinks of himself as white, and holds himself out to be white (though he and everyone else in the locale would deem him to be 'black' were the facts of his ancestry known)." Randall Kennedy, *Racial Passing,* 62 Ohio State Law Journal 1145, 1145 (2001). Mark's conduct is certainly misleading and the disciplinary committee finds it fraudulent. Is it more fraudulent than it would have been if he had not been a law student? Another film that explores racial/ethnic passing is *The Human Stain* (2003), with Anthony Hopkins and Nicole Kidman, based on a novel by Philip Roth.

6. To what extent are gay and lesbian students "othered" by the law school experience? Sketch the screenplay of a Hollywood film about a gay or lesbian student. Could such a film attract a mass audience?

D.   LAW STUDENTS AND ETHICS

As part of their professional education most law students learn to adhere to a code of responsibility known as an "honor code" or a "code of ethics" promulgated by their law school. The code sets out the types of conduct deemed inappropriate for law students. A student reported to the administrative officer responsible for enforcing the code may find herself before a disciplinary board convened for the purpose of deciding whether she should be reprimanded privately or publicly, suspended for a time from attending school, or expelled. A sanction may be recorded on the student's transcript; if sufficiently grave, it may mean that the student might be prevented from taking the bar exam and ultimately from ever practicing law.

The following excerpt provides the most important provisions in one law school's code for its students.

CODE OF STUDENT PROFESSIONAL RESPONSIBILITY
Louisiana State University Law Center
2006

Introduction

Law School is the first step toward becoming a member of the legal profession. Members of the legal profession are subject to the highest standards of professional conduct. The Law Center, therefore, expects its students to adhere to high standards of conduct during their legal education and to avoid even the appearance of impropriety during that process.

Just as lawyer behavior reflects on the bar and the courts even when they are not in Court, student behavior can reflect on the Law Center away from the physical facility. When students represent the Law Center, or when their behavior might closely affect the Law Center or its relationships with other institutions in Louisiana or abroad, students are expected to abide by the professional obligations of the Code of Student Professional Responsibility. It is the obligation of every student to report to the Office of the Vice Chancellor or to a member of the Ethics Committee of the Student Bar Association any violation of this Code of Student Professional Responsibility. Students are expected to live up to the standards set forth in this Code and to assist in its enforcement.

The Code

Lying, cheating, plagiarism, theft, and other forms of student misconduct are prohibited.

1. Lying includes, but is not limited to, the following:

   a. Knowingly furnishing false or misleading information to the administrators, faculty, or other personnel of the Law Center.

   b. Forging, altering, or misusing Law Center documents, records, or identification cards.

   c. Knowingly furnishing false information in any proceedings undertaken pursuant to this Code.

   d. Failing to acknowledge one's presence in class when present and requested by the instructor to recite materials or otherwise participate in class.

   e. Falsifying information on a class roll sheet in any manner, such as by signing or initialing for another student who is not present, by procuring another student to sign or initial for a student not present, or by signing or initialing a roll sheet indicating that the student was present when the student was not actually present in the classroom or was so late that this student missed a substantial portion of the class.

2. Cheating includes, but is not limited to, the following:

   a. Copying from or looking upon another student's examination paper during an examination with intent to give or obtain information relevant to the examination.

   b. Using material during an examination not authorized by the person administering the examination.

   c. Collaborating during an examination with any other person by giving or receiving information without authority.

   d. Stealing, bribing, otherwise obtaining, selling, giving away, or bribing another person to obtain all or part of an unadministered examination or information about an unadminstered examination.

   e. Substituting for another student, or permitting any other person to substitute for oneself, to take an examination.

   f. Submitting as one's own, in fulfillment of academic requirements, a report, term paper, memorandum, brief, or any other written work prepared totally or in part by another person.

   g. Taking time beyond that allowed other students for the completion of an examination, without the expressed permission of the person administering the examination.

   h. Selling, giving, or otherwise supplying to another student for submission in fulfilling academic requirements any report, term paper, memorandum, brief, or any other written work.

   i. Consulting any attorney regarding the specifics of any written or oral presentation, unless authorized by the instructor.

3. Plagiarism is the unacknowledged incorporation of another person's work in one's own work submitted for credit or publication (such material need not be copyrighted).

4. Theft includes, but is not limited to, the following:

   a. The taking or unauthorized use of Law Center property, including any materials from the Law Library.

   b. The taking or unauthorized use of the funds of the Law Center of any student organization.

   c. The taking or unauthorized use of any property of other students while on campus, or of material related to the Law Center while off campus.

5. Student misconduct includes, but is not limited to, the following:

   a. Attempting to commit, or being an accessory to the commission of any of the foregoing offenses.

   b. Committing any misdemeanor on the premises of the Law Center, or on the premises of student residences associated with the Law Center or its programs, or at an official Law Center function, or committing any felony.

   c. Knowingly interfering with any proceedings undertaken pursuant to this Code, including threats directed to students, faculty, or other persons initiating or participating in such proceedings.

   d. Repeatedly attending class without adequately preparing the material assigned by the instructor, unless special arrangements are made with the instructor prior to class.

   e. Refusing to participate in class discussion when requested to do so by the instructor.

   f. Using any other person's work or assistance in the preparation of work to be submitted for credit, unless authorized by the instructor.

   g. Committing any act of vandalism or destruction with respect to Law Center property, the property of a Law Center partner institution, the property of student residences associated with the Law Center or its programs, or the property where a Law Center function is being held.

   h. Intentionally disrupting a class.

   i. Violating any rules established to govern student use of conduct in the Law Library.

   j. Talking with another student during an examination with intent to give or obtain information relevant to the examination.

   k. Utilizing materials submitted in fulfillment of the requirements of a course to fulfill the requirements of another course or courses without first obtaining consent of all faculty members affected.

Rules of Procedure for Disposition of Complaints

1. Any person having knowledge of a violation of this Code shall report the incident to the Vice Chancellor of the Law Center designated by the Chancellor to receive such reports, or to a member of the Ethics Committee of the Student Bar Association. If a report is made to a member of the Ethics Committee, that member shall promptly report the matter to the designated Vice Chancellor.

2. For Law Center programs and activities away from the physical facility, egregious conduct may be the grounds for expelling a student from the program or activity, in the discretion of the Program Director or Law Center representative.

3. The Vice Chancellor shall investigate the complaint. He may appoint a member of the faculty and of the Ethics Committee of the Student Bar Association to assist him. The Vice Chancellor shall determine whether there are reasonable grounds to initiate a proceeding to determine the merits of the complaint. If reasonable grounds are found to exist, the Vice Chancellor shall appoint a committee to determine the merits of the complaint.

4. The committee shall consist of five members: three members from the faculty and two law student members to be appointed by the Chairman of the Student Ethics Committee and the President of the Student Bar Association.

5. The Vice Chancellor shall set forth in writing the grounds of the complaint against the student and shall furnish a copy of the written complaint to the chairman of the committee.

6. The chairman shall designate the time and place for a hearing to determine the merits of the complaint.

7. The Chairman shall provide the student with a copy of the written complaint. The chairman shall prepare a notice containing the following information: (a) the time and place of the hearing; and (b) the date for furnishing the information described in the paragraphs 7, 8, and 9. The notice shall be furnished to the student and to the Vice Chancellor.

8. The Vice Chancellor and the student shall furnish to each other and to the chairman (a) a list of the names and addresses of witnesses whose testimony should be heard by the committee; and (b) a brief statement describing the substance of the testimony of each witness.

9. The Vice Chancellor and the student shall furnish to each other and to the chairman any documentary evidence which should be considered at the hearing.

10. The Vice Chancellor and the student shall furnish to each other and to the chairman the name of any person designated to assist him or her during the hearing.

11. The following may be present at the hearing: members of the committee, the student, the Vice Chancellor, persons designated to assist during the hearing, the witness under examination, and any person authorized by the committee to record the proceedings.

12. At the request of the student, the committee may permit such other persons as the committee deems appropriate to be present during the hearing.

13. All witnesses whose names have been submitted and who are available will be asked to testify unless the committee determines that their testimony would not assist in finding relevant facts or in making a recommendation as to the proper disposition of the case. The committee may also ask witnesses to testify whose names have not been submitted by the Vice Chancellor or the student. When practicable, notice of such witnesses shall be given to the student. The chairman shall notify all witnesses of the time and place of the hearing.

14. The chairman shall determine whether there are any facts which may be agreed upon and the order in which the witnesses shall be heard.

15. Prior to hearing the testimony of a witness, the chairman shall ask the witness whether he or she will truthfully respond to all questions.

16. The chairman will first examine the witness. The members of the committee will next examine the witness. The chairman may then permit the Vice Chancellor (or the person designated to assist him) and the student (or the person designated to assist him) to examine the witness. The order of examination may be varied by the chairman in order to effectively present the testimony of the witness.

17. The committee may receive any documentary evidence which the committee deems helpful in fairly performing its duty. The committee may receive affidavits based upon personal knowledge addressing relevant facts upon a finding that the witness cannot conveniently attend the hearing. If the committee feels that hearing the witness's testimony is necessary to achieve a fair result and disposition, the committee may ask the witness to appear to testify or, if the witness is unavailable, take whatever alternative steps it deems appropriate.

18. The committee may consider any reliable evidence which it deems helpful in fairly performing its duty. The chairman shall decide whether particular evidence should be heard and considered. His or her decision may be overruled upon motion of a committee member by a majority of the committee. A second to the motion to overrule is not required.

19. At the close of the hearing, the committee shall allow the student (or person designated to assist him or her) and the Vice Chancellor (or person designated to assist him) the opportunity to make a closing statement.

20. The student or the Vice Chancellor may request that the committee vary its procedures or grant a continuance and, upon a showing of good cause for such, the committee shall grant the request.

21. At the time of the hearing, the committee shall deliberate privately. The committee will, by majority vote, make and deliver to the Chancellor of the Law Center (a) written findings of fact and conclusions concerning the complaint; and (b) written recommendations concerning the proper disposition of the case. Any concurring or dissenting views of a committee member, including the chairman, shall be included at the member's request.

22. If the committee finds that the student committed a violation included in the complaint, the committee may recommend any appropriate sanction or combination of sanctions, including recommending that the student be:

    a. expelled from the Law Center indefinitely;

    b. expelled from the Law Center with a right to apply for readmission no sooner than a fixed date;

    c. suspended from the Law Center for a fixed period;

    d. publicly reprimanded by the Chancellor, with a copy of the public reprimand sent the Louisiana State Bar Association;

    e. denied course credit or assigned a grade of .7 in a course if the violation involved the student's conduct in a course.

23. The Chancellor shall advise the student of the recommendations of the committee and allow him or her a reasonable opportunity to respond in writing before imposing a sanction.

24. Determination of the sanction shall be at the discretion of the Chancellor. In arriving at the sanction, the Chancellor shall consult with the committee. Modification of a sanction shall be done only after consultation with the committee.

25. Upon the imposition of a sanction by the Chancellor, an announcement shall be placed on the bulletin boards of the Law Center to the effect that: "A student has been found guilty of a violation of (name the section) of the Code of Student Professional Responsibility in that he or she committed (name the offense), defined by that section as (quote the applicable section). The student has been (name the sanction)." The student's name shall be withheld unless the Chancellor determines that a public reprimand is in order.

26. The Chancellor, with or without a recommendation of the committee, may communicate the results of the proceedings to witnesses, faculty, or other interested parties if he determines it is in the best interests of the Law Center or the legal profession. . . .

NOTES & QUESTIONS

1. As the excerpt suggests, Louisiana State University Law Center has rules regarding the conduct of law students that are different and more refined than the rules for other students at the same university. This is a common practice. Why might administrators and faculty members think different or additional ethical rules are necessary for law students?

2. Several of the films discussed in this chapter feature conduct that would, if reported, require at minimum a disciplinary hearing. In *The Socratic Method*, Charles Johnson accepts his employer's offer of a "cheat sheet" with the answers to a forthcoming law school exam. What else does he do that would violate a law school's disciplinary code? What does he do that violates the law and would, if reported, disqualify him as a candidate for the bar? Should his friends report him? Does the fact that they do not report him mean they should be reported to the appropriate law school disciplinary board? Why or why not? Are they fit candidates to practice law? Note that Johnson eventually ends up as a judge, and he hears the case against Kenneth Stafford. Should he have recused himself? What about the accusation Susan Walsh levels at Kenneth Stafford that he razored out an article put on reserve in the law library? The students take matters into their own hands after the library clerk reveals who had the book checked out last, but what do you think they should have done once they discovered the pages they needed to read were missing? Law library staffs have procedures for dealing with missing reserve items. Ask your own law library public services staff what it will do for you if you find yourself in such a predicament, and what sanctions it has in place for dealing with offenders.

3. In *Soul Man*, Mark Watson accepts a scholarship under false pretenses. Some people might think he gets off extremely lightly — he agrees to pay the money to the person to whom the money should have been paid in the first place, and who, it appears by the end of the film, is likely to turn out to be Mrs. Watson. However, he does learn some important lessons about what it means to be judged on appearances alone. Everyone judges him — blacks and whites alike. Do you think Mark Watson's fraud disqualifies him to be an attorney? If you had been on the panel that heard the complaint against him, how would you have decided his case? Why?

4. James Hart in *The Paper Chase* and Elle Woods in *Legally Blonde* make the mistake of attending their first law school classes without completing the assigned reading first. Could they be disciplined under the Louisiana State University Law Center's Code of Student Professional Responsibility? Later in *The Paper Chase*, Hart defiantly tells Professor Kingsfield that he will participate in class only when he wishes. Is this a violation of 5.c of the Code of Student Professional Responsibility? Should it be?

5. The amount of alcohol consumed in law school films is truly stupendous. In *The Socratic Method,* one of the law students (James Rodgers) seems to live at a bar named the "Frolic and Detour," yet he graduates at the top of his class, gets a great job offer, and eventually purchases the bar. Drinking goes merrily along in *The Paper Chase* and *Soul Man*. To what extent might excessive drinking and drunken conduct subject one to law school disciplinary proceedings?

Should law students be free to drink as much as they wish as long as they are not in their law school buildings or in facilities associated with their law schools?

6. While very little has been written about alcoholism as a disability in law school, a 1994 Association of American Law Schools report found that more than 30 percent of law students admitted to abusing alcohol while in school. *See Report of the AALS Special Committee on Problems of Substance Abuse in the Law Schools*, 44 Journal of Legal Education 35 (1994). At a day-long meeting in New York in 2003, several commentators told the assembled law school administrators that things had not really improved. *See* Thomas Adcock, *Despite '93 Report, Substance Abuse Persists in Law Schools,* New York Law Journal, June 27, 2003, at 16.

7. Gambling is a major problem in *Rounders*: Mike McDermott, played by Matt Damon, is a recovering gambler who attends law school. Poker is a pastime for the students in *The Socratic Method*, and Susan Walsh turns out to be quite a player, to the extent that Terry King worries that she will win all his scholarship money. While not much has been written about gambling addictions and law students, the lawyer with a gambling addiction is a recognized danger to his or her client. *See* Carol P. Walhauser, *Lawyers Helping Lawyers: Part of the Solution: Identifying the Addiction: Part I*, 28 Montana Lawyer 23 (January 2003) and Paul R. Ashe, *Lawyers Helping Lawyers: Part of the Solution: Attorneys and the Addiction of Gambling,* 28 Montana Lawyer 30 (February 2003).

Chapter 3

LAWYERS AND LEGAL ETHICS

A. FILMOGRAPHY

The Devil's Advocate (1997)

Jagged Edge (1985)

Liar Liar (1997)

Two Weeks Notice (2003)

The Young Philadelphians (1959)

B. IMAGES OF LAWYERS: GOOD OR EVIL?

Virtually all treatments of law in popular culture present their images of the law through the actions of people involved in the legal system, including lawyers, clients, witnesses, judges, jurors, police officers, legislators, government officials, and ordinary citizens. Most of the chapters of this book will deal with depictions of lawyers in popular culture in both general and specialized practices as "embodiments" of the different ways law can be seen and experienced. Although many depictions of the law are offered through the common genres of mysteries, crimes, and thrillers that most often involve criminal law enforcement, detection, and "bad men" in the Holmesian sense, most people who decide to come to law school have come with an image of "lawyer" imprinted on them by some exposure to a lawyer (usually, unrepresentatively, a trial lawyer) from movies, television, literature or popular culture (except for that minority of law students who have family members who are lawyers). Depending on the era in which you came of age, your image of lawyers might vary from a crusading justice-seeking do-gooder, to involuntary hero (Atticus Finch in *To Kill a Mockingbird*), to greedy profit-maximizer, to sleazy divorce lawyer (Arnie Becker in *L.A. Law*), to crafty and brilliant defense lawyers (*Perry Mason*, the *Defenders,* or the lawyers of *The Practice*), to victimized prosecutor (Rusty Sabitch in *Presumed Innocent*), or flighty Gen-X lawyer (*Ally McBeal).* Though the images of criminal trial lawyers (as prosecutors and defense attorneys) abound, in fact most lawyers are civil lawyers, and most today do not set foot in the courtroom.

Over the last five decades depictions of lawyers from the "Golden Age" of the 1950s of brilliant trial lawyers, seeking truth and justice, have evolved into more complex characters who sometimes violate ethical rules (the lawyers who sleep with their clients or jurors in *Jagged Edge* (1985) or *Suspect* (1987); or a

69

lawyer like Frank Galvin in *The Verdict* (1982), who rejects a settlement offer without discussing it with a client). Lawyers on screen have also diversified almost, but not quite as much, as the legal profession itself. *See* American Bar Foundation, *The Lawyer Statistical Report: The Legal Profession in 2000* (2000). For example, while in 1951 only 3% of lawyers were women, in 2000 27% of the bar was female, with 47% of the law student population being female. *But see* Timothy O'Brian, *Up the Down Staircase: Why Do So Few Women Reach the Top of Big Law Firms?* N.Y. Times, 19 March 2006, 3-1 (Sunday Business) (reporting that partnership rates in major law firms for women still do not match their demographic representation in the profession). Demographic minority representation in the bar has also grown, but not at the same rate. *See* Richard Abel, *American Lawyers* (1989); David Wilkins, *From "Separate is Inherently Unequal" to "Diversity is Good for Business": The Rise of Market Based Diversity Arguments and the Fate of the Black Corporate Bar*, 117 Harvard Law Review 1548 (2004). In 2000 there were 40,000 black lawyers, a twenty-fold increase from 1960. *See* David Wilkins, *A Systematic Response to Systemic Disadvantage,* 57 Stanford Law Review 1915 (2004–05); *see also* Alex M. Johnson, Jr., *The Underepresentation of Minorities in the Legal Profession: A Critical Race Theorist Perspective*, 95 Michigan Law Review 1005 (1997); Clay Smith, Jr. *Emancipation: The Making of the Black Lawyer* (1993); David Wilkins, *Two Paths to the Mountaintop: The Role of Legal Education in Shaping Values of Black Corporate Lawyers,* 45 Stanford Law Review 1981 (1993). See discussions of different kinds of lawyers in modern television depictions in Christine Alice Corcos, *Women Lawyers*, and Michael Epstein, *Young Lawyers*, both appearing in *Prime Time Law: Fictional Television as Legal Narrative* (Robert M. Jarvis & Paul R. Joseph, eds. 1998).

Images of lawyers in popular culture have veered dramatically over the years from extremes of lawyers as heroes to lawyers as villains, with debates among legal and film scholars about whether lawyers are more likely to be considered forces for social good or evil. *See, e.g.*, Michael Asimow, *Embodiment of Evil: Law Firms in the Movies*, 48 UCLA Law Review 1339 (2001); Michael Asimow, *Bad Lawyers in the Movies,* 24 Nova Law Review 531 (2000); Michael Asimow, *When Lawyers Were Heroes,* 30 University of San Francisco Law Review 1131 (1996); Paul Bergman, *The Movie Lawyers' Guide to Redemptive Legal Practice,* 48 UCLA Law Review 1393 (2001); Anthony Chase, *Lawyers and Popular Culture: a Review of Mass Media Portrayals of American Attorneys,* 1986 American Bar Foundation Research Journal 281; Steve Greenfield & Guy Osborn, *The Double Meaning of Law: Does it Matter if Film Lawyers are Unethical?*, in *Law and Popular Culture* (Michael Freeman, ed. 2005); Carrie Menkel-Meadow, *The Sense and Sensibilities of Lawyers: Lawyering in Literature, Narratives, Film and Television, and Ethical Choices Regarding Career and Craft,* 31 McGeorge Law Review 1 (1999); Marvin Mindes & Alan C. Acock, *Trickster, Hero, Helper: A Report on the Lawyer Image,* 1982 American Bar Foundation Research Journal 177; Robert C. Post, *On the Popular Image of the Lawyer: Reflections in a Dark Glass,* 75 California Law Review 379 (1987). Lawyers, of course, have been subject to ridicule and humor from time immemorial, with a compendium of lawyer jokes now collected in Marc Galanter, *Lowering the Bar: Legal Jokes and Legal Culture* (2005). Yet at the same time that lawyers consistently do poorly on polls of sociologists studying who is to be trusted in our society, it is also true that a majority of parents would love to see their children become lawyers. *See* Harris Poll, Feb. 3, 1999. And while you may have heard or read that famous Shakespearean line, "First thing we do, let's kill all the lawyers" (from *Henry VI, Part II, Act 4, Scene 2*), the reason the lawyers were to be killed was because they were considered guardians of justice and freedom (or at least the controllers of tyrants, through the rule of law), not evil, in that important work of literature.

This chapter will explore some of the many depictions of lawyers as forces for good or evil (or more recently, as complicated human beings who may have mixed motives and complex and morally mixed matters to work on). We will consider how we are to judge lawyers — based on their professional roles, individual acts, or "character." Real lawyers are governed by formal rules of professional conduct (the ABA Model Rules of Professional Conduct, which become law when they are formally approved by a state legislature or state Supreme Court, depending on your state), and as a law student, you are now required to learn these rules in Professional Responsibility. These rules are intended to guide some of the choices lawyers make in doing their work, but often the rules may be ambiguous or even contradictory. Lawyers, like all human beings, have to decide how to act, based on their own personal (and professional) moral codes.

This chapter will ask you to think about how lawyers make choices in their professional and personal lives, how they learn from their experiences, and how they form and create their own character(s) from the decisions and choices they make. By watching pop cultural depictions of lawyer activity, we can see how professional work is conducted, make relatively costless moral judgments (by watching others), and learn to construct our own conceptions and values of what it means to be a good lawyer. Philosopher Martha Nussbaum, among others, has argued that by studying the moral lives of fictional characters we can enrich our own understandings of moral and legal activity. Martha Nussbaum, *Poetic Justice: The Literary Imagination and Public Life* (1995). *See also* Robert Coles, *The Call of Stories: Teaching and the Moral Imagination* (1989); Richard Weisberg, *The Failure of the Word: The Protagonist as Lawyer in Modern Fiction* (1984); John Gardner, *On Moral Fiction* (1978); Lionel Trilling, *Manners, Morals, and the Novel* in *The Liberal Imagination* (1976).

As the following excerpts suggest, you might profitably consider the source of your first image of lawyers.

CAN THEY DO THAT? LEGAL ETHICS IN POPULAR CULTURE: OF CHARACTER AND ACTS
Carrie Menkel-Meadow
48 UCLA Law Review 1305 (2001)

Consider these two thought experiments: First, what was your first image of a lawyer and where did it come from? Was the lawyer a "good" lawyer? A "good" person? Did the lawyer do good deeds or commit bad acts? Did your first image of a lawyer come from real life or from a movie, a television show, a popular novel, or literature?

Second, what popular, cinematic, or literary image would you select as being "exemplary" of the good lawyer? Do you imagine a person of good character or one who does good deeds? Who seeks justice, possibly at great personal or professional risk to self, or who is "good or helpful" to other people, including clients and third parties? Is a "good" lawyer a person who performs his or her craft well or a person who is fair, kind, and just? Do you see a courtroom trial advocate, ready with razor sharp questions and pithy — but moving — closing arguments? Do you see a skillful draftsperson or law office counselor advising people to do the right thing or create new and interesting entities?

Many critics of lawyers in popular culture have argued about whether recent images of lawyers in movies, popular novels, legal thrillers, and even more complex "high" literature reveal a declining ethicality, or faith and trust in lawyers. Some separate the heroes from the villains, and see a decline in the heroism of lawyers. Others see a more complicated alternation of good and bad images of lawyers in American history as different periods of American cultural representations reflect the vagaries of historical appreciation or deprecation of lawyers, beginning with the period immediately after the American Revolution, and — most agree — culminating in the zenith or "golden age" of lawyer appreciation in the films of the late 1950s and early 1960s. From a period of virtual or actual canonization of such figures as Atticus Finch, Sir Thomas More, and television's *The Defenders*, we are now in a period that not only creates its own more morally and ethically ambiguous lawyers, but also seems to be engaged in some revisionist re-readings of even such heroes as Atticus Finch. With the vast increase in novels, mysteries, thrillers, movies, and television shows about lawyers, images of lawyers — good, bad, indifferent, complicated, and nuanced — are proliferating. These recent depictions present a greater variety of lawyer images to choose from, which, while perhaps still not "representative" (in a socially scientific way) of all lawyers, present a more accurate choice of complex lawyer images to analyze than ever before. . . .

[T]he greater variety of genres and increasing numbers of lawyers in popular literature and culture present an excellent opportunity for students of legal ethics to examine the work of lawyers in both their "macro" (choice of career, choice of client, role in legal institutions) and "micro" (choice of particular actions and behaviors) contexts, and allow us to examine the many different criteria we might apply to evaluate whether a lawyer is a good or bad actor, or a good or bad person. It is also interesting to ask why lawyers have so frequently been depicted as the repositories of professional morality, and used in critiques of morality in American culture, compared to other professionals with ethical dilemmas such as doctors, architects, police officers, and business managers, not to mention other kinds of workers (such as British butlers or French executioners), and ordinary human beings.

The variations of genre allow different aspects of the lawyer's persona to be developed. Long novels and television series allow "character" to be more fully developed. Movies and superficial thrillers or mysteries tend to focus more on acts and discrete plot turns rather than on character. Thus, the multiplicity of ways in which lawyers are represented allow us to create a sociologist's "four-fold table." We can examine and map examples of expressions of legal ethics or morality demonstrated in popular culture, considering lawyers' characters and acts in positive and negative columns, representing both professional and personal choices. I supply some examples in the following chart:

Lawyer's:	+	−
Act – Professional	Taking Unpopular Client	Lying, Deception
Act – Personal	Caring for Someone	Lying, Cruelty, Adultery
Character – Professional	Mentoring, Integrity	Manipulation, Greed
Character – Personal	Kindness, Commitment	Selfishness, Deceit

Longer treatments of lawyers' actions in serialized television shows and longer novels allow more panoramic, less "snapshotted" pictures of lawyers to be painted than in movies or short stories, which, in turn, can be used effectively to highlight particular decisions. Depictions of lawyers' actions in novels, movies, and television shows allow us to view (from multiple "sight-lines") the beginning of the action (what led up to a particular choice point), the action itself, and the consequences of such actions. Thus we are provided multiple ways of seeing (backward, sideways, and forward) the consequences of a lawyer's action, which are often missing from an appellate case as read in the conventional professional responsibility class. . . .

BAD LAWYERS IN THE MOVIES
Michael Asimow
24 Nova Law Review 531 (2000)

I. Introduction

Seen any lawyer films recently? Chances are, most of the lawyers in those films were bad. They were unpleasant or unhappy human beings you wouldn't want as friends. And they were bad professionals you wouldn't admire or want as your lawyer. In the majority of films involving law, lawyers, and the legal system since the 1970s, the lawyer characters and their law firms were pretty bad. This generalization holds whether the film fits the standard lawyer/courtroom genre, whether it involves legal issues, whether the film is a comedy (black or otherwise) or a drama, or whether it falls into other genres such as romances, mystery stories, or thrillers that just happen to have lawyer roles. . . .

This article examines two phenomena. First, it documents the precipitous drop in the public's perception of the character, prestige, and ethics of lawyers that began during the 1980s and continues to the present. Second, it traces the history of lawyer portrayals in film, concentrating on the sharp turn toward the negative during the 1970s and 1980s that continues to the present.

The article asks whether there is any connection between these phenomena. It asserts that one connection is clear and obvious: the trend in filmed portrayals of lawyers accurately reflects public opinion. But the article also speculates that negative filmed images can lead public opinion as well as follow it. My hope is that this article will cause its readers to treat lawyer portrayals in film seriously and critically, both because such portrayals are an important social datum and because they have real world consequences.

II. The Popular Perception of Lawyers

Polling data demonstrates clearly that the popular perception of the character and the ethics of American lawyers, and the prestige of the profession, have plunged precipitously since the 1970s. Granted, the image of lawyers never approached that of pharmacists, the clergy, or algebra teachers. Lawyers will always be distrusted, in part because their assigned task is to play whatever role and manipulate whatever law a client's interest demands. Lawyers tend to represent the rich and powerful; naturally everyone else who can't afford lawyers resents that.

Even more significant, lawyers are doomed to be unloved because criminal practice is their most public function. As lawyers see it, justice requires that an accused person have the benefit of appropriate process, such as the reasonable doubt rule or the privilege against self-incrimination. This perspective is not shared by most members of the public, especially when it comes to criminal law. Most people think that justice means finding the truth regardless of the adversarial system, procedural technicalities, statutory loopholes, police or prosecutorial misconduct, or lawyers' tricks.

The general public will always associate lawyers with some of life's worst moments. We don't fondly recall our divorce or divorces, the probate of our parents' estates, our dispute with the IRS, our credit problems or bankruptcy, or our brush with the juvenile court. Dwelling on the time we got sued by somebody who slipped on the sidewalk or we needed an attorney to sue an insurance company doesn't evoke warm and fuzzy memories. Lawyers were present at those events. Probably, we resented the opposing lawyer. While we may have liked and trusted our own lawyer, we resented being involved in a situation where lawyers were needed and we were probably shocked at the size of the bill. In all likelihood, whether we won or lost, we weren't really pleased by the outcome.

Thus, our profession has never been loved, but in years past it was at least respected and sometimes admired. Today lawyers are more despised than they have ever been before. This is something we probably knew already from the prevalence of nasty lawyer jokes or talk shows, or from social and professional interactions with laypersons. The polling data proves that this dismal intuition is all too accurate.

In its introduction to polling data released in 1997, the Harris Poll wrote:

> Recent Harris Polls have found that public attitudes to lawyers and law firms, which were already low, continue to get worse. Lawyers have seen a dramatic decline in their prestige which has fallen faster than that of any other occupation, over the last twenty years. Fewer people have confidence in law firms than in any of the major institutions measured by Harris including the Congress, organized labor, or the federal government. It is not a pretty picture.

> In 1977 over a third of the public (36%) believed that lawyers had very great prestige. Today, twenty years later, that has fallen to 19%. In other words, almost half of the people who accorded lawyers great

prestige then do not do so today. No other occupation has fallen so sharply. . . .

For the last thirty years Harris has been tracking the confidence people have in the leaders of various institutions. In the most recent survey, only 7% of the public said they had a great deal of confidence in the people running law firms. This places law firms at the bottom of the institutions on the list. The 7% figure is not only the lowest number recorded for law firms over thirty years, it is actually the lowest number recorded for any institution over thirty years.

In the early 1990s, the American Bar Association commissioned a public opinion poll from the Peter D. Hart Research Organization. It indicated that overall, respondents gave lawyers a 40% favorability rating, while 34% of respondents gave them an unfavorable rating. This placed lawyers far below other professions, since the favorability rating for teachers was 84%, pharmacists 81%, police officers 79%, doctors 71%, and bankers 56%. Only stockbrokers at 28%, and politicians at 21% were lower.

In 1999, the ABA published results of a follow-up poll from M/A/R/C Research. It revealed that while 30% of respondents were extremely or very confident of the United States justice system, only 14% were extremely or very confident of lawyers. In contrast, 27% had slight or no confidence in the justice system but 42% had little or no confidence in lawyers. Lawyers were soundly beaten by state legislatures, prison systems, and the United States Congress; only the media came in behind lawyers. Thus, the public seems to have moderate confidence in its justice system but almost none in the lawyers who make that system function. The same survey also asked about public satisfaction with particular lawyer services they had purchased in the last five years. The satisfaction levels with transactional attorneys (real estate, contracts, or estate planning) were much higher than the satisfaction levels with litigating attorneys (family law, civil, or criminal disputes).

According to the Gallup Poll, high percentages of respondents give pharmacists, clergy, dentists, and doctors high or very high ratings for honesty and ethics. Between 1976 and 1985, 25–27% of respondents gave lawyers high or very high ratings. Then the figure started to slide, falling to 18% in 1988. After a bump upwards in 1989–1991, it fell back to 18% in 1992, 16% in 1993–1995, and 14% in 1998. The public opinion of lawyers is inversely proportional to education; the more education people have, the more unethical they think lawyers are. A study by the Media Studies Center of the University of Connecticut asked whether the respondent trusts members of various professions to tell the truth. As to lawyers, 24% of respondents trusted a lawyer "to tell the truth all or most of the time"; this came close to the bottom of the list behind newspaper reporters (30%), your Congressional representative (30%), and network television news anchors (42%). Only the president (21%) and radio talk show hosts (14%) came in below lawyers.

To go out on a limb: I think lawyers are getting a bad rap. I believe that most lawyers (not all of them, of course) are decent, socially responsible people who work hard for their clients, successfully check government overreaching, take a lot of undeserved abuse, are pretty ethical most of the time, and do not earn inordinate amounts of money. Instead, they hew out a living in an extremely tough, competitive environment.

In general, I believe (although I cannot prove) that most legal services, whether oriented to transactions, personal planning, or dispute-settlement, add value and that most of the things lawyers do are good for society. It may be unfashionable to say so, but I think the ABA was right when it concocted the slogan "[f]reedom, justice, equality — without lawyers, they're just words." So, if a normative position is needed from which to criticize popular legal culture over the last twenty years, my position is that film should treat lawyers in a fair and balanced manner.

As to the negative public opinion polls, your attitude may be — who cares? Life for lawyers, judges and law professors goes on regardless of what the public thinks of the profession. Lawyers are accustomed to people not liking them much. It's easy for lawyers to write off the polling data as misguided or inconsequential. However, I think we should care a lot about the venomously negative public perceptions of the profession. . . .

NOTES & QUESTIONS

1. Do you recall your first image of a lawyer? From where did it come? A book, television show, movie, or real person, such as a parent or other relative?

2. What was your thinking about the lawyer you first encountered? Was the lawyer a "good" lawyer, a "bad" lawyer, or a lawyer of mixed qualities (like most human beings)? On what basis and with which factors do you come to these judgments?

3. Professor Asimow reports that people have some moderate confidence in the legal system, but less in the particular professionals who inhabit it — the lawyers. Is it possible to think that the legal system is basically fair, legitimate, or to be trusted when you think that most lawyers are not honest (as the polling data seems to indicate)? Remember that Jack Cade (in *Henry VI*) wanted to kill all the lawyers because they represented the rule of law and control of tyrants. See Steve Greenfield, *Hero or Villain? Cinematic Lawyers and the Delivery of Justice*, in *Law and Film* (Stefan Machura & Peter Robson, eds., 2002), suggesting that lawyers uphold the rule of law but just as often "stand outside the law" by protecting and standing with those outside the system (such as unpopular clients like Tom Robinson in the classic 1962 film *To Kill a Mockingbird*), thus encouraging ambivalent reactions to professionals who actually play multiple roles within the legal system. What do you think about the tension in the role of the lawyer to represent a client and at the same time to protect the legal system? Can one always do both at the same time? Think about how many depictions of lawyers in popular culture build on this dramatic role tension, what sociologists of the legal profession call "role conflict." Frank Galvin, for example, in *The Verdict,* ultimately achieves "justice" for his client in a medical malpractice trial by committing several ethical violations in case preparation (stealing documents, violating federal postal laws) and witness manipulation. Both the father and daughter Jedediah and Maggie Ward, on opposite sides of a products liability case in *Class Action* (1990), engage in ethical breaches (document destruction, witness harassment, and cruelty) in order to fight for their respective clients. Eventually, in order to achieve "justice," Maggie commits the ultimate act of "role conflict" — she switches sides in a way which clearly violates rules of professional conduct. *See* Model Rules of Professional Conduct, Rules 1.8–1.12 (conflicts of interest). And Teddy Barnes, the successful criminal defense lawyer of guilty John Forrester, takes "justice" into her own hands when she kills her client (in self-defense, but also because she knows the formal justice system has not punished him for the crimes he has committed), while she stays faithful to the ethical principle that she cannot reveal client confidences or "secrets" (his guilt).

4. How do we measure what a good lawyer is? Is there a difference between what you would want from a lawyer and what you would want from a friend? Professor Charles Fried suggested quite famously several decades ago that the lawyer should act as a "special-purpose friend." See *The Lawyer as Friend: The Moral Foundations of the Lawyer-Client Relation,* 85 Yale Law Journal 1060 (1976), arguing that lawyers do things for their clients, legitimately, that might hurt others — the relationship of lawyer-client "friendship" and the loyalty and service it is built on is intrinsically morally valuable. Do you agree? Do you want your friends to "do anything" for you? Lie? Cheat? Steal? Do you want them to give you good, yet honest, advice, or always tell you you are right?

5. In a genre he helped create, Louis Auchincloss (practicing lawyer and author of over 60 novels and collections of short stories) has explored the relationship of lawyers giving advice to clients (usually in non-litigational settings, like corporate or probate law), often when they share the same social circles and class but might have conflicting professional or personal moralities. *See, e.g., Diary of a Yuppie* (1986); *The Atonement and Other Stories* (1997); *The Partners* (1973); and *Powers of Attorney* (1987). *See also* William Domnarski, *Trouble in Paradise: Wall Street Lawyers and the Fiction of Louis Auchincloss,* 12 Journal of Contemporary Law 243 (1987). For another dramatic representation in popular fiction of just how hard it is to "do the right thing" when your client is your friend, business associate, or just plain old long-term client who pays you lots of money, see Arthur Solmssen, *The Comfort Letter* (1975) (chronicling a lawyer's decision to disclose corporate fraud in a public offering). Consider whether Anthony Judson Lawrence in *The Young Philadelphians* is a good lawyer and a good friend, when he advises Mrs. Allen, a very wealthy woman, on how to "avoid" or at least minimize tax payments, and then takes on the criminal defense of his oldest friend Chet (even when he has no criminal experience at all). What do we mean by talking about a "good" lawyer as friend? Loyalty? Use of skill or craft? Good advice even if it is painful to hear? Objectivity? Promotion of client interests?

6. With which particular lawyer roles are you most familiar? The most classic genre of lawyer movies is the trial or courtroom movie, but increasingly fewer and fewer lawyers actually try cases. Less than 2% of all civil cases filed in federal courts are actually tried, and the rates of trial are similar for criminal cases in the federal system. *See* Marc Galanter, *The Vanishing Trial: An*

Examination of Trials and Related Matters in Federal and State Courts, 1 Journal of Empirical Legal Studies 459 (2004); Carrie Menkel-Meadow, *Is the Adversary System Really Dead? Dilemmas of Legal Ethics as Legal Institutions and Rules Evolve,* in *Current Legal Problems* (Jane Holder, Colm O'Cinneide & Michael Freeman, eds., 2004). Criminal trials are more common in state jurisdictions, like California, where "three strikes" legislation forces incarceration after three convictions and there is now less plea bargaining. Why is the trial lawyer the most common depiction of the lawyer, even as the role becomes rarer and rarer in real life? Is it the drama of confrontation in the courtroom? Our need for sports-like winners and losers when we watch movies or television or read mysteries and thrillers? Is real life really so cut-and-dried? Is it easier for us to perceive "good" (skillful) lawyering in the courtroom setting (the classic cross-examinations of *Perry Mason*; the pithy opening and closing statements of the lawyers on *L.A. Law, The Practice,* and *Law & Order)* than in the law office consultations, advice, and drafting of transactional work? Must a lawyer have to defeat someone to be a good lawyer? What about the role of lawyers as peacemakers, mediators, or, as Louis Brandeis made famous, being a "lawyer for the situation" in solving problems for clients, even those in conflict with each other? *See* Clyde Spillenger, *Elusive Advocate: Reconsidering Brandeis as People's Lawyer*, 105 Yale Law Journal 1445 (1996).

7. Is the good lawyer kind? A true "helping professional"? Or is he more likely mean or rude? Consider the depiction in *Liar Liar* of Fletcher Reede, who is selfish and rude with his family, lies in his practice, and flatters (falsely) his law firm colleagues until he is forced to tell the truth, becoming more honest and even ruder when he tells people (and judges and courts) what he really thinks. In *The Devil's Advocate* Kevin Lomax is a smug and selfish lawyer who wins cases and ignores his wife. His boss, John Milton (named for *Paradise Lost* author as the ultimate depiction of lawyer as Satan), is evil incarnate and has come to be the iconic representation of the evil big firm lawyer. John Grisham's many lawyer protagonists are greedy cheats, fronts for the mob, and even vicious killers. *See, e.g., The Firm* (1993). Have you encountered any lawyers who are really this bad in real life?

8. To what extent do you agree with polling data on the untrustworthiness of lawyers? If you think lawyers are evil or not to be trusted, why did you come to law school? If lawyers are so bad, why do we continue to make and see movies and television shows about them? Shows like *Law & Order* have been proliferating, and lawyer shows vastly outnumber doctor shows. Only police and detective shows are greater in number than lawyer shows, and these shows are also about "law." Professor Asimow suggests in the article excerpted above that lawyers are depicted more favorably on television than in the movies. Do you agree? Why might this be?

9. Are lawyers more likely to be repositories of dramatic moral decisions than other professionals? Doctors must treat all and do no harm, but they triage medical seriousness and make life and death decisions everyday. Engineers and architects design products and buildings that have the power to harm millions. Business managers and accountants, as we have learned all too recently, can bilk employees, suppliers, vendors, and the general public out of millions of dollars. Politicians lie and send innocent people to fight wars. Car mechanics and assembly line workers would never get away with some of the things more educated "professionals" do. (Is there more formal or market discipline in less "revered" or "learned" professions?)

10. To return to the "good" lawyer for a moment, why were lawyers so much more likely to be depicted as heroes in times past? Some commentators have suggested that the "golden years" of lawyer movies in Hollywood accompanied important political and social changes, the McCarthy Era, the Cold War, the Civil Rights movement, the early days of the feminist, anti-poverty, and anti-war movements — times filled with demands for justice and clarity of positions and the need for Americans to exalt their way of life in contrast to others. *See* David Ray Papke, *Law, Cinema and Ideology: Hollywood Legal Films of the 1950s,* 48 UCLA Law Review 1473 (2001), and Francis Nevins, *Law, Lawyers and Justice in Popular Fiction and Film,* 1 Humanities Education 3 (1984). This period also made law quite salient for the general public as the Supreme Court ushered in such important decisions as *Brown v. Board of Education* (1954), ruled in important cases on school prayer and the First Amendment, and revolutionized criminal law with such decisions as *Miranda v. Arizona* (1966) and *Gideon v. Wainwright* (1963), radically changing the legal and social landscape and impressing upon a post-war generation that to get things done or changed, law was at least one of the most efficacious means.

11. Ask almost any lawyer who came of age in the 1950s and 1960s (and still some today), and you will find images of Clarence Darrow (a real lawyer, despite the depiction in *Inherit the Wind*) and Atticus Finch as inspirational sources of career choice. Milner Ball has written eloquently about the many modern public interest lawyers who saw their inspiration to fight for justice in these few heroic lawyers. *See The Word and the Law* (1993). Younger lawyers might base their decisions to be "cause" lawyers on Jonathan Harr's non-fictional description of Jan Schlictman as environmental crusader (and plaintiff's lawyer) in *A Civil Action* (1995) or on Gerald Stern's own description of his representation of damaged West Virginia community after coal-mining caused a dam break in *The Buffalo Creek Disaster* (1976). (Both of these books are widely used in modern civil procedure courses to give students a taste of "real lawyers and law" behind the Rules of Civil Procedure.) A more recent possibility is the movie depiction of a class action sexual harassment suit in upper Minnesota in *North Country* (2005), based on the real case described in Clara Bingham and Laura Leedy Gansler's *Class Action: The Story of Lois Jenson and the Landmark Case That Changed Sexual Harassment Law* (the 2003 book, not the 1991 movie of the same name). Do you think there are enough models of "good" cause or public interest-minded lawyers in media depictions? Should there be more? The public interest-minded lawyer Lucy Kelsen (ironically named for noted legal philosopher Hans Kelsen, the author of *The General Theory of Law and the State* (1946), who argued for "pure" positive law?) says in *Two Weeks Notice* that her heroes are Clarence Darrow, Thurgood Marshall, and Ruth Bader Ginsburg. What do these lawyers have in common? What effects on law school enrollment do you think media depictions (good, bad, or more complex) of lawyers have?

12. As we will explore below, when we focus on what lawyers learn from their lives and cases, some modern lawyers could easily be characterized as redeemed "heroes" as well. Michael Brock in Grisham's *The Street Lawyer* (a 1998 novel and never filmed!) goes from being a conventionally ambitious, partnership-seeking, big-firm associate to being a lawyer for the homeless. Joe Miller (Denzel Washington) becomes a reluctant civil rights gladiator for AIDS-stricken and discriminated-against lawyer Andrew Beckett (Tom Hanks) in *Philadelphia* (1992), and Rita Harrison (Michelle Pfeiffer) in *I Am Sam* (2001) learns the true meaning of family when she focuses on her mentally challenged client's desires to be a parent when it takes more than a village and a binary legal system to care for a child.

13. Increasingly, memoirs and descriptions of real lawyers portray the complexity of modern lawyers' choices and lives — their job choices, their decisions in practice, and their personal lives. From Melissa Fay Greene's moving portrayal of real legal services lawyers for the poor in Georgia in *Praying for Sheetrock* (1991), to Abbe Smith's expressed concerns about criminal lawyers, both prosecutors and defense lawyers (*see Can You Be a Good Person and a Good Prosecutor?* 14 Georgetown Journal of Legal Ethics 355 (2001)), to the reported stories of class action lawyers in asbestos, Dalkon Shield, and other products liability cases (*see* Paul Brodeur, *Outrageous Misconduct* (1985); Richard Sobol, *Bending the Law* (1991); Dan Zegart, *Civil Warriors: The Legal Siege on the Tobacco Industry* (2000)), we have many portraits of good lawyers seeking justice and personal fulfillment in hard times. If Professor Asimow is right that depictions of movie lawyers have gotten worse and more evil over time, why do you think we have such a paucity of movies and other popular culture depictions of these more courageous "cause lawyers"? *See* Austin Sarat & Stuart Scheingold, *Cause Lawyers: Political Commitments and Professional Responsibilities* (1998). Do other media portray the complexity of modern lawyers' professional and personal lives more realistically? Consider the richness and depth of Scott Turow's lawyers in *Presumed Innocent* (1989), *The Laws of Our Fathers* (1997), and *Reversible Errors* (2002). All of the major lawyers are dedicated to justice but humanly flawed.

14. Carrie Menkel-Meadow has called the new genre of writing by (mostly) young lawyers about their unpleasant experiences in various forms of practice the "bill and tell" memoir or journalistic account. *See* Carrie Menkel-Meadow, *Telling Stories in School: Using Case Studies and Stories to Teach Legal Ethics,* 69 Fordham Law Review 787, 790, n.6 (2000). Examples of the genre include Paul M. Barrett, *The Good Black: A True Story of Race in America* (1999); Lincoln Kaplan, *Skadden: Power, Money and the Rise of a Legal Empire* (1993) (evidencing a new genre of law firm histories, often written by professional historians); William R. Keates, *Proceed With Caution: A Diary of the First Year at One of America's Largest, Most Prestigious Law Firms* (1997); Cameron Stracher, *Double Billing* (1998); David Heilbroner, *Rough Justice: Days and Nights of a Young DA* (1990); James Kunen, *How Can You Defend Those Guilty People? The Making of a Criminal Lawyer* (1983); and Stephen Phillips, *No Heroes, No Villains: The Story of a Murder Trial* (1977).

15. As you proceed through the readings and viewings suggested in this book, consider how you are making judgments about whether the lawyers depicted and described are "good" lawyers or not. *See The Good Lawyer: Lawyers' Roles and Lawyers' Ethics* (David Luban, ed., 1983); Stephen L.

Pepper, *The Lawyer's Amoral Ethical Role: A Defense, A Problem and Some Possibilities,* 1986 American Bar Foundation Research Journal 613; and Gerald J. Postema, *Moral Responsibility in Professional Ethics,* 55 NYU Law Review 63 (1980).

16. Do you look at lawyers in their professional roles, with all the specialized duties and responsibilities that those roles entail? Or do you judge lawyers by the particular acts they perform (or fail to perform)? Anthony Judson Lawrence, the lawyer played by Paul Newman in *The Young Philadelphians,* tells us those acts sum up to form the "character" of a lawyer.

C. LAWYERS' ACTS

Many depictions of lawyers turn on difficult decisions or actions (or non-actions) that lawyers may take. Some of these "acts" are designed to illuminate the character of the individual (explored more fully in section D below), others are designed to explore the difficult ethical choices that professional roles require of those specially trained, and still others are used to move the plot along or crystallize some statement about the law and legal institutions. Moral and legal philosophers have long debated whether the morality of a professional is to be judged by that person's "role morality" (different standards permitted for differently performed and needed societal functions), the acts he commits (or does not), or a more general assessment of the person's character. Society's need for some division of labor has long justified the separate morality of soldiers who can kill; politicians who can "dissemble"; lawyers, doctors, and clergy who do not have to reveal certain private information; and employees who are expected to be "loyal" (within increasingly diminishing limits) to their bosses or institutions. One commentator has eloquently explored the "professional role morality" of Charles Henri-Sanson who was so good at his craft (that of executioner of Paris) that he was able to survive all of the changes in regime during the French Revolution and keep his job. See Arthur Isak Applbaum, *Ethics for Adversaries: The Morality of Roles in Public and Professional Life* (1999). The legal profession, as well as many others, has drafted ethical rules and standards that are supposed to guide a professional to do the "right" thing. But many acts that lawyers take are not well-regulated or specified in the formal Rules. How does one choose a client or refuse a case? How does one treat another human being when interviewing a potential client about very private and possibly unlawful behavior? How close (socially and physically) can a lawyer and client become? Modern filmic depictions of lawyer activity allow us to take a closer look (even if only in fictional settings) at the choices that lawyers make about what they do. Consider the "chronology" of lawyer acts described below.

CAN THEY DO THAT? LEGAL ETHICS IN POPULAR CULTURE: OF CHARACTER AND ACTS
Carrie Menkel-Meadow
48 UCLA Law Review 1305 (2001)

It is possible to construct a temporal template of ethical issues depicted in the popular media from the beginning of the lawyer-client relationship to the end of an appeal or transaction (or to a murder for those relationships that end really badly). Russell Banks's *The Sweet Hereafter* (1991) tells the fictionalized story of an actual bus accident that killed a number of children and had a great impact on many lives. The story is told from the point of view of many different participants in the story, but from Mitchell Stephens, Esq., we learn how clients are involuntarily solicited, because lawyers are angry and are able to harness their anger to compensate other people. For Mitchell Stephens, "[t]here are no accidents" — someone is always responsible for things that go wrong, and it is the plaintiff's lawyer's job to find someone (with deep pockets) to blame and to pay up so the injured can be compensated. This is class justice and the lawyer must orchestrate it: "I wanted a mean lean team, a troop of vengeful parents willing to go the route with me and not come home without some serious trophies on our spears." As Stephens describes himself, he lives for these "disaster negligence suits. . . . Nothing else provides me with the rush that I get from cases like this. . . . It's almost like a drug. It's probably close to what professional soldiers feel, or bullfighters." Stephens tells us how he ropes in mourning parents and what he does when one of them, Billy Ansel (who has lost two children), resists him, and how he lies to make his case. We also learn how Stephens appears to his clients (from their point of view), as one of the injured children, Nichole Burnell, takes his measure when she is interviewed and prepped for a deposition (which she later deliberately ruins by telling her own truth and seeking justice against another wrongdoer, her own abusive father, rather than against any of the actors in the accident). Although Nichole likes Mr. Stephens, he makes her feel greedy and dishonest by preparing for a deposition to get the money her parents want from her injury. Nichole over-hears a conversation Billy Ansel has with her father about how the lawyers are all suing each other because some plaintiffs have signed up with more than one lawyer, and the reader feels the pain of grieving parents trying to make sense of what has happened and what could happen to them, while the lawyers fight to profit from their misery.

In contrast, Jan Schlichtmann's [in *A Civil Action*] real-life, initially unwilling plaintiffs grow slowly from distrust of a legal system that will not do anything for a widening group of injured people (never big enough for the class action numbers that would have been possible in the Buffalo Creek disaster) to become increasingly committed to their lawsuit, and to see their lawyer as a mixed bag of altruistic and selfish motives.

Atticus Finch is actually pressed into service in representing Tom Robinson [in *To Kill A Mockingbird*] by the judge handling the case, but he tells a good story to his daughter about the responsibility of lawyers to take unpopular clients and cases (the "n" word is used in both the book and the movie, circa 1960–1962). In so doing, he has given us all a model and argument for the importance of *pro bono publico* and even court-appointed work, especially in criminal law. Representing unpopular clients and taking court appointments has continued on *The Practice*, while in past years, paying clients have been more the rule on *L.A. Law* and on the short-lived *Murder One* (a show inspired by the public's hunger for criminal celebrity trials following the coverage of the O.J. Simpson trial). *A Civil Action* made the economics of contingent-fee lawyers clear to the viewing public, and began to address the inevitable conflicts of interest that accompany virtually any payment scheme for lawyers.

From client acquisition, modern films and movies depict a variety of ethical dilemmas in representation (still mostly restricted to the more dramatic world of litigation and courtrooms, rather than transactional lawyering). For example, *The Practice* has several times, in different settings, explored issues of confidentiality — when must or can a lawyer reveal private, confidential information to others? And, when Bobby and Helen were dating, the show explored difficult, but I suspect increasingly common, professional dilemmas when lawyers on opposite sides of cases date or live with each other, hear confidential information in phone conversations, and see messages and papers left lying around the house. The lawyers on *The Practice* have grappled with what to do with physical evidence, when they can "rat" on their own client, and many thorny witness preparation issues. In a modern replay of the now classic client "coaching" scene of *Anatomy of a Murder*, lawyers tell their clients what the law is before learning the facts. A guilty-feeling Helen, as prosecutor, actually testifies against one of her colleagues whom she believes wrongfully suggested testimony to a material witness. Ellenor Frut commits one of the most egregious, but clever, unethical acts (can you think of what ethical rules she violates?) when she advises a client who has been in an accident and has been drinking, to finish the open bottle at the scene of the accident "to calm his nerves" — and thereby destroy the accuracy of any Breathalyzer test. The lawyers of *The Practice* have conflicts of interest galore — they sleep with each other and the judge, they work both sides of a case, they take on civil matters beyond their competence, but at least they have explicit ethical conversations about what they are doing. There is not only talk about the law, possible ethical violations, and consequences to their firm and their clients, but they do in fact get called on some of their questionable behavior.

Competence is questioned in popular culture, whether by the satire of Joe Pesci's performance in *My Cousin Vinny*, by the too-young and inexperienced colleague in Grisham's *The Rainmaker*, by the all-too-common substance abuse of Frank Galvin in *The Verdict*, by the actual Rule 11 motion filed against Jan Schlichtmann for not adequately investigating and supporting his complaint filing, or by the impressionability of a lawyer who believed she was zealously representing her client, but who may in fact have been subject to a "con job" that cost her freedom and her law license. Scott Turow counters these images of incompetence by providing perhaps the most detailed and accurate accounts of the hard work that both prosecutors and defense counsel put into their jobs — in investigation, case preparation, courtroom strategy, and courtroom execution — even if some of the lawyers and judges turn out to be corrupt or worse.

As most popular culture continues to explore the drama of the courtroom, I am personally interested in recent turns to more typical locales of lawyers' work — the bargaining table. Still located mostly in litigation contexts, the ethics and practices of lawyers in settlement conferences present serious ethical dilemmas, hardly responded to by the rules. While *The Practice* lawyers engage in plea-bargaining and tense settlement negotiations every time they take on a medical malpractice or products liability case, the settlement conference is becoming a more common staple of legal drama. My personal favorite is the blatant ethical violation in *The Verdict*, the premise of which is needed to fuel the rest of the film. Frank Galvin turns down a large, and certainly likely to be accepted by his client, settlement offer from the Catholic Church (which controls the hospital which mistreated his comatose client) without even talking to his client (the family of the comatose woman). In direct violation of Rules 1.2, 1.3, and 1.4 (and all of their predecessors that were in effect in Massachusetts at the time of the film), Galvin turns down the offer. Thus, the case (and the film) can proceed to the more dramatic confrontation in the courtroom, where Galvin, overcoming his alcoholism and violating some laws by stealing mail to get information, triumphs over a major and well-staffed law firm.

Michael Brock's lawsuit against the developer who wrongfully evicted his homeless clients [in *The Street Lawyer*] is completed in a settlement conference, this one in a judge's chambers with Brock's own ethical transgressions (deception used to get evidence and confidentiality violations) as part of the negotiation agenda. Similarly, while nothing overtly in violation of the rules transpires, Jonathan Harr's descriptions (from one side only) of the various settlement negotiations (meetings at the Ritz Carlton in Boston and W.R. Grace headquarters in New York) in *A Civil Action* provide us with some entry into the world of lawyer impression management, guarded information exchange, and normal "deception."

Modern treatments of lawyers demonstrate good acts as well — not all is sex, lies, and videotape. Lawyers like Frank Galvin and Jan Schlichtmann, as well as paralegal Erin Brockovich, demonstrate the power of persistence and the necessity of hard, long, and detailed fact investigation. Although in trial movies and television shows it sometimes looks like victory goes to the clever and the articulate, in truth we seldom see anymore the contrived final question of a devastating and surprising Perry Mason-like cross-examination. As discovery has replaced surprise in trial, popular culture is slowly catching up with what makes good lawyers in real life — hard work! Hard work and long hours get their share of criticism, ruining marriages in *The Firm* and *The Street Lawyer*, not to mention adultery on the job with coworkers. No one could accuse modern lawyers depicted in the media as a lazy bunch — even the "you can have it all" glamour pusses of *L.A. Law*. Good lawyering (as well as realistic lawyering) takes hard work, as the "bill and tell" books painfully recount, and virtually all of these modern tales, both fact and fiction, do want us to consider the consequences of hard professional labor on personal lives.

Changes in the practice of law, both in the work done, and in the demographic composition of the legal profession, are beginning to seep into modern depictions of discrimination issues (partnerships, power, decision-making authority for minority and women attorneys, and sexual harassment). In this, *L.A. Law* showed us other kinds of lawyer work, including Arnie Becker's divorce work, tax, and corporate work. Leland McKenzie even served as an arbitrator in what has to be the first depiction of ADR on screen. As creators of popular culture begin to realize that lawyers do many things besides trying cases, I look forward to depictions of some of the equally difficult and dramatic ethical issues that are encountered in other forms of legal work: conflicts of interest in alternative dispute resolution involving repeat players, corporate deal making, disclosure obligations in transactional negotiations and public offerings, lawyers paid with stock options in dotcoms, and now the fall-out from "dot-gones.". . . .

EMBODIMENT OF EVIL: LAW FIRMS IN THE MOVIES
Michael Asimow
48 UCLA Law Review 1339 (2001)

The life of lawyers in big firms is grueling and unglamorous, but what of the moral claims made by the movies? Do lawyers working for big firms lie, cheat, and steal?

1. Ethical Problems of Small Firms

Small firms are more prone to certain kinds of ethical violations than are large ones. The kinds of misbehavior that cause lawyers to be disbarred mostly involve thefts from client trust funds, neglecting or ignoring clients, severe forms of malpractice, or gross forms of ambulance chasing. In many cases, these lapses are traceable to drug or alcohol addiction. At big firms, however, colleagues are likely to realize that a lawyer has a substance abuse problem and take steps to remedy the problem and protect clients. In contrast, a solo practice or very small firm may lack such internal checking mechanisms. Small firms are also more likely to run into cash flow problems that might cause lawyers to raid the trust funds.

Big firms have a great deal at stake in maintaining their hard-won reputations for quality work and ethical behavior. They are less likely than small firms to engage in blatant ambulance chasing or gross forms of malpractice that could cause an attorney to be disbarred. Big firms maintain elaborate computer checking systems to protect themselves against becoming accidentally enmeshed in conflicts of interest, to detect billing irregularities, or to prevent lawyers from missing deadlines. Many have ethics committees to which lawyers can confidentially refer thorny ethics problems. Big firms have the luxury of being choosy about accepting new business; they can afford to decline marginal matters or sleazy clients. Given the surplus of lawyers, however, many small firms or solos are desperate for business; they are more likely to take marginal cases or dubious clients and may feel they have to cheat to survive financially.

2. Ethical Problems of Big Firms

Using the movies as our text, we would assume that big firms cheat big time. In *The Verdict* we find a big firm engaging in numerous forms of creative cheating such as bribing the opponent's expert witness to disappear or planting a sexual spy in the opposition's camp. In *Class Action*, a big defense firm first conceals, then destroys, a critical document. In *The Rainmaker*, the firm plants a bug in its opponent's office and colludes with the client in causing witnesses to disappear; perhaps it also knows that the client has testified falsely and fraudulently altered evidence. In *Regarding Henry* the firm suppressed critical evidence and engaged in discovery fraud. In *Philadelphia*, the firm engaged in various forms of illegal chicanery to get rid of an associate with AIDS and to cover it up afterwards, including perjury. All of these are clear-cut ethical violations that would surely trigger severe professional discipline if detected; some of them are criminal violations.

How much does this sort of thing actually happen in the big firm environment? The answer is elusive. Lawyers who commit major ethical violations keep quiet about it and pray that nobody will ever find out. In my informal Greedy Associate survey, the vast majority of the respondents said that they had never seen anything of the sort and some were offended that I even asked the question. Some remarked that solo lawyers or small firms, desperate to keep business or to keep a contingent fee case going, are more likely to engage in such cheating. Others remarked that clients frequently try to conceal bad documents but that lawyers insist on disclosing them if the client's fraud is detected. For example, an associate who is thoroughly miserable about his own big firm lifestyle responded to my question about gross ethical violations:

> No way, no-how. We chastise clients who ask us to hide bad facts in my practice. Our litigators that I know are good and aggressive but would never cheat or bend rules to suit them. We are way too busy to work with clients who want us to cheat on their behalf and the exposure is far too great. That shit is for desperate lawyers.

A few Greedy Associates did observe gross ethical violations, either in their own firms or in other firms. Some comments:

> — Yes, I lie to the judges, we all do. . . .

> — I have seen lawyers asking staff to sign a proof of service for an incorrect date and I have seen lawyers lying to clients about why work did not get done or about what a judge said.

> — I've heard stories from friends of opposing well-known firms that have destroyed documents or other evidence.

> — In terms of blatant violations, they do happen. I can't go into specifics, this is fairly serious stuff and I can't screw with the confidence of any colleagues or clients.

> — An associate left the firm because she had been told to destroy a document.

Serious ethical lapses do occur, and both big and small firms occasionally get caught engaging in them. No doubt, for every one of these publicized incidents, countless others have gone undetected or were quietly dealt with by the parties involved. Still, random publicized incidents involving big firms do not prove or even suggest that big firms are prone to bad ethics nor that they are more morally culpable than small firms or solos. Of course, there is no way for an outsider to know the answer. I am inclined to accept the repeated responses to the Greedy Associate survey that big firms have little need to commit clear-cut ethical violations and far too much to lose from taking such chances. Thus, the repeated depiction in big-firm movies appears to convey an erroneous impression that such violations are widespread.

3.   The Harsh Realities of Big-Firm Litigation Practice

Numerous films involving law firms have depicted all-out hardball litigation. In these films, big firms seek to exhaust their opponents with overwhelming discovery demands, resist justified discovery demands, file motions with little merit, and engage in other delaying tactics. Lawyers act uncivilly toward one another and treat deponents harshly.

In this respect, the movies accurately portray the realities of contemporary big firm litigation practice — and a great deal of small firm litigation practice as well. Hardball litigation tactics may or may not lie just on the ethical side of the lines laid out in the Model Rules. They do not, however, contribute to the search for truth or justice in the litigation process. While the great majority of the respondents to my Greedy Associates survey stated that gross ethical improprieties were unthinkable in their firms, they were far more ambivalent about other firm conduct. Numerous responses spoke of behavior that most non-lawyers would think was unethical and immoral. This consists of action designed to conceal the truth or to trick or exhaust the opposing side, but by means that seem to fall just short of ethical violations or which violate unenforced ethical standards. One very prevalent hardball tactic is incivility — that is, rude, bullying behavior that is designed to intimidate other lawyers or witnesses. For the most part, the respondents distinguished hardball litigation tactics from serious ethical improprieties. They do not like to behave this way, but regard such tactics as all in a day's work. One cannot survive in the big firm environment without engaging in them.

> I think the small ethical breaches which are most common contribute most to making the practice of law slimy.

> I have been asked to play dumb by partners ("if the other side calls asking where the new draft is, tell them our system crashed or the para made all the wrong changes last night").

> Less obvious ethical breaches occur — e.g., suggestions that associates lie about who they are ("I'm a college student doing research for a report") or who they represent.

> Big firms . . . may flood smaller firms with paper knowing that the first-year grunts and temps they put on the deal will probably miss something . . .

> The most common ethical violations I see are: (1) the contortions some firms/partners go through to determine that there is no conflict of interest in taking a case; (2) lawyers who don't consult their clients; (3) fast and loose arguments; and (4) discovery games.

> When the imbalance between superior game playing and a fair result is stark, then the system is certainly slimy, and if not slimy themselves, the lawyers who participated at least become slimed in the public's eye.

There are all sorts of sharp litigation practices out there:

— producing documents during a deposition, or late the night before, that were requested and/or subpoenaed many months ago. . . .

— misrepresenting the substance of telephone conversations with opposing counsel

— coaching of witnesses before and during depositions

— excessive and sometimes frivolous motion practice, or unduly burdensome discovery

— obstructionist tactics in "answering" interrogatories, requests to admit, and other legitimate discovery requests;

— egregious mischaracterizations of the facts and law in briefs or in oral arguments before the Court.

. . . [D]elaying production of documents until after a motion to compel has been opposed and lost and, sometimes, appealed and lost, all for the purposes of delay and driving up the other side's costs, is immoral.

But that is the game. Make things as difficult as possible for the other side within the bounds of the law.

Do some documents get put on a privileged list that may not be privileged? Sure, but the other side has an opportunity to challenge that.

There's a lot of unconscious violations — just making blanket exceptions in discovery when you know you will have to disclose, just making trouble for the other side. Lawyers spend time arguing bullshit stuff but they may or may not think it's bad faith.

But I can tell you that we have occasionally buried a document in with others in the hope that it, or its significance, is overlooked.

I think people are obnoxious, and it's true that they spend unbelievable amounts of time writing letters accusing the other side of withholding documents and so forth, but I haven't seen anyone violate the Rules. I do know that lawyers frequently "shade" the facts or law to courts and administrative bodies, so much so that I would consider it deceitful, but again, they are not doing it because they intend to lie; instead they are overzealous in their advocacy.

I think sometimes answers to interrogatories and responses to document production requests place too much emphasis on semantics. An artificially narrow reading of requests allows an attorney to avoid stating or producing something in response to a question . . . that is perfectly understandable in the context of litigation. I sometimes wonder how stupid an attorney can play without going over the ethical line. Playing dumb is pretty common practice.

In their depiction of slippery or hardball litigation practices by big firms, the filmmakers are right on the money.

4. Billing Improprieties

Several movies describe law firm behavior that appears to be aimed at inflating the client's bill. In *The Verdict*, for example, Ed Concannon clearly overstaffs the case. More than a dozen associates sit around a table listening to Concannon prepare a witness. In *The Firm*, a mentor partner tells Mitch McDeere to bill everything, even when he is thinking about client matters in the shower.

Numerous accounts of real-life law firm billing improprieties have appeared. According to Deborah Rhode:

> Audits of "legal expenses" have revealed massages during litigation, dry cleaning for a toupee, running shoes labeled "ground transportation," Victoria's Secret lingerie, and men's suits for an out-of-state trial that took longer than expected. Days in which lawyers bill more than twenty-four hours are no longer rare. . . . When heiress Doris Duke died, leaving over a billion dollars to charity, two dozen law firms embarked on what one attorney candidly described as "a feeding frenzy." Some of the nation's leading practitioners, staying at leading hotels, charging at premium rates, managed to duplicate each other's work and keep each other employed, which diverted an estimated $20 million from charitable causes. Deborah Rhode, *In the Interests of Justice: Reforming the Legal Profession* 168–69 (2000).

About half of the Greedy Associates said that their firms never overbilled clients; indeed, they thought that underbilling was more likely than overbilling. But the other half of the respondents reported that bill padding occurs at their firms. According to these respondents, both associates and partners inflate the number of their billable hours. Billable hours are often used to compute bonuses and lawyers must bill minimum number of hours to advance in the firm. As a result, lawyers inflate their hours on time sheets, either because they cannot physically work that many hours, or because there is not enough work to do. Indeed, it is difficult to understand how associates can consistently bill 2400 hours a year or more without cheating on their time sheets if they want any sort of life outside the office.

A number of respondents observed that basing everything on billable hours is perverse. It punishes lawyers who are more efficient and it keeps them working past the point of exhaustion. Others pointed to the assignment of unnecessary or even useless work to "churn" the number of hours billed to a particular matter. A sampling of some of the comments:

> . . overbilling is very troubling. It occurs in many forms. One of the most common forms is the billing of attorney time for work that clearly should be performed by a staff person, whether by a paralegal, at a lower billing rate, or by a secretary or word processor, at no cost to the client. . . . Unnecessary work often is performed and billed to the client, sometimes even when the client expressly has said that it does not want the work performed. . . . multiple people, even multiple partners, read and revise the same drafts of documents, even when a client directs that this should not occur. Duplication of work also is

a problem. This can occur from client to client, as in when the same research assignment is performed for two or more clients from scratch, rather than using the first project as a basis for updating and billing the subsequent clients only for the work necessary to update. It also can occur in the context of only one client, where a partner simultaneously assigns multiple associates to research the same thing, or assigns one associate to "double check" the entire work product of another associate.

The quality of time billed also can be a problem. If an associate works more than 250, more than 300, more than 400 hours in a month, going without sleep for days at a time, what kind of efficiency and accuracy level is the client being billed for by the end of the month?

Institutionally, it is difficult for partners to "write off" time from the bill. . . . Seasoned lawyers encourage junior lawyers to bill "loosely." Although none would openly condone overbilling or padding, many tacitly accept and reward padding. Senior associates who are known not to fill out timesheets for weeks at a time, to leave the office frequently to work out or attend to personal errands, and who mysteriously come up with 250 hour months, are held out as role models and rewarded with partnership. . . .

Unnecessary work is rampant (where I work). It's a combination of the desire to bill and the incompetence of higher-ups. I have spent many hours doing things that are totally pointless. This is often referred to as "churning the file."

Yes, I pad hours, we all do.

The reality is that if hours determine bonus and especially salary — you have to bill 2400 hours to get the big bonus — people have to cheat and pad. You know who they are, though they never admit it. It's an open secret though not discussed. . . . If you add on an extra .25 here and there, it is a lot of hours.

People say if I am going to be there 14 hours I'm going to bill all 14 hours despite personal phone calls; they just bill all the time they are there at the office. . . . If client insists on cut in hourly rate, you just stick them with more hours.

Overbilling? You bet. Unnecessary work? Absolutely. Overbilling is the dirty little secret that no one wants to talk about. It happens, and the billable hours model along with hours-based bonuses encourage it. Anyone who says differently still thinks the world is flat. But because it's almost impossible to prove, no one (at least in my experience) mentions it. . . .

NOTES & QUESTIONS

1. Many films about lawyers depend on the drama of particularly egregious acts — the lies of Fletcher Reede in *Liar Liar* (1997); the sexual improprieties of Teddy Barnes in *Jagged Edge* and Katherine Riley in *Suspect*; the discovery abuse on both sides in *Class Action*; the ruthlessness of Kevin Lomax and John Milton in *The Devil's Advocate* (1997); Frank Galvin's drinking problem in *The Verdict*; the fraud, tax evasion, and other outright criminal activities in *The Firm*; and the murders committed by lawyers in *Jagged Edge* and *Cape Fear* (original 1962; remake 1991). But how common is it for lawyers to commit these evil acts? Professor Asimow contrasts the ethical practices of small-firm and big-firm lawyers and suggests that small-firm lawyers are more likely to be discovered doing incompetent or worse things and to be disciplined for such activity. But at least one scholar has questioned whether small-firm lawyers are actually more likely to commit unethical or disciplinable acts. *See* Manuel Ramos, *Legal Malpractice: The Profession's Dirty Legal Secret,* 47 Vanderbilt Law Review 1657 (1994); Manuel Ramos, *Legal Malpractice: No Lawyer or Client is Safe,* 47 Florida Law Review 1 (1995).

2. Some of the "bad acts" described above do occur in real life. The satirical treatment of Fletcher Reede's lying in *Liar Liar* is both a major trope of pop cultural treatments and one of the things most commonly thought about lawyers — that they are liars. A joke is often made by using a Southern accent to say the word lawyer. *See* Rob Atkinson, *Lucifer's Fiasco: Lawyers, Liars and L'Affaire Lewinsky,* 68 Fordham Law Review 567 (1999). The proper dividing line between "zealous representation," making good arguments, and being honest is not very clear, even in the formal ethical rules. For example, Rule 4.1 of the Model Rules of Professional Conduct categorically states:

Rule 4.1 Truthfulness in Statements to Others

In the course of representing a client a lawyer shall not knowingly:

a. make a false statement of material fact or law to a third person; or

b. fail to disclose a material fact or law to a third person when disclosure is necessary to avoid assisting a criminal or fraudulent act by a client, unless disclosure is prohibited by Rule 1.6 [confidentiality of lawyer-client communications].

Yet, what the black letter rule giveth, the commentary taketh away. Note the following exceptions to the demands for truth above, stated in the commentary to Rule 4.1:

Comment

Misrepresentation

[1] A lawyer is required to be truthful when dealing with others on a client's behalf, but generally has no affirmative duty to inform an opposing party of relevant facts. . . .

Statements of Fact

[2] This rule refers to statements of fact. Whether a particular statement should be regarded as one of fact can depend on the circumstances. Under generally accepted conventions in negotiation, certain types of statements ordinarily are not taken as statements of material fact. Estimates of price or value placed on the subject

of a transaction and a party's intentions as to an acceptable settlement of a claim are in this category, and so is the existence of an undisclosed principal except where nondisclosure of the principal would constitute fraud.

Given these rules, lawyers often exaggerate, "puff," or manipulate their words, especially in lawyer-to-lawyer negotiations, where such "generally accepted conventions" are thought to apply. *See* Carrie Menkel-Meadow, *Ethics, Morality and Professional Responsibility in Negotiation,* in *Dispute Resolution Ethics* (Phyllis Bernard & Bryant Garth, eds., 2002); Carrie Menkel-Meadow, *Legal Negotiation in Popular Culture: What Are We Bargaining For,* in *Law and Popular Culture* (Michael Freeman, ed., 2005). Consider what happens in the legal system when everyone "generally accepts" that not everyone will be telling the truth.

The Model Rules do seem to expect a slightly higher standard of candor when matters are formally in litigation before the court:

Rule 3.3 Candor Toward the Tribunal

   a) A lawyer shall not knowingly:

      (1) make a false statement of material fact or law to a tribunal;

      (2) fail to disclose a material fact to a tribunal when disclosure is necessary to avoid assisting a criminal or fraudulent act by the client;

      (3) fail to disclose to the tribunal legal authority in the controlling jurisdiction known to the lawyer to be directly adverse to the position of the client and not disclosed by opposing counsel; or

      (4) offer evidence that the lawyer knows to be false. If a lawyer has offered material evidence and comes to know of its falsity, the lawyer shall take reasonable remedial measures.

   b) The duties stated in paragraph (a) continue to the conclusion of the proceeding, and apply even if compliance requires disclosure of information otherwise protected by Rule 1.6.

   c) A lawyer may refuse to offer evidence that the lawyer reasonably believes is false.

   d) In an ex parte proceeding, a lawyer shall inform the tribunal of all material facts known to the lawyer which will enable the tribunal to make an informed decision, whether or not the facts are adverse.

Whether a matter is "before a tribunal" or not can itself be quite complicated. Is discovery formally before a tribunal? Is a mediation or arbitration before a tribunal? Is a judge or magistrate-assisted settlement conference before a tribunal? (Hint: See the definitions, e.g., 1(m), in the Terminology accompanying the Preface to the Model Rules.) Consider whether depictions of lawyer activity in the movies clarify or obscure the different rules of candor in different settings. At least one critic of lawyers in popular culture (and a trial advocacy teacher) argues that trial lawyers cannot and should not have to tell the "technical" truth, precisely because, like the auteurs of film, lawyers must create persuasive narratives to convince juries and judges and adequately represent their clients. "[L]awyers often use the techniques of narrative construction to enhance the truth, not to hide it. A fully developed and well-conceived "trial story" may result in an account that is actually "truer" in many respects than the client's uncounseled version of events, even though the narrative was adroitly structured with courtroom victory in mind." Steven Lubet, *Nothing But the Truth: Why Trial Lawyers Don't, Can't and Shouldn't Have to Tell the Whole Truth* 1 (2001).

Though rare, occasionally lawyers are caught in their misrepresentations or failure to be honest enough to satisfy the Rules (both of ethics and of procedure). Consider the divorce lawyer in *Stare v. Tate,* 21 Cal. App. 3d 432, 98 Cal. Rptr. 264 (1971), who knew that the wife's lawyer had made two computational errors in calculating the value of some community property to be divided in the divorce settlement and failed to disclose the error in order to advantage his own client in the property division. The court was so appalled at this behavior (when it was revealed by the stupidly vindictive husband who called his ex-wife to tell her what he and his lawyer had done) that it did more than rescind the divorce settlement as contract law would have suggested (due to unilateral mistake). The court reformed the contract to reflect the correct values, rather than sending the parties back to renegotiate. Rather than "blame" the wife's lawyer for malpractice or incompetence in doing the computation, the husband's lawyer was publicly exposed for his "exquisite" desire to take advantage of the other side and, in effect, misrepresent the property values.

You may recall the national humor (and serious impeachment proceedings) that developed around President Clinton's lawyer-like attempt to get around acknowledging his sexual indiscretions by claiming, in his deposition, "It all depends on what the meaning of 'is' is," and, his lawyer-like definitional dance around whether oral sex was, in fact, "sexual relations." *See* Nan Hunter, *The Power of Procedure: The Litigation of* Jones v. Clinton (2002).

Lawyers are famous for bending words, and Jim Carrey may perhaps have been chosen to play Fletcher Reede in *Liar Liar* because of his uncanny ability to literally bend his face and mouth in so many different directions. Consider the word manipulation that occurred in the famous case of *Washington State Physicians Ins. Exch. & Assoc. v. Fisons Corp.,* 858 P. 2d 1054, 122 Wash. 2d 299 (1993). The Washington state law firm of Bogle & Gates (yes, that is Bill Gates' father's firm) was sanctioned, under the state's civil procedure rule 26(g), for failing to turn over documents in a serious medical malpractice action because of the way it twisted words in responding to a document discovery request. The plaintiffs requested production of any documents having to do with the drug "Somophyllin Oral liquid" as well as theophylline — the drug's more technical name — and were told such documents did not exist. Several years after the injury (serious brain damage to a young child) and ensuing lawsuit, an anonymous person sent the plaintiffs (both the treating doctor who claimed to have been lied to by the drug company and the child's parents) a copy of a letter which indicated the drug company had in fact warned doctors of the danger of the drug theophylline. The drug company did not produce the "smoking gun" document which revealed how dangerous the drug actually was because they claimed the plaintiffs' lawyers had failed to ask for documents relating to the exact drug compound and that these documents were actually filed elsewhere (in a file having to do with a competitive drug). The court found that the drug company's lawyers twisted every word in discovery requests so as not to produce the incriminating letters, and the lawyers were ordered to pay hundreds of thousands of dollars in sanctions, even though they claimed they were dutifully representing a client zealously in an adversarial system (and even though they were supported in this claim by at least one leading law professor who claimed aggressively resisting discovery requests was an ethical norm of discovery.)

3. At least two of the bad acts described above, after portrayals in movies (and reports on the front pages of many newspapers), have now been more formally dealt with by ethical rules (and empirical study). The billing improprieties described above have now been documented by Professor Lisa Lerman and have led to more disciplinary hearings in these cases. *See* Lisa Lerman, *Blue-Chip Bilking: Regulation of Billing and Expense Fraud by Lawyers,* 12 Georgetown Journal of Legal Ethics 205 (1999); Lisa Lerman, *The Slippery Slope from Ambition to Greed to Dishonesty: Lawyers, Money and Professional Integrity,* 30 Hofstra Law Review 878 (2002). And the American Bar Association has at least attempted to regulate information about billing, if not substantive prohibitions on particular practices. *See* Model Rules of Professional Conduct, Rule 1.5 (A lawyer's fee shall be reasonable, with suggestions for when fee arrangements should be in writing and some regulation of contingency fees.).

In the last two decades (coinciding with many depictions of lawyer-client, lawyer-judge, or lawyer-juror personal and sexual relationships in the movies, and also in real life), more and more states have passed formal statutes or regulations prohibiting sexual relations between lawyers and those with whom the lawyer might have a conflict of interest (that includes clients, jurors, and judges), but the particular formulation of the rule and who is included or excluded may still leave lots of opportunity for such "abuses" of relationships. And where, in some cases, consensual relations are still permitted, how are we to know what is really consensual when the power relations may be unequal (and can run in all sorts of different directions)? Many jurisdictions have passed statutes which attempt to regulate sexual or romantic relations between lawyers and clients by prohibiting sex unless the relationship predates the lawyer-client relationship. Does this solve the problem? *See* William Grady, *Legal World Starts to Build Case Against Sex With Clients,* Chicago Tribune, 27 June 1993; Lynda Crowly-Cyr & Carol Caple, *Sex With Clients and the Ethical Lawyer,* 8 James Cook Law Review 67 (2001); Caroline Forell, *Lawyers, Clients and Sex: Breaking the Silence on the Ethics,* 22 Golden Gate University Law Review 611 (1992).

4. Is it ever appropriate to consider acts committed outside of the professional role when evaluating lawyer or professional behavior? Consider the following examples of conduct by lawyers or legal officials:

— John Tower's rejection as Secretary of Defense because of alleged drinking and "womanizing";

— Gary Hart's loss of the Presidential nomination due to dishonesty and deceit about his adulterous affairs;

— President Bill Clinton's impeachment for perjury and obstruction of justice in one sexual harassment case linked to his behavior in a consensual sexual liaison with a White House intern;

— Senator Packwood's forced resignation from office due to many claims of sexual harassment;

— Mayor Giuliani's televised announcement of his plans to divorce his wife while she was recuperating from cancer and spend his future with a partner from an adulterous liaison;

— Posthumous disclosure (widely believed during his lifetime) of President Thomas Jefferson's unmarried sexual (and perhaps loving) relationship with slave Sally Hemings;

— Judge Sol Wachtler's removal from office and incarceration for criminal harassment following termination of an adulterous relationship and for threats made to his former lover and her family;

— Withdrawal of nomination of General Ralston for Joint Chief of Staff following disclosure of an earlier adulterous affair;

— Resignations by members of Congress Livingston and Gingrich and public "apology" of Dan Burton, following disclosures of affairs, children born out of wedlock and "hypocrisy," exposed by *Penthouse* publisher Larry Flynt, following Clinton sex scandals;

— Resignation from Congress of Joseph Kennedy, following a scandal involving his pursuit of an annulment of his marriage of twelve years;

— Disclosure of a variety of sexual liaisons between President John F. Kennedy and a number of paramours;

— The now common knowledge that President Franklin Roosevelt had an ongoing adulterous and loving relationship with his wife's social secretary, both before and after entering the White House;

— Disclosure of President George W. Bush's arrest and conviction for driving while under the influence of alcohol some years before his candidacy;

— The forced resignation of British Secretary of State for War John Profumo, following the disclosure of his adulterous liaison with "model" Christine Keeler (who was rumored to be consorting with Russian spies);

— The failed Cabinet appointments of several appointees, mostly women, such as Zoe Baird and Kimba Wood, for failing to pay social security taxes for childcare workers (otherwise known as "Nanny-gate").

What are we to make of the relationship of personal lives to professional work, responsibility, and morality? What is relevant to the consideration of what makes a good lawyer, both for purposes of admitting a new entrant to the bar and for purposes of disciplining, sanctioning, or removing a member of the legal profession? To what extent must legal professionals be judged by different standards than those applied to other professionals or from those applied to them in their capacity as ordinary human beings? The scope of inquiry into a lawyer's private life has had an accordion-like existence in American history, opening and closing in relation to larger political and social forces. Carrie Menkel-Meadow, *Private Lives and Professional Responsibilities: The Relationship of Personal Morality to Lawyering and Professional Ethics,* 21 Pace Law Review 365 (2001).

The ethical rule which attempts to define professional misconduct for a lawyer states:

Rule 8.3 Misconduct

It is professional misconduct for a lawyer to:

a) violate or attempt to violate the Rules of Professional Conduct, knowingly assist or induce another to do so, or do so through acts of another;

b) commit a criminal act that reflects adversely on the lawyer's honesty, trustworthiness or fitness as a lawyer in other respects;

c) engage in conduct involving dishonesty, fraud, deceit or misrepresentation;

d) engage in conduct that is prejudicial to the administration of justice. . . .

How many of the acts described above or viewed in the movies you have seen about lawyers violate this rule? Clearly the murders committed by Teddy Barnes in *Jagged Edge,* Sam Bowden in *Cape Fear,* and the widespread criminal conduct depicted in *The Firm* are clear violations (unless you do not think these criminal acts "reflect adversely on the lawyer's honesty, trustworthiness, or fitness as a lawyer"). Thus, even this "criminal acts" standard seems to require some nexus to lawyering to constitute an ethical (not criminal) violation. What about all the sexual indiscretions described above or depicted in the movies? Does it matter if the parties are married, or in particular legal relationships? Should anyone care about people's private lives if they perform their "professional" duties appropriately? When are private lives and private acts relevant to assessing professional quality or character?

What about the demonstrations and protests Lucy Kelsen engages in to prevent the demolition of her beloved community center and other properties in New York (for which she is arrested)? Do lawyers have First Amendment rights too? Can a lawyer be disciplined for arrests or even criminal convictions if they have no bearing on the quality of her work as a lawyer? What if, as Lucy would probably argue, her arrests are actually *part of* and integral to her work as a politically active lawyer?

5. Do lawyers who advise their clients to "avoid" or "evade" (do you know the legal difference?) taxes, or who advise about or predict the likelihood of enforcement of the law (when they know clients will use the information to commit unlawful acts) violate this rule? Is Fletcher Reede's habitual lying professional misconduct?

6. Was it misconduct for Anthony Judson Lawrence to intentionally violate Rule 1.1 (A lawyer shall provide competent representation to a client) when he took on the criminal defense of his friend Chet, knowing that he had no expertise as a criminal trial lawyer? Can you pinpoint when in *The Devil's Advocate* Kevin Lomax's zealous advocacy turns into misconduct? Does John Milton commit any acts of lawyer ethical misconduct?

7. Many legal scholars and critics have argued that the use of the lawyer's technical skill to develop "technocratic" interpretations of the ethical rules is precisely what leads lawyers down the "slippery slope" to John Milton's legal hell. From "simple" exaggerations of a few minutes in billing, to "puffing" in negotiations, to "misplacing" a few key documents, to asking a secretary or assistant to lie about your whereabouts, to lying to your spouse and family about your activities or whereabouts, soon the lawyer may not know what is true or good or right in either his/her personal or professional life. *See* Patrick J. Schiltz, *On Being a Happy, Healthy, and Ethical Member of an Unhappy, Unhealthy, and Unethical Profession*, 52 Vanderbilt Law Review 871 (1999); Heidi Li Feldman, *Codes and Virtues: Can Good Lawyers be Good Ethical Deliberators?* 69 Southern California Law Review 885 (1996).

8. What "good" or inspiring acts do you see taken by lawyers in popular culture? Perhaps the most common theme is the representation of an unpopular (but usually wrongly accused) defendant like Tom Robinson in *To Kill a Mockingbird* (1962). But think of some more modern examples. Lucy Kelsen goes to work for the Trump-like real estate developer George Wade in order to preserve the Coney Island community center and encourage her boss to make many important charitable and public interest contributions. Michael Brock in John Grisham's novel *The Street Lawyer* (1998) becomes a lawyer for the homeless after he is held hostage by a homeless person in his swank law firm. Anthony Judson Lawrence demonstrates one of the few examples of good craft lawyering outside of the courtroom by giving helpful corporate and tax advice (even if there might be some unethical activity in his giving advice to an already represented client, *see* Rule 4.2). Scott Turow's lawyers often have trouble in their personal lives, but more often than not they work hard and eventually "do the right thing" with their cases (even disgorging harmful information when they have to). Scott Turow knows first-hand about potential ethical improprieties, having been complained against and acquitted of "assertive" prosecutorial practices. *See* Carrie Menkel-Meadow, *Scott Turow,* in *Yale Encyclopedia of Legal Biography* (forthcoming, 2007).

9. And what do you make of those more complex or "mixed" acts like Atticus Finch's lie at the end of *To Kill a Mockingbird* (1962) to cover the murder committed by Boo Radley to save Finch's children, or the murders by Teddy Barnes in *Jagged Edge* and Sam Bowden in *Cape Fear*? Lawyers (in the movies and probably in real life too) often commit what look like unlawful or "bad" acts to achieve a higher, if not fully "legal," justice. Professor William Simon calls this "moral pluck" when the lawyer commits an act of "transgression and resourcefulness in the vindication of justice." William Simon, *Moral*

Pluck: Legal Ethics in Popular Culture, 101 Columbia Law Review 421, 422 (2001). He suggests that depictions of more complex lawyering (and personal) acts reveal the need for less authoritarian rules and the recognition that we must exercise moral and discretionary judgment when choosing our own acts, as well as judging others'. Ambiguous, ambivalent, or "mixed" motive acts of not-so-clear good or bad, in popular culture as well as in real life, demonstrate that good lawyers need to exercise individual initiative, respond sensitively to different contexts, and be flexible, smart, and morally accountable practical problem solvers. We must be careful not to judge too quickly those single acts, that when accumulated, may form a lawyer's more complex "character."

D. LAWYERS' CHARACTER(S)

Although the dramatic moments in films about lawyers tend to turn on particular acts (the incisive cross-examination question, the discovery of a hidden document, the investigation of an unknown fact, the brilliant closing argument, the suffered-over refusal of a settlement offer, the ruthlessly negotiated contract or divorce settlement, the delivery of brilliant tax advice or good P.R. material, and — most dramatically — the return of a verdict), after the film is over we are more likely to remember the "gestalt" of the character of the lawyer. John Milton (*The Devil's Advocate*) is evil incarnate, and the fictional Atticus Finch (like the real Clarence Darrow) has become an iconic folk-hero of good lawyering, even though anyone who has seen the movie knows Atticus Finch is actually more complicated as a character. Gregory Peck, who is linked in our mind's eye forever with Atticus, is even more complicated in the other role he played in the same year (1962) — Sam Bowden in the first version of *Cape Fear*. In both films the southern lawyer of white suits and professional, legal, and moral "purity" takes justice into his own hands (by lying in *To Kill A Mockingbird* and killing in *Cape Fear*). These acts are morally justified, perhaps, but they are not subjected to the scrutiny of the legal process and the ultimate trial scene on which so many films depend. Less caricatured lawyer characters and those who learn, grow, and are often "redeemed" in films or books about lawyers offer more nuanced and perhaps more accurate reflections of what it actually means to be a lawyer, confronted with complicated and difficult professional, personal, and moral decisions.

At least one commentator has suggested that popular and populist treatments of these more complex characters offers a corrective to overly rigid conceptions of good/moral and bad/unethical lawyering:

MORAL PLUCK: LEGAL ETHICS IN POPULAR CULTURE
William H. Simon
101 Columbia Law Review 421 (2001)

A study of legal ethics in popular culture has two possible payoffs. First, popular culture is a source of evidence about popular moral understanding. The Conformist Moralism of the Bar and the impeachment proponents is based in part on factual premises about popular morality. The Conformists justify their precepts partly as responsive to categorical and authoritarian tendencies in the moral thinking of ordinary people. The evidence to be examined here suggests that these assumptions are mistaken. At least in some moments, popular morality is disposed to a style of moral judgment considerably different from the one Conformist Moralism attributes to it. Second, Moral Pluck is a substantive challenge to Conformist doctrine. The challenge is made, not through an explicit argument, but through dramatic representations of a type of ethical predicament and of styles of response to it. To be sure, these works romanticize lawyering, just as "lawyer jokes" demonize it, but their distortions are no greater than those of established professional responsibility doctrine. While popular culture is utopian about the possibilities of individual initiative, established doctrine is utopian about the reliability of official institutions. . . .

I. The Conformist Perspective

Elite moralism in general and professional responsibility doctrine in particular is strongly categorical and authoritarian. Ethics is categorical when it insists on appraising conduct in terms of rigid rules, with few if any exceptions and excuses. To take the most famous and extreme example, Kant insisted that lying is always wrong, even when necessary to save an innocent life. In the impeachment crisis, the President's prosecutors denied that either the private nature of the conduct involved or its marginal relevance to the Paula Jones case excused or even mitigated his perjury. They insisted that excusing any kind of perjury would threaten the "rule of law."

Professional responsibility doctrine is categorical in its proclivity for rules insensitive to the contingencies of particular situations. Such rules tend to require mechanical judgment or literal application. They frequently mandate that the decisionmaker take actions that she correctly sees as unjust or contrary to important public values. Notoriously, for example, the confidentiality rules require that the lawyer keep secrets even in some situations where disclosure might save an innocent life and the client's interests are trivial.

Ethics is authoritarian when it conflates moral authority with the explicit commands or enactments of government institutions. For the impeachment proponents, it was sufficient that the President had violated a judge's order and the terms of a federal statute. Even if they had been convinced that the judge's order was wrong or that the statute, as applied, would subvert fundamental privacy values, they would not have deemed these considerations relevant. The President's lawyers seemed to concede this authoritarian view by focusing their arguments, not on appeals to the privacy values that were threatened by an inquisition into consensual sex, but on casuistic claims that the President's deceptive answers did not amount to perjury.

The authoritarian disposition appears in professional responsibility doctrine in the tendency to define law and legal authority in terms of the state. The Model Code distinguishes legal authority from moral, economic, social, and political factors that, though sometimes important, must take a back seat. Lawyers are obliged to press for their clients' interests subject only to the constraints of formally-enacted commands. At the same time, lawyers are obliged to respect any norm that qualifies as law by formal enactment, even where such respect contributes to injustice. There is no tolerance, for example, for civil disobedience — principled noncompliance with unjust positive law. The Bar's norms condemn "even minor violations of law by a lawyer." They insist that the only appropriate response to unjust law is to petition institutions with formal legislative authority to enact revisions.

All these themes contribute to a pervasive hostility to independent judgment in professional responsibility rhetoric. This hostility is transparent in the Multistate Professional Responsibility Examination, which in most states is the only testing of legal ethics in connection with admission to the bar. The examination is preoccupied with black-letter disciplinary rules. Since it is multiple-choice and machine-graded, it focuses on situations that lend themselves to glib black-and-white responses. Bar review instructors commonly advise applicants: "What they are testing is your ability to memorize."

In informal legal ethics discussions, a variety of rhetorical tropes are routinely deployed to penalize independent judgment. When lawyers appeal to informal norms of justice to explain either violations of enacted law or refusals to push client interests to the limits of enacted law, they are charged with self-righteousness and self-aggrandizement: "playing God," "arrogating power to herself," "imposing her own values," "undermining the established process." In the academic literature, frequent disapproval of discretionary norms is linked to concerns about "accountability." Although it is not always clear to whom accountability is sought, it usually appears that the authors contemplate control by the state.

The moral premises of popular fictional portrayals of lawyering are often quite different from this Conformist tradition. Popular fiction is anti-categorical and anti-authoritarian. Categorical norms require us to disregard all but a narrow range of the particularities of the situation. But fiction is committed to particularity. These works tend to evoke situations in which general norms are at war with more powerful particularistic intuitions. The authoritarianism of Conformist Moralism implies a consistently benign and reliable state. But popular culture warns that the state is often incompetent or corrupt and draws attention to the frightening and unjust consequences of its failings. . . .

V. Lessons from Popular Culture

This material from popular culture has two potential contributions to ethics: first as a source of evidence about popular moral thinking, and second as a substantive contribution to ethical understanding. . . .

These entertainments usefully remind us that there is a moral orientation with broad popular appeal that is neither categorical and authoritarian on the one hand, nor relativistic on the other. They raise doubts about the view that has influenced both the Bar and the Congressional leadership that moral precepts framed in categorical and authoritarian terms are most likely to be compatible with ordinary moral thinking. For the appeal of these works seems to depend on a capacity for contextual judgment and a principled skepticism toward authority.

The second potential contribution of these works is substantive. They offer an ethical perspective that competes with Conformist Moralism as a source of moral guidance. The tone of this perspective is Emersonian. It is an ethic of self-assertion that encourages us to think of morality as an occasion for creativity. By contrast, the tone of Conformist Moralism is Puritanical and Kantian. It is an ethic of self-restraint that emphasizes the need to curb our more aggressive and destructive impulses through deference to external authority. Moral Pluck insists that ethics is not simply a matter of duties to society, but rather of character and personal integrity. While philosophers have argued for this perspective abstractly, popular culture teaches it by urging us to identify imaginatively with an attractive figure and then confronting us with the damage to the character's commitments and self-conception that deference to authority sometimes would require.

At the same time, these works insist that we take account of situations in which norms of authority are in tension with substantive justice. They remind us incessantly of the widespread ineptitude and corruption of official institutions. At one extreme — in the darker Grisham novels — these institutions are integral parts of a vast criminal conspiracy. The works also remind us of the limitations of categorical norms that arise from their unresponsiveness to vital dimensions of some morally urgent situations. The confidentiality norm is the most prominent example. Many of these works try to demonstrate that the Bar's established norms are potentially incompatible with morally plausible responses to situations with high stakes. These are important lessons, and Conformist Moralism is deficient for ignoring them. Its view of the good lawyer is unattractive in its passivity and complacency.

Nevertheless, the type of popular works we are considering have undeniable limitations as a form of ethical reflection. One familiar complaint is that popular culture oversimplifies. Instead of promoting reflection, it gratifies unconscious desires for self-assertion by abstracting away the most important moral and strategic difficulties of real world ethical dilemmas. Some of us get visceral satisfaction watching Clint Eastwood or Sylvester Stallone blow away bad guys unconstrained by due process or physical limitations, but on reflection we do not regard their characters as role models. These fantasies grossly understate the dangers of transgressive self-assertion and underestimate the importance of institutional authority.

The works considered here are more self-conscious and thoughtful about ethics than the typical Hollywood "action" movie. Still, it has to be conceded that, as ethical discourse, they are unambitious. To begin with, the dilemmas they portray tend to take a Manichean form with implausible frequency. The works mislead by suggesting that, in the situations where lawyers perceive a tension between the dictates of established authority and their conceptions of substantive justice, defiance of authority would usually meet with the approval of most ordinary people (at least if they knew the facts). In fact, popular moral values are strongly divided across a broad range of situations. There are many situations in which many people would find unattractive the substantive values lawyers would assert in good faith defiance of constituted authority. . . .

The attitude expressed in these works toward institutions is also fanciful. The problem is not that they exaggerate the ineptitude and corruption of official institutions, though they probably do. More importantly, they portray Moral Pluck exclusively as an individual matter. The protagonists accomplish their heroic feats by themselves, or with the informal help of a few close friends. And their own transgressive initiatives leave no institutional traces. They do not contribute to new, more satisfactory institutions or alter the basic contours of established ones. . . .

NOTES & QUESTIONS

1. Professor Simon's article explores the "transgressive" ethical choices made by lawyers in John Grisham's novels and the lawyers on television shows such as *L.A. Law* and *The Practice*. He says that these works show lawyers who are more "self-conscious" and "thoughtful about ethics" than "the typical Hollywood action movie." Recall that Professor Asimow suggested above that lawyers are depicted in a more positive light on television programs than in the movies. Why might this be so? How do the different media showcase or develop different aspects of professional behavior? Does the movie format require dramatic action in individual acts where novels and ongoing television programs allow a longer observation of the development of character over time?

Consider that when professional disciplinary committees have to decide how to punish ethical violations they have to consider both "acts" (in determining if there is an ethical violation) and then look to a whole career ("character") in meting out punishments or other remedies.

How do you judge professionals? Based on single acts or ongoing behavior? How do you make judgments about other people in your life? Relatives and family members? Friends? Classmates? Teachers? How much "data" do we need to have about a person or the context in which they act to understand whether what they are doing is worthy or not?

2. While praising the "moral pluck" of some lawyers in popular culture, Professor Simon is also worried that the messages suggested by popular culture overemphasize the romantic power of the individual. Lawyers are seen making "heroic" or brave decisions on their own and are less often shown changing the corrupt or problematic institutions in which they must operate (such as the American legal system, legislative lobbying, corporate decision-making). Other commentators have suggested that individual lawyers of exceptional professional character can positively affect not only their own profession, but the polity at large. See Robert Gordon, *The Independence of Lawyers*, 68 Boston University Law Review 11 (1988) and Anthony T. Kronman, *The Lost Lawyer: Failing Ideals of the Legal Profession* (1993), discussing the lawyer as "statesman."

Can you think of any popular depictions of institutional or collective law reform? (The 1979 film *Norma Rae* dramatized a union organizing campaign.) Lucy Kelsen, in *Two Weeks Notice*, is presented as both an individual and collective law reformer and protester (the daughter of a law professor mother and a civil liberties-seeking father) for anti-poverty, community, environmental, and other legal causes. The lawyers on *The Practice* at least band together as a group to put the state to its proof in the criminal justice system. The prosecutors in all the *Law & Order* shows (even with cast changes) act as if they share an institutional commitment, both to the workplace and to criminal justice. Do lawyers for the state, as depicted in both movies and films, ever make "brave" ethical choices that demonstrate their commitment, not just to convictions, but to justice? Model Rule 3.8 requires more of prosecutors; they must not only represent their clients (the "people" or the State) but also seek justice. Rule 3.8 Comment says a prosecutor has the responsibility of a minister of justice and not simply that of an advocate.

3. How much "control" do you think individuals have over their own moral development in their careers? To what extent does the particular law office or context of practice influence or socialize a lawyer's character? Consider the different law firm cultures depicted on *L.A. Law* (glamorous and diverse, mostly civil, practice), *The Practice* (chummy, committed, diverse criminal defense practice, with many ethical discussions and debates), *Law & Order* (committed long-term colleagues with explicit supervisory and political meetings with bosses, seniors, and juniors), and the large law firms in *Philadelphia* (1992), *The Young Philadelphians* (1959), *The Verdict* (1982), *Class Action* (1990), *Erin Brockovich* (2000), and *The Devil's Advocate* (1997)? How often do films about lawyers depict the full complexity of character development in the crucible of law practice settings, including the economics and personal stress of partnership decisions? *See* Marc Galanter & Thomas Palay, *Tournament of Lawyers: The Transformation of the Big Law Firm* (1991).

4. How are characters formed or influenced by mentors or supervisors in the media? Consider how the classic lawyer and doctor programs of the Golden Era had Dr. Massey advising Dr. Kildare, Dr. Zorba advising Ben Casey, and Lawrence Preston using his senior authority to morally instruct his son and junior partner Kenneth Preston on *The Defenders*. *See* David Ray Papke, *The Defenders*, in *Prime Time Law: Fictional Television as Legal Narrative* (Robert M. Jarvis & Paul R. Joseph, eds., 1998); Harris Dienstfrey, *Doctors, Lawyers and Other TV Heroes,* in 35 Commentary (1963), reprinted in *Television: The Critical View* (Horace Newcombe, ed., 1976). Contrast the depiction of the parental role models of John Milton in *The Devil's Advocate* and Jedediah Ward in *Class Action*. How often do we see senior and junior lawyers grappling with generational differences in ethics, as depicted in Auchincloss' *Diary of a Yuppie* (1986), and dealing with moral character issues by discussing the Model Rules' complex structure of hierarchy and deference to seniors, while requiring reporting of ethical violations by all lawyers (*see* Model Rules 5.1, Responsibilities of a Partner or Supervisory Lawyer, and Model Rule 5.2, Responsibilities of a Subordinate Lawyer).

5. Is character framed, in part, by who the individual is demographically and personally? To what extent do you think your character was framed in your family, in your religious training, in your peer cultures, or by who you "are" (male, female, black, white, Hispanic or Latino, Asian, European, mixed race or nationality, Christian, Jew, Muslim, Zen Buddhist)?

In a debate that has raged for several decades now, many scholars have argued that women may bring a different moral sensibility to the practice of law, "by seeking to do less harm, solve more problems, be more concerned with human relationships of both clients and of those who interact with clients, and to deal with others more honestly and fairly." Carrie Menkel-Meadow, *Can They Do That?*, *supra*, at 1323; Carrie Menkel-Meadow, *Portia in a Different Voice: Speculations on a Women's Lawyering Process*, 1 Berkeley Women's Law Journal 39 (1985); Carrie Menkel-Meadow, *Portia Redux: Another Look at Gender, Feminism and Legal Ethics*, 2 Virginia Journal of Social Policy & Law 75 (1995); Carrie Menkel-Meadow, *The Feminization of the Legal Profession: The Comparative Sociology of Women Lawyers,* in *Lawyers in Society: Comparative Theories* (Richard Abel & Philip Lewis, eds., 1989). See the source for this argument in Carol Gilligan, *In a Different Voice* (1982).

Consider how this debate was humorously depicted in *All of Me* (1984), a classic "transposed bodies" film. In this film, which uses a now standard plot of bump-on-the-head transformation into someone else, Steve Martin, playing a stereotypically aggressive and dishonest lawyer, becomes literally embodied with the soul of Lily Tomlin, a deceased, do-gooding woman. In what has to be one of the funniest and most serious critiques of the character of lawyers, Lily Tomlin and Steve Martin literally, figuratively, and linguistically fight over the control of both body and soul of a lawyer who, in Steve Martin's body, makes a dishonest closing argument, as Lily Tomlin struggles to push the truth out of Steve Martin's mouth. Of course, this scene can be read not only as a gender critique of lying male lawyers but also as the "layperson as moral, lawyer as good professional but bad person" critique found in much moral philosophy. Carrie Menkel-Meadow, *Can They Do That?*, *supra*, at 1323.

Do you think women lawyers are depicted differently than men in popular culture? Are Lucy Kelsen and Teddy Barnes more "moral" or sensitive than Frank Galvin, Kevin Lomax, and Atticus Finch? Consider how tough the female prosecutors in *Law & Order* are or how much more complex the female lawyers of *L.A. Law* and *The Practice* were (Ann Kelsey, Grace Van Owen, Helen Gambel, Ellenor Frutt, Lindsay Dole, and Rebecca Washington). And consider the ethical improprieties committed by Teddy Barnes in *Jagged Edge*, Kathleen Riley in *Suspect*, and Maggie Ward in *Class Action*. Do you think there is anything to the argument that women lawyers are more likely to use "caring" or "morally connected" approaches to practicing law? Why or why not? What might be the reasons for differences in styles, approaches, or philosophies of the practice of law by gender?

There are also occasionally depictions of minority lawyers confronted with issues about their racial, national, or minority identity and how that interacts with the way they make decisions or practice law. Consider Joe Miller, the character played by Denzel Washington in *Philadelphia* (1992), who is not particularly sympathetic to gay rights and initially turns down the representation of Andrew Beckett, a white gay lawyer dismissed from his law firm, discriminatorily, because he has AIDS. Miller, a black lawyer, clearly understands what discrimination is all about, and the film uses his race to "double" track the discrimination story. And consider how *L.A. Law* used (and made the career of) Jimmy Smits as the Hispanic Victor Sifuentes, who initially refused to join the firm because he did not want to become "the Mexican gardener picking up the snails." John Brigham, *L.A. Law*, in *Prime Time Law, supra*, at 29.

Consider the poignancy with which the black lawyer, Eugene Young, on *The Practice*, was depicted as struggling for his parental custody rights when his wife tried to take his son away from him because of the son's exposure to criminals in his father's practice, after the son is arrested for drug possession. Young courageously underscored important lawyer character issues (commitment to justice and equal treatment) and coupled them with sensitivity to the added social dimension of race. His defense of his profession and its purpose is an especially eloquent vindication of the criminal defense lawyer's calling and commitment to justice that has been seen in the popular media in decades. *See* episodes *Cross-Fire,* broadcast ABC, March 4, 1999, and *Target Practice,* broadcast ABC, March 7, 1999. Carrie Menkel-Meadow, *Can They Do That?, supra*, 1323–24.

Perhaps the most troubling of lawyer character issues depicted in the popular media, which replicates the debates among legal philosophers and ethicists, is the tension between commitment to law and commitment to justice in a lawyer of good character. As Americans and lawyers, we argue throughout the world for the sanctity, as well as the instrumental fairness, of the rule of law. Some legal ethicists seek clarity and conformity in the "law of lawyering." Writers of popular fiction, movies, and television mirror the challenge that William Simon and others have posed to the law of legal ethics.

Is lawyer character constituted from ordinary human mettle? Strength of character? Commitment? Loyalty? Honesty? Selflessness and protection of others? Good judgment? Leadership? Or, is good lawyerly character supposed to be faithful to the rules of law, ethics, and procedure? Literary and popular depictions of lawyers dramatize these tensions, as legal philosophers debate the differences between morality and positive law.

In the movies and on television, the good lawyer character just as often demonstrates a departure from the rules of law in the name of a greater justice as it does conformity to it. We may want to question why this is so; do these fictional depictions help us develop role models committed to justice or is there also a danger that good and strong characters might allow us to take justice, and law (as long as we are "worthy" and morally justified) into our own hands"? Carrie Menkel-Meadow, *Can They Do That?, supra,* 1324–25.

How do we feel when we watch Teddy Barnes and Sam Bowden, both lawyers, commit murder to achieve some form of human "justice"?

E.   LAWYERS' CHOICES AND LEARNING: REDEMPTION OF THE LEGAL PROFESSIONAL

Good drama is intended to illuminate our human condition — both the actors in the play and the viewers in the audience should learn something (and, in many forms of drama, "change" as a result of that learning) during the action. The more sophisticated films, novels, and television shows about lawyers demonstrate how lawyers have learned from the actions they have taken and how they can be better, both professionally and personally, as a result of what they have learned. Kevin Lomax (*The Devil's Advocate*) wakes from his Hollywood-provided dream to realize he does not have to work for his devilish father and represent the guilty; he can withdraw from that representation and seek the truth, as well as the just. Fletcher Reede (*Liar Liar*) learns to speak the truth about the love of his son (how this will affect his legal career is not clear at the end of the movie). Lucy Kelsen (*Two Weeks Notice*) finds true love outside her legal aid office when her former boss, George Wade, gives up his ill-gotten fortune to be with her, just as Teddy Barnes (*Jagged Edge*) loses (kills) her ill-gotten romance with her client, while recognizing her own gullibility and lost faith in the criminal justice system. Anthony Judson Lawrence (by narrating his own story in *The Young Philadelphians*) tells us at the beginning of the movie that we will have to wait until the end to judge his full character; he has been an ambitious social climber, but he has been a good lawyer. When he defends his college friend out of loyalty, he is rewarded with the love of a good (and very rich!) woman. Maggie Ward (*Class Action*) sees the error of her big-firm ambitions and joins her father by switching sides in a products liability (car design) case to seek justice for the injured. And, in what is likely to go down in the annals of lawyer films as the ultimate redemption movie, Frank Galvin (*The Verdict*), a dissipated, lazy, and drunken solo practitioner, learns to sober up and do some hard work, both in investigation and trial, and triumphs over the cocky Boston Brahmin law firm representing the Catholic Church's hospital.

These filmic depictions of learning by lawyers offer viewers an opportunity to see acts change characters. By stumbling through law practice or life, these lawyers learn that they can be better than they seem — often after they come to realize that the legal system may not be all that it seems to be.

THE MOVIE LAWYERS' GUIDE TO REDEMPTIVE
LEGAL PRACTICE
Paul Bergman
48 UCLA Law Review 1393 (2001)

The Chinese use two brush strokes to write the word "crisis." One brush stroke stands for danger; the other for opportunity. In crisis, be aware of the danger — but recognize the opportunity.

An enduring film image is the "moment of crisis" that produces the "moment of truth." Ships about to sink or brakeless cars plummeting down steep mountain roads often provide the impetus for dramatic revelations. In such settings, and in line with the policy behind the "dying declaration" exception to the hearsay rule, characters are prone to revealing long-hidden truths. In Filmland, crises can also be very good medicine. Characters who are fortunate enough to survive moments of crisis often emerge with improved happiness and moral values. Forced by crises to confront suppressed realities, movie characters may choose to redeem their lives by committing their futures to performing what audiences are likely to perceive as good works. Thus, filmmakers may use crises as a tool for sending powerful normative messages about what constitutes a morally good and personally satisfying life.

This Essay examines films in which movie lawyers are redeemed by moments of crisis. Just as crises may serve as tools for sending normative messages about what constitutes a morally good and satisfying personal life, so too may crises lead movie lawyers to "redemptive lawyering," or morally good and personally satisfying professional lifestyles. The Essay examines images of redemptive lawyering for reel lawyers and compares those images to the attitudes of real lawyers.

I. Redemption for Reel Lawyers

Redemptive lawyering in films occurs when sudden, dramatic, or even catastrophic events jolt movie lawyers into adopting morally good and personally satisfying professional lifestyles. Images of redemptive lawyering can convey powerful normative images of lawyering ideals, and of what lawyers can be and can do to emerge from frustrating, unsatisfying, and even unethical careers. The subsections below describe three forms of redemptive lawyering that movie lawyers have adopted in response to crises.

A. Problem-Centered Lawyering

"Problem-centered lawyering" is one form of redemptive lawyering. Redemption occurs when a crisis enables a lawyer to realize that ultimate professional satisfaction consists of using legal knowledge and legal experience to craft satisfactory solutions to clients' problems. The idea is that a life devoted to problem solving is personally satisfying. Moreover, because most of us tend to believe that helping people in need is a socially valuable activity, audiences are likely to perceive devotion to clients' problems as morally good.

Counsellor at Law [1933] presents an archetypal example of a movie lawyer who finds redemption in problem-centered lawyering. George Simon (John Barrymore) is an up-from-the-gutter Jew who has become one of New York City's most successful lawyers. Simon's office, where the entire movie takes place, is a jumble of frantic activity. Simon is in his element, juggling a stream of legal and personal problems brought to him by clients, his mother, his partner, his wife, an investigator, various office employees, and others. However, what matters most to Simon is not his law practice, but his non-Jewish trophy wife Cora (Doris Kenyon). He brags about Cora constantly, and is so concerned with preserving Cora's social status that he turns down a case that would have produced a lucrative fee, but that Cora felt would embarrass her in the eyes of her friends. Thus, when Simon finds out that Cora has been unfaithful, the moment of crisis is at hand. For Simon, because law practice was but a means to acceptance by what he considered the social elite, Cora's unfaithfulness robs his practice of its meaning. Simon opens the window of his suddenly dark, quiet office and prepares to jump to his death. But like many a prizefighter, Simon is saved by the bell — in this case, the bell of his telephone. Simon's adoring secretary Regina Gordon (Bebe Daniels) was supposed to have left for the day, but she returned to the office because she was worried about him. Regina answers the phone and tells Simon that the caller is the president of a steel company whose son is in serious trouble. At first, Simon remains in suicide mode; he orders Regina to hang up. In moments, however, Simon reverts to the confident, energetic lawyer we have seen throughout the movie. He excitedly grabs the phone, shouts instructions to the president, and rushes out of the office with Regina to his client's aid.

The moment of crisis enables Simon to achieve redemption by becoming a problem-centered lawyer. In crisis, Simon recognizes that chasing after Cora and her elite society friends is unimportant compared to the personal satisfaction and even the exhilaration of confronting and overcoming challenging legal problems. Moreover, Simon's commitment to problem solving is morally good, as he places himself in the immediate service of a client who, although the president of a steel company, is at bottom a father worried about his son. The film's final scene symbolizes Simon's redemption. As he leaves his office for the first time in the film, so he sheds his old self and what he had falsely valued in law practice. *Counsellor at Law* conjures a strong image of commitment to problem solving as a lawyerly ideal, and suggests that devotion to problem solving is both professionally satisfying and morally good without regard to the status of the client.

B. Client-Centered Lawyering

"Client-centered lawyering" is a second form of redemptive lawyering. Redemption occurs when crisis enables a lawyer to realize that the ultimate source of a satisfactory professional career is bonding with clients. This image depicts clients as weak and in desperate need of protection. It suggests the need for lawyers to empathize with clients in order to provide them with the legal help they deserve. An empathic lawyer is both professionally happy and morally good.

Lawyer Man [1933] is an early and somewhat general example of client-centered redemption. Anton Adam (William Powell) has a small but successful practice serving the largely immigrant population on New York's lower east side. Olga Michaels (Joan Blondell) is Adam's standard-issue adoring secretary. After a significant courtroom victory, Adam closes his store-front office and joins a powerful uptown practice, where he prospers. To Olga's disgust, Adam seems to have turned his back on his former clients. Economic success for Adam comes with a price, however — the mob wants him to do its bidding. When Adam refuses, the mob sets him up and the ensuing criminal charges ruin his lucrative career. Adam's specific moment of crisis emerges when the mob boss offers Adam a judgeship. While this probably would not be a crisis for most lawyers, it is for Adam because he understands that the offer was made with the idea that, because he has been publicly disgraced and has nowhere to turn, the mob will expect to dictate Adam's decisions. Adam does have a place to turn, however — the lower-east-side practice where he started his career. Arm in arm, Adam and Olga happily walk through streets teeming with the politically powerless population to which Adam will devote the remainder of his career.

Adam's bond is not with a specific client, but with a population with which he shares common roots. More typically, personal redemption for movie lawyers comes from the plight of a specific client. In *The Verdict* [1982], Frank

Galvin (Paul Newman) is a boozed-out personal injury lawyer who tries to scratch out a living by soliciting clients in funeral parlors. Galvin has one case of real value, a medical malpractice case against two anesthesiologists and the hospital that employed them. The complaint, which had been filed by Galvin's mentor, Mickey Morrissey (Jack Warden), alleged that the doctors administered an improper anesthetic to a young woman who entered the hospital's emergency room to have a baby. The improper anesthetic left the young woman comatose. Unfortunately for his clients, the comatose woman's guardians, Galvin has done nothing on the case. It's hard to prepare for trial when you're dead drunk most of the time.

Galvin's moment of redemption occurs when he decides to visit the comatose woman in the hospital. As he takes photographs of her lying helplessly in a hospital bed, kept alive by a respirator and feeding tube, he bonds with her though she cannot speak, hear, see, or offer him a drink. For the first time, Galvin realizes the woman's helplessness and his responsibility to bring to justice the doctors who ruined her life. Significantly, Galvin tells the nurses who want to know why he is in the hospital room, "I'm her lawyer." Thereafter, Galvin works relentlessly for his client. Further evidence of Galvin's redemption occurs when he engages in pretrial settlement negotiations with defense lawyer Ed Concannon (James Mason) in the chambers of Judge Hoyle (Milo O'Shea). Judge Hoyle chides Galvin for turning down a large settlement offer, commenting, "your client could walk out of here with a lot of money." "She can't walk," is Galvin's reply. Galvin is so personally connected to his client that he takes the judge's figurative comment as a personal slight. The film's conclusion further signifies Galvin's redemptive transformation. Though the jurors have no legal basis for doing so, they return a huge verdict in favor of the comatose woman. Galvin later receives a phone call from Laura Fischer (Charlotte Rampling) whom Concannon had employed as a sexual spy to report on Galvin's trial strategy. Galvin's refusal to answer the phone suggests that he has renounced his former habits and will devote himself to his clients.

Joe Miller (Denzel Washington) in *Philadelphia* [1992] becomes a client-centered lawyer when he connects discrimination against homosexual AIDS sufferer Andrew Beckett (Tom Hanks) to discrimination against African Americans. Miller is an African American lawyer with a small but successful neighborhood personal injury practice. At the start of the film, Beckett is an up-and-coming star attorney with one of Philadelphia's largest and most prestigious law firms. However, by the time he asks Miller to represent him in an employment discrimination lawsuit against the law firm, Beckett is deathly ill with AIDS. Beckett claims that he was illegally fired because of his illness. Miller initially refuses to take the case, partly because he thinks it unwinnable, but primarily because he wants nothing to do with the AIDS virus or homosexuals.

Some weeks later, Miller and Beckett are doing legal research at adjacent tables in a public law library. Miller's moment of crisis emerges when he notices a white patron staring at him. The patron's disdainful look suggests that as an African American, Miller could only be a client and therefore should not be in a section of the library reserved for lawyers. Miller then observes a librarian rudely trying to convince a noticeably ill Beckett to move to a private research room. At this redemptive moment, Miller recognizes that both he and Beckett are targets of discrimination. After Beckett holds his ground, Miller asks him about the status of his employment discrimination claim. Beckett calls Miller's attention to a portion of a case establishing that Beckett's claim is legally valid. Miller reads the last portion, in which the court refers to discrimination against AIDS sufferers as the equivalent of "social death," and comparable to any form of illegal discrimination in which prejudice is based on the presumed characteristics of a group rather than individual merit. The language cements the personal bond between Miller and Beckett as targets of discrimination. In the next scene Miller is representing Beckett; he serves the senior partner of Beckett's ex-law firm with a complaint for employment discrimination.

The film suggests the redemptive power of client-centered lawyering. Miller had been anti-gay, and his practice seemingly consisted of going through the motions on behalf of clients in whom he had no personal interest in order to earn a good, steady income. After taking on Beckett's case, Miller becomes aware that homosexual relationships are much like his own, and he views gay rights as an important civil rights issue. He tries the case with a zeal that demonstrates that he has a personal, as well as an economic, stake in its outcome. Thus, *Philadelphia* suggests that lawyers can redeem themselves by personally bonding with clients.

The Accused [1988] offers a final example of client-centered redemption. Sarah Tobias (Jodie Foster), who scrapes out a meager living as a waitress, is raped by three men in a bar. Numerous barflies cheer the rapists on. Prosecutor Kathryn Murphy (Kelly McGillis) initially seeks the maximum punishment. However, she soon finds out that Tobias has a spotty past and that just before the rape, Tobias had been drinking heavily and dancing provocatively. Fearful of losing, Murphy agrees to guilty pleas to a lesser, nonsexual charge.

As it did for Frank Galvin in *The Verdict*, Murphy's moment of redemption occurs bedside in a hospital. Shortly after Murphy has plea-bargained away her case, Tobias is in a parking lot when she is taunted by one of the barflies. She furiously rams her car into his truck, and sustains serious injuries which result in her being hospitalized. Murphy's moment of crisis arrives when she visits Tobias in the hospital. Tobias accuses Murphy of treating her no better than did the barflies — both, Tobias says, treated her "like a piece of shit." Recognition of the truth of Tobias's statement produces Murphy's moment of redemption. Murphy insists on prosecuting the barflies for contributing to the rape, over the vehement objections of her boss, the district attorney. Murphy identifies with Tobias personally and tells him, "I owe her." The case goes to trial. Tobias describes what happened, a key witness comes forward to support her story, and the barflies are convicted.

The Accused suggests how easily what may be "business as usual" for lawyers can appear contemptuous to the outside world. After all, Murphy's conduct prior to her redemptive moment is in no way unusual or improper. Prosecutors routinely offer plea bargains when they face weaknesses in proof. From Tobias's perspective, however, Murphy abandoned her and implicitly denied Tobias's worth as a human being. By personally bonding with Tobias, Murphy derives personal satisfaction and punishes immoral behavior.

C. Justice-Centered Lawyering

"Justice-centered lawyering" is a third form of redemptive lawyering. Redemption occurs when crisis enables a lawyer to realize that ultimate professional satisfaction consists of pursuing justice. Like client-centered lawyers, justice-centered lawyers typically represent politically powerless clients. For the latter group of lawyers, however, personal satisfaction and moral goodness result from the positions they advocate rather than personal attachments to individuals.

In *An Act of Murder* [1948], Calvin Cooke (Fredric March) is a strict, letter-of-the-law judge known in the community as "Old Man Maximum" for his harsh sentencing policies. Off the bench, Judge Cooke is devoted to his wife Cathy (Florence Eldridge). Judge Cooke's moment of crisis occurs when he learns that Cathy has a terminal illness. Judge Cooke crashes his car with the intention of killing Cathy in order to spare her a long and painful death. Although the authorities are prepared to assume that Cathy's death was the result of an accident, Judge Cooke confesses that he intentionally killed her. He is charged with murder, and insists on pleading guilty. Over Judge Cooke's objection, the trial court judge appoints defense attorney David Douglas (Edmond O'Brien) to represent Judge Cooke so as to ensure that a factual basis for the plea exists. Douglas asks for an autopsy, which produces surprising evidence: Cathy was dead from lethal poison before the crash occurred. Additional evidence shows that Cathy also knew of her illness, and that she ingested poison before taking the fatal car ride. After hearing this evidence, the judge dismisses the case. The experience redeems Judge Cooke. Acknowledging his moral guilt, Judge Cooke states that if he is allowed to remain a judge, he will have an enlightened view of justice. To do justice, he must look not only at a person's behavior, but also the person's circumstances and the reasons for that behavior. Henceforth, in his court, "a man shall be judged not only by the law, but by the heart as well." Thus, Judge Cooke's personal crisis allows him to recognize that a uniform application of black-letter rules will not necessarily produce justice. Moral application of rules demands that judges holistically evaluate people's backgrounds and circumstances.

A yearning to do justice also characterizes the redemption of Maggie Ward (Mary Elizabeth Mastrantonio) in *Class Action* [1991]. Maggie is an associate in a large civil defense firm, hungry for partnership. As second chair to Michael Grazier (Colin Friels), Maggie defends Argo Motors against a lawsuit filed by her father Jedediah Ward (Gene Hackman), a crusading plaintiff's personal injury lawyer. Jedediah's complaint alleges that design defects in a car manufactured by Argo, the Meridian, caused numerous deaths and injuries. Maggie learns of a "smoking gun": Dr. Pavel (Jan Rubes), an Argo engineer, had submitted a report stating that the Meridian's design would cause it to explode under certain conditions. Argo disregarded the report, figuring that defending a few wrongful death cases would be cheaper in the long run than retrofitting thousands of cars. Rather than turn the report over to Jedediah in response to his legitimate discovery request, Maggie accedes to her firm's plan to mislabel the report and bury it in a truckload of Argo documents given to Jedediah. Her moment of crisis emerges when she realizes that the law firm duped her. The report was not turned over to Jedediah at all, and even the copy that Maggie had in her desk was removed. Maggie redeems herself by responding to her law firm's deceitful conduct with some trickery of her own. She tells Jedediah about the report, tricks Grazier into denying under oath that the report existed, and provides an Argo witness who testifies to having seen the report. Argo's defense collapses and it has to settle Jedediah's claims for millions of dollars. Maggie then joins Jedediah's law firm, happily dancing and reuniting with her father.

An Act of Murder and *Class Action* manifest markedly different conceptions of justice. For Judge Cooke, justice is a process, a method of evaluating individual responsibility. For Maggie, justice requires choosing sides. Automobile manufacturers and the corporate law firms that represent them are evil; individual consumers and the solo and small firm practitioners who represent them are good. Nevertheless, both Judge Cooke and Maggie experience crisis, and both react by committing to justice. . . .

NOTES & QUESTIONS

1. Can you think of other film or fictional depictions of lawyers who are changed or redeemed by particular events or choices they make? Can you think of examples in real life? Bernadine Dohrn, now a clinical law professor at Northwestern Law School, was in her youth a political radical and member of several leftist organizations which advocated revolutionary ideals (The Weather Underground) and committed some violent crimes. She lived underground for many years in the 1960s and 1970s and was on the FBI's Most Wanted List, until the government dropped charges against her. As a result of her activities, several states (New York and Illinois) refused to grant her a license to practice law (she is a graduate of the University of Chicago Law School); she appealed these decisions. *See* John J. Goldman, *Ex-Radical Fights for Bar Status*, L.A. Times, 11 Nov. 1985, 1–4. She is the founder of Sidley & Austin's pro bono program (where she worked as a paralegal in the 1980s) and has been appointed to many lawyer taskforces and committees (including those at the ABA) on juvenile justice. She remains an advocate for many progressive causes. If you were a member of the Bar Admissions Committee, would you refuse to admit to the Bar a very productive lawyer who advocated revolutionary change in her youth? Why or why not? What is the relationship of morally committed civil (or even criminal) disobedience by a lawyer for principled reasons to the practice or "rule of law?" *See* Judith McMorrow, *Civil Disobedience and the Lawyer's Obligation to the Law*, 48 Washington & Lee Law Review 139 (1991).

2. What if a person seeking bar admission killed someone? One individual who committed murder (unrelated to political activities), served his time, was paroled, was then admitted to study law in Arizona (and graduated from a fully accredited law school), and passed the bar examination has never been admitted to the Arizona bar. The bar says that anyone who is on probation for a serious crime cannot be admitted to the bar. What would you do if you were on the committee deciding this admissions issue? Does such a ruling say someone can never be redeemed from a past bad act? Does it make a difference that someone is asking to be a lawyer (who should not violate the law)? Consider that two Presidents have been disbarred (Richard Nixon for his actions in Watergate and William Clinton for his acts of perjury during the Paula Jones litigation). Given the "good acts" of these men, should they have been readmitted to the bar? What does redemption mean in these contexts? Should Teddy Barnes or Sam Bowden be disbarred for the murders they commit? Should they have to prove justified self-defense in a trial or lawyer disciplinary hearing?

3. Stories about lawyers also use the device of coming-of-age stories or *Bildungsroman* (novels of education or formation) to show developments in social and professional character. *To Kill a Mockingbird* tells the story of Atticus Finch and the role of law through the eyes of his daughter Scout (a slightly fictionalized version of the author, Harper Lee), who comes to understand the complexity of community and justice at several junctures in the novel. Professor Simon says that "Most of Grisham's books are coming-of-age novels that chronicle the moral growth of a new lawyer. The hero learns two lessons through participation in a series of adventures. First, you cannot possibly understand legal or professional responsibility norms as the categorical injunctions they purport on their surface to be. To apply them in a manner that would make them worthy of respect requires a flexible, dialectical judgment. Second, to the extent the social order functions, it is not because of a system of promulgated rules more or less routinely enforced by a self-propelling governmental system of checks and balances, but through creative, transgressive moral entrepreneurialism on the part of individuals in crisis." Simon, *Moral Pluck, supra,* at 426. Consider how the young lawyers in Grisham's novels *The Firm* (1991), *The Pelican Brief* (1992), *The Chamber* (1994), and *The Rainmaker* (1995) learn about the legal system from both their elders and their "adventures." What does Kevin Lomax learn from John Milton in *The Devil's Advocate?*

4. Learning about choices in lawyering, law, and legal institutions from acts, adventures, and mentors is also a common theme where there are "learning communities," as one scholar has named them. Carrie Menkel-Meadow, *Can They Do That?, supra,* at 1320. Another element of modern character development is significant to note — the recognition of small worlds of professional communities. Many of the earlier depictions of modern heroes focus on the strength, courage, redemption, or recovery of the individual lawyer. But there are also interesting depictions of some of the lawyers' commitments to each other and to the professional communities they create. Over thirty years ago, one commentator noted the creation of "professional communities" on a variety of the early lawyer and doctor television programs, in which lawyers help and succor each other while performing difficult, but important, public service. Many of the dramatizations of professionals on television in the Golden Era of the 1950s and 1960s involved character development in the training and mentoring of a younger professional by an older and wiser professional — the senior Lawrence Preston (*The Defenders*) guiding his son Kenneth, Dr. Gillespie and Dr. Kildare, Dr. Zorba and Ben Casey. In more recent times, Leland McKenzie sometimes guided the younger lawyers in *L.A. Law*, and an only slightly older, but clearly more experienced Bobby Donnell was a mentor on *The Practice*. Jedediah Ward, as father figure, encourages his daughter, big-firm defender of corporate interests, to become a lawyer also seeking social justice in *Class Action*. These "learning communities" of lawyers (and other professionals) demonstrate that being a professional does require good character (loyalty, ongoing learning, honesty — at least with one's colleagues, if not the system — and devotion to the larger public and to social good). Note what one television critic has said of the television professionals of the 1960s and consider how much of it is still true:

> [T]hey know that without such work the quality of everyday life would plummet, society would flounder. Their jobs, in short, are the best of all possible jobs: they offer both inner meaning and public worth. Television's city-dwelling professionals thus serve as living proof that work in the modern world can be beautiful. . . . The professionals of these programs are not only public servants; they are also spokesmen of society, and their behavior reveals the way society operates to take care of its own. . . . The professionals themselves are tireless, selfless, and profoundly equitable. . . . In the presumably cold, dead heart of contemporary life and society, television's professional dramas have managed to find nothing less than the pulse of the good community. The living there may have its difficulties, admittedly, but in the end the problems are only superficial ones. For this is a place that offers meaningful work, a public devotion to the common good, and secure, vital values.

Harris Dientsfrey, *Doctors, Lawyers and Other TV Heroes*, at 83–85.

More recent professional series demonstrate an even more equalitarian sense of community. Although Leland McKenzie presided over highly fictionalized daily firm meetings, the lawyers of *L.A. Law and The Practice*, like their compatriots on *ER*, mostly soldier on together in relative equality and with unrepresentatively little concern about partnerships and hierarchy. Occasionally there are treatments of partnership and income, but these modern-day professionals mostly help each other through their difficult cases. They seem to be more likely to help and to fall in love with each other (which involves all kinds of conflicts of interest that the shows do not portray with much ethical accuracy) than to engage in the kind of ruthless competition with each other that is the presumed culture and frequent depiction of legal education. Carrie Menkel-Meadow, *Can They Do That?*, supra, at 1320–21.

Do you think that the movies are accurate in their depictions of how much lawyers do or do not help each other through difficult choices or decisions? What do you think happens in real life?

5. Some of the learning or redemption stories show lawyers changing their types of practices (returns to where they "came from," service to the legally needy, commitments to new kinds of cases or new causes). How common is it for lawyers to change fields or specialties within a career? Do you think that you will change what kind of practice you have at different points in your career?

6. What does it take to change your mind? About what is right or wrong? About what kind of a law practice you think you would want? About what kind of a person you think you would want to be? What are the "dramatic events" in real life that change the choices we make or that cause us to seek some form of "redemption" by doing something different or better?

7. What have you learned about lawyers in general and what kind of a lawyer you want to be specifically by studying the depictions of lawyers in popular culture? If you were to write a modern script about lawyering, what would it look like?

Chapter 4

CLIENTS

A. FILMOGRAPHY

The Client (1994)

Miracle on 34th Street (1947)

Nuts (1987)

The Sweet Hereafter (1997)

A Time to Kill (1996)

B. CLIENT-CENTERED LAWYERING: THE MODEL

Although lawyers are very visible actors in movies about law, clients are largely invisible. Many law review articles have been written about lawyers in the movies, but the relationship between lawyers and clients has received little attention, perhaps because clients are minor characters in most movies with legal themes. Lawyers could not practice law without clients, so the lack of meaningful client roles and the invisibility of the lawyer-client relationship are somewhat surprising. In contrast, the clients portrayed in the five movies highlighted for this chapter are key actors in the stories the movies tell about law. These client roles can best be understood through their relationships with their lawyers. These relationships develop not just in the courtroom, where most movies about law are situated, but also outside the courtroom, in a wide variety of interactions: in lawyer offices, in jail cells, in psychiatric hospitals, and at home.

We will first examine these relationships in the context of a theory of lawyering known as client-centeredness. Client-centeredness is an approach to lawyering that puts clients — not lawyers — at the center of legal representation; it stands in sharp contrast to the more traditional lawyer-focused approach. The following two excerpts explain the difference between these approaches to lawyering. The first excerpt sets out the traditional lawyering approach in the context of legal counseling, which is one of the most important activities that a lawyer undertakes on behalf of a client. Counseling is defined as "the process by which you help clients decide what courses of action to adopt in order to resolve problems." David A. Binder, Paul Bergman, Susan C. Price & Paul R. Tremblay, *Lawyers As Counselors: A Client-Centered Approach* 271 (2d ed. 2004).

CLIENT-CENTERED COUNSELING: REAPPRAISAL AND REFINEMENT
Robert D. Dinerstein
32 Arizona Law Review 501 (1990)

Traditional legal counseling reflects an absence of meaningful interchange between lawyer and client. The client comes to the lawyer with some idea about his problem. The lawyer asks questions designed to adduce the information necessary to place the client's problem within the appropriate conceptual box. At the proper time, he counsels the client by essentially conducting a monologue: the lawyer tells the client something of the nature of his actions on the client's behalf and then advises the client about the course of action he recommends. The lawyer may go into great detail about the rationale for his advice. Alternatively, she may provide a relatively terse recitation of technical advice and let the client decide how to proceed. The lawyer is concerned with the client's reaction to his advice but tends not to value client input, for he believes that the client has little of value to contribute to the resolution of his legal problem. Lawyer and client are likely to talk at, rather than with, each other. Any assurance that the lawyer provides to the client — and it could be substantial — is likely to be based on the client's perception that the lawyer is "taking care of matters" rather than on a belief that the lawyer truly tried to understand the client as a whole, complex person.

In general, the traditional legal counseling model assumes that clients should be passive and delegate decision-making responsibility to their lawyers; that ineffective professional service is relatively rare; that professionals give disinterested service and maintain high professional standards; that effective professional services are available to all who can pay; and that professional problems tend to call for technical solutions beyond the ken of laypersons. . . .

Compare the traditional legal counseling model with the client-centered model, described in the following excerpt.

FORTRESS IN THE SAND: THE PLURAL VALUES OF CLIENT-CENTERED REPRESENTATION
Katherine R. Kruse
12 Clinical Law Review 369 (2006)

As a theory of lawyering, client-centered representation has enjoyed unparalleled success. . . . Indeed, the client-centered approach has so thoroughly permeated skills training and clinical legal education, it is not an exaggeration to say that client-centered representation is one of the most influential doctrines in legal education today.

Despite its popularity and influence — or perhaps because of it — there is a growing lack of consensus about what it means to be a client-centered lawyer. As the client-centered approach has grown from its earliest articulation . . . to its current status as well-established bedrock of clinical legal education, it has evolved naturally into what might be called a plurality of approaches, which expand aspects of the original client-centered approach in different directions. Client-centered representation has been perhaps most commonly associated with an approach to legal counseling that seeks to minimize lawyer influence on client decision-making, relying on strategies of lawyer neutrality. However, some proponents of client-centered representation seek to increase client participation in the legal representation, and thus value lawyer-client collaboration over lawyer neutrality. Some client-centered theorists have made connections between client-centered representation, client voice, and narrative theory, placing central value on the importance of preserving or translating a client's story into legal terms. Other proponents of a client-centered approach view it as primarily concerned with effective problem-solving, and favor holistic lawyering approaches that reach beyond the boundaries of the client's legal case to address a broader range of connected issues in the client's life. Still others focus on the notion of client empowerment, and favor approaches that facilitate a client's ability to make decisions by creating a more equal relationship between the client and the lawyer. Finally, some claim a traditional zealous advocacy model as the essence of client-centered representation, equating it with the unmitigated advancement of a client's legal interests. Taken together [these approaches] define a richly elaborated philosophy of lawyering that strives at once to be client-directed, holistic, respectful of client narrative, client-empowering, and partisan. . . .

[These] five client-centered lawyering approaches [are] built around the core values of client-centered representation. Each approach — holistic representation, narrative integrity, client empowerment, partisan advocacy, and client-directed lawyering — begins with a representational value and supposes an approach to lawyering that would pursue that value exclusively. Each approach is "client-centered" in that it puts the client at the center of the representation instead of something else: the client's legal issues, the lawyer's construction of the client, the client's stated wishes, the interests of third parties, and the client's best interests. Each model is also "client-centered" in that it is supported by a reasonable conception of what it means to respect client autonomy. They are intended not as full-blown alternative models of lawyering, but as component parts of a well-rounded client-centered practice. Indeed, adopting or pursuing any one of these approaches to the exclusion of the others would create a caricature of client-centered lawyering.

When faced with a difficult case in the context of actual practice, this value pluralist approach to client-centered representation would change the kinds of questions that lawyers ask themselves. The question "What would a client-centered lawyer do?" is replaced by a series of questions: What would a holistic lawyer do?; What does narrative integrity require?; What would a client-empowering lawyer do?; What would a partisan advocate do?; and What does client-directed lawyering require? . . .

The plural approaches of client-centered representation that I propose are laid out in the following table . . . :

Table 1 Plural Approaches To Client-Centered Representation

Client is at the center of the representation

LAWYERING APPROACH	*instead of:*	*to prevent:*	Autonomy Concern
HOLISTIC	Client's Legal Issues	Lawyer misdiagnosis or narrow legal framing of client's problem	Removal of external constraints to self-actualization caused by lack of options in the world
NARRATIVE INTEGRITY	Lawyer's Construction of the Client	Lawyer distortion of client narrative in legal storytelling	Preservation of client's project of self-authorship
CLIENT EMPOWERMENT	Client's Stated Wishes	Client misdiagnosis of what the client "really wants"	Removal of internal constraints to client self-actualization caused by client's attitudes, beliefs or unrealistic expectations
PARTISAN	Third Parties	Loss of client's legal rights and interests	Preservation of freedom for the client's "future self"
CLIENT DIRECTED	Client's Best Interests	Lawyer paternalism	Negative liberty— client's right to be "left alone"

The Holistic Approach to client-centered lawyering places the client as "whole person" at the center of the representation, in place of the client's legal issues. The primary concern of the Holistic Approach is to avoid the sometimes distorting effects caused by lawyers who, viewing the client's legal issues as the center of the client's problem, fail to take into account the importance of the nonlegal considerations with which the client's legal issues are intertwined. Such lawyers, as the client-centered approach points out, are in danger of misdiagnosing the client's problems by imposing the structure of legal doctrine on the problem without understanding the full scope of the client's situation.

Taking a Holistic Approach, a lawyer will combat the tendencies to view a client's problems too narrowly by attending to the interconnected set of legal and non-legal concerns that the client's situation presents, rather than just the client's legal issues. Hence, a lawyer operating under a Holistic Approach will seek to work outside and around the law to achieve the client's goals by non-legal means. Holistic lawyering may sometimes occur through a lawyer representing a client on multiple and interconnected legal problems. For example, representing a client in a child custody dispute may require a lawyer to address other legal issues, such as getting the client immigration status or resolving a landlord-tenant dispute so that the client has an adequate home for the children. Holistic lawyering may also occur outside the parameters of purely legal strategies — such as helping a client find a job or qualify for assistance — and may sometimes be achieved best through coordinated efforts with other professionals like social workers. . . .

The Narrative Integrity Approach to client-centered lawyering places the client at the center of the representation instead of the lawyer's construction of the client. It focuses on preserving the integrity of the client's own narrative or voice, and seeks to structure the representation as much as possible around the way the client views the world. The primary concern of the Narrative Integrity Approach is to prevent the lawyer from distorting the legal representation by recreating the client's narrative within legal doctrinal categories that fail to capture the client's perspective. . . .

[R]espect for a client's Narrative Integrity may impel a lawyer past neutrality into a more interactive and collaborative process of legal representation. Legal storytelling is formed by an interaction between the client's story, stories that are embedded in legal doctrine, and "stock stories" that express basic conditions of justice. To maintain the client's voice in the legal representation may require the client to participate more actively in decisions and processes that are traditionally thought of as distinctively legal and strategic in nature, such as the formulation of case theory. . . .

The Client-Empowerment Approach of client-centered lawyering is based on the idea that the legal representation needs to move the client in the direction of self-sufficiency and self-actualization. Its primary concern is that a client's stated wishes may not accurately reflect the client's true desires, and that lawyers who too quickly accept the client's stated wishes as "marching orders" will end up working in ways that are at odds with the client's real needs and interests. Hence it puts the client's real, true, or more fully realized interests and values at the center of legal representation, in place of what the client may initially say (or think) that he or she wants.

The idea of client empowerment has been particularly attractive to lawyers working with communities of poor clients or with battered women, where the experience of political or social subordination is seen as having created passive or accommodating patterns of thinking and behaving, which may need to be confronted or changed before a client has the capacity to make truly autonomous choices. The strategies for assisting clients in such situations go beyond the lawyer merely spelling out the alternatives and consequences of different courses of action, and include facilitating the client's connection and solidarity with others, and helping the client sort through the multiple and conflicting narratives that may describe her situation. . . .

The pull of the Client-Empowerment Approach is thus the strongest when the client's autonomy is constrained by internal obstacles arising out of his own attitudes, perspectives or beliefs. But the concern for paternalism is also the strongest in these kinds of situations, placing limits on the strategies that it is appropriate to employ. . . .

The Partisan Approach puts the client in the center of the representation in place of the interests and needs of third parties. It privileges the client's legal rights and interests, and emphasizes the protection of those rights over the rights of others. The primary concern in the Partisan Approach is that the client may give up a legal entitlement: waive a right, forego an available remedy, miss a deadline, or enter into an agreement that will limit actions the client may want to take in the future. . . .

[I]t comes as no surprise that many of the proponents of strong intervention to protect a client's future freedom would come from the realm of criminal defense, where the freedom at stake — freedom from incarceration — is particularly acute. However, intervention to protect future freedom may also be particularly appropriate to situations like divorce, where the client is undergoing a transition between phases of life, and may be either undervaluing or overvaluing interests that will take on different importance as the transition becomes complete. It is in these kinds of situations where extreme deprivation of future freedom is at stake, or where a client is making irrevocable choices at a time of life transition, that protection of future freedom has a strong pull against a client's current desire to give up a legal right or interest. . . .

The Client-Directed Approach picks up on the concern about lawyer domination inherent in more traditional visions of lawyering. Rather than concerning itself strictly with the distortions that arise from interpreting the client's problem through legal doctrinal categories, the Client-Directed Approach is concerned more broadly about the ways in which a lawyer may influence a client's decision based on what the lawyer believes is best for the client. The problem that the Client-Directed Approach addresses is less that the lawyer will be narrow-mindedly legal in his approach; and more that the lawyer will develop his own view of what would be prudent or wise for the client to do — either legally or in non-legal matters — and impermissibly interject that view into the client's decision-making. . . .

The Client-Directed Approach is evident in the client-centered approach's skepticism about lawyer expertise on the non-legal matters that are most vitally important to the client. . . .

NOTES & QUESTIONS

1. Professor Kruse outlines the five cornerstones of client-centered representation: holistic representation, narrative integrity, client empowerment, partisan advocacy, and client-directed lawyering. Which of these cornerstones is most appealing to you? Why? Which of these cornerstones is least appealing to you? Why? In what situations would you employ one approach over the other?

2. Compare these client-centered approaches to the traditional lawyer-centered approach. Does the traditional lawyer-centered approach have any advantages over the client-centered approach? What are the biggest disadvantages of the lawyer-centered approach? Think of your own experience as a law student in a work setting or a clinical setting. Which of these approaches have you observed lawyers using in these environments?

3. The rules of ethics provide some guidance on the allocation of decision-making authority between lawyers and clients. While some decisions, such as the decision about whether to settle a case, or in a criminal case, whether to plead guilty, waive a jury trial, or testify, are clearly reserved for clients, Rule 1.2 of the ABA Model Rules of Professional Conduct does not provide a clear answer to the role of clients in other aspects of their cases. Instead, it simply states: "a lawyer shall abide by a client's decisions concerning the objectives of representation [and] shall consult with the client as to the means by which they are to be pursued." How would you interpret this rule in light of the traditional lawyer-centered approach? How would you interpret this rule in light of the five cornerstones of the client-centered approach? Which of these approaches is most consistent with the letter and spirit of the rule? How should a lawyer proceed if she is convinced that the client is making a really bad decision?

4. Since client-centered lawyering is context-specific, is it appropriate for all types of clients? How relevant is the client-centered approach for lawyers representing wealthy and powerful clients? What are some of the reasons why a lawyer should not take a client-centered approach with a powerful client? How should we go about determining which clients deserve a client-centered lawyer and which do not?

5. None of the clients in the featured movies are wealthy or powerful in any traditional sense. In *The Client*, Mark Sway is an eleven-year-old boy from a single-parent family who pays his lawyer one dollar to represent him. In *Miracle on 34th Street*, Kris Kringle is an elderly gentleman who is represented *pro bono* by his friend. In *Nuts*, Claudia Draper is a prostitute represented by a public defender appointed by the judge. In *The Sweet Hereafter*, the parents of the children killed in the school bus accident are working-class people from a small town in British Columbia whose lawyer represents them on a contingency fee basis. In *A Time to Kill*, Carl Lee Hailey is an African American man who works a blue-collar job in a southern town and who barely scrapes together enough money to hire a lawyer. What version of client-centeredness is appropriate for these clients?

6. In *The Sweet Hereafter*, an angry Mrs. Otto, a parent who is reluctant to join the lawsuit, confronts Mitchell Stephens, the lawyer who is soliciting her business: "So you're just the thing we need? Isn't that what you want us to believe? That we're completely defenseless? That you know what's best?" When Stephens responds: "Listen to me, Mrs. Otto. Listen very carefully. I do know what's best," is he behaving as a traditional lawyer, or as a partisan advocate? Could he be viewed not only as paternalistic but also as fighting hard to protect her future interests in the way that a partisan advocate would by making sure that she does not waive an important legal right?

7. As Professor Kruse explains:

[These] core values of client-centered representation can sometimes come into conflict in situations of actual practice, posing dilemmas for client-centered lawyers about whether — or how forcefully — to intervene into client decision-making. For example, in representing a battered woman who is poised on the brink of leaving an abusive relationship, the goals of client empowerment may push a lawyer into deeper connection with the client or broader involvement in her life than neutral methods of client-directed lawyering would sanction.

When representing an immigrant seeking legal status in the United States, the partisan protection of a client's legal interests may conflict with the goal of gaining full information that would help the lawyer engage in holistic problem-solving, because knowing too much may impair the lawyer's ability to act ethically as an advocate. The desire to give voice to a client's narrative may confound a lawyer's partisan advocacy if the client's story undermines rather than supports a client's goals.

Kruse, *supra,* 372.

8. After viewing the assigned movies, do you think the various approaches to client-centered lawyering rest on the idea of an equal relationship between lawyers and clients? Alternatively, can lawyers and clients be viewed as contributing different types of expertise to the representation? Which is the better fit, and why?

9. Consider how a central tenet of client-centeredness — the idea that clients do not all share the same concerns and approach problems in different ways — plays out in the film *The Sweet Hereafter*:

The film reminds us of the different ways that loss and suffering become part of the life stories of different people, with some people accepting their fate and others insisting that causes be identified, blame be assigned, and compensation be provided.

Austin Sarat, *Exploring the Hidden Domains of Civil Justice: "Naming, Blaming, and Claiming" in Popular Culture,* 50 DePaul Law Review 425, 430 (2000). Describe how each of the plaintiffs (or potential plaintiffs) viewed the lawsuit and its role in their lives. Would you characterize their goals as primarily legal or non-legal? What about other parties? How did the goals of these clients change as the result of interactions with their lawyer?

10. A familiar criticism of class action lawyers is that they often supplement their own agendas for the agenda of their clients. For example, the lawyers in charge of the NAACP school desegregation litigation have been criticized for taking strong pro-busing positions when their African American clients preferred that more resources be directed at schools in their neighborhoods. Derrick Bell, *Serving Two Masters: Integration Ideals and Client Interests in School Desegregation Litigation,* 85 Yale Law Journal 470, 471–72 (1976). If this criticism is warranted in a situation where clients are unified, think about the challenge that a client-centered class action lawyer would face in determining which goals should take precedence in a situation where the clients themselves have conflicting goals.

11. Consider the following excerpt, which relies on empirical research to argue that client values may be different than the values held by their lawyers:

What lawyers consider to be important, proper, and moral may be considerably different from their clients. These differences are likely to cause a gap in understanding, even a difference in morality, which could cause lawyers to be perceived negatively as cold, dispassionate, uncaring, overly logical, fact-driven, aggressive, competitive, ruthless, and even amoral. Lawyers do appear to be more competitive and aggressive, need more dominance, and be driven to succeed more than most adults. Clients may perceive lawyers as cold, uncaring, uncommunicative, disinterested in anything but the "relevant facts," overly rule-oriented, aggressive, competitive, and hard-driving because they actually are more that way than the norm.

Susan Daicoff, *Lawyer, Know Thy Self: A Review of Empirical Research on Attorney Attributes Bearing on Professionalism,* 46 American University Law Review 1337, 1411 (1997). If the author is correct in her characterization of lawyers, what do these qualities say about the ability of lawyers to practice client-centered lawyering? How can lawyers listen to and understand clients whose values and personal traits are so different from their own? Among the various client-centered approaches, which is the best fit for a lawyer with these characteristics?

12. An astute client whose goals and values differ from her lawyer can undermine the lawyer's agenda in sometimes unexpected ways, as the film *The Sweet Hereafter* demonstrates. Nicole, a teenager who survived the bus accident in *The Sweet Hereafter*, testifies in a way that undermines the lawsuit:

> Because her testimony, which the viewer knows to be a lie, places blame on the person with the shallowest pocket it effectively ends the suit. It serves not only both (for us if not for Nicole) as a satisfying act of revenge against [her father], depriving him of the money he so desperately wants, but also as a way of exposing the vulnerability of law. All of Stephens's legal acumen, all of his work, is defeated and derailed by a teenaged girl.

Austin Sarat, *Imagining the Law of the Father: Loss, Dread, and Mourning in "The Sweet Hereafter,"* 34 Law & Society Review 3, 34 (2000). What motivated Nicole to change her story? Was it only revenge, or something else? Do you think that her role as a member of the community of townspeople had any impact on her decision, or was she purely motivated by individual concerns? Should Stephens have anticipated the possibility that Nicole would change her story, or was it completely unexpected? If he had anticipated this possibility, what difference might it have made? How could the lawyer have employed a client-centered approach before the deposition in order to learn the "alternative" story? Professor Lucie E. White describes a similar incident with a client she represented at a welfare hearing, who "came to the hearing well-rehearsed in the lawyer's strategy. But in the hearing, she did not play. When she was cued to perform, without any signal to her lawyer she abandoned their script." Lucie E. White, *Subordination, Rhetorical Survival Skills, and Sunday Shoes: Notes on the Hearing of Mrs. G.,* 38 Buffalo Law Review 1, 46 (1990). Was Nicole well-rehearsed in her lawyer's strategy? Should she have been? How can lawyers in these kinds of situations determine what really happened?

C.   PUTTING CLIENTS AT THE CENTER OF THE REPRESENTATION: THE CLIENT-CENTERED APPROACHES IN CONTEXT

1.   The Client-Directed Approach

Among the client-centered approaches, the client-directed approach provides the starkest alternative to the traditional approach. In the following excerpt, Professor Polikoff describes the classic justification for client-directed lawyering and then describes her effort to implement this model with a client arrested following a civil disobedience action.

AM I MY CLIENT? THE ROLE CONFUSION OF A LAWYER ACTIVIST
Nancy D. Polikoff
31 Harvard Civil Rights-Civil Liberties Law Review 443 (1996)

[Client-directed lawyering] rests upon the conviction that clients bear the consequences of their decisions and are in the best position to understand the full non-legal as well as legal significance of their choices. Accordingly, lawyers counsel clients best by helping them to explore all of the possible consequences of their actions so that the clients can make decisions that best suit their needs. . . .

After the initial paperwork was completed, we learned the name of the protestor whose case would be called first. It was "Jenifer," a friend of mine. As we stood together in the cell block, she and her fellow demonstrators (including my lover and other close friends) behind the bars and me outside of them, she tried every way imaginable to have me make a decision for her. First, she asked directly what I thought she should do. Then she asked what I would do if I were she. Resolutely, I maintained my role as client-centered counselor. I explained consequences and helped her articulate her goals. I engaged in active listening and reflected back what I heard.

My responses were somewhat frustrating to Jenifer. We had common personal and political bonds, but our relationship in this situation was really no different from that of any client trying to get her lawyer to make a decision and any lawyer resisting with the knowledge that it is the client, not the lawyer, who must live with the consequences of that decision. . . .

NOTES & QUESTIONS

1. Should the lawyer in this example have resisted her client's effort to get the lawyer to make the decision? What should a client-directed lawyer do when confronted with a client who wants the lawyer to provide an answer? If, as Professor Dinerstein suggests, one goal of client-centered lawyering is "to provide opportunities for clients to make decisions themselves," Dinerstein, *supra*, 507, is it client-centered for a lawyer to make a decision for a client when that client has decided she wants the lawyer to be the decision-maker?

Is part of client-centered lawyering giving a client what she wants, not forcing a process on the client that she does not want? William Simon notes the dilemma that lawyers face when they "must either acquiesce in the client's choice to put her fate in the lawyer's hands or force her to be free by denying her the advice that she considers most valuable." William H. Simon, *Lawyer Advice and Client Autonomy: Mrs. Jones's Case*, 50 Maryland Law Review 213, 217 (1991). Does a decision to accede to the client's wishes enhance or undermine her autonomy?

2. Do you agree with the lawyer's refusal to tell the client what the lawyer would do if she were in the shoes of her client? Consider an example from a medical setting:

> I recall our pediatrician advising my wife and me as to whether we should have our then two-month-old son vaccinated against whooping cough, several cases of which had occurred in our area. There was a specified small probability of an adverse reaction to the vaccine, and given an adverse reaction, a specified small probability of death, and specified small probabilities of less extreme bad outcomes. Without the shot, there was a specified small probability of contracting the disease, a specified small probability given contraction of death, and specified small probabilities of various bad results short of death. I found this explanation, which went on for several minutes, overwhelmingly oppressive, and I felt a sense of deliverance when she concluded by saying, "In the case of my own child, I decided to give him the shot." I felt, and still do, that that sentence was all that I needed or wanted to know.

Simon, *supra,* 216–17. In what respects is medical advice different than legal advice? Compare the role of statistics and probabilities in the context of patients making medical decisions to their role for clients making legal decisions. Do clients in legal situations have a stake in the meaning of the story that is different than the kind of stake medical patients have in their care? Should doctors and lawyers respond in different ways to these kinds of questions? Why?

3. If the client-directed approach is premised on lawyer neutrality, how realistic is it? Consider the following:

> Even where they think of themselves as merely providing information for clients to integrate into their own decisions, lawyers influence clients by myriad judgments, conscious or not, about what information to present, how to order it, what to emphasize, and what style and phrasing to adopt.

Simon, *supra,* 217.

4. Are there limits on the ability to clients to be the decision-makers in their cases? Should age matter, as in the case of a very young client (*The Client*) or an elderly client (*Miracle on 34th Street*)? Should a mental or cognitive disability (or perceived disability) make a difference, as in *Nuts*? The ethical rules provide:

> When a client's capacity to make adequately considered decisions in connection with a representation is diminished, whether because of minority, mental impairment or for some other reason, the lawyer shall, as far as reasonably possible, maintain a normal client-lawyer relationship with the client.

ABA Model Rule of Professional Conduct 1.14. Given the limited guidance this rule provides, how should lawyers go about negotiating these relationships with clients? Should the role afforded the client depend on the extent of the client's incapacity, the nature of the decision, the consequences to the client, or something else?

5. The client in *Nuts* goes to great lengths to seize control of her case from her lawyer, beginning with her effort to speak on her own behalf in court when represented by her first attorney, who ignores and patronizes her, to her later efforts, both inside and outside the courtroom, when represented by a public defender. While her first attorney is clearly not client-directed, how client-directed is her public defender? How might his actions have been more client-directed? Is there an argument that attorneys should give clients more leeway to direct the course of legal representation outside of formal advocacy settings?

6. Despite his age, Mark Sway in *The Client* clearly views himself as the decision-maker in his case, ignoring his lawyer's advice that he should talk to the FBI, and admonishing her: "You're my lawyer and you have to do what I tell you." Two commentators give Mark a major role in the representation, arguing that while Reggie Love "outsmarts all manner of wicked adversaries," she succeeds only because her client guides her. Michael Asimow & Shannon Mader, *Law and Popular Culture* 186 (2004). Do you agree? Why? How realistic is the character that Mark plays?

7. The classic legal film *To Kill a Mockingbird* (1962) presents the lawyer as an heroic actor while relegating the client to a passive role. Can this juxtaposition be explained solely by the fact that the client was African American, as one commentator argues, *see* Asimow & Mader, *supra,* 37–38, or are there other factors at play? Why do you think Carl Lee Hailey, the African American client in *A Time to Kill*, was a different kind of client?

2. The Narrative Integrity Approach

As Professor Kruse notes, the question of narrative integrity arises most acutely in the context of case theory and storytelling. Indeed, the constructing of case theory is an aspect of lawyering in which lawyers often take very different approaches to questions of client-centeredness. Binny Miller, *Give Them Back Their Lives: Recognizing Client Narrative in Case Theory*, 93 Michigan Law Review 485 (1994). Case theory is the short version of the story that the lawyer tells on behalf of her client. It is not the whole story, but rather the storyline that captures the facts, the law, and all of the surrounding circumstances of the client and her case. The question of who controls case theory, the story that emerges, and how that story is told is a question of ethics and professionalism. Three of the featured films for this chapter (*Miracle on 34th Street*, *Nuts*, and *A Time to Kill*) explicitly raise questions about the content of case theory and the role of clients in constructing a case theory.

The first excerpt sets out a working definition of case theory.

TEACHING CASE THEORY
Binny Miller
9 Clinical Law Review 293 (2002)

As the key means of framing a case, case theory is the central problem that lawyers confront in putting a case together. Case theory drives much of the work in representing clients, from interviewing the client, to fact-gathering and investigation, and finally to negotiation, trial, or some other resolution of the case. Many of the decisions made during the life of a case are decisions that rest on case theory, including the question of which witnesses to call at trial, the content of their testimony, and indeed, the shape of the trial itself. . . .

I teach a concept of case theory that I have developed over years of litigating, clinical teaching, and writing about case theory, in which case theory can best be described as "storyline." A "storyline" is the short version of the lawyer's story of the case that takes into account the context in which it will be told. The case theory is a snapshot, a framework, the essence of the story or what the case is about. It is not the whole story that a video camera filming the event would tell, but rather the coherent meaning that the elements create. Yet it is in stories that storylines are found. . . .

The view of case theory as storyline places law in a narrative rather than an analytic modality. Facts do not serve law in an element-by-element categorical analysis, but rather work side-by-side with law in the story. Case theory provides an explanation for what happened, and in doing so, shapes what happened. Law plays an important role in some explanations, a lesser role in other explanations, and at times, no role at all.

For example, in a case theory that incorporates the idea of self-defense, who did what first, and with what force, matters because the law says that it does. But in some self-defense cases, the credibility of the complaining witnesses might be the key, and the legal definition of self-defense hardly matters. Context, however, always matters, even in cases that might seem to be about legal categories. . . .

The next excerpt, in describing an actual case handled by a student in a law school clinic, provides a good example of what lawyers mean by the term case theory and the role that clients might play in developing a case theory.

LEGAL FICTIONS: CLINICAL EXPERIENCES, LACE COLLARS, AND BOUNDLESS STORIES
Nancy Cook
1 Clinical Law Review 41 (1994)

Last summer, the summer of 1992, a woman was arrested in Albuquerque for disorderly conduct. The statute she was alleged to have violated prohibits ". . . engaging in violent, abusive, indecent, profane, boisterous, unreasonably loud, or otherwise disorderly conduct which tends to disturb the peace." Through connections with the local Public Defender's office, our law school clinic, which provides supervised student representation to a limited number of individuals, acquired the case. I read through the police report, which was virtually all there was to the file we received from the Public Defender, and assigned the case to one of my eight students, Rachel Kolman.

In the beginning, this is all we knew about the case: The police responded to a call "in reference to a male and female fighting" in a motel room on Central Avenue. Central Avenue is the old Route 66, and this particular section is known for having more than its fair share of drug-related activities and prostitution. On arrival, the two responding Anglo male police officers encountered several people in the parking lot, one of whom advised them that "a crazy woman" had come to his room and wouldn't leave.

As the men were conversing, this woman came around the corner. When she saw the police and the man they were interviewing — the man from the motel room — she began screaming at them. The officers attempted to calm her, but she "just got louder and more uncooperative." First the officers merely asked the woman to leave, but when she continued to yell, they advised her that she was under arrest for disorderly conduct. She then went to her car and locked herself in. At this point, under the threat of being forcibly removed from her vehicle, the woman got out and was handcuffed and transported to the detention center.

This information was contained in the police report that served as the basis for the criminal information filed against the woman. Buried in the middle of the report was this sentence: "We couldn't find anyone or find any reason to support her claim of rape."

Subsequent conversations with the police revealed that the man who spoke to them about the "crazy woman" was calm and articulate. The woman had asked him for money which he would not give her. Asked if they had seen any animals around, a fact that was significant to the defendant's version of events, the officers said that they had not. The defendant appeared to be intoxicated, but the officers' main concern was that she had been creating such a disturbance that many of the motel residents were coming outside and shouting back at her.

Rachel arranged to meet with the defendant, Debra, who was out on bond. Briefly, what Rachel learned in the interview was that Debra, a twenty-six-year-old, single, black woman, had recently arrived in New Mexico from the east coast. She and her boyfriend, with whom she was living, had moved to Albuquerque because they had heard that it was a tolerant place. At the time of the interview, Debra was unemployed, having lost her job because of her several days' absence while she sat in the Bernalillo County Detention Center trying to make bail on this charge.

On the day of her arrest, Debra had gone to a bar with a female friend and there flirted with a man whom she thought was very good looking. She had three or four drinks, after which she left, voluntarily accompanying the man to his nearby motel room.

When she left the bar, Debra wasn't sure whether she was "interested" in the man. It was after they were in his room for a while and he started getting "aggressive" that she decided to cut the evening short. She tried to leave, but was stopped by a pit bull that was positioned in front of the door. The man tore off her clothes and raped her. She was yelling, which brought the motel manager to the room. Her assailant opened the door to speak to the manager and when he did, Debra screamed out that she was being raped. The manager left, but after that, the man backed off. She was able to grab her clothes and run from the room.

Debra called the police from a pay phone around the corner, unaware of the fact that the motel manager had already done so. When she returned to the motel, she was surprised to see that a patrol car was already there. She immediately went up to the officers, who were standing with the man who had raped her, to tell them what happened. They wouldn't listen to her, which made her very angry. In the end, they arrested her and let the rapist go. She spent the weekend in jail, during which time she received no medical attention.

This was the point in the semester when we were dealing in the classroom with case planning and investigation. I thought this case provided an excellent opportunity for working through case theory and investigative plans. In class, Rachel presented the "facts" as we knew them and I then divided students into two groups, four representing the prosecution and four representing the defense. As anticipated, the two teams came up with widely different perspectives on the case, both of which were potentially credible to a fact finder, factually supportable, and predictable. The prosecution theory was, she's a prostitute on the run, possibly a drug addict, she didn't get paid for her services, so she cried rape to get back at the john who stiffed her; she had been "violent, abusive . . . , unreasonably loud" and "otherwise disorderly" in the motel parking lot, drawing a crowd and disturbing the other residents at the motel. The defense theory was, two racist, sexist, white cops saw a poor black woman and immediately thought junkie whore and couldn't be bothered to listen to her; under the circumstances (she had just been raped), any disturbance she caused was more than justifiable. . . .

When Rachel spoke to Debra, client, defendant, victim, with our "theory" of the case in mind, Debra, unique, whole, independent individual, balked. She didn't see racism. She didn't see sexism. She didn't see a great social structure built to disadvantage the poor, women, people of color, or poor women of color. What did she see? Her own innocence. A rapist's guilt. Simple injustice. She expected simple justice to prevail in the courtroom. She expected vindication. If we tell the truth, she maintained, motives, class, and race differences won't matter. All that feminist cow dung doesn't mean anything when the truth is so simple.

Was that all she saw? We don't know. After their first several conversations, in which Debra expressed to Rachel her heartfelt thanks that Rachel had been assigned to the case because finally, finally someone was listening to her, Debra changed her mind about having student representation. She had described Rachel as "a godsend," but as the investigation proceeded, she grew distant, she avoided Rachel, and spoke of her boyfriend wanting her to hire private counsel. Privately, Rachel sought to understand why. Had she alienated her with her whiteJewishmiddleclassfeminist "theories"? Was Debra's boyfriend exerting pressure because he didn't trust a woman, a white woman, a student? Had Rachel been naïve? Was the boyfriend Debra's pimp and the whole rape story a scam? . . . .

Rachel's dilemma was, what to do in light of the client's unwillingness to make race, class, or gender an issue? She was uncomfortable about pursuing a theory of discrimination in the courtroom if Debra opposed it. From Rachel's perspective, "part of being an advocate" was allowing Debra's voice to come through, since, as Rachel put it, "it's her story." At the same time, she did not share Debra's faith that simple truth would win out. Having come to law school believing, as Debra apparently did, in "the myth that courts give fairness," and having quickly been disabused of that notion as a first year law student, Rachel searched in vain for a satisfactory way to explain to Debra what she might reasonably expect in a courtroom. "How was I going to tell her story," Rachel asked, "in a way a judge would understand, a jury would believe?" . . .

NOTES & QUESTIONS

1. Professor Miller asserts that viewing case theory as story "has meant a move away from case theory as doctrine towards a view of case theory as persuasive storytelling." Miller, *Teaching Case Theory, supra,* 295. What are the disadvantages of this move? Does this approach to case theory mean that law simply disappears? Consider this question in the context of Debra's case. In what respect do the various case theories take the law of disorderly conduct into account? In what other instances can you imagine that storytelling would be effective in clarifying the law?

2. Does the balance between storytelling and categorical analysis vary depending on the decision-maker? Is one type of analysis more appropriate for juries, another more appropriate where the trier of fact is a judge? Why?

3. In *A Time to Kill,* during a strategy session on jury selection, lawyer Jake Brigance announces, "Now to win this case we need a sympathetic jury, a jury willing to acquit, and a jury that can use the insanity plea as an excuse to do so." In an earlier conversation, Lucien Wilbanks, a wise older lawyer who has fallen on hard times, advised Jake that "Mr. Hailey is as guilty as sin under all legal systems. [The law] does not permit vigilante violence, and he took the law into his own hands. He murdered two people." Is Brigance's response to Wilbank's bleak assessment simply an argument for jury nullification, a means for juries to ignore the law and instead rely on their feelings and emotions or sense of justice apart from the law? What types of client pictures should lawyers paint to persuade juries to acquit under these circumstances? Consider Paul Butler's argument for jury nullification based in part on the race of the client:

> I argue that the race of a black defendant is sometimes a legally and morally appropriate factor for [black] jurors to consider in reaching a verdict of not guilty or for an individual juror to consider in refusing to vote for conviction.

> My thesis is that, for pragmatic and political reasons, the black community is better off when some nonviolent lawbreakers remain in the community rather than go to prison. The decision as to what kind of conduct by African-Americans ought to be punished is better made by African-Americans themselves, based on the costs and benefits to their community, than by the traditional criminal justice process, which is controlled by white lawmakers and white law enforcers.

Paul Butler, *Racially Based Jury Nullification: Black Power in the Criminal Justice System,* 105 Yale Law Journal 677 (1995). What notion of community is embedded in this argument for jury nullification? Can the thesis be extended to other communities besides the African American community? Does law have any role to play in this type of analysis?

4. In the article excerpted above, Professor Miller argues that movies are an especially good vehicle for conveying story-based case theories:

> [I]t is the tendency of movies about lawyering to simplify antagonists' competing versions of a story that makes case theory stand out so clearly. Detailed, legalistic accounts of real life drama are not what sells movies. Colorful accounts of interesting characters do. It is the relative factual richness of movie portrayals of cases, and the rather limited role of law, that makes case theory so vivid. In a medium that "dumbs down" law, story elements become much more powerful.

Miller, *Teaching Case Theory, supra,* 309. Do you agree?

5. Consider the following examples of different story-based case theories developed by students in a law school class after watching *Miracle on 34th Street*:

> The movie tells the story of Kris Kringle, the white-bearded elderly gentleman hired by Macy's department store as the store Santa Claus at Christmas. When the store manager discovers that Kris thinks that he is Santa Claus, a series of events unfold in which the store psychologist seeks to have Kris committed to a mental institution. In a scene that takes place at a mental hospital to which Kris has been sent for examination pending a commitment hearing, Kris meets with a lawyer (who also happens to be a friend) to plot strategy. From this interaction, students quickly identify a number of theories, from the solidly basic to the sublime. These include theories that Kringle is joking or pretending to be Santa Claus, that although he believes himself to be Santa Claus, he's not dangerous to himself or others, that he

doesn't really believe that he's Santa Claus, but that he comes to so closely resemble the role that he identifies as Santa Claus. This last theory has two variations, the first is that helping others is so much a matter of principle to Kris that he is a Santa-like character, the second is that in playing the role at Macy's he has become the fictional character that he cares so much about. Embedded in this last theory is the idea that if someone knows a character is fictional, that person can't really believe himself to be that character. Kris is sincere in telling the world that he's Santa Claus, while at the same time he doesn't believe in reindeer coming down the chimney on Christmas Eve. The claim that "I am Santa Claus" can also be seen as a metaphor representing goodness, generosity, and love of children.

Miller, *Teaching Case Theory, supra,* 311–12. How could Kris Kringle's lawyer work with him to select a case theory from among these many variations? Which of these theories would Kris Kringle prefer? Can you think of other theories that are not included in the excerpt? What do you think of the theory that was ultimately used at trial?

6. Professor Kruse suggests a framework for determining when keeping the legal narrative consistent with the client's own story matters:

[T]he value of Narrative Integrity in legal representation may be most important in situations in which the client's legal story is integrally connected with the client's sense of self. . . . For example, a client who has been charged with drunk driving may simply want to get his driver's license back so that he can keep his job. Likewise, in some cases, the client's sense of self might be better preserved by keeping the client's own story private, rather than submitting it to public scrutiny. But sometimes legal representation is itself an avenue for a client's self-expression in ways that connect the client's project of self-authorship with the telling of her legal story, such as a client who is challenging discriminatory treatment in the workplace. In such cases, the pull of Narrative Integrity is especially strong.

Kruse, *supra,* 555. Discuss how the clients in *Nuts* and *A Time to Kill* wished to be portrayed, and the impact of that portrayal on case theory. What are the various storylines suggested by the clients' situations in these movies? In which of these situations is narrative integrity most important? Least important? How client-centered is the lawyer in each of these movies in allocating decision-making authority to their clients when it comes to choice of case theory? How do these case theories evolve as the relationships between the client and the lawyer deepen?

7. Professor Cook portrays Debra as a client at odds with her student attorney's portrayal of her case. According to Cook, Rachel viewed what happened to Debra in terms of race, class, and gender discrimination, while Debra saw "[h]er own innocence. A rapist's guilt. Simple injustice." Cook, *supra,* 50. Do you agree with Cook that the views of Debra and Rachel are necessarily so far apart? From this excerpt, we do not have much sense of the conversation between Rachel and Debra. How might Rachel have discussed a case theory based on gender without evoking a reaction from Debra that framing the case in these terms was just so much "feminist cow dung"? Rachel clearly respects her client's narrative integrity, but is there another client-centered approach that might have been helpful in understanding her client's goals?

8. In *A Time to Kill,* race as a component of the case theory is embraced by the client, but initially rejected by the lawyer — the reverse of the situation in Debra's case, where the student lawyer embraced a racial theme, and the client rejected it. In representing Carl Lee Hailey, an African American man who killed the two white men who brutally raped and almost killed his ten-year-old daughter, Jake Brigance, a white lawyer, initially defends the case on a fatherhood revenge theme, but by the time Jake delivers his closing argument, race is an explicit theme in his argument. How does Jake come to see the case in this way? Does it matter that the racial animus of the men who raped Carl Lee Hailey's daughter is palpable, while the motivations of the police in Debra's case were unclear? Compare the use of a racial perspective for a case in rural Mississippi, where the events in *A Time to Kill* occurred, to the use of this perspective in city like Albuquerque, New Mexico, where Debra's case arose. What difference might these two locales make to the choice of a case theory?

9. What are the ethics of choosing among different case theories in these three movies? For example, in *A Time to Kill*, the lawyer does not incorporate a racial perspective in the case until after the psychiatrist called as an expert to prove the insanity defense implodes on the witness stand; at that point the lawyer feels that he has "run out of legal arguments." In selecting from among multiple theories does it seem as "if case theories are 'made up' or make-believe, either pulled out of thin air, or fictions conceived by lawyers"? Miller, *Teaching Case Theory, supra,* 303. Would it be more ethical for the lawyer to determine "what really happened" and go with that theory? Is it possible to determine what really happened when it comes to questions of race? Or in any situation? In writing about the novel *The Sweet Hereafter* (1991), on which the film is based, one commentator argues: "[T]his powerful novel is really about the unknowability of 'truth' and 'facts' and what really happened." Carrie Menkel-Meadow, *The Sense and Sensibilities of Lawyers: Lawyering in Literature, Narratives, Film and Television, and Ethical Choices Regarding Career and Craft*, 31 McGeorge Law Review 1, 21 (1999). Do you agree with this characterization?

10. Professor Miller notes that connecting case theory more closely with client experience has "meant a greater focus on the respective rights and responsibilities of the lawyer and the client for the story that is ultimately told." Miller, *Teaching Case Theory, supra,* 295. In moving beyond case theory, clients can play an explicit role in other aspects of their cases, including matters such as witness examinations, which are typically relegated to lawyers as questions of strategy and tactics. One commentator argues that clients should decide whether to call particular witnesses, and whether to cross-examine the opposing party's witnesses. Mark Spiegel, *Lawyering and Client Decisionmaking: Informed Consent and the Legal Profession*, 128 University of Pennsylvania Law Review 41, 123–26 (1979). What is your view about whether clients ought to participate in questions of case tactics and strategy, or even "call the shots" where the lawyer and client disagree?

11. *A Time to Kill* and *Nuts* both offer examples of clients playing a fairly significant role in trial strategy and tactics. In *A Time to Kill*, Carl Lee Hailey pushes his lawyer to ask a prosecution witness a question that his lawyer considers the "one question too many" that lawyers are taught not to ask, and his lawyer resists. Why does the lawyer eventually ask the question? Is he simply following the client's marching orders? Does the witness' answer vindicate the client? What lessons can we draw from this example about the types of expertise clients possess in matters that are traditionally considered within the purview of lawyers? In *Nuts*, Claudia Draper has strong feelings about whether her mother should be called as a witness in the case, and what questions her father should be asked on cross-examination. How does Aaron Levinsky, the public defender appointed by the judge to represent Draper, respond to her? What do you think of his choice to reveal her secret in the courtroom in the interest of winning the case? Can his behavior been seen as a clash between the competing values of narrative integrity and preserving the client's freedom from legal harm? What do you make of his later apology ("I'm so sorry; I got so wrapped up in being a goddamn lawyer.")? Did the lawyer's response to the judge's request at the hearing the next day that his client consent to an independent psychiatric examination show that the lawyer learned anything from the events of the previous day?

3. Holistic Approach

The next excerpt describes the holistic approach taken by a clinical professor who represents domestic violence survivors.

REPRESENTATION OF DOMESTIC VIOLENCE SURVIVORS AS A NEW PARADIGM OF POVERTY LAW: IN SEARCH OF ACCESS, CONNECTION, AND VOICE
Peter Margulies
63 George Washington Law Review 1071 (1995)

Connection invokes the affective style of lawyering — an approach which stresses mutuality, care, and empathy between lawyer and client. Connection also requires spanning disciplinary boundaries, such as the boundaries between law, social work, and psychology. . . .

Connection also breaks down barriers between disciplines. . . . [L]egal services should be available alongside other services such as medicine or education sought by survivors of domestic violence. In addition to the physical location of services, a multidisciplinary approach involves an integration of both knowledge and action on the lawyer's part.

Knowledge of the psychology of domestic violence is important not only to establish connection with a client, but also to assist her in making sound decisions. Discerning "the interplay between emotion and reason" reveals "connections between knowledge and power." Without an understanding of power in abusive relationships and in gender roles, lawyers cannot hope to represent a domestic violence survivor effectively. . . .

Lawyers for domestic violence survivors also move from interdisciplinary knowledge to action. This action may collapse the wall between "law" and "social work." For example, I, on occasion, provide transportation for clients, and people from my office have gone with clients to seek jobs and housing. This also is a part of connection. It may be distinct from lawyering, in the narrow sense, and encroach into the domain of "social work," but often the lawyer is the only person in a position to provide this service. In a contextual vision of lawyering, lawyers help clients as much through getting a job and housing as they do with legal work. . . .

NOTES & QUESTIONS

1. Although Professor Margulies does not label his approach "holistic," what aspects of holistic lawyering are reflected in this excerpt? How can lawyers become experts in all of the areas identified by Margulies, or would it be preferable, as some have suggested, to work closely with other professionals, such as social workers, in a multi-disciplinary practice? *See* David Dominguez, *Getting Beyond Yes to Collaborative Justice: The Role of Negotiation in Community Lawyering*, 12 Georgetown Journal of Poverty Law & Policy 55, 77 n.73 (2005). Is the "go it alone" approach suggested in this excerpt justified only in situations where limited resources mean that clients do not have access to experts in job hunting or other services? For holistic lawyers who seek to collaborate with other professionals, such as social workers or psychologists, what barriers might those lawyers face? Does working with an expert in another field absolve the lawyer of responsibility for understanding the non-legal aspects of the client's problem? Why or why not?

2. In what other areas of practice besides domestic violence law would knowledge of the "psychology" of the client or her situation be important? Does this effort to categorize clients run the risk of stereotyping those clients and thus failing to recognize and value their unique experiences?

3. In the case of Debra, described in the earlier excerpt from Professor Cook's article, Debra's student attorney and the supervising attorney considered other options beyond her immediate case, involving both litigation and other avenues of reform:

> We considered alternatives other than trial that might result in reforms of police procedures as well as in dismissal of the charges against Debra. The Police Department was already under scrutiny for its handling of several investigatory stops that had resulted in the deaths of two young men the previous spring, and this increased the likelihood that, if approached, the press would take an interest in the department's handling of rape complaints. Media pressure might have some desirable effects. There was also the option of filing a civil suit against the police department in either state or federal court. One thing that was appealing about these alternatives was that they focused attention on a problem that was much larger than the charge pending against Debra; they gave Rachel (and Debra) the opportunity to make a difference on a grander scale.

Debra, however, was not interested in discussing these options. She wanted the charges to go away, yes, and she wanted the police to conduct themselves differently, but she did not want to be involved in a major law reform effort. As far as she was concerned, the sooner this mess got cleaned up, the better; she had been inconvenienced enough.

Cook, *supra,* 52. Is the client's reaction somewhat expected? How many clients would have the time and energy to be involved in pursuing options beyond those options that address their immediate needs?

4. The films *The Client* and *A Time to Kill* illustrate holistic lawyering. For example, Jake Brigance helps his client get the money collected at church to get food for his needy family, and Reggie Love similarly brings food and clothes to her client's mother in the hospital. In taking these actions, did they step outside of an appropriate lawyer role? What impact do Reggie Love's maternal instincts have on her ability to practice law holistically? Notice how Reggie first refers to Mark in court as "the child," and only later refers to him as "my client." What is the relevance of these word choices?

4.   Client-Empowerment Approach

This approach is described in the context of a case study from South Africa.

TO LEARN AND TEACH: LESSONS FROM DRIEFONTEIN ON LAWYERING AND POWER
Lucie E. White
1988 Wisconsin Law Review 699

On August 26, 1985, the South African government announced that it would not force the residents — all of them Black — of a small farming community called Driefontein to relocate to resettlement camps in remote rural areas. Rather, the government acceded to the villagers' demands that they be allowed to continue living, farming, and owning land in a region of the country that had been officially designated as the exclusive domain of whites. The reprieve for Driefontein came just a month after the government had placed a large part of the country under a "state of emergency," tantamount to martial law, in an aggressive effort to quell anti-apartheid activism in Black communities. In the context of these emergency regulations and the heightened repression that they signaled, the government's backing down on the Driefontein removal was hard to comprehend. It did not fit within the overall pattern of events in South Africa at the time. What could have compelled the government to give in, at that time, to a few isolated Blacks on an issue as central to the logic of apartheid as Black ownership and occupancy of land?

This Article explores that question by reconstructing the story of Driefontein's opposition to the South African government. It is a case study of the community's resistance, with a focus on how a lawyer and an organizer worked with the community to enable and support that effort. To work effectively with a community which had few clear-cut legal rights, the outsiders — the lawyers and the organizer — had to depart sharply from traditional notions of their proper professional roles. Instead of following established norms for serving clients, the lawyer collaborated with the organizer and the villagers in a joint project of challenging structures of domination that disabled the community, and of creating sources of their own power. . . .

The villagers' victory may not have ended the era of forced removals, but the work they did to achieve their reprieve undermined apartheid in another way. The villagers did not hand their problem over to a lawyer, who then acted for them. Rather, the lawyer and organizer worked with the villagers to help them gain power. With the help of these outsiders, the villagers educated themselves about the removals. They spread that knowledge among themselves and to others. They set up their own facilities when the government withdrew services. They compelled the government to pay the public benefits that they were due. They analyzed the government's position on the removal and devised strategies for responding to it. They negotiated with government and homeland officials. . . .

The lawyer and the organizer took on distinct tasks as the case developed. The lawyer worked primarily with the negotiating committee and the government, devising strategies to block the removal. The organizer worked primarily with villagers, educating them about the removal threat and helping them build independent community institutions. These two efforts were not isolated from one another. Rather, the tasks of the lawyer and the organizer complemented each other in a single advocacy strategy. As the villagers gained confidence in themselves and consolidated their community, the problem of implementing the removal became more difficult for the government. It became more likely that the villagers would move only if direct physical force was used. Similarly, as the lawyer and the organizing committee gained information and got concessions from the government, the villagers' motivation to build their community increased. Thus, the two efforts — of negotiation and community work — built upon one another. They were two aspects of a "lawyering" effort, in which no single actor occupied the "lawyer" role. . . .

The villagers used public support for two purposes. First, active villagers used the events generated by the public interest in the removal — the visits of outside journalists, the press clippings, the play that they produced about the removal — as occasions to motivate their neighbors to get involved in the community building activities. Second, public opinion, both within South Africa and throughout the world, was a central source of leverage that the villagers had against the government. Ultimately, they were able to pressure the government to agree to the land deal because those officials were unwilling to risk the international outcry that might follow a violent removal.

Public opinion — the audience — became a significant source of power to the villagers only because it was cultivated, consciously, through the lawyering effort. The outsiders — the lawyer and the organizer — were indispensable to this effort; they had the connections to the internal and international press, and they knew the psychology of the white world. Yet the villagers themselves gave the accounts that resonated so deeply in the conscience of the "outside" world and even in some parts of the white community inside South Africa. . . .

[Other community] activities include[d] the informal conversations between the organizer and the villagers, the development of the health clinic and the legal clinic, and the strategizing work that the lawyer did jointly with the villagers and the negotiating committee. All of these activities helped the villagers understand the full measure of their own power. . . . Through those activities, villagers found themselves working together effectively and successfully in their own community and against the government. As a result, the community coalesced and resolved that it would not cooperate in another "voluntary" removal. . . .

NOTES & QUESTIONS

1. In the article excerpted earlier in this chapter, Professor Kruse describes the client-empowerment approach as encouraging individual clients to think outside the box of their own world view so that they can make better decisions, using strategies that include "facilitating the client's connection and solidarity with others." Kruse, *supra,* 423. It is this "group" aspect of client-centeredness that is reflected in the Driefontein case study from South Africa. What aspects of the case study demonstrate a client-empowerment approach to the problem of forced removal? What other lawyering approaches might be implicated?

2. Would a client-empowerment approach of the group variety apply to all cultural settings, or was there something unique about the cultural setting of South Africa at that time? Two of the films — *A Time to Kill* and *The Sweet Hereafter* — also present clients situated in close-knit communities. What impact did this connection have on the relationships those clients developed with their lawyers?

3. In contrast, in *The Client,* Reggie Love practices the arguably paternalistic "individualist" form of client empowerment when she chases after Mark after he tries to fire her as his attorney, an action which she sees as not being in his best interests. This may be an easy case for client-empowerment since otherwise Mark would have been without legal counsel, but what about harder cases? What might these be?

4. In *Nuts,* Claudia Draper's lawyer tells her, "If we win the hearing, you get a trial [on manslaughter charges]. If you lose, you could go to jail for twenty-five years." She replies, "I'll take the risk. If I don't, I could end up wearing this nightie until I collect social security." What might a client-empowering type of lawyer have said or done next?

5. Partisan Approach

In making the case for zealous and partisan advocacy in the context of criminal defense lawyering, the next author discusses the views of legal ethicist and criminal defense attorney Monroe Freedman.

THE DIFFERENCE IN CRIMINAL DEFENSE AND THE DIFFERENCE IT MAKES
Abbe Smith
11 Washington University Journal of Law & Policy 83 (2003)

[Monroe] Freedman argues that an essential function of the adversary system is to "maintain a free society in which individual rights are central." As Freedman notes, the rights that comprise the adversary system include the right to personal autonomy, the right to counsel, the right to equal protection of the laws, the right to trial by jury, the right to call and confront witnesses, the right to be free from compelled self-incrimination, and the right to a presumption of innocence. Freedman further notes that the government must bear the burden of proof, and must prove its case beyond a reasonable doubt.

Freedman regards the right to counsel as the most important of all rights because it is inextricably connected to the "client's ability to assert all other rights." Through adversarial advocacy the lawyer functions to uphold the client's rights, and protects the client's autonomy, dignity, and freedom. Thus, to Freedman, an ethical and professionally responsible lawyer is an ardent civil libertarian who, in zealously representing individual clients, also upholds the political philosophy underlying the American system of justice.

In Freedman's view, the central concern of a system of lawyers' ethics is to strengthen and protect the role of the lawyer in enhancing individual dignity and autonomy through advocacy. This is a constant theme throughout Freedman's considerable body of work. To use the phrase currently in vogue, which he himself may have coined, Freedman is an eloquent champion of "client-centered" lawyering. Thus, to Freedman, lawyers do justice when they pursue their clients' interests with devotion and zeal.

My own view of criminal defense lawyering owes much to Monroe Freedman. I agree with his "traditionalist view" of criminal defense ethics as a lawyering paradigm in which zealous advocacy and the maintenance of client confidence and trust are paramount. Simply put, zeal and confidentiality trump most other rules, principles, or values. When there is tension between these "fundamental principles" and other ethical rules, criminal defense lawyers must uphold the principles, even in the face of public or professional outcry. Although a defender must act within the bounds of the law, he or she should engage in advocacy that is as close to the line as possible, and, indeed, should test the line, if it is in the client's interest in doing so. . . .

NOTES & QUESTIONS

1. The author argues that criminal defense attorneys should "engage in advocacy that is as close to the line as possible, and, indeed, should test the line, if it is in the client's interest in doing so." What personal and professional risks does this approach pose for attorneys who practice in this way? Consider this example:

> My client Norman, and his co-respondent, Steve Thomas, were charged with receiving stolen property. The police happened upon Norman and

Steve in an alley transferring a stereo and TV from a junked car into the back seat of a white Pontiac.

The case hinged on whether our clients knew (or should have known) that the property was stolen. . . .

When Norman borrowed his cousin's Pontiac, he told us, he was given only the ignition key, not the trunk key. But when all the evidence was in, no mention had been made of that fact. At Steve Thomas's lawyer's suggestion, we made what was to me, at that time, a novel and shocking argument: obviously Steve and Norman had no idea that the property was stolen, else why would they have been loading it into the Pontiac's back seat, instead of concealing it in the trunk?

William H. Simon, *The Ethics of Criminal Defense*, 91 Michigan Law Review 1703, 1704 (1993), citing James S. Kunen, *"How Can You Defend Those People?": The Making of a Criminal Lawyer* 117 (1983). Would you be comfortable trying to gain an advantage in a case by arguing that the evidence supports an inference that you know is untrue?

2. Professor Smith argues that in the criminal defense context "[s]ometimes even lawyers who see themselves as their clients' friends will scold clients, gang up on them, twist their arms, brow-beat them to do the right thing." Abbe Smith, *Too Much Heart and Not Enough Heat: The Short Life and Fractured Ego of the Empathic, Heroic Public Defender*, 37 U.C. Davis Law Review 1203, 1231 (2004). Are lawyers who practice the partisan advocacy brand of client-centered lawyering more likely than other client-centered lawyers to ignore their clients' stated interest, bullying their clients to "do the right thing" until they give in? Does this behavior respect clients and their viewpoints? What special expertise do lawyers have in helping clients weigh complicated choices which have both legal and non-legal consequences for their lives? Consider the clients in *A Time to Kill* and *Nuts*. While a plea would have helped Carl Lee Hailey avoid a longer prison term than if he had been found guilty of murder, and a finding of incompetency would have allowed Claudia Draper to sidestep a possible murder conviction, neither client was willing to consider these options. Why? What were their life circumstances that made these options unappealing?

3. Professor Kruse has argued that this type of advocacy may be especially applicable in the context of criminal defense work. Kruse, *supra,* 425. Do you agree? Are there other contexts where clients face losses as severe as the potential loss of freedom resulting from incarceration in a criminal case? What might those losses be?

4. To some degree, the lawyers in the featured films for this chapter (with the possible exception of *Miracle on 34th Street*) at times act as partisan advocates with less concern for the niceties of legal rules than the interests of their clients. In *The Client*, the lawyer puts the interests of her client above everyone else, jeopardizing an important federal investigation through actions that could constitute obstruction of justice. In *Nuts*, the lawyer cross-examines witnesses by going for the jugular with a no-holds-barred cross-examination style. In *The Sweet Hereafter*, the lawyer promises potential clients that "in your name and the Walkers' name and the name of whoever decides to join us, I shall sue. I shall sue for negligence until they bleed." In *A Time to Kill,* the lawyer makes a plea for acquittal that arguably has no basis in law. In your view, are their actions justified? Would you have done the same thing if you had been the lawyer for these clients?

5. While the reliance on racial themes seems entirely appropriate in the context of circumstances like those found in *A Time to Kill,* the use of racial case theories to acquit other African American defendants has been criticized when those theories rely on negative racial stereotypes, as in the Reginald Denny trial:

> To win acquittals, the Williams-Watson defense attorneys challenged and ultimately refuted substantial evidence of intent and voluntary conduct available to prove criminal liability for attempted murder and aggravated mayhem in the beating of Reginald Denny and others. Their main defense rested on a "group contagion" theory of mob-incited diminished capacity. Marshaled as a partially exculpatory defense, the theory holds that young black males as a group, and the black community as a whole, share a pathological tendency to commit acts of violence in collective situations. Both Williams and Watson are young, male, and black. Among the victims, Denny is white, and the others are of mixed ethnic and racial backgrounds.

Anthony V. Alfieri, *(Er)Race-ing An Ethic of Justice,* 51 Stanford Law Review 935, 942 (1999). Do you agree that the use of these types of racial themes is inappropriate? Why? Does partisan advocacy require using any and all themes, regardless of the impact on particular groups? Does it matter that the clients in the Denny prosecution were members of the group that is the subject of the stereotype?

6. Given that a partisan advocate will fight like hell for a client, all the while twisting the client's arm, would you want a partisan advocate as your lawyer? How do you think most clients would react to a partisan advocate-type lawyer?

D.　ESTABLISHING THE RELATIONSHIP: TRUST, EMPATHY, AND SHARED EXPERIENCES

Regardless of a lawyer's approach to lawyering, it is important that lawyers be able to gain the trust of their clients, and in turn be able to empathize with the difficult situations that clients find themselves in. The first excerpt was written with public defenders in mind, but it applies to many other types of lawyering as well.

BEYOND JUSTIFICATIONS: SEEKING MOTIVATIONS TO SUSTAIN PUBLIC DEFENDERS
Charles Ogletree
106 Harvard Law Review 1239 (1992)

Although the term "empathy" has been used in numerous contexts, with various meanings, it is a seriously undervalued element of legal practice.

Empathy has been broadly defined as "understanding the experiences, behavior, and feelings of others as they experience them. It means that lawyers must to the best of their abilities put aside their own biases, prejudices, and points of view in order to understand as clearly as possible the points of view of their clients." I use the term to capture two different concepts: first, to require the listener not simply to hear her clients, but to understand their problems, and, second, to have compassion for her clients. This dual concept of empathy is frequently invoked in feminist jurisprudence and in clinical legal scholarship. In both areas, empathy plays a central role in the development of the theory and practice of client-centered lawyering.

My view of empathy has significant implications for the character of the lawyer-client relationship. My relationships with clients were rarely limited to the provision of conventional legal services. I did not draw rigid lines between my professional practice and my private life. My relationship with my clients approximated a true friendship. I did for my clients all that I would do for a friend. I took phone calls at all hours, helped clients find jobs, and even interceded in domestic conflicts. I attended my clients' weddings and their funerals. When clients were sent to prison, I maintained contact with their families. Because I viewed my clients as friends, I did not merely feel justified in doing all I could for them; I felt a strong desire to do so. . . .

I want to emphasize that the quality of a lawyer's representation often will improve when she takes an empathic view of her client. Empathizing with a client necessarily means caring more deeply for the client. The attorney with a deeper understanding of and sensitivity to the client wants to help him, and this desire directly affects both her will to represent the client and the form that the representation itself takes. When she cares about the client as an individual, not only does she want to assist him through the complex maze of our legal system, but she also wants him to succeed; as a result, her defense is zealous.

Additionally, empathy provides defenders with the ability to hear "complex, multivocal conversations." As a result, empathy enhances a lawyer's ability to interview and counsel clients, to negotiate with opposing counsel, and to engage in the numerous other types of communication that are demanded of lawyers. Empathy also improves a lawyer's problem-solving skills, for she is better able to assess the client's goals and to integrate them into an evaluation of potential solutions. This client contact may in turn have positive effects on one's motivation to do the work, for when an attorney sees her success rate in terms of improvements in the overall quality of her clients' lives, she may come to realize that she does much more good on a daily basis than the record of her "wins" and "losses" might indicate. . . .

NOTES & QUESTIONS

1. How is it possible for anyone to "understand the experiences, behavior, and feelings of others as they experience them," as Professor Ogletree urges lawyers do with clients? Or is Delores, the bus driver in *The Sweet Hereafter*, right when she angrily asks Stephens, "How do you know what I've been feeling?" What other difficulties might a lawyer encounter in seeking the type of close relationship Professor Ogletree sought with his clients? Are you troubled by Professor Ogletree's statement that "My relationship with my clients approximated a true friendship"? When Mark refers to Reggie Love as a "friend" in *The Client*, what do you think he means? Can this situation be distinguished from that of clients who were friends with their lawyers before they established a lawyer-client relationship, as in the case of Kris Kringle in *Miracle on 34th Street*?

2. Another aspect of empathy is the emphasis on the client as a whole person, not just a person with legal needs, consistent with a holistic approach to lawyering. In this view, clients are people who had real lives long before they needed to consult a lawyer, and their individual qualities and experiences affect not just case theory, but every aspect of their representation. What role does this emphasis on the life experiences of clients play in the other conceptions of client-centeredness: narrative integrity, client empowerment, partisan, and client-directed?

3. Distinguish the strategic use of empathy with clients from true empathy. For example, Mitchell Stephens in *The Sweet Hereafter* can be viewed as a manipulative and completely non-empathic lawyer, akin to the ambulance-chasing paralegal that Danny DeVito plays in the John Grisham film *The Rainmaker* (1997). As one commentator describes Stephens:

> He is a seducer of the weak, preying on human vulnerabilities and needs that his finely tuned legal sensibilities can sniff out in a minute. To some of the town's parents he offers dignity and status, treating them as the embodiment of the community's values, its respectability, even as he invites them to gossip about their neighbors' debts, their defects, their criminal records. To other people he holds out different hope and he promises different benefits. To the Ottos, the hippie parents of an adopted child, he promises to give voice to their anger.

Sarat, *Loss, Dread and Mourning, supra,* 24. Is Stephens' character more complex than described by this commentator? Is he out for money, or something else? When he solicits the Ottos as clients, telling them "I'm here to give your anger a voice," is this just a manipulative ploy for business, or is he sincere in feeling their sense of grief, loss, and anger? Is he an angry person himself? Is it possible that he sees it as his duty to get money for individuals who have been wronged? If his motives are purely strategic, is there anything wrong with that? Are his actions any different than the actions of Reggie Love in seeking a bond with her client through her familiarity with the band Led Zeppelin?

4. In forging relationships with their clients, lawyers often confront clients with preconceived notions about lawyers and in some cases negative experiences with lawyers. For example, when Aaron Levinsky met his client in *Nuts*, she had just punched her previous attorney in the courtroom, and she greets Levinsky with hostility, sarcasm, and disdain. In *The Client*, when Mark first visits Reggie Love's office, he quizzes her about her experience, her fees, and whether she will actually keep his secrets. How do these clients' views and experiences affect the relationship that is ultimately forged with their lawyers?

5. The lawyers in these films recognize the importance of the totality of their clients' life circumstances in different ways. In *Nuts*, Richard Dreyfuss visits his client's apartment, rifles through her dresser drawers, and looks at her photographs. While ostensibly he may be viewed simply as visiting the murder scene, his behavior suggests something more. What do you think he is looking for? How does the client react to his trip to her apartment? In contrast, Mitchell Stephens, the lawyer in *The Sweet Hereafter*, seeks information about the lives of potential clients by talking to their neighbors. When he discusses the case with the Ottos, he stresses the importance of having "upstanding citizens" as clients, "folks like you who won't come back to haunt us." Is he acting appropriately? Can lawyers screen out clients with poor reputations or a lot of personal baggage? Are these individuals any less deserving of compensation as personal injury plaintiffs because they have committed minor crimes or personal indiscretions?

6. In telling the story of Ms. Parsons, a foster mother who had lost custody of the three foster children she was seeking to adopt, the next excerpt reveals how lawyers' relationships with clients can change based on the lawyer's own life experience.

REFLECTIONS ON A CASE (OF MOTHERHOOD)
Jane M. Spinak
95 Columbia Law Review 1990 (1995)

Twelve years of lawyering in the foster care system organized Ms. Parsons's story into a case file. This was not a case that [a] lawyer wanted. At another time I would have redoubled my efforts to find her counsel, given her some advice, and told her that the office couldn't undertake such a massive job as the end of the semester approached. I was going to have to do that with other prospective clients. But I couldn't say no that day. Her anguish as a mother overwhelmed me: her terror became mine. Her boys became my girl. My shoulders and chest ached under my dress as I listened to her loss. I let myself listen to the client for the first time as a mother and I couldn't say no. . . .

I had thought, when contemplating motherhood, that the central impact on my work would be balancing my need to be a mother to a child with my need to be a teacher to students and a lawyer to clients. Even though I have always urged students to draw on their life experiences for their lawyering, I never considered that becoming a mother would change the way I considered the process of my work. . . .

Ms. Parsons became a foster mother when she was in her early forties. Her goal was to adopt children and taking foster children appeared to be the most effective route. She wanted to be a "pre-adoptive" foster parent, one who accepts foster children already freed or likely to be freed for adoption. The foster care agency knew she preferred two boys, toilet trained but not much older. She anticipated some of the difficulties of being a single mother and had elaborately organized her life, nursing schedule, and home to minimize the chaos of suddenly being thrust into this new role. After more than a year of waiting, three small boys — Juan, Mati, and Michael — appeared at her door one night, aged seven, four and two. One more than expected and one needing a crib and diapers: the first step away from control over chaos. Her joy at beginning her life as a mother was tempered by her fear that her plans were altered. As she recounted the story, I felt that fear. At the time my daughter was born, when I was in my late thirties, I knew the fear of losing the control built over years of professional adult life. Early in my daughter's life, the fluidity of our days unnerved me: What would I have done if our plans had been altered? If I had not had the support of a sharing husband, a maternity leave, financial stability, years of working with children and parents? Ms. Parsons's fear was mine confirmed. She nevertheless plunged into motherhood.

Ms. Parsons is a proud and contained woman. She does not easily share her feelings and rarely finds humor in life's vagaries. When she first told us what had happened, she circled around her despair. The disjointed narrative, her flashes of anger at "the system," her constant vigilance toward our ability to take her side were intended to keep us at a distance from her pain. She wasn't looking for sympathy or compassion. I don't think she cared what I thought of her as long as I could help her reclaim her motherhood. I have helped other mothers who have been separated from their children. With some of them I have developed an easygoing rapport. We like each other, we try to develop a mutual trust, and we share fairly easily in the struggle to reunite their families despite enormous differences in our backgrounds and experiences. Maybe they are better at hiding their pain. Maybe I shut my eyes to it so that I can do this work. Maybe I distance myself from them intellectually so that I can distance myself emotionally. Maybe they take similar actions. Maybe they just act the way they think I want them to. I certainly would not like to feel about all my clients and cases the way I feel about Ms. Parsons. . . .

Here's what I think my clients think about me. I am privileged. I am a white woman lawyer who always has some money for emergency cabs or lunches for them, who wears a gold wedding ring and who doesn't look or act like I have or will ever experience motherhood in the way they do. I have the perquisites which keep poverty, homelessness, dislocation, unemployment, maltreatment, and thus the state from my and my child's door. I know no one will keep the shop locked against me after the briefest look at my skin. I will not live with fear that my sexual orientation could strip me of my parental rights. I do not have to protect myself or my child from domestic violence. I work for pleasure as well as money. The inequality of this existence is so profound that I wonder whether most of my clients realize its true power.

These differences have usually existed between my clients (or, when I represented children, my clients' parents) and me. I treated them as divisions between us which could be intellectualized as much as felt. They were societal injustices which my lawyering skill was supposed to be able to abstract and thus help alleviate. When I became a mother, and returned to practice as a lawyer, something changed. In assuming the responsibility for another life, I had shed something of my insularity. Love and care for another adult — husband, parent, friend — has required various amounts of time, commitment and adjustments. They are part of but do not permeate my entire existence. I do not feel their responsibility incessantly. Whatever kind of mother I am, mother I am. This is what I felt when Lucy first came to my office. We shared — with our differences — this incessant, maddening pull. I hate its strength, its ability to arouse guilt, jealousy, and fear, especially fear. Random harm is a constant part of my consciousness; deliberate or unintentional cruelty a subconscious menace. As I listened to this client — and later to others — her exposure to me became more personal. Her otherness defined and intensified but did not destroy this shared existence . . .

I do not expect that most of this story's readers are mothers or lawyers for mothers nor, even if they were, that their experience of these conditions mirrors mine or my client's. The particulars of our lives remain ours. Something about motherhood, nevertheless, came to center the way in which I worked with this client and its power began to infect the way I thought about lawyering. . . .

NOTES & QUESTIONS

1. The Spinak excerpt shows that lawyer-client relationships are not static. Lawyers have different relationships with different clients, and indeed, their relationships with particular clients change over time. How was the author's relationship with her client different than her relationship with other clients because they each had the experience of being mothers? At the same time, they were separated by differences in race and class. What are the risks inherent in the assumption of a shared experience? Which matters more to the lawyer-client relationship, the shared experience of motherhood, or differences in race and class?

2. In describing how her view of lawyering changed once she became a mother, Spinak also explains how her view of empathy changed:

This did not feel like the lawyerly empathy that enabled me to listen "actively" to a client, both following and conducting the client through her tale. That respectful empathy was a learned construction with clear benefits: the client would provide more relevant information in a shorter time period if the lawyer confirmed her understanding of the client's tale during the client's telling. Empathy's thoughtfulness does not deconstruct the tale or the teller. It does not offer an alternative vision. It does not require the listener to abandon learned knowing. It is polite but not political.

Spinak, *supra,* 2052. How does the author's view of "lawyerly" empathy comport with Professor Ogletree's? How does her new "political view" of empathy comport with his view?

3. Like his client, Jake Brigance, the lawyer in *A Time to Kill,* also was the father of a young daughter, and thus could understand (at least to some extent) the anger and pain that motivated Carl Lee Hailey to shoot the men who raped his daughter. How did the shared experience of fatherhood affect Brigance's relationship with Hailey?

4. At first glance, Mitchell Stephens, the lawyer in *The Sweet Hereafter,* appears to have little in common with the parents whose children were killed in the bus accident. He is a high-profile lawyer from a big city; they are working class residents of a small remote town in British Columbia. The town is vividly described as "populated by 1960s leftovers, hippies, families built around interracial adoptions, disabled people, and Vietnam veterans turned into single fathers and Allman Brothers 'wanna-bes'." Sarat, *Loss, Dread and Mourning, supra,* 23. The parents are members of a tight-knit community; the lawyer is an outsider. But viewers come to learn that he also is a grieving parent, not grieving for the death of his daughter, but for her descent into the world of drug addiction, the loss of the innocence of her childhood, and his connection to that innocence. As one commentator notes: "Running alongside the story of [the lawyer's] efforts to generate a lawsuit on behalf of the victims of the bus accident is his own troubled relationship to his drug-addicted daughter, Zoe," *id.* at 20; thus, "it is hard to tell where Mitchell Stephens the lawyer ends and where Mitchell Stephens the father begins, and whether it is possible to separate the lawyer's public duty, his 'job,' the law itself, from that private agony that marks his life as a father." *Id.* at 22–23. In the beginning, this connection with his clients is not at all evident, but later in the movie he tells Billy Ansel, one of the parents who did not join the lawsuit and is hostile to it, about his daughter's problems. Why do you think he revealed this information? Does Stephens act appropriately in revealing this information? Would his actions be more or less appropriate if Billy were a client?

5. Mitchell Stephens' experience of the case seems to change throughout the film, both in terms of the viability of the lawsuit (which changes following the deposition of Nicole) and his feelings about who is to blame for the accident, as well as his relationship to his clients and other people in the town. How would you describe this change? Is it positive? Negative? Some of both?

6. The identity issues in *The Client* do not involve a lawyer and a client with shared life experiences, but instead deal with a lawyer whose experience in losing custody of her own child affects her relationship with her young client. According to one commentator, "Reggie's motivation to practice family law clearly seems to be a replacement. She misses her biological children and uses her clients as substitutes." Carrie S. Coffman, *Gingerbread Women: Stereotypical Female Attorneys in the Novels of John Grisham*, 8 Southern California Review of Law and Women's Studies 73, 94 (1988). Another commentator notes that the lawyer's "last name, 'Love,' also signifies the mothering she is able to give to Mark — mothering she cannot give to her own children but can now dole out to Mark under the cover of her astute command of the law." Judith Grant, *Lawyers As Superheroes: The Firm, The Client, and The Pelican Brief*, 30 University of San Francisco Law Review 1111, 1117 (1966). Do you agree with these assessments? What are the dangers in confusing her role as a lawyer to her client with a mothering role? Another commentator notes that Reggie, "largely by supplementing her legal judgment with maternal impulses, achieves both a legal advantage for her client and a large measure of personal gratification." Stacy Caplow, *Still in the Dark: Disappointing Images of Women Lawyers in the Movies*, 20 Women's Rights Law Reporter 55, 57 (1988–99). In what respect do Reggie Love's maternal impulses help her client legally? Are legal judgment and maternal impulses mutually exclusive? Is she a better lawyer for having been a mother? For having lost a custody battle to her former husband?

7. When a lawyer has (or thinks she has) experiences in common with a client, how much of her personal life should she reveal to her client? Professor Spinak does not engage in self-disclosure, in contrast to Reggie Love, who tells Mark that she is a recovering alcoholic. Does the motivation for the disclosure make a difference in your answer? What was Reggie's motive in revealing this information to Mark? After hearing his response, do you think her decision to reveal her former addiction was a good one?

8. Consider the various identity groups to which you belong and your own life experiences. How do you think your identity and your experiences will affect your relationship with clients? Are there certain types of clients you would find easiest to represent? Most difficult to represent?

E.   UNBRIDGEABLE GAPS

Despite the promise of the client-centered approaches to lawyering, and the important role that empathy, trust, and shared life experiences can play in bringing clients together with their lawyers, there may be ways in which we can never truly understand the lives and experiences of others. The following excerpt from the interview of a 72-year-old former sharecropper in rural North Carolina reveals the tension between connection and distance. In researching the Head Start program, the author interviewed the great-grandmother and legal guardian of a child participating in the program.

SEEKING ". . . THE FACES OF OTHERNESS . . .": A RESPONSE TO PROFESSORS SARAT, FELSTINER, AND CAHN
Lucie E. White
77 Cornell Law Review 1499 (1992)

In the interview, she gave me a brief account of the highlights of her life. She told me of her father's defiance in sending his daughter to school when the white plantation bosses expected her to be working in the fields. She told of receiving a scholarship to an elite women's college, but turning it down because she could not afford a bus ticket to get there. She told of graduating from an African-American teacher's college and of teaching for fifty years in the public schools. She told me what it was like to teach before the schools were integrated, when her students were given text-books handed down from whites. She also told me what it was like to teach after integration, when white children asked, and were allowed, to transfer out of her class. She referred only in passing to the civil rights movement. I learned from others that she had been one of the movement's many local leaders in the rural counties of the south.

As I contemplated this story, comparing it to what others had told me about the record of racial violence in the county and the courage this woman had shown in combating it, two features stood out. First, throughout the story, she expressed inexhaustible patience, and indeed love, for the white people she had dealt with over the years. Second, although she recounted many injustices, her narrative carefully excluded the details of the violence she had endured. I had noted similar themes in interviews with other African-American Head Start parents.

After the formal interview was completed and the tape recorder turned off, I casually inquired about the woman's older great-grandchild, who, like my own daughter, had recently started kindergarten. When I asked this question, my informant became visibly sad. She told me that when she had dropped this child off at school earlier that morning, a young white child had run up to take her hand. Just as her great-granddaughter reached back, however, a second white child came up to the first and yanked her hand away, explaining that white girls should not touch people who were black.

Then the woman looked hard at me, and said, "The white people will go to any lengths to keep us down, even if it means keeping themselves down as well. They're making Frankensteins of us all."

This encounter could be examined through a Foucaultian lens. Such an examination would reveal an important reality. It would reveal this woman's skillful maneuvers, designed to ensure that our mutual reality was negotiated on her terms. This lens would show a woman who was artful in controlling the pace and extent of her revelations, and in determining how the injuries she had suffered would be named. This lens would reveal a woman negotiating the power between us to shape an account that she wanted me to hear.

Yet this is lens reveals only a partial reality. For when this woman told me of her child's morning at school, she was not merely controlling how that event would be interpreted, and thereby trumping my own power to do the same. She was also speaking to me as another person. Through her brief story, I "felt," for a moment, something of the impossible sadness that eluded our language game. At the same time, I picked up her astute reminder that as one of those whites, I dare not claim to have "felt" her pain. . . .

NOTES & QUESTIONS

1. Note that the author was conducting the interview as a researcher, not as a lawyer for the woman being interviewed. How does the interview compare to the kind of interview a client-centered lawyer would conduct? Do the lessons about empathy and distance also apply to lawyer-client-interactions? How can we reconcile the woman's "love for the white people she had dealt with over the years" despite many injustices, with her statement that "the white people will go to any lengths to keep us down"?

2. According to one commentator writing about Delores, the bus driver in *The Sweet Hereafter*, the fault lies not so much with lawyers, but with the law itself:

When viewers see Delores giving a deposition, recounting the horror of the accident, stating that the bus was "like a huge wave about to break over us," we are reminded of the gap between her world and the world of law. Delores sobs as she particularizes the "us," by naming every child on the bus. The panning of the camera from Delores to Stephens, who sits impassively toying with a ring on his finger, ignoring her distress as he asks matter-of-factly, "and then what happened," suggests that the gap is truly unbridgeable.

Sarat, *Naming, Blaming, and Claiming*, *supra*, 444. What aspects of the world of law are to blame?

3. Similar sentiments are expressed in this excerpt:

The scene is this: In the basement of the Metropolitan courthouse is a small, locked-in, white room where arraignments take place every week day. In the morning, when court is in full swing, the pews in the center of the room are filled with men and women in scruffy, faded, jailhouse blue serge. These people have slept poorly, if at all; they have not bathed. Some are shoeless, some are hung over, some are bloodied. Some are half asleep, while others are frightened and edgy. They are not permitted to speak, and certainly not to move from their seats.

Around the perimeters of the half dozen or so benches are the professional people, the lawyers, sheriffs, and court personnel whose livelihoods all depend, to a greater or lesser degree, on those individuals whose arrests have brought them into arraignment court. They are mostly standing — except for the judge who looks down from her high bench and the clerk beside her — and they are actively engaged in whispered discussions, only some of which are of a professional nature. With rare exceptions, these people moving around at the edges are well dressed, well rested, and comfortable. The contrast between the standers and the sitters is ludicrously obvious, like a lace collar on a used, blue serge jumpsuit.

I am reminded of an important truism: Law is for Lawyers.

Cook, *supra*, 58.

4. How does the fact of a relationship between a lawyer and a client that predates the lawyer-client relationship affect the ability of lawyer to bridge these gaps? In *Miracle on 34th Street*, Fred Gailey, Kris Kringle's lawyer, knew him first as a friend, then as a client. Although Mr. Gailey shared little in common with Mr. Kringle in terms of their personal backgrounds, what aspects of their relationship made it easier for Mr. Gailey to effectively represent Mr. Kringle? In contrast, in *A Time to Kill*, Carl Lee Hailey knew Jake Brigance because Brigance had represented Hailey's brother on a drug charge. What difference did that make in terms of their lawyer-client relationship?

5. Given the limitations of shared experiences and common backgrounds, how, other than through life experience, can lawyers and law students become more culturally competent? How would you design a cultural competence plan for yourself? For an excellent approach to learning cross-cultural concepts and skills, see Susan Bryant, *The Five Habits: Building Cross-Cultural Competence in Lawyers*, 8 Clinical Law Review 33 (2001).

Chapter 5

WITNESSES

A. FILMOGRAPHY

The Accused (1988)

The Crucible (1996)

Witness (1985)

Witness for the Prosecution (1957)

The Wrong Man (1956)

B. PREMODERN WITNESSING

In the American adversary system the role of witnesses is clear. Lawyers for either side might call witnesses to the stand, examine them under oath, and hope through them to influence the presumably neutral adjudicator. But witnesses existed and played important roles in adjudicatory systems long before the emergence of the modern American system. Reflecting on premodern witnessing might serve to clarify the role of witnesses in the present. The most notorious example of premodern adjudication in colonial North America was the Salem witchcraft trials of 1692. As result of proceedings between June and September of that year, nineteen supposed witches were hanged, and one man was pressed to death with heavy stones because he would not concede the court's jurisdiction.

In the following excerpt Professor Jane Campbell Moriarty describes the witnesses and types of evidence in the Salem witchcraft trials and offers summaries of the cases against two of the witches.

WONDERS OF THE INVISIBLE WORLD: PROSECUTORIAL SYNDROME AND PROFILE EVIDENCE IN THE SALEM WITCHCRAFT TRIALS
Jane Campbell Moriarty
26 Vermont Law Review 43 (2001)

We may never fully uncover the reason that the Salem witchcraft trials escalated so dramatically, but one explanation for the growth of the accusations was the discovery by several accused witches that confession and accusation of others was a likely way to avoid the gallows. Indeed, there was much approval of confessions as the surest evidence of guilt. Cotton Mather himself wrote of the importance of confessions in assuring proper convictions, and the renowned witchcraft expert William Perkins had also ordained their utility. The benefit of false confession and false accusation was apparent after the initial wave of convictions and hangings, since those who clung to claims of innocence were executed.

During the trials, witnesses began piecing together historical memories of strange events that occurred after an unpleasant interaction with the accused which, as Perkins had instructed, was evidence of witchcraft. For example, while the victims would come into court and identify the defendant as the specter bewitching them, other witnesses would provide historical evidence of the defendant's witchcraft acts as well. Robert Calef, who wrote scathingly about the trials after their conclusion, summed up the evidence as follows:

> In the Tryals, when any were Indicted for Afflicting, Pining, and wasting the Bodies of particular persons by Witchcraft; it was usual to hear Evidence of matter foreign, and of perhaps Twenty or Thirty years standing, about over-setting Carts, the death of Cattle, unkindness to Relations, or unexpected Accidents befalling after some quarrel.

A. Categories of Evidence

Much of the trial evidence seems to break into a number of discrete categories, although arguably some evidence seems to fit into more than one. These categories are: (1) confessions; (2) reputation evidence; (3) physical evidence; (4) spectral evidence; (5) syndrome evidence; and (6) profile evidence. The first three are discussed as a group; the remaining three are considered separately. . . .

1. Confessions, Physical Evidence, and Reputation

Confessions played a curious role in the Salem witchcraft trials. Some defendants admitted their complicity with the devil — often testifying about "signing the devil's book" — while others steadfastly maintained their innocence. Cotton Mather was firmly convinced that confession was the strongest evidence to support a proper conviction as was Perkins. While many have written about the reasons for these confessions, as well as their importance, it is indeed a curious and much-studied part of the trials that so many people confessed to something most of us do not believe was true.

To determine whether one was a witch, factfinders could also rely on reputation or character evidence of the accused. For example, Cotton Mather wrote that the defendant in the Glover trial, which pre-dated the Salem trials, possessed a poor reputation. Experts such as Perkins opined on the importance of reputation, noting that if a person was defamed as a witch, that yielded a strong suspicion. In certain trials, such as Bridget Bishop's and Sarah Good's, reputation likely added to the reasons for conviction.

Although it most likely played a minor role, physical evidence was apparently also introduced into the trials. This type of evidence would include "poppets" or dolls made for diabolical purposes, along with pins, nails, and other physical evidence of witchcraft.

2. Spectral Evidence

Spectral evidence, of course, is the most vilified and most difficult evidence to comprehend. According to some sources, it was of dubious value for many in 1692 as well. The definition of spectral evidence is somewhat elusive, and it is difficult to imagine this type of evidence ever being admissible in court.

One scholar provides a useful description: "Spectral evidence refers to the common belief that, when a person had made covenant with the devil, he was given permission to assume that person's appearance in spectral form in order to recruit others, and to otherwise carry out his nefarious deeds." Alleged witchcraft victims testified that the specter of a witch would appear to them — often at night in their bedrooms — and urge them to cast their lot with the devil and his followers. For example, in the trial of George Burroughs, Mercy Lewis testified that she witnessed "the apparition of Mr. George Burroughs, whom I knew very well, which did grievously torture me, and urged me to write in his book." There were also claims that these specters would not only attempt to lure the victims into joining the devil's band of followers, but they would also threaten to inflict very real injury on the victims if the victims did not.

Only those self-selected victims with special sight could see specters, although it would be fair to say that many believed it. Spectral evidence was consistently admitted in the Salem trials, as a review of the trial documents establishes. Generally, it was admitted into trials in three different ways: testimony by observers about witnessing victims afflicted by specters; observations in the court of victims apparently being afflicted; and testimony by victims about spectral torment that occurred outside of the court.

In the first type of spectral evidence, there was testimony from observers about fits and strange behaviors of the girls believed to be afflicted by witches. For example, in the trial of George Burroughs, Thomas and Edward Putnam supplied affidavits stating that they heard Mercy Lewis declare that the defendants had appeared to her in a spectral form and that they "also beheld her tortures which we cannot express, for sometimes we were ready to fear that every joint of her body was ready to be displaced."

In the second category were in-court demonstrations of spectrally-caused discomfort, as occurred in the proceedings against Martha Corey and the others accused. Observer Deodat Lawson recorded one scene:

> It was observed several times, that if she [Goodwife Corey] did but bite her Under lip in time of Examination the persons afflicted were bitten on their armes and wrists and produced the Marks before the Magistrates, Ministers and others. And being watched for that, if she did but Pinch her Fingers, or Graspe one hand hard in another, they were Pinched and produced the Marks before the Magistrates, and Spectators. After that, it was observed, that if she did but lean her

Breast against the Seat, in the Meeting House, (being the Barr at which she stood,) they were afflicted.

The third type of spectral evidence admitted was testimony by victims about events that they experienced in places other than the courtroom. They testified about their visions (specters as well as ghosts) and what these visions said or did to them. In George Burroughs' trial, for example, Ann Putnam testified that she was visited by the apparitions of two women who claimed to be Burroughs' [deceased] wives. They told Putnam that Burroughs had murdered them. Mercy Lewis testified that Burroughs had appeared to her and carried her off to a very high mountain, offering to give her his Kingdom, if only she would sign his book. She testified that when she refused Burroughs' offer, he tormented her dreadfully.

Wendel D. Craker argues compellingly that no defendants were tried or hanged on spectral evidence alone, but opines that the trials relied upon more traditional types of witchcraft evidence, what he terms "non-spectral acts of malefic witchcraft." Many of these "non-spectral acts of malefic witchcraft" fit within the definition of syndrome evidence.

3. Syndrome Evidence

There are two categories within the type of evidence here termed "witchcraft syndrome" evidence. In the first, witnesses told stories about cattle dying after the accused had cursed them ("bewitched cattle syndrome"), or children becoming sick and dying after an unpleasant interaction with the accused ("bewitched child syndrome"). In this category the victims truly were afflicted physically, but the causative factor was deemed demonic, not biological; what Craker termed "acts of malefic witchcraft."

The second type of syndrome evidence consisted of observations of the alleged fits and bizarre symptomology of the victims ("spectral syndrome"). These behaviors may have been feigned, or they may have been real (or some of both); there is still no agreement about their cause. Nevertheless, these behaviors are within my definition of witchcraft syndrome evidence. Thus, the claims of "biting, pricking, burning, and poking" along with the writhing, strange movements, and the like, are also collected under this category of witchcraft syndrome evidence.

4. Profile Evidence

The category of evidence that this Article refers to as "witchcraft profile" includes (1) unusual physiological marks known to be characteristic of witches, such as a "witch's mark"; and (2) inexplicable attributes believed to be of demonic origin, such as unnatural strength or the inability to say the Lord's Prayer. As is true in contemporary cases, the use of profile evidence was far more limited than syndrome evidence in the Salem trials. . . .

Sarah Good

Sarah Good, one of the first three women accused of witchcraft by the affected girls, was indicted for acts committed upon Sarah Vibber, Elizabeth Hubbard, and Ann Putnam. The indictment accused Good of practicing "wicked arts" upon Vibber, by which Vibber "was and is tortured, afflicted, pined, consumed, wasted and tormented, and also alleged sundry other acts of witchcraft."

Like Bridget Bishop, Sarah Good lived on the fringes of Salem society, apparently panhandling and moving from household to household performing whatever tasks were provided. Samuel and Mary Abbey testified that they had let Sarah Good live with them, but had to turn her out, since "Sarah Good was so turbulent a spirit." Sarah's own husband had called her a witch and claimed "with tears that shee is an enimy to all good." Sarah Good's four-year-old daughter, Dorcas, confessed to witchcraft, going so far as to claim she had suckled a familiar, from a spot on her hand. Examiners observed a "deep red spot, about the bigness of a flea bite." Thus, the accusations of witchcraft against Sarah Good surprised few and likely upset even fewer.

When Sarah Good was examined in the court, the accusing girls were asked to "look upon her, and see, if this were the person that had hurt them." According to the transcribed testimony, as soon as the girls looked at Good and identified her as one who had harmed them "they were all tormented." Testimony was taken from a variety of witnesses who claimed to see the apparition of Sarah Good, whose torment included biting, pricking, and pinching the victim, as well as choking. In addition, Tituba had confessed to witchcraft and had inculpated Sarah Good, as did Dorcas Good (Sarah Good's daughter), Deliverance Hobbs, and Abigail Hobbs.

Samuel and Mary Abbey testified against Sarah Good. They first informed the court that they had permitted the Good family to live in their house, since the Goods were destitute. However, after they "could not suffer her to live in their howse any Longer," they "began to Lose Cattle, and Lost severall after an unusall Manner, in drupeing Condition and yett they would Eate: and your Deponenets have Lost after that manner 17 head of Cattle within two years, besides Sheep, and Hoggs: and both doe believe they Dyed by witchcraft."

Another witness, Sarah Gadge, told a similar story. After refusing Sarah Good entry into her house, Good began muttering and scolding. The very next morning, one of Gadge's cows died in "A Sudden, terible & Strange, unusuall maner soe that some of the neighbors & said Deponent did think it to be done by witchcraft." Despite their "opening" the cow after its death, Thomas Gadge, Sarah Gadge's husband, said they could find no natural cause for the cow's demise.

Two young men also testified that Good had bewitched their cattle. Henry Harrick testified that after his father sent Sarah Good away from his barn for fear that she would light the barn on fire with her pipe smoking, she replied that it would cost him one or two of his best cows. According to another young witness, fourteen year old Jonathon Batchelor, cattle were removed from their places and several had been set loose in a strange manner.

Sarah Vibber testified about being visited by the spectre of Sarah Good. Vibber claimed that Good had tormented her and her four-year old child. She claimed that her child had had a great fit and was almost impossible to hold. Vibber also testified that she had witnessed the spectre of Sarah Good tormenting Mercy Lewis.

Sarah Good's husband, William, testified that the night before his wife was examined on witchcraft charges, "he saw a wart or tett a little belowe her Right shoulder which he never saw before." Nevertheless, a physical examination of Good by a group of women failed to discover any unnatural findings. Sarah Good was found guilty, the death warrant was signed on July 12, and she was hanged on July 19, 1692. . . .

Rebecca Nurse

Rebecca Nurse and Martha Corey were named by the girls in the second wave of witchcraft accusations. Both Corey and Nurse were older women in good standing in the Salem community. Neither woman was prepared for the accusations, and even "Corey's sarcastic dismissal and Nurse's earnest bewilderment at the charges did not deter the growing number of unofficial witchfinders." Like Bishop and Good, Nurse was indicted for witchcraft as a result of the claims that she had "tortured afflicted consumed Pined wasted & tormented" the four complaining witnesses, Ann Putnam, Abigail Williams, Mary Walcott and Elizabeth Hubbard.

During her initial examination before the court, Rebecca Nurse was accused of tormenting the girls, which was graphically displayed by the complaining witnesses: "Ann Putnam in a grievous fit cryed out that she hurt her." When Nurse exclaimed "Oh Lord help me, & spread out her hands," the "afflicted were greviously vexed." When Nurse turned her head to the side, "so were the afflicted taken."

After the indictments were returned, dozens of residents signed a petition on behalf of Rebecca Nurse, claiming they never had any grounds to suspect her of anything for which she stood accused. Other residents were not of a similar mind. In addition to the standard allegations consisting of visionary spectral evidence, there were several instances of syndrome evidence.

The Reverend Samuel Parris, Nathaniel Ingersol, and Thomas Putnam provided testimony that they had witnessed the torture of Ann Putnam senior, her daughter Ann, Mary Walcott, and Abigail Williams during the examination of Rebecca Nurse. Thomas and Edward Putnam testified that they had witnessed Ann Putnam during and after her fits and saw her "much afflicted, being bitten, pinched, her limbs distorted, & pins thrust into her flesh, which she charged on Rebekah Nurse that she was the Acter thereof & that she saw her do it." They also claimed they observed, during the examination, that when Nurse "did clinch her hands, bite her lips, or hold her head aside the said Putnam Hubbard & Williams was set in the same posture to her great torture & affliction." John and Hannah Putnam related a particularly upsetting incident about the death of their infant, although he had been thriving in the first eight weeks of life. Hannah Putnam testified that after she had "reported" information about Nurse, she was "taken with strange kinds of fits," but recovered quickly. Her child, however, did not fare as well. She stated that quickly after her recovery, "our poor young child was taken about midnight with strange and violent fits which did most grievously affright us, acting much like to the poor bewitched persons, when we thought they would indeed have died." The child's grandmother (also a Putnam), said that she "feared an evil hand upon it." The child's "strange and violent fits" continued on for two days, until he succumbed to "a cruel and violent death."

Sarah Houlton testified about another incident linking death to Nurse's alleged witchcraft. She claimed that one Saturday morning, Rebecca Nurse yelled at Sarah's husband, Benjamin, because his pigs had gotten into her field. Nurse would not be placated, but continued "railing and scolding a great while together." Within a short time, Benjamin Houlton was "taken with a strange fit in the entry, being struck blind and struck down two or three times." He continued to languish through the summer, suffering stomach pains and attacks of blindness. Two weeks before he died, however, he was "taken with strange and violent fits." The implication of this testimony was that Nurse had bewitched him.

As with Bridget Bishop, the examining women found evidence on Rebecca Nurse of a "preternatural excrescence of flesh between the pudendum and anus, much like teats, and not usual in women." However, upon later examination, "instead of that excrescence within mentioned, it appears only as a dry skin without sense [i.e. without sensation]." Nurse was found guilty and she was hanged on July 19, 1692. . . .

NOTES & QUESTIONS

1. In the fall of 1692 — less than a year after the Salem witchcraft trials began — several Puritans publicly criticized the proceedings. Increase Mather, a prominent minister, singled out spectral evidence as a problem. He did not condemn the judges or deny the existence of witches, but he condemned convictions based on witnesses' assertions that the Devil had appeared in the spectral form of the accused. The merchant and scientist Thomas Brattle seconded Mather's condemnation of spectral evidence, and he also complained about the use of a "touching test" in court.

On October 12, 1692, Governor William Phips stopped the trials. He was probably influenced not only by Mather and Brattle but also by allegations that his own wife was a witch. At the time of the Governor's decree 52 accused men and women were awaiting trial. The great majority of them had confessed, no doubt in hopes of saving their lives. All but two of the accused were acquitted, and the Governor granted reprieves to those two.

2. The secondary literature on the Salem witchcraft trials is immense, but one useful volume focusing on just the legal aspects of the controversy is Peter Charles Hoffer's *The Salem Witchcraft Trials — A Legal History* (1997).

3. The Salem witchcraft trials have captured the imagination of not only historians but also artists, most notably the renowned American playwright Arthur Miller. His play *The Crucible* (1953) employed the Salem witchcraft trials as a backdrop and was much acclaimed for its emotional and intellectual power. *The Crucible* was a success on the New York stage and remains popular for community and high school productions.

4. On the surface, Arthur Miller's *The Crucible* is about accusers and defendants in the Salem witchcraft trials, but on a deeper level it concerns the dangers and excesses of McCarthyism. Between roughly 1947–54, aggressive anti-Communists, including but not limited to Senator Joseph McCarthy of Wisconsin, identified, berated, and otherwise harmed thousands of Americans. Indeed, when other citizens who were not Communists refused to "name names" for Congressional committee members and others, these citizens were often humiliated, censored, and jailed. In Hollywood, Communists and Communist sympathizers were "blacklisted" and soon found themselves unable to find work. Later, in an ironic turnaround, some of those who "named names," e.g., director Elia Kazan, were shunned by members of the Hollywood community.

Senator McCarthy's eventual downfall was due in part to a confrontation with attorney Joseph Welch in a televised Congressional hearing. In one of Hollywood's most intriguing casting decisions, director Otto Preminger put Welch into the role of Judge Harlan Weaver in *Anatomy of a Murder* (1959). Welch had no acting credits, but his careful, restrained portrayal of the judge proved quite effective.

Another intriguing film with ties to the McCarthy era is Woody Allen's *The Front* (1976). It presents a picture of the era and features formerly blacklisted actors Herschel Bernardi and Zero Mostel.

5. Arthur Miller himself adapted his play for a film version of *The Crucible*. The film features Winona Ryder in the role of Abigail Williams, a young woman infatuated with a married man named John Proctor, played by Daniel Day-Lewis. Does the film seem a metaphor for a modern society in crisis? What aspects of the Salem witchcraft trials were emphasized in the cinematic version?

6. Suppose that the witnesses had accused the defendants not of witchcraft but rather of child abuse. Would your reaction to them be different? In fact, a number of child abuse prosecutions have been initiated by nothing more than the say-so of witnesses whose stories collapsed when carefully examined. *See, e.g., The McMartin Preschool Abuse Trials: 1987–90*, at http://www.law.umkc. edu/faculty/projects/ftrials/mcmartin.html.

C. EYEWITNESSES

The verdicts in many actual and pop cultural cases depend on the availability of eyewitness testimony. However, as the following excerpt from an article by Robert Hallisey indicates, social and scientific researchers have serious concerns about how eyewitness testimony is received and the extent to which eyewitness testimony can be trusted. Hallisey also discusses the extent to which expert testimony regarding the formation and reliability of the memories of eyewitnesses might be helpful in a trial.

EXPERTS ON EYEWITNESS TESTIMONY IN COURT — A SHORT HISTORICAL PERSPECTIVE
Robert Hallisey
39 Howard Law Journal 237 (1995)

A. The Concern

At the root of our criminal justice system is the premise that "it is far worse to convict an innocent man than let a guilty man go free." Thus, we presume defendants not guilty. They need not testify; and the jury may not draw negative inferences from the defendant's choice not to testify. The prosecution bears the burden of convincing all the jurors beyond a reasonable doubt that an identification is correct.

Yet, "the annals of criminal law are rife with instances of misidentifications." For example, the *Newsmagazine of the Center for Responsive Psychology* describes eight cases in which witnesses confused people who resembled each other with the real subject. Wagenaar and Loftus, Bedau and Radelet, and Rattner all provide samples of recent miscarriages of justice, with erroneous eyewitness testimony playing a central role in most examples. Kassin and Wrightsman describe a typical miscarriage where seven restaurant employees, all white, identified the defendant as the robber, even though he was six feet tall and they had said the robber was five feet, six inches. The defendant had no criminal record, and nine of his co-workers testified that he was at work, fifty miles away, at the time of the robbery. He was nevertheless convicted. The prosecution dropped the charges, after the defendant had already served one year in jail, when four of the original witnesses changed their minds and identified another person.

Although it appears that eyewitness identification provides an especially knotty problem for jury fact-finders, it is nearly impossible to discern how jurors actually analyze witnesses' testimony because of the confidentiality of jury deliberations. Many judges advise jurors not to discuss their deliberations with anyone. Occasionally, however, the course of their deliberations can be pieced together from individual juror's reports concerning a verdict. For example, some reports suggest that jurors often attempt to reenact key events involved in the case. But such juror reports are always incomplete and of uncertain reliability. Consequently, social research involving experiments and statistical analysis of results, usually based on mock juries rather than on actual juries, is the major source of information about jury deliberation.

B. Milestones in Research

Most scholars would cite the research by Professor Hugo Munsterberg at the turn of the century as the first major application of behavioral science methods and theories to eyewitness evidence in this country. In his book, *On the*

Witness Stand, Professor Munsterberg notes that common beliefs, even among judges, have been proven invalid by psychological experiments. "Cases . . . show that the psychological inspirations of the bench are often directly the opposite of demonstrable facts." Honest witnesses often give contrary testimony, but judges refuse to accept evidence from psychologists that could help fact-finders sort out the truth.

Munsterberg found that associations, suggestions, and expectations played a large role in witnesses' recollection and reported observations. He also claimed that psychology could point out the unreliability of some types of testimony such as the sources of sounds (front or back), tastes from different parts of the tongue, estimated distances, and reports of tactile sensation (for example, something wet is often confused with something smooth, cold, and metal).

Munsterberg believed that, without psychological assistance, fact-finders could go astray in many instances. "Confidence in the reliability of memory is so general that the suspicion of memory illusions evidently plays a small role in the mind of the juryman. Justice would less often miscarry if all who are to weigh evidence were more conscious of the treachery of human memory." For example, classic studies of perception and memory, conducted beginning in the 1940s, show that individual experience is not recorded on a clean slate; rather, it is immediately interpreted against the background of the observer's experience, biases, prejudices, and preconceptions. In a famous experiment by Professor Gordon Allport at Harvard University, a photograph was shown to students in which a white man, holding a straight razor, was threatening a black man. Social stereotypes led students to report that the black man held the razor.

Robert Buckhout, a professor at Brooklyn College Center for Responsive Psychology who testified extensively as an expert in cases involving eyewitness evidence, has criticized judges who exclude expert testimony on the grounds that it is an invasion on the province of the jury, and has encouraged experts to continue their efforts to testify. He has also criticized form jury instructions on evaluation of identification testimony. "For the most part, the recommended instructions for judges to give to juries are relatively simplistic, very contradictory and totally devoid of any reference to scientific findings." Referring to *U.S. v. Telfaire*, he somewhat grudgingly describes the recommended instructions as "not bad on the vagaries of initial perception, but they neglect the problems of testing recognition such as in line-ups and contain no reference to date." He thus suggests that "in any trial, a judge who is not close-minded or threatened may allow a psychologist to testify on the problems of eyewitness identification providing that the psychologist is qualified and that the testimony is relevant." But he expresses some pessimism about the widespread use of this "'new' type of expert testimony since it carries with it the threat of reform; [and] reform in the criminal justice system will always be resisted."

Professor Buckhout buttressed his opinions by conducting research involving sixteen factors in three areas that were shown to affect the unreliability of eyewitnesses: (1) with reference to the original situation: significance of the event, shortness of period of observation, and observation conditions; (2) with reference to the witness: stress, physical condition, prior conditioning and experience, personal biases, needs and motives, and desire to be part of history; and (3) with reference to the situation in which the eyewitness's memory is tested: length of time from event to test, filling in details that were not there, suggestions from the test procedure (line-up, photo array), suggestions from test giver, conformity, relation to authority figures, and passing on a theory ("the self-fulfilling prophecy").

Other research has also fortified the attack on the reliability of eyewitness testimony. For example, there exists a common belief that deception can best be discovered by watching the faces and bodies of witnesses, but studies have shown that the most accurate detection occurs when only the witness's words are heard. In addition, research findings show that, frequently, eyewitnesses are simply inaccurate. In "staged" crime events, witness reports varied markedly from the facts, and over half of the relevant details were not reported. Other studies show great disparity in reports of suspect height and duration of an incident. They also reveal that cross-racial identifications are less reliable than same-race identifications, and, furthermore, witnesses are often influenced in what they believe they observe by their subjective expectations. Stereotyping and prejudice also seem to affect reports. These findings, coupled with the effects of memory loss over time, have caused many, including Buckhout, to conclude that research psychologists should be used as expert witnesses in trials.

Elizabeth Loftus is the most publicly visible expert in this country on the strengths and weaknesses of eyewitness testimony. She is best known for studies demonstrating that the presentation of conflicting (and sometimes deliberately misleading) information about a scene or a narrative — for instance, a slide show depicting a traffic accident — can dramatically interfere with peoples' ability to report what they originally observed. For example, asking subjects misleading questions about the presence of traffic signs at an intersection was shown to reduce accuracy on a subsequent memory test from seventy-five percent to forty-one percent.

In another representative study, Loftus and her colleagues questioned thirty-two preschool children after they viewed four short films. The results showed that the children's recollections concerning entities actually present in the films were quite accurate. "Leading" questions involving entities not in the film, however, were mostly answered in the affirmative. The experiment thus confirmed the hypothesis that children are susceptible to suggestion, are affected by leading questions, and are prone to answer in accord with the suggestion.

In *Eyewitness Testimony*, Loftus acknowledges that she developed her consuming interest in the subject by learning of cases where defendants were falsely identified, particularly the case of Edmond D. Jackson. Jackson was incarcerated for eight years before the Second Circuit in 1978 set aside his conviction as fatally flawed by suggestive police investigative procedures.

Loftus challenges, as wholly incorrect, the commonly held belief that information once acquired by the memory system is unchangeable. To the contrary,

Loftus asserts that evidence supports her conclusion "that once memory for some event is distorted by interweaving events, the information acquired during perception of the original event may never be accurately re-acquired." Yet Loftus also contends that, in terms of persuasiveness, "an eyewitness identification and the victim's memory of the incident . . . are far more important than any other characteristics a witness possesses, such as age, race, or level of income." Additionally, the degree of confidence expressed by such witnesses and ability to speak in a forceful tone combined to lend considerable credibility to their testimony.

Loftus also conducted experiments to evaluate the validity of laypersons' beliefs about eyewitness testimony. Overall she found that 45% of the subjects asked to evaluate factors affecting eyewitness testimony were wrong. Thirteen percent thought white persons could identify a black man more easily than they could a white man. Although 90% understood the effects of leading questions on eyewitness accuracy, one-third failed to give correct answers about the effects of extreme stress on reliability. Finally, Loftus' studies revealed that only 40% appreciated the effects of "weapon focus" on reliability and only 18% correctly indicated the effects of the violence of an event on reliability.

In her 1980 book, *Memory*, Loftus wrote that people can come to believe they saw and heard things that never really happened. She also found that memory is malleable and that people use "refabrication" to "supply bits and pieces, largely unconsciously, to fill out fairly incomplete knowledge." In addition, she found that people "tend to rewrite history more in line with what they think they ought to have done than with what they actually did." She cites instances where suggestions from third persons became part of and were incorporated into the listener's memory.

Addressing memory in the courtroom context, she concluded: "According to the cliche, memory fades. In fact, however, it grows! Every time we recall an event, we must reconstruct the new context, suggestion by others, other people's recollections."

The conclusions from a large chorus of behavioral science researchers reinforce doubts about the reliability of eyewitness testimony, and most conclude that expert testimony can be useful. A staunch cadre of scientific researchers, however, is much more skeptical about the utility of conclusions concerning eyewitness memory that are based almost exclusively on laboratory testing.

C. Can Experts Help? The Public Debate Among Psychologists Over the Utility of Expert Testimony

Taking a strong opposing view concerning the utility of expert testimony on eyewitness reliability, Johns Hopkins University Professors Michael McCloskey and Howard Egeth asserted in May, 1983, that "it is by no means clear that expert psychological testimony about eyewitnesses would improve jurors' ability to evaluate eyewitness testimony." They suggested that such testimony could "in fact have detrimental effects." Furthermore, they argued there was no empirical evidence that people in general are ignorant of the problems with eyewitness testimony; and, moreover, recent studies cast doubt on the conclusions reached by Loftus in her 1974 and 1979 studies.

They cite instances in which eyewitness testimony was apparently disbelieved and point out a number of situations in which jurors believed that the defendant was probably guilty, but concluded that the evidence was insufficient for conviction. They showed that the ratio of convictions in cases where there was at least one eyewitness identification of the defendant to convictions in cases without such identification was only 1.1 to 1. They conceded, however, that jurors cannot readily discriminate accurate from inaccurate eyewitnesses.

McCloskey and Egeth also cited a study which found that where witness viewing conditions varied principally by duration from poor to moderate to good, jurors were able to ascribe credibility to the better viewing conditions, indicating that they had taken at least that factor correctly into account. In the study, identifications were 33%, 50%, and 74% accurate; the juror belief rates for each of these identifications was 62%, 66%, and 77%, respectively. McCloskey and Egeth conceded that, while these figures make it "clear that jurors' ability to discriminate accurate from inaccurate witnesses is far from perfect," jurors do take relevant factors into account when evaluating witness accuracy.

Turning to the possible effect of expert psychological testimony on jurors' ability to discriminate accurate from inaccurate eyewitnesses, the authors found only one relevant study that provided a direct comparison between results in a case where jurors received expert advice and a case where they did not. McCloskey and Egeth asserted that this study showed that expert testimony had "absolutely no effect on jurors' ability to discriminate accurate from inaccurate witnesses." The expert testimony only appeared to reduce jurors' overall willingness to believe eyewitnesses.

McCloskey and Egeth then challenged the conventional wisdom that cross-race identifications are more error-prone than intra-racial identifications, as based on overly complex questions. As to "weapon focus" (witnesses' tendency to selectively direct their attention to threatening objects, rather than to the perpetrator) and stress experienced during the course of a crime event, they pointed to research showing that, while ten studies found decreases in eyewitness accuracy under stress, nine studies found that stress increased accuracy or had no effect on accuracy.

Elizabeth Loftus replied to McCloskey and Egeth, re-asserting her argument that the well-documented cases of innocent people wrongly convicted based on faulty eyewitness accounts require experts to educate the jury. Loftus also criticized McCloskey and Egeth for "using experimental evidence to support their views and yet attacking those very same studies when they run counter to their prevailing view."

Loftus reiterated her firm conviction that post-event information can modify a person's recollection and stated that hundreds of experiments demonstrate this phenomenon. She also defended the "battle of experts" that plays out in many courtrooms by arguing that use of experts can often avoid tragic effects —

for example, as in the case of the drug thalidomide in the 1950s. She claimed that science need not be perfect to be useful in the courtroom. . . .

D. Impact of Erroneous Eyewitness Testimony on the Jury

Many American trial and appellate courts have acted as though unreliable eyewitness testimony is not a major threat to the validity of the legal fact-finding process. In comparison to European authorities, American practice includes fewer proscriptions and safeguards concerning eyewitness evidence.

It is not surprising that the roles of professionals involved in the justice system reflect their attitudes toward eyewitness testimony and its "handling" in jury trials. One survey of Florida defense and prosecuting attorneys, county sheriffs, and police departments about eyewitness testimony revealed that prosecuting attorneys and law enforcement officers regard eyewitness identi-fication as generally accurate and believed that judges and juries appropri-ately emphasized its importance. In contrast, defense attorneys surveyed felt that such identifications are often inaccurate and overemphasized by jurors and judges, and that over-reliance on such evidence is a serious problem. Defense attorneys also were likely to endorse the admission of testimony by psychologists and other researchers as expert witnesses.

Deffenbacher and Loftus contended that "the American judiciary have tra-ditionally viewed knowledge of variables affecting eyewitness performance as part of common understanding." They also point out inconsistencies in judicial treatment of expert testimony, with many judges excluding such testimony as invading the province of the jury.

A. Daniel Yarmey and Hazel P. Tressillian Jones also addressed this ques-tion, stating that "jurors have been deliberating about questions regarding perception and memory for over 200 years and there is nothing new a psy-chologist can tell us about these processes." Yet, in a survey they conducted among judges, lawyers, law students, potential jurors, and experimental psy-chologists to test this hypothesis, they found ninety percent of the experts agreed that extreme stress reduces the ability to notice and remember details of an event, whereas few potential jurors thought so. Also, ninety-five percent of the experts agreed that witnesses generally overestimate the duration of crimes, whereas fewer than half of the potential jurors did so. Yarmey and Jones concluded that "the findings of this study strongly support our conten-tion that knowledge about the psychological variables that influence eyewit-ness identification and testimony does not fall within the province of common knowledge." Furthermore, "this study suggests that the adversary system, in and of itself, is not necessarily sufficient to safeguard against miscarriages of justice when the question of the reliability of the eyewitness arises."

In 1980 Reid Hastie wrote: "Granted that there is scientific evidence con-cerning the reliability of eyewitness testimony, there is no evidence that eye-witness unreliability introduces important errors into the trial fact-finding process." In reviewing the extent of literature on eyewitness testimony, he found the prevailing view was "that men perceive visually like a videotape, and remember auditorially like a tape recorder."

Hastie, in conjunction with the author, conducted a study regarding jury evaluations of eyewitness testimony that found seven aspects of eyewitness testimony that were neglected in jury deliberations: (1) selective attention during encoding; (2) the possibility of directly suggestive police behavior (that is, communication of bias through nonverbal or subtle verbal cues); (3) the possibility of the non-independence of two witness identifications (for example, influence of a confident, high status witness on a second witness); (4) the possibility of distortion, elaboration, or additions to witnesses' memories during the retention interval; (5) the significance of witnesses' non-responses to "distractors" or "lures" (non-target individuals) during identification procedures; (6) witnesses' consistent selection of the same individual across identification procedures; and (7) discussion of the characteristics of "lure" individuals presented as "distractors" in identification procedures.

More important, there were two persistent errors of "commission" concerning human memory that appeared repeatedly in jury deliberations. First, a substantial number of jurors argued that high levels of stress and emotionality would create a "flashbulb effect" such that memories from a threatening or violent crime scene would be especially strong, vivid, and accurate. Second, jurors appeared to rely heavily on witnesses who expressed confidence in their testimony, although research has shown that confidence is a relatively poor index of eyewitness identification accuracy.

Hastie concluded that these results provide the "missing link" identified by Wigmore and demonstrate that potentially unreliable eyewitness testimony combined with erroneous beliefs about eyewitness accuracy threaten the validity of jury decisions based primarily on eyewitness testimony. He further argued that the evidence of juror errors in the evaluation of eyewitness testimony supports the claim that expert testimony can aid the fact-finder (jury) in such cases.

William M. O'Barr, in his book *Linguistic Evidence*, concluded that the credibility ascribed to a witness often was not based on factors that judges thought important but was influenced by the language used by witnesses and their manner of delivery. He concluded that narrative answers by calm witnesses using familiar words without long hesitations and exaggerations or qualifications had the most impact. In addition, the use of powerful, active words and analogies carried more credibility. Hyper-correct language also seemed to carry less credibility (for example, "transport" instead of "carry"; "not cognizant" instead of "unaware"). Like Loftus and others cited above, O'Barr was sharply critical of the courts' reliance on experts on blood and handwriting while neglecting to examine the memory report of a witness.

John C. Brigham and Robert K. Bothwell also were concerned with the ability of prospective jurors to estimate the accuracy of eyewitness identification. Using actual empirical studies on eyewitness identification involving "target-present" line-ups, the researchers presented the prospective jurors with scenarios derived from the previously conducted studies and asked the prospective jurors to estimate the eyewitnesses' "hit" rates. They found that respondents overestimated witness accuracy by an average of 83.7%. They concluded that "awareness of the unreliability of eyewitness evidence does not appear to be part of the 'common knowledge' of prospective jury members," and that the data can be interpreted as refuting the claim made by some courts that "expert testimony about eyewitness evidence does not tell the jury members anything they do not already know."

Earlier researchers found approximately two-thirds of the citizen jurors were unaware that eyewitnesses tend to overestimate the length of time involved in a crime; two-thirds of the citizen jurors believed that the police would be superior to civilians as eyewitnesses; and 15% thought that eyewitness memory of faces would be 90–95% accurate several months after seeing the face. Over half were unaware that an eyewitness identification of someone from a set of photographs is likely to later produce an identification of the same person in a lineup (regardless of whether the identified person is guilty or not) and two-thirds of the respondents indicated they "believed in the existence of a positive relationship between eyewitness accuracy and eyewitness confidence." The final conclusion was that "the present data indicate that the testimony of an expert on these matters would not invade the province of the jury. Rather, such testimony would aid the jury in its evaluation of evidence and would thereby further the cause of justice."

Even the U.S. Supreme Court seems to have been in error when, in *Neil v. Biggers*, it recommended that jurors evaluating identification evidence consider, among other factors, the degree of certainty expressed by the witness. Many social research studies following that decision showed it to be in apparent error. For example, a comprehensive review by Wells and Murray of more than thirty studies of the confidence-accuracy relationship found that there were some statistically significant relationships between confidence and accuracy, but that these relationships were practically useless.

Other reports are more negative. For example, Wells, Leippe, and Ostrom found that while degree of certainty was not related to accuracy, the perceived seriousness of the crime and consequent higher degree of attention were. Lindsay, Wells and Rumpel found that witnesses' confidence was unrelated to accuracy and that persons in the position of jurors could not detect the errors on cross-examination. Smith, Kassin, and Ellsworth concurred, finding that "confidence is neither a useful predictor of the accuracy of a particular witness or of the accuracy of particular statements made by the same witness."

E. Post-1986 Research

Following the painful self-examination and heated debate of the early 1980s, researchers responded by returning to more careful empirical explorations of some of the earlier conclusions in ways that made them more readily applicable to the courtroom context. For example, in 1986, The British *Journal of Psychology* published an article exploring different ways in which people encode faces.

Gary Wells and John W. Turtle observed that it was time to move beyond the simple questions that were central in the debate over expert testimony: "We now know, of course, that eyewitness testimony depends on a great number of factors and that it is sometimes quite reliable and that it is sometimes not. Attention should now be given to the question of under what conditions is eyewitness testimony reliable and when is it unreliable?" They explored identification from lineups and photospreads, pointing out that the wording of instructions can influence whether the witnesses chose anyone, even if the actual offender is present — a conclusion reached in other studies as well. They also discussed prior studies by Wells that demonstrated that some eyewitnesses make false identifications when presented with a "lure" lineup (in which no to-be-identified target is present) and that knowing this helps screen out some witnesses. They discussed a 1986 study by Lindsay and Wells in which suspects were presented sequentially rather that simultaneously, producing fewer false identifications. *The Journal of Experimental Psychology* reported research on misleading post-event information showing that post-event misinformation either impaired the original memory or led to confusion about what had occurred during the original event. While memory test results and confidence ratings supported an interference or inaccessibility interpretation, the results could not rule out "overwriting" of the original information in some cases. The results also supported the conclusion that subjects who were misled might not have known what they saw, but they did know what they did not see. Furthermore, they found that subjects are more confident when they are correct than when they are not.

Loftus and Hunter G. Hoffman maintained that "misleading information presented after an event can lead people to erroneous reports of that misinformation." They argued that "erroneous reporting will depend on the conditions of acquisition, retention and retrieval of information" and that "misinformation acceptance plays a major role, memory impairment plays some role, and pure guessing plays little or no role" in the creation of erroneous eyewitness reports. Yet acceptance of misinformation by witnesses, as a phenomenon worthy of sustained scientific investigation, does not receive the attention that it deserves. . . .

NOTES & QUESTIONS

1. Eyewitnesses and challenges to them can be used effectively in pop cultural drama. In Alfred Hitchcock's *The Wrong Man,* several eyewitnesses accuse jazz musician Manny Balestrero (played by Henry Fonda) of being a hold-up man. Although he is innocent, the evidence of guilt appears overwhelming. Yet all of it has been obtained through police work that is at best shockingly sloppy and at worst deliberately deceitful. In one scene, for example, the cops have him write out a note used by the robber. In another, they put him in a line-up with several other men, none of whom look particularly like him, and ask two eyewitnesses to identify the perpetrator (both pick out Balestrero). In a third, they send him into a delicatessen to walk up and down to see if an eyewitness can identify him. The store owner asks Balestrero if he is the man the precinct "sent over."

2. Consider the many ways in which *The Wrong Man* telegraphs the injustice being done to Balestrero, from the limited and focused lighting used in the police station (indicating the intense interest the police have in Manny, their only suspect) to the repeated images of bars (which represent both symbolic and actual imprisonment). How does the film in its own way bear witness to the reality of false accusations brought against the innocent? Also think about the number of times that a reference to Manny's religion (Catholicism) appears in the movie (such as the rosary the desk sergeant tells him he can keep and the woman who asks if he has thought about praying for assistance). Do these also represent a type of "witnessing," albeit not the kind we usually think of in connection with the law?

3. The eyewitnesses in *The Wrong Man* are sure of their identifications, partly because of the way the police arrange the line-ups. Though commonly used, line-ups have come under fire as inherently unreliable. *See, e.g.,* Richard Willing, *Police Lineups Encourage Wrong Picks, Experts Say,* USA Today, 26 Nov. 2002, at 1A. Should they therefore be discontinued (or perhaps used only to exclude suspects)? Consider the physical resemblance between Manny and the perpetrator. How much do they look alike? In the actual case, the similarities were significant. *See* Jay Maeder, *The Stork Club's Most Famous Bull Fiddle Man, 1953,* N.Y. Daily News, 14 Nov. 2005, 34.

4. Alfred Hitchcock always made a cameo appearance in his films. In *The Wrong Man,* however, he deviated from his practice (so as not to trivialize Balestrero's plight) and instead walked onto a sound stage at the beginning of the film and addressed the audience. What effect does this have on the message he is trying to relay?

5. Whether or not eyewitness testimony is reliable, jurors find it remarkably persuasive, and both prosecutors and defense attorneys go to great lengths to find individuals who can provide it. Picking up on this fact, filmmakers often include in their stories a crucial witness who is reluctant to testify. In the movie *Witness,* for example, Detective John Book (played by Harrison Ford) must work hard to win the trust of Rachel Lapp (Kelly McGillis) and her son, whose statement will make or break Book's charges of high-level police corruption. Yet in the real world is such testimony truly necessary?

6. Sometimes a prosecutor wants the jury to know that a witness will not testify. In the article from which the following excerpt is taken, Professor Russell Dean Covey argues that revealing to a jury a witness's refusal to testify may be useful in attacking organized crime. The excerpt itself outlines the chief reasons a witness might refuse to testify.

BEATING THE PRISONER AT PRISONER'S DILEMMA: THE EVIDENTIARY VALUE OF A WITNESS'S REFUSAL TO TESTIFY
Russell Dean Covey
47 American University Law Review 105 (1997)

The reasons for non-cooperation might be as numerous as there are witnesses, but reasons powerful enough to compel a witness to suffer the heavy sanctions resulting from citation for civil contempt and criminal contempt or both are more limited. In most cases when a witness refuses to testify despite lacking a legitimate fear of self-incrimination, non-cooperation is likely to stem from one of four main reasons.

First, a witness might refuse to testify in fear of the defendant. Although understandable, such refusal is not legally cognizable, and the witness will still be subject to civil or criminal contempt charges. If a witness's fear of a defendant is sufficient to compel that witness to violate a court order and place himself in contempt of court, an adverse inference would seem especially warranted. It would be perverse for a defendant's coercive threats to allow the defendant to escape punishment while the victim of that coercion, the witness, goes to jail. The Federal Rules of Evidence already provide for admission of hearsay statements where the unavailability of a witness results from the coercive or obstructive efforts by the defendant. Thus, where a legitimate fear of violent retaliation motivates the witness's refusal to testify, there seems to be ample justification for drawing adverse inferences based on the witness's behavior.

Second, a witness may refuse to testify out of a desire to adhere to a code of silence. The force of the code of silence, or *omerta*, may spring from internal assimilation of a set of values adverse to the duties imposed by the criminal justice system. It also may be enforced from without by other members of the criminal organization seeking to quiet "squealers," perhaps with extreme threats of force and violence. If the fear stems from other members of the criminal organization, an agency theory subjecting each member of the conspiracy to liability for all the other members justifies a finding that the defendant is at least derivatively responsible for suborning the contemptuous act of the witness. As argued below, it is reasonable and consistent with the evidentiary rules to allow inferences adverse to the defendant to be derived from the witness's own internalized refusal in this context.

The fact that the refusal springs not from a realistic threat of retaliation, but rather from the witness's own internalized acceptance of the code against cooperation, does not significantly alter the logic of the argument. Fear that the testimony may diminish the esteem in which a witness is held in his or her community, or may affect the witness's status, is not a legally cognizable basis to withhold testimony. If the witness and defendant both mutually participate in a shared "culture of conspiracy" that valorizes criminal behavior and demonizes cooperation with the legal authorities, the defendant should share responsibility for the creation and maintenance of the ethic against cooperation. While punishing a defendant for participation in a particular culture goes against the grain of a criminal justice system constructed to punish individual culpability, it does not eliminate altogether the doctrine of individual autonomy. In a multicultural society such as urban America, the choice to join and strengthen the culture of conspiracy reflects the autonomous decision of the organization's participants.

Third, a witness may refuse to testify out of fear that he or she may at a later date be prosecuted for perjury. Although the witness has no immediate fear of self-incrimination, he or she could be subjected to criminal prosecution for lying on the stand. The witness might therefore argue that the Fifth Amendment privilege should prevent him or her from providing the grounds for incrimination. Although this argument is made frequently in criminal contempt proceedings, it obviously does not withstand scrutiny.

First, no witness has a right to invent testimony with impunity. Second, because the witness has been immunized, truthful testimony cannot provide any basis for incrimination, and the witness cannot be prosecuted for prior perjured testimony based on contradictory testimony later given under oath. Any remaining incentive to lie must spring, therefore, not from the witness's own fear of self-incrimination, but from reluctance to implicate a conspirator. If that reluctance fuels the defendant's desire to avoid testifying, the adverse influence is again justified.

Finally, the witness simply may have a powerful desire not to incriminate the defendant. It is, of course, this last reason that provides the strongest basis both for allowing the witness's refusal to testify to occur before the jury, for an adverse inference to be drawn against the defendant. If the witness has no real fear of self-incrimination, the willingness to suffer what appears to be the comparatively minor penalty of criminal contempt in hopes of preventing a coconspirator from receiving a long criminal sentence is rational as an organizational or conspiratorial strategy. The tactic of making the witness refuse to testify in front of the jury should be permitted in order to undermine this strategy.

In short, although the ambiguous evidentiary value of a witness's rightful invocation of the privilege makes that evidence less probative of the defendant's culpability, the problem of ambiguity is substantially reduced when the witness no longer possesses the right to refuse to testify. While giving testimony that implicates the witness in criminal activity may be embarrassing to the witness, the refusal to testify in the face of a court order is unlikely to be motivated by mere embarrassment. The removal of this fundamental ambiguity dramatically transforms the underlying context and restructures the logical interferences that naturally flow from the act of non-cooperation.

Some courts, in sorting out the circumstances under which the forced invocation of the privilege can be sanctioned, have distinguished between the "ordinary witness" and those witnesses who are "so closely connected with the defendant by the facts of the case, the pleadings, or relationship, that the inferences of the witness's guilt would likely be imputed to the defendant." While forcing witnesses who fall into the later category to invoke their privilege before the jury might unavoidably prejudice the defendant, "it may well be proper in some cases to have the proceeding in the presence of the jury where the government is dealing with" witnesses of the more ordinary variety. This approach seems logical when the witness invokes a Fifth Amendment privilege, because the very certainty that accompanies the invocation is likely to taint the defendant. If the witness has the right to invoke a privilege, the logic is reversed. When a defendant has no justifiable fear of self-incrimination, the close relationship with the defendant creates a powerful inference that the witness is refusing to testify in order to protect the defendant. An adverse inference therefore becomes much more appropriate. In contrast, "ordinary witnesses" who lack such a relationship with the defendant, yet refuse to testify, are much more likely to have other reasons for refusing to cooperate aside form protecting the defendant. . . .

NOTES & QUESTIONS

1. Do you find a law enforcement animus in Professor Covey's comments? Would his reasoning have less persuasiveness if one did not have the prosecution of organized crime participants in mind?

2. What dramatic potential exists in each of the types of refusal to testify discussed by Covey? How might each type be used in a film or other pop cultural work?

D.   CROSS-EXAMINATION

The aggressive cross-examination of a witness is a mainstay in law-related popular culture. Sometimes this cross-examination seems stylized and phony, as in the Perry Mason television series from the late 1950s and early 1960s. The resourceful Mason had the uncanny ability to detect who was lying and to subject liars to blistering cross-examination. Sometimes the witness turned out to be the perpetrator of the crime and admitted his or her guilt right on the stand. In other pop cultural works, meanwhile, the cross-examination provides the best, most engaging drama. For example, as indicated in Chapter 14 of this text concerning military law, the tense cross-examination of Colonel Nathan Jessup by Lieutenant Daniel Kaffee provides the most powerful scene in *A Few Good Men* (1992).

The next two excerpts critique the cross-examination of Christine Vole, played by the incomparable Marlene Dietrich, in the classic film *Witness for the Prosecution*.

CHARLES LAUGHTON, MARLENE DIETRICH, AND THE PRIOR INCONSISTENT STATEMENT
James Carey
36 Loyola University Chicago Law Journal 433 (2005)

In the movie *Witness for the Prosecution*, Charles Laughton plays a defense barrister in a murder case. On cross-examination, he confronts Marlene Dietrich, a key prosecution witness, with her own letters contradicting her direct testimony. The letters destroy her credibility. The confrontation is the denouement of the trial, but not of the movie. We learn after the trial that Dietrich contrived the letters herself, enabling Laughton to destroy her in front of the jury, thereby gaining an acquittal for the defendant, Tyrone Power, her lover. In a climactic twist, Dietrich kills Power when she discovers that he no longer loves her — before ultimately being represented by Laughton in her own murder trial.

There comes a point in a trial when advocacy skill, knowledge of the law, and professional responsibility uniquely come together. This is also the time when the adversarial nature of our system is clearest. This point occurs when a witness is impeached with a prior inconsistent statement, as portrayed dramatically in the Laughton-Dietrich confrontation. This essay supports the assertion that witness impeachment is an indispensable part of the common law justice system, returning from time to time to the movie, *Witness for the Prosecution*.

Before discussing this technique in detail, I make three preliminary points. First the rationale for the three-step approach is that jurors are limited in the ways they can learn the facts of the case. Typically jurors learn by listening, which is one-dimensional and is made more difficult by their general inability to ask questions. They must therefore listen and hear correctly the first time that the words are spoken, which emphasizes the obvious importance of repetition, diagrams, and photographs. When the examiner impeaches with a prior statement, she expects the jurors to understand an abstraction, or "inconsistency," between the two statements. If the contradiction is "yes" versus "no," or "red" versus "green," it is relatively easy for the jurors to "see" the contradiction. In the world of real trials, however, the contradiction is embedded in phrases and paragraphs and is difficult to "see" just by listening. Thus, the three-step prescription of commit, build up, and confront addresses this problem by building up to and setting off the contradiction.

Second, the approach creates the opportunity for dramatics. Specifically, when the cross examiner confronts the witness with the prior inconsistent statement, she has the chance to "ring the changes" for emphasis. She can raise her voice; she can lower her voice to a stage whisper. The examiner can also slow down the delivery and labor over each word of contradiction (as Charles Laughton does inimitably in confronting Marlene Dietrich), or can pause for dramatic effect. Here then is the high drama of a real trial: making the witness agree to the examiner's damning words.

Third, a skillful examiner will then emphatically confront the witness, because once the witness answers, the impeachment is complete. There is no room for follow-up along the lines of "were you lying then or are you lying now?" Such a question only gives the witness a chance to explain the inconsistency, thereby taking the clear edge off of the effect of the inconsistent statements. . . .

Charles Laughton's use of Marlene Dietrich's contrived letters is a delightful and realistic practice in staging. Laughton asks Dietrich questions about letters he alleges she wrote to a certain "Max." As he asks these questions, he holds a piece of paper, apparently the letter to which he refers. This paper in fact has nothing to do with the letter, but instead is a mere piece of scrap paper that he had retrieved from his briefcase. The real letters that Laughton intended to use to impeach were placed underneath a book on his desk. Dietrich's answers become shrill denials of his assertions. As he waves the paper in front of her, she blurts out, "why that is not even my stationery. Mine is light blue with my initials on it." At this point, Laughton pauses and slowly lifts from the pages of his book the actual letters, in blue with initials on them. He then asked sonorously, laboriously, "like . . . this?"

Thus, Laughton holds back the writing, induces the vehement denial, and then proceeds to produce the writing with a vengeance. Dietrich is reduced to shrieking insults at Laughton ("Damn you!"). In reality, this technique, if not her reaction, is wholly plausible.

One loose evidentiary end remains untied: does it make any difference whether the prior statement is admissible not only for impeachment, but "substantively" as well, that is, as a true statement?

Today many jurisdictions permit some kinds of prior inconsistent statements to be admitted as true statements. Typically, rules which permit such a use require that the person who made the statement be on the witness stand and be subject to cross-examination on the statement, and that the statement be under oath, or be made under equivalent circumstances supporting the conclusion that it was reliable, such as tape recording.

It is up to the examiner whether she wants the jury to accept the statement as true. The statement's admissibility as a true statement does not necessarily mean that it must be used as true. Its use is determined by the examiner's theory of the case. The examiner offers the prior inconsistent statement as true only if the statement helps support her theory. Yet, even if the examiner intends the statement to be taken as true as well as to be used to impeach, she follows the same technique as she would were the statement being used solely for impeachment purposes. This technique provides the best means of emphasizing the making of the statement. To effectively accomplish impeachment with a prior inconsistent statement in a dramatic fashion, the advocate must know the evidence rules related to impeachment and the procedural rules governing cross-examination and impeachment. She must also possess the advocacy skill to isolate and emphasize the contradiction.

So where does professional responsibility come into play? The advocate needs a good faith basis to assert a fact on cross-examination. This good faith requirement is an aspect of the general obligation that the advocate has to be honest with the court, and to not "perpetrate a fraud upon the court." But what does "good faith basis" mean, concretely?

There are two versions of good faith: one strict and one relaxed. A strict view of good faith requires that the examiner have admissible evidence showing that the impeaching fact is true. Under this view, good faith would require that in order to assert to a witness, "you said before that the light was green," the examiner must have admissible evidence that the witness said the light was green. If the examiner has only some indication that the statement had been made, but has no admissible proof, the statement is not in good faith.

The second good faith view treats it as a rule of reasonableness; specifically, as long as the examiner has a reasonable basis for believing the impeaching fact is true (for example, that the previous inconsistent statement was made) he is operating in good faith. Thus, if the examiner's basis for impeachment is a hearsay report, made by someone other than the witness, and the report nevertheless seems authentic and reliable, she may assert the impeaching fact contained in the report.

Which view of good faith to apply depends upon the law of the jurisdiction. In *Witness for the Prosecution*, Laughton possesses letters that contradict Dietrich's earlier testimony. Laughton has a good faith basis to confront Dietrich with the statements, both because of the circumstances of the letters coming into his possession, as developed in the movie, and his expectation that he can authenticate them, through handwriting analysis, and introduce them, if necessary. Thus, he both acts reasonably and possesses admissible evidence. Of course it is the penultimate twist in the movie that the letters are false, created by Dietrich to enable Laughton to discredit her. . . .

Mirjan Damaska, the Sterling Professor at Yale Law School, is a prominent Comparative Law scholar who has compared the differences between the accusatorial and inquisitorial systems. One of his focuses is on the relative degree to which each system is designed to get at the "truth of what happened":

> It is openly stated by some common law lawyers that the aim of criminal procedure is not so much the ascertainment of the real truth as the just settlement of a dispute. . . . In talking about ends of the criminal process continental lawyers place a primary emphasis on the discovery of the truth as a prerequisite to a just decision.

Accepting the distinction Damaska describes for argument sake, how does impeachment with a prior inconsistent statement quintessentially assist a "just settlement?"

It can be argued that impeachment does so in two ways. First, impeachment balances the witness's assertions with his contradictory words, thereby giving the jurors a balanced view of what the witness has said. Ultimately, a judgment based on these balanced assessments is itself more balanced, fair, and thus a "just settlement."

Second, impeachment assists a just settlement in a criminal case by enforcing the burden of proof beyond a reasonable doubt. This strict burden is itself illustrative of Damaska's characterization of the common law system, as "not so much [concerned with] the ascertainment of the real truth." The burden of proof expresses "a fundamental value determination of our society that it is far worse to convict an innocent man than to let a guilty man go free." Impeachment can itself create reasonable doubt. A judgment based solely upon a witness who has been substantially impeached is not beyond a reasonable doubt, and is not a just settlement.

Impeachment is an effective tool in our adversarial system. Specifically, impeachment may be so effective as to create a reason to believe the very opposite of what the witness has asserted. This is the strategy behind Dietrich's set up of Laughton to impeach her on the stand. Although the trial outcome is a false one, we only know that because we are watching the movie. On its face, the trial outcome appears to be a "just settlement."

LEGAL FICTIONS: IRONY, STORYTELLING, TRUTH, AND JUSTICE IN THE MODERN COURTROOM DRAMA
Christine Alice Corcos
25 University of Arkansas at Little Rock Law Review 503 (2003)

In *Witness for the Prosecution*, Robards overlooks the evidence and truths spoken which would explain much of the mystery of Christine's testimony

("She's an actress, and a good one," Leonard has already told him) in favor of speculation. "It's too easy, something's wrong," he tells Brogan-Moore after the acquittal. His own experience tells him that his abilities in the courtroom do not extend to the kind of miraculous outcome the "hopeless" Vole case presents. He prefers to believe in what seems to him to be an ordinary motive carried out through an extravagant plan (that she is in love with another man and frames Leonard) to an equally mundane motive carried out by an even more elaborate plan (that she loves her husband and frames herself).

Christine taunts Robards with the words "the great Sir Wilfred Robards has done it again," and then goes on to explain how her actions were part of a grand design to obtain Leonard's acquittal. Robards's subtlety and chauvinism forced him to seek a motive beyond Christine's love for Leonard in what she has done. He is therefore amazed to discover that a foreign woman untrained in the law, but an astute observer of human behavior, can manipulate the system far more successfully than he. Christine piles irony upon irony in this scene, since both Christine and the observer clearly believe that they have an accurate understanding of the outcome of the trial, although Christine knows more than the observer, while Robards mistrusts the surface but fails to comprehend the reality. Christine's initial story, that she loves her husband, does not convince Robards because she overplays the part intentionally to raise questions about her veracity. Her next story, that she loves another man, seems more likely to him, yet he is still unconvinced. Robards does not re-exert his natural dominance until, in the courtroom, the truth becomes known and the full extent of Christine's plot and Leonard's duplicity is revealed.

As it is revealed, the defendant, Vole, and the primary witness against him, Christine, concocted a defense together. They manipulated the experienced defense lawyer into unwittingly helping them. Christine tells the defense counsel, "the great Sir Wilfred Robards," that her knowledge of English law ("a wife cannot testify against her husband") gave her the idea for the winning defense. Since Christine is not Vole's wife, although initially no one knows this, and because she will not be believed if she appears as an alibi witness, Christine decides to reveal the truths on the stand, knowing that Robards will characterize it as a lie and that the jury will believe that it is a lie. Ironically, the truth does set Leonard Vole (temporarily) free. When he tells Christine the truth at the end of the drama, that he is leaving her for another woman, she stabs him with the knife that earlier he used to kill Mrs. French. Christine becomes an ironist who unconsciously ironizes herself, what Muecke calls the "irony of self-betrayal."

Christine succeeds in misleading Robards because his experience and prior success in the courtroom have made him cocky and over-confident, although his recent heart attack has reminded him of his mortality. Throughout the film he firmly believes that he is fooling the doctors and nurses at the hospital and continues to fool his nurse by concealing cigars in his cane, replacing the hot cocoa in his thermos with brandy, and cadging smoking materials from colleagues and clients. He tests Leonard Vole's veracity with his "monocle test" in which he focuses the sun's light on Vole's eyes via the monocle lens to see Vole's reaction — extreme nervousness that would indicate guilt, or calmness, which would indicate innocence. When his associate Brogan-Moore asks him the result of the test, he admits that Vole did not react to the light (he passed, a circumstance which baffles him, since he suspects that Vole is guilty). Christine, however, refuses to play the game. She and Robards spar over what he considers her rather too cool attitude toward her husband's very real danger of conviction. "I want to help Leonard," she responds, "and I want to help you, Sir Wilfred." As the light reflected from the monocle continues to bother her, she gets up and adjusts the curtains, saying as she does so, "Now, isn't that better?" The dual meaning of the phrase may escape him, as it initially escapes the observer. Vole's reaction represents his ability to take circumstances and rules as they are in life and change his own behavior to manipulate the reaction of the observer. Christine's action in closing the draperies shows her willingness to manipulate perceptions to prevail. Leonard initially and repeatedly lies to Robards. Christine tests the waters, and when she finds that the truth disguised as a lie will be more convincing than a real lie which follows the lines Robards expects, she tells the truth-as-lie. As Robards points out, the danger to his client lies in the fact that the jury does not like Christine, but they believe her. They like Leonard, but they do not believe him. The failure of Robards's previously surefire "monocle test" is the first intimation to the observer that truth will be an elusive creature in this story.

NOTES & QUESTIONS

1. Is Carey correct that an attorney bent on impeaching a witness will never follow up with questions such as "Were you lying then, or are you lying now"? Does such a question open the door to an objection by opposing counsel? If so, what objection and with what result? Notice also that Christine Vole is a hostile witness, is not married to the accused, and has (arguably) already perjured herself.

2. What does Robards' monocle test represent to him? When both Christine and Leonard pass it, what do those events symbolize? Are Christine and Leonard even aware that they have passed the test?

3. A recurring motif in many films is that of the attorney who browbeats a witness as opposing counsel ineffectually tries to object. Often the witness spills the beans right on the spot. The motif is so familiar that its disruption or alteration of it can be used to garner laughs, as in Woody Allen's hilarious *Bananas* (1971). In the film, Fielding Melish, played by Woody Allen himself, calls himself to the stand and delightfully runs back and forth from the defense counsel's table while conducting an aggressive examination.

4. Regardless of how the judge rules, the loud-mouthed lawyer examining a witness routinely seems to score points with the jury. However, aggressively cross-examining certain kinds of witnesses (such as a child) is tricky. In the movie *The Accused*, the defense must be careful in how it approaches the complainant and rape victim Sarah Tobias (Jodie Foster). If its questions are too confrontational, Tobias will gain extra sympathy from the jury.

E.   QUESTIONS ABOUT THE WITNESS'S CHARACTER

Sometimes attorneys attempt to expose not inconsistencies in a witness's testimony but rather personal flaws in the witness. However, there are limits as to how the examining attorney might proceed and what he or she might reveal. The most discussed limitation involves the prior conduct and sexual promiscuity of a rape victim. State statutes are not uniform, but in different ways the states have attempted to "shield" the rape victim's sexual history.

The following statutes constitute California's attempt to prevent the rape victim's past sexual conduct and arguably flawed character from being presented in court.

CALIFORNIA EVIDENCE CODE
Divisions 6 and 9 (2005)

§ 782. Evidence of sexual conduct of complaining witness; Offer of proof; Affidavit; Procedure

(a) In any prosecution under Section 261, 262, 264.1, 286, 288, 288a, 288.5, or 289 of the Penal Code, or for assault with intent to commit, attempt to commit, or conspiracy to commit any crime defined in any of those sections, except where the crime is alleged to have occurred in a local detention facility, as defined in Section 6031.4, or in a state prison, as defined in Section 4504, if evidence of sexual conduct of the complaining witness is offered to attack the credibility of the complaining witness under Section 780, the following procedure shall be followed:

> (1) A written motion shall be made by the defendant to the court and prosecutor stating that the defense has an offer of proof of the relevancy of evidence of the sexual conduct of the complaining witness proposed to be presented and its relevancy in attacking the credibility of the complaining witness.

> (2) The written motion shall be accompanied by an affidavit in which the offer of proof shall be stated. The affidavit shall be filed under seal and only unsealed by the court to determine if the offer of proof is sufficient to order a hearing pursuant to paragraph (3). After that determination, the affidavit shall be resealed by the court.

> (3) If the court finds that the offer of proof is sufficient, the court shall order a hearing out of the presence of the jury, if any, and at the hearing allow the questioning of the complaining witness regarding the offer of proof made by the defendant.

> (4) At the conclusion of the hearing, if the court finds that evidence proposed to be offered by the defendant regarding the sexual conduct of the complaining witness is relevant pursuant to Section 780, and is not inadmissible pursuant to Section 352 of this code, the court may make an order stating what evidence may be introduced by the defendant, and the nature of the questions to be permitted. The defendant may then offer evidence pursuant to the order of the court.

(5) An affidavit resealed by the court pursuant to paragraph (2) shall remain sealed, unless the defendant raises an issue on appeal or collateral review relating to the offer of proof contained in the sealed document. If the defendant raises that issue on appeal, the court shall allow the Attorney General and appellate counsel for the defendant access to the sealed affidavit. If the issue is raised on collateral review, the court shall allow the district attorney and defendant's counsel access to the sealed affidavit. The use of the information contained in the affidavit shall be limited solely to the pending proceeding.

(b) As used in this section, "complaining witness" means the alleged victim of the crime charged, the prosecution of which is subject to this section.

§ 1103. Evidence of character of victim of crime

(a) In a criminal action, evidence of the character or a trait of character (in the form of an opinion, evidence of reputation, or evidence of specific instances of conduct) of the victim of the crime for which the defendant is being prosecuted is not made inadmissible by Section 1101 if the evidence is:

(1) Offered by the defendant to prove conduct of the victim in conformity with the character or trait of character

(2) Offered by the prosecution to rebut evidence adduced by the defendant under paragraph (3).

(b) In a criminal action, evidence of the defendant's character for violence or trait of character for violence (in the form of an opinion, evidence of reputation, or evidence of specific instances of conduct) is not made inadmissible by Section 1101 if the evidence is offered by the prosecution to prove conduct of the defendant in conformity with the character or trait of character and is offered after evidence that the victim had a character for violence or a trait of character tending to show violence has been adduced by the defendant under paragraph (1) of subdivision (a).

(c) (1) Notwithstanding any other provision of this code to the contrary, and except as provided in this subdivision, in any prosecution under Section 261, 262, or 264.1 of the Penal Code, or under Section 286, 288a, or 289 of the Penal Code, or for assault with intent to commit, attempt to commit, or conspiracy to commit a crime defined in any of those sections, except where the crime is alleged to have occurred in a local detention facility, as defined in Section 6031.4, or in a state prison, as defined in Section 4504, opinion evidence, reputation evidence, and evidence of specific instances of the complaining witness' sexual conduct, or any of that evidence, is not admissible by the defendant in order to prove consent by the complaining witness.

(2) Notwithstanding paragraph (3), evidence of the manner in which the victim was dressed at the time the commission of the offense shall

not be admissible when offered by either party on the issue of consent in any prosecution for an offense specified in paragraph (1), unless the evidence is determined by the court to be relevant and admissible in the interests of justice. The proponent of the evidence shall make an offer of proof outside the hearing of the jury. The court shall then make its determination and at that time, state the reasons for its ruling on the record. For the purposes of this paragraph, "manner of dress" does not include the condition of the victim's clothing before, during, or after the commission of the offense.

(3) Paragraph (1) shall not be applicable to evidence of the complaining witness' sexual conduct with the defendant.

(4) If the prosecutor introduces evidence, including testimony of a witness, or the complaining witness as a witness gives testimony, and that evidence or testimony relates to the complaining witness' sexual conduct, the defendant may cross-examine the witness who gives the testimony and offer relevant evidence limited specifically to the rebuttal of the evidence introduced by the prosecutor or given by the complaining witness.

(5) Nothing in this subdivision shall be construed to make inadmissible any evidence offered to attack the credibility of the complaining witness as provided in Section 782.

(6) As used in this section, "complaining witness" means the alleged victim of the crime charged, the prosecution of which is subject to this subdivision.

NOTES & QUESTIONS

1. Why do you think the California lawmakers used the phrase "complaining witness" in the statutes? Is the rape victim best understood as a witness? If we understand the rape victim as a witness, should we have the same skepticism regarding her eyewitness testimony as the materials in section C of this chapter suggest we should have for eyewitness testimony in general?

2. *The Accused*, starring Oscar-winner Jodie Foster as Sarah Tobias, nicely dramatizes the rape victim's dilemma. Tobias's promiscuous past initially turns even the prosecutor Kathryn Murphy, played by Kelly McGinnis, against Tobias. However, through the course of the film Murphy comes to appreciate Tobias' victimization and also develops a degree of "sisterhood" with Tobias. To what extent can sisterhood truly bridge socioeconomic gaps? To what extent does Hollywood want us to think sisterhood can bridge socioeconomic gaps?

3. *The Accused* is based on an actual case from New Bedford, Massachusetts. In 1983, a 22-year-old mother of two was raped by three young men on a pool table in Big Dan's Bar. Other bar patrons cheered on the rapists. The defendants and defense witnesses testified that the victim was drunk and had "come on" to the perpetrators. The Portuguese community in the area strongly supported the defendants and held rallies on their behalf. Why might the film-makers have left this ethnic dimension of the actual case out of the film version?

4. In the trial in the actual case the three rapists were convicted and sentenced to nine to twelve years in prison. Two onlookers who had cheered on the rapists during the rape were acquitted. After the trial the victim moved to Florida, where she died a few years later in a car crash. How do the lessons that might be taken from the actual case differ from those viewers are invited to take from the film? What do these differences suggest about the goals of the typical Hollywood filmmaker who retells the story of an actual case in a film intended for mass audiences?

Chapter 6

JUDGES

A. FILMOGRAPHY

First Monday in October (1981)

Judgment at Nuremberg (1961)

The Life and Times of Judge Roy Bean (1972)

The Pelican Brief (1993)

The Star Chamber (1983)

B. THE ROLE OF THE JUDGE

What do we want in a judge? When it comes to judicial images in film, audiences seem schizophrenic. We want a profoundly thoughtful, moral judge like Spencer Tracy's character in *Judgment at Nuremberg*, but we also enjoy a good old rascal like Paul Newman's Judge Roy Bean. We want a judge who is deeply principled and committed to following the letter of the law, like Jill Clayburgh's Supreme Court Justice in *First Monday in October*, but we can sympathize with Michael Douglas' compulsion in *The Star Chamber* to take the law into his own hands when he believes justice has not been done.

Perhaps our ambivalence concerning judges has a very down-to-earth explanation: judges are only human, but we place them in a superhuman role. To judge another human being is a god-like act. All the trappings of power that surround a judge in a courtroom (the somber black robes, the physical layout of the courtroom, the formalities of address) support the judge's role as majestic law-giver. A judge embodies the law in his or her own person — small wonder, then, that so many judicial characters, from the real-life Wild West Judge Roy Bean to comic book characters such as Judge Dredd, intone the fateful words, "I am the Law!"

In movies centering on judges, a central theme often is the tension between the judge's allegiance to the system versus his or her desire for justice. How do real-life judges balance doing justice with the daily pressures of getting through the docket? Read the following two excerpts by judges for a glimpse into the different perspectives judges themselves have on their changing institutional roles.

WHAT IS THE ROLE OF THE JUDGE IN OUR LITIGIOUS SOCIETY?
Hon. Marjorie O. Rendell
(United States District Judge, Eastern District of Pennsylvania)
40 Villanova Law Review 1115 (1995)

The inquiry which is the subject of this discussion, namely, "What Is the Role of the Judge in Our Litigious Society?," can be interpreted in as many ways as there are listeners. To one, it may be perceived as asking whether Judge Ito did a good job; to another it may be viewed as inquiring about judicial activism or "legislation" by judges; yet to others, it may echo the cry for help of a harried, overworked benchsitter — not unlike the question, and I quote: "What's a mother to do?" These differing interpretations of the question illuminate the immense difficulty of divining an answer. The role of the judge as one who presides over trials and assists the jury in understanding legal issues is of course the most popular and usual depiction. While sometimes donning a wig (as in the British courts) or a southern accent (as in *My Cousin Vinny*), but always donning the robe, the universal view of judge as trial overseer is as a character larger than life, above the fray, exuding dignity and dispensing justice for all.

The statue of Justice — regal, impartial, literally blind to any outside influence on her measured judgment — is a familiar symbol of judicial demeanor. Professor Judith Resnik has described how this personification of Justice represents the traditional view of the neutral judiciary:

> The goddess herself — aloof and stoic — represents the physical and psychological distance between the judge and the litigants. . . . Justice is unapproachable and incorruptible. The scales reflect evenhandedness and absolutism. The sword is a symbol of power, and like the scales, executes decisions without sympathy or compromise. Finally, the blindfold protects Justice from distractions and from information that could bias or corrupt her. Masked, Justice is immune from sights that could evoke sympathy in an ordinary spectator.

Federal judges, seen in the light of this image of justice, have traditionally been presumed to play their most important role at trial. The judge is overseer and umpire. However, the traditional role of the federal judge was never limited to that of a mere umpire. Instead, the judge has always been "the governor of the trial for assuring its proper conduct." In the exercise of this power, the trial judge has the prerogative and, at times, the duty of eliciting facts necessary to the clear presentation of issues. To this end, she may examine witnesses who testify, as long as she preserves an attitude of impartiality and guards against giving the jury the impression that the court believes that one side or the other should prevail. The blindfold on the statue of Justice symbolizes this impartiality, a necessary element in an adversarial system. The integrity and independence of the judiciary is mandated and assured, its separateness from the executive and legislative branches a hallmark of our system. This was thought important by the framers of the Constitution as a safeguard against government tyranny over people, their rights, and their property. Justice's blindfold represents not only an attitude of impartiality in the case at hand, but also an institutionalized blindness to outside influences from other branches and other sectors.

The perception of the judge as isolated and removed has historically carried over into the reality of what a judge does, day to day, in connection with the matters before her. Traditionally, judges have remained above and removed from the more unseemly aspects of litigation — the filing of papers, trial preparation and discovery, settlement negotiations, and other attempts to resolve cases amicably or short of a full-blown trial by jury. The traditional judge was aloof and isolated, holding the scales at arm's length. Due to the adversarial nature of our system, the parties controlled the pace and shape of litigation. They defined the case or controversy; the judge merely acted as listener, observer and occasional inquisitor. The macro aspects of the system — the number of cases filed or the progress of cases before them — were not the judge's concern. It was in most chambers anathema to urge a resolution of disputes other than by a constitutionally-guaranteed trial by a jury of one's peers.

All that has changed. To say that the discrete role of judges in 1995 is to preside over trials is like saying that the role of women in the 1990s is to care for the home. Surely, we do that, but we do so much more. Analogies can easily be made between the expansion of the roles of judges and of women, especially those with children, in these fast-moving, no-holds-barred times. The complexity of society, the awakening of individuals to ever-increasing needs, rights, and desires, the advent of technological advances, to say nothing of the countervailing pressures of time and money, make the role of a judge, and that of a parent today, challenging indeed. The teenager was content to wear sneakers until someone called them Nikes, said you had to have them and slapped a $130 price tag on them. Counsel were content to correspond and informally exchange information in preparation for trial with little or no judicial involvement until someone enacted the Federal Rules of Civil Procedure and discovered you could charge fees not only for trial but for hours spent in pretrial discovery. Judges and parents must moderate these influences. I belittle neither of these callings by the foregoing remarks, just note the reality of life in our times.

With the advent of the Federal Rules of Civil Procedure, the judge joined the fray. Justice no longer merely holds the sword as a symbol of power, but wields it actively through involvement at every turn. She monitors not only the trial, but all aspects of litigation — especially the discovery phase and pretrial proceedings.

At the same time as the procedures have been expanded, the basic rights of individuals for which there are remedies, and citizens' awareness of these rights and readiness to seek recourse in the courts, have increased greatly. The number of civil cases has doubled in the last twenty years, with 239,000 civil cases filed in 1995. This reflects an increase of 15% in the last four years alone. Criminal cases in the federal courts have increased as well — filings in 1994 were 58% higher than in 1980. The average district court judge's caseload in 1994 consisted of 396 civil and 58 criminal cases. . . .

While shepherding the cases along, careful that none stray from the fold, the judge must make room for the determination of motions in her copious free time. The roles of speed reader and juggler are thus added, as well as that of interpreter of foreign tongues. Summary judgment is now in favor, and summary judgment motions of six inches or more in thickness predominate. The court's ruling on an issue rarely depends upon a clear legal principle, but rather upon whether defendant's mound of evidence will meet plaintiff's mound of evidence, and raise it one. In fact, I find it curious that summary judgment motions are thought to be an economical way of avoiding trial when they, in and of themselves, are costly undertakings indeed: costly to litigants in terms of attorney hours devoted to their preparation, and costly in terms of the expenditure of judicial time and effort. Once the motion, the answer, the reply, and the surreply have been filed, the judge then examines the four corners of the 1500 pages of deposition testimony and determines whether there are genuine issues of material fact — any one of which would thwart the entire motion — and whether movant is entitled to judgment as a matter of law. You might scoff at this and suggest that this is law clerk's work (and sometimes it is, but usually because of the press of other matters, not because the judge prefers it this way). Pennsylvania Superior Court Judge Spaeth commented on his modus operandi in addressing appellate cases before him:

> I have four clerks. That is too many to permit proper supervision. I ask each clerk to draft at least six opinions a month. That asks more than is wise; only the ablest and most diligent clerk can meet such a norm and still do good work. I rarely read the entire record of the trial testimony and documents, usually reading only those parts that seem from the briefs or my clerk's draft opinion likely to be critical. In reviewing a draft opinion, I often accept the clerk's exposition, so that my revisions are mostly stylistic. Sometimes I do not read the record at all. In deciding whether to join the opinion of another judge, I often accept the judge's statement of the record, on my clerk's assurance that the statement is accurate. In ruling on motions, I usually rely on summaries and recommendations prepared by the staff attorneys and my clerks. . . . I assent to every criticism that may be made of this breakneck way of doing things. I am sure that I should have decided some cases differently had I proceeded in a more deliberate and thorough way. But what else can I, or any judge like me, do? The cases keep piling up. They must be decided.

NOTES & QUESTIONS

1. "Speed reader," "juggler," and "interpreter" are not perhaps the first qualities we might think of as essential for a judge. Yet, as Judge Spaeth notes, "The cases keep piling up." Are the daily pressures of the litigation docket realistically reflected in popular culture? Do judges in popular culture have plenty of time to ruminate thoughtfully over the finer points of a case? As various methods of Alternative Dispute Resolution (mediation, arbitration, mini-trials, etc.) become more and more common, will judges no longer be necessary? Could a computer program do what a judge does?

2. Can any judge ever be as impartial and aloof as the blindfolded symbol of Justice seems to require? Do we hope a judge will rule fairly, but fear he or she will rule based on political ties?

3. What kind of assumptions do we make about the nature of the ideal judge? How do race, gender, ethnicity, religion, and sexual orientation come into play in our image of the "ideal" judge? Many lawyer films and television series now feature minority or women judges in the courtroom scenes. Does this visibly changing face of the judge in popular culture reflect real progress toward social justice, or is it just window dressing?

4. In the next article, Judge Richard Posner (a renowned Law and Economics scholar) suggests an economic explanation for the role of the judge. He argues that although economic incentives for a judge to rule a particular way are largely non-existent (because of such factors as set salaries and lifetime tenure), there are other deeper, less tangible incentives that can help us understand how a judge decides cases and how he or she plays the judge's role.

WHAT DO JUDGES AND JUSTICES MAXIMIZE? (THE SAME THING EVERYBODY ELSE DOES)
Richard A. Posner
3 Supreme Court Economic Review 1 (1993)

A difficult question remains — that of the judge's motivation, when all monetary punishments and rewards have been stripped away and a choice between work and leisure is not in the offing, to vote for one side rather than another, or to vote for one interpretation of a statute or legal doctrine rather than another, or to adopt one judicial philosophy (such as "conservative," "liberal," "activist," or "restrained") rather than another. The traditional objection to the secret ballot — that it promotes, or at least protects, irresponsible voting — has carried the day with respect to voting by judges. Every judicial vote is public, although sometimes a judge will tell his friends that he joined an opinion with which he disagreed because he didn't think the issue important enough to warrant a dissenting opinion. The public character of judicial voting facilitates criticism, which can be expected to have a greater effect on behavior when ordinarily more powerful incentives, such as money, are not in play. Yet most judges in fact are relatively insensitive to criticism other than by other judges, believing conveniently that most of it is motivated by political disagreement, envy, ignorance (willful or otherwise) of the conditions under which judges work, and self-promotion. Moreover, public comment on judicial decisions other than by the Supreme Court is rare. Only a tiny fraction of the tens of thousands of other appellate opinions published each year receive any sort of critical attention that might get back to the judge and alter his future behavior.

Choices of the kind that face a judge who must vote in a case — choices that cannot be made on the basis of wanting to increase one's pecuniary income, leisure, fame, or other forms of utility — are common in other areas of living. They are for example the choices we make when watching dramatic or cinematic performances. Athletic contests are different, mainly because of the built-in "bias" in favor, normally, of the "home" team, a bias that makes the judicial analogy strained. The bias is highly relevant to state court adjudication, however, and can help explain not only the federal diversity jurisdiction but also the exclusive federal jurisdiction over many types of cases that pit a state resident against federal taxpayers.

The audience for a play or movie is detached, having no tangible stake in the outcome of whatever struggle is being depicted on stage or screen. Yet ordinarily it is induced to "choose" one side or the other. Usually the choice is manipulated by the author — he "tells" us as it were to side with the hero against the villain. But in dramatic works of deep ambiguity, which often are highly popular among intellectuals on that account, such as *Hamlet,* or *Measure for Measure*, or *Pygmalion,* the choice offered to the spectator is a real one, because the author either has not resolved in his own mind the central tension in the situation dramatized or has not been able (or desired) to communicate the resolution clearly. This explains the popularity of revisionist interpretations of literature, such as arguing that the real hero of Paradise Lost is Satan. The spectator, or, in the last example, the reader (but a "live" performance provides a closer analogy to the judicial process, though today many cases are submitted for decision without any oral argument or other hearing — much as when a play is read rather than performed), has to weigh the evidence and come to a decision. The position of the judge is similar. If spectators get consumption value out of such choices, it is not surprising that judges do.

Spectators make choices about the meaning of a play or movie by bringing to bear their personal experiences and any specialized cultural competence that they may have by virtue of study of or immersion in the type of drama that they are watching, and often by discussing their reactions with friends who may have a similar competence. The judge brings to bear on his spectatorial function not only a range of personal and political preferences, but also a specialized cultural competence — his knowledge of and experience in "the law." And if he is an appellate judge he will often discuss with his professional colleagues the proper outcome of the contest before making up his mind.

Of course not every case has the rich ambiguities of *Hamlet*. Many cases involve puzzles soluble with the technical tools of legal analysis — here the judge is like the reader of a detective story. The jury as fact-finder performs a similar function. It is a different kind of spectatorship from the one I am stressing here, that of the appellate judge asked to decide not where truth lies but which party has the better case. But in either case the choice, like that of the theater audience, is a disinterested one; the judge's or jury's income is not affected by it. A further point is that the less informed the tribunal is, the more "dramatic" the trial must be to hold the "audience's" attention. It is not surprising that Anglo-American trials, historically dominated by juries, are far more dramatic than Continental trials, historically dominated by professional judges.

The voting and spectatorship analogies to judicial decision-making are similar. This is most easily seen by comparing applause to voting — for in a large audience the clapping of a single spectator contributes little more to the overall decibel level than a single vote in an election contributes to the outcome. The voter is the spectator in a contest between candidates, much as the reader or viewer of *Antigone* is the spectator of a contest between Antigone and Creon. It is no surprise that voter turnout is higher, the more publicized and the closer an election is, just as the audience for a heavily advertised, highly dramatic play is likely to be larger than the audience for a meagerly advertised, undramatic play.

Why has the spectatorship analogy to judging been overlooked? One reason is the piety in which the public discussion of judges is usually clothed. The analogy seems to give judging a frivolous air. But serious engagement with the arts as reader or viewer is not a frivolous activity; nor is "play" (contrasted with work) incompatible with adherence to rules. A chess player would reduce rather than enhance the pleasure he received from playing the game if he violated its rules, and so would the theatergoer who refused to enter into the lives of the characters on the stage, on the ground that they were not real people; and likewise the judge who violates the rules of the judicial game. Sports fans, theater fans, movie fans, and opera fans often develop a degree of connoisseurship which enhances their pleasure. In other words, they learn the rules (broadly understood) of the game they are watching, and respond in accordance with those rules. It is the same with judges, but with the important difference that some of the rules of the judicial game are uncertain and contested.

A second reason why the spectatorship analogy to judging has been overlooked is the domination of analyses of judicial behavior by legal academics. The academic is a spectator too, but he is a spectator not of the little drama that the judge witnesses — the trial or other contest that the judge resolves — but of the judge's opinion. He usually does not attend oral argument or even read the briefs in the cases that he discusses. Naturally, therefore, he tends to ascribe more importance to the opinion, to its reasoning, its rhetoric, etc. than to the decision itself. Yet these are secondary factors for most judges. For the judge, as for Hamlet, "the play's the thing." When judges got busy, the first thing to be delegated was opinion-writing; yet even today it would be considered a scandal if judges delegated the hearing of testimony or argument (though there is in fact some delegation of these functions to magistrates and masters).

The analogy to spectatorship can help us see how judicial outcomes reflect both the judges' preferences going in and the quality of the briefing and argument in particular cases. It can also help us understand the function of confirmation hearings in enabling legislators to ascertain a judicial candidate's policy preferences, since those preferences can be expected to guide or at least influence a judge's decisions. We might also expect that "ideologues" would be appointed to judgeships at an earlier age on average than other candidates. Not only may it be difficult to determine the trajectory of the non-ideologue's views save by a process of inference from behavior over a long career, but to the extent that an ideologue is inherently more predictable there is less worry that if appointed young he will have a long time to change his views.

Contrary to appearances, this analysis does not justify complacency about judicial performance. To eliminate by means of rules governing conflicts of interest all personal stakes from the judge's decision-making increases the weight (by reducing the cost) of ethical consideration, including the ethical duty to follow legal rules, but at the same time, as with the nonprofit enterprise, it reduces the penalty for careless, erratic, inattentive, or willful decision-making. The problem is deeper. We can see it by returning to the analogy between political and judicial voting, and by examining more critically than before the analogy between judicial and theatrical spectatorship. Most political campaigners appeal primarily, though not exclusively, to the voter's self-interest. The judge, in contrast, like the theatrical spectator, is asked to cast a disinterested vote. It is easy to see why the spectator's vote is likely to be disinterested; what has he — being powerless — to gain by refusing to play the spectator's game? But a judge has some power. Supposing that the conflict of interest rules are effective in insulating his decision from any consequences for his personal or family wealth, one can still imagine a host of inappropriate considerations that might enter into his utility function: personal dislike of a lawyer or litigant in the case, gratitude to the appointing authorities, desire for advancement, irritation with or even a desire to undermine a judicial colleague or subordinate, willingness to trade votes, desire to be on good terms with colleagues, not wanting to disagree with people one likes or respects, fear for personal safety, fear of ridicule, reluctance to offend one's spouse or close friends, and racial or class solidarity. These are common factors in the decisions of everyday life — why not in the decisions of judges, unless we ascribe to them a utility function different from that of the ordinary person, which would be inconsistent with treating them as ordinary persons?

Such factors do influence judicial decisions, but less often than the suspicious layman might suppose. The reason is not that judges have different utility functions from other people but that the utility they derive from judging would be reduced by more than they would gain from giving way to the temptations that I have listed. It is the same reason that many people do not cheat at games even when they are sure they can get away with cheating. The pleasure of judging is bound up with compliance with certain self-limiting rules that define the "game" of judging. It is a source of satisfaction to a judge to vote for the litigant who irritates him, the lawyer who fails to exhibit proper deference to him, the side that represents a different social class form his own; for it is by doing such things that you know that you are playing the judge role, not some other role, and judges for the most part are people who want to be — judges. This is consistent with most judges' not wanting to work too hard, for working as hard as a lawyer in private practice is not one of the rules of the judicial game. It is also consistent with judges' often voting their policy preferences and strong personal convictions. For in our system the line between law and policy, the judging game and the legislating game, is blurred. Many cases cannot be decided by reasoning from conventional legal materials. Such cases require the judge to exercise a legislative judgment, although a more confined one than a "real" legislator would be authorized to exercise.

The analogy to playing games is worth pursuing a bit. Rules are not always irksome restraints. They are often constitutive. It is difficult to write a sonnet, because the sonnet is a genre with rigid rules; but without the rules, there would be no sonnets, and this would be a loss not only for the reader but for the sonneteer. And similarly with a game, for example, chess. If you decided that your bishops should be allowed to make the same moves as your queen, or that some of your pieces should be allowed to make moves off the chessboard, you would no longer be playing the game of chess. It is true that people sometimes cheat at games when they think they can get away with it. But that is because the pleasure of the game is not the only argument in their utility function. A person might cheat at tennis (this is very common in fact) because he saw an advantage from winning, but if at all reflective he would realize that his pleasure from playing the game itself was diminished, that he was trading off that pleasure against another source of utility. The judicial "game" has rules that lawyers learn in law school and then in practice or teaching, and both self-selection and the careful screening of federal judicial candidates help to assure that most lawyers who become federal judges will be lawyers who enjoy this particular game. They are therefore likely to adhere, more or less, to the rules limiting the materials and considerations that enter into their decisions. The rules, it should be noted, are not the rules of substantive law, to which the community is subject but to which judges in their judicial capacity relate differently, as law givers and law appliers; they are the institutional rules of judging, to which only judges are subject. These rules, as I have said, are not altogether clear or uniform, especially in application; they are probably less clear and uniform, at least in the United States, than the substantive law. Some judges play by "activist" rules, more by rules of "restraint" because those rules are more congenial to the legal profession's self-image; and judges, like game players, sometimes bend or break the rules for the sake of other values, such violations being in fact rather common because detection and sanctioning are difficult. Nevertheless most judicial decisions do have a "ruled" quality, and the analogy to games helps to show how this property of decisions is consistent with utility maximization and how therefore it does not presuppose — what would be contrary to the assumptions of my analysis — heroic self-abnegation on the part of the judges.

Another aspect of rules makes it reasonable to expect most judges to abide by the rules of the judicial game. In creating games, as in creating art, people create a reality in which they can find temporary refuge from, by imaginative transformation of, the sinister realities of ordinary life, the realities of hatred, disease, crime, betrayal, war, and so forth. The judicial game has aspects of this refuge and transformation. Its raw materials are the ugly realities of life, but they are transformed in the judicial game to intellectual disputes over rights and duties, claims and proofs, presumptions and rebuttals, jurisdiction and competencies. And that is a comfort; it spares the judge who inflicts or upholds the death penalty from having to think of himself as a killer. But to get to this comfort the judge must play by the rules of the judicial game, because the rules constitute the game.

Elected judges play the judge game too, and legislators play a related game called statesmanship or public service. But unlike life-tenured federal judges, these players face higher costs (and obtain no greater benefits) from abiding by the rules of the game and therefore break them more often. Not always, which is why many and indeed most decisions by non-elected judges have a ruled quality and why much legislation has a genuine public-spirited character — not necessarily because the voters are public-spirited but because legislators derive satisfactions from acting in the public interest that may outweigh the costs when those costs are small.

NOTES & QUESTIONS

1. If judges are largely insulated from most economic incentives, what other incentives do they have to rule one way or the other? Moral righteousness? Intellectual satisfaction? Aesthetic satisfaction? Do you agree with Judge Posner's judge-as-spectator and judge-as-gamester models? What are the pleasures of judging?

2. Judges (like many of us) may have too lofty of a notion of their social and cultural position. Should every judge periodically visit the courthouse in disguise, to see how ordinary people are treated? The next reading shares insights from feminist criticism on the power structure of the judicial role.

ON THE BIAS: FEMINIST RECONSIDERATIONS OF THE ASPIRATIONS FOR OUR JUDGES
Judith Resnik
61 Southern California Law Review 1877 (1988)

After [Malcolm Lucas] completed his statement, Lucas was asked [by the Commission on Judicial Appointments] only one question — whether he had preconceived ideas about any issue that might go before him. He said he had none. [Thereafter, Lucas was sworn in as an Associate Justice on the California Supreme Court.] [As reported by Dan Morain, *Lucas Sworn in as High Court Justice*, Los Angeles Times, April 7, 1984, Part 2, at 1, Col. 1.]

Question No. 4: "Do you think women judges will make a difference in the administration of justice?" . . .Well, I answer honestly, "What does my being a woman specially bring to the bench? It brings me and my special background. All my life experiences — including being a woman — affect me and influence me. . . . My point is that nobody is just a woman or a man. Each of us is a person with diverse experiences. Each of us brings to the bench experiences that affect our view of law and life and decision-making. . . . " [The Honorable Shirley S. Abrahamson, *The Woman Has Robes: Four Questions*, 14 Golden Gate Law Review 489, 492–94 (1984).]. . . .

IV.   A. THE VOICES OF WOMEN

In addition to quoting coments by Malcolm Lucas, of the California Supreme Court, I began this essay by quoting Shirley Abrahamson, a Wisconsin Supreme Court Justice, who has written a good deal about the act of judging. "What does my being a woman specially bring to the bench? It brings me and my special background. All my life experiences — including being a woman — affect me and influence me. . . ." Notice that her comments are "in a different voice," for, unlike the tradition of distance, Shirley Abrahamson accepts her history and rejoices that her life informs her work. But, just as Carol Gilligan has been accused of a selection bias, so can I be challenged. A few phrases out of context. Those of one woman, compared to those of one man.

But listen to more from Justice Abrahamson. In an address to the National Association of Women Judges (NAWJ), Abrahamson urged judges to visit — essentially incognito — courtrooms in other cities. She described her experience in one courtroom, where she, "dressed in my t-shirt, wrap-around jean skirt, and sandals." The clerk was abrasive and "unfriendly," the lawyers condescending, the legal activity taking place in chambers, outside the public purview. Justice Abrahamson's request that judges enter into the world of litigants and the public was, in essence, a plea that judges attempt not only to understand the perspective of another, but to be an other (when possible), to experience the meaning of being a person in a courtroom who lacks the first name "Judge." By going to the courtroom unrobed, and therefore temporarily powerless, Shirley Abrahamson was able to understand more clearly how much her position of power affects her own construction of courtroom reality.

Justice Abrahamson also exhorted her sibling jurists to speak to the public and to participate in community organizations. Contrast this view with the Code of Judicial Conduct, which worries about extrajudicial activities that will "detract from the dignity" of the judicial office. The judicial canons have been used as the basis for criticism of judges who have participated in too many public activities. Felix Frankfurter made statements about judicial distance from the fray, all the while engaging in backroom politicking. Unlike Frankfurter, Shirley Abrahamson's views unify theory and practice and provide a very different conception of the judicial.

Listen also to Judge Patricia Wald, now Chief Judge of the United States Court of Appeals for the District of Columbia. Judge Wald joined Justice Abrahamson and Deans John Ely and Jesse Choper on a panel entitled "Judicial Review and Constitutional Limitations." Judge Wald commented on the academic vogue of considering the question of judging in the context of constitutional jurisprudence. "I am not at all sure that the debate among the judicial review jurisprudentialists is really aimed at affecting the behavior of ordinary judges at all. . . . The point is simple: constitutional cases for most federal judges are a rarity — gourmet fare, definitely not the bread and butter of our everyday worklives." Her criticism was deeper than the problem of irrelevance. Judge Wald argued that the academics failed to take into account the experienced reality of judging:

> [F]ew judges I know reach out for or even want to decide constitutional issues. Such reticence does not stem from innate humility alone; but from a weary recognition that anytime you reverse some governmental action on constitutional grounds, it almost inevitably means en banc review, or certiorari granted and probable reversal. The prognosis, of course, is quite different if you decide that challenged action is constitutional. I suggest there is institutionally and experientially a very strong built-in bias in the lower courts against holding laws or actions violative of the federal constitution.

In short, Judge Wald argued that the "big" academic questions — the creation of new rights and the judicial usurpation of legislative and executive roles — are uninformed by, and irrelevant to, the reality of judging. Judge Wald argued for an appreciation of the daily experiences of judging and for a jurisprudence of judging built upon the experience of judges, rather than imposed from theory.

Compare Judge Wald's voice to that of Antonin Scalia, Associate Justice of the United States Supreme Court. Like Judge Wald, Justice Scalia has commented on the everyday work of judges. In a recent speech, he deplored the drudgery of a federal judge, "processing many . . . less significant cases," such as "many routine tort and employment disputes." Justice Scalia spoke of his understanding, in 1960, when he graduated from law school, of the task of federal judges. "When I had the unrealistic ambition of being a federal judge, back in 1960, I did not want to dispose of predominantly routine cases. . . ." Justice Scalia suggested that "trivial cases" — explicitly defined as many social security claims and implicitly defined as those of little dollar value — be removed from the federal courts. Note that the commentary of Judge Wald and Justice Scalia have a similar basis — the experience of being a judge. Both Wald and Scalia remark on the distance between the reality of judges and the rhetoric of judging. Judge Wald seeks to have the reality inform the rhetoric, while Justice Scalia wants to change the reality to conform to his view of what judges "should" do; important men do not engage in routine tasks.

In addition to individual voices, there is a bit of information about how women judges speak in the aggregate. The National Association of Women Judges (NAWJ) provides some data. "As a large national organization, we can speak out on those issues — often controversial ones such as discriminatory clubs or federal judicial appointments — that individual judges, with all their ethical restrictions, do not feel they can appropriately address." The NAWJ addressed the issue of discriminatory clubs because of a perceived link between behavior in the world at large and the task of judging; the NAWJ opposes membership by judges in clubs that practice invidious discrimination. The NAWJ argues for an appreciation of the connection between what a judge does "on the bench from 9:00 a.m. to 12:30 p.m. supposedly making decisions without regard to race or sex" and what the judge does at lunch "at a social club which excludes women and blacks from its dining room."

I do not want to overstate the distance between female judges and the NAWJ, on the one hand, and male judges and the canons of judicial ethics, on the other. Like the NAWJ, the American Bar Association's Code of Judicial Conduct acknowledges that a relationship exists between the person on the bench and the person off the bench. The Code is replete with prohibitions on certain kinds of "extrajudicial activities" and with acknowledgments that, while a judge can engage in civic activities, a judge must not do so in a manner that "detracts from the dignity" of the judicial office. Moreover, the American Bar Association recently adopted a change in the commentary to the Code to recognize that membership in discriminatory clubs was problematic, insisting that individuals withdraw from such institutions. And, unlike Justice Shirley Abrahamson, the Code does not embrace the obligations of judges to leave their protected role and attempt to experience the judicial systems as do those without robes.

I also do not want to leave the impression that the few female voices on the bench all exemplify what could be seen as the "upside" of feminism. Another bit of collective information, provided by a statistical analysis of decisions made by federal judges, reminds us that some traditions of women — subservience and deference to a patriarchal culture — may also come with women to the bench. Thomas Walker and Deborah Barrow wanted to learn whether black and female federal judges appointed by the Carter administration decided cases differently from their white, male colleagues. Using a "pairing" device, the researchers compared opinions of twelve female/male pairs and ten black/white pairs. One of the study's findings was that "female judges were . . . more prone to rule in favor of the government in federal regulatory disputes. . . . Female judges exhibit a much greater tendency to defer to positions taken by government than do male judges."

How are we to interpret this information? Putting aside possible methodological complaints such as sample size, a first problem is that the researchers' analysis assumed that appropriate behavior was displayed by the male judges. Women were compared to men, and women were found wanting — found to be more deferential than were men. Perhaps the women's behavior was appropriate and the male judges were simply displaying male arrogance and a lack of humility. Alternatively, if the women were, in Sara Ruddick's terms, engaging in a learned but undesirable behavior, obedience to the "actual control and preferences of dominant people," then how do we explain the women judges who rise above such obedience? The real difficulty is thinking about how, over time, a person could hold the position of judge, retain humility and yet be able, when necessary, to challenge the powers of government. Responses to this problem must come in part from learning how judges experience their power and whether those experiences of power change over time. Learning from the practice of judging will teach us lessons about ourselves, as well as lessons about how we might transform our understanding of judging. . . .

NOTES & QUESTIONS

1. Does gender affect the way a judge experiences and administers power? How does popular culture treat women judges? In *First Monday in October*, Jill Clayburgh plays the first woman Justice of the Supreme Court. The film tries to have it both ways, presenting an ostensibly feminist subject matter, but also sexualizing Jill Clayburgh's character (in our first glimpse of her, she is attired in skimpy tennis shorts and tight top). She is supposed to be a bit of a prude (Walter Matthau, playing a liberal Justice, calls her "the Mother Superior of Orange County"). At her confirmation hearing, she addresses the issue of her childlessness (something we would not expect to hear a male nominee discuss about himself): "The FBI is wrong in reporting I have no children. I have hundreds. . . . We are the parents of our ideas. My children [are] my opinions." This little exchange highlights her intelligence, but the scene also suggests a personal lack. Again, the film seems a bit double-edged, exhibiting a progressive veneer, but also a reactionary underpinning.

Interestingly, the film picks up an aspect of feminist theory that has been very influential — it suggests that because of the material conditions of their lives, men and women may "see" the world differently. Walter Matthau's long-suffering wife leaves him after asking him to describe the wallpaper in the house he has lived in for years. He cannot do it because, as she tells him, "you can't memorize what you don't even see." Later, Matthau's character tests Jill Clayburgh at a Chinese restaurant by covering her eyes and asking her,

"What's on the wall?" She describes in great detail the wallpaper, which she has seen only once. The positive spin on these scenes is that perhaps our life experiences help us see the world in different ways, and that men and women can learn from each other. The negative spin is that women notice "trivial" details while men pay attention to the "important" things in life. But who decides what counts as trivial?

C. WHO ARE THESE PEOPLE? IMAGES OF JUDGES FROM HOLMES TO JUDGE JUDY

1. "Only Human" — Judges in Love, Judges in Trouble, and Troublemaker Judges

The next set of readings takes judges off their pedestals and focuses on the human factor. Perhaps we expect more of judges because we have given them power over us and we desperately hope they will use it wisely. We want them to be more fair, more humane, more righteous than we ever could be. But judges, like the rest of us, are only human.

JUDICIAL FICTIONS: IMAGES OF SUPREME COURT JUSTICES IN THE NOVEL, DRAMA, AND FILM
Laura Krugman Ray
39 Arizona Law Review 151 (1997)

The Supreme Court as Battleground: *First Monday in October*

The most prominent Supreme Court play since *The Magnificent Yankee* is *First Monday in October* by Jerome Lawrence and Robert E. Lee, first produced on Broadway a generation later in 1978 and prophetic of Sandra Day O'Connor's appointment to the Court by President Reagan in 1981. Although *First Monday in October* anticipates history by placing a woman on the Court, it is scarcely an innovative or radical work. Like *Talk of the Town*, it draws heavily on the conventions of romantic comedy; unlike the earlier film, however, it has little interest in the institution of the Court except as a new setting for its traditional story.

Although the authors characterize their play as "a comedy-drama," it might more appropriately be described as an exercise in polarity. The first woman appointed to the Court is Ruth Loomis, a youthful circuit court judge from California who is athletic, orderly, and outspokenly conservative in her jurisprudence. Her opposite number is Dan Snow, the Court's senior Associate Justice, a dedicated liberal who cultivates a messy desk and, when not climbing mountains, exercises his sharp tongue. The play is organized around their mutual antagonism, which includes more than their basic ideological disagreement; she finds him arrogant, while he finds her priggish. In the first act, they spar over a First Amendment case, and Ruth questions Dan as he plays the part of the distributor of a pornographic film. In the second act, the disputed case is a shareholder suit against a large corporation, and this time Dan questions Ruth as the missing corporate president. Even the stage set emphasizes the characters' opposition. It consists principally of their judicial chambers, set "back to back," with a foreground area that serves as all of the other Court settings.

Despite its legal trappings and debates, *First Monday in October* is a variant of a familiar romantic comedy pattern: the man and woman meet in unusual circumstances, recognize their differences, and bicker relentlessly until they realize what the audience already knows, that they are a perfect match. Dan, who has been considering retirement from the Court, is energized by the news that Ruth has been appointed. He begins sniping at his new colleague even before she arrives, calling her "Lady Purity" and the "Mother Superior of Orange County" and preparing for battle. At their first meeting, in the Justices' robing room, they size each other up, and the stage directions make clear the future course of their relationship: "They look at each other with a full awareness of the gulf between them. Cryptic smiles cross each face: boy, are these two going to have a donnybrook!" Ruth rises to the occasion, challenging Dan's approach to First Amendment cases and accusing him of behaving "like a burlesque comic." By the end of the first act, Dan has acknowledged that she is "a worthy adversary," and he pays her the serious compliment of finding her "dangerous."

In the conventional comedies perhaps most perfectly embodied by the films pairing Katharine Hepburn and Spencer Tracy, the protagonists inevitably move toward a romantic resolution. Lawrence and Lee stop short of providing such an ending for their play, but they do give the relationship of Ruth and Dan some sexual overtones. By the second act, both Justices are romantically available; Ruth is a widow, and Dan's wife has filed for a divorce. In a conversation with Dan's law clerk, Ruth asks several increasingly suggestive questions: what does Dan do for recreation, what is his wife like, and, most revealingly, "[d]oes he ever talk about me?" Dan himself answers the last question when he describes for Ruth his wife's suspicions about the Justices' relationship:

> Dan. I think she thinks I spend so much time being furious at you I don't have enough energy left to be furious at *her*. You know — love-hate, hate-love. And I suspect she's got a hunch that I consider you attractive.
>
> Ruth. Well, there's no evidence to support *that* contention.
>
> Dan. I wouldn't be too sure.
>
> Ruth. I hope you'll assure Mrs. Snow that the mere fact one of your colleagues happens to be a woman. . . .
>
> Dan. That's no "mere" fact — it's a *towering* fact!

Ruth is sufficiently unsettled by this exchange to misinterpret Dan's movement toward her as an advance, but the stage directions make clear that he is only reaching for a book. Although the scene ends not with an embrace but with Dan's collapse from an apparent heart attack, it teases the audience by bringing to the surface the romantic subtext of the legal arguments between the Justices.

The audience remains, however, unclear about the nature of the relationship between Dan and Ruth because the play treats the "towering fact" of a woman Justice with ambivalence that borders on confusion. At her confirmation hearing, Ruth acknowledges that her gender will affect her opinions and that "[p]erhaps it's time for the majority of the population to have one voice in nine in the rulings of the Supreme Court." At the same time, she rejects the term "lady" and asks the senators "[w]hat has sex got to do with being a judge?" Dan seems similarly confused about how to treat a woman colleague, worrying when five Justices sit for the Court's annual photograph while Ruth stands; he has no difficulty, however, in asserting his seniority when the Justices march into the courtroom. The play adds another layer of confusion by identifying Dan with a jurisprudence of compassion and concern for the individual, while Ruth insists that Justices should be "dispassionate" in their search for "broad legal principles." It is hard to imagine within this framework what role Ruth envisions for the woman's voice on the Court, and the play offers no explanation.

Although Lawrence and Lee retreat from a romantic reconciliation of their protagonists, they provide instead the professional equivalent. When Ruth, having learned that her late husband was involved in misconduct connected with a pending case, decides to resign from the Court, Dan insists that it is her public duty to remain. He tells her that the "Court changes people" from flawed individuals to honorable judges; whatever their ideological and personal differences, they share a professional bond that is meant to replace or overshadow the romantic bond that has been dangled before the audience and withdrawn. The play ends with the two Justices cheerfully anticipating their battles over future cases and agreeing only, as Ruth says, that "[y]ou and I make each other possible." In place of the conventional kiss, there is a handshake before Ruth and Dan proceed, in order of seniority, into the courtroom; the scene might have been scripted as a deliberate contrast to *Talk of the Town*, where the couple instead escapes from the Court. There is, however, an even more important difference between the two resolutions. In the earlier work, Lightcap's chilly rationalism has clearly been moderated by his brush with emotion; in the later play, there is only a brief hint from Dan that Ruth's dispassionate approach to the law may have been softened by Dan's compassion. The point of the final scene is that the antagonists remain just that, what Dan has earlier described as "a pair of flying buttresses" which, supporting "opposite sides of a Gothic cathedral . . . keep the roof from caving in."

First Monday in October is less a play about the Court than it is an attempt to transpose the conventions of romantic comedy into the judicial workplace. This is made clear by the film version, adapted by the playwrights and released in 1981, which softens Ruth somewhat and contributes two new characters to the romantic aspect of the plot. Ruth is now courted by her late husband's law partner, while Dan's wife is present to demonstrate his lack of interest in their marriage. A gentler Ruth rides in the ambulance with Dan after his heart attack and, when he rejects her resignation, gives him a chaste kiss. While its romantic elements are enlarged, the legal elements of the plot are less clear and less accurate than in the play. The authors are understandably confused about the certiorari process, but they might on that ground have given less prominence to the battle over bringing the corporate misconduct case to the

Court. Although both the play and the film treat the Court as an honorable and powerful institution, they are principally interested in it as a novel setting for a familiar story, a setting that defeats their intentions. As Supreme Court Justices, Dan and Ruth remain in a kind of dramatic limbo: too elevated for the ordinary resolution of romantic comedy, but too conventional for a plausible version of collegial relations at the Court. . . .

The Supreme Court as Target: *The Pelican Brief*

John Grisham's 1992 suspense novel, *The Pelican Brief*, is the first to hinge a plot on the composition of the Supreme Court and the first to locate the solution to murder in the Court's docket. Writing a decade after Truman [*see* Margaret Truman, *Murder in the Supreme Court* (1981)], Grisham had several advantages in basing a plot on the Court. As a lawyer, he brought to his novel a more sophisticated understanding of the Court's role than the typical layperson, even an experienced Washington observer like Truman. More importantly, Grisham wrote after the defeat of Robert Bork's nomination to the Court had educated the public about the significance of a single Justice's vote. Not since Owen Roberts' celebrated "switch in time [that] saved Nine" helped to derail Roosevelt's court-packing plan had the nation been forced to consider how the viewpoint of a single Justice might alter the legal landscape.

A national audience watched Robert Bork's confirmation hearings on television in September 1987 with the sense that the Senate Judiciary Committee was about to make a choice that was not merely important but momentous. Bork had been nominated to fill the seat of Justice Lewis Powell, a moderate Justice generally considered a swing vote between the liberal and conservative wings of the Court, and thus it was generally assumed that his vote would determine the Court's direction. In the overheated rhetoric of such Bork opponents as Senator Edward Kennedy, the confirmation of Bork would threaten the basic civil liberties of all Americans. Bork's supporters inside and outside the Reagan administration countered that Bork's confirmation was essential to restrain the Court's dangerous and illegitimate tendency to rewrite the law in accord with its members' liberal policy preferences. The televised spectacle of the nominee responding to the senators' questions was accompanied by a fierce media campaign that insisted on the apocalyptic nature of the battle: the lives of all Americans would be directly affected by the confirmation or rejection of Robert Bork. Four years later, the confirmation hearings of Justice Clarence Thomas created another media spectacle, though this time the focus was less on the Court's balance than on the credibility of the nominee. Together the Bork and Thomas nominations dramatized for the American public the turbulent emotions and high stakes surrounding the selection of Supreme Court Justices.

Although *The Pelican Brief* is largely a novel of pursuit, the chase is set in motion by the problem of the Supreme Court's composition. Grisham's premise is that a wealthy entrepreneur appealing the injunction that prevents him from drilling for oil in a wildlife refuge has ordered the assassination of the Court's two environmentalist Justices in order to secure a more favorable bench. The entrepreneur, a heavy contributor to the incumbent President's election campaign, accepts the advice of counsel that two new conservative appointees will ensure a favorable decision worth millions of dollars. The novel's plot is a variation on the Bork scenario — the motive is financial rather than ideological — but it relies on the same assumption that a shift in Court membership will have immediate and predictable consequences. Grisham makes the point with some emphasis at the start of the novel, when a crowd of 50,000 angry demonstrators rings the Supreme Court on the first Monday in October, and we learn that "[t]hreats, serious ones, against the justices had increased tenfold since 1990." The link between individual Justices and the decisions of the Court is well established in the public mind.

The target of eighty percent of the death threats against the Court is Justice Abraham Rosenberg, a ninety-one year old liberal who, though paralyzed and weak after two strokes, still writes his own opinions and refuses to resign until a Democrat is elected President. Rosenberg's position on environmental issues is unequivocal: "the environment over everything." Justice Glenn Jensen, sixth among the Justices in death threats, is an erratic conservative who has drifted toward the left since his close confirmation vote six years earlier and who is now "fairly consistent in his protection of the environment." Jensen also has a secret life in which he takes Prozac for his depression and frequents a theater specializing in gay pornographic films. Although his fear of exposure has been largely replaced by the pleasure he takes in the challenge of evading detection, Jensen, like several of Truman's Justices, has a part of his life that he wants to keep from the public. In the violent political climate surrounding the Court, all of the Justices are closely guarded by FBI agents, though not well enough to prevent the assassinations of Rosenberg and Jensen by a highly skilled professional.

In the aftermath of the assassinations, the most perceptive detectives are not the law enforcement experts but the amateurs who understand the roles played by Rosenberg and Jensen on the Court. Justice Ben Thurow, a former federal prosecutor, tells his colleagues that the victims "'were murdered for a reason, and that reason is directly related to a case or an issue already decided or now pending before this Court.'" Thurow proposes using the Court's law clerks "to solve the killings" by having them review the cases pending in the circuit courts, though the other Justices are skeptical. In fact, Thurow is on the right track. The case is solved by a second-year law student at Tulane, Darby Shaw, who examines the pending appellate cases and finds one with the crucial element: not a strong ideological issue, but simply "a great deal of money." The angry protesters and the death threats against the Justices turn out to be red herrings. The motive is greed, that staple of detective fiction, though the solution is found in electronic data bases by someone who knows how to read the jurisprudence of the victims.

The Pelican Brief is thus a highly conventional novel that casts the Supreme Court as a source of financial benefits, much like the victim's will in a mystery novel by Agatha Christie or Ngaio Marsh, and a law student as the detective. What is new in Grisham's fiction is the grounding of motive in the substance of the Court's decisions and the related idea that the Court can be easily redirected by the expedient of substituting more congenial Justices for hostile obstructionists. In Rosenberg and Jensen, Grisham presents two varieties of obstacle. Rosenberg, the committed liberal, is determined to control his seat by withholding his resignation from a conservative President; Jensen, the erratic conservative, has become unpredictable and therefore a business risk for the entrepreneur who seeks certainty and control. The murders, carried out on advice of counsel, are thus a carefully researched business strategy. Grisham is a good deal less interested in working out the implications of this novel's premise than he is in detailing Darby Shaw's ingenuity in evading her pursuers, and the novel does not linger long over the Court and its docket. Nonetheless, *The Pelican Brief*, together with its popular film, has brought to a vast audience an image of the Court not as a powerful protector of constitutional rights but rather as a vulnerable institution subject to manipulation by sinister external forces bent on furthering their own financial interests through their mastery of the Court's jurisprudence.

NOTES & QUESTIONS

1. In a post-*Bush v. Gore* world, does a film like *First Monday in October* seem hopelessly outdated, with its idealized picture of quirky but highly principled Justices always trying to do the right thing? Or does the film still have a potent message about the difficult but possible path toward justice? Does your answer to this depend on your own jurisprudential philosophy?

2. In *First Monday in October*, Walter Matthau plays a stalwart liberal dissenter on the Supreme Court. When a conservative fellow Justice dies, Matthau gives the eulogy, and says, "Stanley and I were like a pair of flying buttresses. Leaning against opposite sides of a Gothic cathedral, we helped keep the roof from caving in." (He adds that "you don't have to agree with a man in order to respect him.") Is this kind of balance a good description of the role of the Supreme Court today?

3. In the next excerpt Professor Kimberlianne Podlas comments on a study of 241 individuals reporting for jury duty in Manhattan; Washington, D.C.; and Hackensack, New Jersey. She reports that regular watching of reality-based courtroom television shows such as *Judge Judy* encourages viewers to take as the norm behavior that in real life would constitute gross judicial misconduct. As you read, consider how popular culture shapes our perceptions of "proper" judicial behavior.

BLAME JUDGE JUDY: THE EFFECTS OF SYNDICATED TELEVISION COURTROOMS ON JURORS
Kimberlianne Podlas
25 American Journal of Trial Advocacy 557 (2002)

Findings suggest that syndi-court [syndicated television courtrooms] "teaches" the public about the law, but that its teachings may be flawed. A significant portion of frequent viewers believe that judges should be active, ask questions during the proceedings, hold opinions regarding the outcome, and make these opinions known. Frequent viewers, unlike non-viewers, stated a desire to look for clues to a judge's opinion and interpreted judicial silence as indicating a clear belief in one of the litigants. Moreover, the prior personal experience of viewers and non-viewers with the justice system exhibited no discernible effect on these measures.

When these frequent viewers become jurors, the ramifications are profound. Not only might these individuals enter the courtroom with a diminished respect for judges and a perverted sense of the trial process, but they may also actively search for clues to a judge's opinion, impute opinions where they do not exist, and draw mistaken inferences from judicial behavior or silence. Consequently, trial advocates should craft strategies to address these potential biases and misunderstandings. Some mechanisms include juror orientation, voir dire on the issue, and requests for instructions upon impaneling the jury and as part of the main charge.

I. Television's Influence on Public Opinion *About* the Law

. . . In the last decade, networks have added the "reality programming" of the syndicated television courtroom, or syndi-court, to their repertoire. As of this writing, there are eleven syndicated courtroom shows airing, including *Judge Judy*, *Judge Mathis*, and *The People's Court*. These courts add to the stream of information feeding "law" to the American populace. Although individuals within the legal profession may disregard these forums as aberrational or embarrassing, they are a key source of information about judges and the law for many citizens.

In contrast to other televised, reality law, syndi-court's ratings demonstrate that the public systematically tunes into these shows: One year after the show's 1996 debut, *Judge Judy* boasted the nation's top syndicated ratings and continues to enjoy significant popularity. Additionally, this slate of television programming follows a remarkably similar format. Hence, syndi-courts exude the consistency and repetition required for cultivation and social learning. Their metaphors and images are repeated both within each individual show and among the slate of syndi-court programs. What one sees on *Judge Judy* is confirmed by what is seen on *Judge Mathis*. And, because these are broadcast daily instead of sporadically (as the trial arises), they create a unified body of information. One criticism of the typically televised trials, including those on Court TV, is that they are too unique to actually educate the public. High-profile trials may excite interest, but viewers tend to fixate on the political lure of the trial and not the legal issues. This is not true of syndi-court.

Furthermore, syndi-court is accessible to the average person in a way and to a degree that other televised legal proceedings are not. In terms of availability — how easy it is to find a syndi-court on the dial — anyone with a television set can find at least one syndi-court telecast on any weekday. Cable is not a prerequisite. Finally, the production style of these shows ensures that their stories are easily digestible, their conflicts clear, and their resolutions swift. The end of the program always brings closure. Whereas real trials may confuse viewers with procedural and strategic issues and can drag on for a number of days, syndi-courts are intellectually accessible. At five hours per week, fifty-two weeks per year, viewers of only one show are exposed to 260 hours of syndi-court programming. Consequently, these shows possess a tremendous potential for impacting mass public opinion regarding the justice system. Even New York's Chief Judge has posited that knowledge and direct experience with the court system, even if that experience is "sitting in front of a television, watching Judge Judy . . . play(s) a huge role in public perceptions of the justice system." . . .

The Primacy of the Judge in Law and Syndi-Court

A primary symbol of law is the judge. Judges are the most important figures in our legal system in light of the responsibility and discretion they are given to orchestrate the proceedings before them. In fact, empirical evidence suggests that a judge can direct a jury to a verdict, even one the jury feels is unjust, as long as the jury believes the decision is legally correct. This prominence also makes judges important figures to society in general, carrying "multiple resonating meanings and associations, under-and-over-tones of mystic power."

The primary focus in syndi-court is also the judge: Judy, Gerry, Joe, and Mathis. Not only are most shows named after the judge (rather than the types of disputes or the venue), but the judge monopolizes much of the airtime. Yet, the role and authority of the syndi-court judge is one of the most significant points at which the line between law as pop culture and law as a means of regulating human affairs becomes blurred. Many individuals are not aware that syndi-court is not a real court of some type, that television brethren are not acting in the role of true judges, and in fact, that these "moral judges" are not real judges at all. To illustrate: One member of the California Commission on Judicial Performance has reported that "the public regularly submits complaints about Judge Judy and other TV judges," not "understand(ing) that Judge Judy and most of her cohorts are not present members of any judiciary." This confusion among the viewing public is hardly surprising, given that the tag-line of many of these shows intones that these are "real people, real cases." Thus, both types of judges play a critical role in the public's perception of justice. . . .

III.   Discussion: The Influence of Syndi-Court

. . . The study's results demonstrate that syndi-court cultivates in frequent viewers beliefs that judges: are (and should be) an aggressive, expressive, opinionated, inquisitive lot; should indicate their opinion about the evidence or witnesses obviously and often; and are doing so even when silent. This may impact the public and potential jurors in a number of ways. First, the behavior of television judges may "diminish the brand" in the eyes of the public. Negative opinions about television judges may be extended to a negative view of the bench generally, the outcomes with which they are associated, and the justice system that they represent. Second, the television bench may alter the public's expectations of the justice system regarding what its functions are and how its successes are measured. Third, syndi-court may alter the behavior of viewers in response to the law. They may become prone to litigation, act out television litigant behavior when they appear in court, or seek to represent themselves pro se believing they know the law. Finally, the actual behaviors exhibited by the television bench may imply to the public the appropriate behavior of the true bench and the meaning of certain behaviors. Thus, judicial syndi-court behavior becomes an unintentional interpretive guide to be (mis)used by jurors in real-life trials. Jurors may actively look for clues, misinterpret behavior, or weigh innocuous behavior in real courtrooms. Ironically, while syndi-court viewing seems to have a significant impact on viewers' perceptions of judges, study results also suggest that actual, personal experiences seem to have little impact. . . .

NOTES & QUESTIONS

1. Popular court "reality" shows can be misleading because they overemphasize the judge's role and simplify procedural issues. But is there any benefit from the popularity of such shows? Does popular culture make us smarter about the legal system?

2. What impact does Judge Judy's gender have on her persona as a television judge? Does her often harsh behavior seem more surprising because she is a woman? Traditionally, assertive women have been viewed as "unfeminine" or "bitchy." Is Judge Judy playing into that stereotype, or playing with that stereotype? Compare Judge Judy with some of her male counterparts. What kind of judicial personae do you see in Judge Joe Brown, Judge Mathis, or the male judges on *The People's Court* or *Divorce Court*? How do real-life judges cultivate their own personae for the public eye?

JUDICIAL CONFIRMATION WARS: IDEOLOGY AND THE BATTLE FOR THE FEDERAL COURTS
Sheldon Goldman
39 University of Richmond Law Review 871 (2005)

I. Why the Focus on Ideology?

Ordinarily, with the exception of the nomination of U.S. Supreme Court Justices, the nomination and confirmation of federal judges is not a subject of extensive media attention and consequently not on the minds of most Americans. During recent presidential election campaigns, including the most recent one in 2004, the opposing sides have raised the issue of the appointment of federal judges. The major party platforms adopted by each party's national convention mention judicial selection, and it is clear that the party division over judicial selection is profound. The 2004 Democratic Party platform is succinct in what it has to say about the selection of judges: "We support the appointment of judges who will uphold our laws and constitutional rights, not their own narrow agendas."

The 2004 Republican Party platform is more expansive in what it has to say about judges and judicial selection. In a special section of the ninety-two page platform, titled "Supporting Judges Who Uphold the Law," the platform states in part:

> In the federal courts, scores of judges with activist backgrounds in the hard-left now have lifetime tenure. Recent events have made it clear that these judges threaten America's dearest institutions and our very way of life. In some states, activist judges are redefining the institution of marriage. The Pledge of Allegiance has already been invalidated by the courts once, and the Supreme Court's ruling has left the Pledge in danger of being struck down again — not because the American people have rejected it and the values that it embodies, but because a handful of activist judges threaten to overturn common sense and tradition. And while the vast majority of Americans support a ban on partial birth abortion, this brutal and violent practice will likely continue by judicial fiat. . . . President Bush has established a solid record of nominating only judges who have demonstrated respect for the Constitution and the democratic processes of our republic, and Republicans in the Senate have strongly supported those nominees. We call upon obstructionist Democrats in the Senate to abandon their unprecedented and highly irresponsible filibuster of President Bush's highly qualified judicial nominees, and to allow the Republican Party to restore respect for the law to America's courts.

In another section of the platform there is a clear statement of the use of ideological litmus tests for the appointment of judges: "We support the appointment of judges who respect traditional family values and the sanctity of innocent human life."

The core constituencies of both parties, as well as scholars of law and courts, understand that judging is an art and not a science. It is a process of applying the provisions of statutes or constitutions — which may be vaguely worded — to a specific set of facts. The judge must figure out for herself what the words of the Constitution, the statute, or the precedent mean as applied to the case at hand. The study of the use of discretion by judges and how that judicial discretion impacts the claims of the parties is the study of judicial behavior, a major facet of the public law subfield within the Political Science discipline.

Studies of judicial behavior have identified judges who are judicially liberal in their willingness to give a generous interpretation to those asserting their civil rights, political liberties, or due process rights. Other judges have been identified as judicially conservative in their willingness to support government's claims that regulation of rights and liberties is in the greater public interest. And there are judicial moderates who by definition fall somewhere in between the judicially liberal and the judicially conservative. . . .

Federal judges can and do rule on almost every facet of life in the United States. Indeed, it matters who sits on the Supreme Court of the United States and on the lower federal courts. And Justices and judges are not fungible, something very well understood by advocacy groups on the right and left who have mobilized their forces and resources in the judicial confirmation wars seeking to influence presidents and senators.

NOTES & QUESTIONS

1. Lately, judges have been cast as troublemakers (Republicans complain of liberal "activist judges," and Democrats bemoan the narrow agendas of judges who must pass conservative ideological "litmus tests"). What role should ideology play in judicial confirmations?

2. Is being a judge dangerous? If you are a judge, are you in physical and spiritual peril? In popular culture, judges frequently are portrayed as powerless victims in dire peril from the profaning world of politics and money. (In *The Pelican Brief*, a hit man kills two Supreme Court Justices who were going to rule against a developer.)

3. Death is not the only peril for those involved in the power plays of judicial selection. Moral and spiritual corruption are possibilities, too. In *The Seduction of Joe Tynan* (1979), Alan Alda plays a Senator who becomes embroiled in the political machinations surrounding the nomination of a Supreme Court Justice. The judicial nominee made a racist speech some twenty years ago, and a film of that speech has recently come to light. Meryl Streep, playing a civil rights lobbyist, seductively tells Alda, "Senator, I think you are the most exciting political figure in this country today, and when I think of the splash you could make if you had this film, I get weak in the knees." She adds belatedly, "And, of course, it's the right thing to do." But is it in fact the right thing to do? The problem is that Alda's friend and mentor, an elderly Senator, has asked Alda to support this nominee because the elderly Senator does not want the nominee running against him in the next election. The question of who is the best nominee for the Supreme Court quickly becomes subsumed in backroom deals and the exchange of political favors or political threats (if you don't go along with my nominee, that favorite bill of yours will be stuck in committee forever, etc.). Ultimately, Alda betrays his old friend and abandons his family. Alda convinces himself he is doing everything for an ultimate greater good, but he fails to recognize his own corruption.

Is the judicial selection process inherently political? Is that necessarily a bad thing? What is the best method of choosing judges — periodic elections, political appointments, rotation of candidates, or other methods?

2.   The Outlaw Judge

Judges who break the law are an unsettling group in popular culture. Some, like Paul Newman's Judge Roy Bean, blithely and unconcernedly break laws left and right. Others act only after a deep moral struggle and extensive soul-searching. Does the disturbing figure of the Judge-as-Lawbreaker reflect our societal anxiety that those we "allow" to have legal power over us through our societal institutions may not have the requisite moral authority? The following excerpt describes the real Judge Roy Bean.

LAW IN TEXAS LITERATURE: TEXAS JUSTICE — JUDGE ROY BEAN STYLE

Shawn E. Tuma

21 Review of Litigation 551 (2002)

"Hear ye! Hear ye! This honorable court is now in session, and if anybody wants a snort before we start, step up to the bar and name your poison, hod-ziggity dog."

– Judge Roy Bean

I. Introduction

The mention of the name Judge Roy Bean causes most people to think of "the Hangin' Judge." Roy Bean is one of Texas's most infamous jurists. He gained his reputation by dispensing "law, of a sort, in the dusty country west of the Pecos River." It was this reputation that gave rise to his becoming known as "The Law West of the Pecos."

Roy Bean had no legal training, but he played a judge in real life; using his saloon for a courtroom, he dispensed justice while serving and consuming beer. Judge Bean, whose real name was Phantly Bean, was technically a justice of the peace who, according to some, appointed himself to office. Bean relied on one law book — a copy of the 1879 Revised Statutes of the State of Texas — and a six-shooter for the basis of his judicial decisions.

Bean's decisions were "witty, unorthodox, prejudiced, but sometimes wise decisions, defying higher courts and scandalizing jurisprudence." Frequently, he would fine culprits a round of drinks for the crowd and require lawyers to "cover" beers for Bruno — the beer guzzling black bear he kept in his saloon.

Although Bean is a legitimate historical figure, his reputation has made him mythical to such a degree that it is often impossible to distinguish between what is fact and what is fiction. According to Jack Skiles, one of the few biographers of Roy Bean:

> Numerous stories have been told about Roy Bean and many were true, or at least based on truth, but just as many were tall tales. It was only natural that the truth would be stretched, for he was a colorful character and many of the genuine stories about the old judge were strange and interesting enough to be fiction.

His colorful character is what makes Judge Roy Bean suitable for studying in the context of law and literature. Judge Bean was such a notorious jurist that many of the stories associated with him, be they fact or fiction, are widely recognized in contemporary culture. The legendary stories surrounding Bean serve as good indicators of what is on many people's social conscience. Moreover, the many character traits exemplified by stories about Judge Bean serve as good examples for the people with whom lawyers come into contact. . . .

IV. Judge Roy Bean — What a Character!

A. Bean's Respect for the Law

The legend of Judge Roy Bean has had a profound impact on giving the Old West the image with which it is saddled. Modern day authors continue to make analogies to Roy Bean to convey to their readers a rough and rowdy image or one lacking fairness and basic procedure.

Bean cared very little for the substantive law. Early in his career, he decided cases based upon the "law" as he thought it should be as he had no legal training and no law books. However, to make his decisions seem more dignified, he had a blank book in which he had written his own "staoots" in addition to his poker rules: "Cheating and horse theft," he recorded, "is hanging offenses if ketched." On another page he wrote, "A full beats a straight unless the one holding the full is not straight or is himself too full." Bean later obtained a law book, but little changed.

As Bean's career progressed, it became clear that his authority rested squarely on his one law book — though only when it supported his decision — and his six-shooter, with the latter carrying more weight. He didn't pay much attention to technicalities and ran his court on common sense principles; he simply did not see the need to keep up with the current laws. In his words, "They sent me a new book every year or so . . . but I used them to light fires with."

Even when confronted with a valid law, Bean wouldn't let it sway his decision. In one story, Bean and an attorney were debating whether there was a statute governing the attorney's case. The attorney requested to see Bean's Revised Statutes and, upon finding the statute for which he was looking, replied to Bean: "Here it is — you may start reading, Section F, Article 48." Bean looked it over carefully and ripped the page out. "It's a bad law — it's been repealed — you're still a thief."

Bean didn't always ignore laws; sometimes he would just "interpret" them to support the result that he desired. In what is perhaps Bean's most famous decision, he once ruled that he could find no Texas law prohibiting killing a "Chinaman." "I find the law very explicit on murdering your fellow man, but there's nothing here about killing a Chinaman. Case dismissed." Bean's inaccurate construction of the law may be attributed to the fact that an Irish railhand killed the Chinese worker and the Irishman was accompanied in court by a large group of fellow Irishmen there to ensure that their countrymen was treated fairly. It was only after Bean surveyed the "tough crowd" that he made his decision.

In addition to ignoring laws, Bean was not opposed to making up laws when it suited his purposes. In another of Bean's better known cases, he held an inquest over the body of a man who had fallen to his death while working. Bean searched the man's body and found a six-shooter and what is believed to be approximately forty dollars, and then he said, "I will have to fine this man $40 for carrying concealed weapons and that's my rulin'." There remains little doubt that the fine influenced Bean's decision more than the law. Bean's respect for procedure was no different than his respect for substantive law — he wasn't going to let technicalities interfere with the business of his court.

Bean is said to have "considered it a personal affront if a defendant hired a lawyer, and he chose to use jurors only on rare occasions — then selecting them from his best customers." Bean's court usually resembled an inquest, but it has been said that on occasions he actually heard evidence and decided serious cases.

The rough and rowdy way that Bean implemented his own justice demonstrates that a "system of justice" need not follow even its own rules. This system has been called "a legal system only in the Pickwickian sense that a void contract is one kind of contract." For example, one of Bean's more famous literary quotes is, "I always give 'em a fair trial before I hang 'em." In literature he was understood to be a strong proponent of stern and swift justice — justice as he saw it: "He sentenced a number of supposed horse thieves and cattle rustlers to death, sometimes on the flimsiest evidence, and these sentences were carried out. 'Give him a drink and tie him to the nearest limb! Well, what'll you have feller?' And that was all."

NOTES & QUESTIONS

1. What is appealing about a character such as Judge Roy Bean? What is subversive about an outlaw judge? Most practitioners know at least one hard-nosed, "hanging" judge. Apocryphal stories circulate about such judges, and newly minted practitioners quake in their shoes if they must make an appearance before the hanging judge. Do modern-day judges ever attempt to play into the "cowboy justice" style of judging? Is this a judicial persona that is limited to white males?

2. In his portrayal of Judge Roy Bean in *The Life and Times of Judge Roy Bean,* Paul Newman embodies the law, even draping himself in the American flag. He puts up a sign on a former brothel — "Law West of the Pecos" — and tells the itinerant preacher played by Anthony Perkins, "I am the new law in this area." However, his law is very much grounded in his perception of individual justice, and when he comes to a law he does not like, he simply rips it out of the statute book. (When a lawyer points to a statute, the Judge says, "That's a bad law. I just repealed it." He then threatens to feed the lawyer to a pet bear.) Ironically, he says, "I know the law, since I have spent my entire life in its flagrant disregard." In one of his final battles, when the Judge comes to fight by the side of the daughter he has abandoned, he clarifies that his role as a judge is to pursue justice. "Who are you?" asks a puzzled ruffian during the fight. "Justice, you sons of bitches!" the judge replies from horseback, before beginning one last rampage.

3. In *The Star Chamber*, Judge Stephen Hardin, played by Michael Douglas, feels all too keenly the disjuncture between law and justice and agonizes when he lets two alleged child molesters go on a technicality. The murdered child's father confronts Hardin in the hallway and tries to get him to look at his son's school photo. The father says, "Look at the photo. That was my boy, not a plaintiff or a statute!" Hardin protests, "I can only deal with law." The father responds, "What about justice? Do you ever deal with that?"

Near the breaking point, Hardin confesses his doubts about the system to his wife: "First day of law school, looking at law books in the library, it was like I was looking at the truth . . . in all those rows . . . The truth. The law. Nothing is right or wrong. It's either the law or it's not the law. Turns out that right and wrong count. See, the bad guys, they get hold of one of those books, they find something and I give them the prize. Doesn't matter that it wasn't put there for them, it was put there for that little kid and the five women, it doesn't matter. What happened to right and wrong? It's gotta be somewhere in one of those books."

After yet another child is murdered, Hardin contacts Judge Benjamin Caulfield, a mentor played by Hal Holbrook, who convinces Douglas to join a secret group of vigilante judges who hire hit men to kill defendants they believe to be guilty. As Caulfield says, "*We're* the goddamned law. . . . *We* are accountable, we are the judges, for Christ's sake. We are the law. . . . Someone has kidnapped Justice and hidden it in the law. Now who's better qualified than we are to find it, you tell me that?"

A revenge fantasy fuels the thirst for justice we feel as an audience, but those emotions dissolve once we learn, along with Judge Hardin, that the wrong men are going to be executed. Does the film "cheat" by making the defendants actually innocent? Would *The Star Chamber* have been a better, more honest film if the guilt of the defendants was never in doubt?

4. Can we split off our professional lives from our personal lives? What are the costs of doing so? Many of us know judges or lawyers who, like the lawyer Wemmick in Dickens' *Great Expectations* (1860), are coldly professional at work and warm and loving at home. Wemmick takes this trait so far that if you ask him the same question at work and then again at home (where he cares lovingly for his aged father), he will give two completely different answers.

Similarly, Fredric March's Judge Cooke in *An Act of Murder* (1948) is a loving husband and father at home, but his daughter (who is a first-year law student) complains that Dad stops being a human being and becomes "a talking law book" in the courtroom. (The Judge's first name is "Calvin," a name resonant with a sacred and uncompromising belief system.) When he learns his wife is terminally ill, Judge Cooke struggles with the relentless overlap between the world of law and the world of the home. He lies to his wife about her condition, the first breach of his moral code. "It's only a lie of omission," says the doctor. The Judge wretchedly responds, "[T]he thing that has always made our life so good is the truth between us." His wife's condition dramatically worsens, and Judge Cooke purposely crashes the car in which they are riding, unaware that his wife has already taken an overdose of pills. The Judge then asks the District Attorney to issue an indictment for murder, although he doesn't want a lawyer: "I've committed an act of murder, and I must be tried for it." His rigidly rule-oriented solution is that he must be punished for his actions. However, his refusal to consider the nuances of judgment shows him as a judge who may know the letter of the law, but lacks an understanding of the spirit of the law. After his trial, Judge Cooke has been educated into being a better judge. He has learned that the law is not simply the letter, but also the spirit. As he says, "A man's heart must be considered."

D. WHO JUDGES THE JUDGE?

Law or justice — where does a judge's highest duty reside? And who decides when a judge oversteps his or her prescribed boundaries, and strays too far into one realm to the neglect of the other? At one extreme we have the image of a secret vigilante Star Chamber lawlessly meting out punishments according to its own private notion of justice. At the other extreme we have the horrors of the Nazi judges in the Nuremberg trials, who followed the letter of the law and sent innocents to extermination.

The film *Judgment at Nuremberg* invites reflection on how people, even judges, come to do evil. Dan Haywood, played by Spencer Tracy, is a judge at the Nuremberg tribunals who desperately wants to understand how a seemingly moral judge such as Ernst Janning, played by Burt Lancaster, could have become so inhumane. The answer seems to lie with the distinction between law and justice. One of the defendants makes the following statement in his own defense: "I followed the concept that I believe to be the highest in my profession. The concept that says to sacrifice one's own sense of justice to the authoritative legal [oath]. To ask only what the law is, and not to ask whether or not it is also justice. As a judge, I could do no other." As a judge sitting in judgment on other judges, Tracy says, "The real complaining party at the bar in this courtroom is civilization," and condemns those "men who sat in black robes in judgment on other men, men who took part in the enactment of laws and decrees the purpose of which was the extermination of human beings."

As the next excerpt makes clear, although the Nazi judges literally are on trial, Judge Haywood also will be tried during the course of the hearings. How does one acquire the moral authority to judge the judges? Which is the higher good, law or justice? And how does a storyteller best encapsulate such wrenching real life dilemmas in a fictionalized form?

THE CONFLICTS OF LAW AND THE CHARACTER OF MEN: WRITING *REVERSAL OF FORTUNE* AND *JUDGMENT AT NUREMBERG*

Suzanne Shale
30 University of San Francisco Law Review 991 (1996)

This essay is about the collision of two worlds, the world of the law and the world of drama in the form of cinema. In it, I consider the process of writing a trial movie based on real life events. Tracing the creation of the feature film from legal and life facts helps us to understand a little of how knowledge of law moves from the legal to the popular domain, how the dramaturgy of the law itself influences popular culture, and, further, how the conventions of popular culture form the structure of popular legal knowledge. What message, to recall Marshall McLuhan, is the medium of film? I will discuss the writing of two films, *Reversal of Fortune* and *Judgment at Nuremberg*, to show how the demands of film as a narrative medium affect the stories that films tell about law. I shall argue that some movies represent far more of the nature of law than we acknowledge. But I shall also argue that Hollywood movies are bound to represent law in what might best be described as an epic form. . . .

Judgment at Nuremberg was originally a television play written by Abby Mann, who adapted his own work into an Academy-Award-winning screenplay. Directed by Stanley Kramer, and acerbically described by one critic as an "all-star concentration-camp drama with special guest victim appearances," *Judgment at Nuremberg* is based upon the trial of a group of German judges and legal officials by the United States Military Tribunal in Nuremberg in 1947. The judges (ten in Nuremberg, but only four by the time they got to Hollywood) were charged with various offenses, including crimes against humanity, complicity in the degradation of the German legal system, and denial of due process of law to defendants. All were convicted of one or more offenses and were imprisoned by the American occupying forces. Along with many other minor war criminals, they were subsequently released by the Americans only a few years after the trial ended. . . .

In preparing the screenplay of *Judgment at Nuremberg*, Abby Mann read thousands of pages of trial transcript, corresponded with the legal principals, consulted other legal authorities with knowledge of the Nuremberg war crimes tribunals, and visited Germany, where he conducted research into the Nuremberg trials. The screenplay quotes verbatim from American law and jurisprudence, and some of the characters' speeches bear traces of the Nuremberg pleadings.

To understand fully the processes by which . . . the Nuremberg trial [was] transmogrified into a satisfying feature film, we need to look on three levels at how film narratives are constructed. First, we must consider the narrative conventions that structure the paradigmatic Hollywood movie, shaping it into a tale of heroic odyssey. Second, we must look at the way in which a screenwriter creates a story from the life-stuff of events. In asking how a story emerges, I am asking how the writer creates a meaningful, thematic narrative rather than an inconsequential, flat recitation of occurrences. Third, we need to turn our minds to the problem of plot — that is, how the meaningful story is presented to the audience as a series of discrete events. Having a meaningful story in the life events, the screenwriter must still establish a satisfying way of telling it.

II. The Foundations of Form

Hollywood requires stories to embrace a distinctive principle of causality and to be plotted according to certain conventions. Hollywood stories are ones in which the leading characters are propelled into some personal odyssey, in pursuit of something they desire. By the journey's end, their experiences will have changed them in a significant way. As David Bordwell has summarized it:

> The classical Hollywood film presents psychologically defined individuals who struggle to solve a clear-cut problem or to attain specific goals.

In the course of this struggle, the characters enter into conflict with others or with external circumstances. The story ends with a decisive victory or defeat, a resolution of the problem and a clear achievement or non-achievement of the goals. The principal causal agency is thus the character, a discriminated individual endowed with a consistent batch of evident traits, qualities, and behaviors.

Bordwell argues that the principles of the conventional Hollywood narrative are not unique to the cinematic medium, but are, rather, the specific application of a "canonic" story form in American filmmaking. Research into story comprehension has identified a story structure widely used in western culture. This "canonical" story format embraces six elements: introduction of setting and characters, explanation of a state of affairs, complicating action, ensuing events, outcome, and ending. This is not so different from the three-part narrative structure embraced by Hollywood: the set up, complication, and resolution. This principle is most graphically articulated in Root's advice to "get your man up a tree," "throw stones at him," and "get him down out of the tree." If we compare the European cinematic narrative with the Hollywood product, however, it would appear that while the canonic story is widespread, it is most markedly in Hollywood that these principles of narration have been refined, exaggerated, and elevated to a hegemonic position.

Hollywood movies are stories about "character" and how character determines the outcome of life events. "Character" is the sum of a human being's personhood: biography, memory, virtues and vice, reactions, capabilities, potentiality, and weakness. In movies, we learn about such character when it is expressed in the actions which emerge from human conflict: conflicts between people, conflicts within a person, and conflicts between persons and their environments. Human lives and, perhaps even more so, movie lives, are littered with incompatible goals and incommensurate values. In the movies, it is the task of "character" to resolve the human conflicts that our goals and values create. It is always a character who takes steps, a character who makes choices, a character's responses that drive the story forward or spin it around in new directions. It is a character who overcomes, a character who changes or learns. . . .

In *Judgment at Nuremberg*, Abby Mann emphasizes the importance of character early in the film. In *Judgment at Nuremberg*, the protagonist is Judge Haywood, a man who is possessed, we learn early-on, with all of the down-home, plain-speaking, salt-of-the-earth, and man-of-the-people American virtues. His antagonist — and in many respects his antithesis — is the German judge Ernst Janning: a repressed Teutonic archetype — intellectual, aristocratic, austere. Herr Rolfe, Janning's defense counsel, bespeaks the crux of the matter at the very outset of the case. (Note that it is Ernst Janning's character that is on trial at Nuremberg. Hence, for the movie audience, it is Judge Haywood's character that will be tried in the film.) Rolfe stated:

> The avowed purpose of this Tribunal is broader than the visiting of retribution on a few men. It is dedicated to the reconsecration of the Temple of Justice. It is dedicated to finding a code of justice the whole world will be responsible to. How will this code be established? It will be established in a clear, honest evaluation of the responsibility for

the crimes in the indictment stated by the prosecution. In the words of the great American jurist, Oliver Wendell Holmes, "This responsibility will not be found only in documents that no one contests or denies. It will be found in consideration of a political or social nature. It will be found most of all in the character of men."

What is the character of Ernst Janning? Let us examine his life for a moment. He was born in 1875. Received the degree of Doctor of Law in 1907. Became a Judge of East Prussia in 1914. Following World War One, he became one of the leaders of the Weimar Republic and was one of the framers of its democratic constitution. In subsequent years, he achieved international fame. Not only for his work as a great jurist but also as the author of legal text books which are still used in universities all over the world. He became Minister of Justice in Germany in 1935.

In Ernst Janning, Abby Mann has rendered the real defendant Schlegelberger a much more sympathetic character. The real Schlegelberger played a significant role in executing the savage "Nacht und Nebel" ("Night and Fog") plan, whereby the civilians of occupied countries involved in resistance activities would be dispatched to face summary justice in secret trials in Germany. Schlegelberger was also responsible for drafting laws for the occupied territories which imposed the death sentence on Jewish and Polish citizens for nothing more than speaking out against Nazi occupation. Ironically, the Schlegelberger that the Law Reports portray, a man who acted with unmitigated inhumanity, would have been a character for cinematic purposes too stark, too villainous, and too quaintly melodramatic. The fictitious Janning, on the other hand, a smoldering amalgam of shame, pride, and repression, is the far more plausible character.

Whether hero or anti-hero, if the movie is to succeed, the audience must find itself able to identify with the protagonist. How? The most compelling invitation to identify oneself with the screen character is offered when the protagonist is forced by the narrative to make hard choices and difficult decisions. This is the moment when the audience recalls the agony of minds we would rather not make up, and are generous with our sympathy for characters who cannot avoid doing so. In the courtroom, the advocates and the judges, who must decide from moment to moment how to conduct the case, are the decision-makers. In courtroom drama, therefore, the protagonist is frequently an advocate, and if not an advocate, a judge. . . .

III. The Search for Story

Within the opportunities and constraints of the canonic structure, there is still an infinity of story choices to be made.

I want to move on now to consider the creation of story from life events. E.M. Forster illustrated the difference between flat narration and meaningful story as the difference between recounting "the king died, and then the queen died" and "the king died, and then the queen died of grief." The difference between story and a simple series of events is a principle of causality that permits us to ascribe some meaning to what happened. Story is therefore the outcome of a writer's point of view and the events with which she is concerned. Events are given story meaning by a writer's beliefs and values, and her own ethical sense of the material with which she is working.

It is the power of both law and drama that they operate analogically. In the telling of one story, we can be commanded or encouraged to bring to mind another. In some courtroom movies, as in *Reversal of Fortune*, the trial we see fought on the screen invites us to reflect only upon itself and its own meaning. In others, the trial in the movie may also argue, by implication, a quite different case. In *Judgment at Nuremberg*, the trial is ostensibly a tale about the evils of the Nazi legal system. But Mann wrote it in such a way that in the conflicts between moral right and logic and between justice and political expediency, the movie recalls not only Nazism and the Nuremberg trials, but also McCarthyism and Hollywood's complicity in it.

Many stories could have been written about the Nuremberg trials, and the story Mann told reflected his own beliefs. He constructed the courtroom scenes so that they would lead the audience toward his own views about Nazi law, rather than point ineluctably toward the Tribunal's stated conclusions. Mann felt that the judgment of the Nuremberg tribunal over-emphasized the importance of denial of due process and under-emphasized the depravity of the substantive laws under which the victims of Nazi racial ideology were tried. In his movie courtroom, Mann chose to emphasize the intrinsic inhumanity of Nazi laws. In one scene, Petersen, a confused and not very clever laborer, testifies about the proceedings that led to his sexual sterilization. When Petersen is cross-examined, Herr Rolfe has no difficulty in establishing that Petersen is indeed mentally incompetent and could legitimately have been sterilized under the eugenic laws. But Rolfe's legal "victory" brings him little satisfaction, and the audience is left with no doubt that Mann believes such laws to have been morally wrong in and of themselves, however correct the procedure by which they were enforced.

But Abby Mann also wanted to write a screenplay that reflected his concern for the state of America, as well as his compassion for the victims of the Holocaust:

> It was very much on my mind [that] there were writers like Dalton Trumbo and John Howard Lawson, writers who had been blacklisted. . . . I came after that and I tried to help them, I tried to get them jobs. And so the fact that this could happen, could have taken more steps . . . that was very important. And the big thing that was bugging me too was . . . I wanted to pierce the lie; the big lie [in Germany] was, "we didn't know about it." . . . There were certain emotional feelings that I had, I don't think that I violated the basis of the trial . . . but these things were very much on my mind.

Judgment at Nuremberg is a serious attempt to explore the significance of the Nuremberg trials, but Mann's initial outline of the film suggests a depth and sophistication diluted in the process of preparing the commercial presentation. It is this author's opinion that it was Kramer who was responsible for injecting into the movie the sentimental liberalism of which some commentators were so critical. The first outline Mann submitted to Kramer was an exploration of many more of the moral conundra of the war crimes trials than are discussed in the resulting film. Straightforwardly, there was more law in Mann's outline: more explanation of the difference between the German and American legal systems and their conceptualizations of the role of the judge; more discussion of the nature of the charges being brought against the defendants; more concern with the legitimacy of the military tribunals. The figure of Judge Haywood, too, was drawn more complex and ambivalent, an exploration of the character of a man of modest esteem as he rises, unexpectedly, to the occasion of judgment. Judge Haywood appeared in Mann's outline with a wife and daughter who served the narrative by drawing it into the sexual and material chaos of Nuremberg, in images of defeat which were to be juxtaposed against the sanitized order of the trials. The novelistic complexities that these characters introduced appear to have been sacrificed in pursuit of the entrenchment of Judge Haywood in the role of the lone protagonist, an approach that was perhaps more appropriate to the condensed cinematic form. . . .

IV. Presentation and Plot

Both Abby Mann and Nicholas Kazan had as their first creative task to discover what was, for them, the true story of the events about which they wrote. Only then could they organize events from the months and months of trial and pre-trial work into a plot capable of illustrating the aesthetic and factual truths in which they believed.

How is it possible to compress the human action of twelve months into two hours? The writer must make a highly restricted selection from factual material. He may choose to adapt the strict reality of facts to suit the needs of the emerging screenplay, or he may invent entirely new, fictitious material. . . .

[I]t seems that Abby Mann had to be persuaded to create a conventional romantic drama around the figure of his Nuremberg judge. The character of Madame Bertholt, Judge Haywood's "love interest," was born quite late. She came into existence sometime between the outline Mann initially submitted to Kramer and his first draft of the screenplay. While the love interest seems a harmless enough element in the film, it elicited vigorous complaint from the film's legal advisors. They objected that if the story was a true one, Judge Haywood's liaison would have been highly unethical. In their view, the fictional romantic subplot was defamatory to the real Nuremberg judge upon whom Haywood was based. . . .

In the earlier discussion of *Twelve Angry Men*, I touched upon that distinction, so central to art, between factual truth and dramatic truth. Plot, no less than story, may embrace the same distinction. In an early scene in *Judgment at Nuremberg*, Ernst Janning refuses to concede the jurisdiction of the tribunal:

> Haywood (addressing Janning): How do you plead to the charges and specifications set forth in the indictment against you — guilty or not guilty?

[Janning refuses to speak]

Rolfe: Your Honor. May I address the court?

Haywood: Yes.

Rolfe: The defendant does not recognize the authority of this tribunal and wishes to lodge a formal protest in lieu of pleading.

Haywood: A plea of not guilty will be entered. The prosecution will make its opening statement.

While Schlegelberger himself did not challenge the jurisdiction of the tribunal, many of the war criminals did refuse to acknowledge it. The issue of jurisdiction was discussed in the Alstotter trial, and legal scholarship was cited in judicial opinion. One member of the tribunal, Judge Blair, entered a dissenting opinion regarding the extent of the jurisdiction that the military tribunals claimed for themselves. Haywood's response, to formulate a legal answer from a refusal to speak, acknowledges an important truth about the obduracy and inescapability of trial procedures. There was, therefore, much legal truth in that fictional exchange, although Mann maintains that he wrote the scene for purely dramatic reasons. . . .

NOTE

1. The fall of a judge is particularly tragic (per Aristotle's classic definition of tragedy), for it implicates a person of great social significance, and by extension, the judge's fall from grace implicates the fall of an entire society. Spencer Tracy's character in effect judges the whole of German society during the Nuremberg trials. (That is why Marlene Dietrich's character is so eager to show him the art, music, and architecture of Germany — she desperately hopes he will weigh such things in the balance.)

E.   THE SUPREME COURT AND POPULAR CULTURE

The Supreme Court holds a strangely ambiguous place in the popular imagination. The Court is the source of ultimate judicial power and still commands great respect in the public eye. However, as the next reading points out, more people can name three of the Three Stooges than can name three Supreme Court Justices. Does popular culture care about the Supreme Court?

PAY NO ATTENTION TO THE MEN BEHIND THE CURTAIN: THE SUPREME COURT, POPULAR CULTURE, AND THE COUNTERMAJORITARIAN PROBLEM

Adam Burton

73 University of Missouri-Kansas City Law Review 53 (2004)

II. THE COURT AND POPULAR CULTURE: DEFERENCE OR IGNORANCE?

Justice Frankfurter surely was correct in his assessment of the source of the Court's authority — "sustained public confidence in its moral sanction." A separate, though overlapping, explanation of the source of the Court's authority is Barbara Perry's assertion that the Court's remoteness, its mystery, gives it power. With either explanation, the image of the Court as presented to the American public assumes heightened importance for the body's popular institutional validity within the context of the countermajoritarian difficulty. Indeed, one key factor in the confinement of the countermajoritarian to academic circles, as opposed to popular debate, is the public's continued perception, rooted in nineteenth-century jurisprudence, of the Court as a vindicator of objective Constitutional rights but not merely as a collection of power brokers interested in profiting from their positions or bluntly advancing their political agendas in a manner completely divorced form the Constitution. In this view, the public tolerates judicial review in part because it respects the judgment and independence of the Court as an institution and perceives the Justices as arbiters of law free from political entanglements in their interpretation of the Constitution.

Commentators traditionally have described the Court's public image as revered and august, remote if not mysterious. In this view, the Court appears in various guises: as a collection of Delphic oracles, Olympian gods, wizards of Oz, or as the transubstantiated incarnation of the Constitution itself. To determine whether the public really views the Court as such, it is useful to examine the ways in which the Court has been depicted in popular culture, especially in recent years, when the popular culture has become less deferential to authority figures.

Popular culture not only reflects popular views and tastes, but also informs and instructs. If the members of the Court were depicted as ordinary politicians (or worse than ordinary politicians because they cannot be voted out of office), and not as constitutional scholars, the Court's legitimacy might suffer, as Frankfurter predicted. A hagiographic popular culture, on the other hand, would reinforce the Court's authority. A popular culture that ignores the Court might fortify the Justices' ability to "skillfully avoid public accountability.". . . .

B. The Court, Jerry Springer, and *Bush v. Gore*

In recent years popular culture has assumed an increasingly prurient face — the face of Jerry Springer. The staggering success of Springer's glorified carnival freak show cum "talk show" has spawned a cultural revolution of sorts, with exhibitionist "reality" shows dominating television and pornographic film stars gracing the advertisements of once respectable corporations. Somewhere, P.T. Barnum is smiling, or perhaps lamenting the fact that he did not live in the era in which his genius could be fully exploited and appreciated.

Today's popular culture celebrates the zeitgeist of iconoclasm; reverence and restraint are passe in a culture that holds almost nothing sacred, and sarcasm and excess appear to have replaced them. The private lives of public figures are flaunted as never before, satisfying a public that seems to want to know everything about its celebrities. The change in the treatment accorded to politicians by the media and other purveyors of popular culture is illustrative of the general trend. It is impossible to pinpoint the exact moment when the culture became less deferential to authority figures and more exhibitionist in its tastes. But as late as the early 1960s, the media, by gentlemen's agreement, refrained from publishing stories concerning the private or personal affairs of President Kennedy. Most critics of culture contend that the culture changed because of the loss of trust in government, and authority figures in general, following Vietnam and Watergate.

At any rate, by the 1990s, restraint in popular culture had all but evaporated. In the most obvious example, the salivating media devoured and propagated the most lascivious details of the allegations put forth in the Starr Report, and President Clinton's sexual practices became a staple of popular culture, inspiring countless *Saturday Night Live* sketches, Monica Lewinsky Halloween costumes (complete with stained blue dress), and Monica internet fan pages, to name only a few indicators of popular culture's obsession with the story. That the most intimate details of the President's encounters, and not merely the simple fact of the encounters, could be revealed in the government's official reports is a testament to the lack of regard that our popular culture holds for the privacy of public figures. While the degree of detail might have been thought of as excessive and in poor taste in earlier times, and may have inspired sympathy for the President's situation and repulsion for his attackers, the architects of the Starr Report calculated that exposing the salacious minutiae of the President's sex acts would fascinate the American public in the age of Jerry Springer. And the new tools of information technology were quickly utilized to allow the public to satisfy its desire to know. In addition to garnering widespread television coverage, the Starr Report was available on the Internet within minutes of its official publication.

The Clinton-Lewinsky scandal is the most obvious example of the exposure of the private life of a political figure, but by no means the only one. Exposure is not limited to circumstances of scandal, sexual or otherwise. Even before the Lewinsky scandal, the private lives of the Clintons were subject to scrutiny; an audience member at a 1992 campaign speech famously asked the future President what style of underwear he preferred. The inspection of the Clintons was not limited to the family's patriarch. Chelsea's braces garnered unwanted attention, even inspiring a scene in the film *Beavis and Butt-Head Do America*. In the same vein, the arrest of President Bush's daughter, Jenna, for underage drinking also generated headlines and is manifest in expressions of popular culture.

How has the Supreme Court fared in an age of no restraint? If the Court's power is, as in Oz, equivalent to mystery, what are the implications of this culture of exposition for the Court's ability to maintain its distance from the public, and therefore its institutional clout? Or, if, as in Frankfurter's estimation, the Court's authority rests on its "moral sanction," can the Court retain its aura of moral righteousness when purveyors of popular culture pander to public tastes, coveting scandal, eager to expose and exaggerate the deficiencies of any public figure?

The Court has, even in our age, remained largely immune from attack in the avenues of mass visual popular culture. Novelists and journalists have, at times, closely scrutinized, if not excoriated, the Justices and the Court as a whole. Bob Woodward and Scott Armstrong examined the inner workings of the Berger Court in their best-selling non-fiction book *The Brethren*, in which the Justices were depicted as a body of men who engaged in petty politics not only to advance their policy preferences, but also to gratify their personal jealousies. Edward Lazarus published a similar tell-all expose of the Rehnquist Court in *Closed Chambers*. However, the Court as an institution has generally remained below the radar of representational popular culture and the more general audience it attracts, except in extraordinary circumstances, after which it again fades into relative obscurity. As I will show below, the Court's decisions sometimes frame the background of fictional productions exploring controversial social issues, such as abortion or capital punishment, and the Court has as such been portrayed as a tangential "character," sometimes without ever actually "appearing" on-screen. The Court itself, however, rarely is depicted as a subject worthy of exploration: The real Justices rarely appear on television, in the national media, or in fictitious representation. The lack of publicity can be explained in part by the Court's protection of its anonymity. Thus, "[n]o American institution has so . . . controlled the way it is viewed by the public," although that control is neither absolute nor complete.

The Court as an institution allows itself to be presented before the public in two situations: at televised confirmation hearings, over which it has no control, and in published opinions. Confirmation hearings predictably register more forcefully in popular culture, as they highlight personalities as well as issues and sometimes produce indelible images. Tellingly, the only *Saturday Night Live* sketches ever dealing directly with the Supreme Court or any Justice have been parodies of candidates in high profile confirmation hearings: Douglas Ginsburg, Robert Bork, and Clarence Thomas. The Thomas hearings, in which the circumstances presented the rare opportunity for a sex scandal, particularly registered in popular culture, and the *Saturday Night Live* skit lampooned Thomas' alleged predilection for pornography as discussed in the actual proceeding.

One might have expected that at least after Thomas was confirmed, the hearings would have damaged the Court's image — its "moral sanction" — before the American public and that, according to Frankfurter's formula, the legitimacy of the Court to render constitutional decisions would be at least somewhat compromised. Or, that the hearings would undermine the mystery behind the Court by reaffirming, in a most sensationalistic way, that the Court is composed of flawed men and women. The images of Thomas answering questions on television about pornography never have vanished from popular consciousness, and Hollywood relived the hearings in the 1999 made-for-television film *Strange Justice*. Although the films portraying the hearings continue to question Justice Thomas' moral character, the character of the Court as an institution has never been called into question as a result of the Thomas confirmation debacle.

The second type of circumstance in which the Court may raise the public's interest and figure more prominently in popular culture is when it decides a high profile, controversial, or unpopular case. The Court's widely criticized opinion in *Bush v. Gore* was arguably all three. The Court's result and, more importantly, the manner in which it reached its decision, opened the door to the serious charges that the Court improperly engaged directly in partisan politics to interfere in the 2000 election, frustrating the victory of the popular vote winner and giving the election to President Bush. While the Court had decided politically sensitive cases before, the judicial vote had never before been so evenly and predictably split on party lines and never before raised such disturbing questions regarding the Court's impartiality. In his dissent, Justice Stevens strongly recalled Frankfurter's warning about the Court's role in democracy and the possibility that *Bush v. Gore* would erode the source of the Court's authority:

> Time will one day heal the wound to that confidence that will be inflicted by today's decision. One thing, however, is certain. Although we may never know with complete certainty the identity of the winner of this year's Presidential election, the identity of the loser is perfectly clear. It is the Nation's confidence in the judge as an impartial guardian of the rule of law.

To some extent, Stevens' fears concerning the tarnished public image of the Court were realized. On January 15, 2002, just on the heels of the *Bush v. Gore* decision, CBS aired the pilot episode of *First Monday*, the first television show about the Supreme Court ever produced. ABC followed with *The Court* on March 26, 2002. Both shows, which I will discuss below, portrayed the members of the Court as squabbling politicians, not as principled interpreters of the Constitution. But neither show lasted long enough to cause a serious dent in the Court's image; *First Monday* flamed out after only one season, and *The Court* was cancelled after only three episodes. Since the cancellation of these shows, no television or movie producer has risked any project with the Supreme Court as the subject.

C.   O Brethren, Where Art Thou?: Why the Court Remains Invisible

What accounts for the Court's near invisibility in terms of recent mass cultural depictions and for the short shelf life of those depictions when they do exist, even after the unprecedented negative publicity of *Bush v. Gore*? Below, I will suggest and explore several hypotheses supporting or refuting these possibilities, using examples from the limited canon of popular culture works that depict the Court.

1. The "People" Do Not Know the Nine Justices from the Three Stooges

Public opinion polls historically show a profound lack of public knowledge about the Supreme Court and the Justices who compose it. A 1989 poll showed that 54% of the respondents could name Judge Wapner, the presiding judge on the television show *The People's Court*, while only 9% could name Chief Justice William Rehnquist as a member of the Court. In 1995, more people could name The Three Stooges (59%) than could name three Justices (17%).

If these polls accurately reflect the public's knowledge of and interest in the Court, then the traditional absence of the Court from the channels of mass culture is no mystery. Hollywood could easily predict from the numbers that the public is disinterested in the institution and that television shows or movies about the Court likely would inspire equally little interest and generate correspondingly low box office figures or Nielsen ratings. On this view, the Court's image is protected from the searching and distorting glare of popular culture by a lack of public interest and awareness: to modify Perry's calculus, ignorance equals power.

Of course, that may be putting the cart before the horse. Awareness of the Court may be low precisely because of the body's absence from popular culture. As the Court itself recognized in *Dickerson v. United States*, popular culture often serves as an educator, and a successful and prolonged representation of the Court in mass culture would probably spark public awareness in the institution. . . .

2. The Court Is Removed from the Concerns of the People

A related explanation for the limited coverage of the Court in popular culture is that the people do not care what the Court does because they do not believe it affects their lives. Indeed, apathy toward the Court would be consistent with the public's apparent view toward politics in general, if historically low voter turnout is any indicator. The view that the Court does not in fact affect people's lives, even through monumental cases such as *Brown v. Board of Education*, has some academic support, although the empirical consequences of such cases is [*sic*] a matter of debate.

However, whether or not the Court has any actual effect on people's lives is a different question from whether people perceive the Court as such. The Court frequently serves as a minor character in films that touch on the implications of the Court's decisions for ordinary Americans, underlining the importance of the institution for the general public. The Court's decision in *Brown* was and is widely viewed as an important step in the civil rights movement, especially among Southerners who vented their opposition to segregation by displaying "Impeach Earl Warren" signs. Notwithstanding the views of segregationists, *Brown* continues to stand as a landmark of racial justice in the American consciousness and was lionized as such in the critically acclaimed 1991 television movie *Separate but Equal*, starring the archetypically classy Sidney Poitier.

Furthermore, the Court's abortion decisions constantly remind Americans of the Court's power to affect their most important life choices. Every year on the anniversary of *Roe v. Wade*, or when the Court decides a case calling *Roe v. Wade* into question, advocates on both sides of the abortion controversy demonstrate their views on Maryland Avenue and around the country. Representational popular culture supports the assertion that the Court is perceived as powerful and important. The Court's power to sustain or withdraw the right to abortion has resonated in film, inspiring a litany of films about the decision. The latest television movie on the subject, *Swing Vote*, shows the inter-chambers political maneuvering behind a fictional Supreme Court's crafting of a moderate abortion decision.

The Court's capital punishment jurisprudence also has spawned a number of films depicting the effect of the decisions on society. Following the Court's decision striking down the death penalty in *Furman v. Georgia*, *Terminal Island*, co-starring a young Tom Selleck, appeared in movie theaters. After the Court in the movie strikes down California's death penalty, voters pass an initiative to exile all first-degree murderers (both male and female) to the island of San Bruno, where they are free to do whatever they like except leave. Predictably, the rule of law breaks down, and the movie degenerates into an orgy of sex and violence. But the point is made that the Supreme Court's "liberal" death penalty decision paves the way for the breakdown of orderly society.

More recently, *The Pelican Brief* reestablished the "link between individual Justices and the decisions of the Court . . . in the public mind." Starring Denzel Washington as reporter Gray Grantham and Julia Roberts as law student Darby Shaw, *The Pelican Brief* centers on the assassination of two Supreme Court Justices. Like any diligent and crafty law student, Darby figures out that the culprit is a shadowy millionaire oilman who will do anything to protect his billion dollar oil fields from the grasping green hands of an environmentalist Court. The lesson is that big money turns on the Court's pen strokes.

Thus, it does not appear that the public underestimates the power of the Court to rule on issues that affect large segments of society.

3. The Court Really Is Revered

The third possibility for the general lack of treatment of the Court in representational popular culture is that the traditional explanation for the Court's legitimacy, namely, that the public reveres the Court as it does the Constitution, is accurate. Thus, the public's view of the Court as an unassailable paragon of virtue is exceptional in an otherwise irreverent age, and people leave the Court alone or depict it in glowing terms because, despite periodic criticism of judicial opinions, "residual Court-worship" and "judge-worship" exist among the American public.

The depictions of the Court in the 1930s might seem to draw this argument into question. However, even though the decisions of the Court were unpopular, and the popular culture reflected the public's disfavor with the Court, the public remained supportive of the institution and never seriously questioned either the legitimacy of judicial review or the commitment of the Justices to the principles of the Constitution. Even the Court's image as "nine old men" had been repaired in 1943, when MGM released *A Stranger in Town*. In that film, a small town attorney trying to break a ring of corrupt officials runs for mayor. His attempts to clean up the town's political system are frustrated until he gets help from a visiting fisherman, who turns out to be vacationing Supreme Court Justice Jon Josephus Grant. Thus, the Court, represented by the fictional Justice Grant, is a secretive and anonymous but benevolent force, a deus ex machina saving justice from politics.

Other films have portrayed the Court's most popular decisions, promoting the Court as a guarantor of justice. As noted above, the 1991 television movie *Separate but Equal* celebrated the Court's decisions ending segregation. In 1980, Henry Fonda and Jose Ferrer co-starred in *Gideon's Trumpet*, a well received television film dramatizing the litigation of *Gideon v. Wainwright*, in which the Court interpreted the Sixth Amendment as guaranteeing the provision of counsel at state expense for anyone accused of a felony.

More recently, the Court has been portrayed in reverential terms in *The People vs. Larry Flynt*. This Sony Pictures' 1996 film dramatizes the life of pornographer Larry Flynt and culminates in his successful First Amendment battle before the Court in *Hustler Magazine v. Falwell*. While feminist critiques attacked the film for making a hero out of Flynt, director Milos Forman claimed that the film was a "love letter to the Supreme Court" and that "the real hero of [the] film is . . . the Supreme Court of the United States." Following from Forman's vision, the on-screen Court is portrayed as serene and dignified, if not heroic. Even the on-screen Flynt, who throws oranges and spews profanities at lower court judges throughout the film, acts with relative decorum in the Supreme Court while his lawyer argues his case. The Court and its members, as the impartial, ultimate expositor of the Constitution, are thus automatically worthy of a respect that the lower court judges do not enjoy, and the film celebrates the Court as a defender of the Constitutional rights of even unpopular causes or despicable characters.

a. The Justices as People, Not Oracles

The People vs. Larry Flynt comports with Professor Westin's claim that residual "Court-worship" and "judge-worship" exist among Americans. Although unquestioning and exalted respect for the Court is certainly one strain in popular culture's representations of the body, it is not the dominant strain. Professor Laura Krugman Ray has demonstrated that most judicial novels featuring the Court have shown the Justices as normal people, not as legal shamans or deities, and that some authors have even reveled in the commonplace deficiencies of the Justices, especially since the publication of *The*

Brethren. Professor Ray's claim that the publication of The Brethren "altered irrevocably the public perception of the Supreme Court" may be overstated, but she accurately points out that most modern representations of the Court have not portrayed it or the Justices who compose it in an aura of "impenetrable dignity and rectitude." *First Monday in October* employed the Court as a backdrop for a romantic comedy, portraying the members of the Court as regular and accessible, not as uptight and unapproachable. Even more to the point, the continued fascination with the Thomas hearing illustrates popular culture's unwillingness to let a scandal drop even when the subject of that scandal is a Supreme Court Justice. Thus, respect for the individual Justices as stony guardians of the law is no longer automatic.

b.   The Justices as Political Manipulators

Works depicting Justices as flawed characters have arguably distinguished between the individual member of the Court and the Supreme Court as an institution, sometimes showing the Justice in an unflattering light while simultaneously upholding the Court as "an institution of dignity and authority." Showing the idiosyncrasies of personal disputes among the Justices as individuals is different from showing that these quirks result in arbitrary decisions or that Justices tailor their decisions to spite their colleagues, either of which might call into question the legitimacy of the institution. Likewise, showing that an individual Justice has personal political opinions and fixed moral guideposts is a far cry from accusing the Justices of regularly engaging in partiality in rendering decisions — this is the familiar academic distinction between high politics and low politics, and it in part explains why maintaining mystery is not essential for the Court to retain its authority.

However, showing the Justices as compromisers and dealmakers and not as principled decision-makers, i.e., showing the institutional processes of rendering a decision as no different in timbre than Congressional or Presidential legislative processes, might undermine respect for their decisions. Mr. Dooley long ago commented on the Court's tendency to engage in political decision-making. But *Bush v. Gore* opened the Court to more severe institutional criticism, as it appeared to many that the Republican-majority Court was engaging in low politics, rather than valid and well-reasoned constitutional analysis, when its decision resulted in the appointment of George W. Bush as President. *Bush v. Gore* and the attendant controversy inspired new interest in the Court, and both CBS and ABC premiered television shows about the Court as an institution in 2002. Both networks believed that public interest in the Court would support television shows illuminating the inner workings of the Court, dispelling the mystery of the tribunal's proceedings and exposing the Court's decision-making process as both a highly political and highly personal affair. *First Monday* producer, Donald P. Bellisario, explained the premise of the show: "I really wanted to pull the ol' curtain aside like Toto did and show the wizard behind it. Or in this case, the nine wizards." In this way, *First Monday* and *The Court* were poised to become fictional television versions of *The Brethren*, propagating the themes of that book to a more widespread and general audience and in the process damaging the Court's prestige.

Neither show quite lived up to *The Brethren* in style or critical acclaim. *First Monday* starred Joe Mantegna as the recently appointed, politically moderate Justice Joe Novelli and James Garner as mean-spirited conservative Chief Justice Thomas Brankin. *First Monday* portrayed the Court as the ultimate arbiter on serious issues, although it often addressed them in clichéd terms or with inappropriate caprice. In only thirteen episodes, the Court decides cases on capital punishment, teenage abortion, and the "three strikes law." CBS' impish Court also hears cases on whether dwarves are protected by the ADA and whether the First Amendment protects polygamists.

First Monday attempted to depict the Court's decision-making process in the style of NBC's popular drama about the President, *The West Wing*. *First Monday* portrayed the Court as unabashedly political, suggesting that the Justices' chambers are but settings for cigar smoke-filled backroom deals and that politics, not legal reasoning or precedent, is the only relevant factor in the resolution of a case. Furthermore, *First Monday* overemphasized the roles of the law clerks, who are portrayed as sexy, glamorous, and cocky.

Producer Don Bellisario admitted to taking liberties with accuracy in the interests of creating dramatic plots: "[Q]uite honestly, you're creating a TV series. You're trying to entertain." But the inaccuracies of the show were more than subtle, leading one television critic to quip, "Nothing about . . . *First Monday* is believable except the set." For example, *First Monday* implausibly shows one of the clerks discovering a botched autopsy report in a death row case, as if the clerks' job approximated that of Columbo or Magnum P.I., and the Justices ask obnoxious and arrogant questions directly of the parties, instead of the lawyers. But these factual inaccuracies were the least of the show's flaws. Most critics found the show's writing lacking, at times even laughable, and *First Monday* was cancelled on May 13, 2002, due to low ratings.

ABC's *The Court* fared even worse, even though critics favorably compared the show's writing to that of *First Monday*. Starring the likeable Sally Field as Justice Kate Nolan, a recently appointed moderate in an ideologically divided Court, *The Court* attempted to focus more on the inner workings of the Court than on the flurry of Constitutional issues dealt with in *First Monday*. The first episode of ABC's show dealt with the appointment of Kate Nolan to the Court. The popular governor of Ohio, Nolan is appointed in only six hours despite her lack of a judicial record and her refusal to answer questions regarding her position on important issues. But the implication is that we can trust her to vote with her conscience and that we can trust her judgment. After all, this is no ordinary stealth candidate; this is Sally Field.

Like *First Monday*, *The Court* portrays the Justices as politically motivated actors, separating the Justices into "teams" of conservatives and liberals. *The Court* also raises questions concerning the important role of law clerks, although the young, good-looking, and competitive law clerks are portrayed as having "far too large an effect on the outcome of the cases." In the second episode, Justice Nolan makes a decision in an important case based on the misleading information of her ambitious young clerk, raising questions about who is really in charge of important Supreme Court opinions. Despite Ms. Field's best efforts, the show was cancelled after only three episodes and declining ratings. . . .

4. Popular Culture Stifles Public Debate

A fourth possibility for the dearth of treatment for the Court in popular culture is that the tawdriness of the culture itself discourages producers and consumers from paying attention to the institution. The Supreme Court cannot slake the public appetite for scandal and sex except on bizarre occasions, so producers turn elsewhere for subject matter. The world of the Court is filled with thinking and writing, which is not exactly the stuff of Perry Mason, or even Judge Judy. The Supreme Court and its discussion of arcane legal matters, which take time and concentration to grasp, fail to provide satisfying material for the culture of instant gratification. Popular culture could therefore only discuss the institutional values of the Supreme Court in a most cursory (or worse, inaccurate) fashion. The mission of Hollywood, and television in particular, is to entertain (and thereby keep the attention of consumers), not to educate.

There may be something to the claim that the culture of instant gratification has decreased the quality of public debate. But the major flaw of this argument is that we have not seen a major drop-off from production of shows with the Court as subject matter in relation to earlier time periods with different cultural backdrops. Indeed, the popular culture of earlier time periods featured the Court no more often than today's. The popular culture media of earlier times were, of course, much different, but within those media the Court was not prominently featured.

5. Popular Culture, Social Utility, and Democracy

The social utility of popular cultural depictions of the Court in the modern mass media remains questionable. Exposing the Court as a policy-making body and increasing the general level of knowledge about the Court's proceedings might benefit democracy by fostering debate about the Court's place in the government. However, such depictions might also misinform the public about the Court in the interests of making it seem more dramatic, exaggerating the deficiencies of the body and its members. The public might also become more knowledgeable about the fictional Court than about the real Court and blur the line between the two. As Richard Sherwin put it, "[w]hatever the visual mass media touch bears the mark of reality/fiction confusion." Neither exaggerating the heroism or deficiencies of the Court nor blurring the line between fact and fiction would serve to inform the public about the Court or inspire greater public accountability from the Court. There are two negative possibilities that might result from the exaggeration of the role that personal ideology plays in Court decisions. The first possibility is to legitimize the role of "low politics" in judicial decision-making. As Judge Harry Edwards has argued with regard to lower court judges, if the public expects the Justices to decide cases according to blunt partisan ideology, the Justices may be tempted to conform to this perception; the inappropriate politicization of the Court would thus become a self-fulfilling prophecy. This outcome is not likely, however, among Justices who take their role seriously. The second, and more likely, possibility is that Senators or the President might use widespread public perceptions of a Court run amok, propagated and dramatized in fictional images, to further their own careers at the expense of the judiciary. In 1968, President Nixon's Law and Order campaign played on popular discontent at the perceived overreaching of the Warren Court, especially in the field of criminal procedure. Today's Senate also vigorously pursues judicial appointments as a political and electoral issue. The point here is not to pass judgment on the propriety of increasingly politicizing judicial appointments — the Constitution surely anticipates such an outcome, and political struggle over appointments does not in itself decrease the likelihood that quality jurists will be appointed to the Court. Rather, the point is to illustrate the possible negative effects of distorted popular culture depictions of the Court to that process. Moreover, if the Court's appearances in popular culture mostly are limited to the rare occasions when the Court is involved in scandal, and popular culture serves as a tracker for the Court's mishaps, then maybe the absence of the Court from fictional television is a good thing.

Some critics argue that the Court might receive more public attention, and possibly more attention in popular culture, if oral arguments were televised. Then, the Court would receive fuller treatment in public discourse, as opposed to appearing only on the rare occasion of public scandal or other sporadic treatment. However, like C-SPAN for Congress, a C-SPAN for the Court's arguments is unlikely to attract a wide audience. To the extent that television news might air portions of oral arguments, it would likely dilute the arguments into ten-second sound bites, taking arguments out of context.

III. CONCLUSION

Popular culture has not yet injured the legitimacy of the Court. While the age of deference is apparently over, and Supreme Court Justices sometimes are depicted as real people with political agendas and moral flaws, Hollywood has yet to raise the issue of whether and how an unelected and unaccountable Court should be making important decisions that affect society. Popular culture, and television in particular, has difficulty portraying such issues in an appropriate manner without distorting facts and arguments in its efforts to entertain. And the failure of recent programs about the Court has ended the body's brief run in the spotlight of popular culture for the time being, returning the Court to its familiar place behind the curtain.

The Court's retreat from popular culture following its short appearance in the spotlight after *Bush v. Gore* has not, however, lowered the curtain entirely. The momentum of public interest has surely shifted away from the Court for the time being, and it will likely be a long time (if ever) before the Court decides another opinion [sic] that matches the controversy of *Bush v. Gore*. However, it is clear that the Court is not an inherently inappropriate subject for today's popular culture, and it would take only good dramatic writing to capture rating shares or box office figures. We have not yet seen any well-conceived movies that focus on the Court or the Justices as their subject. But the critical acclaim of several television movies about the Court, the Justices, or important cases, such as *Separate but Equal* and *Gideon's Trumpet*, suggests that successfully portraying the Court in a big screen movie would not be an impossible task and likely would be easier than doing so in a weekly television show.

NOTES & QUESTIONS

1. Should Supreme Court arguments be televised? Would the educational value of televising oral arguments outweigh any potential negative effects (such as grandstanding by lawyers or perhaps by Justices, a "media circus" atmosphere, the reduction of complex arguments to sound bites on the evening news, etc.)?

2. What would it take to have a successful television series about the Supreme Court (along the lines of *The West Wing*)? Do you agree with Adam Burton's hypothesis that the Supreme Court is all about thinking and writing, and may not encompass enough "sexy" material for a hit show?

Chapter 7

JURIES

A. FILMOGRAPHY

12 Angry Men (1957)

The Juror (1996)

Jury Duty (1995)

Runaway Jury (2003)

Trial by Jury (1994)

B. WHAT THE JURY MEANS TO US

A juror's lot is a hapless one in most popular films. Everything starts inno-cently enough, with a naïve citizen dutifully responding to a summons for jury duty. The situation, however, degenerates speedily, with the juror being threatened, harassed, and assaulted by mafia hit men and various and sundry criminals. Soon, the hapless juror is forced to sway the deliberations in the defendant's favor or else her child will be killed by the defendant's goons. Finally, unable to trust anyone, our beleaguered juror has to single-handedly kill the villain with an ice-pick in an isolated mansion while she is seductively dressed like Rita Hayworth in a glamorous evening gown. (See *Trial By Jury* and *The Juror* for suitable examples.) Alternatively, in *The Devil and Daniel Webster*, a classic film from 1941, the jury actually consists of a group of damned souls — evildoers called up from their sufferings in hell to sit on a trial for the soul of a New Hampshire farmer. (It must have been a toss-up as to which was worse — jury duty or hell.) In perhaps the most unspeakable option, the juror can suffer the indignity of being Pauly Shore (*Jury Duty*). No wonder we look forward to jury duty with all the eager anticipation we give to a root canal.

In real life, even if you respond to a jury summons, dutifully sit through a lengthy trial, and work hard in deliberations to reach a verdict, there is always the chance the media will reduce the whole complex trial to a 30-second sound bite and talking heads will gleefully ask, "What were the jurors thinking?"

It is all about power. The jury is a powerful, profoundly democratic institu-tion at the heart of our system of jurisprudence. Perhaps the imperiled juror in popular culture reflects a cultural anxiety not that jurors are powerless, but that they in fact can be extremely powerful. (A juror in *Runaway Jury* brings the entire gun industry to its knees.) The type of power is deceptively ordinary — it is the power of talk. "I just want to talk about it," says Henry Fonda as the lone juror holding out against a guilty verdict in a murder case (*12 Angry Men*). That talking, that idea of the give and take of discourse among a group of citizens, resonates strongly as an American ideal. In the next readings, consider what the jury stands for in contemporary American culture.

INTRODUCTION TO THE JURY AT A CROSSROAD: THE AMERICAN EXPERIENCE
Nancy S. Marder
78 Chicago-Kent Law Review 909 (2003)

Introduction: Popular Portrayals of the Jury

The American jury is an institution that has proven resilient in the past and yet remains vulnerable in the future. Although national polls show that the American populace continues to think highly of juries, that citizens who actually have served on juries give high marks to their experience, and that judges, for the most part, agree with decisions rendered by juries, the jury remains under attack in the popular press and many legislatures.

Over the past few years, press coverage of jury trials has been somewhat critical, at least in several high-profile cases. In press coverage, criminal juries have been faulted for reaching erroneous verdicts and civil juries have been chastised for awarding excessive damages. The press typically has attributed the erroneous verdicts to juror bias or sympathy and the excessive damages to juror incompetence or sentiment.

Just a few of the high-profile jury trials that garnered headlines in recent years serve to illustrate the press's generally critical portrayal of these juries. For example, the juries in the state criminal trial of police officers Stacey Koon and Laurence Powell for the beating of motorist Rodney King and the state criminal trial of O.J. Simpson for the murders of Nicole Brown Simpson and Ronald Goldman received largely negative treatment in much of the press. Both juries failed to convict the defendants. In both cases, much of the press portrayed the jurors as having reached the wrong verdict out of prejudice against the victim or sympathy for the defendant.

Civil juries have been portrayed in an unflattering light as well. One of the best known civil cases in which the jury came under blistering attack was the McDonald's coffee cup case. In that case, the jury awarded Stella Liebeck, the elderly woman who scalded herself on McDonald's coffee, punitive damages of $2.7 million. The jury was lambasted for this award in almost every newspaper account of the case. What received little attention in the press, however, were the facts of the case including the following: McDonald's served coffee that was significantly hotter than that of other eateries; it previously received hundreds of complaints by people who had been burned, but nevertheless, McDonald's chose not to lower the temperature of its coffee or to warn customers; Ms. Liebeck, who had been severely burned, required skin grafts, yet McDonald's had refused to pay her medical expenses, which was all that she initially had sought; and the damage award was likely to be reduced by the trial judge through remittitur, which it eventually was.

Although the McDonald's jury became emblematic in the press for much that was wrong with the civil jury system, this jury was not alone in receiving condemnation for its damage award. Numerous other cases in which the jury awarded damages that the press depicted as excessive contributed to this view of the civil jury as having gone awry. Indeed, if one were to read only newspaper accounts of civil jury trials, one would conclude that most juries award excessive damages, and that they do so because they sympathize with the plaintiffs at the expense of corporations. Coverage of cases involving tobacco, asbestos, and other types of product liability paint this picture. Yet, empirical studies indicate otherwise.

Legislatures, both at the state and national levels, are intent upon responding to the so-called crisis in jury behavior. A number of state legislatures have limited the types of cases that civil juries can hear and have capped the damages that civil juries can award, at least for pain and suffering. Recently, the U.S. House of Representatives passed a bill that would cap at $250,000 the damages that civil juries could award for pain and suffering in medical malpractice suits, although the Senate refused to consider the bill. The issue, though temporarily defeated, is likely to resurface because "President Bush has made jury award caps a central piece of his agenda for tort law changes."

The press's portrayal of the jury as an institution in need of fixing, and the interest of the executive and legislature in fixing it quickly, should raise concerns for those who care about and study the jury. Although press coverage of the jury is certainly not monolithic and not every article is a critique, many articles, particularly in high-profile cases, paint a picture of an institution that is unreliable and erratic at best, and biased and extreme at worst. Legislatures, too, have shown a deep distrust of the jury and have responded with mechanisms that would further limit the power of the jury, such as capping civil jury awards, or would further limit the power of the individual juror, such as abandoning the unanimity requirement in criminal jury verdicts. Although press depictions of and legislative reactions to the jury are not the only sources of popular images of the jury, they certainly contribute to some of the more powerful portrayals.

I.   Possible Explanations for Unflattering Portrayals of the Jury

Why do the press and legislatures view the jury as an institution in need of repair? The press could be reporting, and legislatures responding to, problems that actually exist. There is no doubt, for example, that high medical malpractice insurance premiums for doctors are real and driving some doctors to reexamine whether they can afford to remain in practice. Whether jury awards are responsible for the high insurance premiums or whether other factors, such as insurance practices, are at work, is still unknown, though many members of Congress have concluded that the jury is to blame.

Another explanation for the critical press coverage is that a more sensational view of the jury will sell newspapers, and so the press focuses on that story. After all, a jury gone awry makes for a more interesting, dramatic story than a jury that is functioning properly and doing its job. The press's emphasis on what is wrong with the jury helps to persuade legislators and the public that the jury needs to be "fixed."

Yet another explanation for the critical view of juries expressed by the press and legislatures alike is that the jury is a convenient scapegoat. Juries consist of laypersons who are summoned for jury duty and who serve for one trial and then return to their private lives. They have no particular stake in defending the institution. Thus, the jury can be criticized and there is no repeat player to come to its defense. Individual jurors might speak out after a trial and defend their verdict, if it has been criticized, but then they return to their private lives and any further criticism goes unchallenged. Judges cannot comment on cases that might go up on appeal, and in any event, they usually are quite restrained in making statements outside of their judicial opinions. Lawyers, especially those on the winning side, could speak out in the jury's defense, but their views would be seen as those of self-serving advocates, not disinterested observers.

Finally, another explanation might be that the press and legislatures, consisting of professional journalists and politicians respectively, distrust an institution consisting entirely of laypersons. Although, on one level, the fact that the jury is an institution of ordinary citizens temporarily summoned to serve is a source of national pride, on another level, jury composition is a source of national distrust. How can laypersons perform the tasks with which they are charged in this increasingly specialized world in which we usually depend on professionals or experts?

II. Potential Harms from Such Portrayals

Critical press coverage and legislative distrust of the jury can lead to a number of harms to the jury. One harm is that press and legislative focus on perceived weaknesses of the jury may deflect attention from weaknesses of other institutions. For example, the high medical malpractice premiums, currently attributed to excessive jury awards, actually may be the result of insurance practices. The jury may simply be a convenient target. However, there is no one to defend the institution of the jury on an on-going basis, or to look after its interests as lobbyists are paid to do for other institutions and interest groups, such as the insurance industry.

Moreover, the press's and legislatures' focus on some perceived weaknesses of the jury system may obscure more serious shortcomings of the jury that are worthy of attention, but are not receiving it. Unfortunately, the jury weaknesses that both the press and legislatures focus on are likely to be driven by vocal or influential constituencies rather than by the needs of jurors, or even parties to litigation.

A third harm is that legislatures, at least with respect to the jury, tend to look for quick-fix solutions. Such reforms are not finely calibrated to intrude as little as possible into the workings of the jury, nor are they developed from the jury's perspective. Rather, these remedies tend to take power away from the jury. Legislators do not seem to consider a less blunt approach, such as providing jurors with the tools they need to perform their tasks more effectively. For example, in the debate over whether juries have the expertise to decide certain kinds of cases, the legislative response in some states has been to take the cases away from the jury, rather than to consider whether juries should be permitted to take notes, to ask questions, and to take written copies of the jury instructions into the deliberation room. Although these practices would help juries in all cases, they would be particularly beneficial in complex or highly technical areas of the law.

A fourth harm in focusing solely on what juries are doing wrong is that it distracts both the press and legislatures from considering what juries are doing well. Perhaps this is an unfair criticism because it is not the press's job to provide "good news" or the legislature's job to commend institutions for good performance, but to fix institutions that fall short. One consequence, however, is that critical coverage and debate dominate and obscure the virtues of the jury. What is lost from public consideration is the way in which the jury works properly in the myriad jury trials that never find their way into press stories. What is lost in the legislative debate is the way in which the jury can be made into an even stronger institution by giving jurors the tools they need to do their job more effectively.

Finally, another harm is that the press and legislatures, in framing the debate about the jury, focus on very narrow functional roles for the jury. Neither the press nor legislature has the luxury of exploring the aspirational goals for the jury, of articulating a vision of the jury; rather, this is the province of academics.

NOTES & QUESTIONS

1. Mark Twain wryly commented, "We have a criminal jury system which is superior to any in the world; and its efficiency is only marked by the difficulty of finding twelve men every day who don't know anything and can't read." *Fourth of July Speech* (1873). Is a verdict too important to be left up to, as the old saw goes, twelve people who weren't smart enough to get out of jury duty?

2. Why are there so many negative portrayals of juries in the media? Is it simply a case of the media ignoring the vast majority of cases where juries do a good job? Or have juries (particularly civil juries) become obsolete and ineffective in this age of complex litigation and highly specialized cases? If the jury at one point in history served a vital democratic purpose, is that function still necessary? Consider the following reading.

ECHOES OF THE FOUNDING: THE JURY IN CIVIL CASES AS CONFERRER OF LEGITIMACY
Victoria A. Farrar-Myers & Jason B. Myers
54 SMU Law Review 1857 (2001)

I. THE JURY AS A POLITICAL INSTITUTION

The Framers of the United States Constitution developed a political system to protect American citizens against tyranny. To guard against tyranny by a minority, the Framers adopted a system of majority rule. To protect against tyranny of the majority, they developed an elaborate system of checks and balances in which political power and authority were split among various political institutions. This framework, coupled with the Bill of Rights added to the Constitution during the first session of Congress, created a limited government that flows from the popular sovereignty of the American citizenry and at the same time protects that sovereignty.

After Alexis de Tocqueville traveled throughout America, he compiled his insights on the still-new American political system in the classic *Democracy in America*. At the end of his discussion of "what tempers the tyranny of the majority," Tocqueville distinguished the jury system as a political institution as compared to a judicial one. In terms of the jury's role in "facilitating the good administration of justice," he acknowledged, "its usefulness can be contested." But in terms of the jury as a political institution, he insisted that it "should be regarded as one form of the sovereignty of the people." The jury system provided a means by which the American citizenry could participate in and make decisions regarding the political system: "There is always a republican character in it, inasmuch as it puts the real control of affairs into the hands of the ruled, or some of them, rather than into those of the rulers." For Tocqueville, the jury's role represented as important an expression of popular sovereignty as voting.

Tocqueville also noted that the use of the jury system is "bound to have a great influence on national character" and that such "influence is immeasurably increased the more [juries] are used in civil cases." Among the ways in which Tocqueville saw the jury system enhancing the national character:

> "Juries, especially civil juries, instill some of the habits of the judicial mind into every citizen, and just those habits are the very best way of preparing people to be free."

> "It spreads respect for the courts' decisions and for the idea of right throughout all classes."

> "Juries teach men equity in practice. Each man, when judging his neighbor, thinks that he may be judged himself."

> "Juries teach each individual not to shirk responsibility for his own acts, and without that manly characteristic no political virtue is possible."

"Juries invest each citizen with a sort of magisterial office; they make all men feel that they have duties toward society and that they take a share in its government."

"Juries are wonderfully effective in shaping a nation's judgment and increasing its natural lights. That, in my view, is its greatest advantage."

"I regard it as one of the most effective means of popular education at society's disposal."

For Tocqueville, jurors were more than just participants in the legal process. They served as a vital component of the American political system.

Let us now fast-forward approximately two centuries from the framing of the Constitution and Tocqueville's travels. The American experiment in guarding against tyranny has proved successful, and the country has grown up from the youthful nation that Tocqueville experienced. One change that has accompanied America's growth is that the jury system's role as a political institution seems to have receded into the background. Instead of the positive benefits that the jury system provides, news stories on juries focus more on their excesses and the ways in which jurors pervert the legal process. Most Americans probably are familiar with the jury that awarded $2.7 million to an elderly woman who, after spilling coffee on herself, sued McDonald's for serving the drink too hot; or with the jury in Florida that arguably ignored the judge's instructions in awarding $145 billion in a suit brought against tobacco companies. Juries are often seen as out of control and in need of being reined in.

As hinted at by the reference to the McDonald's and tobacco litigation, this criticism is levied largely against the use of juries in civil proceedings. But it is not a recent development. Tocqueville's words of praise aside, ever since the days of America's Founding and continuing today, many have questioned the need for juries in civil cases. If the jury system does help educate the citizenry and "gives them added confidence in democracy," as Judge Jerome Frank asked, "can that contention be proved? Do not many jurors become cynical about the court-house aspects of government? And should education in government be obtained at the expense of litigants?" For critics of the jury system, one of the best ways to rein in juries would be to limit the role of the jury in resolving civil disputes. . . .

NOTES & QUESTIONS

1. Is the political role of the jury still a viable goal? Or is the potential for a miscarriage of justice too steep of a price to pay for the benefits of civic education?

2. Does the jury system still retain a moral authority in popular culture? The next reading suggests that we must not unduly romanticize the role of the jury system as a democratic institution, nor unduly demonize it in popular culture. Rather, the significance of the jury is in its very ordinariness. Both good and bad, jury verdicts are among the most visible workings of democracy in our justice system.

"THE IMAGE WE SEE IS OUR OWN": DEFENDING THE JURY'S TERRITORY AT THE HEART OF THE DEMOCRATIC PROCESS
Lisa Kern Griffin
75 Nebraska Law Review 332 (1996)

I. INTRODUCTION: THE JURY IN THE SPOTLIGHT

Public disenchantment with the criminal justice system increasingly centers on the jury. Sensational stories, like the Simpson, King, and Menendez trials, undermine the legitimacy of jury verdicts and call into question the compatibility of the institution with the ideal of the rule of law. Such controversial verdicts have prompted reforms to limit the jury's power and to restructure the jury system. While the parade of celebrity trials attracts the spotlight, 1.2 million people participate in jury deliberations each year, and they generally reach a verdict that the presiding judge considers correct. Moreover, rather than subverting legality, the jury nurtures it by allowing for community input within the framework of the rule of law, and by linking the public to the institution of the courts.

The jury system operates under a complex mandate: Jurors must affirm that laws appear legitimate to the community, protect the interests of individual defendants, and strive for an accurate verdict. The jury, like the rule of law, negotiates the "tolerable accommodation of the conflicting interests of society." Where the jury sacrifices degrees of certainty, it also enhances flexibility and individualized justice; when public condemnation of an individual influences a verdict, the individual suffers, but there is a corresponding gain in community cohesion and the perceived legitimacy of the system. Many verdicts generate criticism about the balance the jury strikes between these competing interests. To those most concerned about the harm to the community, a jury that fails to convict an unpopular defendant appears unjust. Because the jury's consideration of the evidence is mediated through an adversarial process, fairness to the individual does not always produce the result the public expects. The jury represents the public's interests, but the deliberative process also tempers the anger and fear of the community and protects individual defendants from hasty judgments.

The language used by both critics and defenders of the jury system reveals tensions between democratic values and countermajoritarian fears of tyranny by the people. William Blackstone called the jury "the palladium of liberty," Thomas Jefferson deemed it the touchstone of our peace and safety, and Patrick Devlin praised it as "the lamp that shows that freedom lives." But critics of the jury emphasize its tensions with founding principles like the rule of law rather than its compatibility with democratic foundations like liberty and equality. Judge Jerome Frank considered the jury incompetent, prejudiced, and lawless. He cited jurors as obstacles to legal certainty because they apply "laws they don't understand to facts they can't get straight." Judge Frank responded to the champions of the jury system's democratic origins that what "was apparently a bulwark against an arbitrary tyrannical executive, is today the quintessence of governmental arbitrariness. . . . If anywhere we have a 'government of men,' in the worst sense of that phrase, it is in the operations of the jury system."

Although some of our romantic ideals about jury service are mythical, many popular criticisms of the jury are also misguided. Jury verdicts give effect to beliefs held by a substantial portion of the public. When those beliefs are deemed illegitimate, efforts at change should focus not on the jury system, but on the underlying sources of the disjunction. Moreover, when the jury appears to falter, forces beyond its control often cause the failure. It is only the most visible component of a complex system, and criticisms of the jury reflect failings in other workings of the court as well. The public, however, takes a results-oriented view of the law, and "clues to the legitimacy of courts are not to be found in the structure of doctrine, or in the formal texts of jurists, but in the broad messages traveling back and forth between the public and the organs of popular culture." Popular culture portrays the criminal justice system as an obstacle course of legal rules that prevent police and prosecutors from doing their jobs. Because of both fictional depictions and the increasing coverage of real cases, many believe that all defendants have the opportunity to go to court and that high profile jury trials constitute typical cases.

The jury system lies at the heart of our democratic system, but it has lost much of its moral authority in the popular legal culture. . . .

II. DEMOCRATIC IDEALS

The direct and raw character of jury democracy makes it our most honest mirror, reflecting both the good and the bad that ordinary people are capable of when called upon to do justice. The reflection sometimes attracts us, and it sometimes repels us. But we are the jury, and the image we see is our own.

Jeffrey Abramson, *We, The Jury* (1994). . . .

NOTES & QUESTIONS

1. What is your response to Judge Jerome Frank's suggestion in the preceding excerpt that jurors apply "laws they don't understand to facts they can't get straight"? Are jurors too incompetent to handle the complexities of a trial? Should we hand the trial process over to professionals? Or are these the wrong questions to ask, because a jury's purpose is not efficiency of judgment? How might we re-think the jury for the twenty-first century?

RETHINKING THE JURY
Phoebe A. Haddon
3 William & Mary Bill of Rights Journal 29 (1994)

III. THE CASE FOR JURY DECISION-MAKING

What are the distinctive values of civil jury decision-making? Often "[e]nthusiasts of the jury have tended to lapse into sentimentality and to equate literally the jury with democracy," without more clearly delineating what are decision-making qualities and distinguishing truth-determining features which justify its use. Litigators, even when supportive of the jury guarantee, often cast jurors as pawns in a litigation game. Conscious that prejudice in their communities runs high, citizens, when asked, express serious doubt about whether the jury promotes socially just results in civil trials; yet they also respond that they want juries to decide their cases.

There is much disagreement about whether and how the jury serves the interests of social justice in civil litigation. Legal commentators who favor its use emphasize the importance of the community's presence in legal decision-making and the significance of the collective's expression of popular will. Critics who are more skeptical of the community's decision-making role disparage the capacity of the jury to grasp the legal issues or move beyond individual self-interest, often questioning whether there should be any policy-making or law-making function for the jury. Many critics argue that the jury is expensive, unpredictable, and inefficient as well as incompetent.

Essentially the competing arguments concerning the civil jury trial guarantee suggest that there are differing conceptions of social organization and its impact on law. One view stresses the importance of community and shared values and beliefs, conceiving the community as potentially greater than the number of its constituents and treating positive law as but one of the ways to find expression of community values. An alternative view emphasizes the more formal process of law making; law becomes not so much a reflection of shared social values as the product of procedures adopted by the individual or group in control of law-making.

Preferring the first conception, I seek to identify what is significant about jury decision-making as distinguished from decision-making by judges and legislators. This significance historically was located in the capacity of members of the jury to provide local knowledge from experience and community connection, knowledge unavailable to the judge or other expert. It can be argued that the significance of jury decision-making today can be drawn from an understanding that truth is socially constructed and that the interchange of views of members of diverse communities not only meaningfully contributes to the derivation of truth, but that the interchange can be important for the many communities to feel a part of the larger lawful enterprise.

In our multicultural society of often estranged individuals and communities, jury duty can be a useful opportunity for citizens to come together in a public setting which promotes exchange. Jury deliberation can be a time for the exercise of authentic self-government by ordinary citizens who, through conversations, expose their differences and provide opportunities for others to understand them. Jury decision-making need not pale against either a model of political majority rule or expert decision-making by judges. Rather, the jury can be distinguished by its small-group, collective capacity to explore competing or emerging normative understandings and to achieve consensus through deliberation. Consensus reached by the group of individual jurors representing diverse communities who have engaged in dialogue is important since through their deliberation these participants can learn from and about each other. In short, jury deliberation can help individuals through their resolution of public controversies to realize the meaning of citizenship, thereby claiming a role in government.

A. The Value of Juries

Debate about the jury has centered on five principal areas of disagreement about its strengths: (1) its law-legitimating features; (2) its role as "little parliament"; (3) its truth-determining and decision-making competency; (4) its ability to foster good citizenship; and (5) its educational value. In the following sections, I will present competing arguments concerning the benefits of jury decision-making related to these areas and suggest how a model which emphasizes the representative and deliberative, participatory potential for juries strengthens the case for the jury.

1. Legitimacy

The jury has been said to forge public acceptance of court decisions by legitimizing them. This legitimacy feature holds great promise, particularly if the jury can reflect the social makeup of society in light of the explosion of common law and statutory rights in the late twentieth century. Traditionally, the legitimizing function has had two aspects. First, the fact of popular participation through the jury makes tolerable certain decisions which the litigants or the public would otherwise find unacceptable, because the jury verdict is seen as the product of the group, and thus the legitimacy of the result is supported in a manner that might not be attainable if one person, the judge, decides. Second, the transitory nature of the jury, though often characterized as a weakness of the jury system, can also protect the court: the jury can serve "as a sort of lightning rod for animosity and suspicion which might otherwise be directed on the judge."

This account, emphasizing two legitimizing features of the jury, however, minimizes the creative, deliberative possibilities of decision-making by the collective. Historically, proponents of this account have made use of the no-name, "black-box" quality of jury decision-making which implies that no one need assume responsibility for decisions. Perhaps as a consequence of this responsibility, to protect the independence of the jury but limit its abuse, we developed procedures to circumscribe the areas where the jury's impact could be felt.

The transient, informal nature of the jury could be looked upon as an extraordinary opportunity for individuals who are normally preoccupied with the mundane, private affairs to "redefine as private citizens, our collective identity," while recognizing that no citizen can live a wholly public political life.

In support of that conception of the community's role, we could, in fact, explore ways of making the jury more accountable for its decisions. One means, one which is connected with the desirable objective of having the decision-making be a product of the diverse views of the citizenry, is to permit those with minority views to feel confident to challenge the assumptions and perspectives of the majority.

2. Little Parliament

The jury is often characterized as "a little parliament," protecting the public against tyranny, or, in modern times, abuse of government. That characterization suggests that the jury device is useful to ensure that we are governed by the spirit of the law and not merely its letter; but it also implies that, like the legislature or other politically motivated institution, in the jury lies the propensity for self-interested decision-making. This view minimizes the fact that the jury's peculiar value lies in its capacity for dialogue and deliberation. The capacity to arrive at socially acceptable resolution of disputes is enhanced by the presence of multiple perspectives. But I also stress the importance of fostering accountability through exchange between jurors and other participants in the litigation process. Thus, rather than limit the jury function, we should seek ways to expand its contribution, by giving it more of an interactive, participatory role in legal decision-making. The fact that the jury is not electorally accountable should not be a reason for marginal treatment, or for its decision-making to be viewed as effectuating "justice beyond law." The resolution of factual controversy and application of law supported by knowledge communicated by jurors in the exchange of life experiences and reflections of jurors is law making.

3. Truth-Determining and Decision-Making Competency

Much of the criticism about jury participation concerns issues of competency. Critics focus on the superior intelligence of the judge, her training, discipline, and social experience in handling other cases, and conclude that the jury is superfluous or, by comparison with other expert decision-makers, incompetent. Earlier this century, some legal realists depicted jury decision-making as irrational and manipulable, sometimes reflecting shifts in norms while often not consciously appreciating such normative turns. A reconceived jury model not only must more fully underscore the peculiar deliberative function of the jury, it must also respond to charges of unpredictability.

In addition to disagreeing with the view held by legal realists, that the jury is an irrational group with limited potential for contribution, I question the importance placed on predictability which generated the critique of juries and which led to a preference for other expert decision-makers. Laypersons are able to view the context of the controversy with freshness lost to the experts and with insight built on cultural and social knowledge. There is a significant role for the community both in the interpretation of law and in delineating the application to a controversy of generally recognized legal standards. A focus on scientific — professional — expertise ignores the reality that bias arises out of any human's personal experience and can accumulate over the course of time. Through dialogue among diverse community members, bias can be exposed and checked. A focus on lay decision-making potential reaffirms the value of the personal perspective which, when offered through dialogue with other community representatives, can blunt bias. Deliberation by a representative jury drawn from a cross-section of the community provides special meaning and insight. Of course, this conclusion contests the legal realists' premise of

scientifically derivable and objective truth, instead viewing the resolution of
disputes as social and the claim of neutrality in law as contestable.

4. Citizenship

Among the recognized advantages of jury participation is that it provides an
important civic experience for citizens. For many citizens, jury duty may be
their only experience with the law and government beyond the exercise of a
local or federal vote. Thus the opportunity for citizens through jury participation to come together and "enter into the heart of a public matter" should not
be lost. Ideally the jury institution can afford diverse citizens the chance to join
other citizens in a common enterprise that can be transformative. In my view,
that enterprise is concerned with achieving an approximation of truth through
the exchange of ideas by diverse people, thereby meting social justice.

The reality is, however, that exposure to jury duty at present is often disen-
chanting and causes citizens to lose confidence in the administration of justice
and to be cynical about their role. The disenchantment experienced by citizens
may in part be the result of the failure of the other principal participants to
communicate with the community's representatives with civility and in an
engaging way. It can stem from a sense of alienation — of not meaningfully
being a part of the system of administering justice. Through orienting instructions given by the judge, and other information made available by the judge
at the outset of trial, including efforts to educate jurors about the function of
all the actors and reasons for procedures which may be unfamiliar to laypersons, this feeling can be allayed. These steps, which some but not all judges
perform, can engage the jury and communicate to the other participants the
value of the jury's work. Similar to the judge's ability to enlighten and explain
matters to the jury through instructions, the attorneys in their arguments and
case presentation can enlighten the jury.

Disenchantment among jurors may also be a product of diminished expectations about the quality of the administration of justice, pertinently, the level
of representation and case management. Moreover, jurors' images of trials
may be largely drawn from fictionalized court-room drama portrayed in movies and television programs. The development of rules and procedures which
emphasize the value of active citizen participation in adjudication can both
contribute to a more productive role for jurors and can result in a better-
educated pool of participants. The one-day, one-trial movement, responsive to
overburdened caseload conditions, can also meet these objectives. Note-taking,
question-asking, and even interviewing of witnesses are other reform efforts
which promote active participation and interest.

Jurors have complained of the passive role that they play in litigation as a
principal reason for viewing the experience as tedious and ultimately unappealing. Critics of assertive juror activity like taking notes, asking questions,
and interviewing witnesses, however, argue that these steps transform the
trial process from an adversarial one to one of inquisition, where the fact
investigator becomes combined with the fact-finder. This conclusion preempts
an assessment of the benefits which could flow from a power-sharing emphasis
on community participation. It promotes the image of the trial process as

combative and the jury as a group of strangers confronting the judge and litigants in an alien and alienating environment.

Reform measures which emphasize decentralizing control by the judge and power-sharing with the jury build upon the understanding that dialogue and decision-making by lay participants have distinctive value important in adjudication. The citizenship building quality is meaningful if full representation of communities and opportunity for meaningful participation in deliberation by community representatives is promoted.

A focus on nourishing citizenship through jury participation might be said to reflect an instrumental conception of jury participation which does not properly focus on the kind of decision-making that directly benefits the individual litigants. Emphasizing this individualistic posture, some critics have also argued that jury service imposes an unfair tax and social cost on those forced to serve.

My reconceived model assumes that the citizen has a stake in resolving public controversies. It begins with the proposition that any dispute worth pursuing in court and thus utilizing the resources of the state has a significant public dimension, and that the use of courts for the resolution of disputes is an aspect of self-government which has transformative potential for the citizen and, ultimately, for the law. The jury's civic responsibility, however, extends beyond its principal duty of resolving the dispute for individuals in a particular case. The jury role can be seen as providing the citizen with opportunities to develop a relationship with other citizens and with the state. The significance of adjudication also lies in defining public values and in identifying the interests of the political community in defining rights and obligations of citizens that has effects beyond the boundaries of an individual dispute. This conception reflects the general democratic principle "that people should be represented in institutions that have power over their lives."

Moreover, the citizens' participation does directly benefit litigants involved in the trial process. The justice-seeking goals of adjudication in a diverse society can be served by recognizing the distinctive capacity of the community's representatives to bring their perspectives to bear on the legal stories presented in court. The value of the jury's participation in terms of enhanced administration of justice lies in the jury's size, limited life, and deliberative quality. Finally, the jury's truth-defining function should be understood in terms of its members' distinctive capacity to engage in the social construction of truth.

5. Education about Differences

The jury's coming together can have an impact on the ability of its members and other participants in the trial — including the judge — to perceive differences among themselves and to reflect upon whether those differences have social significance affecting judgment. My construction of the arguments favoring jury participation has emphasized that the involvement of citizens with different perspectives in resolving public disputes, including their opportunity to converse and to deliberate, has educational potential both in and beyond the particular trial. That educational potential arises from evaluating the stories of the parties and their witnesses, from voir dire, and from evaluating the other jurors by reflecting on their capacity for judgment.

The jury has the potential, moreover, for causing the judge to reflect upon whether his responses are drawn from a too narrowly situated perspective and to benefit from the alternative social experiences offered by the jury-participants. Another aspect of the jury's role has to do with exposing the judge and other professionals to their insulation and to the effects of repetition experienced by these experts. This proposition reflects the view that "[w]e come to know who we are — our authentic selves, what sort of person we want to be, and what we should want — only through deliberation and dialogue with others." A civic objective of reconceiving the jury, emphasizing its representative potential, can be cultural exchange benefiting traditional dispute resolution objectives but also contributing to the fertilization and growth of normative understandings affecting other participants. . . .

NOTES & QUESTIONS

1. If you agree that the jury system has value (because of its citizenship-building qualities, its community-based conception of social justice, or other reasons), how can it be improved? Should jurors have a more active role during trial? (Should they be allowed to take notes? Should they be allowed to ask questions?) Should jurors be paid more for jury service? Are there any other incentives the system should offer potential jurors? (Child care, perhaps?)

C. AVOIDING JURY DUTY

In the next reading, Judge Patricia D. Marks, Supervising Judge for Criminal Courts in the Seventh Judicial District of New York, comments on real-life excuses made by potential jurors and intersperses these with her own analysis of pop cultural images of jurors. Truth still proves itself stranger than fiction, but popular culture definitely appears to influence jurors' understanding of their roles.

MAGIC IN THE MOVIES — DO COURTROOM SCENES HAVE REAL-LIFE PARALLELS?
Hon. Patricia D. Marks
New York State Bar Journal, Vol. 73, No. 5, 40 (2001)

As the 100 prospective jurors walked into my courtroom for the next trial, my mind wandered: Does real life imitate film? Are there jurors anxious to find the excuse that will get them off of jury duty as Dennis Quaid did in *Suspect* (that was, until he learned the defense attorney was Cher)? Will a single mom like Valerie Alston in *Trial by Jury* come into the courthouse worried about the danger to her and her son if she serves on a jury? Is there a Pauly Shore in *Jury Duty* angling to escape jury duty on a short trial in favor of a notorious case where the jury is sequestered throughout the trial? Is there someone looking for romance, like Dennis Morgan and Ginger Rogers found in *Perfect Strangers*? Is there a Henry Fonda here about to re-enact *Twelve Angry Men* and turn the tide of jury deliberations?

The entertainment industry has long had a fascination with the law and courtroom drama. A search on the internet readily discloses hundreds of movies with courtroom themes. The growth of television shows depicting courtroom scenes is extraordinary — *Judge Judy*, *Judge Joe Brown* and *The People's Court* are flanked by *The Practice*, *Law & Order* and *Ally McBeal* to name a few. Those depictions, of course, include jurors from time to time, but this article looks at juries and jurors as they are depicted in the movies and suggests that in some way the fictional portrayals may or may not influence the way real jurors look at their role in the system. . . .

A Place to Sleep

Pauly Shore was truly amusing in *Jury Duty* as he went from trial to trial seeking the one that would provide him with a place to sleep. He pulled a fake prosthesis from his arm in jury selection for a medical malpractice case involving an orthopedic surgeon. He feigned recognition of a defendant during an embezzlement trial, and finally he posed as the perfect juror in the trial of a homicidal maniac so he could be selected and sequestered for a lengthy period of time.

Pauly Shore is not unique in his clever excuses to be disqualified from jury duty. Throughout New York State there are reports of the tactics employed by jurors to get excused. A news anchor arrived for jury duty in New York City wearing a NYPD t-shirt and carrying a beach chair and portable radio. Another juror reported that he could not come to court because "my summons was taken by aliens." Excuses vary, from "my cat just had kittens and I have to stay home with them for six weeks" to the man in the process of becoming a woman who wanted to know whether he should dress for court as a man or as a woman. In another case involving a defendant charged with driving while intoxicated, a mistrial was called during jury selection when a juror told the court that he and the accused used to drink together.

Valerie Alston portrays a juror in *Trial by Jury*. She endures the rigors of voir dire and is retained as a juror in a murder trial even though she describes the defendant as Mafia-related and known as "the Big Spaghetti-o." In an assault trial in upstate new York, a juror who described the defendant as a "Mafia hit man" but assured the court that she would try to set aside her preconceived notions and be fair, did not fare as well. She was not selected as a juror. The case was ultimately reversed because the trial court denied an application for a challenge for cause.

Character Development

I have saved the best for last. Who can forget Henry Fonda's memorable portrayal of a juror in *Twelve Angry Men*? Of course, the accuracy and completeness of the evidence are subject to some challenge, but who would quibble with a jury being told to "separate facts from fancy" or with the simplified reasonable doubt charge: "If there is a reasonable doubt of guilt you must acquit the defendant. If there is no reasonable doubt you must find the defendant guilty." In fact there are jurisdictions that recommend such a simplified charge.

What is unique in *Twelve Angry Men* is the way the characters of each of the 12 jurors — all male — are developed and their approaches to the deliberations. The accountant was quite reluctant to give an opinion and preferred the comfort of his numbers. The successful businessman, on the surface, was a self-assured juror who made reasonable and logical arguments, but as time went on he began to unravel and show signs of instability. The juror who openly voted guilty because of the defendant's background was the most troublesome. The immigrant watchmaker was provoked to anger by the indifference of another juror. It is remarkable that this film can succeed in providing an intelligent plot and developing 12 distinct and interesting characters. It succeeds in reminding us of the uniqueness of each juror in a real trial and how each personality contributes to the ultimate verdict.

The initial vote is 11 to one to convict but as the discussion progresses it is apparent that the reasons for the votes are not what they should be. One juror votes to convict because his anger toward his son gets in the way of an objective view of the guilt of the defendant, who is charged in the death of his father.

An experiment in the jury room influences some votes. The unique knife is not so unique after all when juror Henry Fonda produces a knife similar to the murder weapon and displays the angle of the death-producing wound. He finds the knife when he goes for a walk in the neighborhood where the defendant lives and where the crime occurred.

While experimentation is not permitted, the books are full of cases where such experimentation has occurred. During the overnight sequestration in one trial, a juror adjusted the lighting conditions and opened the curtains in her hotel room to simulate what she believed to be the conditions of the crime scene, based on the victim's testimony. She then asked another juror to walk in and out of the room, wearing clothing similar in color to that worn by the attacker, so that she could determine whether the victim would have been able to make a reliable identification. The contrived experimentation was not approved by the courts and the conviction was reversed.

Application of everyday experience is acceptable. When the defense counsel suggested that the jurors place the gun in the pocket of their shorts during their deliberations, the court held that jurors are not precluded from applying their everyday experiences and common sense to the issues presented in a trial. Was it contrived experimentation, an application of everyday experience, or a little of both? I'll leave that to you.

As the 100 members of the group before me were reduced to 14 jurors and they prepared for deliberations, I had satisfied myself that jurors would not be influenced by the movies or television. And then I saw on the Internet an entry by a juror who was summoned to jury duty in California and immediately did his "homework" by watching the following videos: *Jury Duty*, *Trial by Jury*, and *Twelve Angry Men*.

NOTES & QUESTIONS

1. Can popular culture serve an educational function for jurors? What are the benefits and the dangers of relying on popular culture to educate citizens about juries? Should prospective jurors be required to watch a movie such as *12 Angry Men* before serving on a jury? Many jurors are puzzled about how to go about their task of deliberating. (While they do receive instructions about the law, instructions about the mechanics of how they actually are supposed to deliberate are sparse to non-existent.) Is the proper spirit for deliberations best taught through entertainment? *12 Angry Men* definitely gets the spirit of the process right, but some aspects of the film (such as Henry Fonda going out to purchase a knife similar to the murder weapon) are beyond the pale as juror experimentation.

In *Jury Duty*, Pauly Shore plays a slacker who, needing a free place to live, maneuvers to be a juror on a lengthy murder trial. (Jurors get put up at a hotel and also get the princely sum of five dollars a day.) After listening to a fellow juror and new citizen describe how, in his former country, no one had the right to a trial by jury, Shore has a change of heart and decides to take the trial seriously. Shore prepares himself for serious deliberations by renting and watching a number of classic law-related videos, including *12 Angry Men, Judgment at Nuremberg, And Justice for All,* and *Witness for the Prosecution*. (He also reads the Cliffs Notes of *Law for Beginners*.)

2. Jury duty is serious business. Yet movies about jury duty, such as Peter Bogdanovich's *Illegally Yours* (1988) and *Jury Duty*, the Pauly Shore vehicle, are broadly farcical comedies. The next excerpt suggests that comedy is a good fit for stories about law because (1) comedy has a strong truth-seeking potential (laughter can be subversive) and (2) comedy helps make the law accessible to laypersons. As you read, consider whether you agree with these propositions.

TRIAL AND ERRORS: COMEDY'S QUEST
FOR THE TRUTH
Rajani Gupta
9 UCLA Entertainment Law Review 113 (2001)

Comedy is a social phenomenon, a reflection, if not critique of the prevailing (or narrow-minded) beliefs of a given culture. It develops as a community out-growth, a moment of light attack on the existing norms of a given population. Comedy finds its way into the smallest forms of human communication and expression, extending from tiny witticisms or ill-mannered jokes to the full-blown parodies or comprehensive satires of human existence often found long-form in the mediums of novels or films, or, in other words, through the outlets of pop culture itself.

Comedy defines itself in relation to social categories; directed as an often derisive attack on the status quo, it situates itself as a disrespectful observer of a given situation, society, culture, or even a particular human behavior. While comedy consists of universal components attributable to many facets of human interaction and activity, its true thrust (and intended goal) depends on its ability to delve into a communal understanding of its intended comedic "victim" as a sort of foil for its alternative proposition. This alternative is a model of possibilities, a substitute to the current approach that could potentially replace the generally accepted prototype. In a manner of speaking, comedy presents a playful challenge to traditionally held notions of social behavior by way of a light approach to the serious; it pokes fun at current conduct through parody or exaggeration while always depicting the existence of a different manner of acting in that particular situation.

The legal system itself is a social construction, the epitome of social categorization of acceptable behavioral norms. Varied from culture to culture, law represents the classification of proper moral values according to the body politic (depending on the particular political structure) along with its complementary enforcement mechanism. Through and within its malleable structure, an aggregation of laws creates a hierarchy of social values that attempts to define proper human deeds in relation to an overarching ideology. The courtroom has come to represent the battleground of these values. It presents a forum for conflicting notions of proper social behavior. Borrowing from a Rousseauian theory of the social compact, the courtroom can be seen as the constant renegotiation of the terms of the communal contract. In this theoretical analysis of the ideal, the lawyers represent opposing approaches to the same situations, testing their philosophies of justice against the sounding board of the community — a jury composed of twelve members who, in the ideal, represent a cross-section of the community and its component values.

Now the question that arises here is: Where do the two intersect? What are the possibilities when law merges with comedy and exposes a connection through the medium of popular culture?

The links between comedy and the law are endless. Both depend upon a categorization of social norms; however, whereas law defines these customs, comedy exists as a foil of them, creating an alternative community with different possibilities that could work within the existing community. Where law is the epitome of social structure, comedy functions as the anti-structure, the breakdown of hierarchy and order and the comic subversion of dominant ideas. Comedy presents breaks in traditional logic, demonstrating a play upon form that produces humor through its unconventional pattern. In addition, both comedy and the law depend on a sort of community consensus to attain their ends. One seeks order through the creation of social parameters; the other seeks laughter and social critique through the destruction of constraints. Both are, however, the construction of worlds that encapsulate a certain notion of behavior while attacking that which is outside of it, "the other."

Together, comedy and the law present great possibilities of truth-seeking. Comedy has been often considered a truth-seeking mechanism with its constant consideration of that which challenges the status quo. Of all social creations, the law requires such a challenge in order to evolve towards a stronger understanding of truth and the proper means that should be exercised in order to attain those ends. Since popular culture has come to define and characterize the general public's understanding of justice and the legal process, a comic portrayal of the law can become a strong vehicle for social criticism (and eventual change) of the legal process. . . .

III. Law and Community: How Do They Work Together?. . . .

A. Comedy That Makes the Law More Accessible

Comedy, being a medium that is accessible to a broad spectrum of the population, has the unique ability to make the subjects it covers more accessible to its target audience. In the legal context, this is especially clear. In the first instance, legal comedies are almost always delivered through inherently comedic actors. While this observation seems brutally obvious, it is important in the context of the law because these actors generally appear to be more approachable and closer to "real" people. Comedic actors have an already established comic persona and a pattern of humorous gestures which the audience then recognizes. The comic personality of the character is then laid on top of this persona. When the movie star glamour of an actor can be more easily separated from the character he is portraying, the situation and the subject becomes more lucid and authentic to the viewer.

Aside from the actor, the characters themselves are notably accessible to the public and often intentionally created to pattern real people. . . .

Yet another perspective of the legal system is shown in the utterly awful movie *Jury Duty*, starring Pauly Shore as Tommy Collins, an unemployed trailer park resident who seeks jury duty as a source of income and guaranteed room and board. Throughout the entire film, Collins seeks to delay the trial, using every tactic possible to turn around a guilty verdict by eleven of his twelve fellow jurors. Despite his own abuse of the system, even Collins seeks out the truth and finds it, resulting in the release of a man falsely accused of murder. Eventually Collins discovers the mastermind behind the whole plot to frame Carl Wayne Bishop (Sean Whalen) and justice prevails. Although the casting alone makes the film's message accessible (who does not feel superior to Pauly Shore?), the fact that the truth was secured through an unskilled and seemingly unintelligent man such as Collins places a certain responsibility upon the average person in their search for truth from the jury box. In addition, if Pauly Shore can discover the truth and have it be recognized in a court of law, then the court system is certainly accessible to the average person. . . .

NOTES & QUESTIONS

1. What connections do you see between law and comedy? Literary scholar Northrop Frye notes that law in comedy serves as a blocking force which must be overcome before the lovers can be united in a happy ending. The paternal (legalistic) figures in charge of society at the beginning of a comedy must give way to the young lovers who will represent a new, more free social order. Frye succinctly notes, "The action of comedy in moving from one social center to another is not unlike the action of a lawsuit, in which plaintiff and defendant construct different versions of the same situation, one finally being judged as real and the other as illusory." Northrop Frye, *Anatomy of Criticism* 166 (1957).

2. Why must juror-heroes so frequently break the law in films? *Runaway Jury, The Juror, Illegally Yours* (1988)*, Jury Duty,* and *Trial by Jury,* among others, all feature juror protagonists who lie, cheat, steal, or even kill. Of course, in comedy most lawbreaking is played for laughs, but what kind of message does a film send about our legal system when the one sure-fire way to achieve justice is through breaking the law?

Illegally Yours and *Jury Duty* feature plenty of law-breaking by jurors. The films are romantic comedies of the so-bad-they're-good variety. Bogdanovich seems to be channeling a Zen version of *What's Up, Doc?* (1972) in the genuinely weird *Illegally Yours*, in which a very young Rob Lowe plays a character named Richard Dice who rolls a pair of dice to help him make big decisions. *Jury Duty* features Shelley Winters, Tia Carrere, and Pauly Shore, plus a cute miniature dog. (How could anyone resist?) Both films center on a hapless juror-hero who saves the defendant and finds love.

Both Rob Lowe and Pauly Shore's characters break the law left and right. Dice is a dorky guy who lies during voir dire when he denies knowing the defendant in a murder trial. (In fact, he has been in love with her since first grade.) Convinced she is innocent, Dice's law-breaking investigations escalate to include breaking and entering, impersonating a judge's wife, stealing, assault, etc. (The only thing that really troubles his mom is when he tells her he is considering law school. "Richard," she tells him, "We've done a lot of stupid things over the years, but we've never been boring people.") Dice muses to himself that he is the only one who can save Molly (the defendant), "and yet everything I was doing was completely against the law. . . . Still, there were the laws of love to consider."

The laws of love seem as inexplicable and chancy as the laws of the legal system, but fortunately for Dice, he lives in a romantic comedy. He gambles on love, and the legal system be damned. As Johnny Cash sings "Love is a gambler" on the soundtrack, Dice kisses Molly, while the police read them their Miranda rights.

Pauly Shore's juror character, of course, breaks or bends the law every few minutes in *Jury Duty*, including such visual gems as dressing up as the defendant's "girlfriend" to visit him in jail to investigate the case. However, unlike Dice in *Illegally Yours*, Shore's character has a genuine change of heart about the legal system, fueled in part by his education in pop culture. (He watches videos of *12 Angry Men, Judgment at Nuremberg,* and the like.) He uses actual dialogue from *12 Angry Men* in his arguments with other jurors. Ultimately, with the help of Peanut, his trusty dog, he saves the innocent defendant. (Of course, since the film is a Pauly Shore vehicle, the movie ends with Peanut competing on *Jeopardy*.)

D. JURY CONSULTANTS

Can we scientifically predict whether certain jurors will be pro-plaintiff or pro-defendant? If we can make such predictions, should we? Do attorneys who use jury consultants skew the very spirit of the jury system? Is this "cheating"? Of course, every attorney tries to pick a favorable jury panel during voir dire. (At the very least, attorneys try to keep off the panel prospective jurors who seem to have pre-judged a case or a defendant.) But not every client can pay the fee for consultants. The whole topic of jury consultants raises key questions about human nature (how predictable are people?) and issues of equity (because of the vastly different resources clients can afford to spend on jury selection).

TWELVE CAREFULLY SELECTED NOT SO ANGRY MEN: ARE JURY CONSULTANTS DESTROYING THE AMERICAN LEGAL SYSTEM?
Maureen E. Lane
32 Suffolk University Law Review 463 (1999)

Then the jury consultants from both sides took their positions in the cramped seats between the railing and the counsel tables. They began the uncomfortable task of staring into the inquiring faces of 194 strangers. The consultants studied the jurors because, first, that was what they were being paid huge sums of money to do, and second, because they claimed to be able to thoroughly analyze a person through the telltale revelations of body language. They watched and waited anxiously for arms to fold across the chest, for fingers to pick nervously at teeth, for heads to cock suspiciously to one side, for a hundred other gestures that supposedly would lay a person bare and expose the most private of prejudices.

They scribbled notes and silently probed the faces. Juror number fifty-six, Nicholas Easter, received more than his share of concerned looks. He sat in the middle of the fifth row, dressed in starched khakis and a button-down, a nice-looking young man. He glanced around occasionally, but his attention was directed at a paperback he'd brought for the day. No one else had thought to bring a book.

More chairs were filled near the railing. The defense had no fewer than six jury experts examining facial twitches and hemorrhoidal clutches. The plaintiff was using only four.

For the most part, the prospective jurors didn't enjoy being appraised in such manner, and for fifteen awkward minutes they returned the glaring with scowls of their own.

John Grisham, *The Runaway Jury* 27 (1996). . . .

B. The Role of Jury Consultants in the Selection of Jurors

Jury consultants provide a variety of services to attorneys in both criminal and civil cases, ranging from jury selection to actual trial strategy. Most jury consultants are psychologists, sociologists, or attorneys by training. They attempt to utilize a variety of tools to predict jury behavior. Generally, jury selection consultants construct a model of a potential juror favorable to their client's case, use this knowledge to chose a jury panel to fit this characterization, predict the outcome of the case, and instruct attorneys on the best way to present evidence during trial.

1. History of the Jury Consulting Industry

The jury consulting industry began in the early 1970s when social scientists volunteered their services to anti-Vietnam War activists on trial for various acts of civil disobedience. In *United States v. Berrigan*, the first notable criminal trial utilizing jury consultants, consultants utilized telephone polls to predict how potential jurors would view the case and to obtain information on what types of people shared the defendants' anti-war beliefs. A hung jury in the highly conservative area of Harrisburg, Pennsylvania acquitted the Berrigan defendants, thus announcing the birth of the consulting industry.

First motivated by political views, the jury consulting field soon moved into the commercial setting, creating a multi-million dollar industry. In particular, large corporations engaged the services of a variety of new companies created specifically for jury consulting. Along with these new jury consulting firms came various methods for studying potential juror reactions to a case, such as the use of paid "shadow juries," who observe an actual trial and provide insight as to what the actual jurors perceived. Not long after corporations began using consultants, wealthy criminal defendants began employing them as well.

2. Methods Jury Consultants Use in Selecting a Jury

In an attempt to identify an ideal juror for a particular case, jury selection consultants employ a variety of "scientific jury selection methods" derived from the social sciences. The methods chosen may vary depending on the particular consultant, case, and available funds. During voir dire, attorneys then use this information to strike jurors whom the jury consultant determines are not ideal for the particular case.

Consultants commonly conduct community attitudinal surveys. Generally conducted through telephone polls or in person, community surveys attempt to ascertain attitudes and biases in the demographic area from which the court selects the jury pool. Consultants analyze the data obtained from the polls and construct a profile of an ideal juror, meaning a juror who favors their client's position. Attorneys utilize the profile to remove jurors possessing characteristics that render them unsympathetic to their client's case. Consultants may also investigate potential jurors through methods such as home surveillance, handwriting analysis, and by checking credit, property, and tax records.

In addition, consultants observe juror behavior during the selection process, noting body language and interaction with other jurors.

Jury consultants also offer an array of services to assist attorneys during the actual trial. Consultants may arrange for attorneys to present the case issues to a focus group or a mock jury to gauge their reaction to the evidence and issues of the case. Consultants also employ "shadow juries" to observe the trial as it unfolds, thus providing attorneys with valuable insight regarding the actual jury's comprehension of the evidence and overall perception of the case.

3.   Who Are Jury Consultants?

Although jury consultants come from a variety of educational and professional backgrounds, the majority of consultants have training in the social and psychological sciences. Jury consultants, however, do not need a specific education, training, or professional license to practice as a consultant. The American Society of Trial Consultants, a voluntary organization for jury consultants, does not require that its members possess specific credentials or follow any guidelines in their advertising and practice. In addition, the Model Rules of Professional Conduct do not bar or place any restrictions on attorneys using jury consultants. Consequently, many commentators, both proponents and critics of jury consultants, advocate for some type of regulation in the jury consulting industry. Despite the prominence of the jury consulting industry in the American legal system, legislatures and bar associations across the country have largely ignored the subject of regulating jury consultants. In 1995, however, Illinois state senator James Philip introduced Senate Bill 1225, which proposed a ban on the use of all non-lawyer jury consultants in Illinois. The Illinois state Senate, nevertheless, failed to pass this proposal, leaving jury consultants unregulated in Illinois as well as in the rest of the country.

4.   Rising Use and Costs Associated With Jury Consulting Services

The use of jury consultants is now standard practice in most large civil and significant criminal trials. In 1997, the American Society of Trial Consultants had over 450 members, compared with only 19 members in 1983. As of 1994, jury consulting constituted a $200 million dollar per year industry, with Litigation Sciences, Inc., the industry leader, claiming $25 million in sales. Consultants charge approximately $250 per hour, and fees on an individual case may range from $10,000 to $250,000.

Commentators argue that jury consultants are accessible only to the rich because of the high price tag associated with consultants' services. In *Spivey v. State*, the Georgia Supreme Court held that the court's refusal to appoint jury selection experts on behalf of an indigent defendant did not violate his constitutional rights. Although not the standard throughout the country, some judges, in an attempt to level the playing field, have appointed consultants to assist indigent defendants.

5. Impact of Consultants on American Judicial System

While jury consultants often claim high success rates in predicting the outcome of a trial, no empirical data exists to demonstrate that scientific jury selection methods really work. Litigation Sciences Inc., a market leader in the field, claims a ninety-six percent accuracy rate in predicting the outcome of a case and claims that eighty percent of their clients receive a favorable verdict. Such claims, however, appear to constitute nothing more than consultants' marketing tools, as numerous scholars assert that the data does not support their claims. Although consultants' advice modestly assists their clients during the jury selection phase, in many instances, attorneys are better served by using their own instincts because of their familiarity with the case and its evidence. In addition, studies indicate that the evidence presented at the trial, not the composition of the jury, controls the outcome of the case. Some commentators, however, assert that the dramatic growth in the consulting industry suggests that, at some level, the advice gained from consultants must assist attorneys.

Critics also assert that while research demonstrates that jury consultants cannot effectively predict juror behavior, such claims by consultants nonetheless undermine the public's confidence in jury verdicts and the jury system as a whole. Both attorneys and the media are quick to attribute a successful verdict to the jury selection experts, often ignoring the evidence presented at trial and failing to interview jurors after the verdict to ascertain the reasoning behind their decisions. By crediting the consultants with such victories, the public may view the jury as a group easily manipulated by those litigants who can afford the services of jury consultants.

Legal scholar Jeffrey Abramson examined six high profile trials where jury consultants claimed credit for obtaining a favorable verdict for their clients. After reviewing the evidence and post-trial interviews with jurors, Abramson concluded that the verdicts resulted mainly from the evidence and not from the personal characteristics of the jurors. Despite studies such as Abramson's, attorneys continue to use jury consultants when selecting juries, and the media, the public, and many in the legal profession continue to believe the claims of these consultants. . . .

NOTES & QUESTIONS

1. Are high-priced trial consultants ruining it for everyone but their well-heeled clients? "Trials are too important to be left up to juries," says Rankin Fitch, the unscrupulous jury consultant played by Gene Hackman in *Runaway Jury*. Fitch is an expensive and thoroughly venial jury consultant, a cunning mastermind hired to help a group of gun manufacturers ensure no victim of gun violence ever wins a suit against them. He has thoroughly researched the prospective jurors (including putting them under surveillance), finding and sometimes even creating blackmail material to bring pressure to bear on the jurors. (One juror has had an abortion, one is HIV positive, and Fitch has made sure that one juror's husband is set up with a shady real estate deal.)

Fitch's disdain for the jury process is apparent. He tells Wendell Rohr, the plaintiff's attorney played by Dustin Hoffman, "You think your average juror is King Solomon? No, he's a roofer with a mortgage, he wants to go home and sit in his Barcalounger and let the cable t.v. wash over him, and this man doesn't give a single solitary droplet of shit about truth, justice, or your American way."

Rohr has his own jury consultant, who is young and idealistic, but Rohr trusts his own instincts as often (or more) as he trusts his consultant's. Although the film paints Fitch's over-the-top behavior in a negative light, the message seems to be that jury consultants might be tolerable as long as they do not take over the lawyer's job. How do popular culture portrayals of jury consultants affect public respect for the jury system? Does popular culture make it seem too easy to manipulate the system?

2. "We love fat women, people! They're tight-fisted, unsympathetic," says Fitch to his workers in *Runaway Jury*. But of course people are not machines. Such one-size-fits-all judgments are dangerous stereotypes. Fitch himself is a stereotype — the villainous and unprincipled jury consultant. Why does Hollywood film depend so heavily on stereotypes?

E. THE WORK OF A JURY

1. Jurors as Storytellers — "I guess we talk."

Contrary to suggestions in the previous section, one hopes the evidence rather than the characteristics of the jurors is the key to a verdict. How does a jury use evidence to reach its collective determination? In a key scene in *12 Angry Men*, the jurors take a preliminary vote, and it is 11-1 for a guilty verdict. A juror asks, "What do we do now?" and Henry Fonda's character responds, in his classic laconic style, "I guess we talk." What kind of talk is jury talk? Is jury talk always purely and coldly rational? How do emotions affect the process of jurors working toward a decision? And what about the internal talk, the cognitive process inside a juror's head as he or she listens to and tries to understand the evidence at trial? Most commentators today believe that jurors use a story model in the way they decide. Consider the following excerpts from an article by Reid Hastie, one of the preeminent researchers into juror decision-making.

EMOTIONS IN JURORS' DECISIONS

Reid Hastie

66 Brooklyn Law Review 991 (2001)

I. THE JUROR'S DECISION-MAKING PROCESS

Most conceptions of the juror's decision assume that the process is primarily cognitive, even rational in character. Descriptive psychological theories all focus on cognitive information processing functions, and none of the currently popular models include an explicit account of the role of sentiments, moods, emotions, and passions in the process.

Normative theories also assert that legal decisions should be predominantly rational. For example, the Advisory Committee's note on Federal Rule of Evidence 403 comments that one consideration in deciding whether to exclude evidence should be to avoid "unfair prejudice," defined as "an undue tendency to suggest decision on an improper basis, commonly, though not necessarily, an emotional one."

There is an apparent contradiction between the conception of the ideal juror as a logical reasoning machine and also as a source of community attitudes, sentiments, and moral precepts. Robert Solomon noted this discrepancy when he commented that "[t]he idea that justice requires emotional detachment, a kind of purity suited ultimately to angels, ideal observers, and the original founders of society, has blinded us to the fact that justice arises from and requires such feelings as resentment." This apparent contradiction may be resolved by distinguishing between the several functions required of the jury, some of which (for example, fact-finding) demand cold rational assessments, while others (for example, determining the moral egregiousness of a defendant's conduct) require a more passionate evaluation. Nonetheless psychologists know of no satisfactory normative analysis of the relationship between cognitive and emotional functions in the decision-making process.

Theoretical analyses provide extremely cognitive versions of the jurors' decision-making processes, but any realistic assessment concludes that jurors experience varied emotions and that these emotions sometimes influence their decisions. First person reports of jury service invariably mention emotional experiences: anxiety or irritation produced by jury service, reactions of anger, fear, and sympathy evoked by the events that led to the trial or by participants in those events or the trial, and sometimes dramatic evidence exhibits that evoke strong emotions. It is also likely that emotions caused by events outside the trial may be carried into the jury box and that even these irrelevant events may influence a juror's decision. . . .

This Essay starts with an overview of the three major cognitive theories of juror decision making.

Many scholars claim that jurors' judgments are best described by algebraic models of mental processes like those proposed by philosophers and mathematicians as rational belief revision principles. A popular choice is Bayes Theorem, which describes the judgment process as starting from a prior probability of guilt and then adjusting from that initial point by multiplicatively integrating the implications of new evidence according to the laws of mathematical probability theory. The other popular algebraic process model supposes that jurors form their initial beliefs about guilt (analogous to the Bayesian prior probability) and then adjust using an averaging, rather than multiplying, information integration process. Empirical studies favor the statistically robust linear, averaging model over the Bayesian model as a description of jurors' decision-making processes.

A second, more complicated theoretical description comes from research on cognitive judgment heuristics. The reigning metaphor is that the juror carries a "cognitive toolbox" of useful inference heuristics in long-term memory, and selects relevant judgment tools, algorithms, or strategies to solve the problem of making a legal decision. . . .

The third theoretical description is of the juror as a "naive reporter" who constructs a narrative summary to explain the evidence, concluding with the verdict that is most consistent with that story. The primary cognitive activities in the decision-making process are inferences made to serve the goal of creating a coherent, comprehensive story to summarize the situation implied by credible evidence. The final stage of the decision-making process involves classifying the constructed story into one of the legal criminal verdict concepts or relying on the story for premises to infer causation and responsibility to decide many civil cases.

None of these approaches is a unique winner in the competition for "best theory" status, although the Story Model provides the most valid description of a typical juror's decision-making process. It includes many of the heuristic judgment strategies as sub-components, and it is intended to describe cognitive processes that could, at a general level, be captured by the parameters of an algebraic equation. This Essay will review what is known about the influence of emotions on juror decisions and conclude with an interpretation of those effects, in terms of the Story Model, as it provides the most systematic, detailed, and empirically-supported account of the juror decision-making process. First, this Essay will further describe the Story Model.

II. THE STORY MODEL OF THE JUROR'S DECISION PROCESS

The Story Model proposes that the central cognitive process in juror decision making is story construction — the creation of a narrative summary of the events under dispute. Applications of the Story Model to criminal jury judgments have identified three component processes: (1) evidence evaluation through story construction, (2) representation of the decision alternatives (verdicts) by learning their attributes or elements, and (3) reaching a decision through the classification of the story into the best-fitting verdict category. . . .

The distinctive claim is that the story the juror constructs determines the juror's verdict. More generally, the approach proposes that causal "situation models" play a central role in many explanation-based decisions in legal, medical, engineering, financial, and everyday circumstances . . . .

IV. EMOTIONS IN JURORS' DECISIONS

. . . Three important categories of emotional experience most relevant to the decision act are "incidental emotions," "decision process emotions," and "anticipated emotions." What is known about the effects of these emotional phenomena on the outcomes of decisions? There is no scientific research on "decision process emotions" in legal contexts, but there are a few studies demonstrating the effects of incidental emotions and anticipated emotions on jurors' decisions.

The extant empirical research literature does not provide us with a comprehensive list of emotional phenomena that occur in jury decisions. The most important examples include: reactions to jury service, primarily anxiety and irritation; reactions to the events that led to the trial, primarily anger; reactions to participants involved in the trial, primarily anger, sympathy, and fear; and reactions to evidentiary exhibits, primarily disgust and horror.

If a juror's general decision-making strategy follows the stages described by the Story Model, we can locate the various effects of emotions within that framework. Since, according to the Story Model, the story is the central determinant of the decision, the Essay suggests that most of the effects of emotions will be manifested in characteristics of the juror's story.

Where do jurors' stories come from? The initial stages of story retrieval and creation can be biased by simple associative or appraisal processes. Sometimes, while trying to comprehend the evidence, the juror is reminded of another story, and that story is used as a template for comprehension of the current case. The original story may come from a television show, a movie, a novel, the news, or everyday conversations. Or perhaps the juror knows of a generic story schema or story skeleton such as a "script" for a kidnapping, an oil spill, or a traffic accident. Under these conditions, the jurors' emotional states will influence the reminding process and bias the selection of a relevant story from memory.

In other cases, no related story comes to mind, and the juror constructs a story from background knowledge. We liken this process to deduction from a database of facts and inference rules. Again, it is likely that associative or appraisal-based influences of incidental and anticipated emotions will affect the nature of the "premises" that are salient, those that come to mind when a juror attempts to construct a story de novo. For example, if a juror is in an angry emotional state, he or she is likely to attend to, or retrieve from memory, information that is negative, perhaps exaggerating the egregiousness of the defendant's alleged conduct or the severity of the injury to a plaintiff or victim or constructing a story for the instant case from another story that produced an angry reaction. . . .

NOTES & QUESTIONS

1. It is common to speak of lawyers as storytellers. However, we forget that jurors, too, are storytellers. They use stories as cognitive tools to help process, sort, balance, and understand the evidentiary story they hear at trial. Additionally, as they talk to each other during deliberations, they consider the alternative possible stories presented at trial and must decide which story makes the most sense. How might the stories that circulate in popular culture affect jurors' processing of a trial story?

2. What role should emotion play in a jury trial? Hastie is right to point out that Federal Rule of Evidence 403 frowns on the use of unfairly prejudicial, i.e., overly emotional, evidence. But the key is "unfair" prejudice. Jurors do expect emotional testimony at trial (in accord with what they see in popular culture), and jurors themselves experience a great many possible emotions (boredom, anger, sympathy, etc.) In fact, anecdotal stories abound suggesting that jury duty is so emotionally stressful it is actually bad for your health. One formal study found mixed results, but concluded that serving on a traumatic trial can have a negative health effect in the area of depression. Daniel W. Shuman, et al., *The Health Effects of Jury Service,* 18 Law & Psychology Review 267 (1994).

2. Doing the Work of Community Justice

In addition to deciding in individual cases, juries help constitute the type of community in which we live. How does their work help answer the questions of who we are and who we want to be? The next reading, by Professor Milner S. Ball, suggests that a jury's work is the communal work of telling stories to create something, finally, like justice.

JUST STORIES
Milner Ball
12 Cardozo Studies in Law & Literature 37 (2000)

"For [Paul] Ricoeur, the justice that sought to be the aim of responsible politics is one that is always in the making. It calls for an ongoing conversation about justice itself, a conversation that always calls upon and contests both convictions and the criticisms of them."
                                      – Bernard Dauenhauer, *Paul Ricoeur*

"A juror's decision between competing narratives is, moreover, a definition of public identity. Because he is taking public action through public institutions, his judgment is inevitably determination, in a strong sense, of the nature of his community."
                                      – Robert Burns, *A Theory of the Trial*

Richard Weisberg says public discourse is in disarray, and he is clearly right. But I imagine a possibility within it. I imagine an accessible public discourse about justice whose central activity is telling and contesting stories. Narrative is the primary medium for talking together about who we are — and would be — as a people, and this is the talk in which conversation about justice chiefly subsists. Notwithstanding disarray and continued academic belief in theories rather than stories of justice and a lingering assumption that justice is — or should be — practically separated from law, the American story is regularly performed in law. The current version invites the critique of other stories and therefore a public discourse richly arrayed.

I. Justice, Story, and the People

There are various ways to approach these things. Augustine, for example, urged that justice is a less adequate gauge of a people than are the objects of their love. A people is greater or lesser, he thought, depending on the greatness of what they love, and he therefore took up the conversation as one about love. I would not divide the terms, for to talk about justice is to talk about love.

As Paul Lehmann said, "justice is the political form of love." But, primarily as a matter of rhetorical strategy for the time being, I judge that dialogue about justice has a better chance of making headway than disciplined public discussion about the politics of love.

What is true of love is true also of righteousness: It is companion to justice as a measure of a people, but it is generally unfamiliar in contemporary discourse about political fundamentals. The alignment of justice with righteousness is embodied in the Hebrew Bible's employment of mishpat and tzedaka as synonyms and in the use of "justice" and "righteousness" as alternative translations for both mishpat and the Greek diakaiosyne in Christian scripture. Notwithstanding the efforts of people like Aviam Soifer and Stephen Wizner to re-familiarize us with the valid relation of justice and righteousness and the need for righteous acts by lawyers and judges, Justice Antonin Scalia employed "righteousness" as a term of disparagement in his dissent from the Court's opinion in *Romer v. Evans*. He dismissively accused the majority of placing "heavy reliance upon principles of righteousness rather than judicial holdings." I think that the Justice on righteousness reflects a general attitude, for although fidelity in constitutional interpretation is familiar enough at least to academics, I have seen no symposia on righteousness. "Righteousness" must wait until public discourse has been better prepared for its return. For present purposes, then, I turn primarily to "justice" rather than to "love" or "righteousness."

As a rule, when we talk to each other about who we are and would be, as the American people that is, when we talk about justice, we tell stories — about pilgrims, about July the Fourth, about the frontier, about wars we have fought, about struggles for rights, about our own political experiences. It may be that there is an inherent connection between narrative and justice. Melvyn Hill, for example, proposes that storytelling in general "must be understood not just as the primary form of thinking about experience, but also as the primary form of communicating with each other about experience. . . . Stories tell us how each one finds or loses his just place in relation to others in the world. And the communication of the story is confirmed when justice has been recognized."

Certainly stories of origin orient us in the world and in justice, but, like all stories, they are forgotten unless they are retold. In the retelling, the story continues to constitute a living community of remembrance. Consider, for example, the gathering effect, then and now, of the story that begins: "We were Pharaoh's slaves in Egypt and the Lord brought us out of Egypt with a mighty hand . . . that he might bring us in and give us the land which he swore to give to our fathers."

Ricoeur observes that "the identity of a group, culture, people, or nation is not that of an immutable substance, nor that of a fixed structure, but that, rather, of a recounted story." A fresh, multi-layered experience of narrative communal identity was offered by a version of the mystery play *The Nativity* recently produced by the Royal National Theater in London in its small, experimental Cottesloe theater. The primary subject of the production was the biblical story of Jesus's birth and the gathering of shepherds and wise men at the manger. Another was the telling of the story by the community of tradesmen, as acted, who had originally performed the play and whose lives in England had been shaped by the biblical stories. But the present actors and audience, too, became a community, a fact uniquely underscored by the absence of seats and a separate stage and by the continuous movement of the action through the playgoers. I found it deeply affecting to be drawn thereby into a community of witnesses with the present actors, the medieval trades-men, and the ancient shepherds and wise men. The community that a story constitutes is not limited by divisions between past and present.

Arendt noted that the incessant talk that saves deeds and experiences and their stories from futility will itself remain "futile unless certain concepts, certain guideposts for future remembrance, and even for sheer reference, arise out of it." And she noted that a loss of bearings has accompanied "the 'American' aversion from conceptual thought." Concepts do play necessary, valuable roles as prompts for memory or as analytical tools for testing stories, but their end lies in service to the underlying story. It is the story that counts.

Of course narrative has limits and defects. It does not create the conditions for its realization and interpretation. It is not immune to monopolization or aggressive use. And it may bear no helpful relation to the story-less, those whose world is consumed by pain or oppression. Memory, too, has limits and defects. Aviam Soifer points out that, while forgetting what happened can have grievous consequences, "too much remembering may also be dangerous," as the grim, revengeful violence of ethnic conflicts in Rwanda and the former Yugoslavia exemplify. And in conjunction with a reflection on legal responses to unspeakable horror, Martha Minow reminds us of the complex need for remembering what to forget.

More and other stories do not cure narrative — it cannot save itself — but they do compose a corrective response. The story of the founding of America is (would be) improved by different versions, especially the versions of those excluded from, or harmed by it. By bringing alive the story of slaves, Toni Morrison's *Beloved* offers readers a contesting experience of the story of American origins. "Recounting differently," Ricoeur observes, "is not inimical to a certain historical reverence to the extent that the inexhaustible richness of the event is honored by the diversity of stories which are made out of it, and by the competition to which that diversity gives rise." Moreover, as Bernard Dauenhauer says, even if it is only symbolic, participation in the founding stories of other nations as well as our own and in the stories or origin of vari-ous ethnic minorities and religious confessions "not only teaches us about one another's cultures but also [helps to free] capabilities for renewal . . . trapped within our own dead traditions."

The telling and hearing of stories — the participation, the giving and receiv-ing, the performance — "is really a matter of living with the other in order to take that other to one's home as a guest." In this way and for this reason, the process enacts something like what Richard Weisberg refers to as "poethics," and what James Boyd White calls "justice as translation": "Good transla-tion . . . proceeds not by the motives of dominance or acquisition, but by respect. It is a word for a set of practices by which we learn to live with differ-ence, with the fluidity of culture and with the instability of the self. It is not simply an operation of mind on material, but a way of being oneself in relation to another human being."

One of White's central points is that the practice of law is the practice of translation. The lawyer constantly moves between languages, mediating between them, between the stories of clients and the arguments of law, and, crucially for the democratic character of law, she makes "the ultimate translation [of law] into the ordinary language of the citizen." Lawyers come to public discourse about justice already engaged in it.

II.   Justice, Story, and the Law

Some decisive national occasions precipitate community willingness "to reassess fundamental beliefs and commitments as few events in political life do." "Constitutional moments" are an example of the phenomenon, and one seems to be in progress in Britain just now. Another is show trials in transitions from administrative massacre to democracy as may be illustrated by the prosecution of military juntas in Argentina. Such singular occasions concentrate the mind of the polis on fundamentals.

The civil rights movement may have precipitated an American constitutional moment. An obituary for Federal Judge Frank Johnson of Alabama celebrated his opinions during that time and described him as one of the "courageous men and women asking Americans to decide what kind of people they wanted to be." His courtroom joined the streets of Birmingham and Montgomery as a site for raising the issue of justice.

The question of who Americans would be, however, is not reserved for such extraordinary times. It is regularly before us, and answers to it are routinely in formulation in law. A photographic study of courthouses, those landmark centers of community life, makes a successful visual argument that "they are our history" and that the study of them is a "way of reconstructing the American people's story." The structured telling and contesting of stories that takes place in trials and to some extent in appeals and that lies at the heart of law is an ongoing performance of our story of justice. As White says, law is "a way in which the community defines itself, not once and for all, but over and over, and in the process it educates itself about its own character and the nature of the world." The participants are working out our story.

Robert Burns helpfully observes that the trial structure of competing stories "assures that the jury will not act on the basis of One Big Story authorized by a state official. . . . It reflects a distinctly Anglo-American approach that the inability to agree on one story to be told is precisely what brings the parties to trial." There is no "metanarrative that resolves the differences." The jury's decision in that tension between competing stories "decisively shapes what the community is becoming." Trials are one of the ways in which we determine and perform our story of justice. . . .

———————

3.   Jurors Behaving Badly

The jury has a major role in what Ball calls the performance of our story of justice. But what happens to justice when jurors fail to perform correctly? And how would we even know, given the general secrecy surrounding deliberations? The next excerpt discusses some of the myriad ways jurors can misbehave.

CONTAMINATING THE VERDICT: THE PROBLEM OF JUROR MISCONDUCT
Bennett L. Gershman
50 South Dakota Law Review 322 (2005)

Bias and misconduct by jurors have been demonstrated in several different ways. Instances of jurors violating their oath and engaging in improper conduct have produced a significant body of case law analyzing the juror's conduct, the nature and seriousness of the impropriety, the extent to which the conduct may have prejudiced the trial, and the appropriate methods available to the trial judge to remedy the problem. The kinds of misconduct include the following: contacts by third parties with jurors; exposure by jurors to extra-judicial non-evidentiary materials; efforts by jurors to conduct experiments and reenactments to test the evidence; untruthful statements by jurors during the voir dire; conduct by jurors that evinces bias and prejudgment; physical and mental impairment of jurors; pre-deliberation discussion by jurors; and efforts by jurors to repudiate the trial court's instructions on the law.

A. Third-Party Contacts

It is fundamental that "the 'evidence developed' against a defendant shall come from the witness stand in a public courtroom where there is full judicial protection of the defendant's right of confrontation, of cross-examination, and of counsel." Violations of these protections occur when third parties engage in private contacts or communications with jurors concerning matters pending before the jury. The leading case involving juror exposure to external influences is *Remmer v. United States*. There, the jury foreman was contacted by an unknown caller and offered a bribe to acquit the defendant. Without advising the defense, the judge asked the FBI to investigate the matter and concluded that the approach was harmless. The Supreme Court remanded for a hearing, holding that a "presumption of prejudice" should apply to any extra-judicial contact with a juror about the case. The Court stated:

> In a criminal case, any private communication, contact, or tampering directly or indirectly, with a juror . . . about the matter pending before the jury is, for obvious reasons, deemed presumptively prejudicial, if not made in pursuance of known rules of the court and the instructions and directions of the court made during the trial, with full knowledge of the parties. The presumption is not conclusive, but the burden rests heavily upon the Government to establish, after notice to and hearing of the defendant, that such contact with the juror was harmless to the defendant. . . .

B. Exposure to Extra-Judicial Materials

A jury's exposure to extraneous information not presented as evidence in the courtroom can contaminate a verdict as readily as third-party contacts. When such extrinsic information relates to a material issue in the trial, it can seriously impair a defendant's right to a fair trial and an impartial jury. Such information may reveal a defendant's guilt, prior criminal record, prior misconduct, reputation for violence, or a co-defendant's guilty plea. Extrinsic information may come from a juror's personal knowledge, the jury's exposure to mid-trial publicity, or from official documents and records made available to the jury. The distinction between intrusions from extra-judicial contacts by third parties and exposure to extra-judicial information ordinarily has no bearing in determining whether the verdict was tainted by the event. The nature of extra-judicial information to which jurors have been exposed ranges from the very prejudicial to the insignificant. Exposures to external information that required a new trial included knowledge by one juror that was imparted to other jurors that the federal defendant had been convicted in state court for the same conduct; jurors' pre-existing knowledge of specific facts surrounding the crime and defendant's connection to it; an opinion by two jurors who had professional expertise in medicine on whether defendant's explanation for blood loss was credible; and the trial court's acceding to the jury's request, after the close of the evidence and during deliberations, to return to the courtroom to observe the defendant's ears, which were covered during the trial for Spanish translation through headphones.

Jurors also may acquire extraneous information relating to the facts of the case or the meaning of certain legal principles by engaging in extra-judicial research. A juror's acquisition of extra-judicial, non-evidentiary knowledge, particularly when the juror disseminates the information to the other jurors, may produce sufficient prejudice to require reversal. Moreover, the ready accessibility of the Internet makes such research not only easy, quick, and extremely informative, but also potentially highly prejudicial. Examples of jurors engaging in extrinsic research include consulting an encyclopedia to confirm that a blood type is rare, researching law treatises to ascertain the meaning of legal concepts such as "malice," or the possible penalties for first and second degree murder, and gaining access to a dictionary to define prominent terms associated with the case, such as "enterprise" in a RICO prosecution, or "callous" and "wanton" in a homicide trial. *People v. Wadle* is a recent example of a jury verdict being tainted by a juror's unauthorized use of the Internet to acquire information relevant to the case. The defendant was charged with the shaking death of her 4-month-old step-grandchild. The prosecution presented evidence that the defendant was taking the anti-depressant Paxil for stress and holiday season depression. During deliberations, a juror who had training as an emergency medical technician told the other jurors that Paxil was a "very strong drug" that was "used for people who are antisocial, violent, or suicidal." Despite the trial judge's denial of the jury's request to consult a pharmacological reference, a juror downloaded form the Internet a description of Paxil and the next day read the description to the jury. The description stated that the drug is used to treat "mental depression, obsessive-compulsive disorder, panic disorder, and social anxiety disorder."

Following a conviction, and learning of the jury's action, the trial court conducted an evidentiary hearing and concluded that the juror's use of the
Internet constituted misconduct, but denied the defendant's motion for a new
trial on the ground that there was no reasonable possibility that the extraneous information affected the verdict. The appellate court reversed, finding that
the juror's use of the Internet, in direct violation of the trial judge's order,
tainted the verdict. The court noted that given the sharp conflict in the testimony, the jury may have used the specialized and complex terminology from
the Internet to assess the defendant's motive, state of mind, and credibility as
a witness. The fact that the defendant was taking an anti-depressant, anti-
anxiety medication for panic attacks may have been a determining factor in
the jury's verdict. Recognizing the problems created by the availability and
widespread use of the Internet, the court instructed trial judges to emphasize
to jurors that they "should not consult the Internet or any other extraneous
materials" during the trial and deliberations. . . .

C.   Experiments and Reenactments

Jurors do not live in capsules. It is not expected that jurors should leave
their common sense and cognitive functions at the door before entering the
jury room. Nor is it expected that jurors should not apply their own knowledge, experience, and perceptions acquired in the everyday affairs of life to
reach a verdict. However, a juror's procurement of new knowledge gained
through extra-judicial means may contaminate the deliberations and upset
the verdict. The line between the two sources of information, needless to say,
is not easily drawn.

Courts are much more likely to recognize as appropriate a juror's knowledge
gained from ordinary life experiences. For example, there is no impediment to
a juror's knowledge gained from personal experience that a particular neighborhood is busy all night, drawing a map to show the location of buildings in
a certain area, or describing a person's ability to make an accurate identification from a moving automobile. These mental processes involve no more than
the application of everyday observations and common sense to the factual
issues in the trial. By the same token, the application by a juror, trained as a
professional engineer, of his technical knowledge of physics to refute an opinion offered by a defense witness also was permissible.

By contrast, a juror's deliberately contrived investigation or experiment that
relates to a material issue in the trial ordinarily undermines the integrity of
the verdict. Acquiring relevant factual information in this manner puts the
jury in possession of evidence not presented at the trial and not subjected to
confrontation and cross-examination. Examples of improper juror experimentation include a juror who placed a heavy load in the trunk of his car as a
conscious way to determine whether such weight in a trunk would have
imparted knowledge to the defendant of the presence of drugs, a juror's experiment in attempting to fire a weapon while holding it in a position consistent
with the defendant's account, clocking how long it would take to drive a certain distance, and simulating a witness's use of binoculars to determine
whether the witness could possibly have seen what he claimed he saw. The

same principle that forbids jurors from acquiring specialized knowledge through extra-judicial means also accounts for the prohibition against jurors making unauthorized visits to locations described in the trial testimony. . . .

Reenactments in the jury room based on the jury's recollection of the testimony are usually allowed as an application of the jury's common sense and deductive reasoning to determine the truth of the facts in dispute. The reenactments by jurors portrayed in the classic film *Twelve Angry Men* illustrate the use of critical analysis by jurors of the evidence based on their knowledge and experience. One of the reenactments in the film involved a juror who, based on his experience as an adolescent familiar with the use of a switchblade knife, described the manner in which a switchblade knife ordinarily would be opened and thrust outward, thereby contradicting a key theory of the prosecution. Another reenactment in the film portrayed a juror simulating the time it would take for an elderly, crippled witness to go from his bedroom to the door of his apartment in order to determine whether the witness's estimate of the time it took to travel the distance — a critical issue in the trial — was accurate and believable.

However, if the reenactment is not merely a more critical analysis of the evidence but puts the jury in possession of extraneous information that might be based on flawed and irrelevant conclusions, the reenactment may be found improper. For example, a juror engaged in improper conduct by biting another juror to observe the resulting bruises. Also improper was a reenactment by a juror with machinery that had been admitted into evidence but was operated under conditions wholly unlike the conditions relevant to the charges.

D.   Untruthful Statements During Voir Dire

The Sixth Amendment and the Due Process Clause guarantee a defendant the right to an unbiased jury. The voir dire of prospective jurors serves to protect a defendant's right to an impartial jury "by exposing possible biases, both known and unknown, on the part of potential jurors." Bias of prospective jurors may be actual or implied. Actual bias is a bias in fact; implied bias is a bias that is presumed as a matter of law. Actual bias may be established by showing that a juror failed to respond honestly to questions during voir dire and that a truthful response "would have provided a valid basis for a challenge for cause." As the Supreme Court observed, "[t]he necessity of truthful answers by prospective jurors if this process is to serve its purpose is obvious." Bias also may be presumed or imputed to a juror by establishing from the circumstances that the juror is unable to exercise independent and impartial judgment. Proof of juror bias necessitates a new trial.

There is a presumption that prospective jurors answer the voir dire questions truthfully. There is also a presumption that a juror's failure to respond honestly during voir dire is indicative of bias. Prospective jurors for various reasons may give deliberately untruthful answers. Deliberate concealment or misleading responses also may impair a party's right to meaningfully exercise challenges to the juror's ability to serve and ordinarily provide a basis for relief. However, only intentionally dishonest or misleading responses provide a basis for relief. Forgetfulness or honest mistakes, by contrast, do not establish dishonesty and are not grounds for a new trial. As the Supreme Court noted, "[t]he motives for concealing information may vary, but only those reasons that affect a juror's impartiality can truly be said to affect the fairness of a trial." . . .

E. Bias and Prejudgment

Apart from showing that a juror gave dishonest or misleading answers during voir dire, a party still may be entitled to relief by demonstrating that a juror harbors an actual bias or that a bias may be imputed to the juror based on the juror's conduct and the surrounding context and circumstances. As noted above, the ability to substantiate a claim of bias may be hampered by the rule against impeaching a juror's verdict, which would probably disallow testimony by jurors concerning negative or inappropriate comments made by a juror during deliberations. In *Smith v. Phillips*, the Supreme Court suggested that only proof of actual bias could be the basis for a new trial. The Court stated: "This Court has long held that the remedy for allegations of juror partiality is a hearing in which the defendant has the opportunity to prove actual bias." In *Smith*, a juror submitted during the trial an application for employment as an investigator with the same district attorney's office that was prosecuting the case. At a post-trial hearing on whether to grant a new trial for juror bias, the trial court found that the letter "was indeed an indiscretion" but that the letter did not demonstrate bias or prejudgment. Thereafter, on a petition for habeas corpus, the federal district court granted the writ by imputing bias to the juror as a matter of due process, finding that "the average man in [the juror's] position would believe that the verdict of the jury would directly affect the evaluation of his job application." The Court of Appeals for the Second Circuit affirmed. However, the Supreme Court rejected the conclusion that bias should be imputed to this juror and made the following observation:

> [D]ue process does not require a new trial every time a juror has been placed in a potentially compromising situation. Were that the rule, few trials would be constitutionally acceptable. The safeguards of juror impartiality, such as voir dire and protective instruction from the trial judge, are not infallible; it is virtually impossible to shield jurors from every contact or influence that might theoretically affect their vote. Due process means a jury capable and willing to decide the case solely on the evidence before it, and a trial judge ever watchful to prevent prejudicial occurrences and to determine the effect of such occurrences when they happen. . . .

F. Physical and Mental Incompetence

A necessary corollary of the right to an impartial jury is the right to a jury in which all of its members are physically and mentally competent. Proof that a juror was mentally impaired, intoxicated, or unconscious would appear to cast grave doubt on the integrity of the verdict. When such claims are raised during the trial, the judge is in a position to correct the problem and permit the trial to continue. When such claims are raised after the verdict, attempts to take corrective action become much more difficult. As noted earlier, the courts are reluctant to allow a post-verdict inquiry into a juror's mental state. The rule against admitting juror testimony to impeach a verdict is based on several policy considerations: the need for finality of the proceess, the interest in encouraging "full and frank discussion in the jury room," the interest in encouraging jurors to return an unpopular verdict without fear of community resentment, and the interest in inspiring the "community's trust in a system that relies on the decisions of laypeople." These interests routinely prevent jurors from giving testimony to invalidate a verdict based on allegations that jurors considered prejudicial and irrelevant matters, may have engaged in bizarre behavior during trial, were inattentive during the testimony, did not understand the judge's instructions, or disregarded those instructions. These policy reasons are often strong enough to overcome post-verdict proof that a juror was mentally impaired and to justify a court's refusal to conduct any formal investigation into her condition.

The same policy considerations supported the Supreme Court's decision in *Tanner v. United States*, upholding the trial judge's refusal to conduct an investigation into broad allegations that a jury "was on one big party" and numerous claims alleging jurors' excessive use of alcohol and drugs. The Court rejected the defendant's contention that substance abuse constituted an improper external influence. According to the Court, "drugs or alcohol voluntarily ingested by a juror seems no more an "outside influence" than a virus, poorly prepared food, or lack of sleep." As an internal matter, ingestion of drugs and alcohol was within the rule prohibiting juror testimony to upset a verdict.

G. Pre-Deliberation Discussions

Whereas some courts and commentators have argued that it should be permissible for jurors to have intra-jury discussions about the case during the trial, it is well-settled that jurors are forbidden to discuss the case before they have heard all of the evidence, closing arguments, and the court's legal instructions, and have begun formally deliberating as a collective body. Judges routinely admonish juries at the outset and throughout the trial to not discuss the case among themselves prior to deliberations. There are several reasons for this admonition. Premature discussions are likely to be unfavorable to a defendant, incline jurors who expressed opinions prematurely to adhere to those opinions, impair the value of collective decision-making, lack the context of the court's legal instructions, prejudice a defendant who may not have had the opportunity to present evidence, and benefit the prosecution by reducing the burden of proof. . . .

H. Nullification

Jury nullification is understood as a refusal by a jury to apply the law as instructed by the court. Nullification has been condemned as "lawless," an "aberration," and a "denial of due process." As one court observed, "[a] jury has no more 'right' to find a 'guilty' defendant 'not guilty' than it has to find a 'not guilty' defendant 'guilty,' and the fact that the former cannot be corrected by a court, while the latter can be, does not create a right out of the power to misapply the law." The dangers of nullification were described by Judge Simon Sobeloff in an oft-quoted statement:

> To encourage individuals to make their own determinations as to which laws they will obey and which they will permit themselves as a matter of conscience to disobey is to invite chaos. No legal system could long survive if it gave every individual the option of disregarding with impunity any law which by his personal standard was judged morally untenable. Toleration of such conduct would not be democratic, as appellants claim, but inevitably anarchic.

It is commonly recognized that juries have the power to nullify the law, although they do not have the right to do so. It has thus been the settled rule in federal courts and virtually all state courts for over a century that the jury's function is to accept the law that is given to it by the court and to apply that law to the facts, and that no instruction should be given to a jury that it has the power to nullify. Counsel's invitation to a jury during summation to disregard the law is misconduct and subject to contempt. Jurors who engage in the practice may be removed.

A trial judge has the power to remove jurors who become incapacitated or otherwise become unavailable during the course of deliberations. Whether a court has the power to remove a juror who refuses to follow the law has received much less attention. However, the few cases that have addressed the question emphatically support the judge's power of removal. The major difficulty in administering this power is being able to conduct an appropriate investigation into the allegation of misconduct without jeopardizing the traditional rule of secrecy in jury deliberations. . . .

NOTES & QUESTIONS

1. What examples of juror misconduct can you pinpoint from popular culture? Dennis Quaid plays a juror who has an affair with defense counsel, played by Cher, in *Suspect* (1987). (Bias, anyone?) Pauly Shore's character lies during voir dire in order to get on the jury in *Jury Duty*, as do Richard Dice, played by Rob Lowe in *Illegally Yours* (1988) and Nick Easter, played by John Cusack in *Runaway Jury*. There are outside threats and violence against jurors in *Trial by Jury* and *The Juror*. It is surprisingly easy to find examples of juror misconduct in popular culture. Why is this? Surely the films had legal consultants. Are these incidents just inserted for dramatic effect, to tell a good story? Or is there something more insidious at work? Does popular culture exhibit a certain cynicism or distrust toward the jury system, suggesting jurors are generally corrupt or capable of corruption?

F.   THE JURY AND POPULAR CULTURE

1.   How Does Popular Culture Affect the Jury?

Jurors, like the rest of us, are immersed in a sea of popular culture on a daily basis. Television, films, the internet, magazines, billboards — how do such aspects of contemporary culture affect the way a jury decides a case? The next two excerpts suggest that savvy lawyers tap into popular culture in order to tell stories that jurors will find compelling.

"DESPERATE FOR LOVE II": FURTHER REFLECTIONS ON THE INTERPENETRATION OF LEGAL AND POPULAR STORYTELLING IN CLOSING ARGUMENTS TO A JURY IN A COMPLEX CRIMINAL CASE
Philip N. Meyer
30 University of San Francisco Law Review 931 (1996)

During 1990 and 1991, I attended criminal trials in the state and federal courts of Connecticut. It had been many years since I had attended trials as a young attorney specializing in litigation. Over the course of observing several high-profile criminal trials I noticed several developments.

To begin with, I observed that the nature of lawyering practice and storytelling at trial is changing rapidly. Many of these changes are the result of new technologies, especially the use of aural and visual "paratexts" at trial. These new technologies include computer simulation, visual aids, and other "storytelling" devices. The impact of this new storytelling technology at trial is profound. The use of these paratexts has permitted reinvention of the ways that stories are now told, and often the types of stories that are told. Evidence is often presented aurally and visually. These are "present-tense" simulations of voices and images, rather than past-tense testimonial evidence. This adjustment enables, and perhaps compels, a radical reinvention of the types of stories told at trial.

Secondly, the law is increasingly complex. Evidentiary details accumulate over weeks and even months. This legal and factual "complexification" of the trial provides additional room for narrative invention and ultimately severs the trial from the events that the storytellers purport to describe. Furthermore, the storytelling at trial often "slows down" some events that led up to the trial, as the past is re-imagined and reconfigured from multiple perspectives. Consequently, the storytelling at trial takes far longer than the events themselves. Crucial moments in the dramatic action of the trial can be examined through multiple media and from multiple perspectives (audio and visual tapes, witness testimony, inventive storytelling). At other times, the storytellers can skip over vast spaces of time, especially in the back story that frames the action, and choose to focus on crucial moments of criminality or drama.

Additionally, lawyers' work has become popularized and narrativized in the popular imagination through the media, including television and film. These stories incorporate artistic and aesthetic patterns embedded in the cultural imagination.

As a result of these changes, a phenomenon has occurred that is notable in the high-profile and complex criminal trials I observed: jurors seem to make sense out of increasingly complex situations through references to other imagistic stories. The new media world at trial evokes other cinematic stories of popular culture. There is an apparent interpenetration between popular stories and the stories that lawyers tell at trial. No longer does popular culture merely reflect the stories told by lawyers at trial — popular culture creates these stories. . . .

REALITY PROGRAMMING LESSONS FOR TWENTY-FIRST CENTURY TRIAL LAWYERING
Gary S. Gildin
31 Stetson Law Review 61 (2001)

[T]wo interrelated changes are occurring as we enter the new millennium that must affect the way trial lawyers present their cases to the jury — the evolution in the demographics of the jury pool and the revolution in technology that has transformed how our new breed of juror receives and is presented out-of-court information.

A spate of recent articles has documented that Generation X has arrived not only to populate, but to dominate, the jury pool. Jury consultants Elizabeth Foley and Adrienne LeFevre offer that, in the year 2000, thirty percent of all jury panels will be composed of representatives of the 78.2 million Americans born between 1966 and 1976. Projecting that Generation X will make up forty-one percent of the jury pool in the year 2000, Sonya Hamlin updated her seminal work *What Makes Juries Listen* — newly minted as *What Makes Juries Listen Today* — on account of "[t]he fundamental changes in the jury and how people get information." Michael Maggiano, in his article "Motivating the Modern Juror," cites data predicting that, in the next five years, fully half of the jurors will be members of Generation X. All who have recognized Generation X's invasion of the venire agree that trial lawyers must adapt both the substance and manner of their presentations to the contemporary juror. For members of Generation X, life experiences have not only given rise to a unique set of values and biases, but also have imbued these jurors with ways of receiving and evaluating information that differ vastly from preceding epochs.

Invariably, the assessment of new strategies for shaping trial presentations to Generation X jurors is accompanied by acknowledgment of the second galvanizing change in society — the rapid rise of new technologies to accumulate and convey knowledge. Indeed, most commentators cite an interrelationship between the technology that may have been instrumental in affecting the thought processes of Generation X and the metamorphosis that the ascension of that generation has mandated in trial advocacy. Hence, while the ultimate object of the trial has remained constant, the twenty-first century lawyer must adapt his or her advocacy to accommodate the new audience, as well as to employ new means of information delivery.

While consultants and trial lawyers are in the nascent stages of pondering how to adjust to the new jurors and technologies, other disciplines have already changed the way they go about the business of informing and persuading. This Article proposes that television is the medium that currently serves as the most useful guide for informing and persuading the new generation of jurors about the truth of past events — more particularly, its two species of reality programming.

II. How Television Can Help Us Learn Modern Trial Techniques

Like examining movies and theater, studying television may lend insight into precisely how jurors will process information offered at trial. In his recent, fascinating book, *When Law Goes Pop: The Vanishing Line Between Law and Popular Culture*, Professor Richard K. Sherwin cautioned how the media affects the manner in which jurors will interpret reality:

> Popular culture, especially through its chief agency, the visual mass media, also contributes to law by helping to shape the very processes of thought and perception by which jurors judge. . . . Each generation learns a new set of skills for making sense of experience. These meaning-making skills make up what may be called a "communal tool kit."

> For most people the source [of the tool kit] is not difficult to ascertain. It is the visual mass media: film, video, television, and to an increasing degree computerized imaging. This vast electronic archive provides us with the knowledge and interpretation skills we need to make sense of ordinary reality. . . . In a sense, we "see'" reality the way we have been trained to watch film and TV. The camera is in our heads. . . .

NOTES & QUESTIONS

1. What are the implications of Philip Meyer's comment that popular culture creates the stories lawyers tell at trial? Should every law school require a course in popular culture? If jurors have certain expectations about trial stories based on popular culture, the wise lawyer will be familiar with popular culture.

2. How would the type of Gen X juror Gary Gildin describes compare to a Baby Boomer juror raised on images of Raymond Burr as Perry Mason and Henry Fonda in *12 Angry Men*? If television is the key medium for Gen X jurors, is the internet the key medium for Gen Y? How might the internet affect jurors' storytelling expectations at trial?

2. What Kind of Stories About Juries Can Popular Culture Tell?

Consider again the issue of power and the juror. There seem to be two threads, two divergent types of power stories about juries in popular culture: the story of the imperiled, powerless juror or the story of the strong, powerful juror. In one type of popular dramatic story about jurors, the juror-hero spends much of the film as an almost completely powerless pawn (see, for example, the characters Valerie Alston in *Trial by Jury* and Annie Laird in *The Juror*). The imperiled juror is caught in the clutches of evil men and forced to "throw" the jury deliberations in order to protect herself and her family. Not until the end of the film does she take on power, and she often does so at the expense of her integrity and perhaps the integrity of the system.

Another kind of dramatic story about jurors also is about power, but it features the opposite kind of story: a juror who is so powerful he can by talking alone direct the course of a verdict (see, for example, *12 Angry Men* and *Runaway Jury*). Henry Fonda's character in *12 Angry Men* evidences this power in a positive way, through integrity and courage, while John Cusack's more problematic Nick Easter in *Runaway Jury* uses manipulation and mind games to direct the course of deliberations. (Additionally, it is noteworthy that the most imperiled juror characters tend to be women, while the most overtly powerful are men. How does gender impact the juror story in popular culture?)

Why is there this tension between power and lack of power in juror movies? Are juror movies enabling or disabling for viewers who themselves are potential jurors? Is there another possibility, a different kind of jury story that you can imagine?

THE JURY AND POPULAR CULTURE
Jeffrey Abramson
50 DePaul Law Review 497 (2000)

Ours has not been a culture that likes to tell stories about juries out-of-school. Whether from respect for the sanctity of juries, the awe of their oracular mystery, or just plain fear of what lay inside Pandora's box, the law regards the jury room as virtually off limits to journalists and outside observers. Even screenplay writers and novelists rarely make jury deliberation central to the drama. There are exceptions of course, John Grisham's *The Runaway Jury* being the most famous contemporary example, the teleplay *Twelve Angry Men* is an older exhibit. However, deliberation is still largely a subject waiting for its dramatist. In fiction, as in real trials, the jury remains on the sidelines, an audience rather than an actor, passive rather than active.

In contrast, we have vast popular literature about jury selection devoted to all types of lore about the cunning of lawyers and the strategies of that already legendary figure, the paid scientific jury consultant. A familiar feature of trial coverage is the running tally that reporters offer about how many accountants versus social workers, women versus men, whites versus Hispanics have been selected to date. This box score is updated daily and repeated throughout trial coverage, resonating with the prevailing view that the real drama in jury trials is played out during jury selection.

Legal thrillers offer rich and nuanced portraits of victims (the heroes and the fakes), lawyers (the crusaders and the parasites), communities (their prejudices and their sufferings), whistleblowers (their fates and their fortunes), witnesses (their fears and their foibles), the cop (the crooked and the honest), and the reporter (the insider and the outsider). However, jurors appear mostly in stock and supporting roles such as the bribed or intimidated juror in a Mafia trial, the planted juror in a big tobacco lawsuit, the juror in mid-vendetta or love affair, and the juror out of his league or over his head.

If we look behind the stock-in-trade jury characters, however, popular portrayals of civil jury trials do capture great public debates about injury and claiming in America, as well as debates about blame and responsibility. "I'm having a hard time understanding why we're supposed to make this woman a multimillionaire," a Grisham juror says of a smoker suing the tobacco companies. The remark resonates with the struggle jurors frequently go through to reconcile the deep cultural norms about work and reward with the legal norms about liability and compensation. Jury work is about constituting and reconstituting those norms, and the best of the courtroom dramas at least place us, the audience, in the position of the jury. . . .

V. CONCLUSION. . . .

Populists tell stories from the bottom up, victims recouping their honor by taking on the giant corporations destroying their communities. Lawyers are rarely the driving forces in populist narrative, they are more likely to be saved and uplifted by the company of ordinary people than the other way around.

Hamiltonians tell a mirror-image story, about victimized corporations and fraudulent plaintiffs served by the big industry of trial lawyers. The undeserving poor in popular welfare legends easily translate into the undeserving plaintiffs in popular jury lore. "Popular justice" is an oxymoron for Hamiltonians. Lawyers are no better than are pickpockets who like their pockets deep.

Wilsonians believe that law, lawyers, and trials can force and direct social change by pushing for new norms. Law never floats free of public opinion and cultural practices, but trials and juries can reconstitute norms in ways that energize social forces ready to apply the norms in practice.

There used to be a fourth narrative about juries and civil litigation. It was the story Alexis de Tocqueville told about the American jury, a more robustly democratic story than is told by any of the three surviving narratives. I close by recounting Tocqueville's democratic discourse on the civil jury, as a way to show the limits of contemporary aspirations for the civil jury.

Tocqueville purposely refrains from defending the jury, whether civil or criminal, as a way of deciding cases. "If it were a question of deciding how far the jury, especially the jury in civil cases, facilitates the good administration of justice, I admit that its usefulness can be contested." Indeed, already in the 1830s, the French visitor had heard arguments that the complexity of modern lawsuits outstripped the competence of jurors as fact finders. The jury arose "in the infancy of society, at a time when only simple questions of fact were submitted to the courts." Adapting the jury "to the needs of a highly civilized nation, where the relations between men have multiplied exceedingly," is "no easy task."

However, "arguments based on the incompetence of jurors in civil suits carry little weight with me," Tocqueville continued. Partly he thought the concern with "the enlightenment and capacities" of jurors was misplaced, as if the jury were merely a "judicial" institution to be judged narrowly by its use to litigants. More crucially, Tocqueville saw the assessment of juror qualifications as too static, unmindful of the moral uplift and civic education that comes from investing citizens with responsibility for justice. This is the part of the Tocquevillian narrative that has wholly dropped out of contemporary conversation about the civil jury. Ultimately, the jury for Tocqueville was rightly as much a political as a legal institution. The jury was as characteristic of democracy as universal suffrage. Juries took an abstract ideal such as "popular sovereignty" and "really puts control of society into the hands of the people."

Applied to the criminal jury, Tocqueville's emphasis on the jury as a political institution is familiar. Even today, we continue to value the criminal jury as a forum for popular input into the law. However, descriptions of the civil jury as a "political body" are far more jarring to the contemporary ear. Nevertheless, Tocqueville believed the civil jury was more important than the criminal jury as a way of empowering and educating citizens for self-government. The civil jury of the 1830s was "one of the most effective means of popular education at society's disposal." The jury was "a free school which is always open," a place where ordinary citizens rub elbows with the "best-educated" and gain "practical lessons in the law." Service on civil juries was the principal reason a broad segment of the American public came into "political good sense."

Criminal trials involve the people only "in a particular context," but civil litigation "impinges on all interests" and "infiltrates into the business of life." Few people can imagine themselves a defendant in a criminal trial. However, "anybody may have a lawsuit." Therefore, "[e]ach man, when judging his neighbor, thinks that he may be judged himself." In this way, civil juries "teach men equity in practice."

Far from fomenting class divisions and rich versus poor adversary relations, civil juries moderate popular passions by establishing the judge as legal tutor for jurors. Law is the only aristocratic force left in America, Tocqueville thought, and via the jury, it extends its empire over the common person. "[T]he legal spirit penetrate[s] right down into the lowest ranks of society."

Tocqueville's republican narrative of the civil jury as a crucible of democratic learning is fairly unspoken in America. Hamiltonians scoff at the idea that ordinary people can be brought up to speed by some ritualistic recital of legal instructions. Wilsonians agree that law is a matter for professional elites, not amateurs. Only populists remain enticed by the ideal of participatory democracy. Ultimately, populists lack patience to practice the ideal; they would rather stay home and are aroused to wrest control back from elites only when betrayed. Therefore, the populist tells great stories about muscular juries delivering an occasional blow for the people. However, they do not tell Tocqueville's kind of story, the republican story about the daily, undramatic work of juries and the slow ways jury duty inculcates habits of persuasion and deliberation, the civic virtues of collective argument upon which self-government depends. For all the popularity of the courtroom drama, there remains no drama since *Twelve Angry Men* that centrally portrays the dynamics of jury deliberation.

NOTES & QUESTIONS

1. Are there any popular culture examples of Professor Abramson's fourth type of narrative — Alexis de Tocqueville's idea of the civil jury as ideal democratic institution? Is there yet a story to tell about the civil jury as political institution?

Or is this too old-fashioned or too un-dramatic of a notion? *12 Angry Men* seems to fit the bill best, except for the fact that it is a criminal rather than a civil trial. But are there more recent examples you can identify?

3.   Images of the Jury in Popular Culture

THE UNSEEN JURY
Bill Nichols
30 University of San Francisco Law Review 1055 (1996)

The films *Twelve Angry Men* and *Inside the Jury Room* both belong to the sub-genre of the courtroom movie that address the theme of the wrong man. What separates these two films from the rest of the sub-genre is their singular focus on the process of jury deliberation. My nomination of these two films stems from the rarity with which jury deliberations receive representation and from the insights the two films offer into the complexities of the process.

The open courtroom trial is the outward and visible sign of legal justice. Many works, from the Perry Mason television series to films like *Inherit the Wind*, *To Kill a Mockingbird*, and *Reversal of Fortune* celebrate the process by which the legal skills, argumentative strategies, and psychological acumen of great lawyers can so arrange evidence that the work of the jury becomes an invisible afterthought, a mere ratification of the truth already discovered or revealed by prosecution or defense. During the careful process of in camera deliberation, the image of guilt or innocence registered in the grain of courtroom evidence and argument develops into a clear, decisive verdict. Popular culture often presents jury deliberation as a largely technical and somewhat mechanical process, similar to film developing. Evidence, argument, and verdict should correspond closely with one another, almost in the same spirit of correlation as that between symptom and disease or barometric pressure and weather.

Twelve Angry Men and *Inside the Jury Room* reverse this underlying assumption; the jury's job is not done for it by heroic courtroom lawyers. The deliberation process has an autonomy of its own. It leads to verdicts that seem in flagrant violation of both evidence and law. What strategies both prosecutors and defense lawyers should adopt to take the distinctiveness and autonomy of jury deliberation into account is not pursued in either film, but the two trials of the Los Angeles police officers who beat Rodney King and the O.J. Simpson murder trial are vivid reminders of the importance of doing so.

Twelve Angry Men opens with a judge who can barely keep awake as he delivers his instructions to the jury. The self-evident verdict appears so foregone as to require no effort. We never see the lawyers or hear their arguments. If there is drama to be found here, it will have to come from the jury itself. . . .

Trial by jury may be a legal right, a "buffer between the accused and the power of the state," as the narrator of *Inside the Jury Room* intones, but it also testifies to a philosophical dilemma. Since antiquity, trials have provided a prime example of how to decide the undecidable. What really happened stands in doubt; no scientific procedure exists that can render a conclusive determination. The result is that someone must decide, following one or another set of criteria. Our trial process relies on the jury's verdict to arrive at a sense of an ending — but not at an incontestable conclusion (except by convention). Trial by jury is a social ritual by which we dispel certain forms of uncertainty about the past. We confer on a jury the obligation to put a stop to debates in which accuser and accused can both claim to uphold the truth, based on the terms and assumptions used to make their case. Two different arguments would string the same set of evidence into narrative chains endowing fact with meaning, doubt with certainty. And yet these meanings and truths diverged from, if not contradicted, each other. Guilty or innocent? It all depended on the adopted premises, rhetorical skill, and point of view. Both sides of such debates rely on language; verbal (and sometimes visual) representations. But as Richard Lanham notes:

> [Language has an] imperfect correspondence to the 'outside world,' whatever one might think that world to be. . . . It is from this accommodation to antithetical structure that Anglo-Saxon jurisprudence descends: we arrange social issues into diametrically opposed questions, arrange a dramatic display of their conflict, and (since the law cannot afford aporia [radical doubt] as a conclusion to social disputes) accept the jury-audience's verdict as a defining truth. . . .

Rather than continue courtroom debate indefinitely, jury deliberation has a different dynamic. As Henry Fonda asserts in *Twelve Angry Men*, "I don't have to be on a side, I'm just asking questions." One of the citizen-jurors in *Inside the Jury Room*, a doctor, shares this view: "I have lots of questions; we need to talk." The social dynamics of consensus building prevails over the public rhetoric of argumentation. What allows consensus to arise? What dynamics come into play? Anna Deveare Smith's play, *Twilight: L.A. Uprising 1992*, gives some insight into how this process involves a mix of psychodrama, personal confession, and the forging of a common resolve through narrative revision — telling yet another story with the same set of evidence. This "final" story puts a stop to argumentation not simply by choosing prosecution or defense as right or true, but by conforming the facts to a somewhat different frame. If the jury were to admit that "what really happened" is undecidable, it could not reach a verdict, but if it reaches a verdict, "what really happened" must be decidable after all. This double bind can be resolved by changing the frame. Consensus arrives not when the jury agrees on a common sense of what truly happened, but rather when it agrees on a common interpretation of what happened. This interpretation escapes the double bind by invoking a higher criterion of truth than the question of what really happened in a literal sense, namely justice.

Twelve Angry Men and *Inside the Jury Room* present complementary views of the process by which jurors base their verdicts on a sense of justice rather than conclusive truth. Common to both films, and abundantly evident in the Rodney King and O.J. Simpson trials, is that juries must undergo a reasoning process of their own, regardless of the argumentative clarity of prosecution or defense. Juries resist wholesale rubber-stamping of others' arguments and conclusions. As one juror from *Inside the Jury Room* puts it, in a highly individualistic version of this sentiment, "I am not a computer. I won't accept everything I'm told just because I'm told it is true. I can't do that as a thinking, breathing human being." This resistance provides the entry point for assumptions and arguments external to the courtroom phase of the trial. Resistance introduces personal predispositions and values, social biases and goals, and cultural differences and ideals acquired long before the trial began. It is between the hammer of cultural ideals and the anvil of ideological practices that consensus must be forged.

Twelve Angry Men dignifies the principle of the jury as buffer and of the arduous process of consensus-building as its central theme. The jury's charge is to determine the guilt or innocence of a teen-age male accused of murdering his father with a knife after an argument. The defendant belongs to a minority group and is probably Puerto Rican. Supporting the charge is the testimony of two eyewitnesses, countered only by an apparently weak alibi. The boy had a similar knife, but he had lost it, and he was at the movies at the time of the crime, but he could not remember the movie's title.

The jury initially votes eleven to one guilty. The sole holdout is our questioning, open-minded hero, Henry Fonda. Reprising his role from *Young Mr. Lincoln*, Fonda's function is to serve as the great unifier, dispelling prejudice, faulty reasoning, and uncommon haste to allow others to discover the truth they would have otherwise never seen. As in *Young Mr. Lincoln*, which pivots on Fonda's performance as a lawyer who discovers that a key witness has lied to hide his own guilt, Fonda again ferrets out the truth others fail to see. In this case, he exposes the vindictive hatred that poisons fellow juror Lee J. Cobb's judgment, driving him to insist intransigently on a guilty verdict against a rising tide of doubt. The penultimate vote is eleven to one not guilty with Cobb the now isolated and ostracized holdout.

In *Twelve Angry Men* Fonda ensures justice by rising above the presumptions and prejudices of his all too susceptible peers. At first the other jurors display astonishment that he is willing to doubt what they regard as settled. To dramatize the point, *Twelve Angry Men* attributes haste to selfish indifference (one juror, Jack Warden, hopes to finish quickly enough to get to a ball game that night) or personal bias (holdout Lee J. Cobb wants to punish the defendant unjustly as a surrogate for his own rebellious son). The jurors begin by almost humoring Fonda's hesitation but gradually come to see that his questioning spirit is right and their own rush to judgment is wrong; their willingness to accept testimony at face value jeopardizes the defendant's right to a fair trial. Another holdout, E.G. Marshall, insists on the use of cold logic. He shares none of Cobb's vitriolic hatred or the glib indifference of Jack Warden's baseball fan. Marshall finally comes around when the group discovers vital flaws in the testimony of the two eyewitnesses. Marshall's flaw was not haste but a failure to scrutinize evidence rigorously enough.

Fonda embodies a spirit of doubt aligned with the higher truth of justice and the spirit, not the letter, of the law. He opposes easy solutions, biased assumptions, prejudicial convictions, and faulty reasoning. To eliminate such limitations does not guarantee guilt so much as make doubt possible. His character's mission bears noticeable hints of a Christlike quality in the mise en scene and iconography of the film through such aspects as leaving him nameless until the very end, setting him physically apart, dressing him in white, and bestowing on him an air of transcendent serenity. Fonda puts a stop to debate, less by arriving at conclusive certainty, than by eliminating the proclivity to easy answers and quick fixes in a complex, divided world.

In *Twelve Angry Men* Henry Fonda works to make a verdict of not guilty serve justice when guilt initially seemed beyond doubt. He instigates a process, resisted by the others, of throwing the evidence back into doubt, dissolving the argumentative cohesiveness of the prosecution's case, and catalyzing the discovery of another story, another point of view, unveiling what haste and bias — in essence, the failure to scrutinize apparent facts with sufficient rigor — had hidden. Consensus emerges. Even though the truth cannot be known, justice can be done. Lumet gives us a close-up shot of the defendant as he hears the not guilty verdict; his look of innocence and vulnerability confirms the triumph of justice. (The film uses its own narrating authority to affirm what Fonda intuited.) Fonda prompts others to conclude that doubt is indeed *reasonable,* not simply in an absolute or philosophic sense, but in a historical sense, in *this* specific case. . . .

NOTES & QUESTIONS

1. *12 Angry Men* is perhaps the most well-known of jury films, and Henry Fonda's character is the juror as hero (his all-white suit, his courage, and his deep integrity all operate to code him as a Christ figure). We feel good about the system after watching *12 Angry Men*. Fonda's character had been a powerful juror. But what about the other thread of juror films, those films that tap into our anxieties about the powerlessness of the juror?

In *The Juror*, Demi Moore plays a single mom who does not try to get out of jury duty, because she thinks she needs "a little excitement." Her wish is granted, as a psychotic hit man (Alec Baldwin) bugs her home, murders her best friend, threatens to kill her young son, and generally makes her life hell. He insists on the impossible — that she manipulate the jury deliberations to get an acquittal, not just a hung jury. He also makes her wear a necklace containing an eavesdropping device so he can make sure she is doing her best during deliberations. Some kinky mind-games are going on, too. Moore's character is an artist, a sculptor who makes art in boxes. (You are supposed to feel the art, not see it.) Moore describes the process of viewing her art as "reaching up and feeling her private stuff." Baldwin buys some of her art, and tells her they are "kindred spirits," both artists in their own fields.

Baldwin's enforcer character makes Moore's helplessness crystal-clear early on in one scene where he takes her for a car ride and threatens to kill her son, who is riding on a bicycle ahead of them. Baldwin says, "The grey suits want you to love the law, justice. . . . But can the grey suits shield you from somebody like me?"

But are films with imperiled jurors really about the lack of power of the juror? Or are they perhaps about our cultural anxiety that an individual juror may in fact have too much power and abuse that power? Are these films the flip side of *12 Angry Men*? In *The Juror*, Demi Moore manages to single-handedly sway the other jurors to vote for acquittal. She does whatever it takes to get each juror to vote her way. She flirts with one juror who finds her attractive. She verbally beats down any arguments for guilt with a relentless emphasis on reasonable doubt. She even convinces one grandmother on the jury that letting this killer go free will make children safer. Listen carefully to the irony in this speech, where Moore desperately (and disingenuously) argues for the rule of law in order to save her son's life: "[I]f you twist the law even just a little for the best of reasons, then the law loses whatever power it's got and then my child is in even more danger than before, and so are your grandchildren." The jury votes for acquittal.

Similarly, in *Trial by Jury* the single mom played by Joanne Whalley-Kilmer is coerced into helping a murderer go free. In this film the mob-enforcer and former cop, played by William Hurt, merely wants her to hang the jury (not get a complete acquittal). After she does the job, Hurt tells her not to fret about the jury's decision. She asks, "And when he kills again?" Hurt replies, "It won't be nobody you'd have to dinner."

Both Demi Moore and Joanne Whalley-Kilmer get revenge, of course. They kill the bad guys. (Whalley-Kilmer does it most memorably. Dressed up as the glamorous kind of '40's pin-up that the mobster Armand Assante likes, she seduces him and then kills him with an ice-pick.) But such "happy" endings do not make us eager to sign up for jury duty.

Popular culture seems to suggest that jurors are at one and the same time devoid of power and filled with power, and neither state seems especially desirable. What do you make of this? Why is there this ambivalence?

2. In the next reading, Carol Clover uses cinematics to help explain the jury's ambiguous role in popular culture. She hypothesizes that, in many trial films, the audience becomes the jury. As you read, consider not only what we see but what we do not see when it comes to the role of the jury in films.

MOVIE JURIES
Carol J. Clover
48 DePaul Law Review 389 (1998)

Let us begin with a simple question: how does the camera look at juries in trial movies? A "trial movie" can provisionally be defined as a plot in which the significant action bears directly or indirectly on a specific trial, in which some important part plays out in a courtroom, and in which the outcome of the trial coincides with the climax of the film. The form is overwhelmingly Anglo-American, and, given its popularity, it is no surprise that academic lawyers have looked to it for an understanding of "popular legal culture." Most discussions of trial movies have been thematic, treating films in the same terms as they might treat novels or stage plays. But what happens if we look at such films, and more particularly their juries, cinematically? What do the cinematics in trial movies tell us that we do not already know about the place of juries in the public imagination?

The some two hundred Anglo-American trial movies that I have reviewed (in connection with an in-progress book on trials and entertainment) are remarkably consistent in their inventory of jury shots. The run-of-the-mill trial movie shows us images of the jury filing in (and/or out), listening attentively, occasionally registering some emotion (disgust, horror), and, in the person of the foreman, rendering a verdict. The "listening attentively" shots are the most common, if only because Hollywood cinematographic protocol calls for establishing shots and reaction shots in certain set-ups, and in the courtroom, the jury is an indicated position and "listening attentively" fits the bill. More telling, perhaps, is what we do not see. We seldom see jurors individually (when the camera does single one out, it is in a reaction shot, and the demeanor of the juror is understood to represent that of the group as a whole). We seldom see them anywhere but in the courtroom — not in hallways, elevators, or jury room. We almost never see them doing anything but being normally attentive; shots of the jury are remarkably contentless (in keeping with their function as reaction and establishing shots). We almost never see the jury close up; on the contrary, it is typically viewed at a distance and even indistinctly (because focus is on a lawyer in the foreground). Finally, and most significantly, we do not see the jury at any length. Most jury shots are held for three or four seconds at most, and in the standard trial movie, no more than a minute or two. There are some minor exceptions to these rules, but they are remarkably few and far between. The first and most important thing to be said about trial-movie juries, then, is that they barely exist. In the courtroom, juries are seen only briefly, and the work they do, their deliberation, is with very few exceptions avoided altogether. Within the film's universe, the jury is a kind of visual and narrative blank, viewed as so much human furniture when present, but mostly just absent.

This habit of avoiding the jury may seem a little odd in light of our public commitment to the institution and also in light of the ongoing discussion about its value. It seems odd that a culture as manifestly obsessed with jury trials as ours is (that obsession measured by film and television alone) should have so little interest in the actual decision process. It seems no less odd that our trial movies are so often critical of lawyers, judges, and law enforcement generally, but so rarely question the institution of the jury. (On this point, trial movies echo the bias of law jokes; lots about lawyers, almost none about juries.) *So* odd is the patterned avoidance of the jury as both a narrative issue and a visual subject that it wants an explanation. Is this a new development, or is it an abiding feature of the form?

One very early trial movie, the 1915 film *By Whose Hand?*, suggests an answer. In it, a woman is on trial for murder, but evidence keeps emerging that casts doubt on her guilt, and the film closes with a title exhorting the film audience to determine the truth: "YOU ARE THE JURY! YOU DECIDE!" Question mark endings of one sort or another are not as unusual as one might think in trial movies, and early examples like this one put the lie to the common claim that the unclosed or "contingent" text is somehow postmodern. What interests us here, however, is the apostrophizing of the film viewer as trier of fact. Film scholars distinguish between diegetic and extradiegetic effects, the former located in the fictional world of the film (like the music Sam plays in *Casablanca*) and the latter somewhere beyond it (like the Phillip Glass score in *The Thin Blue Line*). What the ending of *By Whose Hand?* suggests is that we should extend our search for the missing jury beyond the diegetic out into the realm of the extradiegetic. . . .

[E]ven rule-obedient trial movies have ways of gesturing toward an extradiegetic jury. One such gesture is the empty jury-box topos, dramatically used in recent times by *Presumed Innocent*. The film opens with the shot of the vacant courtroom. Our vision pans ever so slowly to the right until it arrives at the jury box. We pause. Then, at an almost imperceptible rate, we start moving forward. The empty, ornate chairs of the jury loom ever larger in our vision, and as the credits crawl over them, we hear a man's voice intone:

> I am a prosecutor. I am a part of the business of accusing, judging, and punishing. I explore the evidence of a crime and determine who is charged, who is brought to this room and tried before his peers. I present my evidence to the jury, and they deliberate upon it. They must determine what really happened. If they cannot, we will not know whether the accused deserves to be freed or punished. If they cannot find the truth, what is our hope for justice?

What is most striking about the voiceover is its incantatory tone. It is as though we, the spectators, are being ushered into the empty courtroom, directed to the empty chairs, and sworn in. Two hours later, we will revisit this scene — same shot of the empty courtroom and jury seats, voiceover in the same monotone. The time in between we spend not in the courtroom, but following the fortunes of the speaker, District Attorney Rusty Sabich (Harrison Ford) as he investigates the murder of his colleague Carolyn Polhemus (Greta Scacchi) with whom, it emerges, he had been having an affair. In fact, the finger of suspicion begins to point to him: the blood type matches his and a wineglass found in her apartment has his fingerprints on it, as well.

The visualized story roams into Sabich's obsessive relationship with Carolyn, into his home life with wife Barbara (Bonnie Bedelia), a woman angry about her husband's affair with Carolyn and dissatisfied with her role as bedmaker (she is at work on a dissertation but it's slow going), into his relation with his own lawyer, and into the District Attorney's political ambitions and shady connections. Even when we finally arrive in the courtroom, some eighty minutes into the film, our narrative and cinematic focus remains stubbornly on Rusty and his lawyer Stern (Raoul Julia) as we approach the bench with them, go to chambers with them, and so on. When it comes down to it, Sabich's own "work" is pretty much the work of the jury, which is to say pretty much our work — at least until some point in the last third of the film, when something seems to dawn on him that does not dawn on us. At that moment, he splits off from us, leaving us behind with the (unseen) diegetic jury, with whom we "vote," in the end, for a verdict of not guilty — not because we positively know otherwise, but simply because the prosecution did not meet the standard of reasonable doubt. The fact that we subsequently learn who really did it (Sabich's wife) does not mean that we have finally transcended our role as jurors in the rhetorical economy of the film; it only means that we are jurors who learned more after the fact, as jurors sometimes do. (*Presumed Innocent* lets us off easier than films like *Anatomy of a Murder*, in which we realize we are jurors who may have screwed up, or *Witness for the Prosecution*, in which we learn we are jurors who surely *did* screw up.) Our position and our predicament are slammed home in the film's closing scene, which returns us to the scene (same courtroom, same empty jury seats) and the sound (same flat voiceover) of the opening, the only difference being that this time the voice tells us, in effect, that the search for justice sometimes fails. At no time during the film's two hours do we so much as catch a glimpse of the jury actually trying the case — an omission all the more striking in light of the attention lavished on the empty seats in the beginning and again at the end. The point could hardly be clearer: *we* are it. *Court TV* and CNN viewers will recognize the empty jury-box as an image routinely used to advertise and to introduce coverage of current trials.

But let us turn from Mercedes strategies to Hyundai ones. Most trial movies and trial television dramas neither address us directly nor present us with a yawning jury box. But if we watch closely, we see that even the most run-of-the-mill examples have their own cinematographic strategies for positioning us as an outboard jury. Consider, to pick a couple of examples almost at random, *The Accused* and a trial sequence from the television serial *Law & Order*. Here we see the workaday strategy of trial movies. In both cases, the lawyers, in their closing arguments, look not quite at the camera, but just below it, shifting their gaze methodically between a point very slightly to the right of the camera and a point very slightly to the left of it, and so on, back and forth. In short, they come as close as one can to looking at us, without actually doing it — off just enough to meet the terms of the invisible-camera rule. Lest we miss the point, we see the backs of heads in our foreground — the heads of our fellow jurors in the front row. No one looks at us or calls us jurors, but we are jury-boxed as squarely by this "not quite" strategy as we were by the blunt strategies of *The Trial of Mary Dugan, Free, White, and 21*, and a host of other films, starting in 1906, that reach out directly to put us in our place.

But what, then, are we to make of *12 Angry Men*, a trial movie that not only shows the jury, but shows almost nothing *but*? It should be clear by now that for all of the respect that film enjoys, it is something of an oddball in the tradition. Three facts may bring its difference into focus. The first is that it based on a French original, *Justice est faite*. A film about jurors' overdetermined reactions in a mercy killing case, *Justice est faite* played the U.S. art-cinema circuit first in 1950 and again a couple of years later. (Reginald Rose's teleplay of *12 Angry Men* aired in 1953 and the film version was released in 1957.) A second fact to keep in mind about *12 Angry Men* is that it was hardly a success in its day. Indeed, it was a box office mediocrity, not even close to the top ten grossing films of that year. Reviews were mixed, and not a few venture some version of the opinion that it was not a proper trial movie. Finally, the idea did not start a trend. There have been a few remakes and takeoffs (recognizable as such) but no new subgenre of jury dramas. The fact that it was cloned but never produced offspring attests rather eloquently to its problematic hybridity as far as genre is concerned. As a public, it seems, we prefer trial dramas that do not disturb our role as triers of fact, even if they are less smart and less well acted, and so it is that after this very small blip on a very long horizon, we reverted to the security of the traditional arrangement. In short, *12 Angry Men's* jury-focus was an experiment conducted under the sign of European art cinema, and the film's present reputation is to a considerable extent the creation of academics and intellectuals after the fact. That reputation may be deserved, but I daresay it has somewhat deformed our perception of the place of the jury in cinema.

In the beginning of this presentation I proposed a definition of the trial movie as a plot in which the significant action bears directly or indirectly on a specific trial, in which some important part plays out in a courtroom, and in which the outcome of the trial coincides roughly with the climax of the film. To that definition we can now add that the trial movie is also a plot that both rhetorically and cinematically positions its audience as extradiegetic triers of fact. In his classic work on the rise of the English novel, Ian Watt proposed that the "novel's mode of imitating reality may be . . . well summarized in terms of the procedures of another group of specialists in epistemology, the jury in a court of law. Their expectations, and those of the novel reader, coincide in many ways. . . . The jury, in fact, takes the 'circumstantial view of life,' which [may] be the characteristic outlook of the novel."

As with the novel, so with film, even more obviously so. The jury system has provided Anglo-American popular cinema with a subject matter and with a rhetorical geometry that is fundamental not only to trial movies, but to a variety of genres (notably the detective thriller) that are trial-derived but stand at some remove from the courtroom. When German film director Uli Edel, assigned to a trial movie in Hollywood, tells how he "had to learn to set up the courtroom scenes in such a way that the whole film audience participates as the jury would," he put into words a procedure that is normally just performed as a matter of course. (His remark also acknowledges either a different practice in Europe or, just as tellingly, no experience making trial movies there.) The cinematics of trial movies not only bear him out, but gesture toward a silent contract of sorts between film and audience, an ongoing deal whereby we enter the theater prepared to double as audience and as outboard triers of fact, and, for better or worse, ready to judge the film both as a piece of cinema and as a piece of law.

It must be the film's presumption of an extradiegetic jury that explains why diegetic juries are so little seen and the process of their deliberation so consistently avoided in Anglo-American cinema: *we* are the jury, and any sustained representation of an opposite number within the diegesis would interfere with our habitual relation to the text. This analysis may also make some sense of the oft-lamented tendency of jurors to perceive real-life courtroom proceedings through the lens of scenarios from popular culture. (One could argue, given how many of those scenarios were born in the courtroom and, more generally, how deeply our most popular narrative forms have been imprinted by adversarial logic, that the chickens are merely coming home to roost. Call it reverse migration.) Finally, this analysis may explain why it is that in the world of law and politics, the jury can be the subject of critical debate, but in the world of popular culture, it remains for the most part serenely untouchable.

NOTES & QUESTIONS

1. Why do juries, as Clover notes, "barely exist" in so many trial movies? Is Clover correct in her point that in many trial movies, the film audience is the jury? How could such a cinematic positioning affect popular critiques (or the lack of critiques) of the jury? Does this "I, the Jury" stance we find ourselves in make us reluctant to criticize the portrayals of juries in popular culture?

2. Clover suggests a "reverse migration" effect, whereby jurors in real life expect certain things to happen at trial based on popular culture. Think back to our *Blame Judge Judy* reading in the previous chapter of this text concerning judges. What are the negative ways popular culture affects juror perceptions? Are there any positive effects?

PART III:

LEGAL SUBJECT AREAS

Chapter 8

TORT LAW

A. FILMOGRAPHY

A Civil Action (1999)

Class Action (1991)

Erin Brockovich (2000)

Philadelphia (1993)

The Verdict (1982)

B. THE PARTICIPANTS

1. Plaintiffs' Attorneys

Previous chapters have noted that law-related popular culture often empha-sizes lawyers' stories, and popular culture related to tort law is no exception. As you consider the plaintiffs' attorneys portrayed in the films discussed in this chapter and other popular culture with which you are familiar, think about whether the story being told about each character reflects the way in which society views personal injury lawyers.

REVERSALS OF FORTUNE: HOW HOLLYWOOD MAKES HEROES OUT OF LAWYERS
Patrick Keefe
Legal Affairs, March/April 2003, 48

John Grisham's band of wide-eyed and good-hearted rookies notwithstand-ing, lawyers nowadays tend to be typecast as morally vacuous opportunists, practitioners of a black art that is inaccessible to the average Joe yet utterly capable of ruining his life.

But Hollywood being Hollywood, there is always room for redemption, even in a jaundiced age, even for lawyers. *The Verdict* is one of a handful of court-room dramas in which lawyers are allowed to be heroic, not in the born-heroic manner of Gregory Peck's Atticus Finch, but in classic Hollywood redemption style, where heroism must be mustered at a crucial juncture.

The Verdict and a series of films that have followed its lead over the last two decades chronicle the lives of down-and-out attorneys who have been lulled by the routines of their practices into risk-averse lawyering for profit — and

289

along the way, have lost the ability to make moral judgments. But in the end, they are redeemed through a Big Case.

In *A Civil Action* and *Erin Brockovich*, lawyers who have lost touch with the nobler aspects of the profession are instilled with the desire to see the justice system dispense justice. These films adhere to a fairly strict formula. The lawyers, often personal injury lawyers, are jolted out of their parasitic and banal existence by the novelty of an innocent and deserving client. While profit might lead them to take on the case, a moral awakening persuades them not to settle, and to proceed to trial in the face of staggering odds.

These films seem to argue that the law itself, in its cold objectivity and its refusal to make exceptions, is somehow antithetical to justice. These films start with the assumption that if lawyers are generally rotten people, then it's the study and practice of law that made them that way. The lawyers have lost their humanity in their immersion in the law, but these deracinated souls manage to find new resolve by representing innocent clients and placing the demands of justice over profit, practice, even the law itself.

And they pull it off — handsomely. In several of these cases, redemption comes with a big check. You have to love the have-your-cake-and-eat-it-too dynamics of Hollywood storytelling. Frank Galvin [of *The Verdict*] lives in a basement flat and doesn't fool anyone when he says his secretary has just stepped out. While Ed Masry seems to have a steady practice and a decent strip-mall office in the opening scenes of *Erin Brockovich*, he is living day-to-day. It is only when these characters embrace idealism that they find big money.

These movies suggest that on some occasions, a jury will do what's right and pay the redeemed lawyer handsomely to boot. A simple tale, and not a very realistic one. In real life, outside the prescribed arc of a Hollywood narrative, most lawyers are probably more scrupulous than these characters are at the beginning of a film and less scrupulous than they are at the end. But who couldn't love a story that allows Paul Newman [in *The Verdict*] to sidle down the bar to a ravishing Charlotte Rampling and utter what is surely one of the great pick-up lines: "I changed my life today. What'd you do?"

NOTES & QUESTIONS

1. How accurate is this description of plaintiffs' lawyers in the movies? If Patrick Keefe is correct about the transformation of these lawyers from people corrupted by the law to heroes redeemed by a meritorious case, what role does that assign to the victims of the tort? Do they merely serve as the catalyst to the lawyer's redemption? Compare the structure of these movies' narratives — centered around the lawyer (or, in Erin Brockovich's case, the paralegal) — to the way an ethical attorney should practice law. In reality, should a case ever be about the lawyer?

2. Similarly, should lawyers guard against being "transformed" by their cases? Think realistically about what would happen if you let every case you take on influence your life and morals so deeply. On the other hand, is it truly better to remain unmoved by the plight of those one represents?

3. In *Film and the Law*, the authors argue that

> [f]or us there is little to be gained from comparisons between the real and the image. We all know that lawyers are not normally the son of Satan (*Devil's Advocate*) or drunken ambulance chasers (*The Verdict*). But we also know that they are definitely not Atticus Finch nor Henry Fonda (*Twelve Angry Men*). The difference is that it is lawyers that have contributed to the myth of law; they have become the role models to which not only lawyers but the public "should" aspire or, rather, expect. The crucial point is that this applies even though we know that it is not real. The proper comparison to make is between the cinematic portrayal of law with the cinematic myth of law. How far do our lawyers measure up against the ideal not in real life but in popular culture?

Steve Greenfield et al., *Film and the Law* 27 (2001). If films do indeed present idealistic portrayals of lawyers and justice, is it fair to expect the same heroics from real lawyers and the real system? Does accepting that popular portrayals are apt to be more satisfying than reality suggest that we should expect less from our real justice system and the people who work in it? Should we settle for less when it really matters?

4. Is there a difference between the idealism of plaintiffs' attorneys portrayed in popular culture and the ethical ideals created by the legal profession itself? Consider, for example, any scenes in which plaintiffs' attorneys speak out in the media on behalf of their wronged clients. Now read Rule 3.6 of the ABA Model Rules of Professional Conduct:

> A lawyer who is participating or has participated in the investigation or litigation of a matter shall not make an extrajudicial statement that the lawyer knows or reasonably should know will be disseminated by means of public communication and will have a substantial likelihood of materially prejudicing an adjudicative proceeding in the matter.

How often do lawyers in popular culture violate this Rule? Should such action be considered an ethical violation? Is justice ultimately better served when the public is presented with the facts of a tort case in a manner that is more accessible to them than the way evidence is presented at a trial? Is it realistic to maintain such a sharp distinction between the "real" law and the way the public perceives it?

5. Do you find anything wrong with popular culture portraying lawyers violating ethical rules? Is any harm done if the majority of the viewing public doesn't know that the lawyer's actions violate a code of ethics? Conversely, is the public's perception of attorneys adversely skewed when they regularly witness fictional lawyers acting in unethical ways without repercussions?

6. Consider the actions of Frank Galvin in *The Verdict*:

> The movie begins with Galvin breaking the rules, as he deviously crashes funeral services of complete strangers, intending to solicit

cases. This is a clear violation of Rule 4-7.4(a), "Direct Contact with Prospective Clients," which states that "[a] lawyer shall not solicit professional employment from a prospective client with whom the lawyer has no family or prior professional relationship, in person or otherwise, when a significant motive for the lawyer's doing so is the lawyer's pecuniary gain." Although the general public may not be aware of the restriction against solicitation, Galvin's behavior is no doubt considered despicable by most people. Such behavior reinforces the public's view that lawyers are predatory, selfish, and incessantly in search of the almighty buck. These perceptions are intensified by the endless law firm advertisements that bombard viewers day in and day out on television, a practice that is now being strictly regulated by the Florida [and other states'] Bar.

David M. Spitz, *Heroes or Villains? Moral Struggles vs. Ethical Dilemmas: An Examination of Dramatic Portrayals of Lawyers and the Legal Profession in Popular Culture*, 24 Nova Law Review 725, 745 (2000). Is it fair of Professor Spitz to suggest that the viewing public does not distinguish between fictional portrayals of attorneys and real attorneys who advertise on television? Or is there a correlation between the two?

7. State ethical rules also require attorneys to forward and discuss all settlement offers with their clients and to let their clients make the final decision whether to accept. How commonly does popular culture portray lawyers dramatically turning down settlement offers without first consulting their clients? Consider, for example, Frank Galvin in *The Verdict*, whose moment of personal redemption occurs when he turns down the settlement offer. Are his actions justifiable or self-serving? Compare Jan Schlictmann's efforts in *A Civil Action* (based on a real case) to persuade his clients to accept an offer because of his own financial difficulty maintaining the case. Is Schlictmann's course of action — which does not violate ethical rules — preferable? Why? Should the fictional Galvin have to follow the same rules that bound the real-life Schlictmann?

8. Rule 11 of the Federal Rules of Civil Procedure states, in pertinent part, that:

(b) By presenting to the court (whether by signing, filing, submitting, or later advocating) a pleading, written motion, or other paper, an attorney or unrepresented party is certifying that to the best of the person's knowledge, information, and belief, formed after an inquiry reasonable under the circumstances,

(3) the allegations and other factual contentions have evidentiary support or, if specifically so identified, are likely to have evidentiary support after a reasonable opportunity for further investigation or discovery.

How many plaintiffs' attorneys in popular culture should be sanctioned under Rule 11 for filing lawsuits with insufficient facts to support their complaint allegations? Bear in mind that most of the information about the corporate defendant's actions will be accessible only through discovery, after the commencement of the action. Compare this reality of litigation to the world of television and film, where corporate wrongdoing can be portrayed prior to the victim's knowledge of it. Consider as well the dramatic devices used to reveal corporate malfeasance post hoc in popular tort narratives. Does the popular desire for dramatic and obvious revelations impede the task of real plaintiffs' attorneys, who often have little more than their client's story to support the complaint allegations?

9. Can female plaintiffs' attorneys be as "heroic" as their male counterparts? Are they more heroic? In *Erin Brockovich*, the lead character is a tenacious paralegal who goads her lawyer boss into representing their deserving clients. Would her portrayal be as positive if she were a lawyer herself? Compare her to Maggie Ward in *Class Action*, a woman lawyer who plays hardball with the men. According to Professor Carole Shapiro, "[g]rafted onto the social and political landscape of our particular era, [films like *Class Action*] played to men's fears about the loss of male dominance in the workplace as men faced competition from women." Carole Shapiro, *Women Lawyers in Celluloid: Why Hollywood Skirts the Truth*, 25 University of Toledo Law Review 955, 961 (1995). Do the female protagonists of popular culture related to tort law fit within this dynamic? If they do not seem particularly threatening, are they as successful as male attorneys?

10. What impact does Denzel Washington's race have on the character of plaintiff's attorney Joe Miller in *Philadelphia*? Does it change the portrayal of the plaintiff's attorney as "hero"? Who is the hero in this movie — Miller or Andrew Beckett, his white attorney client fighting his law firm's decision to dismiss him because he has AIDS? Is there a difference between Beckett's status as a white gay lawyer and Miller's as a black straight lawyer when considering the "plaintiff's attorney as hero" paradigm?

11. If you disagree that lawyers in popular culture related to tort law are portrayed as heroes, consider the connection between a negative portrayal and real life. Do negative images of lawyers in popular culture adversely affect the profession? The *Film and the Law* authors argue that it makes no difference how negatively lawyers are portrayed:

> One of the claims of the profession is that lawyers are the subject of overly critical portrayals and that the great hero lawyers have been replaced by a less salubrious contemporary version. If this is true, does it much matter? Do we think any worse of our lawyers because Al Pacino, as a lawyer, is the devil (*Devil's Advocate* (1997))?

Steve Greenfield et al., *Film and the Law* 27 (2001). Do you agree?

12. Are real lawyers less than heroes if they fail to take the kinds of risks cinematic lawyers do for a meritorious case? Consider the actions of Arnold & Porter, a large law firm that took on pro bono representation of the victims of the Buffalo Creek disaster — the 1972 collapse of a massive coal-refuse pile in the mountains of West Virginia that "unleashed over 130 million gallons of water and waste materials. The flood devastated Buffalo Creek's sixteen small communities," killing 125 people, destroying 1,000 homes, and leaving roughly 4,000 survivors with emotional trauma and heavy personal losses. Gerald M. Stern, *The Buffalo Creek Disaster* ix (1976). The firm's Assignment Committee initially advised against taking on the case, but recalling founding partner

Paul Porter's favorite saying — "When in doubt, do the right thing" — the firm's Executive Committee rejected the advice. *Id.*, 20–21. Is Paul Porter a hero? Would his actions be considered heroic if portrayed in a film? Or would it take more to ensure that the audience views him as the hero of the piece? If it does take more, do portrayals of lawyer-heroes in popular culture detract from the heroics of real lawyers?

13. It is possible, of course, that we give too much credit to Hollywood writers to for creating memorable fictional lawyers. Read on for a description of the "real King of Torts."

THE REAL KING OF TORTS: FAMED SAN FRANCISCO LAWYER WAS MORE ENTERTAINING THAN FICTION
The Rodent
ABA Journal e-Report, 8 Feb. 2003, 8

Have you read John Grisham's latest novel, *The King of Torts*? I haven't. And not reading the book would normally stop me from writing a review. But this is not a book review. What caught my attention about the Grisham book is its title.

The King of Torts is a thriller about mass tort attorneys. But those who know about lawyers know the real (and only) King of Torts is famed San Francisco attorney Melvin Belli.

Belli, who died in 1996 at the age of 88, is perhaps most famous for his courtroom tactics. He was a pioneer with his work in illustrating the nature of his clients' injuries to the court. This included early use of photographs, movies, and scale models. He is even better remembered for bringing human skeletons and animals into the courtroom. He also once asked a client to remove a prosthetic limb and show it to the jury. As a result, he was dubbed "The Father of Demonstrative Evidence" and, more memorably, the "King of Torts."

Among Belli's clients were Jack Ruby, Errol Flynn, Jim and Tammy Faye Baker, Zsa Zsa Gabor, Tony Curtis, Lana Turner, Mae West, the Rolling Stones, and Muhammad Ali. But among his most famous trials was his own. He was accused of having sex with one of his clients. In his own defense, Belli explained, "It wasn't very good, and she didn't serve me breakfast."

The King of Torts was the founder of the American Trial Lawyers Association. He recovered more than $700 million for his clients. He played a villain in an episode of the original *Star Trek* series. He wrote more than 60 books. He married six women.

His active law practice and love life had their impact at the end of Melvin Belli's career. Late in life, Belli was ordered to pay $15 million in a divorce settlement. At about the same time, he and his law firm advanced $5 million to doctors and expert witnesses on behalf of a client, and then the corporate defendant filed for bankruptcy. Belli did the same himself one year before his death.

Melvin Belli was also well-known for collecting mementos from his many historic court battles. He used these to decorate his office. I know this because

I saw the inside of his office. I was never invited inside, but his office on Montgomery Street in downtown San Francisco was on the map for many tour companies. The building itself is a historic landmark and, night or day, you could look directly into Melvin Belli's office from the sidewalk. I once saw him inside and watched him give a wave to the tourists.

"King of Torts" is engraved on Melvin Belli's tombstone. It is worth noting that he earned a C in his torts class at Boalt Hall.

For you law students out there reading this article, keep in mind that getting a C in a particular law school course will not necessarily make you the king (or queen) of that particular subject. If it did, I, too, would be the King of Torts. Constitutional law, civil procedure, and evidence would also be among my kingdoms.

NOTES & QUESTIONS

1. In John Grisham's *The King of Torts* (2005), to which the author refers, Clay Carter II leaves his position as a public defender to pursue a class action lawsuit against a drug company whose product causes bladder tumors. The suit is meritorious, but Carter also takes on other class action suits that are more likely to be lucrative for him personally. In the end, Carter recognizes the error of his ways, files for bankruptcy, and leaves the country with his true love. Note that Carter's story follows the path of redemption discussed in Chapter 3 of this text. Do you suppose Melvin Belli achieved redemption through his own bankruptcy? How do lawyers in popular culture about torts achieve their redemption?

2. Do you think Melvin Belli represents the general public's perception of real tort lawyers? Or is he so much larger than life that he could get away with actions that only fictional characters can? Does he reflect on the plaintiff's bar as a whole, or can the public recognize an unusual person when they see one? Even if they can recognize the difference, are some people apt to see a little bit of Belli in every plaintiff's attorney they encounter?

3. Belli's self-lionizing autobiography (written with Robert Blair Kaiser) suggests an almost desperate need for attention. *See* Melvin M. Belli, *Melvin Belli: My Life on Trial* (1976). Should lawyers be allowed to publicize themselves in this manner? Do you think those who wish to do so are influenced by popular culture? For a review essay comparing Belli's autobiography to other lawyers' autobiographies from the 1970s, see David Ray Papke, *Advertisements for the Legal Self: A Review of Contemporary Lawyers' Autobiographies*, American Legal Studies Association Forum, Fall 1979, 57.

2. Defense Attorneys

According to Professor Patrick Keefe, in Hollywood dramas, "we need someone to root against. If you want to have your lawyer be a hero, says the producer to the screenwriter, the story had better be on the David and Goliath model, and Goliath had better be a lawyer for the other side." Patrick Keefe,

Reversals of Fortune, supra, 49. Consider whether you agree as you read the following excerpt.

EMBODIMENT OF EVIL: LAW FIRMS IN THE MOVIES
Michael Asimow
48 UCLA Law Review 1339 (2001)

Movies accurately reflect the public's dismal opinion of law firms. During the seventy years of the sound era, filmmakers have often presented lawyers in solo practice as decent human beings and as excellent lawyers, although that is much less true in the last thirty years than in the first forty. Once movie lawyers join together into law firms, however, they are portrayed quite negatively, regardless of the era. In film lawyers who practice in small law firms are worse than solo lawyers, and big firms are much worse than small firms. Judging by what we are taught in the movies, lawyers in firms (especially large ones) are miserable, bigoted, materialistic people. Despite their wealth and beautiful cars and homes, they have mostly unhappy personal lives and dysfunctional families. As lawyers, they are greedy, heartless, predatory, unethical, and often buffoonish or incompetent.

The only half-way decent law firms we encounter in films of the last thirty years are small ones that oppose much bigger firms. Even filmmakers understand that a solo lawyer cannot possibly muster the resources to fight big firm scorched-earth tactics. Even in these small firms, lawyers' ethics are sometimes dubious, and the lawyers sometimes treat their clients badly. Aside from these Davids in combat with Goliaths, just about the only good lawyers we see in this period are the ones who practice by themselves. . . .

NOTES & QUESTIONS

1. Does the solo-practitioner (David) versus big firm (Goliath) framework make sense in cinematic terms — making it exciting and fulfilling for audiences to root for the underdog? How realistic is it? It is extremely difficult for solo practitioners to litigate against large firms with greater resources. Do cinematic portrayals of small plaintiffs' firms winning big jury awards against much larger, well-funded firms give laypersons a false sense of the odds of winning their own lawsuits?

2. Consider the fact that few individuals who have been injured can afford the services of large law firms and instead opt for small firms or solo practitioners, many of whom will take cases on a contingency fee basis. The corporate defendants they are suing, on the other hand, tend to be represented by large law firms for a range of matters. Does this disparity in the resources of the parties' representatives have any impact on the ultimate outcome of most tort cases? Is any such disparity reflected in popular culture related to tort law?

3. Rule 34(a) of the Federal Rules of Civil Procedure allows either party to inspect and copy documents or tangible things in the possession, custody, or control of the opposing party, as long as the items are not privileged and are "relevant to the claim or defense of any party" as required by Rule 26(b). The latter addresses the scope of the parties' discovery rights. How might these Rules affect the parties in a real lawsuit? Do monetary considerations affect discovery? Does popular culture take into account the monetary considerations? Certainly Frank Galvin in *The Verdict,* Jan Schlictmann in *A Civil Action,* and Ed Masry in *Erin Brockovich* garner audience sympathy when they have to deal with the discovery tactics of large defense firms which can bury them in both requests and produced documents. Do these portrayals overstate the case? Are such portrayals likely to scare meritorious victims away from litigation? To pressure them into settling?

4. How do popular portrayals of civil defense attorneys affect the public's attitude toward the defense bar and the companies and individuals they represent? Jerome Facher, the attorney representing one of the defendants in *A Civil Action,* "is portrayed by Robert Duvall as a bundle of Dickensian eccentricities who retreats to the dusty stacks of the firm library to eat brown-bag lunches and listen to the Red Sox on transistor radio [and] banters with . . . Judge Walter Skinner, also a Harvard man." Patrick Keefe, *Reversals of Fortune, supra,* 50. Similarly, "[i]n *The Verdict,* James Mason's Ed Concannon is a consummate insider. Though he works for a fictional firm, the stature and trappings are old school, and his cohort of young associates all have the scrubbed and tweedy Harvard look about them." *Id.* Consider too the contrast between the high-powered law firm that dismisses Andrew Beckett after discovering he has AIDS in *Philadelphia* and the shabby solo practitioner who represents him in suing them; the sleek firm where Maggie Ward works in *Class Action* versus the down-to-earth small firm where her father represents the plaintiffs suing her client; and the strip-mall firm where Erin Brockovich works in contrast to the offices of the Pacific Gas & Electric's attorneys.

5. Is the negative portrayal of defense attorneys even more marked when the law firm is the defendant rather than simply its representative? In *Philadelphia,* we learn more about the law firm that Andrew Beckett sues for firing him than about the lawyer representing it at the trial:

> Throughout the trial, the law firm is shown in the worst possible light. On the stand, the partners falsely deny suspecting that Beckett had AIDS and they lie about the quality of his work. Their lawyer, Belinda Conine (Mary Steenburgen), adopts a condescending manner and she criticizes Beckett's lifestyle choices — just the wrong approach in a case in which the jury's sympathy lies with the plaintiff. Thus we learn that big firms are viciously homophobic, even turning against their best lawyers when they are found to be gay or to have a fatal disease. Naturally, they do not hesitate to lie in order to cover their tracks.

Michael Asimow, *Embodiment of Evil: Law Firms in the Movies,* 48 UCLA Law Review 1339, 1355–56 (2001). Does the portrayal of the law firm as defendant reflect on its portrayal as representative of the defendant? In other words, is it any accident that the homophobic-defendant employer in *Philadelphia* is a large law firm?

6. Are tort defendants really the villains they are made out to be in popular culture? Consider this observation:

> Most harm compensated by the tort system is negligently caused and not intended by the defendant. These negligent actors are not, as a class, despicable villains out of central casting. When our inevitable human lapses in concentration or judgment cause harm to others, it is we who become tort defendants. That which separates those of us who negligently cause harm from those of us who do not is often fate or chance, not higher intelligence or moral superiority.

Daniel W. Shuman, *The Role of Apology in Tort Law*, 83 Judicature 180 (2000). Even if this statement is true, are popular portrayals of tortfeasors justifiable as necessary to tell an interesting story? What is the harm in such portrayals if, as Professor Shuman asserts, any one of us could become a defendant in a civil suit? Does that possibility protect against harmful stereotyping?

7. Notice that in these films, the defense attorneys are almost always white men — with the notable exceptions of Maggie Ward in *Class Action*, who ultimately finds she has too much compassion and too great a sense of justice to zealously represent her client, and Belinda Conine in *Philadelphia*, who states that she hates her job after cross-examining the sympathetic and ailing plaintiff in court. Do portrayals of women lawyers accurately reflect gender differences — women as more nurturing and justice-oriented; men as capable of representing any client zealously in a way that supports our system of legal representation? Or do popular portrayals of women lawyers perpetuate such gender stereotyping? Below, Professor Carole Shapiro presents her take on pop cultural portrayals of women lawyers.

WOMEN LAWYERS IN CELLULOID: WHY HOLLYWOOD SKIRTS THE TRUTH
Carole Shapiro
25 University of Toledo Law Review 955 (1995)

While the woman lawyer is generally shown as smart and talented, she is rarely portrayed in such a way that a woman, never mind a woman lawyer, would ever want to be (like) her. Unlike Katherine Hepburn's character in *Adam's Rib*, who both wins her case and keeps her man, the modern-day women lawyer films punish their professional heroine for her independence.

They do this, in large part, by depicting her as unhappy in her personal life, or even from time to time by killing her. The movies show that the seemingly self-sufficient lawyer, despite her assured and independent exterior, turns out to be just another woman who primarily needs a man. Whether she knows it or not, what will make her life complete is some dashing white knight who can save her personally and sometimes even professionally. In the absence of the man who alone can rescue her from the regrettable consequences of her career decisions, the poor thing will arouse the audience's pity or, alternately, its contempt for her unfortunate plight. . . .

Movies about women lawyers generally play out male fears and fantasies about "strong" women. Although the Hollywood lawyer films made since the

1980s show women in a new professional role, they incorporate traditional messages about them and their roles in society. These films may be particularly effective in perpetuating backlash ideas against women because they purport to depict the new woman of our time although they in fact do something quite different. While their portrayal of women as lawyers undeniably reflects changes in social reality, the movies largely depict these professionals in a way that echoes decades-old conventions of female characters in Hollywood film-making. . . .

The substance of the message most of these movies deliver is a distinctly conservative one. For female viewers, it is a cautionary one, designed to encourage traditional gender roles, even in the face of women's new professional emergence. It warns women whose jobs may take them outside the home not to allow ambition to seduce them away from the family hearth. It warns that by ignoring this cautionary warning, they risk the personal unhappiness many of these movie characters experience. Viewers see overreaching women lawyers on the screen punished by their failure with men and their ensuing loneliness. By contrast, some movies show that if the woman character behaves properly, she can either find — or keep — a man and be saved from life-long misery. . . .

NOTES & QUESTIONS

1. If Professor Shapiro is correct in her assessment of how women lawyers are portrayed, does it make any difference if they are defense attorneys? If the defense lawyer happens to be a woman — like Maggie Ward in *Class Action* — is she being punished for being a woman or being a defense attorney?

2. How accurate is Professor Shapiro's account? Have portrayals of women lawyers changed since 1995, when she wrote her essay? For example, Erin Brockovich — while not a lawyer — is a strong, likeable woman who seeks and gains greater empowerment through the law. What about Maggie Ward, who achieves happiness by the end of *Class Action* when she quits her job and reunites with her father?

3. Do gender stereotypes ever help make women defense attorneys more likeable? Consider Belinda Conine, the defense attorney who cross-examines plaintiff Andrew Beckett in *Philadelphia* and ultimately brings about his collapse. She is plainly affected by her job; does this fact help complicate the narrative or does it make her more despicable for carrying on despite her misgivings? Is *Class Action*'s Maggie Ward a more satisfying character because she ultimately finds herself unable to be both a big-firm defense attorney and a woman and daughter?

4. When lawyers of color are portrayed in popular culture, do they tend to represent the plaintiff (like Joe Miller in *Philadelphia*) or the defendant? Are they "insiders" or "outsiders"? If they represent large corporate defendants, what is their role? Are they the lead attorney, or the dark face at the counsel table? Are they "tokenized" in the same way as women? In a different way?

3.　Tort Victims

In popular culture related to tort law, justice for the victims almost always comes in the form of a large monetary reward, usually in the courtroom, sometimes in settlement. Hollywood — and perhaps the public in general — seems to assume that the victims are best served by such compensation. The following excerpt provides a different perspective.

THE ROLE OF APOLOGY IN TORT LAW
Daniel W. Shuman
83 Judicature 180 (2000)

Tort plaintiffs often claim that what they really wanted was an apology and brought suit only when it was not forthcoming or that when they received an apology it "was the most valuable part of the settlement." If these claims are not merely public posturing to avoid appearing greedy, they may provide important clues about helping people recover from emotional wrongs and avoiding unnecessary litigation. Given the turmoil over tort litigation and compensation for emotional harm, the prospect of an alternative that helps the injured to recover and reduces tort claims demands serious consideration. . . .

What does an apology accomplish in the adjustment of harm, and might that benefit mental or emotional losses addressed in the tort system? When people receive a sincere apology, does it play a role in helping them to recover from the emotional consequences of negligently or intentionally caused harm? If sincere apologies play an important role in the healing process, how might the law encourage or avoid discouraging apology?

At a time when the tort system is under attack as costly and inefficient, exploration of the role of apology may provide powerful clues for tinkering with the tort system to achieve more at less cost. . . .

Tort damages for intangible loss such as pain and suffering, loss of consortium, indignity, and grief are both a practical and a theoretical problem. Practically, tort damages for these intangible losses defy the formulation of an empirically grounded metric that can be used to assist lawyers in settling cases, communicate appropriate damage calculation to juries, or assist judges to review jury damage findings.

No valid psychological tests exist to measure these intangible losses nor are there valid formulas to determine their dollar value. No market based standard exists for these intangible injuries. We have no way to measure whether awards for intangible injuries are valid or reliable; it is not possible with any degree of scientific precision to say that these awards are too high or too low, or to compare awards across cases. While we can precisely calculate the amount of money necessary to make whole the loss of a year's worth of wages or a year's worth of nursing care, we cannot precisely calculate the value of a year of pain or grief. And these costs are significant; damages for intangible loss constitute the largest element of tort damage awards and are the most difficult to control.

At a theoretical level, damage awards for these intangible losses are difficult to justify or explain as an award of compensatory damages. While the award of damages to compensate tangible out of pocket losses caused by another's tortious acts enjoys firm support in the case law and commentary, the award of tort damages to compensate for intangible harm such as grief, loss of consortium, and pain and suffering has been much criticized. We award compensatory damages to wrongfully harmed plaintiffs to restore them to their pre-accident condition, to make them whole. If a negligent driver crashes into another's car, the owner of the damaged car is entitled to damages that will permit her to repair it or, if necessary, to purchase an equivalent one. If a negligent driver causes another to be hospitalized and lose a month's income, the injured person is entitled to damages that will pay for the expenses of hospitalization and lost income.

In a limited sense, damages for tangible loss undo the harm; damages for intangible loss cannot make a similar claim. Although the emotional pain that results from the loss of a child or spouse, for example, is undoubtedly horrific, it is difficult to understand how monetary damages paid by or on behalf of the party that caused the loss should be expected to salve that emotional pain. No amount of money will permit a plaintiff whose spouse or child died in an automobile accident to be restored to his or her pre-accident psychological condition, to be made emotionally whole for that loss. . . .

NOTES & QUESTIONS

1. Is providing an apology as the primary award in a tort action viable? Consider the clients in *A Civil Action* or *Erin Brockovich*, who are more interested in an apology than monetary compensation. Are they merely cinematic portrayals designed to make the victims look more deserving?

2. Certainly, a "big win" translates to a happy ending in cinematic and novelistic terms, but is there a cost to feeding popular conceptions of what constitutes a legal victory? What happens to the real victims of torts when they encounter the realities of the system they expect to provide substantial compensation for their injuries? Kathleen Sharp reports many plaintiffs in the actual Hinkley case thought *Erin Brockovich* misrepresented them. "Far from being the populist victory the movie depicts, the Hinkley lawsuit was a case study in how the rise of private arbitration, as an alternative to costly public trials, is creating a two-tiered legal system that not only favours litigants who can afford it over those who cannot, but is open to potential conflicts of interest and cronyism. The case never went to trial, because Pacific Gas and Electric, the utility accused of polluting Hinkley, and the plaintiff's lawyers agreed to private arbitration before a panel of for-hire judges, some of whom had socialized with the plaintiff's attorneys." Kathleen Sharp, *"Erin Brockovich": The Real Story*, Salon, http://www.salon.com.html. Does the movie's different ending set real victims up for disappointment? Skew public perceptions of tort suits?

3. For many people, injunctive relief seems the best way to remedy the situation, particularly in mass tort cases such as those portrayed in *A Civil Action* and *Erin Brockovich*. To someone who has not experienced the real costs of litigation — monetary, emotional, and practical — injunctive relief might seem to provide a happier ending than compensatory damages. For example, at the end of *A Civil Action*, the audience sees the Environmental Protection Agency using its substantial resources to resolve the case that Jan Schlictmann could not. However, Dan Kennedy, a reporter for the *New Republic*, points out that this ending is pure Hollywood:

> It makes for an uplifting conclusion to a decidedly downbeat story. It is also completely and utterly false. But, unlike most of the fictionalizations, exaggerations, and dramatizations in the transition from Jonathan Harr's best-seller to the Hollywood screen, the tale of Schlichtmann and the EPA is likely to have a lasting — and distorting — effect on the moviegoers who saw the film over the past few months. The notion that it took one lone ranger to force an uncaring, unresponsive government bureaucracy to act may resonate. But it's not true — or, at least, it wasn't in Woburn.

Dan Kennedy, *Civil Inaction*, New Republic; 15 March 1999; 13. Do such happy endings dangerously skew public views about the reach of the law and the ability of lawyers to enact social justice? Or is this belief justified, even if it does not always come to fruition?

4. When a work of popular culture revolves around the lawyer, rather than the victim, the victory resounds as much — if not more — to the lawyer as to the victim of the tort, whatever the remedy. For example, in *Film and the Law* the authors argue that Andrew Beckett, the plaintiff in *Philadelphia*, loses narrative power because, although he is a lawyer, his role in the story is that of the victim:

> Unfortunately, it is as the bearer of AIDS rather than as a lawyer in his own right that we encounter Andrew Beckett. The lawyers active in the courtroom in *Philadelphia* are Joe Miller [Beckett's attorney] and, to a lesser extent, Belinda Conine [defense counsel]. Interestingly, the first major portrayal of a gay lawyer shows him as a victim and he [figures] only as a witness to the action.

Steve Greenfield et al., *Film and the Law* 90 (2001). Another film theorist has argued that:

> Joe is the central character. The narrative of *Philadelphia* is less about being gay and living with AIDS then about being heterosexual and homophobic. Joe comes to understand how his homophobia, which he regards as integral to his manhood, underlies his fear and loathing for people with AIDS. But *Philadelphia* is a breakthrough film, not only because it deals with AIDS and homophobia, but because it is the first major non-action Hollywood movie in which a black man personifies mainstream America. Joe's homophobia is a sign of his normality (he's a regular Joe): Andrew's white skin privilege is cancelled by his homosexuality and his disease.

Amy Taubin, *The Odd Couple*, Sight & Sound; March, 1994; 24. Are the authors correct that *Philadelphia* is centrally about Joe Miller, the

African American attorney, rather than Andrew Beckett, the gay white man with AIDS? Is there anything wrong with this narrative focus? Consider the dynamics of other popular culture about torts and compare the race, sex, and sexual orientation of the attorneys to the victims they represent. Do these narratives replicate troubling power structures in our society? If so, are popular tort narratives responsible for real social disparities?

5. These authors suggest that the turning point for Joe Miller occurs when he sees the discrimination Andrew Beckett suffers as a gay man — presumably because, as an African American man, Miller can empathize with being the victim of prejudice. How useful is this narrative for a white audience? For any audience member, is the film about using the law to correct injustice? Or is it about the persistence of discrimination in our society? Could it be about Beckett's injury or about Miller's recognition that his injury is real?

6. According to Professor Patrick Keefe, "[t]he suffering of the clients in [tort] films is important, but the clients occupy supporting roles. The ability to recognize the clients' plight is a mere precondition for Galvin's [in *The Verdict*] and Schlichtmann's [in *A Civil Action*] coming to terms with their own depravity." Patrick Keefe, *Reversals of Fortune, supra,* 50. How do you feel about the victims serving merely as a plot device to bring about the lawyer's redemption? Does this subordinate role translate to popular understandings of the roles of real lawyers and their clients?

7. Consider ABA Model Rule of Professional Conduct 1.2(a): "[A] lawyer shall abide by a client's decisions concerning the objectives of representation, and, as required by Rule 1.4, shall consult with the client as to the means by which they are to be pursued." How realistic is this ethical rule? Even if it does operate as intended, does it have any effect on popular perceptions of lawyers and the power they wield?

8. One real context in which the tension between the client's right to make decisions about her own case and the power of the lawyer in conducting the litigation on her behalf becomes quite clear is the use of "settlement class actions," in which one plaintiff represents the interests of an entire class of victims during the settlement of a tort suit. Some practitioners argue that settlement class actions threaten to render the individual victims of a tort silent and powerless parties to the litigation conducted entirely by the lawyers and judge. *See* Steve Bauman Jensen, *Like Lemonade, Ethics Comes Best When It's Old-Fashioned: A Response to Professor Moore*, 41 South Texas Law Review 215 (1999). Might such judicially created aspects of litigation be in part a by-product of the way we see tort victims portrayed in popular culture? Does the lawyer-as-hero paradigm — where the victim is a passive plot device rather than an active protagonist — allow us to adopt the same structure in real litigation? Do you think popular portrayals of tort victims contribute to the rise of such litigation devices as settlement class actions? Is that a bad thing?

9. Is the popular portrayal of the tort victim as secondary to the plaintiff's attorney in part a result of public perceptions of personal injury plaintiffs? According to Patrick Keefe,

... the good client in *The Verdict*, *A Civil Action*, and *Erin Brockovich* is a rare breed: the truly wronged personal injury client. When we think of personal injury law, we think of fender-bender survivors strapping on the old neck brace and of the doubly parasitic lawyers who encourage ("Have you been hurt on the job?") and enable the injured to sue. The portrayal of personal injury law in the opening moments of these films plays on this preconception, leaving the viewer suspicious of plaintiffs and defendants.

Patrick Keefe, *Reversals of Fortune, supra,* 49. Are such movies and other similar popular portrayals of personal injury plaintiffs responsible for this view? Or does the fault lie with real personal injury lawyers, such as the ones who place cheap advertisements on late night local television? Is it possible to control the barrage of such images to which the public is constantly exposed? Should we care?

C.   THE ELEMENTS OF THE TORT

When it comes to the actual litigation of a tort claim within popular culture, evidence must be conveyed in a more cinematic mode than it would normally be in the courtroom. When the point is entertainment, the rules of evidence are not as important as the most dramatic way to tell a story. The question then becomes how the elements of a tort are "proven," and what impact such portrayals have on common understandings of the law.

1.   Breach of Duty of Care

In the following excerpt, Professor Leslie Bender presents a feminist alternative to the traditionally understood duty of care. As you read the excerpt, consider how the feminist alternative would affect a work of popular culture — which requires a recognizable villain — and whether popular conceptions of tortfeasors might interfere with the adoption of her duty of care.

FEMINIST (RE)TORTS: THOUGHTS ON THE LIABILITY CRISIS, MASS TORTS, POWER, AND RESPONSIBILITIES
Leslie Bender
1990 Duke Law Journal 848

"Responsibility" and "responsible" have several different meanings. I want to suggest that the meaning of "responsibility" in tort law is too thin. We can improve the tort system by rethinking the values underlying legal responsibility and making legal responsibility more multi-dimensional, more contextual, and more informed with insights from feminist theory. . . . I recommend the expansion of our legal account of responsibility to include a holistic, needs-based, caregiving response. . . . In order to achieve this end, the meaning of responsibility in law would include a commitment, in advance of harm, to protecting and caring about the health and safety of other people. . . .

Tort law has been weighted down by a language and value system that privilege economics and costs. Every time there is an injury, we determine legal responsibility by asking about the dollar and efficiency costs of paying for the harms and/or of avoiding them. Questions of cost have consistently been our first or second inquiry in cases of mass torts by corporate defendants.

As harms from mass tort have become more widespread, legal analysis in tort law has become desensitized to the individuals and groups of people harmed. The more people who are injured or subjected to the risk of injury, the more tort law dehumanizes people generally, views them as statistical risks, and sees their injuries as costs of economic growth and progress. If this kind of legal thinking is inconsistent with our core values, we must reject it outright as violative of human dignity and equality. Instead, we can require corporate defendants, corporate officers, and courts to be more socially and personally responsible.

A. Meanings of Responsibility

Responsibility can be divided temporally into two types of categories: pre-event (prevention-based) responsibility and post-event (response-based) responsibility. . . .

The pre-event account of responsibility is important because it indicates who ought to be held responsible if something occurs. Pre-event or prevention-based responsibility is tied to the notion of power. The power to decide and take action entails a responsibility for the decisions made and action taken (or not taken). With power comes responsibility. They are inseparable. Prevention-based responsibility in mass tort derives from the power to choose (in a human agency sense) to impose risks on the health and safety of others or to perform activities that cause harm. One who "responsibly" exercises this power chooses to prevent harm, to minimize or eliminate risks to others created by activities or products, to gather information, to advance learning about the consequences of corporate actions, and to stress the values of health, safety, and human dignity. In wanting people to act more responsibly, we want them to choose to act with more care and reflection about the possible effects of their conduct and decisions on others. This is particularly true in dealing with potential harms caused by the actions of corporations. For-profit corporate activities are conducted with considerable input and pre-planning, which affords corporations more opportunities for intervention before harm is caused. We want this exercise of power to occur before there is harm (pre-event), so that there will be no harm. . . .

To compel people imbued with this power to take responsibility for the consequences of their actions and decisions, mass tort law as well as criminal law must be constructed in a manner that imposes personal liability on the individuals with the power to make decisions or select among actions. The process of requiring people to take responsibility also requires that the corporation as a whole be held responsible. . . .

Post-event responsibility ought to mean more than making reparations. A different notion of responsibility arises out of our interconnectedness as human beings, and it has to do with responding to the needs of someone through interpersonal caregiving — it means "taking care of." Although this account of responsibility seems completely absent from the law, it remains central to our life experiences. . . .

[C]orporate harm-causer/mass-tort victim relationships are analogous to those within the family to the extent that they involve responsibility.

Family members have an initial interpersonal responsibility of care for one another. At a minimum we understand this responsibility as an obligation to take care of or care for a family member who is unable to care for herself. Likewise, once the legal system determines that a corporation is liable or responsible for a harm, it has an obligation to remedy the harm and to take care of the people harmed. By shifting to a post-event meaning of responsibility that includes both a reparations sense and a caring sense, we can alter the way that the legal and corporate worlds function. . . .

NOTES & QUESTIONS

1. Which model of responsibility better facilitates storytelling — pre-event or post-event? Think about this question first in terms of popular culture. How does the narrative set up the villain? Specifically, how do we know in *A Civil Action* that Grace and Beatrice are "bad" corporations, rather than simply businesses that made a mistake? Would it have been enough for Pacific Gas & Electric to have inadvertently polluted the town in *Erin Brockovich*? Why is it important in *Class Action* that Maggie Ward's client intentionally ignored information about the dangers inherent in the design of its cars? How does *The Verdict* manage to make the Catholic Archdiocese a "bad guy," and why? Why are defendants portrayed as not caring about the people they have injured?

2. Now think about the difference between pre-event and post-event responsibility in terms of an actual trial. Put yourself in the shoes of the plaintiff's attorney. Your job is to tell the jury a story that moves them to punish the defendant and award substantial damages to your client. How would this goal best be accomplished — by trying to prove that the defendant violated its pre-event responsibility to the victims or by focusing instead on its post-event responsibility of care-giving? Is the trial narrative compatible with the popular one?

3. Consider Professor Bender's assertion that corporate officers who make crucial decisions should be held personally liable for their actions. How well would this construct work in popular culture? What about a real trial? Is the difference clear in any of the movies examined in this chapter or any other works of popular culture with which you are familiar? Does it matter to the audience whether the corporation or individual is financially responsible? Could the ending of any of the movies be satisfying for an audience if it were clear that the individuals who were responsible for the injuries are likely not to be considered legally responsible? How does the need for an identifiable villain affect the public's notions of tort responsibility?

4. If you believe that one of the goals of our tort system is (or ought to be) prevention of future injury, how do you think popular culture contributes to this goal? In particular, do the ways in which these narratives portray the defendants as having breached a duty of care positively or negatively influence real people? Or does popular culture have no influence on real people?

2. Causation

Often, the most difficult part of a tort case is proving that the defendant's breach of her duty of care was the proximate cause of the plaintiff's injury. The following article examines the root of some of the legal difficulties, particularly in toxic tort cases, such as those portrayed in *A Civil Action* and *Erin Brockovich*.

GUARDING THE GATE TO THE COURTHOUSE: HOW TRIAL JUDGES ARE USING THEIR EVIDENTIARY SCREENING ROLE TO REMAKE TORT CAUSATION RULES
Lucinda M. Finley
49 DePaul Law Review 335 (1999)

Vigorously exercising their role as evidentiary "gatekeepers" — a task assigned to them by the United States Supreme Court in *Daubert v. Merrell Dow Pharmaceuticals, Inc.*, 509 U.S. 579 (1993) — federal trial judges in products liability cases have been doing far more than screening proposed expert testimony to determine admissibility. The *Daubert* gatekeeper power has become a potent tool of tort lawmaking. Under the guise of admissibility determinations, federal judges have been making significant substantive legal rules on causation by substantially raising the threshold of scientific proof plaintiffs need to get their expert causation testimony admitted, and thus survive summary judgment. While the decisions purport to be no more than deferential nods to the criteria of science, judges have actually been making legal rules about what types and strengths of scientific evidence are necessary in order to prove causation. The emerging legal rule is that plaintiffs' experts must be able to base their opinions about causation on epidemiological studies, and that these studies standing alone must show that the population-wide risk of developing the disease in question, if exposed to defendants' products, is at least double the risk without exposure.

In the process of developing this legal rule, judges in products liability cases have been making profoundly normative judgments about the social allocation of risk and who should bear the burden of scientific uncertainty or controversy — injured people or manufacturers of the products alleged to have caused those injuries? Few of the opinions announcing or applying this emerging causal proof standard acknowledge awareness of the normative nature or implications of their decisions. Thus, an important underlying policy debate remains submerged. Should the rules of the tort system put the onus for uncertainty about the risks of a product on the manufacturer who has marketed it, perhaps without sufficient testing or warning? By doing so, causation rules would enhance the tort policies of deterring marketing of relatively untested products and promoting expanded research on both the effectiveness and hazards of drugs and medical devices. The tort system would also align itself more with the public health protective values that govern the FDA regulatory arena, where a drug is presumed not safe for marketing unless the manufacturer can prove its safety. Or, should the tort system instead embrace the conservative values of the scientific discipline of epidemiology, whose internal disciplinary standards start with a hypothesis of lack of risk, and demand stringent statistical proof of a doubling or tripling of the risk of a disease before entertaining the possibility of a causal association? Judges have been using their evidentiary gatekeeper power to squarely align tort law with the conservative causal normative principles of epidemiology, thus moving the law sharply away from the more consumer protective social policies about risk embodied in the safety regulatory system.

While adopting substantive changes in causation law through the rubric of evidentiary admissibility decisions, judges have also frequently conflated admissibility decisions and sufficiency of evidence decisions. This has effected another profound but concealed change in tort law. Judges have applied *Daubert* to subject each item of expert proof proffered by plaintiffs to substantive causation law scrutiny, to see if it, standing alone, would prove both general and specific causation. If the scientific studies underlying an expert's opinion are not alone sufficient, then the expert's testimony is deemed inadmissible. This stands in stark contrast to traditional and proper practice, which sees the admissibility of evidence as a question quite distinct from the sufficiency of evidence to meet a plaintiff's burden of proof. The sufficiency inquiry is supposed to view plaintiffs' evidence in its entirety to see if, taken as a whole, it would support a conclusion that causation is more likely than not. By calling what is really a sufficiency of the evidence determination an admissibility decision, judges are using their evidentiary gatekeeper power to close the gate on plaintiffs' opportunities to have their proof evaluated as a cumulative whole. This subtly but substantially increases plaintiffs' burden of proving individual causation, and it also furthers the trend in toxic tort cases to shift the allocation of power away from juries to judges. Because a trial judge's decision to exclude evidence is reviewed under the lenient abuse of discretion standard of review, this new heightened substantive standard of causation and judges' applications of it are largely insulated from meaningful appellate review. . . .

NOTES & QUESTIONS

1. What exactly is the problem Professor Finley describes? Is it truly a "problem," or simply an inherent and correct part of the plaintiff's burden to prove causation in a tort case? Now consider the "problem" in works of popular culture which center on the story of the plaintiff's attorney gaining justice for his or her clients. Do you find the plaintiff's higher burden more fitting in a dramatic context? Less?

2. According to Professor Finley, judges now tend to demand that expert testimony establish that the defendant's actions caused twice the risk that the

THE ELEMENTS OF THE TORT

plaintiffs develop a specific disease than the risk faced by the general population. Do works of popular culture seem to provide a higher or lower standard? In other words, do the stories make the proof of causation so strong that it seems as if the defendant made it even *more* than twice as likely that the victims would contract illness because of the defendants' activities? Or is the story furthered by lesser evidence, which is still taken as enough to satisfy the legal case being portrayed?

3. What effect, if any, might these cinematic standards of proof have on actual legal cases? Consider the role of jury instructions in a court case and whether a jury understands the legal standards well enough to apply them correctly. Might it be just as easy for a jury to turn to the "knowledge" they have acquired from popular culture? Might a juror think she is applying the standard articulated by the judge but really substitute the one she thinks she already "knows" from popular culture? Or are people able to distinguish easily between fiction and reality?

4. Professor Finley asserts that judges are unaware of the normative implications of their high admissibility standard for expert testimony in tort cases. Does the entertainment industry face the same sort of normative implications in its depiction of torts in popular culture? If so, does its ignorance pose a greater or lesser problem than judges'?

5. Is Professor Finley's "consumer protection" model attractive to you? Should popular culture act as a consumer protector? Can it? Consider movies like *Erin Brockovich* and *A Civil Action*, where causation seems obvious, and how they raise public awareness of the problems. Is such a portrayal harmful to real tort cases, where the evidence of causation tends to be less obvious? What about movies like *Class Action*, *The Verdict*, or *Philadelphia*, where defendants show deliberate indifference to the victims or cover up evidence of their negligence? Is it too dangerous to rely on popular culture to set the tone for consumer protection? Does the entertainment industry have sufficient checks on its power to persuade?

6. In *A Civil Action* and *Erin Brockovich*, causation is quite plainly an important component of the narrative tension — the plaintiffs' attorneys must prove it to win their cases. How important is it in the other movies? For example, in *Philadelphia*, is it important to prove that Andrew Beckett's injury (discharge from his job) was directly caused by his firm's discrimination against him as a gay man with AIDS? In *Class Action*, does the primary narrative tension center on Jed Ward proving that the design of the Meridian automobile was the cause of the plaintiffs' injuries?

7. How does popular culture dramatize the causation problem? Generally, causation is the most tedious part of a case because it often relies heavily on dry expert testimony. Thus, in *A Civil Action*, the defendants strike a fatal blow to the plaintiffs' case by convincing Judge Skinner to bifurcate the proceedings so that the jury must sit through weeks of testimony about how contaminants might enter a drinking water supply and find causation before they ever hear the more sympathetic and moving stories of the victims themselves. How do the filmmakers avoid boring the audience in the same way the lawyers bored the jury? In finding other ways to dramatize the plight of the plaintiffs to the movie audience, do the filmmakers do a disservice to real tort plaintiffs by making laypeople more accustomed to seeing the victims' tragedy portrayed cinematically?

8. According to Professors Graham and Maschio, "[p]opular film serves as a cultural text. When we look at a group of films on any given subject, we are also viewing a record of the culture that produced those films. Generally, films produced for mass or popular consumption reflect the dominant culture's ideology." Louise Everett Graham & Geraldine Maschio, *A False Public Sentiment: Narrative and Visual Images of Women Lawyers in Film*, 84 Kentucky Law Journal 1027, 1028 (1995–96). Is this statement correct? Does a film "reflect the dominant culture's ideology"? If it does, does every audience member take away the same meaning? Would everyone who saw it describe the story the same way? By the same token, should every juror who views the evidence "correctly" come to the same conclusion about the defendant's culpability? If so, why do we have juries?

3. Injury and Compensation

Both in real cases and in popular culture, one of the most important things a plaintiff's attorney must do is encourage the fact-finder to feel sympathy toward her client. In an excerpt in the previous chapter of this text, Professor Jeffrey Abramson discussed various jury stories available in popular culture. In the following excerpt, he contemplates two distinct narrative treatments of tort compensation that might differently affect a jury's — or an audience's — perception of tort victims as deserving of compensation.

THE JURY AND POPULAR CULTURE
Jeffrey Abramson
50 DePaul Law Review 497 (2000)

Let me call the first narrative the populist or Jacksonian story. In this narrative, as much as the common people would prefer to stay out of politics and off juries, sometimes they are simply needed to clean out a corrupt system. The common person responds to the moral heroism of deserving victims whose water, air, or lungs have been poisoned by corporate giants. The moral claims of the victims are so overwhelming, the behavior of the corporations so arrogant, that even lawyers are transformed by civil litigation from sleazy sharks into crusaders for a cause. This populist depiction of the morality tale inside many a civil trial has been the central story line in a cluster of recent hits. The first example is *A Civil Action*, a nonfiction account of the jury trial of W.R. Grace and Beatrice Foods for causing the cases of childhood leukemia in Woburn, Massachusetts, by contaminating the town's wells with carcinogenic chemicals. The second is *Erin Brockovich*, about one woman's discovery of how Pacific Gas and Electric Company poisoned the water of a California town and then conspired to cover up its torts. The third example is *The Runaway Jury*, the Grisham novel about corrupt Big Tobacco executives trying to buy a jury in an anti-smoking trial.

The timing of these "David and Goliath" books and movies on civil trials is itself interesting. Since the 1970s, a second narrative, the Hamiltonian one, has told the most popular stories about civil litigation. This story is all about the stupidity of setting economic policy through jury trials. Victims are rarely deserving and always litigious, lawyers prey upon the unfortunate, jurors are in over their heads, junk science breeds junk lawsuits, damage awards are a crap shoot, and the rich just cannot get justice. Hamiltonian stories are the mirror image of populist ones: the corporation or the doctor is the victim of unsavory lawyers serving shoddy victims. As to juries, the reigning Hamiltonian punch line is that "the only difference between TV juries and real juries is 50 IQ points.". . . .

Mark Galanter and others have pointed out that the Hamiltonian story about civil justice is often impervious to empirical evidence that civil juries are not as anti-business and anti-doctor as the plot line demands. The narrative has some of the staying power of folklore, anchored into a deep belief structure about the essential immorality of damage awards that sever the connection between work and reward. . . .

NOTES & QUESTIONS

1. Is Professor Abramson's characterization of *A Civil Action* and *Erin Brockovich* as "Jacksonian" correct? What exactly makes them so? Can you imagine a Hamiltonian take on the stories in these films?

2. Is it possible for popular culture to be evenhanded, or must it take one side or the other? Compare works of popular culture to real trials, where both sides have the opportunity to present their side of the story to the jury. Is there a danger in one-sided works or popular culture about torts?

3. How would you characterize the other movies discussed in this chapter or other works of popular culture about torts — Jacksonian or Hamiltonian? Consider when the works appeared. Do you discern any trends? Can such an analysis of popular culture tell us anything meaningful about widespread attitudes toward compensation in real tort cases? If you were an attorney representing one of the parties in a large tort suit, would you be concerned with such trends?

4. Professor Abramson cites research indicating that real juries are not influenced by the Hamiltonian narratives they receive in popular culture because they continue to award significant damages to plaintiffs. Is this reasoning sound? He goes on to argue that the Hamiltonian narrative has "the staying power of folklore." Is Abramson suggesting that people recognize and embrace it as pure fiction? If so, does that mean that people can also distinguish between the fiction of the Jacksonian narrative and the reality of an individual case?

5. How do the films discussed in this chapter or other popular culture about torts portray the victims' injuries? Be specific about how they are communicated. Is it in a scene of the victim talking to her lawyer? Where does such a conversation take place? Is she shown testifying in front of a jury? Or is the incident portrayed visually? What reasons might the filmmakers have for these choices? Does the different mode of communication adversely affect jury trials, where it is impossible to render a real-time depiction of the injury for the jurors?

6. If the narrative is centered around the lawyer as protagonist, how do the filmmakers account for the fact that the lawyer becomes involved well after the actual injury has occurred? In other words, if the movie starts with the lawyer, by the time we meet the victim, the incident is already past. How does an injury inflicted in the past fit into the narrative of the litigating the case?

7. Do filmmakers manipulate audience sympathy to make up for a perception that the victims themselves are really responsible for their own injuries? If this assertion seems far-fetched, consider the following:

> Perhaps no assumption about the civil jury is so universally accepted as the belief that juries are highly sympathetic to injured plaintiffs. Opinion surveys, business and insurance industry briefs, and court opinions reflect beliefs that juries naturally take the side of the injured plaintiff. Research on civil juries, however, provides evidence that jurors and the public are inclined to question the credibility and claims of plaintiffs who bring personal injury lawsuits.

Valerie P. Harris & Juliet Dee, *Whiplash: Who's to Blame?* 68 Brooklyn Law Review 1093, 1094-95 (2003). Where do these popular views of plaintiffs come from? Are jurors able to distinguish the tort victims portrayed in films from the ones they see in the courtroom? What about films based on true stories, like *A Civil Action* and *Erin Brockovich*? Could the secondary role of the victims in popular culture have something to do with juries' dismissal of real plaintiffs' injuries? Or does popular culture lead jurors to feel more sympathetic even to victims of less sensationalistic torts?

8. Does the focus on sympathetic plaintiffs bypass the larger social considerations at stake in popular culture? Think about the types of tort cases that are likely to be considered interesting enough to be made into mass entertainment. They tend to have some larger social impact: toxic pollution that threatens entire communities (*A Civil Action* and *Erin Brockovich*); product liability suits that cause grievous injury to many people (*Class Action*); discrimination (*Philadelphia*); health care negligence (by the Catholic Church, no less) (*The Verdict*). Are these stories about the plaintiffs or about greater social harms that affect all of us?

9. According to the authors of *Film and the Law*, relying on the stories of individual victims to build narrative sympathy for the plaintiffs' attorney-protagonist can cause us to ignore remedies with a more widespread and positive social impact. "One issue that comes to the fore in both *A Civil Action* and *Erin Brockovich* is the question of remedies and the weakness of the law in providing some defence [sic] for the community. This is shown by the concentration on individual cases and monetary compensation as the prime remedy wants. There is [a] tension between what the law can provide, in terms of a remedy, and what the community wants." Steve Greenfield et al., *Film and the Law* 93 (2001). Does popular culture have a responsibility to present remedies with a broader social impact?

10. The same authors claim that the movies' reliance on monetary remedies to the exclusion of other forms of compensation parallels corporate thinking, wherein the costs of tort liability are calculated against the profits to be obtained by engaging in tortious activity. Do you agree? If audiences become accustomed to seeing tort cases resolved with financial remuneration, are they likely to begin viewing all injuries as monetarily compensable? Are they? How else can one make reparations for causing bodily or emotional injury?

11. Think about the use of "bean counting" in *Class Action*. Recall that Maggie Ward, one of the attorneys for the defense, discovers that her client's chief risk-assessment manager was aware of a design flaw in the car they manufactured whereby if the car were rear-ended while engaging its left-turn signal, its gas tank would explode. The risk-assessment manager had determined that the cost of fixing the flaw would exceed the cost of paying victims of the likely explosions. This information, along with other ethical lapses by her colleagues, causes Ward's transformation from a hard-nosed defense attorney to a woman with a conscience who deliberately throws the defense's case. How realistic do you find this portrayal of corporate practices? If you find it plausible that corporations let the cost of compensating an injured public drive their actions, where does your knowledge of such corporate practices come from? Is it influenced by popular culture? By media scrutiny of one or two particularly high-profile cases? Are law-abiding large corporations themselves the victims of popular attitudes derived from portrayals of tort cases in popular culture that need an identifiable villain?

D.   THE IMPACT OF TORT MOVIES ON THE LAW

In this section, we consider the connection between popular culture depicting tort cases and the current trend toward tort reform.

THE AMERICAN CIVIL JURY FOR AUSLÄNDER
(FOREIGNERS)
Neil Vidmar
13 Duke Journal of Comparative & International Law 95 (2003)

Legal practitioners and scholars whom I encounter in my travels outside the borders of the United States frequently challenge me to explain the "crazy," "outrageous" system by which we allow groups of untutored laypersons to decide civil disputes. Invariably, they bring up *Liebeck v. McDonald's Restaurants, P.T.S. Inc.*, 1995 WL 360609 (D.N.M. 1994), the McDonald's case in which a civil jury in New Mexico awarded a woman $160,000 in compensatory damages and $2.7 million in punitive damages just because she spilled coffee on herself. My inquisitors are frequently surprised to learn that for years McDonald's had kept its coffee many degrees hotter than home-brewed coffee or the coffee of its competitors; that for over five years it had been aware of the problem of serious burns resulting from the coffee through over 700 complaints but had never consulted a burn specialist, reduced the temperature of its coffee, or warned consumers; and that the seventy-nine-year-old woman who was injured suffered second and third degree burns to her private parts. They are also surprised to learn that the plaintiff had tried to settle the suit for a much more modest amount before trial, initially around $20,000 to cover her medical expenses, and that the jury's punitive damage award was equal to two days' worth of the McDonald's corporation's profits from selling coffee. Finally, almost everyone is ignorant of the fact that the trial judge subsequently reduced the punitive damage award to $480,000 for a total award of $640,000, and that the case was later settled for an undisclosed, presumably lesser, amount.

One source of misunderstanding in the McDonald's case is incomplete media reporting about the details of the case. This problem is endemic with media coverage of jury awards. A number of studies have carefully documented the fact that mass media newspapers and television tend to report jury awards selectively, focusing on large awards, ignoring small awards and defendant verdicts, and not providing complete details about issues put to the juries or matters preceding trial or following the jury verdict. In addition, industry groups generally opposed to the tort system frequently distort information about jury awards in order to further their political agendas. Moreover, some legal commentators who have made claims about the legal system may be less than informed about the empirical realities of jury behavior. . . .

Assessing Damages

It is jury damage awards that get the attention of the news media and the public. It is safe to say that the McDonald's case would have gained no attention from the media if the award had only been several thousand dollars. Studies indicate that media coverage is heavily skewed toward cases involving large damage awards. Of course, this skews public perceptions of the jury. . . .

In a major study of 1992 verdicts in a sample of the largest urban state courts, Brian Ostrom and his colleagues concluded that the typical jury award was "modest." The median jury verdict, including punitive damages, was $52,000; however, because of some very high awards, the arithmetic mean of those awards was much higher, $455,000. About eight percent of awards exceeded $1 million and the mean amount of the awards varied by case type, with malpractice, products liability, and toxic torts generating the largest awards on average. In contrast, automobile and premises liability cases had much lower awards.

Many of the same jurisdictions were assessed again in 1996. The median amount of the jury award for plaintiffs who won at trial was $35,000, with about nineteen percent of winners receiving over $250,000, and an estimated seven percent receiving $1 million or more. Of a total of 5060 jury trials in which the plaintiff prevailed, there were only 212 cases (about four percent) that resulted in punitive damages. Of these, about twenty-two percent involved intentional torts and forty-nine percent involved contract cases. In tort cases considered as a whole, the median punitive award was $27,000 compared to a median punitive award in contract cases of $76,000. . . .

C. Jury Consideration of Insurance and the Effects of Damage Awards

Is there any validity to the claim that jurors are profligate with defendants' or their insurers' money? Critics of the jury system might argue that juries are irresponsible because the jurors see the money award coming from the rich person or corporation and do not consider the aggregate impact of large awards on financial costs that must be borne by all of society. As a general rule, these claims about jury profligacy are not only unsupported by systematic research, but findings suggest just the opposite — that juries tend to be very skeptical of plaintiffs' claims about damages. . . .

IV. Conclusion

A substantial body of systematic empirical studies indicates that the American civil jury system is not as erratic or unreasonable as portrayed in the media. Whether it involves issues of liability, responses to experts, attention to the judge's instructions, or damage awards, the civil jury performs much better than many people believe. If this were not so, surely the civil jury would have been abandoned, or at least drastically curtailed, despite the guarantee of the right to jury trial in the U.S. Constitution and the constitutions of individual states. American society could not afford the caprice and craziness ascribed to juries. Examined from this pragmatic perspective, it should not be surprising that the empirical research into the performance of the civil jury yields a generally positive picture, especially when considered in the context of the formal and informal controls on errant verdicts. . . .

NOTES & QUESTIONS

1. What might account for the downward trend in amounts of jury awards noted by Professor Vidmar? In making this assessment, be as specific as you can. For example, if you believe political factors are primary, consider what might have generated and contributed to the political movement. If you believe it is a product of popular culture, try to identify specific examples. Be as critical as you can about the role of popular culture in the decline of tort plaintiffs' awards.

2. Is the news media entirely to blame, as Professor Vidmar suggests? Is it more at fault than popular culture, such as the movies examined in this chapter? How do you distinguish between the news accounts of the McDonald's case and film versions of real cases like *A Civil Action* and *Erin Brockovich*?

3. Despite the downward trend in tort damages noted by the author, tort reform continues to enjoy substantial political support. For example, some members of Congress have supported a large surtax on lawyers' contingency fees and/or the federalization of virtually all class actions. Constituents have lobbied to replace jury awards for certain types of injuries with compensation funds set up by acknowledged mass tortfeasors. For a discussion of these reforms and the concomitant attacks on tort plaintiffs from the perspective of the Association of Trial Lawyers of America, a plaintiffs' bar advocacy group, see David S. Casey, Jr., *A Time to Fight*, Trial; Sept. 2003; 9. What do you make of such tort reform proposals, especially in light of Vidmar's claim that tort awards are actually on the decline? If popular perceptions of tort awards are skewed, how did they get that way? Is it irresponsible of Hollywood to produce entertaining movies about huge jury awards? Or is it up to movie-goers to distinguish between fact and fiction? What about other forms of popular culture?

4. Stephen Daniels and Joanne Martin argue that "[t]he future of punitive damages is in doubt because of the political success of the interest groups wanting changes in the civil justice system" even though "a punitive damages explosion . . . does not in fact exist." Stephen Daniels & Joanne Martin, *Punitive Damages, Change, and the Politics of Ideas: Defining Public Policy Problems*, 1998 Wisconsin Law Review 71, 71–73. If the authors are correct that there is not a problem of outrageous punitive damage awards, what is driving the political interest groups? Why rally behind a cause that does not really exist? What role does popular culture play in this political movement?

5. How important is the actual size of the award in works of popular culture about torts? In *A Civil Action*, the jury finds no liability on the part of Beatrice. The plaintiffs settle with co-defendant Grace for a total of $8 million — of which each family receives $375,000, with an additional $80,000 payable after five years. Legal expenses eat up $2.6 million of the settlement and legal fees are $2.2 million. Jonathan Harr, *A Civil Action* 453 (1995). The Reverend Bruce Young, who advised some of the victims, was furious and disgusted with the settlement. "This was a case I thought would have some real importance," he said. "It never happened." *Id.*, 452. Does Rev. Young's reaction affect whether you believe the plaintiffs were victorious? Do you think he was happy with the hugely successful book and movie that brought the case to the attention of a large audience? Should we have to rely on popular culture for this aspect of justice?

6. For a different perspective, put yourself in Maggie Ward's shoes in *Class Action*. What are the consequences for her, personally, in contributing to her client's loss by deliberately exposing corporate and legal malfeasance? Does this brand of morality exist in daily practice? Should it? Do knowing tortfeasors deserve zealous representation? Consider again how the tortfeasors are portrayed in popular culture and contrast these portrayals with your own perception of reality.

7. Read on for a discussion of how jurors view the claims of tort victims and see if it affects your views on the interaction between popular culture and the tort reform movement.

WHIPLASH: WHO'S TO BLAME?
Valerie P. Hans & Juliet Dee
68 Brooklyn Law Review 1093 (2003)

A central task of the civil jury is to assess the competing claims of the defendant and the plaintiff. However, in retrospective accounts of their own decision making, civil jurors seemed to focus more on the plaintiffs, and their scrutiny was often extraordinarily intense. "Jurors' suspicions about plaintiffs' claims led them in most cases to dissect the personal behavior of plaintiffs, with seemingly no limits. Jurors criticized plaintiffs who did not act or appear as injured as they claimed, those who did not appear deserving, and those with preexisting or complicated medical conditions." Juror interviews also reflected concerns about money-hungry plaintiffs: "I just thought they felt they were going to come into a big sum of money and just live the rest of their life on easy street" or "I think, probably, looking at these medical claims, (the plaintiff) said, 'well, maybe I can cash in on this knee injury.'"

Of course, jurors' reactions to the plaintiffs in their cases could have as much to do with the facts of the case and the individual parties to the lawsuit as with jurors' predispositions toward plaintiff blame. The factual circumstances of the event, the causal actions of the defendant, any contributory fault on the part of the plaintiff and the presence of extenuating circumstances will figure centrally in how jurors judge the responsibility for an accident. Yet, Neal Feigenson and his colleagues conducted experimental studies confirming that, in certain cases, people ascribe some responsibility to legally blameless plaintiffs. They conducted a scenario experiment in which the plaintiffs' blameworthiness varied between conditions. They found that, even when the plaintiff was completely blameless as a legal matter, some participants still held him accountable. For example, one condition involved a worker who obeyed all the rules, and thus did not appear to deserve blame, yet study participants judged him to be 22% responsible for his accident. In another scenario, study participants allocated to a homeowner 14% of the blame for injuries stemming from a faulty valve on a propane gas tank in his home that was the property of the gas company.

Questions about credibility in individual personal injury cases reflect larger doubts about the general merits of plaintiff claims in civil litigation. Recent polls indicate that most people believe that many lawsuits are worthless. In one recent national survey, 92% of the respondents agreed with the statement: "There are far too many frivolous lawsuits today." In fact, 76% of respondents said that they "strongly agreed" with the statement, suggesting an emotionally laden endorsement. Beliefs in frivolous lawsuits are ubiquitous. Public opinion polls expose a common concern about the amount of illegitimate litigation today. There is widespread agreement among the public that many people who sue are not negligently injured; instead, they are just trying to blame others for their problems. Plaintiff lawsuits are seen as attempts to violate the important principle of individual personal responsibility. Indeed, President George W. Bush recently exploited this widespread perception of frivolous lawsuits in advocating his administration's plan to limit jury awards in medical malpractice cases: "We're a litigious society," the President proclaimed, "(e)verybody is suing, it seems like."

At the same time that members of the public believe that jurors are highly sympathetic to civil plaintiffs, they hold a concomitant view that fraud among claimants is rampant. Respondents in one national poll estimated which was likely to be more frequent, an insurance company denying a valid claim or a person attempting to bring a fraudulent claim. Over half of the poll respondents thought that an individual was more likely to bring a fraudulent claim.

Although the extent of fraudulent claims is unknown, practitioners in the insurance industry consider false claims a major problem. The Insurance Research Council reported that people submitted $42 billion worth of claims for auto accident injuries in 1997, and estimated that as many as 40% of these claims ($16.8 billion) could have been fraudulent. The Coalition Against Insurance Fraud asserts on its Web site that insurance fraud is an $80 billion problem. It is difficult to assess the validity of these estimates. A separate but related question is the extent to which false legal claims result in lawsuits, since personal injury attorneys provide an additional layer of scrutiny before filing a lawsuit. . . .

NOTES & QUESTIONS

1. Choose one of the movies discussed in this chapter or some other work of popular culture about a tort claim with which you are familiar and consider how it might influence and be influenced by the tort reform movement. Push yourself to be as critical and specific as possible: Could the work on its face support a tort reform argument? Could it support such an argument when contrasted with the vast majority of tort claims? Does the secondary role of the victims in the work make real tort victims less important to jurors? If real victims do not act and look like the paid actors who portray them in film and television, are jurors less likely to sympathize with them?

2. Now consider the chosen work as an attack on the tort reform movement. Is this political role a fair one for mass entertainment? Does popular culture stack the deck too strongly against the tortfeasors in portraying their corporate power, lack of sympathy for their victims, and greed? Does the portrayal of one egregious case — either entirely fictional or at least partly fictionalized for dramatic effect — unduly skew public perceptions against large corporations and in favor of tort victims? Do the roots of our increasingly litigious society lie at least in part in the mass consumption of popular culture such as the films discussed in this chapter?

3. If you believe that popular culture predisposes the public against large corporations, how do you account for the statistics cited by the authors? If they are correct in their assessment of public attitudes toward tort plaintiffs, is it safe to say popular culture has no effect on public perceptions?

4. In *Film and the Law*, the authors describe the trial in *The Verdict* as an example of how justice triumphs when movie juries ignore the strictures of the evidence presented and apply their own understanding of justice to the evidence that is admitted:

> [T]he rules relating to the submission of evidence in a trial are unlikely to quicken the beat of many hearts, but in *The Verdict* they become a vital feature of the case. The crucial part of the plaintiff's claim is struck out by the judge, as it falls foul of the procedural rules. The issue then switches to the morality of the plaintiff's claim and the ability of the jury to deliver justice, as they see it, regardless of the paper evidence.

> The rules of law here are being shown as a barrier to the pursuit of a just cause, and the issue at stake is not the narrow one of whether the evidence should be admitted but a broader one of achieving justice in spite of the rules.

Steve Greenfield et al., *Film and the Law* 20–21 (2001). Do the trials in popular culture portraying tort claims boil down to nothing more than whether the jury does the "right thing" as it has been set up for the audience — regardless of the evidence? Does this role for the trial heighten the sense of dramatic tension in the film, or would a more realistic portrayal be equally exciting? What about jurors who are faced with the considerably less stirring performances of lawyers and witnesses in a real trial? Are they more or less likely to follow the law as it is explained to them rather than doing what they, individually, think is "just"? Which should they do?

5. What accounts for the difference — if there is one — between works of popular culture about torts and reality? What impact might portrayals of the legal system as a barrier to justice have on popular perceptions of law in reality? Are people less likely to expect a just outcome in real life if they receive the message from popular culture that the legal system impedes justice?

6. How much does the concept of "justice" have to do with how the stories are actually presented? In other words, think about all the ways in which the popular culture you have encountered "teaches" what the just result should be — its portrayals of the plaintiffs' attorneys, the defendants and their attorneys, the victims and their injuries. Do the same rules apply to "teaching" fact-finders the just result in real cases? Does real justice for tort victims depend on whether the plaintiff's attorney is attuned to current popular culture? Does this expectation place an acceptable burden on tort attorneys?

Chapter 9

CRIMINAL LAW

A. FILMOGRAPHY

I Want to Live! (1958)

The Ox-Bow Incident (1943)

A Place in the Sun (1951)

Presumed Innocent (1990)

The Thin Blue Line (1988)

B. INTRODUCTION

Initial reactions to the materials in a law school course in Criminal Law are often different than the initial reactions to the materials in other courses. Students have been subjected to innumerable stories about criminal law and criminals, and as a result they perceive the cases presented in law school as somehow familiar. The cases capture students' imaginations, and students frequently begin their criminal law studies eager to read "real" stories about crime.

Yet students' hunger is often not fully satisfied by the appellate opinions in their criminal law casebooks. Students perceive something is missing in these edited and fragmented texts about criminal law doctrine. Students rightfully believe that lurking beneath the surfaces and edges of appellate opinions are powerful, complex, and consuming stories which are usually not well served by the partial renderings in the facts presented in the opinions. These stories have numerous themes: stories about guilt and innocence; punishment, revenge, and redemption; whodunits and mysteries — some solved, others not; stories about notions of guilt and innocence that are more shaded and subtle than the law often allows; meanings more literary than legal; stories about character and motivation; stories about behaviors caused by environments; stories that provide fuller comprehension of the unfolding of events; stories about integrity and strength; and stories about systemic corruption, about the probabilities and possibilities of justice, and about justice gone haywire too. These are narratives that the opinions seldom reach.

Further, the appellate cases studied in law school purposefully minimize the drama of engrossing, complex, and often ambiguous narratives at the core of many criminal law stories. This dumbing-down of facts is often strategic; the narrow legal issues reviewed on appeal must not be subsumed by the compelling power of narrative. Appellate opinions dissect fragments or cross-sections of a story, and appellate judges parse out from their opinions complex renderings of "character," "plot," "settings," "style," and "narrative time." The strange is made familiar; the story, intentionally flattened. It is the law and the doctrinal analysis that are placed in the foreground; the factual narrative is merely a springboard for legal analysis.

Pop cultural storytelling, especially in quality commercial films, routinely turns the legal world upside down. The plot-driven and character-based stories are now crucial. The law and the precise cataloging of facts in terms of legal doctrine are suspended; narrative is no longer subservient to doctrine. The lens of the story widens literally and figuratively. Constraints, conventions, and limitations placed upon storytelling in judicial opinions fall away; the popular storyteller attempts to capture a different truth than the appellate judge. Narratives emerge from beneath doctrine, and seem to take shape attempting to capture the imagination of the reader or viewer.

This chapter looks at several of these popular versions of law stories. It is divided into three main sections: The Players as Legal Actors, Legal Storytelling in Criminal Trials, and Punishment and the Death Penalty. The excerpts may assist readers to better explore systematically the discrete and characteristic aspects of popular storytelling about criminal law.

C. THE PLAYERS AS LEGAL ACTORS

1. Defendants and Criminals

LEGAL FICTIONS: IRONY, STORYTELLING, TRUTH, AND JUSTICE IN THE MODERN COURTROOM DRAMA
Christine Alice Corcos
25 University of Arkansas at Little Rock Law Review 503 (2003)

Apart from pointing out the easy manipulation of the legal systems available to such unscrupulous defendants as Leonard Vole [*Witness for the Prosecution*] and Frederick Manion, [*Anatomy of a Murder*] the author or filmmaker can also criticize the legal system by demonstrating that it fails from the beginning in its quest for justice by bringing the "wrong defendant" to trial. The "wrong defendant" may be a totally innocent person, or he may be someone whose morality is immediately apparent to the observer, and who, though he may be literally guilty, is ethically innocent of the charges.

Presumed Innocent and the Lawyer as the Accused

With the choice of defendant, particularly when the defendant is a lawyer, the conflicts of fact merge with the conflicts of belief to create a dramatic whole. Both the lawyer as ethical chameleon and the lawyer as defendant are popular choices for the author wishing to examine the contrast between law and justice in the legal system.

The image of the lawyer, expert in the manipulation and control of the legal system, as the accused in a criminal trial (particularly murder) is an obvious choice for the author wishing to present an ironic situation. . . .

The confusion of roles is a major component of the dramatic irony present in *Presumed Innocent*, and the spectacle of the lawyer-manipulator as accused-manipulated is a particularly striking one. From the cynical title (Rusty Sabich is clearly not presumed innocent by anyone except the real killer and arguably his lawyer) and his opening "I am a prosecutor" voice-over in the film, Sabich swings between the extremes of judge and judged, between accuser and accused. Sabich's superior, Raymond Horgan, assigns the murder case to him because "you're the only guy I can trust." In reality Sabich is "the only guy" likely to be loyal enough to him to cover up Horgan's involvement with the dead woman. Horgan equates "trust" with blind loyalty: the prosecutor who should be assigned the case is Horgan's political enemy — an enemy who ironically becomes the prosecuting attorney in Sabich's case. Yet Horgan does not trust Sabich enough to tell him the truth about the dead woman or about his and the dead woman's involvement with the judge. Further, Horgan lies on the stand in a final effort to cover up his own involvement and implicate Sabich.

Rusty's experience as a prosecutor seems to lead him completely astray once he becomes the defendant. His very definite opinions about how to obtain a conviction should alert him to the dangers of his own appearance on the stand, yet he insists to Sandy Stern, his attorney, that "the jury wants to hear me say I didn't do it." Stern is reluctant; defense attorneys in general prefer not to let their clients testify because the client may say something in an unguarded moment that the attorney cannot control, allowing the prosecutor an opportunity to attack the defense's entire case. Stern's own choice is for Rusty's wife, Barbara, to plead his case, but Sabich indicates that he believes his wife will not be a good witness. His sixth sense about testimony seems to guide him clearly but inexplicably here. Although Rusty believes (ironically) that his wife would not be a good witness because she is emotionally unstable, the truth is that she would not be a "good witness" because she committed the crime. Although Stern tells the judge that Sabich is "an integral part of our defense," Sabich loses every tactical argument that he has with Stern. Stern controls the defense completely, like a good attorney. Sabich the wily prosecutor becomes Sabich the client unable to make effective decisions in his own defense.

Rusty's voice-over in the opening scene establishes the irony of his situation: "I am a part of the process of accusing, judging, and punishing." Normally, he can only do the first — accusing; as the defendant, first accused, then exonerated, he ends by doing the second — judging — because the first is denied to him. Like a jury that "can't decide on truth," because of the identity of the real killer, Rusty can never do the third — punishing. Without that decision, no resolution is possible. Sabich's entire experience demonstrates that the very system to which he has devoted his life cannot uncover the truth necessary to resolve the question of guilt. Others (Sabich's lawyer, his police officer friend, the real killer, the district attorney) intervene to prevent crucial evidence from being presented to that jury. What does his ordeal teach Rusty? That the system works only for those who know how to manipulate it. The presumption of innocence is not merely untrue; it is irrelevant. . . .

NOTES & QUESTIONS

1. One often-exploited "stock" story in popular culture concerns the wrongfully accused defendant. The film *Presumed Innocent*, as Professor Corcos observes, provides one version of this story. Here, this narrative theme is given an ironic spin as the prosecutor becomes the wrongfully accused defendant, and feels the force of betrayal by the system which he has, until this time, used to his strategic advantage. Other versions of this story are numerous and prevalent in pop cultural storytelling and especially in popular films, including several suggested for this chapter. *The Ox-Bow Incident*, for example, is a gripping World War II-era film in which a posse of men in the early American West reconstitutes itself as judge and jury. The group votes 21-7 to hang three men for the murder, only to learn the supposed murder victim is still alive and those who shot and wounded him have been captured. Overall, the film is a cautionary tale about disregarding the rule of law. For a provocative discussion of the film, see Robert Louis Felix, *The Ox-Bow Incident*, 24 Legal Studies Forum 645 (1999).

The approaches to the theme of the wrongfully accused defendant and the tonality of the storytelling are diverse. Contrast, for example, the humor of *My Cousin Vinny* (1992) with the realism of the fictional *12 Angry Man* (1957) or the mystery of Hitchcock's *The Wrong Man* (1956), which is based upon a real case and considered at length in Chapter 5 of this text. Despite their fundamental differences, these films compel our imaginative attention. Why do you think there is still such a recurring power and narrative satisfaction in retellings of this basic tale? Do we believe or suspect that the systematic processes of the law often do not work effectively, and that we wrongfully convict innocent defendants or let the guilty go free?

2. Reflect upon your personal experiences: Have you ever been accused of committing a wrongful or criminal act that you did not commit? Have you ever been wrongfully punished? How did you respond? With anger and indignation? What, if anything, did you learn from your experiences? Does this story still stay with you? Does it affect your perceptions about whether there is usually fairness and justness, or are results often random and outcomes often unjust?

3. Corcos observes that when Rusty Sabich, the prosecutor, is placed on trial for murder in *Presumed Innocent* and becomes the defendant, he desires to tell his story to the jury and testify in his own behalf. His shrewd defense attorney, Sandy Stern, does not want Sabich to testify, and advises even this court-savvy defendant against it. Juries usually want to hear the defendant's side of the story, and are disappointed when the defendant chooses not to testify. Nevertheless, criminal defendants usually are passive, and defendants do not usually testify at trial. Defendants characteristically rely upon the presumption of innocence and the inability of the prosecutor to prove the defendant's guilt beyond a reasonable doubt. This strategy, however, often makes for a less-than-satisfactory resolution in popular culture. Consequently, we are far more likely to see defendants testifying in films. Are the narrative certainties of film and the closure usually provided by most popular culture more satisfying than the problematic resolutions of many criminal trials?

4. In *Presumed Innocent* we learn that it is Barbara, Sabich's calculating wife, who has plotted and carried out the murder of Carole Polhemus. Likewise, the documentary *The Thin Blue Line* provides the satisfaction of narrative closure and resolution by strategically placing the dramatic confession of David Harris at the end. Without the careful selection and placement of these narratively structured and plot-driven events, assuming some component of uncertainty and irresolution remained, would we be compelled and drawn in by these stories? Does this suggest any strategies that a criminal defense attorney should follow in telling the defendant's story at trial?

5. In *Presumed Innocent*, defendant Sabich acts on his own behalf outside the courtroom. He is not a passive defendant. He participates actively in an independent investigation of the crime and draws upon his friends, e.g., Detective Lipranzer, to better understand the circumstances of the crime. Akin to a private investigator in a detective story, Sabich gradually develops his own theories of what happened and why. Note that this investigative function is not an activity usually undertaken by criminal defendants. It is the job of many defendants merely to remain largely passive, to not speak to the authorities without their attorney's permission, and to carefully follow the instructions and advice of their attorney, allowing their character and identity to be shaped by the attorney's storytelling at trial; the narrative strategies at trial depend upon the investigations undertaken by the attorney. Contrast, for example, the investigation undertaken by Sabich in the fictional *Presumed Innocent* with the investigations undertaken by the defense attorneys in *The Thin Blue Line*. Randall Adams, the defendant, is passive, a defendant as wrongfully accused victim trapped in a television-program nightmare over which he has no control. Does this discomforting imagery suggest the plight of the defendant in a typical criminal case, subjected to the power of the machinery of the state?

CONVICTS, CRIMINALS, PRISONERS AND OUTLAWS: A COURSE IN POPULAR STORYTELLING
Philip N. Meyer
42 Journal of Legal Education 129 (1992)

In "The Outlaw as Eve," the first of two papers, student ("C") uses anecdotal material to engage the reader in her analysis of popular cultural depictions of women as murderers, criminals, and outlaws in course materials. . . . There is the power of a student's discovering the authority of a first-person storytelling voice grounded in the particularity of experience rather than in the abstraction of theory. The journal begins:

> I went to school with a murderer. Two weeks before graduation, the police discovered the mother's body in the trunk of the family car, where it had rested while my schoolmate commuted to class each day. I attended a private Catholic girls' high school. The student was convicted and sentenced to Niantic Prison for Women, from whence

presumably she received a high school diploma. My story has a point — the only murderer I ever knew personally was female, and very much like me, yet in the literature of criminality, women infrequently appear as direct or deliberate, as so-called cold-blooded murderers.

In her analysis, C observes that although female murderers are occasionally portrayed as "queens or warriors, pseudo-males, operating in their stead," female roles in criminality are generally archetypal and fall into two categories. There is the "evil stepmother of fairy tales, grasping and jealous," who "dominates the night psyche of many a child." And there is "Eve the primal temptress [who] preserves women's roles as both 'helpmate and temptress' and accounts for female evilness while maintaining her dual status as desirable and subservient. . . . Eve evokes ambivalence at once attractive and repugnant, compelling a response to our very nature." C places the female characters in course materials within her framework. Her journal is replete with subtle observations and a deftly accurate analysis of plots and characters.

Other students perceived and analyzed gender issues in their journals. In an untitled seminar journal, "H" explores sexual stereotyping, comparing the characters of Barbara in Turow's *Presumed Innocent*, Daisy in Fitzgerald's *Gatsby*, and Maria in Wolfe's *Bonfire*. H puts some nice vitriolic salsa on her prose, distinguishing characters in a voice often heard in a courtroom but seldom in classroom discussions of appellate cases. She contrasts Barbara, prosecutor Rusty Sabich's melancholy wife, with Daisy and Maria:

> The misogyny evident in the picture of Barbara, however, is of a newer, more invidious type than that found in the other novels. Daisy and Maria are the classic bimbos who find definition in their attractiveness to men. Barbara is a new stereotype: the "have it all" woman who is miserable.

Unlike Daisy and Maria, Barbara is capable of plotting and carrying out a murder: Barbara's crime is planned and motivated. She puts her prodigious brain power to work and plans the killing, "a byzantine scheme[,]as a way to both free and punish her husband." Barbara's physicality also distinguishes her from Daisy and Maria: "She is first seen laying on her bed with sweat clinging to her back after an aerobics workout. Our first view of Daisy, by contrast, finds her languishing on a couch which she has not left for hours. Maria, encumbered by her tight clothes and teetering on her high heels is likewise not a picture of vigorous physicality."

Nevertheless, H concludes that ultimately Barbara is just as sexist a creation as Maria and Daisy:

> Although Barbara, with her brains, her middle-class work ethic, and her independence from her husband seems far removed from the bright young things that Daisy and Maria become, she still is much like them in that she will never have to face justice. This could be due to a certain squeamishness on all three authors' part with the idea of women suffering for their crimes. Such an attitude is grounded in paternalistic notions of protecting women from life's rigors and with the idea that women, like children, are not really responsible for their actions and thus should not have to answer for them.

The course materials (stories) crystallize analysis that, I think, would be far more abstract and diffuse in, for example, theoretical discussions in a seminar on "Feminism and the Law." *Presumed Innocent* provides an excellent basis for thoughtful and animated discussion of sexuality and sexual conduct in the professional environments that law students and practicing attorneys inhabit. Again, academic purists and traditionalists might denigrate the propriety of allowing such discussion to take place within the law school curriculum. I doubt, however, that these discussions would take place elsewhere. . . .

NOTES & QUESTIONS

1. Professor John Denvir, a long-time law and popular culture scholar, observes: "Students better understand this new language [of popular film] than their book-bound teachers. While legal scholars are more adept in reading written texts than their students, we quickly find that our video-sophisticated students are much better trained in 'reading' films. Therefore, film helps to level the pedagogical playing field to the advantage of teacher and students alike." John Denvir, *Legal Reelism: The Hollywood Film As Legal Text*, 15 Legal Studies Forum 195, 196 (1991).

2. Do you agree with the student comments in the previous excerpt regarding gender stereotyping in popular culture? Are these stereotypes especially prevalent and pernicious in depictions of women criminals and defendants? Do you believe that, similarly, attorneys in courtroom storytelling at criminal trials rely upon stereotypical notions of defendants' character, grounded in stereotypical notions of behavior and archetypal models of character and behavior? Do the evidentiary and temporal limitations upon storytelling in the courtroom, e.g., rules of evidence pertaining to relevance and limitations upon character evidence, facilitate and encourage the use of stereotypes that engage jurors' preconceptions?

3. Student "C" in the previous excerpt observes that, in the particularities of her experience, a female classmate at a private girls' Catholic school who murdered her mother was "female, and very much like me." Yet in popular culture, female criminals are depicted as "other," and seldom appear as deliberate and cold-blooded murderers. Perhaps we are more comfortable with female murderers who fall into certain categories that offer comforting distance. "C" identifies three archetypes: "the queen or warrior, pseudo-male"; "the evil stepmother of fairy tales, grasping and jealous [who] dominates the night psyche of many a child"; and "Eve the primal temptress." Do you agree that most female murderers can be conveniently slotted into one of these three categories? How might you categorize the character or identity of Barbara Graham in *I Want to Live!*? Does she fit neatly into one of the categories suggested by "C" in her journal? How might you describe her character and identity? Note that *I Want to Live!* is, purportedly, largely a fact-based dramatization, and perhaps a dramatic precursor to *The Thin Blue Line*. It is based upon the real trial and conviction of Barbara Graham for a murder occurring in 1953. Note that, as in the film, Graham was tried and convicted of murder. Her conviction was affirmed by the California Supreme Court, and the U.S. Supreme Court refused to hear the case. Graham was executed on June 3, 1955.

4. Student "H" perceives that the stereotyped depictions of defendants and criminals in popular storytelling result from the fantasies and projections of male authors and filmmakers. Implicitly, there is misogyny, intentionality, and a certain gendered pleasure at work in these artistic renderings of character. Do you agree? Are these characters versions of male fantasies? Or is the depiction of these characters as defendants and criminals aesthetically compelling because they are psychologically accurate? Do you think that attorneys representing defendants at trial rely on similar stereotypical notions?

GOOD GUYS AND BAD GUYS: PUNISHING CHARACTER, EQUALITY, AND THE IRRELEVANCE OF MORAL CHARACTER TO CRIMINAL PUNISHMENT
Ekow N. Yankah
25 Cardozo Law Review 1019 (2004)

Criminal law . . . continues to maintain the rigid dichotomy of good guys and bad guys. It is crucial that there be a clear allocation of virtue within the conflict. The state can impose punishment only if there is a clear dichotomy of good and evil. The state maintains the position of good guy. Placing the defendant within the realm of bad guys justifies the imposition of punishment.

Criminal law cannot recognize the moral ambiguity of film noir. If the criminal defendant's common humanity or the state's moral uncertainty were illustrated, the state would lose its moral right to punish. Witness the last minute loss of nerve in the scheduled execution of Timothy McVeigh. The Federal Bureau of Investigation committed a blunder by failing to disclose 3000 pages of relevant material. No one in the Justice Department or the general public thought this material might exonerate the confessed terrorist McVeigh, but the image of professional incompetence made the Justice Department feel uneasy about taking a life. Only the virtuous have the right to execute.

Conceptualizing the state as good and the criminal as bad does more than justify our imposition of punishment. Imagining criminal offenders as a class of bad guys, cinematic villains who are living threats to all of us, allows us to distance ourselves from them. This image severs our common bond of humanity with the criminal defendants. . . .

Being human, we are given to making moral judgments about others' character. We base a great deal of our personal affections, admiration and blame on these judgments. We harbor cravings for a simple world where there are good guys and bad guys; a world where we know that good people do good and that the bad are punished.

When we translate our personal blaming practices into the criminal law, however, things go horribly awry. We begin to assume that those who are punished are unifaceted bad people and that the awesome power of the state should, replicating the personal sphere, make them pay for being bad people.

We ignore the critical difference between what is legitimate in personal moral judgment and political morality. We ignore the nagging truth that the state ought not permanently segregate and punish people because they are bad. When we premise punishment on character we give in to our thirst to get the bad guys. Though it is only too human, it quickly allows us to forget the common humanity of those we punish.

NOTES & QUESTIONS

1. Professor Yankah perceives the practice of criminal law, and, presumably, storytelling in criminal law cases, as a form of melodrama. In melodrama, plot is shaped to the conventions of a genre, and conflict is usually reduced to a battle of good against evil. There are clear heroes and villains. We identify with the hero and root for the hero to emerge triumphant at the end of the story. Do you agree that this form of narrative is at the core of criminal practice? If so, then the defendant would be cast in the role of either protagonist/hero or antagonist/villain depending upon what legal actor (defense attorney or prosecutor) is telling the story. Is Yankah's position overstated? Do the compressions and simplifications of melodramatic plot lines provide adequate templates for narratives in the courtroom?

2. Some cultural works, traditionally the novel but occasionally some films, focus upon careful investigations of character of the defendant. The question is not "whodunit" but why. In some criminal cases, determining the complexity of the thought processes, motives, and intentionality (*mens rea*) of the defendant is determinative in assessing culpability. For example, in the film version of Theodore Dreiser's novel *An American Tragedy* (1925), George Stevens' *A Place in the Sun*, the determinative issue is whether George Eastman (Montgomery Clift) intended to murder Alice Tripp (Shelly Winters) when they went boating together on Loon Lake. The trial focuses exclusively upon George's specific intent to murder Alice. Now recall your first-year criminal law course. Are there other relevant legal issues in addition to whether George acted with the premeditation and deliberation required for first degree murder? For example, did he commit any voluntary act that caused the harm? Was there concurrence between the *mens rea* and an action that resulted in her death? Knowing that Alice could not swim, and having taken her boating, and given the special relationship between Alice and George, did George have a duty to rescue Alice after she accidentally fell into the water? Is there sufficient circumstantial evidence to serve as the basis for Eastman's conviction and overcome the presumption of innocence that was so important in *Presumed Innocent*? The film and the arguments presented in the cinematic trial do not address these complex legal issues or explore the evidence of various levels of culpability that may result in conviction of lesser included offenses: second-degree murder, voluntary manslaughter, involuntary manslaughter, negligent homicide. Why does this flattening or compression into melodrama take place? Is it crucial to reduce the narrative to the simplest issues and heighten the drama and conflict in the story to compel the imaginative attention of the audience?

We posit that trial storytellers, similar to Hollywood storytellers, often attempt to tell compressed stories about crimes, avoiding subtle explanations of conduct based upon complex literary understandings of the character of the defendant or of environmental factors upon the defendant. Why is such evidence often inadmissible at trial as "irrelevant," or determined to be more "prejudicial than probative"? How do evidentiary rules operate as constraints upon telling the defendant's story at trial?

3. Assess the "character" of defendant Rusty Sabich in the film *Presumed Innocent*. He appears as neither melodramatic hero nor villain. How would you describe his character? Do the simple categorizations of melodrama fit? Rusty is a complex and flawed man. Nevertheless, he is a man of fundamental decency, and seemingly less corrupt than other legal actors in the drama (the judge who dismisses the case so that testimony will not emerge implicating him in bribery, the ruthless yet ineffectual prosecutors, and the victim of the murder who sleeps her way up the career ladder). In relationship to the other characters, it is the defendant with whom the viewer identifies. His valence is clearly more positive than negative, and we are relieved when he is found not guilty. As we shall explore in the section on legal storytelling, many fine defense attorneys believe that the jury must have a similar relationship to a sympathetic defendant as the pop cultural audience does with a complex protagonist such as Sabich.

2.   Adversaries: Defense Attorneys and Prosecutors

DEFENDING THE INNOCENT
Abbe Smith
32 Connecticut Law Review 485 (2000)

The truth is a complicated thing in criminal defense. I learned this early on as a public defender. During the initial training for new defenders, one of the senior lawyers shared a story. He was representing a man who maintained innocence about a series of thefts. The man claimed that he had nothing to do with the crime — instead, an enormous talking chicken had done it. The lawyer thought the client had a mental health problem and referred the case to the office's social services unit. Fortunately, he also asked an investigator to look into it. By doing so, the lawyer learned that on the day of the thefts there had been a promotional event for a newly opened fast-food restaurant specializing in fried chicken. As part of the event, the restaurant had hired a man to wear a chicken suit and hand out flyers. Several witnesses confirmed that they saw this "chicken-man" in possession of several of the stolen items near the location where the thefts had occurred.

I understood this anecdote to be a broad institutional lesson, the sort that gives rise to a number of maxims: Truth is stranger than fiction; don't be too quick to judge; you never know; and, most importantly, investigation is central to good defense work. I also understood it to suggest that the truth may not always be the most convincing or credible story, and, while the truth in this case led to the client's vindication, there may well have been other effective defense theories that could have been employed.

The best criminal defense lawyers have some sense of what the truth is, but are not hamstrung by it. Good criminal trial lawyers know how to use various aspects of the truth in order to construct a compelling narrative — one that jurors will accept, or one that will at least raise reasonable doubt. But, generally, criminal defense lawyers cannot and must not spend much time or energy worrying about the truth. After all, most criminal defendants are not innocent, and the truth is usually not helpful to the defense. When a crime is caught on videotape, this usually means a guilty plea.

By and large, I find the defense lawyer's relationship to the truth liberating. I like being unfettered by what "really happened." I like being free to craft my own story. I like putting the evidentiary pieces together in a puzzle of my choice. Criminal defenders are not mere lawyers; we are creative artists. Good defenders can make something of nothing and nothing of something. . . .

As defenders construct a theory of the case, much of their energy is spent trying to put the "truth" out of their minds. It can be disheartening to look at a police report with its damning account of your client's commission of a crime. You want to throw up your hands and say, how the hell am I supposed to defend against these charges? But, then you remind yourself: These are simply the allegations; they don't have to be taken at face value; there are many ways to raise questions and doubts about what is being alleged.

In some cases, the theory of defense may be that the truth of what happened is an existential question. Life is complicated. People are complicated. Memory is complicated. Motive is complicated. Sometimes defenders start believing that truth is itself illusory. No one can ever know what really happened in anything. Life is the movie *Rashomon*. . . .

When one undertakes a professional obligation to represent criminal defendants — the vast majority of whom are probably guilty — it seems quaint at best to suddenly start talking about innocence. After all, only Abraham Lincoln built a career representing only innocent clients. It is no easier for the factually innocent client to profess his or her innocence.

Of course, the problem with the defender's new-found embrace of truth in this posture is that truth is no simpler when a client is factually innocent than in a more typical case. The truth — even when it supports innocence — is often murky and complicated and may not make a very good story. . . .

Defending the innocent is no more noble than defending the guilty, no more honorable, no more virtuous; the calling of criminal defenders is to represent the guilty and innocent alike. But, the burden of defending the innocent is an extraordinary burden. It is constant and unrelenting. It is both a professional burden and a deeply personal one. It poses a challenge to everything I believe in, including myself.

NOTES & QUESTIONS

1. Criminal defense attorneys have ethically and morally complex professional relationships with "the truth" and, simultaneously, with their clients. In the preceding excerpt Professor Smith says of the defense attorney's relationship to the "truth": "The best criminal lawyers have some sense of what the truth is, but are not hamstrung by it." Smith finds this relationship "liberating." Is there something troublesome about the characterization? What, precisely, is the source of the discomfort for you, if any? Do the ethics of defense practice, or rationales about systematic checks and balances, provide sufficient insulation so that truth-telling takes a backseat to the interests of the client and to the primacy of the defense attorney's obligation to serve the client's interests without being "hamstrung"?

2. The defense attorney's complex role with respect to "the truth" is occasionally captured in popular culture. Scott Turow's Sandy Stern (played by Raul Julia in the movie version of *Presumed Innocent* and depicted in numerous Scott Turow novels) is a professionally competent and, usually, "ethical" defense attorney. Yet, in the film and novel versions of *Presumed Innocent*, Stern crosses ethical boundaries to prevent the truth from emerging at trial and to shape the evidence that does emerge into narrative. For example, in addition to conducting masterful cross-examinations of prosecution witnesses that disassemble the prosecution's case, in an *ex parte* conversation Stern threatens Judge Lytle, who presides over Sabich's trial, with the disclosure of a criminal investigation file that implicates the Judge in accepting bribes in complicity with the murder victim. This threat may compel the Judge to dismiss the charges against Sabich after the close of the prosecution's case, and before Stern attempts to present the "B File" (including evidence of Lytle's corruption) as evidence to the jury. Why would an attorney risk his career in order to vindicate his client, especially a client whom he may not believe is innocent of murder? Why would Turow bend his plot upon the unethical conduct of his sympathetic and heroic defense attorney? Is this an exaggeration to push the plot forward? Are all criminal attorneys criminal when the stakes are sufficiently high? Does Turow exaggerate for the sake of dramatic effect? But is Stern's conduct really an exaggeration that is so far-fetched in the high-stakes games of legal storytelling in the courtroom in notorious criminal trials? Note that risky and professionally suspect conduct may not be limited exclusively to the actions of defense attorneys. Some prosecutors have equally complex and suspect relationships with "the truth." Prosecutor Douglas Muldur, recently a distinguished member of the Texas defense bar and sometimes featured on Court TV, is quoted by Adams' attorney in *The Thin Blue Line* to the effect that any good prosecutor can convict a guilty man, but it takes a great prosecutor to convict an innocent one.

3. The complexities of defense attorneys' roles and their professional relationships with the truth and with clients are often not explored in the flat and simplified entertainment of commercial melodramas pervasive in popular culture. Television programs, especially serials such as *Perry Mason*, come immediately to mind. These provide formulaic plots and consistent characters to viewers desiring heroes and villains, and unproblematic, untroubling themes and plotting. These stories are, perhaps, merely the stuff of entertainment incorporating the inherent drama and conflict of the courtroom. For example, defense attorney Perry Mason is skillful, not corrupted; he is a truth-teller, a heroic and virtuous attorney. There is never anything problematic or troubling in Mason's relationships to his clients or to the truth; it is "the truth" that invariably emerges in the courtroom drama. Likewise, consistently heroic defense attorneys are often depicted in popular films.

PROFANE LAWYERING
James R. Elkins
http://www.wvu.edu/~lawfac/jelkins/mythweb99/profane.html

Webster (in the Seventh New Collegiate) says of profane: not concerned with religion or religious purposes — secular; not holy because unconsecrated, impure, or defiled — sanctified; serving to debase or defile what is holy — irreverent; not among the initiated; not possessing esoteric or expert knowledge. The verb profane means to treat (something sacred) with abuse, irreverence, or contempt, to desecrate, violate. To debase by a wrong, unworthy, or vulgar use.

Criminal lawyers, one suspects, are most accustomed to profane speech. Jerry Kennedy, the working man's lawyer in George Higgins's novel, *Kennedy for the Defense*, in his first meeting with Emerson Teller, a young man charged with homosexual solicitation of a police officer. . . . Emerson tells Kennedy he was framed by the police officer. And Kennedy responds:

> Right. . . . And I was sculpted into my present graceful shape by a maniacal genius of a topiary gardener. Now, I did not haul my ass up here this morning [from his vacation] to hear you tell me how you got framed and you're innocent and so help you God, you are the victim of a malevolent society. I came up here so you can tell me what happened. You tell me what happened. I will tell you whether you were framed, or whether there is some way I think maybe you got a shot at getting off, or whether you should hang down your head and cry and tell the judge that you ain't gonna do it again and you don't know what possessed you, you did it this time. I will also tell you what any one of those things is liable to cost you, and you will give me some money, and I will proceed. Or else you won't, and I won't. Clear?

Lawyers are sometimes profane in speech, but they can also live profane lives. When lawyers tell stories about irreverent machinations of law, and their own lack of concern for justice, they become part of this profane world. The pull of this world and stories that defile are common in the hallways of buildings devoted to law.

Consider novelist and lawyer George V. Higgins' introduction to Jerry Kennedy, the protagonist in *Kennedy for the Defense*:

> I have a client named Teddy Franklin. Teddy Franklin is a car thief. He is thirty-two years old, and he is one of the best car thieves on the Eastern Seaboard. Cadillac Ted is so good that he is able to support himself as a car thief. He has been arrested repeatedly, which is how he made my acquaintance, but he has never done time. That is because I am so good. It is also because Teddy is so good.

This is the way, Mack, Jerry Kennedy's wife describes her husband, according to Jerry Kennedy:

If you ask Mack what kind of lawyer I am, she will tell you that I am the classiest sleazy criminal lawyer in Boston, even if I am standing right there. This is not flattering, perhaps, but she knows I will not argue with her. I go to my office to make a living, not to make a life. My life is at home.

George V. Higgins, *Kennedy for the Defense* 1, 13 (1981).

Jerry Kennedy is not a bad man or a bad lawyer but he is working with some profane notions about lawyering, notions that may get him into trouble before all is said and done.

To profane law, to tell its profane stories, to treat law in a debased, irreverent way violates one myth of professional life even as it identifies and configures another myth — that of the street-smart realist.

We profane only that which can be held sacred. Profanity of language is made possible by the beauty and inventiveness of language. If we had no poetry, no poetic rendering of experience, no word-shaped image of world and human sentiment, we could utter no profanity. In the absence of sacred sensibilities we would not experience outrage when we speak of what lawyers do in the name of law.

NOTES & QUESTIONS

1. Professor Elkins provides illustrations of how, at least in popular legal fiction, the defense attorney's language begins to adapt to the world that he inhabits. He begins to sound like the criminals and defendants he represents, as if he is an insider within this world, able to see deeply into the thought processes of his clients and "speak their language." In doing so, the defense attorney in contemporary popular culture may begin to embody or inhabit the shadow world or underworld of the defendant. The compelling dialogue and street language of George V. Higgins' defense attorney Jerry Kennedy provide vivid examples. Like Sandy Stern, Jerry Kennedy is a recurring protagonist in a series of popular, successful and critically well-reviewed novels. Higgins is regarded as a master of dialogue and vernacular. It is unsurprising that in addition to his life as a novelist, Higgins practiced as both a prosecutor and defense attorney in Boston prior to his death. (He was also co-owner of a favorite bar and lawyer's hangout in Cambridge, Massachusetts.) Is Kennedy's street language (profane language) merely the fancy of a fiction writer or the idiosyncratic personal style of one novelist/attorney? Do criminal defense attorneys (and indeed other practitioners) tend to adopt the cultural coloration of the clients they serve?

2. A significant question is whether criminal defense attorneys adopt more from their clients' identities and through their professional relationships with their clients than merely language and style. Do they begin to assume moral ambiguity, if not engaging directly in the criminal activities of their clients? Is this perception embodied in a relatively recent shift in popular perceptions of defense attorneys in popular film? Is it also a characteristic of criminal law practice? Professor Richard Sherwin perceives the shift in identities of the defense attorneys in recent films from the idealizations of the heroic defense attorneys in earlier times. For example, in Martin Scorcese's *Cape Fear* (1991), defense attorney Sam Bowden is transformed from the heroic protagonist attorney and moral family man in the original film adaptation of J. Lee Thompson's novel (1961) into a far more complex and morally ambivalent character, who has suppressed evidence that would assist his client, engaged in adulterous behavior, and attempted to cover up his personal and ethical lapses and criminal misconduct. This may fit audience expectations in a different age. Richard K. Sherwin, *Cape Fear: Law's Inversion to Cathartic Justice*, 30 University of San Francisco Law Review 1023 (1996). Do you believe that this transformation of cinematic identity of criminal defense attorneys in popular culture anticipates cultural transformation in the identity of the typical criminal defense practitioner?

3. Professor J. Thomas Sullivan observes, "What is likely is that, for the most part, the inherent goodness of [Abraham] Lincoln and Atticus Finch is reserved for history, both in films and in our collective consciousness. This might mean that the adversarial system is due for reconsideration, if not revision. It may also mean that we have lost our innocence as an audience and society or that the problem of moral and legal guilt will remain a difficult one for clients, lawyers, and filmgoers struggling to understand how the defense attorney can represent a guilty defendant." J. Thomas Sullivan, *Imagining the Criminal Law: When Client and Lawyer Meet in the Movies*, 25 University of Arkansas at Little Rock Law Review 665, 680 (2003). Unlike Sherwin, Sullivan locates our unease with the role and tactics of the defense attorney in the fact that not only does the criminal defense attorney represent clients who are guilty, but that the defense attorney knows this to be so. Do you agree with Sullivan's observation? Has this always been the case? Why do you think our popular perceptions of the defense attorney have changed in recent years? Can you recall notorious criminal trials that may have reshaped popular perceptions of the role of the criminal defense attorney?

4. It may be that the defense attorney can speak no language except the profane language of the criminal client. However, it may also be that the successful defense attorney may be remarkably adept at translating this language into the embedded narratives of the trial and into the language of the law when the time is appropriate. In 1991, the reputed mobster Louis Failla was accused in a RICO conspiracy prosecution of plotting the death of the father of his grandson (Tito Morales) under orders by the capo of the Connecticut faction of the Patriarca crime family (Billy "The Wild Guy" Grasso). Various incriminating conversations between Failla and the mobsters had been recorded on surveillance tapes by the FBI. Failla's attorney was Jeremiah Donovan, a former federal prosecutor. Donovan's task was a difficult one. He developed the theory that Failla only pretended to go along with the mobsters and pointed to a "subtext" in Failla's interactions with the mobsters. In his two-hour closing argument Donovan spoke the voices of various characters, including the gravelly voice of the defendant-turned-protagonist Failla, while quoting from transcripts of surveillance tapes. He literally created a new story. In the end, he had something that sounded "like a movie plot." Jeremiah Donovan, *Some Off-the-Cuff Remarks About Lawyers as Storytellers*, 18 Vermont Law Review 751, 756 (1994).

PROSECUTORS, PREJUDICES, AND JUSTICE: OBSERVATIONS ON PRESUMING INNOCENCE IN POPULAR CULTURE AND LAW
Christine Alice Corcos
34 University of Toledo Law Review 793 (2003)

In Scott Turow's world, prosecutors are the individuals least likely to presume anyone innocent as a matter of law or as a matter of fact — even though they are required by the canons of legal ethics not to prosecute anyone they believe might not in fact be guilty. Indeed, Turow's novel sketches for us the archetypal prosecutors who represent the best and worst of both real and fictional district attorneys (DAs), all of whom struggle with the question to some degree. In each archetype there is enough truth to cause some real concern about whether justice can be done, and seen to be done. In addition, *Presumed Innocent* presents us with a world in which many prosecutors intentionally or unintentionally, backed by the force of the state, destroy lives. They are not the heroes they should be; the heroes that Rusty thought he recognized when he first became a prosecutor. Only by leaving the world of the prosecutor does he fully discover this, although at the beginning of the novel he has his suspicions.

If we compare Turow's characters to prosecutors we hear and see in daily life, then the concern whether justice can be done deepens. Thus, *Presumed Innocent* continues to be relevant in any examination of both real and media justice. The film, of course, compresses many of Turow's complicated written images into more easily digestible visual chunks, but I would argue that it does not lessen the novel's impact. Fifteen years after its publication, *Presumed Innocent* remains an indictment of the legal system and suggests that one of our most honored principles — the presumption of innocence — is honored more in the breach than in the observance. . . .

NOTES & QUESTIONS

1. Prosecutors and defense attorneys may not have precisely parallel roles or obligations. The defense attorney represents the interests of his client. The prosecutor, however, represents "the people" or "the state." What is the meaning of this distinction? Does it suggest that the prosecutor has a higher calling, and theoretically a greater interest in truth-telling than the defense attorney? That his obligations are not to effective storytelling but to doing justice? Pragmatically, the resources available to the prosecutor, e.g., police investigators, ability to question witnesses, etc., are vast compared to the investigatory resources available to the typical defendant. This often results in an imbalance of power. Does the prosecutor have an obligation of fair dealing and full disclosure in criminal cases? Or may a prosecutor properly adhere to a gamesmanship model as long as he does not violate ethical rules of conduct?

2. Like George V. Higgins, Scott Turow was a former federal prosecutor before becoming a popular novelist and sometime criminal defense attorney. He speaks with the authority of his experiences. His depictions of prosecutors in *Presumed Innocent* and, indeed, in all his novels, are at best ambivalent. In

Presumed Innocent, prosecutors are often careerist (the cold-hearted and venal Carole Polhemus comes to mind) or willing to cut corners and readily engage in ethically suspect conduct to obtain a conviction (Nicco della Guardia). Prosecutors are willing to sell out loyal subordinates to advance politically, or for revenge for personal or professional slights (Raymond Horgan). Further, they are often blatantly incompetent and lazy in their investigatory work and even in their courtroom practice (Tommy Molto). At least in Turow's Kindle County, prosecutors are often deeply entrenched in the shadows of criminality. Given these images, do you agree with Professor Corcos' assessment that, "if we compare Turow's characters to prosecutors we hear and see in daily life, then the concern whether justice can be done deepens"? Do you agree that *Presumed Innocent* "continues to be relevant in any examination of both real and media justice"? Or are these depictions of prosecutors in both the novel and film versions of *Presumed Innocent* merely fabrications, creating fictional antagonists to fuel popular narrative and propel stories forward toward dramatic and surprising resolutions that are not possible in the world of legal practice where, in fact, most criminal defendants brought to trial are guilty?

3. There is clearly a counter-trend in popular culture as well. There are heroic prosecutors who, unlike the prosecutors in Turow's Kindle County, are committed to the emergence of truth, protectors of the public and cognizant of the rights of defendants. *Law & Order*, one of television's most popular and longest-running series, tells the stories of heroic prosecutors with great moral integrity and legal acumen. These prosecutors are, and remain, remarkably attractive characters psychologically, professionally, and physically (despite the passage of time). These prosecutors seek truth and justice, and practice the law with scrupulous ethics. Unlike Turow's Kindle County prosecutors, seldom, if ever, do the trustworthy prosecutors on *Law & Order* cross ethical boundaries or sacrifice to expediency, avarice, or careerism in their noble calling to obtain the truth ethically. Why do these images still appeal to the viewer as consumer of television images? Why are they still so persuasive and compelling? Is it simply that we need these heroic archetypes in our popular melodramas, as counterpoint to the dark stories of revelation and exploration of the shadow world of criminal practice? Further, the legal issues in *Law & Order*, although dramatically transformed, are well researched, and some law professors even employ episodes as texts in their classes. Does this program, and the images of truth-telling prosecutors in it, suggest more accurate representations of truth-telling prosecutors of competence and integrity and provide more accurate storylines for dramatization of what usually transpires within the criminal law system?

D.   LEGAL STORYTELLING IN CRIMINAL TRIALS

As previously observed, films provide a unique mechanism for critical reflection on the dynamics of legal cultural storytelling, especially storytelling in criminal trials. That is:

> Lawyers are popular storytellers who operate in an aural and visual storytelling culture. Lawyers tell imagistic narratives constructed upon aesthetic principles that are closely akin to the principles that

control the formulation of plot-structure in commercial cinema. We tell stories with hard driving plot-lines and clear themes that are readily distilled. We shoot our films from the fixed perspective of protagonist-clients.

Philip Meyer, *Visual Literacy and the Legal Culture: Reading Film as Text in the Law School Setting,* 17 Legal Studies Forum 73 (1993).

Here, we explore these perceptions: (1) through the theoretical concerns of a law professor analyzing Errol Morris' *The Thin Blue Line*; (2) through the observations of a "skeptical" law student in a seminar on "Law and Popular Storytelling" imagining the work of a criminal lawyer in relationship to the work of the filmmaker Errol Morris in *The Thin Blue Line* and to the work of the detective in Roman Polanski's film noir masterpiece *Chinatown* (1974); (3) through observations on how a skilled attorney in a "real" criminal case converts evidence into cinematic images in a narrative closing argument that intentionally implicates and draws upon "mob" stories from popular film; and, finally, (4) through the perceptions and wisdom of Jeremiah Donovan, a shrewd and self-reflective criminal law practitioner formulating his closing argument, who is profoundly aware of the interpenetration of legal and popular culture in criminal trial practice. Donovan further observes how and why he strategically attempts to incorporate popular storytelling practices at trial to the advantage of his client.

LAW FRAMES: HISTORICAL TRUTH AND NARRATIVE NECESSITY IN A CRIMINAL CASE
Richard K. Sherwin
47 Stanford Law Review 39 (1994)

When truth defies certainty and becomes complex, justice requires difficult decisions on the basis of that doubt. The struggle between shifting cognitive needs and legal duty is commonplace, and without a way to question how a given narrative shapes and informs our desire for certain and tidy justice, that desire, and competing ones, cannot be adequately understood. As a result, the kind of justice operating in a particular case at a given cultural juncture may remain confused or hidden from view. The emergence in our time of a post-modern narrative of justice, one that is spontaneous, contingent, and irre-pressibly messy, provides a case in point. The challenge is to tap the salient cultural storylines, both familiar and newly emerging, that give meaning and coherence to uncertainty, so that when a case demands, we can feel sure enough in our reasonable doubt.

In some of what follows, I shall be arguing uphill, in favor of complexity, insinuating ambivalence about the kind of order legal stories typically create. I shall approach the disorder that lurks beyond the bounds of these well-told tales. Perhaps more unforgivable, I shall question whether the specific tale of Randall Dale Adams might be less tidy than we'd prefer. What if the modern-ist penchant for dichotomies that produces starkly polar choices like guilt/ innocence, frameup/frameup undone, injustice/injustice corrected — the very mindset that gives us such satisfaction in seeing justice's scales finally bal-anced — were part of the problem? I want to suggest that the simplicity of these polarities, and the calm they induce, are at least partly responsible for making us leave things out. The messy things. The things that leave a sense of disorder and lack of control, the unsettling things we refuse to see or discuss. These are the things that make it hard to make legal decisions, decisions that can have irrevocable effects upon the body and soul of a person: prison, prison life, perhaps even death. No less grave, they are decisions that could lead to erroneous acquittal and the recurrence of violence by the liberated defendant. It is precisely because the stakes are so high that I want to examine how we might guard against facile resolutions without getting mired in indecision and meaninglessness. In particular, I want to explore a form of postmodern legal storytelling that can serve a sustainable sense of justice as well as order. But to follow this path we must learn to question our own complicity in making truth appear overly neat and coherent. Thus, rather than share in the triumph of having seen the system set straight, we must ask ourselves whether we are not accomplices in a form of reality-making that let the Adams frameup occur in the first place and that could let similar frameups occur in the future.

Uncontrollable disorder within the criminal justice system is an admittedly disturbing topic, and I don't enjoy dwelling on it any more than you do. But surely it is a good thing to increase our awareness of how we deal with the omnipresent possibility of disorder, as well as the possibility that conflicting legal stories may simultaneously be true. This sort of knowledge helps us guard against deception by others, and by ourselves, and better enables us to distinguish credible from incredible narratives. In criminal law, where lives hang in the balance of a tale, this ability is critical. . . .

NOTES & QUESTIONS

1. Professor Sherwin speaks of a tension or struggle between a desire for a "certain and tidy justice" and an "emergence of postmodern narrative of justice" that is "spontaneous, contingent, and irrepressibly messy." What, exactly, does Professor Sherwin mean? Can you translate Sherwin's observation into an example that makes the abstract generalization come alive? Often, the word "postmodernism" appears in critical and scholarly writings on law practice. What is "postmodernism"? Do you believe that there is tension between "modernist dichotomies" such as "guilt/innocence" required for legal determinations in the courtroom, and how we now perceive stories as relativistic, "spontaneous, contingent and irrepressibly messy"? Are legal outcomes in trials often a function of the power of the storyteller to construct and tell an effective and compelling narrative that matches the evidence introduced at trial? Could we say this has always been the role of the trial attorney in our advocacy system?

2. Do you believe that trials are about the possibility of "objective" understandings that are not dependent upon the perspective and skill of the storyteller? Are courtroom battles in our system about unearthing and determining the truth? Or are you already a hardened and cynical postmodernist, comfortable with the notion that determinations of guilt and innocence are often based primarily upon who is the more effective storyteller, and who has the most resources to engage in investigations for evidence connected to artful and manipulative narratives?

3. The stories that emerge at trial depend upon evidence that is developed in factual investigations. How are these investigations undertaken? Does the selection of a narrative theme shape the facts uncovered by the investigation that will be converted into evidence at trial? For example, consider the police investigation and prosecutorial decisions that resulted in the conviction of Randall Adams for murder in *The Thin Blue Line*. The reinvestigation by the filmmaker Errol Morris as developed in the movie points to a different culprit (David Harris). As you sit as a viewer sits as if upon a jury, and observe the powerful storytelling practice of Errol Morris, are you persuaded that David Harris is clearly the murderer? How does Morris shape his story? What narrative and strategic choices does he make? What is the powerful theme that drives his construction of the narrative? Is it, as Professor Sherwin suggests, a story about "a frameup"? Is it a story about "actual innocence"?

4. In *The Thin Blue Line*, what forces or presumptions shape the investigation by the police, anticipate the prosecutor's theory of the crime, and shape the trial story? Is it important that David Harris is an adolescent who cannot receive the death penalty? Or that he is a soft-featured and well-spoken young man from Texas while Randall Adams is a drifter from the Midwest? That the police desire to close the case quickly and condemn a cop killer to death for the murder? That the prosecuting attorney desires to maintain his excellent winning percentage (his "batting average") in jury trials?

5. Once the investigation targets Randall Adams, police and prosecutors seem intransigent and unwilling to change their theory of the case. What are the psychological and pragmatic forces that prevent the police and prosecutor from acknowledging the possibility that Randall Adams may not be the culprit?

6. Assume, as Sherwin suggests, that Morris' version of the story is about a "frameup." The new evidence uncovered by Morris (often first-hand testimony from the various legal actors, including the testimony of David Harris confessing to the crime placed at the end of the picture as the denouement) is extremely powerful. Why do the defendant's attorneys not conduct a similarly efficient and thorough investigation? How are they blocked and thwarted in their efforts by the prosecutor and the police? Is their failure to uncover evidence based upon a lack of resources? Did the prosecutor act unethically in the trial and investigation, or was he merely acting in accord with the gamesmanship model of adversary proceedings?

7. Assume you are now the prosecutor, and Randall Adams seeks post-conviction relief. Would you challenge the authenticity of the confession by David Harris? Would you attack his credibility? Assume Harris' "confession" on the tape recording was introduced as new evidence at an evidentiary hearing. What, if any, counter-story might you tell? What, if any, counter-arguments would you make against reopening the case based on Harris' alleged confession?

8. Are any crucial narrative pieces of the story omitted from Morris' version of the story? For example, is there a time on the night of the killing that is not accounted for by either the testimony of Randall Adams or David Harris? What, if anything, do you think occurred during this missing "gap" in time? Why is the time line of events not fully developed?

VISUAL LITERACY AND THE LEGAL CULTURE: READING FILM AS TEXT IN THE LAW SCHOOL SETTING
Philip N. Meyer
17 Legal Studies Forum 73 (1993)

Skepticism

I proposed hypothetical questions to contextualize our viewing of several films: Do trials ever reveal the "truth" of the past? Is this their primary function? Or are lawyers merely narrativist tricksters? Is it, as one seminar participant observed, only "God who really knows what happened?" Does the trial serve primarily other functions, " . . . such as resolving the controversy, releasing emotions, providing a sense of coherence — not necessarily between the event and the outcome, but between the outcome and what happened at the trial itself[?]"

Alternatively, as the cognitive theorist Jerome Bruner has argued persuasively, is the storytelling (narrative) mode discrete from the empirical (paradigmatic) mode of proof? Are stories formed by clever and devious aesthetic arrangements connected by the aesthetic tissue of verisimilitude? Although events may "happen," are the causes (the hows and whys of events) ever "knowable"? Can we, for example, ever look inside someone's mind to determine "intent" or "state of mind"? Do rules of procedure and evidence unduly circumscribe and artificially constrain trial narratives? Are lawyers an ethnocentric sub-culture of popular storytellers particularly subject to the professional self-delusion that cognitive theorists have termed "the original attribution error"?

In exploring this constellation of discussion questions and themes, thoughtful participants reveal in their journals additional features of visual literacy. Doug C. titles his exploration of the storytelling role of the lawyer "Truth In and Out of Chinatown." The journal compares *Chinatown* and Errol Morris' *The Thin Blue Line* as presenting visual metaphors for the lawyer's role in the storytelling process. "Chinatown" is the title of Roman Polanski's movie; it is also Doug's elliptical reference and response to conflicting images of the lawyer's storytelling role.

Initially, Doug's introduction states, somewhat apologetically, that his paper reflects a "familiar" seminar discussion theme:

> . . . [C]an the truth of a past event be known? Is an "objective" reality possible, or is every past occurrence only possible of interpretation within the context of the observer's unique unrepeatable perspective of the event?

Doug discusses this theme with a certain detachment and indignation, reflective of the attitudes of many bright seminar participants. That is, Doug's answer to this question is, implicitly, obvious. Stories, especially aural and visual stories, can not and do not reveal truth. We live in an imagistic, fragmentary and subjective world and our "stories" are intrinsically imaginative reconstructions.

> . . . [S]ince there is no recount[ing] of events that we can accept as absolutely true . . . we are forced to create systems of "truth substitutes" as alternatives and thus "truth" becomes definable only within the systems that we create. . . .

"Truth" is literally dependent upon the placement and angle of the camera:

> A popular example: last spring Tate George propelled the UCONN Huskies basketball team into the NCAA Final Eight by a "buzzer beating" last second shot. But was the shot "good"? The best view provided by CBS cameras "Super Slo Mo" replays appears to indicate that Tate's hand touching the ball when the shot clock on the same screen indicated no time was remaining . . . this replay became the "truth substitute" to which the announcers latched onto and their pronouncement was that UCONN stole a victory. But in the case of Tate's shot, accepting a camera replay as the best "truth substitute" probably doesn't get us any closer to the absolute truth than the version espoused by any random ticketholders. Perhaps if God were a Husky fan, He might inform us that two molecules that connected Tate's hand to the basketball ceased to "touch" one another (in some atomic sense) with a nanosecond of time remaining in the game. However, anything short of such a divine vision will contain all the inherent defects that "truth substitute" systems suffer from. That is, belief in the truth becomes synonymous with belief in the system.

Doug's observations reflect a knowing cynicism that he shares with many seminar participants about the nature of their chosen profession and the limited possibilities of such a narrative-based system's providing "justice" that is ultimately any more than narrative resolution or denouement:

> . . . As a general rule, the justice system seems to favor the "knowable" version of the truth. Lawyers tend to believe the opposite. By their behavior and their beliefs, lawyers view the truth as "unknowable" and as an unapproachable ideal. Thus a lawyer might say that the judicial system is not a search for truth but a forum for the exposition of competing versions of what-the-hell happened in a given event.

Doug states his belief that "leaving aside examples where it is so clear that an account of an event is 'true' or at least so clear that no one wants to bother arguing about it — 'the truth' is 'unknowable.' Since there is no way 'truth' can be definitively proven, the role of the lawyer is not to aid in the search for truth, which according to him is an oxymoronic phrase anyway, but to arrange any and all facts available to produce the story that best suits his client's needs." Errol Morris's *The Thin Blue Line* is a "persuasive illustration" of how easily stories are manipulated and how readily we succumb to the call of our own stories:

> In the movie, truth is not static or fixed, but is malleable enough to bend according to the teller of the story.... The movie's premise achieves the effect of creating horrible unease in the hearts of viewers.

Detective mysteries, particularly cinematic detective stories, provide an effective visual metaphor for a contrasting idealization of how the "justice" system (a "truth-substitute" system) supposedly works.

> How do detectives fit into this scheme? ... Each is faced with a past event that is open to dispute; a crime, mystery, or confusing or unexplained incident. Both must "reconstruct" the event for an audience. But here the detective and lawyer part company. The lawyer's motivation is not necessarily to find the truth; instead he is motivated to come up with a reasonable version of a story, consonant with the facts, that best serves his client's needs and in turn his own. In contrast, the ... detective traditionally wishes to find the truth, or the least distorted version of truth available.

Detectives can be "roughly categorized into two groups; those that primarily ponder on the past and those that act within the present." In the first "genre" — akin to the way truth is uncovered in the judicial system — passive truth-finders "parse through all available information and establish not the best but the only explanation":

> ... [A]n event leaves behind facts that are indelible and unique as a fingerprint. The mere inspection of existing clues would expose a wolf-hound, a poisonous snake climbing a rope bellringer, or a murderous orangutan. Though cloaked in enticing packaging, this view of the the way the world operates is mostly stage theatrics and ... borders on campiness.

A second type of truth finder is an "active participant" in the process. Jake Gittes in Polanski's *Chinatown* is an example of a detective in this genre:

> Gittes is quick-witted and bright but not of [Sherlock] Holmesian intellect. Instead, Gittes' genius appears to be not in finding out what the hell happened but in making things happen. Since the case before him is not laid out like an intricate puzzle, Gittes must resort to old-fashioned investigative work and during his meddling, dames scream, punches are thrown, and guns blaze in the night. Gittes is a human monkey wrench and despite being confused as to what his role should be, since he isn't sure of anything including why he was initially hired, he throws himself into a vague conspiracy hidden against the gauzy southern California landscape

> Jake seems to be aware that he will not always find clues merely by obtaining a superior vantage point but that clues must be dislodged by his very presence.... In *Chinatown* Jake is as much a part of the overall plot as the crime itself.

> As much as *Chinatown* tends to resemble how truth is actually unearthed, the movie is still faithful to, and thus somewhat limited by its adherence to the notion that, truth is "knowable." This commitment to a clean, tidy universe is understandable in a commercial

sense, since moviegoers are unlikely to flock to see a movie with no resolution, or worse, one whose conclusion is that truth is unknowable. Although *Chinatown* challenges commercial orthodoxy in certain ways, its iconoclasm is limited to sending the message that the search for truth and justice is not rewarded (can it be its own reward?) and the act of doing good will only result in getting your new girlfriend killed in the end.

Errol Morris' *The Thin Blue Line* presents a contrasting metaphor about the "nature of truth" although, Doug observes, the movie's ending is "at odds with the overall message":

> Morris sets out to show that all stories are hopelessly subjective, and that truth cannot be found, except in the ending of the movie Morris betrays his own thesis. By concluding his film with David Harris's vague, ambiguous "confession," Morris has arranged the facts and interviews to produce the inevitable conclusion that Randall Adams is innocent and Harris is guilty. While I do not argue with the merits of this conclusion (anyone who saw the movie would have to agree that Harris is guilty as sin), the overall point of the movie is lost. Morris sets out to establish that all interpreters of events rely on their particular perspective; this is why no two accounts of an event can be absolutely similar and why the past only exists according to the storyteller's will. But by choosing to place Harris' confession at the end, Morris has made a conscious decision to have the story come to a conclusion that points to an obvious "truth"; that Harris is guilty. The theme of storyteller as creator of truth becomes an incestuous one, as Morris appears to fall prey to the same folly as those that he tries to expose.

Other participants, like Doug, revealed similar attitudes about stories, particularly visual and aural stories. Participants were deeply skeptical about the possibilities of such stories' revealing "truth" especially when these stories were embedded in the formulaic procedural maze and evidentiary constraints of the judicial process. This cynicism is, perhaps, partially a product of three years of immersion in the exclusively paradigmatic culture of law school that devalues and deemphasizes narratives. Simultaneously, participants — subjected to a continual barrage of visual and aural stories in a popular culture filled with advertising, television, radio, politics, sound-byte news — often felt deceived by stories and popular storytellers. Although extremely thoughtful and perceptive, they were sensitive to manipulation and tended to disbelieve their eyes and ears. The heightened awareness and critical acuity of many students was often accompanied by a hardened detachment, cynicism, and refusal to suspend disbelief. Many participants, like Doug, are truly suspicious of all visual narratives including "actual" video shots of such events as the Tate George shot or the Rodney King beating. These images, often edited into fragments and sound bytes that are deceptive and decontextualized from the events themselves, are perceived as "truth substitutes" that do not capture or reflect externalities or totalities. Many upper-level law students no longer trust narrative explanations; they are frozen into narrative disbelief. The filmic texts provided an opportunity to reflect systematically on this deep skepticism.

Passivity, detachment, cynicism and, I fear, resentment and anger, are also deeply ingrained features of the new visual literacy. . . .

NOTES & QUESTIONS

1. As the preceding excerpt suggests, Professor Sherwin is not alone when he speculates that the process of narrativization of evidence in the criminal trial through legal storytelling may not always lead to discovery of "the truth." Doug C. and other law students in a "Law and Popular Storytelling" class likewise perceived inherent limitations on legal storytelling in criminal trials, and shared the postmodernist cynicism or skepticism identified by Sherwin. Do you share Doug C.'s belief that "truth" is often dependent upon "the placement of the camera" (perspective) or the shrewdness of attorney-storytellers' tactical and rhetorical strategies and the theatrics of the courtroom?

2. Doug C. also argues that, in attempting to provide a clear narrative resolution by selecting David Harris' confession as the final piece of the narrative puzzle, Errol Morris "falls prey to the same folly as those that he tries to expose." That is, in attempting to fulfill the narrative expectations of his audience, and provide a clear resolution and message, Morris betrays his underlying "postmodernist" message. How might Morris have restructured his story to more fully convey this message? How do you think the audience might have responded to a film without a clear narrative resolution?

3. Stylistically, Errol Morris blends "real" interviews with reconstructions akin to a low-budget television program and clips from fictional movies. Why is there an intentional montage of fictional and non-fictional material in the narrative mix? Why does Morris employ an intentionally eloquent Phillip Glass musical score? Do all these seemingly irreconcilable aesthetic pieces clash or fit together? What do you think Errol Morris is trying to "say" with this strangely eclectic mix of source materials, and through his visual style and editing choices? Do these choices intentionally draw the viewer's attention to the interpenetration of legal and popular culture and, simultaneously, invite reflection upon how we construct our stories and meanings on the storyboards of our own imaginations?

4. Richard Pryor, the late African American comedian and storyteller, observed, "I went down to the courthouse looking for justice, and that's what I found: Just us! I went to the jails, and who's serving time? Just us! So who gets justice in this country? Right again? Just us!" Richard Pryor, *Is It Something I Said?* (Reprise Records 1975). Statistically, there seems to be evidence supporting Pryor's observation regarding prosecution, conviction, and incarceration of black Americans. For example, the likelihood of an African American (male or female) being imprisoned is 16.2%, but the comparable figures are 9.4% for Hispanics and 2.5% for whites. U.S. Department of Justice, Bureau of Justice Statistics, *Lifetime Likelihood of Going to State or Federal Prison* (Mar. 1997, NCJ-160092). Note that the films discussed in this chapter generally pertain primarily to white (Caucasian) attorneys telling the stories of white (Caucasian) defendants. African American storytellers are seldom lead characters in pop cultural stories, especially commercial entertainment films marketed to mass audiences. Why is there a shortage of stories featuring these characters in popular films? Are commercial audiences less able to understand fully narratives outside of their own experiences or to empathize fully with characters whose ethnicity, personal circumstances, and experiences are unlike their own?

WHY A JURY TRIAL IS MORE LIKE A MOVIE THAN A NOVEL
Philip N. Meyer
28 Journal of Law & Society 133 (2001)

Converting Evidence and Argument into Story

In trials to a jury, effective advocates often convert the more fragmented structures of rule-based analytical arguments into unitary and focused narratives. The analytical arguments are structured through logic and inference. Clinical paradigms for teachers of trial advocacy accurately articulate the sequence of steps that the trial attorney employs to create the analytical structure of a trial argument. First, the advocate converts the more abstract terminology and categories of legal elements into factual propositions. Some of these factual propositions are crucial and highly problematic and contested. Others are not. The advocate in structuring argumentation and proof at trial must establish the linkage between evidence introduced at trial and the crucial and relevant underlying factual propositions by identifying generalizations that connect the evidence to the factual propositions.

For example, I analyzed the trial of a federal criminal case (brought under the federal RICO conspiracy statute) charging a defendant with conspiracy in the attempted murder of another person. The problematic element of the charge was whether the defendant, a reputed mobster and member of a crime family, intended to murder that person. That is, the crucial legal issue was the question of defendant's "intent," the *mens rea* component of the crime. The most probative evidence of defendant's intent was his promise to the head of the crime family that he would kill the third person. The "logical" or "inferential" legal argument presented by the prosecution may be diagrammed in accordance with the clinical model presented for analyzing inferential arguments by Moore, Bergman, and Binder as follows:

Evidence: Defendant promised the mob boss that he would kill the third person.

Generalization: When a defendant promises another person that he will kill a third person, the defendant usually intends to kill the third person.

Especially when:

1. The defendant is a member of a "crime family."

2. The defendant is "deathly afraid" of the person to whom he has made the promise.

3. The defendant knows that the person to whom he has made the promise has a compelling motive for wanting the third person dead.

4. The defendant conspires with other members of the "crime family" about how to accomplish the killing.

The defendant responds with counter-propositions ("except whens") that make the prosecution's argument less likely to be true. These counterpropositions must also be supported by evidence submitted at trial. Thus the logic of defendant's counter-argument may be set forth as follows:

Defendant's "Except Whens":

1. Defendant is not receiving much benefit from being a member of the crime family and does not participate in the family's day-to-day activities.

2. Defendant has a close personal relationship with the third person.

3. Defendant does not really mean what he says and is lying about his true intentions to buy time for the third person.

4. Defendant is prone to hyperbole and exaggeration about his criminal intentions.

5. Defendant has failed to carry out the execution even when he has been alone with the third person and has had the opportunity to do so.

The attorney, hypothetically, could have presented evidence at trial, and structured his argument in just this way, as a series of logical counter propositions. Like many, perhaps most, effective attorneys these days, however, he did not choose to do so. Instead, he converted the "except whens," and the evidence supporting these propositions, into an aesthetically compelling narrative similar in tone, structure and content to many hard, linear, protagonist-driven Hollywood cine-myths. The evidence introduced at trial had been presented as if "story-boarded" and was then recapitulated in closing argument in the form of a three-part structure of a popular, compelling, and entertaining "Mafia movie." Theme, character, conflict, and narrative structure were intentionally proximate to filmic counterparts about the mob, and the story of the tender-hearted mobster had numerous historical, cinematic antecedents. Furthermore, the attorney nested his storytelling in these cinematic models. The story had many of the characteristics of a popular Hollywood mob fable filled with irony and humor, and attempted to fulfill the audience's expectations and understandings about American crime families derived from popular film.

Evidence is converted into story on the spine of a hard narrative structure that is "thematic." The theme is like the "stock" themes and repetitive stories of Hollywood entertainment fables. Here the theme is that of a redemption plot, where the protagonist moves from selfishness towards selflessness and ultimately sacrifices himself to a larger cause. The classic Hollywood version of redemption story is, perhaps, *Casablanca* where the protagonist, Rick, a strong but selfish man, moves from cynicism to romantic love and then, at the moment *of* crisis, sacrifices himself in service of a larger cause.

I have called the "title" of the defendant's version of the thematic trial story "Desperate For Love" and explained the plot as the story of a weak but kind man torn between the love of his Mafia family on the one hand and the love of his "real" family on the other. His dilemma and his internal psychological conflict and the outer plot conflict are resolved at the denouement. Like Rick, the protagonist in *Casablanca* who moves from great selfishness towards love of another and then towards self-sacrifice within the confines of three hard narrative acts, the protagonist, defendant Louie Failla, moves through a similar psychological arc, along the well-trodden character through-line and narrative progression of the contemporary almost-hero.

The perspective of the storyteller, the defendant's attorney, like the director's perspective in *Casablanca,* is focused upon Louie's psychological transformation that is intimated through his responses to the pressures of external events. Like the audience in *Casablanca,* the jurors respond to Louie's psychological transformation. Also, in the end, like Rick in *Casablanca,* Louie, the protagonist/defendant, a weak but kind man, gains strength and sacrifices himself, stringing along his adopted mob family and pretending to participate in the murder conspiracy while, in fact, protecting his son-in-law from the mob. . . .

It is my belief that trial storytelling genre conventions — the rules of evidence, the time constraints of the trial itself, the focus on arranging testimony and events into clear narrative progressions that complement juror expectations, and the focus upon events taking place on a shared and external narrative landscape — all shape the defendant's character in the trial story to take the imaginative form of the protagonist in a Hollywood genre film. . . .

NOTES & QUESTIONS

1. Attorneys construct arguments based upon evidence entered at trial. Attorneys are very careful about the evidence that is entered and carefully shape the way their audience derives inferences from this evidence. Trial attorneys do not have the opportunity, outside of opening statements and closing arguments, to speak directly to their audience and explain the significance of the evidence. It is up to the audience (jurors or judges sitting as fact-finders) to ascribe meaning through inferences. How, precisely, does the audience make these inferences? Professor Richard Sherwin identifies such terms as the "schema" and "script." A script, for example, is a model of behavior embodying our normative expectations (how people go about their "normal" everyday lives and activities). Sherwin illustrates the "script" for ordering a meal in a restaurant. *See* Sherwin, *supra,* 50. The plots of stories, however, are typically about "conflicts" that are violations or breaches of customary or normative cultural scripts and explorations of the consequences of these violations.

2. Sherwin further identifies "metaphors, stereotypes, narrative genres, and recurrent plot lines" as additional cognitive tools that jurors employ to decode meaning through customary patterns. *Id.* at 51. Recently, there has been an expansive and rapidly developing interdisciplinary literature by legal academics decoding how jurors interpret and convert the evidence at trial into meaning, and then formulate these stories to match verdict categories. For example,

Professor Neal R. Feigenson draws upon work in social psychology and observes:

> Connecting the schematic analysis and the particular story are the cognitive frameworks we use to understand the social world. These implicit knowledge structures and inferential habits constitute the audience's "common sense" about how the world works and why people behave as they do. They shape the audience's cognitive and emotional responses to the facts and thereby guide the audience's interpretation of both the facts and their legal significance. . . .

Neal R. Feigenson, *On Social Cognition and Persuasive Writing*, 20 Legal Studies Forum 75, 75 (1996).

3. Pop cultural stories, especially film stories, may provide (or illustrate) the "macro" templates upon which attorneys graft or "storyboard" evidence at trial. These stock stories are often "mythic." Can you identify one or more of these popular "stock" stories and identify the controlling myths that have been used in recent notorious criminal trials by both defense attorneys and prosecutors?

4. In Errol Morris' *The Thin Blue Line* various witnesses testify for the movie audience, and the director intentionally splices in (cuts to) internal images that are television-like reconstructions or "clips" — sequences of images — from old movies. These internalized narrative templates reveal a great deal about how the various witnesses reconstruct "reality" and imaginatively configure events into narratives that often seem like part of familiar movie plots. What are your core myths, and are they embodied in popular films? Do films similarly influence your world view? How might these stories influence you and predispose you to accept certain types of narratives?

SOME OFF-THE-CUFF REMARKS ABOUT LAWYERS AS STORYTELLERS
Jeremiah Donovan
18 Vermont Law Review 751 (1994)

This two-month trial provided an enormous amount of material to work from. If you listen to the tapes used in this trial, you would say to yourself, "This is not real life — this was written by a radio writer." The FBI intercepted a mob initiation ceremony, but it sounded as if it had been written for radio. It was responsorial, much like the old Latin mass, "Io voglio . . . io voglio . . . entrare . . . entrare . . . in questo orginazione . . . in questo orginazione." It sounded like a Latin prayer. When they burned the picture of the saint, you could hear the crackling of the fire on tape. I mean, this ceremony has been handed down from sixteenth century Sicily so you expect it to be dramatic. However, what was equally dramatic was all the activity surrounding it. Afterwards, after all the cleaning up and goodbyes, you hear the steps of the final participant going to the door, the door squeaks open, and then, to the empty room, you hear someone say, "No one will ever know what went on here today — except for us and the fucking Holy Ghost." Then you hear the door slam, and you imagine fifty FBI agents in the surveillance van shouting,

"Hurray!" Louis and Jack would reminisce not only about all the things that got the other defendants in trouble at trial, but also about their young days. These included some of the most wonderfully tender but obscene reminiscences about adolescent life such as going out on dates in the late 1930s and early 1940s. They were just wonderful pieces of evidence.

This extraordinary evidence caused a divorcement between reality and what was portrayed in the course of the trial, between what happened in the real world and the evidence that the jury saw. Professor Sherwin talked earlier today [at a Vermont Law School conference devoted the consideration of narrative and the law] about taking a videotape, computerizing it, and looking at it over and over and over until the reality begins to change. In this trial that is exactly what happened. The evidence was so dramatic and so interesting that one got the sense that these things did not take place in the real world at all and that Billy Grasso was a character rather than a real dead person.

This struck me most strongly after the Government introduced an exhibit of a board with about a hundred human bones mounted on it. These tiny little bones, some of them, but not all, were alleged to be the remains of some poor guy who had the indiscretion to engage in an affair with the wife of an unindicted co-defendant on the lam. After the bones were introduced, I walked by the clerk's table one day where the bones were laying underneath all the other exhibits: videotapes, papers, documents, and boxes on top of this fellow's bones. Nobody had any sense whatsoever that these were once a man.

One of the corporeal acts of mercy is to bury the dead. I got a plastic bag, covered the bones, and put them in a corner of the courtroom. I realized at this point that nobody was thinking of reality, nobody was thinking, "These are a person's bones." They were props in a drama. That realization helped me with my final argument because I could make that argument into a story, something that sounded like a movie plot.

When I talk to juries in my closing argument I think back to my bachelor days, and the jury is my date. We just saw a movie and we're drinking coffee and talking about the movie. I talk about the trial as if it were the film we saw. "Do you remember the part where Sonny Castagno was testifying? Remember he said. . . ." As I do this, I talk directly to a particular juror. It doesn't seem to embarrass the juror. "Remember the part where Sonny Castagno said that he was going to give Jackie Johns a call that night? Do you know why that was so important? Do you know why? Did you follow it? Well, wait a second, before I get to that, let's talk about something else," and then I'll talk about something else. Now the jurors are dying to know why I think what Castagno said was so important. At the end, when I finally come back to it, they will be all ears.

These final arguments always have three parts, just as my talk to you today has three parts, because final arguments must be very carefully structured. The problem is, if you are not talking from notes it is hard to keep the structure of the argument in your mind. But if they always have three parts, you will always know where you are. So if you get carried away at some point, you nevertheless remember, "I'm still in part two."

Professor Meyer finds my storytelling cinematic. I never thought or realized that it was cinematic; however, I now see that he is right. I don't necessarily tell the story chronologically, rather I tell portions of the story or simply a dramatic segment of the story in order to illustrate a point. What happens once I begin telling the story is that I can relax since I know it. I've just watched the movie, and spent the last two months trying this case. The little details that I need to make the story vivid, to make the story come alive, are those details I've struggled with for the last two months to get in through my witnesses or through cross-examination of the Government's witnesses. Since these things are fresh in my mind I can relax during the course of retelling the story. I notice that juries tend to relax as well: they sit back and seem to enjoy the story that I'm retelling. After all, they've just seen the movie too.

NOTES & QUESTIONS

1. Jeremiah Donovan contrasts appellate arguments with closing arguments to a jury. Describing trial argumentation when the attorney speaks to the jury in a closing argument, Donovan employs the analogy of a conversation with a girlfriend on a date after a movie. Donovan stresses that his conversation is intentionally interactive or "dialogic," and the tone is intimate. That is, the attorney is retelling the story as if to his date, the juror. But he has another purpose in mind — he is not simply telling the tale for entertainment. Thus Donovan presents implicitly the image of the trial attorney as seducer. Do you find this image troubling or problematic? If so, identify the source of your discomfort.

2. Donovan also speaks of the "divorcement between reality and what was portrayed in the course of the trial, between what happened in the real world and the evidence that the jury saw." In addition, he emphasizes the visuality of the evidence converted into images in a trial narrative, presented to evoke the "real" world. Donovan bifurcates what occurs in the courtroom (what is admitted into evidence) from some more objective determination of what may have happened outside the courtroom. Implicitly, this assessment affirms law student Doug C.'s skeptical postmodern perspective, and his belief that the attorney's quest at trial is not for truth, but rather for a form that achieves a purpose and provides a "truth substitute" that affirms the system and serves his client's interests. Do you agree?

3. Donovan speaks of a three-part narrative structure that undergirds, and is characteristic of, his closing arguments. Such a structure is also characteristic of other popular narratives, including traditional three-act plays and the three-part movements of the typical popular Hollywood film. According to Donovan, reliance upon this structure liberates him from the limitations of a strict and literal chronology. Stories can then seemingly move more freely in time, e.g., through flashbacks and flashforwards, within the set pieces of this structure. Likewise, events can be revealed to fit the rhythms of the storyteller and the needs of the story, rather than shaped artificially or limited by chronology. That is, narrative time in courtroom storytelling is not "real" time. Likewise, chronology is not the primary ordering principle in movies. Narrative time is more complex than in the stories presented in appellate cases, or how students are typically allowed to retell the facts of a case in the law school classroom. Why do you think there is this difference?

4. What interesting or unusual narrative strategies or techniques do law-realted films employ to convey or reveal the passage of time? Do these techniques help or hinder the viewer to better understand the story? Do they make the story more compelling or persuasive? How might some of these techniques be useful to the legal storyteller in a criminal trial?

E. PUNISHMENT AND THE DEATH PENALTY

I WANT TO LIVE! FEDERAL JUDICIAL VALUES IN DEATH PENALTY CASES: PRESERVATION OF RIGHTS OR PUNCTUALITY OF EXECUTION?
Teree E. Foster
22 Oklahoma City University Law Review 63 (1997)

I Want to Live!, a 1958 film which recounts a few years in the brief life of Barbara Wood Graham, tells an arresting story. The film is a 1950s drama classic, a period piece that reflects the established social mores of that era. Nevertheless, considered from a near-millennium perspective, *I Want to Live!* defines modern systemic paradigms that provide insight into the relationship between the judiciary, the criminal justice system, and the society that these institutions influence and shape. . . .

Principal among the film's motifs is a compelling reminder that, at least in criminal cases, it is essential that an impartial entity interpose itself as a barrier between the accused and the unfettered force of governmental, prosecutorial power. This buffer role is an integral component of the guarantee that procedures used to gather incriminating information and to build a case "beyond a reasonable doubt" against an accused comport with due process and substantial justice. When Barbara Graham was tried in California in the mid-1950s, the judiciary had not yet assumed this insulating role. Thus, although her conviction was tangibly dependent upon the testimony of the ironically-named Ben Miranda, the undercover police officer who adopted the guise of friendship, and extracted from Barbara a ruinously incriminating — and possibly unreliable — statement, Miranda's testimony evoked little judicial comment.

Barbara Graham's trial occurred almost a decade prior to the assault of the Warren Court on a plethora of egregious police tactics that had become accepted as the *sine qua non* for vigorous law enforcement. During the 1960s, the Supreme Court breathed vitality into constitutional protections for criminal accuseds found in the Fourth, Fifth, Sixth, and Eighth Amendments. Decisions of the Warren Court during this period revolutionized the substance and focus of criminal procedure. A touchstone of Warren Court jurisprudence was the shielding of suspects from coercive law enforcement tactics; an interposition function was assumed with vigor and alacrity by the federal judiciary and the United States Supreme Court. . . .

Whether or not the imposition of capital punishment is morally defensible or desirable, it is apparent that in reviewing convictions in capital cases, the Supreme Court has abdicated, actively and absolutely, its role as insulator of the individual from the force of governmental, prosecutorial power. The Warren Court's position was that a federal court, in considering a habeas corpus petition from a state prisoner, should independently consider the merits of the constitutional challenge, notwithstanding the previous state court adjudication. State court rulings were entitled to the respect ordinarily afforded to opinions of a court of another jurisdiction, but did not preclude federal review of constitutional claims raised in a habeas corpus application.

A series of recent cases demonstrates that values of efficiency, expediency, and finality predominate over any obligation to consider potentially meritorious claims on behalf of the condemned. No longer is habeas corpus readily available to defendants incarcerated under state authority, even defendants convicted of capital offenses, as a device to challenge the constitutionality of their confinement. Instead, the Court has transmuted habeas corpus into a mechanism by which federal courts are permitted to do little more than ascertain whether state courts properly considered all constitutional challenges raised by the defendant during direct appeal. Above all, the Court, in its current preoccupation with punctuality in the execution of state-condemned capital defendants, has transmogrified its own role from shielding protector to detached timekeeper. . . .

That finality, efficiency, and expediency are legitimate and valuable goals for the criminal justice system cannot be gainsaid. Yet, these concerns must not eviscerate substantive interests in preserving individual liberties. If Barbara Graham was, as portrayed in *I Want to Live!*, an innocent victim of circumstance, the governmental termination of her life is an unspeakable perversion of justice. If Barbara Graham was guilty of Mrs. Monaghan's murder, premising her conviction for that crime upon information acquired by illegal, abusive and reprehensible law enforcement tactics sabotages fundamental principles of respect for the dignity of the individual — even the individual criminal — and for her inviolable constitutional rights. . . .

NOTES & QUESTIONS

1. The movie *I Want to Live!* cinematically adapts real events from a high-profile murder trial that resulted in the conviction and execution of Barbara Graham in the gas chamber in California. Unlike Errol Morris' *The Thin Blue Line*, the screenwriters and director have readjusted some of the facts to suit a popular audience. The movie is akin to the contemporary docudrama developed from real events rather than, for instance, *The Thin Blue Line*, which is a narrative documentary. In the movie, Susan Hayward's Graham is a feisty, extremely attractive and, in many ways, deeply sympathetic character, and is also apparently innocent. In the "real" case, however, the character of Graham is darker, and there is stronger evidence of her complicity in the murder of Mabel Monahan. Graham was not merely a passive observer; she allegedly asphyxiated the victim — a 64-year-old invalid — by placing a plastic bag over her head. And her jailhouse confession to the police informer included incriminating knowledge of details of the crime that would have been difficult for a non-participant to know. These details, however, are omitted from the movie. Why did the moviemakers find it necessary to tweak crucial facts, especially since the opening to the film specifically states that it is a "real" story based upon the articles of a Pulitzer Prize-winning journalist and Barbara Graham's own letters?

2. Is *I Want to Live!* truly an exploration of capital punishment? Or is the film a reworking of a more traditional Hollywood theme about the wrongful punishment of an innocent defendant? Here, unlike many predecessors, the innocent victim is not released at the end, but instead maintains stoic and "heroic" dignity in the face of injustice. Would a film audience have been interested in the film (or the story) if Graham was depicted as a less attractive or sympathetic protagonist? If she was guilty rather than innocent?

3. *I Want to Live!* details realistically (or at least what is possible within the constraints and limitations of a two-hour movie format) many of the procedural details of death penalty practice such as the multiple appeals and petitions for stays of execution and requests for clemency. The movie also explores the psychological effects upon the convicted defendant of these protracted proceedings and accurately details the workings of the machinery of death by depicting the physical preparations for, and the execution of, a prisoner in the gas chamber, right up to the moment the fumes from cyanide tablets are dropped into sulfuric acid and the prisoner inhales and struggles for life. (In Graham's case, this execution was a public enactment of the biblical admonition of "an eye for an eye," as the type of execution paralleled the form of the murder Graham purportedly committed by asphyxiation of another woman.) How, if at all, do these scenes compel you as viewer to respond emotionally? How, if at all, is the film persuasive to you? Does it change or reinforce your attitudes about capital punishment?

4. Does it matter that Barbara Graham is a woman? That is, is the story and the film's cinematic argument against capital punishment made more compelling because of Graham's gender or the fact that she is a mother with a young child? (In fact, Barbara Graham was the mother of three children.) Is there anything more troubling to you about executing a woman convicted of murder than a man? How do factors such as race, economic circumstance, and the physicality or attractiveness of convicted defendants affect the probability of imposition of the death sentence? Are Richard Pryor's earlier observations about the "justice" and "just us" (race and probability of prosecution and incarceration) equally applicable to the imposition of the death sentence?

5. In a more recent film based upon a "real" story, *Dead Man Walking* (1996), a subtext is the attraction and sublimated sexual relationship between a convicted murderer and a nun. In this sense, *Dead Man Walking* is truly a Hollywood "love and redemption" story rather than an argument against the death penalty. Are Hollywood films attempting to make rhetorical arguments compelled to include stock themes and stories with traditional plot ingredients (characters, conflict, plot)? How does the documentary *The Thin Blue Line* include such ingredients?

THE CULTURAL LIFE OF CAPITAL PUNISHMENT: RESPONSIBILITY AND REPRESENTATION IN *DEAD MAN WALKING* AND *LAST DANCE*

Austin Sarat

11 Yale Journal of Law & the Humanities 153 (1999)

Punishment, as Nietzsche reminds us, makes us who we are and constitutes us as particular kinds of subjects. The subject constituted by punishment is watchful, on guard, fearful, even if never directly subject to the particular pains of state-imposed punishment. One of the primary achievements of punishment, to use Nietzsche's vivid phrase, "is to breed an animal with the right to make promises," that is, to induce in us a sense of responsibility, a desire and an ability to properly discharge our responsibilities. Dutiful individuals, guilt-ridden, morally burdened — these are the creatures that punishment demands, creatures worthy of being punished.

Punishment constitutes subjectivity through the complex juridical mechanisms that put it in motion, as well as the moral tenets and legal doctrines that legitimate it. Here too, we can see the centrality of responsibility. The state will only punish responsible agents, persons whose "deviant" acts can be said to be a product of consciousness and will, persons who "could have done otherwise." As Blackstone put it, "to constitute a crime against human laws, there must be, first, a vicious will, and, secondly, an unlawful act consequent upon such vicious will." Thus, the apparatus of punishment depends upon a modernist subject and a conception of the will that represses or forgets its "uncertain, divided, and opaque" character.

In addition, because most citizens are not, and will not be, directly subjected to the state's penal apparatus, punishment creates a challenge for representation that is deepened to the point of crisis when the punishment is death. Punishment is inscribed in both our unconscious and our consciousness. It lives in images conveyed, in lessons taught, in repressed memories, in horrible imaginings. Some of its horror and controlling power is, in fact, a result of its fearful invisibility. "Punishment," Foucault reminds us, "[has] become the most hidden part of the penal process." He argues that:

> This has several consequences: [Punishment] leaves the domain of more or less everyday perception and enters that of abstract consciousness; its effectiveness is seen as resulting from its inevitability, not from its visible intensity; it is the certainty of being punished and not the horrifying spectacle of public punishment that must discourage crime. . . . As a result, justice no longer takes public responsibility for the violence that is bound up with its practice.

It may very well be, however, that the more punishment is hidden, the less visible it is, the more power it has to colonize our imaginative life. We watch; we seek to conjure an image of punishment; we become particular kinds of spectators, anticipating a glimpse, at least a partial uncovering of the apparatus of state discipline.

And what is true of all punishment is particularly true when death is a punishment. That the state takes life and how it takes life insinuates itself into the public imagination, even as the moment of this exercise of power is hidden from view. This particular exercise of power helps us understand who we are and what we as a society are capable of doing. And as Wendy Lesser so skillfully documents, the hidden moment when the state takes the life of one of its citizens precipitates, in an age of the hypervisual, a crisis of representation. This crisis occurs as we confront the boundaries of our representational practices, where we must determine who decides what can and cannot be seen, and whether particular representations of the "reality" of the pain on which the penal apparatus depends are adequate.

The modern execution is carried out behind prison walls. In these semi-private, sacrificial ceremonies a few selected witnesses are gathered in a carefully controlled situation to see, and by seeing to sanctify, the state's taking of the life of one of its citizens. As Richard Johnson suggests:

> In the modern period (from 1800 on), ceremony gradually gave way to bureaucratic procedure played out behind prison walls, in isolation from the community. Feelings are absent, or at least suppressed, in bureaucratically administered executions. With bureaucratic procedure, there is a functional routine dominated by hierarchy and task. Officials perform mechanistically before a small, silent gathering of authorized witnesses.

Richard Johnson, *Death Work: A Study of the Modern Execution Process* 5 (1990).

Capital punishment becomes, at best, a hidden reality. It is known, if at all, by indirection. "The relative privacy of executions nowadays (even photographs of the condemned man dying are almost invariably strictly prohibited)," Hugo Bedau notes, "means that the average American literally does not know what is being done when the government, in his name and presumably on his behalf, executes a criminal."

While executions have been removed from the public eye for more than fifty years, in most states capital punishment still must be witnessed by members of the public in order to be legal. It is this linkage between violence and the visual that Lesser explores when she notes that witnesses are "there not just to ensure that the deed is actually done . . . but to represent and embody the wider public in whose name the execution is being carried out." Thus the state's power to kill is linked to the imperatives and privileges of spectatorship. Whatever the means chosen, execution is always a visual event. . . .

NOTES & QUESTIONS

1. Professor Sarat argues that the power of punishment, and its hold over our imaginations, is based upon its secrecy. That is, "punishment is inscribed in both our unconscious and our consciousness. It lives in images conveyed, in lessons taught, in repressed memories, in horrible happenings. Some of its horror and controlling power is, in fact, a result of its fearful invisibility." Further, "what is true of all punishment is particularly true when death is a punishment." Do you agree? If so, how might the televising of executions affect or change public attitudes about how we respond to this punishment? Would it diminish the imaginative power of the punishment? Do you believe that it would cause us to recoil in horror? Or are we already so deadened to the effects of violence that we would not have any response, or find the presentation of ceremonies of death another type of entertaining reality programming?

2. *I Want to Live!* depicts in graphic detail how the death penalty is carried out in California in 1953; the images documenting the externals of an execution in the gas chamber are presented with precision. Yet, for many viewers, these images may have little sway or power over our imaginations. The story may seem dated to some viewers. Why is this so? Reflect upon your own responses to *I Want to Live!* in the context of Sarat's observations about punishment.

3. Today, in many jurisdictions, death by injection is often a seemingly antiseptic practice without the obviously horrific imaginative external dimensions of other forms of execution, e.g., firing squad, hanging, the electric chair, or the gas chamber. The images of the gurney and of lethal injections do not carry the visual freight of earlier forms of execution. In Sarat's words, it is less of a "visual event." Some of the power of the ritual of the "sacrificial ceremony" described by Sarat may have been lost — its power to colonize the imagination made less compelling. Does this diminish the effectiveness of the punishment as a deterrent?

4. Hugo Badeau notes that the "relative privacy of executions nowadays (even photographs of the condemned man dying are almost invariably strictly prohibited)" means "that the average American literally does not know what is being done when the government, in his name and presumably on his behalf, executes a criminal." Do you agree or disagree with Badeau's observation? Explain and reflect upon the reasons for your responses.

READING DEATH SENTENCES: THE NARRATIVE CONSTRUCTION OF CAPITAL PUNISHMENT
Christopher J. Meade
71 New York University Law Review 732 (1996)

[S]upport for the death penalty persists despite seemingly overwhelming counter-arguments. Utilitarian arguments, based on the evidence that the death penalty does not deter murder, fail to stimulate death penalty opposition. Indeed, research suggests that when death penalty proponents are presented with mixed evidence about the deterrent effect of the death penalty, they disproportionately credit the data that supports their position, so that the mixed evidence actually results in more hardened support. Moral arguments similarly fail to change people's minds. . . .

Despite the ineffectiveness of these arguments, there are indications that death penalty support is not as monolithic as it might appear. Poll data indicates that a majority of people prefer alternatives to the death penalty, such as life imprisonment without the possibility of parole plus restitution to the victim's family. Significantly, even a majority of those who "strongly" favor the death penalty abandon their support for capital punishment when presented with such an alternative. Research also indicates that there is an underlying ambivalence among death penalty supporters.

What is it about the death penalty that causes so many Americans to express support, despite the contradictions underlying this support? And since utilitarian and moral arguments have proven to be ineffective, how can those who oppose capital punishment most effectively fight against it?

This Note addresses these questions by analyzing narratives about the death penalty, focusing on films that are based on true-life stories. Since these true-life narratives recount actual occurrences, they provide examples of how reality is shaped into narratives. Narrative is one of the primary ways in which people make sense of the world, and as Robert Cover notes, "[n]o set of legal institutions or prescriptions exists apart from the narratives that locate it and give it meaning." As such, these popular culture narratives help illuminate the role that the death penalty plays in America. In addition, they offer insights into how death penalty opponents can use narrative to erode capital punishment's high but unstable support. Analyzing how a particular narrative tells the story of an actual defendant may therefore provide insight for those who tell real-life stories to juries, to commutation boards, and to the media. . . .

An understanding of narrative is critical for the death penalty lawyer in attempting to persuade the public or particular jurors to vote against the death penalty. Although utilitarian and moral arguments are ineffective in changing public opinion about capital punishment, narrative may provide an effective tool. This possibility is especially encouraging given the public support for alternatives to the death penalty, as well as the ambivalence about capital punishment among its supporters. Similarly, because jurors structure their understanding of cases through narrative, a lawyer's effective use of narrative may help shape jurors' understanding of the facts and the law and ultimately determine the jurors' verdict. . . .

NOTES & QUESTIONS

1. In an initial excerpt from his law review note, Christopher Meade, a law student at New York University School of Law, makes some broad assertions regarding the death penalty. First, he asserts that the death penalty exists despite "seemingly overwhelming counter-arguments." Based upon your perceptions, readings in criminal law, exposure to law programs in the media, and work experiences, is Meade's observation correct? Further, Meade asserts that "when death penalty proponents are presented with mixed evidence about the deterrent effect of the death penalty, they disproportionately credit the data that supports their position." Is this perception accurate? Finally, Meade asserts that moral arguments "fail to change people's minds" about the death penalty. Do you agree? Does Meade's rhetoric remind you of "talking heads" on television talk-show programs? If you were writing a note about popular storytelling practices and the death penalty, how might you begin your argument?

2. Meade also asserts that "popular cultural narratives help illuminate the role that the death penalty plays in America" and that "narrative may provide an effective tool" to change popular attitudes about capital punishment. Again, do you agree with these assertions about the potential power of popular stories to reshape public opinion? Do you believe movies such as *I Want to Live!* and *The Thin Blue Line* effectively change popular perceptions, beliefs, and public attitudes about the death penalty? Explain your answers.

3. Do you agree with Meade that close analysis of popular stories may provide "insight to those who tell real-life stories to juries, to commutation boards, and to the media"? Reflect upon what you have learned thus far from studying pop cultural storytelling in viewing and analyzing the films in this chapter. What insights, if any, have you gained that might be of assistance to you in law practice?

FICTIONAL DOCUMENTARIES AND TRUTHFUL FICTIONS: THE DEATH PENALTY IN RECENT AMERICAN FILM
David R. Dow
17 Constitutional Commentary 511 (2000)

When it comes to death, most Hollywood movies cheat. They cheat by tinkering with the truth, because the truth as it actually is, is too complex or too disturbing to confront honestly. (The so-called happy ending is the most famous form of such cheating.) They cheat because people generally prefer happiness and simplicity to darkness and complexity, especially where their entertainment is concerned, and filmmakers tend to give people what they want. . . .

Death penalty movies cheat as well. . . . [T]hey cheat by featuring an innocent inmate: someone who, by nearly anyone's estimation, deserves to be living. This focus is their mode of distraction, their mode of avoiding moral complexity. Death penalty movies that focus on innocence cheat because they allow the viewer to be certain that the protagonist ought not to be killed; such movies permit viewers to oppose a death penalty without opposing the death penalty. In real life, we do not have that indulgence.

When death penalty movies cheat, they obscure the fundamental moral questions that the death penalty involves. One might expect documentaries to be more real and Hollywood productions to be less so, but one would be wrong. Exactly the opposite is true. Documentaries cheat much more than Hollywood movies. Most (though not all) documentaries cheat by focusing almost exclusively on the issue of innocence, whereas many Hollywood movies willingly grapple with moral complexity by featuring at least one guilty inmate. Moreover, although the focus on innocence might seem innocuous, it is in fact rather pernicious, because it contributes to the increasingly widespread view that there is no great harm in violating a person's rights as long as we are certain that the person is guilty. . . .

I am not urging that documentary filmmakers and lawyers and journalists cease their efforts to identify individuals who have been wrongfully convicted; I am suggesting that the recent obsession with claims of innocence has obscured the fact that innocence is a symptom of a larger, systemic corruption.

Thus, *The Thin Blue Line*, a film that led directly to Randall Dale Adams's release from death row, has nothing to do with the philosophical issue of the death penalty's moral legitimacy. Similarly, *Fourteen Days in May*, which details the final two weeks of the life of a death row inmate who suffered nearly every injustice that the capital punishment regime can serve up, ultimately elects to focus on the inmate's claim of innocence, thereby blunting the force of, and even obscuring, all else. . . .

Someone who believes that the death penalty is inherently wrong cheats by focusing solely on innocent inmates. Worse, this cheating tends to legitimate the increasingly entrenched legal doctrine that holds that unless an inmate can prove that he did not actually commit the crime for which he was sentenced, then virtually any constitutional violation can be overlooked. Surely innocence should matter, but it should not be all that matters. Constitutional values and moral norms are not applicable only to the wrongly accused. . . .

NOTES & QUESTIONS

1. Dow emphasizes that "Hollywood" movies about the death penalty — and non-Hollywood documentaries including *The Thin Blue Line* — "cheat" by focusing upon claims of innocence, rather than challenging the moral legitimacy of the death penalty. Do all narratives "cheat"? That is, as we observed in the previous section on legal storytelling in criminal cases, narratives convert the complex stuff-of-life into tightly ordered forms. Narratives turn upon clear themes. Events are carefully selected, shaped, and ordered to create purposeful and forward plot-driven stories. Players then become characters (protagonists, antagonists, secondary characters). Surroundings are transformed into settings. Time is modified into "narrative" time that seldom is equivalent to literal clock time or simple chronology. Stylistic choices including perspective and point of view control and shape what is seen and heard, from where the action is viewed, how it is viewed, and how the audience responds to the events that are depicted.

2. Post-conviction relief practice in death penalty cases is also primarily a writing practice, as well as a storytelling practice. Unlike the testimony provided by witness participants in Errol Morris' *The Thin Blue Line*, the attorney usually tells the convicted inmate's story in a written "brief." She is not entitled automatically to an evidentiary hearing. Instead, the attorney representing a condemned inmate must persuade a judge in writing that she should be afforded an opportunity to re-present witnesses and testimony. The brief is, of course, a fact-specific and legally specific story; it is not a theoretical argument against the "moral legitimacy" of the death penalty. That is, the core of the brief is narrative; it must retell the story that has already been certified as truthful in an appellate opinion affirming an inmate's conviction. To do this requires powerfully retelling the story anew, as a different story that requires a new ending. There are, of course, constraints upon this storytelling practice, e.g., the story must be true; certain facts are given; there is an opposing storyteller; parts of the story certified to be true must be changed; the audience is a judge rather than a jury; etc. To change the story, after reinvestigating the crime, the attorney sometimes tells stories of an innocent defendant (actual innocence) akin to the story told by Errol Morris in *The Thin Blue Line*. But there are clearly other story themes depending upon the procedural posture and the requirements of the law. For example, stories with a theme of "betrayal" are common in post-conviction relief briefs. Here, the state actors or, perhaps, the convicted inmate's own attorney, have betrayed him and made it impossible to tell his story accurately and completely in a fair initial proceeding. For example, the state has withheld information about a plea agreement with a crucial witness testifying against the defendant. Alternatively, the story may be about the law itself. For example, in a petition for certiorari the confused interpretation of a previous case or statute may be characterized as "the trouble," arriving to disturb a peaceful "steady state" in the law. The Supreme Court is then cast in the role of the hero to step in and to resolve the trouble, restoring order in the legal community. The form of the storytelling is akin to the mythology of a popular film about the Wild West. These written stories, as Dow observes about *The Thin Blue Line*, convert or transform legal arguments into thematic and plot-driven stories. Not all issues are given full consideration.

3. Finally, we conclude this chapter by asking whether your law school legal writing courses have taught you sufficiently what you need to know about developing these skills and placed sufficient narrative tools in your professional toolkits. We hope some of the films you view while discussing popular culture engage your imagination and begin to develop the vocabulary and concepts for the narrative practice that is especially crucial to the practice of criminal law.

Chapter 10

CONSTITUTIONAL LAW

A. FILMOGRAPHY

Boys Don't Cry (1999)

Guess Who's Coming to Dinner (1967)

The People vs. Larry Flynt (1996)

The Siege (1998)

Whose Life Is It Anyway? (1981)

B. THE PARTICIPANTS

Because constitutional claims may be directed only at government (not private) action, popular culture concerning constitutional questions generally must present two stories: one about a private individual's fight to vindicate her own constitutional rights, and one about the triumph of constitutional rights for the public. In this section, we consider how those stories interact by focusing on the narrative roles of the parties involved.

1. Individual Litigants

WHY PUNITIVE DAMAGES ARE UNCONSTITUTIONAL
Martin H. Redish & Andrew L. Mathews
53 Emory Law Journal 1 (2004)

Our society draws a fundamental distinction between public and private authority to assure that the private autonomy so essential to attainment of the goals of liberal democratic theory is not undermined by subjecting it to the constitutional and political structures to which the state, in the exercise of public power, is subjected. Thus, the state action requirement preserves the public-private dichotomy that is central to liberal democratic theory by assuring that the constitutional constraints imposed on public power do not spill over into and restrict the scope of free choice within the core private sphere. But by the same token, our constitutional structure must prevent private power from invading the public sphere, at least in situations in which the two do not necessarily overlap.

For the very reason that society wants to preserve some level of private autonomy to assess, choose, and pursue personal goals, it correspondingly must keep purely public power out of the hands of those whose primary focus is not pursuit of the public interest. This is not necessarily to suggest either that the private and public spheres are mutually exclusive in scope or that drawing the distinction will always — or even usually — be an easy task. The point, rather, is that as a matter of normative political theory the distinction on occasion must be drawn, to ensure the continued viability of liberal democracy. It is liberal theory's recognition of the independent vitality of private interests, separate and distinct from the public interest, that necessarily implies the need to have the public interest directly enforced only by those who are free from the potentially conflicting influences of private interests. This is especially true of the adversary system, where private litigants are permitted to pursue and protect their private interests within the framework of the adjudicatory structure. . . .

[I]n deciding whether to file suit, what remedy to seek, and how to conduct the litigation, government attorneys are restrained by their moral and ethical obligations to the public interest and by exposure to democratically based public review in ways that private attorneys and clients are not. In short, the practice of government attorneys vested with authority to enforce the public interest may be described — paradoxically — as a type of "adversarial neutrality.". . .

As advocates within the adversary system private litigants cannot be held to the extremely high standards of constitutional neutrality that have been imposed on public adjudicators. While there may well be legitimate debate on exactly where those lines are to be drawn, there can be no doubt that the vesting of power to sue on behalf of the government in the hands of attorneys who possess a strong financial interest in the success of their actions and in clients who possess both a financial and often personal interest in imposing punishment on defendants falls below that line. When one adds to the mix the important fact that neither attorney nor client is directly or indirectly accountable to the electorate, the fairness of the exercise of public power becomes even more severely compromised. . . .

NOTES & QUESTIONS

1. Given the authors' argument, does it make sense to resolve constitutional issues that affect the public through litigation by a private individual with a personal claim? Does the law-related popular culture with which you are familiar recognize the distinction? Does it represent the story of one individual or the championing of constitutional rights on behalf of all Americans?

2. Consider the trial in *The People vs. Larry Flynt*. The Reverend Jerry Falwell files the suit against Larry Flynt that gives rise to the constitutional issue. The suit includes claims of libel and intentional infliction of emotional distress caused by a satiric piece about Falwell published in *Hustler* magazine. Falwell loses the libel suit because of the jury's finding that no reasonable person could believe the content of the piece. He is, however, awarded $200,000 for his emotional distress claim. Flynt appeals this ruling, arguing that the availability of a libel and intentional infliction of emotional distress claim places an unconstitutional restriction on his First Amendment right to respond to statements Falwell had previously made against *Hustler*.

Is Flynt acting to preserve the First Amendment rights of all citizens? Or is he motivated by anger at Falwell to vindicate his own personal interests? Which motivation works better in terms of cinematic storytelling? Which makes Flynt appear more heroic? Is it fair of the filmmakers to present Flynt as a proponent of the public's First Amendment rights? Is it harmful for them to do so?

3. Similarly, in *Whose Life Is It Anyway?* Ken Harrison fights for his private right to refuse medical treatment even though without it he will surely die. Should the moving story of a particularly self-reflective and intelligent man be used to argue more generally for a constitutional right to die? Or do individual circumstances play too important a role in such a determination to allow the movie judge's ruling in favor of one individual to stand for the right of the public generally? In other words, because Harrison has a right to die, does anyone?

4. In *The Siege*, there is no trial because the government's arguable violation of citizens' constitutional rights occurs under martial law, where constitutional rights may be suspended. The film's protagonist, FBI Special Agent Anthony Hubbard, is both a representative of the government — an FBI agent — and a private individual who is opposed to the government/military's actions. Does Hubbard oppose the military's actions as a private individual fighting for his own rights, or is he still acting as a government agent representing the public? Which makes the narrative more compelling?

5. In *Guess Who's Coming to Dinner?* Dr. John Prentice, a black man, and Joanna Drayton, a white woman, announce their intention to marry — an act that was considered illegal in sixteen states at the time the film was released in 1967. Although the film does not depict any overt legal battle by the couple, Joanna's father recognizes that they are implicitly raising a legal challenge to antimiscegenation laws. Is the point of the movie the couple's pursuit of their own individual happiness or their vindication of the public's constitutional right to marry regardless of race (recognized by the U.S. Supreme Court the same year the film was released in *Loving v. Virginia*, 388 U.S. 1 (1967))? Can a deliberately provocative film simply be about private individuals? Can a story about two individuals fairly present an argument for the public interest?

6. *Boys Don't Cry* tells the story of a transgendered individual, yet the Supreme Court has never recognized a violation of the constitutional rights of transgendered individuals as a class. Do you think the filmmakers' motivation in telling the story of Brandon Teena's mistreatment by the legal system, rape, and subsequent murder was to relate the struggle of one individual or to make a statement about the rights of all citizens? Does presenting him as a hero make the audience members more likely to support constitutional protections for transgendered individuals? If so, are the filmmakers engaging in political propaganda? Is it dangerous for them to do so? Is it possible for them to do otherwise in telling this story?

2. Attorneys and Judges

In much law-related popular culture lawyers are heroes. Consider whether lawyers play the same role in popular culture specifically related to constitutional law as you read the following piece about Thurgood Marshall's life as a constitutional lawyer and Supreme Court Justice.

A TRIBUTE TO JUSTICE THURGOOD MARSHALL
Owen M. Fiss
105 Harvard Law Review 49 (1991)

From the beginning, Thurgood Marshall fought for what was right, even when the chances of success were minute and the hardships great. He began the practice of law during the Great Depression, when he opened a one-man law office in Baltimore. Soon he started handling civil rights cases, although there was virtually no law in his favor and, of course, no prospect of a fee. He won a number of important victories, including one against the University of Maryland, and in 1936 he moved on to the national headquarters of the National Association for the Advancement of Colored People (NAACP) in New York. Two years later he became its chief counsel. At the time the NAACP was, to put it charitably, a fledgling organization. It had a shoestring budget and a minuscule staff — one or two lawyers and a secretary. Marshall once confessed that after a number of years he received a raise, but spent the entire amount — such as it was — on a single lunch at Luchow's. Things improved for the NAACP after Marshall's victory in *Brown* and the subsequent confrontation with Governor Faubus in Little Rock, Arkansas. But for Marshall, the struggle continued.

I clerked for Marshall in 1964–1965, when he was a judge on the Court of Appeals for the Second Circuit, and I witnessed first-hand his extraordinary capacity to stand up for what he believed was right. At that point, the struggle stemmed from the reluctance of his colleagues to implement fully the reforms in criminal procedure being developed by the Warren Court. Unlike the battles of his early years, in these confrontations Marshall could invoke the formal authority of the Supreme Court. But in the early 1960s, the Court was at the center of controversy and criticism; it needed support and had little to confer. His years as Solicitor General and his early years on the Supreme Court, when he sat in the company of his heroes, were something of a respite, for by 1967 the Warren Court had achieved considerable power. But soon the tide shifted.

In 1968 Richard Nixon campaigned for the presidency by attacking the Warren Court, and upon winning, began to make appointments to alter radically the Court's direction. Justice Marshall soon began to feel under siege. In 1970 he was hospitalized with pneumonia, and, as he tells the story, was informed by a doctor one day that President Nixon had been inquiring about his health. Instantly, Marshall instructed the doctor to tell the President, "Not yet." In the end, he proved true to his word, although this resolve meant that he would spend the next twenty years — almost his entire career on the Supreme Court — in battle against the counterrevolution led by Justice, later Chief Justice, Rehnquist.

On the Justice's retirement, one law professor trying to summarize Marshall's years of service on the High Court aptly referred to him as "the Great Dissenter." In his dissents, he continually tried to remind us how far short we have fallen from our ideals. Justice Marshall made a career of protesting the roll-back in school desegregation, the dismantling of procedural protections for the accused, the erection of new barriers to affirmative action, the disregard for free speech, and the reinstitution of the death penalty. On his last day on the bench, Justice Marshall dissented from a Rehnquist decision permitting the admission of victim impact evidence in capital cases, and he concluded his opinion and his career on this worrisome note: "Cast aside today are those condemned to face society's ultimate penalty. Tomorrow's victims may be minorities, women, or the indigent."

Sitting in the Supreme Court's exalted offices, one does not need great courage to speak out, only strong convictions and a will to resist. Much more than that, however, was needed when Marshall began his career as a civil rights lawyer. Marshall loved telling stories of those early years — and he retold those stories so often that they must be true. During my clerkship year, I heard many tales of his travels in the South, especially in the late 1930s and 1940s when he criss-crossed the region by car and train, lived out of a suitcase, and confronted the crude and violent racism of the day. . . .

Once he recalled this encounter in a small Mississippi town:

> I was out there on the train platform, trying to look small, when this cold-eyed man with a gun on his hip came up. "Nigguh," he said, "I thought you oughta know the sun ain't nevah set on a live nigguh in this town." So I wrapped my constitutional rights in cellophane, tucked them in my hip pocket — and caught the next train.

Marshall's modesty in reciting these tales was admirable, but it did not mask the immediacy of the danger he faced. We do not often think that great lawyering requires courage, but it does, and Thurgood Marshall has plenty. . . .

NOTES & QUESTIONS

1. Is Professor Fiss' description of Justice Marshall consistent with the portrayal of attorneys in popular culture related to constitutional law? Consider also Justice Sandra Day O'Connor's remembrance of Justice Marshall:

> Although all of us come to the Court with our own personal histories and experiences, Justice Marshall brought a special perspective. His was the eye of a lawyer who saw the deepest wounds in the social fabric and used law to help heal them. His was the ear of a counselor who understood the vulnerabilities of the accused and established safeguards for their protection. His was the mouth of a man who knew the anguish of the silenced and gave them a voice.
>
> At oral arguments and conference meetings, in opinion and dissents, Justice Marshall imparted not only his legal acumen but also his life experiences, constantly pushing and prodding us to respond not only

to the persuasiveness of legal argument but also to the power of moral truth.

Sandra Day O'Connor, *Thurgood Marshall: The Influence of a Raconteur*, 44 Stanford Law Review 1217 (1992). Is it possible for a real person to be more heroic than the fictional or fictionalized attorneys in popular culture about constitutional law? Or do you think Justice Marshall has become larger than life in the personal narratives of the people remembering him?

2. Justice Marshall was largely responsible for school desegregation through his work as an NAACP attorney on *Brown v. Board of Education*. Does the popular culture discussed in this chapter present lawyers as heroes responsible for important social change? Who specifically is presented as the hero? If there are no lawyers in a given work, why not? What considerations drive the filmmakers' decisions about whom to make the heroes?

3. In his article *Bad Lawyers in the Movies*, Professor Michael Asimow begins by asking, "Seen any lawyer films recently? Chances are, most of the lawyers in those films were bad. They were unpleasant or unhappy human beings you wouldn't want as friends. And they were bad professionals you wouldn't admire or want as your lawyer." Michael Asimow, *Bad Lawyers in the Movies*, 24 Nova Law Review 533 (2000). Is Asimow's assessment correct for films involving constitutional law? If so, what accounts for the negative portrayal of the lawyers, especially given the reality of true heroes like Justice Marshall? How does such a negative characterization compare with the portrayal of lawyers in popular narratives involving other types of law? If constitutional law narratives are different, what might account for the difference? Consider the demands of storytelling, historical accuracy, legal accuracy, political rhetoric, and other aspects of filmmaking in addressing any such differences.

4. Are attorneys or the individuals whose cases give rise to the constitutional challenge the real advocates for constitutional rights? How realistic is it to think a layperson could accurately recognize a violation of her constitutional rights? For example, in *Inherit the Wind* (1960), the dramatization of the "Scopes Monkey Trial":

> The skillful and philosophical defense attorney wins his case by losing; his client is obviously guilty of having defied the law, but by the end of the film the viewer and some of the characters believe that the statute is wrongheaded and should be repealed. The judge imposes the least possible sentence (a fine of one hundred dollars) to signal his disapproval of the proceedings. By defying the law and appealing to a higher authority — the power of human reason — Drummond's client reaffirms the spirit that animates the First Amendment to the Constitution.

Christine Alice Corcos, *Legal Fictions: Irony, Storytelling, Truth, and Justice in the Modern Courtroom Drama*, 25 University of Arkansas at Little Rock Law Review 503, 581–82 (2003). Is the true advocate for the Constitution the schoolteacher who dared to teach Darwinian Theory in violation of the law or his attorney, a fictionalized version of the real-life Clarence Darrow? When does the heroic act of invoking the Constitution occur? When the individual engages in some activity that implicates an arguably unconstitutional statute or when her attorney recognizes the constitutional argument?

5. *The People vs. Larry Flynt* presents Alan Isaacman as a young attorney fresh out of law school when he first represents Flynt. In reality, the character is a composite of many different attorneys who have represented Flynt. According to the real Isaacman:

> When I started to represent Larry back in 1978, I had been practicing law for ten years or so. The movie made Edward [Norton]'s character look like he was just out of law school. I had tried a lot of cases before I ever represented Larry and I thought it was not believable that Larry Flynt, who could afford to hire experienced counsel, would pick some green attorney, some attorney who really did not have experience and say, "Go in there and fight for my liberty." I expressed that to Milos Forman [the director], but he told me the movie really wasn't about me. It was about Larry, so don't worry about it.

Clay Calvert & Robert D. Richards, *Alan Isaacman and the First Amendment: A Candid Interview with Larry Flynt's Attorney*, 19 Cardozo Arts & Entertainment Law Journal 313, 343 (2001). Is Forman correct that the movie was not about Flynt's attorney? If so, why change the character? Why construct a story about Flynt around a Supreme Court decision? If the public, like Forman, perceives lawyers as relatively unimportant in these films, do they also perceive lawyers as relatively unimportant in the development of First Amendment jurisprudence? Is there any danger in a public perception that the meaning of the First Amendment is not necessarily shaped by the arguments of the attorneys representing parties like Larry Flynt?

6. In *Whose Life Is It Anyway?* Ken Harrison is represented in his quest to refuse medical treatment by Carter Hill, an insurance attorney. Hill is plainly ambivalent about representing Harrison; he tells Harrison that, "This is a case I could stand to lose." Indeed, Harrison is the only character in the movie who seems determined to see his wish to die fulfilled. Yet it is Hill who styles the case as a petition for writ of habeas corpus, thus avoiding Dr. Emerson's strategy of having Harrison involuntarily committed as mentally incompetent based on his desire to die. Who is the hero in this film? Is it Harrison or Hill who best champions the right to bodily integrity?

7. Can any of the characters in *Guess Who's Coming to Dinner?* be characterized as "attorneys"? Consider Monsignor Ryan, who eloquently advocates on behalf of the interracial couple's right to marry. Why might this position be taken by a Catholic priest rather than an attorney? Take into account the fact that the movie is a comedy. Is there something funny about having a priest take this position? Or does his vocation make him particularly persuasive? Does he have greater moral authority than an attorney would? Is moral authority more important in fighting for constitutional rights than legal authority? Which is likely to appeal more to a movie audience?

8. In *The Siege*, is it important that FBI Agent Anthony Hubbard has a law degree? Hubbard does not use the courts to challenge martial law; indeed, he uses extralegal measures to subvert the military's plans. Is he acting as a heroic lawyer or simply a heroic person? Is he the real hero, or is his friend and colleague Frank Haddad the hero for quitting his job as an FBI agent in protest of the military's detention of all men of Arab descent living in Brooklyn? Does the fact that one of the detainees is Haddad's son affect your answer?

9. Does anyone play the role of lawyer in *Boys Don't Cry?* Consider Lana Tisdel, who defends Brandon when the other characters question and attack him. She also bails Brandon out of jail, where he is housed with the female inmates. Is Lana acting heroically? Or is Brandon the hero? Can Lana fairly be characterized as advocating for Brandon's constitutional rights? If so, can laypersons play the role of attorney in popular narratives, or is legal training necessary? Is there a danger in popular portrayals of unschooled laypersons subverting laws that they personally find unfair?

10. Professor Burt Neuborne argues that the "new democratic hero is the constitutional judge whose job it is to guard the liberties that are necessary for a true democracy." Jeffrey Rosen et al., *Panel Discussion: Brennan's Approach to Reading and Interpreting the Constitution*, 43 New York Law School Law Review 41, 42 (1999). Do you agree? How heroic are the judges in the popular culture relating to constitutional law with which you are familiar? If the judges who make the constitutional rulings play only a minor role — or if there are no judges and no rulings at all — is the real role of judges being undervalued? Should popular culture make the public more aware of the important role of judges in interpreting the Constitution? Or do judges and their rulings really have little impact on people's daily lives?

11. The limits of a constitutional lawyer's heroics are recounted with a healthy dose of self-deprecation in the following anecdote of Jack Greenberg, one of the NAACP attorneys who argued and won *Brown v. Board of Education*.

> [In] the days shortly after the decision in *Brown [v.] Board of Education* . . . there arrived in our office two members of the New York City Police Department. . . . They arrested our office boy on the charge of grand larceny. They took him away; and as he went out the door we said, "Ronny can we help you?" He said, "No," and he was gone. We called him at the police station; he would have nothing to do with us. We called his mother; she said, "It's not necessary. I don't want to have anything to do with it." And we despaired. The next morning Ronny came to work again, bright and early and chipper. . . . Finally I got up the courage to go up to him and say, "Ronny, what happened?" He explained that he had a girlfriend and he had given her a ring and things weren't going so well. So he took back the ring and she, rather than going into the streets, decided to go to the courts. She filed a charge of grand larceny against him. He explained this all to a lawyer from Legal Aid Society who arranged his release immediately, and so he was out and was in jail just only for a few hours. And I said, "Ronny, we could have done that. You've seen us go to the Supreme Court of the United States. You've seen us in Brown against Board of Education yet you didn't come to us when we wanted to help you — you went to the Legal Aid Society?" He said, "Mr. Greenberg, I didn't want to go to the Supreme Court. I just wanted to get out."

Jack Greenberg, *A Crusader in the Court: Comments on the Civil Rights Movement*, 63 UMKC Law Review. 207, 208 (1994).

C. CONSTITUTIONAL RIGHTS

The films discussed in this chapter concern a number of constitutional rights widely recognized by the public. As you consider these films and others that address the same issues, think about the relationship between the public's understanding of certain constitutional rights and how much of that understanding derives from popular culture.

1. The First Amendment and Free Speech

THE CONSTITUTIONAL CONCEPT OF PUBLIC DISCOURSE: OUTRAGEOUS OPINION, DEMOCRATIC DELIBERATION, AND *HUSTLER MAGAZINE v. FALWELL*
Robert C. Post
103 Harvard Law Review 601 (1990)

For centuries the kind of ridicule represented by the *Hustler* parody [of Jerry Falwell] was regulated by the common law tort of defamation. Communications were deemed defamatory if they exposed an individual "to hatred, contempt, or ridicule." The object of the tort was the protection of reputation, which is to say the standing of a person in the eyes of others. . . .

The relationship between dignity and reputation is complex, but the essential idea is that our sense of identity and "worth" depends to a significant degree upon what others think of us. Because individual identity evolves from forms of social interaction, we incorporate into our personality, into our very sense of self-worth and dignity, the institutionalized values and norms to which we have been socialized. This insight was most acutely formulated by George Herbert Mead, who observed that "what goes to make up the organized self is the organization of the attitudes which are common to the group. A person is a personality because he belongs to a community, because he takes over the institutions of that community into his own conduct."

More recently, the sociologist Erving Goffman has demonstrated how the very stability of human personality depends upon the continual reaffirmation of community values and attitudes through the enactment of forms of civility, which Goffman calls rules of "deference and demeanor." In his most famous work, for example, Goffman documented how certain "total institutions," like mental hospitals, prisons, or the military, deliberately violate ordinary rules of deference and demeanor in an attempt to unhinge and alter the identity of new initiates. This strategy works because a person's "self" can be "disconfirmed" if a person is not permitted to participate in the forms of mutual respect which he has been socialized to expect. The dignity and integrity of individual personality thus depend to no small degree upon the maintenance of this respect. . . .

Defamatory communications may be defined as those whose content is not civil, because their meaning violates the respect which we have come to expect from each other. They thus threaten not only the self of the defamed person (causing, among other things, symptoms of "personal humiliation, and mental anguish, and suffering"), but also the continued validity of the rules of civility which have been violated. These rules represent the "special claims which members of a community have on each other, as distinct from others," and hence they embody the very substance and boundaries of community life. The definition and enforcement of these boundaries create for each community "its distinctive shape, its unique identity." The common law's regulation of defamation contains numerous features that attempt to preserve the integrity of these rules of civility, and thus to safeguard not only the dignity and personality of defamed persons, but also the identity and values of the community.

NOTES & QUESTIONS

1. Does this explanation of common law defamation conflict with popular perceptions of the First Amendment right to free speech? Is a film audience likely to know the difference? Is there a danger in their learning about any such difference from a film like *The People vs. Larry Flynt*?

2. If Larry Flynt's portrayal in *The People vs. Larry Flynt* were not favorable, should Flynt be able to sue for defamation? Or are the filmmakers protected by the First Amendment? Does it make any difference that his attorney, Alan Isaacman, has said that, "the movie portrayed him very accurately"? Clay Calvert & Robert D. Richards, *Alan Isaacman and the First Amendment, supra,* 343.

3. Based on the way the movie posits Larry Flynt as a hero of First Amendment jurisprudence, is it possible for audience members unschooled in this area of the law to make a reasoned decision for themselves about whether the ruling was fair? Note that the film never presents the full and exact content of the parody for which Falwell sued *Hustler* magazine. As you read it, consider whether the film presents an unbalanced picture of the dispute when it omits an explicit presentation of the parody's contents.

Hustler's version [of a fake advertisement for Campari] was entitled "Jerry Falwell talks about his first time." The spoof followed the usual Campari format; it featured a thoughtful photograph of Falwell, beneath which was set forth the following "interview":

FALWELL: My first time was in an outhouse outside Lynchburg, Virginia.

INTERVIEWER: Wasn't it a little cramped?

FALWELL: Not after I kicked the goat out.

INTERVIEWER: I see. You must tell me all about it.

FALWELL: I never really expected to make it with Mom, but then after she showed all the other guys in town such a good time, I figured, "What the hell!"

INTERVIEWER: But your mom? Isn't that a bit odd?

FALWELL: I don't think so. Looks don't mean that much to me in a woman.

INTERVIEWER: Go on.

FALWELL: Well, we were drunk off our God-fearing asses on Campari, ginger ale, and soda — that's called a Fire and Brimstone — at the time. And Mom looked better than a Baptist whore with a $100 donation.

INTERVIEWER: Campari in the crapper with Mom . . . how interesting. Well, how was it?

FALWELL: The Campari was great, but Mom passed out before I could come.

INTERVIEWER: Did you ever try it again?

FALWELL: Sure . . . lots of times. But not in the outhouse. Between Mom and the shit, the flies were too much to bear.

INTERVIEWER: We meant the Campari.

FALWELL: Oh, yeah. I always get sloshed before I go out to the pulpit. You don't think I could lay down all that bullshit sober, do you?

At the bottom of the parody, in small letters, was the disclaimer "ad parody — not to be taken seriously."

Reprinted in Robert C. Post, *The Constitutional Concept of Public Discourse, supra,* 606–07. Does seeing the full content of the parody affect your view of whether Flynt should have been able to publish it? If so, what is the impact of the filmmakers' decision to leave it out? If you do not think it makes a difference, why do you think they left it out?

4. Reassess your view of Flynt's right to publish the parody in light of his attorney's later statement that Flynt "said that he intended to cause emotional distress, that he intended to assassinate the character of Falwell. He knew it would hurt him in his profession and that's what he intended." Clay Calvert & Robert D. Richards, *Alan Isaacman and the First Amendment supra,* 337. Do the filmmakers have a responsibility to make this fact clear? Can a magazine publish a piece with such malicious motives and still deserve the protection of the First Amendment? Does the nature of *Hustler*'s content enter into the equation?

5. Do the filmmakers stack the deck in their portrayal of Flynt? On the one hand, the opening of the film establishes him as motivated by money. Not long into the film, however, Flynt declares that his publishing of *Hustler* magazine is "about breaking taboos." When the arrests for obscenity begin, he is portrayed as a crusader for the vendors of the magazine, at one point asking, "Why do I have to go to jail to protect your freedom [to sell porn]?" Do you think Flynt truly was an advocate for the public's First Amendment rights or an opportunist out for his own monetary gain? Is a publisher of pornography a particularly compelling advocate for First Amendment rights? Does it matter, given the broad impact of the Supreme Court's ruling in his favor?

6. In *Hustler Magazine v. Falwell*, the Supreme Court opined:

> [I]n the world of debate about public affairs, many things done with motives that are less than admirable are protected by the First Amendment. . . . There is no doubt that the caricature of respondent and his mother published in *Hustler* is at best a distant cousin of the political cartoons [plainly protected by the First Amendment], and a rather poor relation at that. If it were possible by laying down a principled standard to separate the one from the other, public discourse would probably suffer little or no harm. But we doubt that there is any such standard, and we are quite sure that the pejorative description "outrageous" does not supply one. "Outrageousness" in the area of political and social discourse has an inherent subjectiveness about it which would allow a jury to impose liability on the basis of the jurors' tastes or views, or perhaps on the basis of their dislike of a particular expression.

Hustler Magazine v. Falwell, 485 U.S. 46, 53-55 (1988). Do you agree? Can you think of any examples from popular culture that cross the line? As a legal matter? As a moral matter? Is there anything wrong with letting a jury steeped in the mores of popular culture determine what is "outrageous" and therefore beyond the protection of the First Amendment?

7. Consider the following example, related by Alan Isaacman, Larry Flynt's attorney, who recalls seeing it on television the night before oral argument in the *Hustler Magazine* case.

> I was watching Jay Leno. He was doing a monologue that involved Douglas "K, for Kilo" Ginsburg [during 1987 confirmation hearings from which the Senate declined to confirm Judge Ginsburg's nomination to the Supreme Court]. Leno talked about Ginsburg and his smoking of marijuana, and the show did a little skit that talked about Ginsburg running into this fellow who used to work in the Reagan White House, Michael Deaver. It was very humourous and it made Ginsburg look very silly and Deaver look like a drunk. It was a very ridiculous kind of thing. If I were Deaver or Ginsburg, I would balk at that. I wouldn't want anybody doing that to me. But it was funny, at least if you're not one of those people connected to it.

Clay Calvert & Robert D. Richards, *Alan Isaacman and the First Amendment,* *supra,* 334. Is it disingenuous of Isaacman to say he would be offended by such a spoof of himself when he argued in favor of Larry Flynt publishing much more hurtful statements about Jerry Falwell? If you believe that the Leno skit was protected by the First Amendment, is your opinion at all affected by the knowledge that Judge Ginsburg ultimately was not confirmed to the Supreme Court, in large part because of public reaction to his admission that he had smoked marijuana? Could such media parodies have affected the Senate's decision not to confirm him? If so, should there be any limits on popular discourse about public figures when it could directly harm their public careers?

8. How much impact does popular culture have on the public's understanding of constitutional issues? According to Flynt, the *Hustler Magazine* case received "a minimal amount of [media] coverage," despite the fact that mainstream journalism benefited from Flynt's position. Only with the release of the film *The People vs. Larry Flynt* did the public become widely familiar with the case. *See* Clay Calvert & Robert Richards, *Larry Flynt Uncensored: A Dialogue with the Most Controversial Figure in First Amendment Jurisprudence*, 9 Comm. Law Conspectus 159, 163 (2001). If the public learns more about law from television and films than from newspapers, do filmmakers have a responsibility to correctly and objectively educate them about constitutional rights like those protected by the First Amendment? Is a layperson familiar primarily with just the film likely to have a firm grasp on the meaning of the First Amendment? Does it matter?

9. Are there any limits to the First Amendment's protection of artistic expression? At the Super Bowl halftime show in 2004, popular singer Janet Jackson bared her breast during her performance on live national television. The Federal Communications Commission (FCC)'s Chairman Michael Powell issued the following statement in response:

> I am outraged at what I saw during the halftime show of the Super Bowl. Like millions of Americans, my family and I gathered around the television for a celebration. Instead, that celebration was tainted by a classless, crass, and deplorable stunt. Our nation's children, parents, and citizens deserve better.

Statement of FCC Chairman Michael Powell, issued Feb. 2, 2004 (press release) (*available at* http://www.fcc.gov.html.). Should Jackson's performance be regulated by the government, or is it protected by the First Amendment? If you believe that publicly broadcast television should be regulated, what standards should be used to determine what content is acceptable? Is Jackson, as a recording artist who depends on the public buying her records, in the best position to correctly decide whether her act was acceptable in the current popular culture? Does the FCC's regulation of her performance impede the free development of public attitudes toward women's bodies, or does it protect women's rights?

10. In a 2004 episode of the television series *Law & Order*, a newspaper publishes the name and address of a baseball fan who interfered with a foul ball and caused the Yankees to lose the World Series. The episode was inspired by a comparable incident involving a real-life Cubs fan in a playoff game in Chicago's Wrigley Field. While the real fan escaped with his life, the fictional fan in *Law & Order* was murdered. Did the fictional newspaper have a First Amendment right to publish the information that led to the fan's murder? What about the subsequent discovery by the police of an internet site devoted to tracking the fan's movements? Is such a website protected by the First Amendment?

2.   The Fourteenth Amendment: Equal Protection and Due Process

"WE MUST BE HUNTERS OF MEANING": RACE, METAPHOR, AND THE MODELS OF STEVEN WINTER
D. Marvin Jones
67 Brooklyn Law Review 1071 (2002)

In *Guess Who's Coming to Dinner*, Sidney Poitier, the Denzel Washington of his day, portrays a black male who attempts to break through the barbed wire of an age old racial taboo: he wishes to marry a white woman.

Sidney is a young black doctor in love with the willful, colorblind daughter of an old school white businessman (Spencer Tracy). Wearing a Brooks Brothers suit and a smile as his armor, Sidney comes to the white family's dinner table both as guest and as would be harbinger of the modern age of race relations.

The film thematizes not merely the moral anxiety over the sexual designs of black males. It posed, dramatically, the social and political question of the place of the black male in the new world order following the dismantling — officially at least — of segregation and the racial ideology on which it rested.

Sidney's black male is affluent, culturally hip, and doomed. Striving to be American and black, a rugged individualist and a representative of his race, Sidney lives split between worlds, and split inside himself.

Sidney is, as the black male in the white mind always is, an abstraction: in this case the embodiment of a modern liberalism. This liberalism, rising like a phoenix out of the ashes of World War II — a war against Nazism — dreamed in the colors of the rainbow. This new liberalism rejected the idea that race in a biological sense determined who one was. Anthropologists like Franz Boaz and Otto Kleinberg began unbuilding the myth that intelligence and other mental characteristics had anything to do with heredity: "Culture not racial inheritance was the principle shaping force in determining mental character-istics of a people." Where classical sociology had attributed the poverty of blacks to innate laziness and instability, E. Franklin Frazier, and Charles Johnson, standing on the shoulders of W. E. B. Dubois, began to trace black economic inferiority to environmental causes involving racism. Of course the most pivotal work here was that of Gunnar Myrdal, whose post-war bombshell of a book *An American Dilemma* was cited in the *Brown v. Board of Education* decision itself. Myrdal argues that the practice of segregation was inconsistent with America's own creed and in effect was an obstacle in the road of America's national destiny. . . .

If the black male is always merely a product of the white society's gaze, Sidney is its product as it looks at the black male through the lens of the melt-ing pot story. Through this lens the image of Sidney looks "right." He is well dressed meticulously pronouncing all the endings on his words, trying hero-ically in his behavior to overawe the degraded image of his phenotype. Sidney is a doctor, who happens to be a black male. Thus, it was not Sidney's race or gender that defined him. It was the values he had chosen as reflected by his Ivy League degrees and his Brooks Brothers suit.

In these terms, Sidney's character personified a social proposition: race was like a national costume and could be taken off and exchanged for an American identity. It was axiomatic of cold war liberalism — this was the essence of the *Brown* decision, I think — that not only was the assimilation of blacks possible, but a moral imperative. As Myrdal wrote in his classic *An American Dilemma*: "If America in actual practice could show the world a progressive trend by which the Negro finally became integrated into modern democracy, all mankind would be given faith again — it would have reason to believe that peace, progress and order are feasible.". . .

NOTES & QUESTIONS

1. Professor Jones suggests that *Guess Who's Coming to Dinner* — a film in which no lawyers, courtrooms, or judges appear — is about the United States' post-World War II legal effort to address systemic societal racism. He cites *Brown v. Board of Education*, 347 U.S. 483 (1954), as emblematic of a postwar change in attitude toward race. Does this view of racial change seem correct? Can a Supreme Court opinion change cultural attitudes? Or is it the other way around?

2. How much of a practical impact do Supreme Court interpretations of the Constitution have on popular culture? While the legal right of interracial couples to marry is no longer questioned, how much has it been accepted culturally in the decades after the *Loving* decision? How often are interracial couples portrayed in popular culture narratives? What does the fact that they are particularly rare on television say about popular attitudes toward interracial marriage? Are certain racial pairings more culturally accepted? What might account for this fact?

3. Writing about the film *Snow Falling on Cedars* (1999), Professor Keith Aoki makes the following observation about the relationship between a popular film narrative and the rule of law:

> While the film tries to evoke the pervasiveness of the systemic anti-Japanese prejudice of the day, ultimately it grounds its depiction in a disturbing partial vision of what racism is. The courtroom part of this story really is about the ultimate vindication of the legal system and an optimistic post-war legal liberalism. This viewpoint perceives racism as essentially an aberration, an irrationality, in a system that otherwise works generally well and justly.

Keith Aoki, *Is Chan Still Missing? An Essay About the Film* Snow Falling on Cedars *and Representations of Asian Americans in U.S. Films*, 7 Asian Pacific American Law Journal 30, 35 (2001). Does this criticism apply to *Guess Who's Coming to Dinner* and other popular culture that deals with the legal treatment of race? Does such popular culture suggest that the proper legal outcome will redress what is merely an "aberration" of systemic social racism? If so, is there a danger in presenting this message to the public?

4. Many theorists have criticized film and television shows confronting racial issues for presenting the stories through a white character, thus subsuming the racial issues under the primary concerns and actions of white people. Professor Margaret M. Russell explains that:

> In viewing Hollywood movies as texts about race and the law, one might productively start with questions about origin and perspective. Whether one draws upon *Gone with the Wind* or *Glory* for insights about the Civil War and Reconstruction, the issue of authorial control of the narrative is essential in gleaning a full understanding of this "legal" text as it is with regard to more traditional legal materials such as cases and statutes. Whose story is being told? From whose perspective? Whose experiences are being excluded or distorted, and why?

Margaret M. Russell, *Rewriting History with Lightning: Race, Myth, and Hollywood in the Legal Pantheon*, in *Legal Reelism: Movies as Legal Texts* 178 (John Denvir, ed., 1996). Think about specific works of popular culture that deal with race. Is Russell correct? Do they use a white character to tell the story of the nonwhite characters? If so, is this choice problematic? Does it make the message more accessible to the general public? Or does such a narrative structure perpetuate the very inequality the producers seek to remedy?

5. Professor Russell suggests that questions about authorial control in popular culture "might also serve to highlight the subjectivity of judicial constructions of racial issues in cases often read as objective doctrinal analyses." *Id.* Do you agree? Does the exercise of critically examining how a film tells a story have any bearing on one's reading of judicial opinions? How do the economic and artistic pressures faced by producers compare to the ethical and legal constraints placed on judges? Are the different systems, with their different goals, all that different in the role they play in the social constructions of race?

6. Television in particular has been criticized for its underrepresentation of nonwhite characters. In 1999, a number of civil rights groups, including the NAACP, called for a boycott of network television in protest:

> In 1998, the United States Census Bureau estimated that African Americans comprised 12.7% of the populace; Latinos (designated "Hispanic origin" in Census data) comprised 11.2%; Asian and Pacific Islanders comprised 3.9%. The Screen Actors Guild (SAG), using casting data for 1998 covering 43,686 roles on television, found a continued lack of people of color on television. African Americans were best represented numerically, obtaining 13.4% of all roles on television. Asian American and Pacific Island actors garnered only 2.1% of all roles cast, while Latinos accounted for 3.5% of the acting roles for that year. The SAG report was prescient regarding the controversy over the 1999-2000 network television schedules, noting that "[e]very ethnic minority except Asian/Pacific Americans saw a slight decline in the number of roles they captured."

Gary Williams, *"Don't Try to Adjust Your Television — I'm Black": Ruminations on the Recurrent Controversy over the Whiteness of TV*, 4 Journal of Gender,

Race & Justice 99, 105–06 (2000). How can television be so unrepresentative of the public who watches it? Does legal progress seem unconnected to social progress? Do the statistics Professor Williams cites suggest that the law or popular culture is more progressive? Which should we rely upon to achieve racial equality?

7. However society may deal with race, the Supreme Court has recognized that any government action drawing distinctions between citizens on the basis of race are inherently suspect. *See Korematsu v. United States*, 323 U.S. 214, 216 (1944). The legal status of gay men and lesbians, however, does not receive the same level of constitutional protection. As you read the following piece, consider how important you find this difference given the growing acceptance of gay men and lesbians in popular culture.

SANCTIONING SODOMY: THE SUPREME COURT LIBERATES GAY SEX AND LIMITS STATE POWER TO VINDICATE THE MORAL SENTIMENTS OF THE PEOPLE
Gary D. Allison
39 Tulsa Law Review 95 (2003)

Perhaps as a result of the attention given to the gay community in light of AIDS, gay men and lesbians have achieved a much higher and more positive cultural profile since 1986. The United States Postal Service twice issued commemorative stamps with gay themes — one in 1989 commemorating the twentieth anniversary of Stonewall, and one in 1993 depicting a red ribbon stamp to encourage AIDS awareness.

In 1997, Ellen DeGeneres' character on her prime time television show "[came] out as a lesbian," which was a first for network television. Subsequently, the television networks substantially increased the number of gay characters depicted in their programs. Shows prominently featuring gay characters included "MTV's *The Real World*, . . . NBC's *Will & Grace*, [and] Showtime's *Queer as Folk*." This trend has persisted despite the unsuccessful attempt of the Christian Action Network in March 1999 to force broadcasters to attach an HC (homosexual content) rating to every show with gay characters. In 2003, VH1 aired an infotainment documentary entitled *Totally Gay*, "an explosive, sexy, fast-paced take on the new openness of sexuality in the twenty-first century [that explored how] lines are blurring and [documented] the dramatic changes that have turned the mainstream into the mixed-stream."

American movies portrayed gay men and lesbians in a much more favorable light during the 1990s and into the twenty-first century than they did in the 1980s. In 1994, Tom Hanks won an Academy Award for best actor for his role in *Philadelphia*, in which he played a gay lawyer dying of AIDS who sued his law firm after it fired him upon learning he had AIDS. The film depicts the lawyer and his lover as dignified, loving, well-adjusted individuals triumphing in the face of death and homophobia. Then, in 1995, Whoopi Goldberg played a strong lesbian character who nurtures two heterosexual women through the trials and tribulations of relations gone wrong in *Boys on the Side*. In 2000,

Hilary Swank won an Academy Award for best actress for her portrayal of a transgendered murder victim in the film *Boys Don't Cry* (1999). . . .

[I]n May 1993, *New York* magazine published a cover story "declaring the advent of 'lesbian chic,' which presented female same-sex relationships as glamorous, slightly exotic alternatives to heterosexual relationships." Perhaps this view of lesbianism has become the pop cultural view, for during the 1990s popular singers k. d. lang, the Indigo Girls, and Melissa Etheridge came out as lesbians without much impact on their careers.

The literary world has also become much more accepting of gay men and lesbians. Many bookstores now have gay and lesbian sections. Mainstream presses are publishing many more works by gay men and lesbians. . . .

NOTES & QUESTIONS

1. To what extent do these cultural changes reflect changes in the legal treatment of gay men and lesbians? To what extent is the law influenced by this growing cultural acceptance?

2. Obviously, there are many instances of public rejection of popular representations of gay and lesbian culture. For example, Professor Allison offers a description of how homoerotic art led to an intense local controversy:

> In 1990, the curator of the Cincinnati [Contemporary Arts Center] was charged with obscenity after displaying the controversial homoerotic photographs of Robert Mapplethorpe. The curator was acquitted, but he subsequently left the museum, and the aftermath led Congress to reduce National Endowment of the Arts grants to artists and organizations perceived as supporting homoerotic works.

Gary D. Allison, *Sanctioning Sodom, supra,* 132–33. What accounts for this different treatment of the Mapplethorpe exhibit, in contrast to the growing acceptance of gay and lesbian characters in film, television, and literature? Is it the sexual subject matter of the photographs? The portrayal of a type of gay lifestyle that is deliberately antithetical to the mainstream? Or is it something about the medium in which homosexuality is depicted?

3. Should a politically created fund for the support of the arts like the NEA be influenced by popular cultural attitudes?

4. In 1986, the Supreme Court declared that the Constitution afforded no protection for private, consensual sexual acts between members of the same sex. In *Bowers v. Hardwick*, Justice White, writing for a majority of the Court, reasoned:

> [P]roscriptions against that conduct have ancient roots. Sodomy was a criminal offense at common law and was forbidden by the laws of the original thirteen States when they ratified the Bill of Rights. In 1868, when the Fourteenth Amendment was ratified, all but 5 of the 37 States in the Union had criminal sodomy laws. In fact, until 1961, all 50 States outlawed sodomy, and today, 24 States and the District of Columbia continue to provide criminal penalties for sodomy performed

in private and between consenting adults. Against this background, to claim that a right to engage in such conduct is "deeply rooted in this Nation's history and tradition" or "implicit in the concept of ordered liberty" is, at best, facetious.

Bowers v. Hardwick, 478 U.S. 186, 192–94 (1986). In dissent, Justice Blackmun wrote:

> The Court concludes that [the Georgia statute criminalizing sodomy] is valid essentially because "the laws of . . . many States . . . still make such conduct illegal and have done so for a very long time." But the fact that the moral judgments expressed by statutes like [Georgia's] may be "natural and familiar . . . ought not to conclude our judgment upon the question whether statutes embodying them conflict with the Constitution of the United States." *Roe v. Wade*, 410 U.S. 113, 117 (1973). Like Justice Holmes, I believe that "[i]t is revolting to have no better reason for a rule of law than that so it was laid down in the time of Henry IV. It is still more revolting if the grounds upon which it was laid down have vanished long since, and the rule simply persists from blind imitation of the past."

Id. at 199 (Blackmun, J., dissenting). Who has the better argument? Should the Court interpret the Constitution according to long accepted cultural mores? Or does the meaning of the Constitution change as popular culture changes?

5. In 2003, the Court reconsidered *Bowers* in *Lawrence v. Texas*, 539 U.S. 558 (2003). Justice Kennedy wrote for the majority:

> It must be acknowledged, of course, that the Court in *Bowers* was making the broader point that for centuries there have been powerful voices to condemn homosexual conduct as immoral. The condemnation has been shaped by religious beliefs, conceptions of right and accept-able behavior, and respect for the traditional family. For many persons these are not trivial concerns but profound and deep convictions accepted as ethical and moral principles to which they aspire and which thus determine the course of their lives. These considerations do not answer the question before us, however. The issue is whether the majority may use the power of the State to enforce these views on the whole society through operation of the criminal law. "Our obligation is to define the liberty of all, not to mandate our own moral code." Holmes, *The Path of the Law*, 10 Harv. L. Rev. 457, 469 (1897).

Lawrence, supra, 571. To what extent do you think popular culture influenced the Court's decision to overrule *Bowers* only seventeen years after it was issued? Did the rise of representation of gay men and lesbians in popular cul-ture contribute to the Court's ability to recognize the due process rights of these people? Or did the rise in representation make the general public more accepting and did the Court rely on public perceptions rather than their own beliefs? Is either course an acceptable way to interpret Constitutional rights?

6. *Boys Don't Cry* tells the true story of a transgendered individual, Brandon Teena, who is raped and subsequently murdered after it is discovered that he is biologically female. Brandon's murder seems largely, if not entirely, attributable to Sheriff Laux's treatment of him after he reports being raped. Laux did not issue warrants for the arrest of rapists John Lotter and Tom Nissen for nearly a week, during which time they killed Brandon for reporting the assault. Both the film and the documentary *The Brandon Teena Story* (1998), on which the film is based, include Laux's insensitive and aggressive questioning of Brandon, much of which focused on Brandon's sexuality rather than the assault itself. In 2001, the Nebraska Supreme Court held that as a matter of law Sheriff Laux's conduct toward Brandon Teena was extreme and outrageous and therefore supported Brandon's mother's tort claim against him for intentional infliction of emotional distress. *See Brandon v. County of Richardson*, 624 N.W.2d 604 (2001).

Is it fair to judge Laux by the cultural standards of a public which has been exposed to and is subsequently more comfortable with people who express a sexuality different from the mainstream? Should transgendered status receive heightened constitutional protection in the same way as race in order to account for negative popular attitudes toward transgendered individuals as a class? Or should the Constitution be used to reinforce majority culture?

7. Consider the community in which Laux lived, the town of Falls City, located in southeastern Nebraska, population 4,756 in 1998, when the documentary was made. In the documentary, townspeople refer to Brandon, whom they believed to be a man and were shocked to discover was biologically female, as a "monster," "animal," "fag," and "dyke." The current sheriff repeatedly notes that Brandon was arrested and jailed for forging checks, a sign, in addition to his "misleading" people about his gender identity, that he could not be trusted. Can a film or documentary with a particular and obvious point of view fairly convey the story and the point of view of its participants? In other words, are the real people featured in the documentary treated fairly by the filmmakers?

8. Brandon clearly states at the beginning of *Boys Don't Cry* that, "I'm not a dyke," suggesting that the filmmakers quite explicitly want the public to understand the difference between transgendered individuals and gay men and lesbians. Given the greater cultural acceptance of gay men and lesbians, is this a wise decision? Would encouraging the public to see transgendered individuals as gay be justifiable if it led to greater legal protection for them, even at the cost of a correct cultural understanding of this identity?

9. In *Littleton v. Prange*, 9 S.W.3d 223 (Tex. 1999), the Texas Supreme Court held that Christie Littleton, a transgendered individual, could not file a claim for the wrongful death of her husband because she was born a man and because Texas does not recognize marriages between two individuals of the same sex. Should the court have considered information from nonlegal sources to better understand the difference between transgendered and gay/lesbian identity? Should the sources be limited to purely medical and psychological literature? Or would popular culture such as *Boys Don't Cry* better convey Christie Littleton's situation? If courts rely on popular culture, how should they determine if it is reliable? Is there a sound argument to be made for demarcating a clear distinction between legal decisions and popular beliefs?

10. Professor Julie Greenberg criticizes the *Littleton* opinion for its choice of cultural sources:

> Because the Texas legislature had not provided any guidelines on how to determine a person's sex and Texas case law on the subject did not exist, the court had the opportunity to look at case law and legislation from other jurisdictions, and guidance from experts in other fields, such as medicine and psychology. The court should have based its holding on an examination of the developments in other disciplines, an analysis of the policy concerns that arise in cases involving sex deter- mination, and a comparison of the justifications for the contrary results reached in other jurisdictions on similar cases. Instead, it chose to rely on religious rhetoric, and ruled that when God created Christie Littleton, God created a man that neither the law nor the medical community could turn into a woman.

Julie A. Greenberg, *When Is a Man a Man, and When Is a Woman a Woman?* 52 Florida Law Review 745, 746 (2000). Why shouldn't courts rely on religious beliefs in their decisions? Religious beliefs comprise a distinct and longstand- ing subset of popular culture — one with more stability than the constantly changing attitudes of popular entertainment. Should they be entirely dis- counted in legal reasoning?

11. Phyllis Randolph Frye has used the film *The Cider House Rules* (1999) as a template for how to change the law through extralegal action when it fails to address the cultural reality of transgendered individuals. She explains:

> John Irving's book *The Cider House Rules* and the movie by the same name serve as a clear parallel to the jurisprudential approach we must take toward [a hostile] legal environment. In *The Cider House Rules*, the experiences of Homer and Candy, both at the actual cider house and at the orphanage in St. Cloud, reveal a profound theme that can- not be ignored. In life, we are confronted with sets of rules that are legally imposed or socially ingrained. If these rules are absurd or inap- plicable, we must ignore them to live our lives until we are able to change the rules or create new ones. Similarly, so long as the laws and social mores of society are absurd or inapplicable, transgenders must ignore them and continue to work toward having the rules changed or removed.

Phyllis Randolph Frye, *The International Bill of Gender Rights vs.* The Cider House Rules*: Transgenders Struggle with the Courts over What Clothing They Are Allowed to Wear on the Job, Which Restroom They Are Allowed to Use on the Job, Their Right to Marry, and the Very Definition of Their Sex*, 7 William & Mary Journal of Women & Law 133, 137 (2000). Do you agree? Who decides which groups should ignore the law in order to change it? What about the democratic and legal processes?

12. Where should we draw the line between respect for the rule of law and ignoring it to bring about social and, ultimately, legal change? Bear in mind the difficulty of changing the law, especially the Court's interpretation of the Constitution. As Justice O'Connor has explained:

The obligation to follow precedent begins with necessity, and a contrary necessity marks its outer limit. With Cardozo, we recognize that no judicial system could do society's work if it eyed each issue afresh in every case that raised it. Indeed, the very concept of the rule of law underlying our own Constitution requires such continuity over time that a respect for precedent is, by definition, indispensable. At the other extreme, a different necessity would make itself felt if a prior judicial ruling should come to be seen so clearly as error that its enforcement was for that very reason doomed.

Planned Parenthood of Southeastern Pennsylvania v. Casey, 505 U.S. 833, 854 (1992). Justice O'Connor made this observation in declining, with a majority of the Court, to overrule the Court's 1972 decision in *Roe v. Wade*, 410 U.S. 113 (1973), that a woman's right to choose to terminate her pregnancy is protected by the due process clause of the Fourteenth Amendment. Is there a good reason for *stare decisis*? For the rule of law? Should a rule change with changes in popular attitudes? Does the context in which the question arises — the legal right at issue — influence your answer?

3. The Fourteenth Amendment: Due Process and the Right to Privacy

In its opinion in *Washington v. Glucksberg*, 521 U.S. 702 (1997), the Supreme Court relied on the history of state laws regulating suicide to determine whether physician-assisted suicide is protected by the due process clause of the Fourteenth Amendment. As you read this portion of the Court's opinion, consider the role of popular attitudes in determining unenumerated due process rights.

WASHINGTON v. GLUCKSBERG
521 U.S. 702 (1997)

Chief Justice Rehnquist.

We begin, as we do in all due process cases, by examining our Nation's history, legal traditions, and practices. . . .

[F]or over 700 years, the Anglo-American common-law tradition has punished or otherwise disapproved of both suicide and assisting suicide. In the 13th century, Henry de Bracton, one of the first legal-treatise writers, observed that "[j]ust as a man may commit felony by slaying another so may he do so by slaying himself. The real and personal property of one who killed himself to avoid conviction and punishment for a crime were forfeit to the King"; however, thought Bracton, "if a man slays himself in weariness of life or because he is unwilling to endure further bodily pain . . . [only] his movable goods [were] confiscated." Thus, "[t]he principle that suicide of a sane person, for whatever reason, was a punishable felony" was . . . introduced into English common law. Centuries later, Sir William Blackstone, whose Commentaries on the Laws of England not only provided a definitive summary of the common law but was also a primary legal authority for 18th- and 19th-century American lawyers, referred to suicide as "self-murder" and "the pretended heroism, but real cowardice, of the Stoic philosophers, who destroyed themselves to avoid those ills which they had not the fortitude to endure. . . ." Blackstone emphasized that "the law has . . . ranked [suicide] among the highest crimes," although, anticipating later developments, he conceded that the harsh and shameful punishments imposed for suicide "borde[r] a little upon severity."

For the most part, the early American Colonies adopted the common-law approach.

Over time, however, [they] abolished these harsh common-law penalties. William Penn abandoned the criminal-forfeiture sanction in Pennsylvania in 1701, and the other Colonies (and later, the other States) eventually followed this example.

The movement away from the common law's harsh sanctions did not represent an acceptance of suicide; rather, as Chief Justice Swift observed, this change reflected the growing consensus that it was unfair to punish the suicide's family for his wrongdoing. Nonetheless, although States moved away from Blackstone's treatment of suicide, courts continued to condemn it as a grave public wrong.

That suicide remained a grievous, though non-felonious, wrong is confirmed by the fact that colonial and early state legislatures and courts did not retreat from prohibiting assisting suicide. Swift, in his early 19th-century treatise on the laws of Connecticut, stated that "[i]f one counsels another to commit suicide, and the other by reason of the advice kills himself, the advisor is guilty of murder as principal." And the prohibitions against assisting suicide never contained exceptions for those who were near death. Rather, "[t]he life of those to whom life ha[d] become a burden — of those who [were] hopelessly diseased or fatally wounded — nay, even the lives of criminals condemned to death, [were] under the protection of the law, equally as the lives of those who [were] in the full tide of life's enjoyment, and anxious to continue to live."

The earliest American statute explicitly to outlaw assisting suicide was enacted in New York in 1828, Act of Dec. 10, 1828, ch. 20, § 4, 1828 N.Y. Laws 19 (codified at 2 N.Y. Rev. Stat. pt. 4, ch. 1, Tit. 2, Art. 1, § 7, p. 661 (1829)), and many of the new States and Territories followed New York's example. Between 1857 and 1865, a New York commission led by Dudley Field drafted a criminal code that prohibited "aiding" a suicide and, specifically, "furnish[ing] another person with any deadly weapon or poisonous drug, knowing that such person intends to use such weapon or drug in taking his own life." By the time the Fourteenth Amendment was ratified, it was a crime in most States to assist a suicide. The Field Penal Code was adopted in the Dakota Territory in 1877 and in New York in 1881, and its language served as a model for several other western States' statutes in the late 19th and early 20th centuries. The code's drafters observed that "the interests in the sanctity of life that are represented by the criminal homicide laws are threatened by one who expresses a willingness to participate in taking the life of another, even though the act may be accomplished with the consent, or at the request, of the suicide victim."

American Law Institute, Model Penal Code § 210.5, Comment 5, p. 100 (Official Draft and Revised Comments 1980).

Though deeply rooted, the States' assisted-suicide bans have in recent years been reexamined and, generally, reaffirmed. Because of advances in medicine and technology, Americans today are increasingly likely to die in institutions, from chronic illnesses. Public concern and democratic action are therefore sharply focused on how best to protect dignity and independence at the end of life, with the result that there have been many significant changes in state laws and in the attitudes these laws reflect. Many States, for example, now permit "living wills," surrogate health-care decisionmaking, and the withdrawal or refusal of life-sustaining medical treatment. At the same time, however, voters and legislators continue for the most part to reaffirm their States' prohibitions on assisting suicide.

Attitudes toward suicide itself have changed, but our laws have consistently condemned, and continue to prohibit, assisting suicide. Despite changes in medical technology and notwithstanding an increased emphasis on the importance of end-of-life decisionmaking, we have not retreated from this prohibition.

The history of the law's treatment of assisted suicide in this country has been and continues to be one of the rejection of nearly all efforts to permit it. That being the case, our decisions lead us to conclude that the asserted "right" to assistance in committing suicide is not a fundamental liberty interest protected by the Due Process Clause.

NOTES & QUESTIONS

1. Does the historical evidence of how the law has treated suicide cited by the Court reflect popular attitudes toward the act? Consider the goal of a democratic society to represent the interests of the electorate. Is it possible for assisted suicide to be accepted in popular culture if state legislatures prohibit it?

2. As the *Glucksberg* opinion explains, the Court determines what rights are protected by the due process clause by examining whether there has been a tradition of recognizing the right legally. Should rights be determined by reference to existing law? If so, what check exists on the law itself; what is to prevent legislatures from enacting laws that do not reflect the attitudes of the public? While the democratic process anticipates that the people will elect new representatives who will change the law, is this process realistic politically? Is it possible for such a process to account for our rapidly changing popular attitudes? Think about how quickly information is disseminated and attitudes influenced in our age of Internet dependence and satellite-dish television. Can the democratic process keep up?

3. In *Whose Life Is It Anyway?* Ken Harrison, a thirty-two-year-old man who becomes a quadriplegic after a car accident, rationally decides that he would rather not live in the dependent state in which he finds himself. When Harrison asks to be discharged from the hospital where he receives constant care, including crucial dialysis, Dr. Emerson, the head physician, refuses, contending that death is the "enemy" and he will not allow Harrison to discontinue his own treatment when it will inevitably lead to his death. According to Professor G. Steven Neeley:

> The present state of the law is ill-equipped to deal with Harrison's plight. Although the common law has long recognized the right to refuse life-saving medical treatment, it has simultaneously prohibited suicide. The two traditions were able to co-exist harmoniously until recent technological advances forced them to battle in the medical arena. Harrison is not a terminal patient who could readily refuse medical intervention. Intervention has already taken place, and he can expect to live forty years or more if he remains hospitalized. Withdrawal of life support at this point may well be viewed as suicide — especially if Harrison appears eager to die. The principal reason for his decision to die is his concern for human dignity, which he conceives to be antithetical to a life of total dependence. Even though he concedes that "many people with appalling physical handicaps have overcome them and lived essentially creative, dignified lives," he insists that "the dignity begins with their choice. It would be an indignity to force the others to die against their will, but an equal indignity to force him to remain alive, as a kind of 'medical achievement' against his will. Human dignity is not possible without the acknowledgment of personal sovereignty."

G. Steven Neeley, *Chaos in the "'Laboratory' of the States": The Mounting Urgency in the Call for Judicial Recognition of a Constitutional Right to Self-Directed Death*, 26 University of Toledo Law Review 81, 90 (1994). Is there a popular distinction between refusing medical treatment and committing suicide? If not, is it up to the law to make that distinction? Or should constitutional due process reflect popular mores, however mistaken or ill-examined they might be?

4. In an area like assisted suicide, should popular beliefs carry as much weight as they do? According to Professor Neeley:

> The law surrounding death and dying has failed to keep pace with medical technology. Research and technological innovations in the medical sciences have granted us a higher quality of life than ever before. A mounting concern, however, is the effect this same technology is having upon the quality of dying. Until this century, decisions concerning medical intervention to prolong life probably appeared more straightforward, as physicians had a limited range of effective therapies. Today, in contrast, a diagnosis of serious illness no longer connotes imminent death. "Between 1900 and the present, the causes of death have changed dramatically: communicable diseases have declined sharply while chronic degenerative diseases have become much more prominent." At the turn of the century, the leading causes of death were influenza and pneumonia, followed by tuberculosis and gastritis. By 1976, the leading causes of death were heart disease, cancer and cerebrovascular disease — illnesses which typically occur later in life and are ordinarily progressive for some years before death.

"Consequently, those facing death today are more likely to be aged and to be suffering from one or more ailments for which at least some potentially therapeutic interventions exist." Indeed, the American Medical Association recently estimated that "approximately 70% of all Americans will face a decision to refuse life-sustaining treatment for themselves or a family member at some point in their lives."

Id., 85-86. Given these medical changes, should the opinions only of terminally ill people and their caretakers — people who understand the realities of the situation — be taken into account in determining whether we have a constitutionally protected right to assisted suicide? Is it the responsibility of the media to introduce the general public to the realities of such a politically contested subject so that they can make informed arguments?

5. In *Whose Life Is It Anyway?*, Harrison ultimately seeks a writ of habeas corpus to force the hospital to discharge him, arguing that Dr. Emerson is holding him against his will and inflicting deliberate cruelty in violation of the Eighth Amendment. Would his case be as compelling to the audience if he were not presented as a highly intelligent and articulate person? What if he were not someone who so obviously had considered his options and come to a reasoned decision to end his own life? Is it unfair of the filmmakers to portray him in this way — even choosing the popular actor Richard Dreyfuss to play him? What about the fact that as a sculptor Harrison needs to use his hands in order to do what he loves? Do the filmmakers have a responsibility to present a more balanced story on which to frame this difficult issue?

6. The film *Whose Life Is It Anyway?* is based upon a stage play of the same name. Is there a difference in the responsibility of a playwright, whose work is likely to be seen by a much smaller and more circumscribed audience, versus that of a filmmaker, in presenting politically loaded subjects? Is the responsibility greater when dealing with an issue like constitutional due process, wherein courts determine the substantive parameters of the right by reference to popular beliefs reflected in the law? In other words, if the existence of a due process right to refusing medical treatment needed to keep one alive depends on whether such a right has traditionally been recognized at law, and a popular film could influence popular attitudes toward acceptance of this right enough to cause state legislatures to recognize it, might the filmmakers ultimately be responsible for defining the constitutional right itself?

7. In an episode of the television series *Law & Order* entitled "Painless" (2004), the District Attorney's office uses New York's assisted-suicide statute to prosecute a doctor who supports individuals considering suicide via a website and provides the insulin used by one woman to kill herself. The first jury nullifies the state statute and acquits the defendant. When the defendant is retried based on new and more conclusive evidence, the jury deadlocks, with only a single juror holding out for conviction. Given the potential for such jury nullification, how useful is the Court's reliance in *Glucksberg* on the existence of state statutes to determine there is no constitutional right to assisted suicide? If popular culture about the issue is likely to influence potential jurors, should there be some regulation of the entertainment industry to ensure that the public receives accurate information? Or is the possibility of jurors nullifying on mistaken information simply part of the jury system?

8. In *Whose Life Is It Anyway?*, Dr. Emerson tells Harrison's lawyer, Carter Bell, that Bell's wish to represent Harrison means that "you believe in capital punishment. That's what you're recommending." Is his claim correct? Is it fair to introduce this notion through a villainous character? Is there any way for popular culture to deal with the death penalty neutrally?

9. Is the responsibility of the media greater in dealing with a due process right that is politically contested but not recognized by the Supreme Court? In 1962, a decade before the Supreme Court recognized a woman's right to terminate a pregnancy as protected by the due process clause, the television series *The Defenders* aired an episode entitled "The Benefactor" that advocated for the right. It tells the story of Dr. Montgomery, a physician who began performing abortions after his own daughter's death as the result of a botched abortion. The episode even included the testimony of a sociologist who presented cogent reasons for legalized abortions. The series' creator, Reginald Rose, defended the writers' choice to present their political views on such controversial topics, stating that "Good drama always projects a writer's moral values." *See* David Ray Papke, *The Defenders*, in *Prime Time Law: Fictional Television as Legal Narrative* 5 (Robert M. Jarvis & Paul R. Joseph, eds., 1998).

Is Rose correct? Should television writers be allowed to present such blatantly political views to a loyal audience? What about the fact that many people are not as critical when viewing a fictional story as they might be when watching a documentary or a news show? Are the writers taking advantage of the viewing public?

4. Civil Liberties and Counter-Terrorism

RACE, CIVIL RIGHTS, AND IMMIGRATION LAW AFTER SEPTEMBER 11, 2001: THE TARGETING OF ARABS AND MUSLIMS
Susan M. Akram & Kevin R. Johnson
58 New York University Annual Survey of American Law 295 (2002)

Commentators have observed how popular perceptions of racial and other minorities influence their treatment under the law. As with other minority groups, this proves to be true with respect to Arabs and Muslims.

Feeding on existing stereotypes in U.S. society about Arabs and Muslims, media and film have found a ready audience for dangerous and one-dimensional images. Such depictions contribute to the racialization of Arabs and Muslims.

One-sided film portrayals omit images of Arabs and Muslims as ordinary people with families and friends, or as being outstanding members of communities, scholars, writers, or scientists. Few U.S. movies have depicted Arabs or Muslims in a favorable light, and even fewer have included them in leading roles. Commentators rarely criticize the unbalanced depiction of Arabs and Muslims. The stereotyping and demonizing of Arabs and Muslims by American films may well have gone largely unnoticed because they are entirely consistent with widespread attitudes in U.S. society.

Reinforcing the anti-Arab, anti-Muslim stereotypes portrayed in film public officials have openly used intolerant speech toward Arabs and Muslims — speech that would be deemed clearly unacceptable if directed at other minority groups. For example, a mayoral candidate distributed a campaign brochure in Dearborn, a suburb of Detroit, Michigan, in which he claimed the city's Arab Americans "threaten our neighborhoods, the value of our property, and a darned good way of life." In 1981, the governor of Michigan proclaimed that Michigan's economic woes were due to the "damn Arabs." Such statements by public officials fuel the perception that prejudice and animosity directed at Arabs and Muslims are socially acceptable.

The stereotyping of Arabs and Muslims historically has had a dramatic impact on immigration law and policy. Separate procedures and the selective enforcement of the immigration laws has adversely affected the civil rights of Arabs and Muslims in the United States. The most recent "war on terrorism" has built on previous anti-terrorist measures.

NOTES & QUESTIONS

1. Do you agree with the authors that negative portrayals of Arabs and Muslims in popular culture have contributed to the government's targeting of them in its efforts to combat terrorism? What accounts for public support of government actions that violate the constitutional rights of members of these communities? Is it entirely based on the ethnicity of members of al-Qaeda? Or have past images in popular culture prepared the public to condemn all members of these ethnic groups for the crimes of a few?

2. Are popular portrayals of Arabs and Muslims really so negative? Professor Jack Shaheen claims that they are:

> What is an Arab? In countless films, Hollywood alleges the answer: Arabs are brute murderers, sleazy rapists, religious fanatics, oil-rich dimwits, and abusers of women. . . .
>
> Mythology in any society is significant. And, Hollywood's celluloid mythology dominates the culture. No doubt about it, Hollywood's renditions of Arabs frame stereotypes in viewers' minds.

Jack G. Shaheen, *Reel Bad Arabs: How Hollywood Vilifies a People*, 58 Annals American Academy of Political & Social Science 171, 172 (2003). Is his assessment accurate? Provide specific examples to support your opinion.

3. Professor Shaheen finds the movie *The Siege* "especially alarming. In it, Arab immigrants methodically lay waste to Manhattan. Assisted by Arab-American auto mechanics, university students, and a college teacher, they blow up the city's FBI building, kill scores of government agents, blast theatergoers, and detonate a bomb in a crowded bus." *Id.* at 178. Is the film's portrayal of these actions unfounded? Justified? To what extent is a film like *The Siege* responsible for its negative portrayal of an ethnic, racial, or religious group if it bases this portrayal on real events? *The Siege*, released in 1998, for example, was quite apparently inspired by the 1992 bombing of the World Trade Center. After the September 11, 2001, attack, should the film be read differently?

4. *The Siege* also prominently features the sympathetic Frank Haddad, an FBI agent of Lebanese descent. A close friend of the film's hero, Anthony Hubbard, who is African American, Haddad is instrumental in combating both terrorism and the government's curtailment of the civil liberties of Arab-American citizens. Is it fair of Professor Shaheen to criticize the film for its negative portrayals when the filmmakers included the Haddad character?

5. In *The Siege*, the President ultimately declares martial law in New York City in order to apprehend a terrorist cell attacking within the city; he thereby subordinates the civil liberties of private citizens to the demands of the military. How realistic is this scenario? If it seems unrealistic, how harmful is the film? Can it be seen as harmless Hollywood entertainment dreamed up by writers envisioning an unlikely action spectacle? Consider the pre-9/11 opinion of Major Kirk Davies, a member of the Staff Judge Advocate of the U.S. Air Force:

> Unfortunately, some time in the future, life may imitate art and America's experience with martial law may extend outside the movie theater into reality. It seems obvious that a number of anti-American groups exist both within and without our borders that would not hesitate to employ terrorism and other tactics that could result in upheaval and, perhaps, anarchy within our country.

Kirk L. Davies, *The Imposition of Martial Law in the United States*, 49 Air Force Law Review 67, 111–12 (2000). Do you agree with Major Davies? Is the scenario made more likely by depictions in popular culture of the declaration of martial law? Does a film like *The Siege* make the concept less foreign and more easily accepted by the public?

6. Seemingly as unlikely as the declaration of martial law is *The Siege*'s plotline about the military's internment of all men of Arab descent living in Brooklyn. Does the implausibility of this scenario prevent the film from fueling dangerous popular support for such a notion? Consider the internment of Japanese-Americans during World War II, a practice found constitutional by the U.S. Supreme Court in *Korematsu v. United States*, 323 U.S. 214 (1944). According to the *Korematsu* Court:

> [H]ardships are part of war, and war is an aggregation of hardships. All citizens alike, both in and out of uniform, feel the impact of war in greater or lesser measure. Citizenship has its responsibilities as well as its privileges, and in time of war the burden is always heavier. Compulsory exclusion of large groups of citizens from their homes, except under circumstances of direst emergency and peril, is inconsistent with our basic governmental institutions. But when under conditions of modern warfare our shores are threatened by hostile forces, the power to protect must be commensurate with the threatened danger.

Korematsu v. United States, 323 U.S. 214, 219-20 (1944). To what extent might negative portrayals of Japanese in the "patriotic" films of the era have contributed to the Court's decision? Could the same thing happen today, given the wealth of popular culture about Middle-Eastern terrorists living in the United States?

7. To what extent might stereotypes of Arabs and Muslims contribute to a similar acceptance of internment now? According to Professor David Cole:

> [W]e have not, it is true, interned people solely for their race, but we have detained approximately two thousand people, mostly through administrative rather than criminal procedures, and largely because of their ethnic identity. In addition, we have subjected Arab and Muslim noncitizens to discriminatory deportation, registration, fingerprinting, visa processing, and interviews based on little more than their country of origin. We have not, it is true, made it a crime to be a member of a terrorist group, but we have made guilt by association the linchpin of the war [on terror]'s strategy, penalizing people under criminal and immigration laws for providing "material support" to politically selected "terrorist" groups, without regard to whether an individual's support was intended to further or in fact furthered any terrorist activity.

David Cole, *The New McCarthyism: Repeating History in the War on Terrorism*, 38 Harvard Civil Rights-Civil Liberties Law Review 1, 1–2 (2003). Are these measures the result, at least in part, of how Arab and Muslim people are portrayed in popular culture?

8. In *The Siege*, FBI Agent Anthony Hubbard, played by Denzel Washington, opposes the military's efforts to apprehend a terrorist cell. The audience is told several times that Hubbard has a law degree. Does the depiction of the lawyer opposing the military suggest to audiences that the law (and the Constitution) is the hero and that the military's detention of Arab-American men based on nothing more than their ethnicity is wrong? Does this dynamic prevent the film from fueling public support for similar treatment of real citizens? Or is this theme too subtle in contrast to the action and hysteria of the film's plotline about Arab terrorists attacking New York City?

9. *The Siege* contains scenes in which American military and CIA personnel threaten suspected terrorists with cigarette burns, beat and douse a naked prisoner with cold water as he sits in a freezing bathroom, and even summarily execute a suspect. Do such portrayals of authoritative violence inure audiences to it? Consider the popularity of television shows such as *The Shield* or *NYPD Blue*, in which the police officers/protagonists regularly employ excessive force in order to serve the greater good of law enforcement. Do these "heroes" fuel public acceptance of civil liberties violations in the name of crime prevention? Is there anything wrong with presenting the view that such a use of force may be justified in certain circumstances? Do these shows have their own crime-deterrent effect?

10. If you believe that popular culture depicting with approval state violations of citizens' civil liberties is dangerous, should it be regulated? What role should the government play in policing the media when it may be damaging

the public's respect for constitutional rights? What if the narratives potentially interfere with the government's ability to combat terrorism by stirring
up public sentiment against any curtailment of civil liberties?

D. JUDICIAL ACTIVISM

The Supreme Court radically broadened the scope of rights protected by the
Constitution during the years that Chief Justice Earl Warren presided, 1953–
69. Drawing on your developing understanding of the interaction of law and
popular culture, think about how the Court determines the existence of rights
that were not only unenumerated in the Constitution but also unheard of
when the Constitution was ratified.

THE WARREN COURT AND AMERICAN POLITICS
Richard L. Sippel
48 Federal Lawyer 55 (2001)

Earl Warren, a Republican governor of California, was appointed chief justice by President Eisenhower in October 1953. Chief Justice Vinson had died
after a heart attack with *Brown v. Board of Education* pending, so it was necessary to reargue the case before the Court and its new chief justice. Thurgood
Marshall, the NAACP Legal Defense Fund's chief advocate, won a unanimous
decision that gave meaning to the Civil War. Only 11 pages in length, the decision had to be primarily political in order to take into account the predicted
emotions of the South, where the decision would have its greatest impact. But,
while succeeding as a political argument, it was not a perfect legal opinion,
and from the outset it failed to persuade the South of its legal or moral correctness. Certainly, the Court need not have relied on troublesome sociological
evidence that young African-Americans needed integrated education in order
to succeed. It would have been better for the Court simply to have voided state
segregation statutes by recognizing an equal right for African-Americans to be
free from legislation intentionally directed against them.

But the larger problem that needed to be addressed was institutionalized
segregation in the South, which *Plessy v. Ferguson* had upheld as separate but
equal. Under that entrenched apartheid system, equality could never be
achieved. Granted, through hard work and persistence, the Legal Defense
Fund was succeeding on a case-by-case basis in showing that facilities of
higher education were deliberately made unequal. Unfortunately, such litigation was lengthy, frustrating, and impractical to use against regional segregated secondary school systems. Broad relief from the Supreme Court
presented the only chance to challenge white supremacy in the school systems.
Justice Jackson stated at oral argument why *Brown* was before the Court:
because no relief could be obtained from Congress. Jackson was absolutely
right: at the time, Congress could not even pass anti-lynching legislation.
Brown became the century's flagship case.

After *Brown*, the Warren Court embarked on a crusade to remove obsolete
state laws that interfered with individual rights. But the Court deferred taking up the miscegenation issue so as not to hinder implementing *Brown II*.

And the Republicans' success in portraying Democrats as soft on communism (remember Richard Nixon's slurs on his opponent Helen Gahagan Douglas?) restrained the Court in the domestic security area.

Obscenity passed a watershed when the Court ruled that a work of literature had to be viewed in its entirety and evaluated on the basis of a community's standards, and not just on someone's puritanical impulse. In *Poe v. Ullman*, married couples and a doctor sued to void an 1879 law prohibiting the use of, or advice about, contraceptives. The case was dismissed as not justiciable because no one had been prosecuted, but the issue was later resolved in *Griswold v. Connecticut*, when two counselors were fined for giving advice about contraceptives to married couples. In 1953, there was no right for speedy arraignment of suspected criminals. Nor did convicted criminals have a right to obtain copies of trial transcripts for use in their appeals, let alone the right to counsel. By the early 1960s, those rights were in place, from arraignment through appeal. The Warren Court also took up the apportionment of voting rights, prayer in public school, and the poll tax.

These [Justices] were pragmatists who were survivors of the Great Depression and of World War II — not just constitutional theorists. They believed that they could successfully tackle problems. A feeling of national pride had set in with the election of John Kennedy, a bona fide hero of a good war. That spirit remained even for a time after Dallas, until Lyndon Johnson and Richard Nixon crippled a generation with a bad war.

For Warren, the mantra charge of legislating from the bench was regularly heard, and "Impeach Earl Warren" bumper stickers and billboards were commonly seen. The Court was hardened to it, but those smear campaigns affected voters. The public's reaction to the "liberal" Warren Court was seen in Richard Nixon's successful law-and-order campaign. Nixon won and appointed Warren Burger as his chief justice, and by 1969, the Warren era was over. But the Warren Court had left its mark and the Burger Court could do nothing to upset the bulk of what the former had accomplished. While the Warren Court continues to be criticized in some circles, there is no political movement to return to the constitutional landscape of 1952. Political reality plus *stare decisis* should protect those revolutionary decisions for posterity. . . .

NOTES & QUESTIONS

1. To what extent was the Warren Court likely influenced by the popular attitudes of the times? Do you agree that the Justices' personal experiences living through the Depression and World War II colored their reading of the Constitution?

2. Judge Patricia Wald has written:

[A] judicial hero is different from a military hero whose heroics usually involve acts of physical courage, or a political hero whose heroism may involve daring leadership or a charismatic ability to attract the devotion of crowds of followers. The judicial hero walks a high wire between his natural terrain of declaring and interpreting laws made by others and the jungle of constitutional crises where decisive action may be required to preserve the nation, some groups of citizens within it, or the constitutional pact itself. The judicial hero needs caution and humility on the one hand and boldness on the other and the judgment to recognize when to use either.

Patricia Wald, *Remembering a Constitutional Hero*, 43 New York Law School Law Review 13, 27–28 (1999). Should judges act "heroically" in the way Judge Wald describes and the Warren Court did? Or is their job strictly to interpret the law as it is written? Would it be harmful for the public to be exposed to popular culture in which the judges are credited with changing or expanding the law in a way few do? Or is it important only that trained lawyers understand the true limits of judicial authority?

3. Is the Supreme Court truly an arbiter of change, or is that view itself merely a product of popular perception? Professor John Brigham writes that, "[T]he U.S. Supreme Court . . . is an elemental icon for American law. From the purple curtain behind the bench to the constant flow of traffic in (and almost immediately out) the back door, what we experience of the Court contributes to its considerable authority." John Brigham, *Representing Lawyers: From Courtrooms to Boardrooms and TV Studios*, 53 Syracuse Law Review 1165, 1172 (2003). Do you agree? To what extent is this perception derived from portrayals of the Court in popular culture? Does it make a difference that news cameras are not allowed inside the Supreme Court, so most people have never actually seen it?

4. According to Professor Michael Klarman:

[T]he romantic image of the Court as countermajoritarian savior is shattered by historical reality. The Supreme Court sanctioned rather than attacked slavery, legitimized segregation for much of the Jim Crow era, validated the Japanese-American internment during World War II, sanctioned McCarthyism, and approved sex discrimination until after the emergence of the modern women's movement.

The most celebrated examples of the Court's supposed countermajoritarian heroics are less than compelling. The *Brown* decision was the product of a broad array of political, social, economic, and ideological forces inaugurated or accelerated by World War II; by the time of the Court's intervention, half the nation no longer supported racial segregation. Similarly, *Roe v. Wade* was decided at the crest of the modern women's movement and was supported by half the nation's population from the day it was handed down. Finally, the Court protected gay rights for the first time in *Romer v. Evans* only after a social and political gay rights movement had made substantial inroads against traditional attitudes toward homosexuality.

Michael J. Klarman, *What's So Great About Constitutionalism?* 93 Northwestern Law Review 145, 161 (1998). Is Professor Klarman correct? If so, where do popular notions of the Supreme Court as arbiter of social change come from? Why do even nonlawyers view *Brown v. Board of Education* as the case that brought an end to racial segregation? Is the Warren Court's reputation unearned? If so, why did the public support Richard Nixon in his campaign to reign in the Warren Court?

5. In 1819 Thomas Jefferson wrote that unelected judges had the power to "twist and shape" the Constitution as they wished. The following year, he referred to the judiciary as a "subtle corps of sapper sand miners constantly working under ground to undermine the fabric of our confederated republic." *See* Anthony Chase, *Movies on Trial: The Legal System on the Silver Screen* 18 (2002). Were Jefferson's fears well founded? Is there a danger in judges interpreting the Constitution with no more than *stare decisis* to guide them? Or should the judiciary reflect the tenor of the times?

6. Was the Warren Court justified in influencing and accelerating slowly changing public attitudes, given the important rights it recognized? Or should constitutional law and popular culture remain separate?

Chapter 11

FAMILY LAW

A. FILMOGRAPHY

Baby M (1996)

Kramer vs. Kramer (1979)

Losing Isaiah (1995)

Mr. and Mrs. Loving (1991)

War of the Roses (1989)

B. MARRIAGE

The American style of marriage originated in the Anglo-Saxon tribal society. It included a betrothal through which the bride's family agreed to transfer the bride to the bridegroom in return for property ranging from token amounts to the truly substantial. After the Norman conquest and the increase in Christianity's importance, marriage passed into the hands of the church. Marriages through the church were also standard in the North American colonies, but after the founding of the American republic, civil marriage and common law marriage supplemented Christian ceremonies and covenants. In the present, Americans remain extremely fond of marriage. Nine out of ten say "I do" at least once during their lifetimes, and even the percentage of divorced Americans who remarry is on the rise.

American enthusiasm for marriage, meanwhile, does not mean the states have allowed their residents to marry whenever and whomever they want. Certain of the common state restrictions are uncontroversial. Few would quarrel, for example, with requirements that those entering into marriage be sane or at least sixteen years of age. But other restrictions on marriage have generated controversy. These restrictions invite both actual litigation and pop cultural narratives about overcoming legal impediments to marriage.

1. Interracial Marriage

Some western states barred marriages between whites and Chinese, and most of the southern states had statutes barring marriages between whites and African Americans. "More statutes banned miscegenation than any other form of racially related conduct." Kermit L. Hall, *The Magic Mirror: Law in American History* 157 (1989).

In the post-World War II era and especially after the rise of the Civil Rights Movement in the 1950s and early 1960s, state legislatures began eliminating antimiscegenation statutes. However, as recently as 1967, seventeen states, mostly in the South, continued to prohibit marriages between whites and African Americans. Virginia's statutory scheme dated back to its Racial Integrity Act of 1924, which not only prohibited a "white person" from marrying anyone other than another "white person" but also directed local registrars to maintain "certificates of racial composition" for Virginia residents. *See* Walter Wadlington, *The Loving Case: Virginia's Anti-Miscegenation Statute in Historical Perspective*, 52 Virginia Law Review 1189 (1966). Richard Loving and Mildred Jeter Loving sued, arguing that the Virginia antimiscegenation statute was unconstitutional.

LOVING v. COMMONWEALTH OF VIRGINIA
388 U.S. 1 (1967)

Warren, C.J.

This case presents a constitutional question never addressed by this Court: whether a statutory scheme adopted by the State of Virginia to prevent marriages between persons solely on the basis of racial classifications violates the Equal Protection and Due Process Clauses of the Fourteenth Amendment. For reasons which seem to us to reflect the central meaning of those constitutional commands, we conclude that these statutes cannot stand consistently with the Fourteenth Amendment.

In June 1958, two residents of Virginia, Mildred Jeter, a Negro woman, and Richard Loving, a white man, were married in the District of Columbia pursuant to its laws. Shortly after their marriage, the Lovings returned to Virginia and established their marital abode in Caroline County. At the October Term, 1958, of the Circuit Court of Caroline County, a grand jury issued an indictment charging the Lovings with violating Virginia's ban on interracial marriages. On January 6, 1959, the Lovings pleaded guilty to the charge and were sentenced to one year in jail; however, the trial judge suspended the sentence for a period of 25 years on the condition that the Lovings leave the State and not return to Virginia together for 25 years. He stated in an opinion that:

> Almighty God created the races white, black, yellow, malay, and red, and he placed them on separate continents. And but for the interference with his arrangement there would be no cause for such marriages. The fact that he separated the races shows that did not intend for the races to mix.

After their convictions, the Lovings took up residence in the District of Columbia. On November 6, 1963, they filed a motion in the state trial court to vacate the judgment and set aside the sentence on the ground that the statutes which they had violated were repugnant to the Fourteenth Amendment. The motion not having been decided by October 28, 1964, the Lovings instituted a class action in the United States District Court for the Eastern District of Virginia requesting that a three-judge court be convened to declare the Virginia antimiscegenation statutes unconstitutional and to enjoin state officials from enforcing their convictions. On January 22, 1965, the state trial judge denied the motion to vacate the sentences, and the Lovings perfected an appeal to the Supreme Court of Appeals of Virginia. On February 11, 1965, the three-judge District Court continued the case to allow the Lovings to present their constitutional claims to the highest state court.

The Supreme Court of Appeals upheld the constitutionality of the antimiscegenation statutes and after modifying the sentence, affirmed the convictions. The Lovings appealed this decision, and we noted probable jurisdiction on December 12, 1966.

The two statutes under which appellants were convicted and sentenced are part of a comprehensive statutory scheme aimed at prohibiting and punishing interracial marriages. The Lovings were convicted of violating sec. 20-58 of the Virginia Code:

> Leaving State to evade law. — If any white person and colored person shall go out of this State, for the purpose of being married, and with the intention of returning, and be married out of it, and afterwards return to reside in it, cohabiting as man and wife, they shall be punished as provided in sec. 20-59, and the marriage shall be governed by the same law as if it had been solemnized in this State. The fact of their cohabitation here as man and wife shall be evidence of their marriage.

Section 20-59 which defines the penalty for miscenegation, provides:

> Punishment for marriage. — If any white person intermarry with a colored person, or any colored person intermarry with a white person, he shall be guilty of a felony and shall be punished by confinement in the penitentiary for not less than one nor more than five years.

Other central provisions in the Virginia statutory scheme are s. 20-57, which automatically voids all marriages between 'a white person and a colored person' without any judicial proceeding and ss. 20-54 and 1-14 which, respectively, define 'white persons' and 'colored persons and Indians' for purposes of the statutory prohibitions. The Lovings have never disputed in the course of this litigation that Mrs. Loving is a 'colored person' or that Mr. Loving is a 'white person' within the meanings given those terms by the Virginia statutes. . . .

In upholding the constitutionality of these provisions in the decision below, the Supreme Court of Appeals of Virginia referred to its 1955 decision in *Naim v. Naim*, 197 Va. 80, 87 S.E.2d 749, as stating the reasons supporting the validity of these laws. In *Naim*, the state court concluded that the State's legitimate purposes were "to preserve the racial integrity of its citizens," and to prevent "the corruption of blood," "a mongrel breed of citizens," and "the obliteration of racial pride," obviously an endorsement of the doctrine of White Supremacy. *Id.*, at 90, 87 N.W.2d at 756. The court also reasoned that marriage has traditionally been subject to state regulation without federal intervention, and, consequently, the regulation of marriage should be left to exclusive state control by the Tenth Amendment.

While the state court is no doubt correct in asserting that marriage is a social relation subject to the State's police power, *Maynard v. Hill*, 125 U.S.

190, 8 S. Ct. 723, 31 L. Ed. 654 (1888), the State does not contend in its argument before this Court that its powers to regulate marriage are unlimited
notwithstanding the commands of the Fourteenth Amendment. Nor could it do
so in light of *Meyer v. State of Nebraska*, 262 U.S. 390, 43 S. Ct. 625, 67 L. Ed.
1042 (1923), and *Skinner v. State of Oklahoma*, 316 U.S. 535, 62 S. Ct. 1110,
86 L. Ed. 1655 (1942). Instead, the State argues that the meaning of the Equal
Protection Clause, as illuminated by the statements of the Framers, is only
that state penal laws containing an interracial element as part of the definition of the offense must apply equally to whites and Negroes in the sense that
members of each race are punished to the same degree. Thus, the State contends that, because its miscenegation statutes punish equally both the white
and the Negro participants in an interracial marriage, these statutes, despite
their reliance on racial classifications, do not constitute an invidious discrimination based upon race.

Because we reject the notion that the mere 'equal application' of a statute
containing racial classifications is enough to remove the classifications from
the Fourteenth Amendment's proscription of all invidious racial discriminations, we do not accept the State's contention that these statutes should be
upheld if there is any possible basis for concluding that they serve a rational
purpose. The mere fact of equal application does not mean that our analysis of
these statutes should follow the approach we have taken in cases involving no
racial discrimination where the Equal Protection Clause has been arrayed
against a statute discriminating between the kinds of advertising which may
be displayed on trucks in New York City. *Railway Express Agency, Inc. v.
People of State of New York*, 336 U.S. 106, 69 S. Ct. 463, 93 L. Ed. 533 (1949),
or an exemption in Ohio's ad valorem tax for merchandise owned by a non-
resident in a storage warehouse, *Allied Stores of Ohio, Inc. v. Bowers*, 358 U.S.
522, 79 S. Ct. 437, 3 L. Ed. 2d 480 (1959). In these cases, involving distinctions
not drawn according to race, the Court has merely asked whether there is any
rational foundation for the discriminations, and has deferred to the wisdom of
the state legislatures. In the case at bar, however, we deal with statutes containing racial classifications, and the fact of equal application does not immu-
nize the statute from the very heavy burden of justification which the
Fourteenth Amendment has traditionally required of state statutes drawn
according to race.

The State argues that statements in the Thirty-ninth Congress about the
time of the passage of the Fourteenth Amendment indicate that the Framers
did not intend the Amendment to make unconstitutional state miscegenation
laws. Many of the statements alluded to by the State concern the debates over
the Freedmen's Bureau Bill, which President Johnson vetoed, and the Civil
Rights Act of 1866, 14 Stat. 27, enacted over his veto. While these statements
have some relevance to the intention of Congress in submitting the Fourteenth
Amendment, it must be understood that they pertained to the passage of specific statutes and not to the broader, organic purpose of a constitutional
amendment. As for the various statements directly concerning the Fourteenth
Amendment, we have said in connection with a related problem, that although
these historical sources 'cast some light,' they are not sufficient to resolve the
problem; at best, they are inconclusive. The most avid proponents of the post-
War Amendments undoubtedly intended them to remove all legal distinctions

among "all persons born or naturalized in the United States." Their opponents, just as certainly, were antagonistic to both the letter and the spirit of the Amendments and wished them to have the most limited effect. *Brown v. Board of Education of Topeka*, 347 U.S. 483, 489, 74 S.Ct. 686, 689, 98 L. Ed. 873 (1954). *See also Strauder v. State of West Virginia*, 100 U.S. 303, 310, 25 L. Ed. 664 (1880). We have rejected the proposal that the debates in the Thirty-ninth Congress or in the state legislatures which ratified the Fourteenth Amendment supported the theory advanced by the State, that the requirement of equal protection of the laws by penal laws defining offenses based on racial classifications so long as white and Negro participants in the offense were similarly punished. *McLaughlin v. State of Florida*, 379 U.S. 184, 85 S. Ct. 283, 13 L. Ed. 2d 222 (1964). . . .

There can be no question but that Virginia's miscegenation statutes rest solely upon distinctions drawn according to race. The statutes proscribe generally accepted conduct if engaged in by members of different races. Over the years, this Court has consistently repudiated '(d)istinctions between citizens solely because of their ancestry' as being 'odious to a free people whose institutions are founded upon the doctrine of equality.' *Hirabayashi v. United States*, 320 U.S. 81, 100, 63 S. Ct. 1375, 1385, 87 L. Ed. 1774 (1943). At the very least, the Equal Protection Clause demands that racial classifications, especially suspect in criminal statutes, be subjected to the "most rigid scrutiny," *Korematsu v. United States*, 323 U.S. 214, 216, 65 S. Ct. 193, 194, 89 L. Ed. 194 (1944), and, if they are ever to be upheld, they must be shown to be necessary to the accomplishment of some permissible state objective, independent of the racial discrimination which it was the object of the Fourteenth Amendment to eliminate. Indeed, two members of this Court have already stated that they "cannot conceive of a valid legislative purpose . . . which makes the color of a person's skin the test of whether his conduct is a criminal offense." *McLaughlin v. Florida, supra*, 379 U.S. at 198, 85 S. Ct. at 292, (Stewart, J., joined by Douglas, J., concurring).

There is patently no legitimate overriding purpose independent of invidious racial discrimination which justifies this classification. The fact that Virginia prohibits only interracial marriages involving white persons demonstrates that the racial classifications must stand on their own justification, as measures designed to maintain White Supremacy. We have consistently denied the constitutionality of measures which restrict the rights of citizens on account of race. There can be no doubt that restricting the freedom to marry solely because of racial classifications violates the central meaning of the Equal Protection Clause. . . .

These statutes also deprive the Lovings of liberty without due process of law in violation of the Due Process Clause of the Fourteenth Amendment. The freedom to marry has long been recognized as one of the vital personal rights essential to the orderly pursuit of happiness by free men. . . .

These convictions must be reversed. It is so ordered.

NOTES & QUESTIONS

1. The opinion in *Loving* is noteworthy for forcefully ending racial restrictions regarding marriage and for clarifying features of emerging equal protection doctrine, but in a more abstract sense the opinion is a typical appellate opinion. Chief Justice Warren begins with a statement of the facts, reports on the decisions of the lower courts, reviews the relevant statutes, explores the central arguments and precedents, and enunciates a holding. What might Richard Loving and Mildred Jeter Loving have said about the text of the opinion? Might they have been surprised by what the Supreme Court emphasized? Would they have felt certain important features of their relationship and case were left unmentioned?

2. In part because legal impediments have been removed, interracial marriage has become common in the United States. While 1960 Census figures showed only 149,000 interracial marriages, 2000 Census figures reported 1.5 million. Almost half of the nation's interracial couples live in four states with large minority populations — California, Florida, New York, and Texas — and nearly one in every four interracial marital partners live in California. Latinos and Asians, the two minority groups that are growing the most quickly, marry members of different races at three times the rates of African Americans and five times the rates of Caucasians. Asian women and African American men are more than twice as likely to marry members of other races than are Asian men and African American women. The likelihood of interracial marriage increases with education levels for all racial groups. Tony Pugh, *Interracial Marriages Becoming Commoner*, Indianapolis Star, 24 March 2001, A11.

3. The film industry, like the news industry, has long perceived dramatic potential in the struggles of men and women of different races to overcome societal biases and marry. However, in an earlier era the film industry's self-censorship actually prevented stories of miscegenation from making their way to the big screen. The so-called "Hays Code," named after Will Hays, the head of the Motion Picture Producers and Distributors of America, provided lists of what could not appear in the movies, and the Code was strictly enforced from 1934 until it fell into disuse in the 1960s. This resulted in the laughable absence of toilets in movie bathrooms as well as the less laughable absence of interracial couples. For general discussions of the Hays Code and Hollywood's attempts to censor itself, see Gerald Gardner, *The Censorship Papers: Movie Censorship Letters from the Hays Office, 1934 to 1968* (1987) and Leonard J. Leff & Jerold L. Simmons, *The Dame in the Kimono: Hollywood, Censorship, and the Production Code from the 1920s to the 1960s* (1990).

4. With the Hays Code no longer operative, interracial couples and marriages are routinely seen in the movies and on prime-time television. The Showtime/Hallmark production of *Mr. and Mrs. Loving* (1991) dramatized the *Loving* case itself, with Timothy Hutton taking the role of Richard Loving and Lela Rochon playing Mildred Jeter Loving. The acting is captivating, with Hutton conveying a simple, rough man of few words, and Rochon suggesting how a countrified African American, who had never heard of Martin Luther King, Jr., might develop a political consciousness. Were these portrayals faithful to the real-life Richard Loving and Mildred Jeter Loving? Perhaps, but a film's accuracy is less important than its viability as a pop cultural artifact. Most Hollywood productions are character-driven. These characters need not be complex or conflicted, and, indeed, many film portrayals are stock, that is, we recognize them as types or subtypes and journey with them through the plot. "It is always a character who takes steps, a character who makes choices, a character's responses that drive the story forward or spin it around in new directions. It is a character who overcomes, a character who changes or learns." Suzanne Shale, *The Conflicts of Law and the Character of Men: Writing "Reversal of Fortune" and "Judgment at Nuremberg,"* 30 University of San Francisco Law Review 991, 999 (1996). "The classical Hollywood film presents psychologically defined individuals who struggle to solve a clear-cut problem or to attain specific goals. In the course of this struggle, the characters enter into conflict with others or with external circumstances. The story ends with a decisive victory or defeat, a resolution of the problem and a clear achievement or non-achievement of the goals." David Bordwell, *Narration in the Fiction Film* 157 (1985).

5. How are law and legal institutions presented in *Mr. and Mrs. Loving*? Attention to statutes, rules, and Constitutional Law doctrine is almost completely absent, but there are brief scenes of (1) the Lovings being arrested by Virginia sheriffs, (2) the Lovings being sentenced in the Virginia trial court, (3) Attorney Bernard Cohen of the American Civil Liberties Union interviewing the Lovings in a Washington, D.C. apartment, and (4) Cohen arguing before the United States Supreme Court. Screenwriter and director Richard Friedenberg might be said to have used law to enhance rather than define this dramatic narrative.

2.   Same-Sex Marriage

Some have argued that the issue of same-sex marriage is the modern-day equivalent of interracial marriage in an earlier era. In 2003 the majority of the Massachusetts Supreme Court concluded that same-sex couples in Massachusetts must be allowed to marry.

GOODRIDGE & OTHERS v. DEPARTMENT OF PUBLIC HEALTH
798 N.E.2d 941 (Mass. 2003)

Marshall, C.J.

Marriage is a vital social institution. The exclusive commitment of two individuals to each other nurtures love and mutual support; it brings stability to our society. For those who choose to marry, and for their children, marriage provides an abundance of legal, financial, and social obligations. In return it imposes weighty legal, financial, and social obligations. The question before us is whether, consistent with the Massachusetts Constitution, the Commonwealth may deny the protections, benefits, and obligations conferred by civil marriage to two individuals of the same sex who wish to marry. We conclude that it may not. . . .

We are mindful that our decision marks a change in the history of our marriage law. Many people hold deep-seated religious, moral, and ethical convictions that marriage should be limited to the union of one man and one woman, and that homosexual conduct is immoral. Many hold equally strong religious, moral and ethical convictions that same-sex couples are entitled to be married, and that homosexual persons should be treated no differently than their heterosexual neighbors. Neither view answers the questions before us. Our concern is with the Massachusetts Constitution as a charter of governance for every person properly within its reach. . . .

The individual liberty and equality safeguards of the Massachusetts Constitution protect both "freedom from" unwarranted government intrusion into protected spheres of life and "freedom to" partake in benefits created by the State for the common good. Both freedoms are involved here — whether and whom to marry, how to express sexual intimacy, and whether and how to establish a family — these are among the most basic of every individual's liberty and due process rights. And central to personal freedom and security is the assurance that the laws will apply equally to persons in similar situations. "Absolute equality before the law is a fundamental principle of our Constitution." *Opinion of the Justices*, 211 Mass. 618, 98 N.E. 337 (1912). The liberty interest in choosing whether and whom to marry would be hollow if the Commonwealth could, without sufficient justification, foreclose an individual from freely choosing the person with whom to share an exclusive commitment in the unique institution of civil marriage. . . .

The marriage ban works a deep and scarring hardship on a very real segment of the community for no rational reason. The absence of any reasonable relationship between, on the one hand, an absolute disqualification of same-sex couples who wish to enter into civil marriage and, on the other, protection of public welfare, suggests that the marriage restriction is rooted in persistent prejudices against persons who are (or who are believed to be) homosexual. Limiting the protections, benefits, and obligations of civil marriage to opposite-sex couples violates the basic premises of individual liberty and equality under law protected by the Massachusetts Constitution. . . .

NOTES & QUESTIONS

1. The *Goodridge* decision had been preceded five months earlier by a decision of the United States Supreme Court striking down a Texas statute that criminalized sodomy. *See Lawrence v. Texas*, 539 U.S. 558 (2003). Although this earlier decision did not speak to the question of same-sex marriage, the decision accorded full respect to same-sex relationships. According to Linda Greenhouse, the *Lawrence* decision "was a strikingly inclusive decision that both apologized for the past and, looking to the future, anchored the gay-rights claim at issue in the case firmly in the tradition of human rights at the broadest level." Linda Greenhouse, *Supreme Court Paved Way for Marriage Ruling With Sodomy Law Decision*, New York Times, 19 Nov. 2003, A19.

2. Three of the seven members of the Massachusetts Supreme Court dissented in *Goodridge*. A dissent by Justice Cordy, in which Justices Spina and Sosman joined, concluded by stating:

> While the Massachusetts Constitution protects matters of personal liberty against government incursion as zealously, and more so, than does the Federal Constitution, this case is not about government intrusions into matters of personal liberty. It is not about the rights of same-sex couples to choose to live together, or to be intimate with each other, or to adopt and raise children together. It is about whether the State must endorse and support their choices by changing the institution of civil marriage to make its benefits, obligations, and responsibilities applicable to them. While the courageous efforts of many have resulted in increased dignity, rights, and respect for gay and lesbian members of our community, the issue presented here is a profound one, deeply rooted in social policy, that must, for now, be the subject of legislation not judicial action.

Goodridge & Others v. Department of Public Health 798 N.E.2d 941, 1004 (Mass. 2003).

3. The *Goodridge* decision does not mean same-sex couples may be married in Massachusetts and then expect their home states to recognize those marriages. To begin with, Mitt Romney, Governor of Massachusetts at the time of the decision, informed local officials that same-sex couples should not be allowed to visit Massachusetts and marry during the visit. "Massachusetts should not become the Las Vegas of same-sex marriage," he said. Pam Belluck, *Romney Won't Let Gay Outsiders Wed in Massachusetts*, New York Times, 25 April 2004, A1. Furthermore, the federal Defense of Marriage Act, signed into law in 1997, says states do not have to extend full faith and credit to same-sex marriages from other states, and as of 2004 thirty-eight states had specific statutes saying they would not recognize same-sex marriages from other states. Outline a screenplay for a made-for-television film about a same-sex couple from a state other than Massachusetts and the couple's efforts to marry. Recall from previous discussions that most films are character-driven. How would you portray the same-sex partners? Who would be your "dream actors" for the lead roles? Recall as well that almost all made-for-television films achieve closure: the featured characters succeed or fail. How would your film end?

C. DIVORCE

DIVORCE IN THE MOVIES: FROM THE HAYS CODE TO *KRAMER vs. KRAMER*
Michael Asimow
24 Legal Studies Forum 221 (2000)

Marital trouble and divorce are unpleasant but ever-present realities of modern life. These days, approximately one of every two first-time marriages ends in divorce, and the prospects for later marriages are even worse. Similar patterns apply throughout the first world. But this is nothing new. During the twentieth century, divorce has been a social and economic phenomenon of epic proportions. The divorce rate has advanced steadily, particularly after World War I and throughout the 1920s. It fell during the Depression, but spiked after World War II, stabilized (though at a much higher rate than before the War) during the 1950s, and shot upwards throughout the 1960s, 70s, and 80s. Divorce law reform was a subject of constant controversy during most of the century.

The reasons for the relentless advance in the divorce rate are not difficult to discover. The social stigma attached to divorce diminished steadily; the more people that got divorced and survived the experience, the more others wanted to follow in their footsteps. Divorce laws were liberalized. Perhaps most important, in the early part of the century and especially between WWI and WWII, a new paradigm for marriage took hold. In the old days, most people viewed marriage as a matter of social status and a lifetime commitment to furnish mutual financial and homemaking support. Long-term love and happiness might be an unexpected and welcome byproduct, but few people thought such things were essential. Under the new paradigm, people came to believe that marriage should bring happiness and personal fulfillment. Since marriage frequently fails to provide happiness and fulfillment to one or both partners, a great many marriages fail to meet expectations. Such marriages are doomed to disintegrate, and divorce generally follows.

At the same time, women reevaluated their roles and came to believe that they were socially and economically equal to men; they rejected the idea that men and women inhabited their own spheres, the woman at home and the man in the world. Women's economic opportunities improved, making divorce a realistic option for many more women. Women renounced the sexual double standard. They believed they were entitled to escape from dreary, loveless, or abusive marriages, and they thought they could manage economically without male support. As more and more women internalized these feminist sentiments, more of them decided to leave their marriages.

The eternal process of marital breakdown and divorce is full of dramatic possibilities. During the pre-divorce phase, the parties become increasingly incompatible and unhappy in their lives together. Frequently, there are complex and clandestine love affairs outside of marriage; deception, jealousy, and betrayal; emotional upheaval; disruption of the lives of children; and economic warfare. The routine of everyday life is shattered. During the post-divorce phase, one or both parties may find themselves physically and emotionally isolated; others turn to promiscuity. Forced out of the shelter of the household, many women find satisfying new careers; others find that the world of work holds nothing for them. Often one ex-spouse's standard of living rises while the other's plummets. One partner's true personality blooms when freed from the stifling constraints of marriage; another's joy of life is snuffed out. A high divorce rate insures that there are plenty of complex blended families with multitudes of stepchildren and ex-spouses.

This sort of highly dramatic material should be the subject of countless film scenarios, right along with such staples as romance, love, marriage, and childbirth. After all, a high percentage of adults have been divorced at least once;

everyone else has friends or relatives that have been divorced. A substantial percentage of young people have experienced their parents' divorce. All of these people can empathize with the travails of fictional characters whose marriages disintegrate. And they should, therefore, be willing to buy tickets to dramatic or comedic movies that center on divorce.

These days, movies routinely dwell on the emotional and financial prequels and sequels to divorce. Divorce is the obvious and natural platform for numerous modern film stories: *Living Out Loud* (1998) focuses on the loneliness of a divorced woman; *Husbands and Wives* (1992) explores the struggles of two newly divorced couples. *As Good As It Gets* (1997) deals with the difficulties of single parenthood; *Music of the Heart* (1999) features a divorced woman who, by necessity, starts a fulfilling new career; *Mrs. Doubtfire* (1993) centers on a father's unusual tactics to live with his kids; *Stepmom* (1998) deals with the travails of two moms, the kids, and the dad; *The First Wives Club* (1996) features a group of embittered ex-wives out for a little revenge; a black woman is abandoned by her husband for a younger white woman in *Waiting to Exhale* (1995). And there are countless others. . . .

NOTES & QUESTIONS

1. Would you add to or subtract from the reasons Professor Asimow gives for the rising divorce rate? In a widely discussed history of twentieth-century American divorce, J. Herbie DeFonzo maintains that the passage of no-fault divorce laws grew out of an effort to channel divorces into the therapeutic environment of urban family courts. *See* J. Herbie DeFonzo, *Beneath the Fault Line: The Popular and Legal Culture of Divorce in Twentieth-Century America* (1997).

2. One of the divorce-related films Asimow does not mention specifically is *The War of the Roses* (1989). In the following excerpt, Ira Lurvey, a California divorce lawyer, and Selise E. Eiseman, a Hollywood screenwriter, argue that the film is an especially revealing portrayal of the modern-day divorce process.

DIVORCE GOES TO THE MOVIES
Ira Lurvey & Selise E. Eiseman
30 University of San Francisco Law Review 1209 (1996)

If the multitude of divorce films produced during the past century has shown Hollywood to be ahead of reality, the quintessential divorce movie may be *The War of the Roses*. It shows not only the current state of the divorce process, but the illogic of continuing without meaningful change.

From its brilliant title, which can be interpreted to mean various things, to its black satire on Yuppie materialism and its devastating climax in the chandelier scene, *Roses* seems to sum up the present bleak state of the divorce process. If war is hell, *Roses* says, then divorce is worse!

Not without small irony, Danny DeVito, one of Hollywood's most talented and versatile character actors, elects here not only to serve as the film's director, but as the divorce attorney as well. As director, he presumably has put his imprint on the production. As the divorce attorney cum narrator, he tells us in effect that the process was totally outside his control.

It did not have to be that way. Instead of just shrugging away at various times in the plot when his increasingly hysterical client, Oliver Rose, requested legal acts or advice, DeVito could have tried to return moderation to the matter. The movie does not even try to suggest such a possibility. DeVito is a hired gun. Perhaps a wiser, more sensitive and perceptive gun than the usual stereotypic divorce lawyer, but a total mercenary nevertheless.

For those who may have forgotten, *Roses* is a story about the sheer horror of an uncontrolled divorce. As Oliver and Barbara Rose, Michael Douglas and Kathleen Turner show how wonderful it was to be young and beautiful and falling in love in the 60s. The days were filled with sunshine and promise; the lovers were filled with one another. Life was dreams and romance and soft strings of background music so well integrated to the whole that you only hear it when you listen closely. This was how boy-girl movies used to end.

In *Roses*, however, it is just the beginning. Marriage, the movie tells us, is just the overture to tragedy.

With time but seemingly little effort, Oliver becomes a successful lawyer. Barbara becomes an extraordinary housekeeper. At this point, it is *Stepford Wives* revisited. The couple has two children, who grow normally and healthfully and eventually move away to school or adulthood. It has been a "marriage of long duration."

Barbara now "awakens." Selling some of her "wonderful" liver pate to a neighbor, she realizes that true independence lies in self-employment as a caterer. Somehow, because there is a lot more plot yet to cover in only a short remaining time, this discovery leads Barbara to tell Oliver that she wants a divorce as well as the house and furnishings that she says she created during the marriage. Oliver presumably can keep his law practice.

As in reality, however, it does not end that simply. What follows is a series of escalating interactions between Oliver and Barbara so vicious and mean-spirited that it has made *Roses* a classic of what is wrong with the divorce process.

When the "war" is over, with the Roses swinging like pre-Darwinian apes from their prized chandelier, scorched earth as a policy of battle is made to seem a term of endearment.

The movie often is billed as black comedy. It has been critiqued as a satire on materialism. According to DeVito, no marriage ever is happy for long.

There may be a larger, and more constructive, message as well. Viewing the horror for the absurdity it is may teach that divorce is survivable if each spouse is willing to compromise.

Barbara states that she just wants the house because it represents her adult achievement. She remodeled it and picked the furniture. Oliver says the house should be his because he earned the money that permitted its purchase and development. *Roses* says that both are right and neither is: if spouses cannot share, neither will get anything.

The moral is both accurate and Draconian. It is accurate because it portrays what all too often is the result of modern divorce. It is Draconian because it discounts as worthless to mitigate human nature, both the role of the intelligent divorce lawyer and the entire legal process.

For example, what if Barbara was correct? What if she should have received the house and furnishings? What if Oliver was being unreasonable in seeking to deny them to her? Was the message of *Roses* that there is no recourse when one spouse is being unreasonable?

Perhaps that is why *Roses* has become so classic an example of the genre. Perhaps we face now an era (hopefully temporary!) when most persons have lost faith in any process mitigating the horrors of their personal lives and emotions. DeVito as the seemingly hopeless divorce lawyer can do no more than stand by at the beginning and end to tell us the story, smoking a big, comforting cigar. Has a fascination with greed and self-absorption so clouded thinking that even the mythmakers of Hollywood cannot break through?

After one hundred years of examining the issue, is the ultimate message the movies have for us on the subject of divorce that clients will fiddle while lawyers' cigars burn? We moviegoers may have a right to expect much more from our beloved silver screen. . . .

NOTES & QUESTIONS

1. Lurvey and Eiseman seem to assume that Hollywood filmmakers have an obligation to critically contemplate divorce, divorce law, and divorce law reform. They speak of Hollywood's "clouded thinking" and suggest "moviegoers may have a right to expect much more from our beloved silver screen." What are the responsibilities of the film industry with regard to legal education? What might viewers legitimately expect of their films? Hollywood's ultimate goal might be the production of dramatic, engaging films that will attract viewers and generate profits. As a result, Hollywood could be expected not to make a pitch for divorce law reform but rather to portray divorce in ways that capture viewers.

2. Lurvey and Eiseman suggest *The War of the Roses* might be best understood as a "black comedy," that is, a work in which naïve, inept, or pernicious characters find themselves part of a tragic farce that is both comic and horrifying. Why might black comedies be especially appealing to present-day filmgoers? *See* Max F. Schultz, *Black Humor Fiction of the Sixties* (1980).

3. As Lurvey and Eiseman mention, Danny DeVito's Gavin D'Amato in *The War of the Roses* is both Oliver Rose's divorce lawyer and the film's narrator. He is frustrated when his suggestions are ignored and the Roses' battle escalates. In reality, many real-life divorce lawyers take firm, managerial control of their divorce cases. Is this part of the reason that when the divorce process is complete, clients often end up disliking their own lawyers?

4. The best-known pop cultural divorce lawyer of the late-1980s and early 1990s was Arnie Becker. A conniving practitioner and insatiable womanizer, Becker was one of the featured lawyers in the popular prime-time series *L.A. Law* (1986–94).

TAKING *L.A. LAW* MORE SERIOUSLY
Stephen Gillers
98 Yale Law Journal 1606 (1989)

Today, an informal group of teachers of legal ethics, I among them, periodically meet to discuss how to teach the course. Inevitably, our discussions include scenes from *L. A. Law*.

My favorite episode is one in which Arnie Becker, the film's sometimes shallow (but always adept) divorce lawyer, meets with Lydia, a woman nearing forty who has decided to accept her husband's settlement offer. Lydia has come to Arnie because her original lawyer, Julia, had qualms about the settlement and urged Lydia to talk to Arnie about it. Lydia tells Arnie she does not want a fight. "I just don't want to get into an ugly, pitched battle with name calling and recriminations," she insists. *L.A. Law* (NBC television broadcast, Sept. 15, 1986).

On the very morning of the day he meets Lydia, a gun-carrying former client threatened Arnie because he had not stopped her from accepting a settlement she now realized was too low. In the interim, the former client had learned that her husband had "another woman" and that they were living in Bel Air while Arnie's former client was living out in Van Nuys. With the memory of that assault still painfully present and based on his years of experience as a divorce lawyer, Arnie tells Lydia that her husband surely has another woman. He urges Lydia to be more aggressive in protecting her economic interests. Lydia does not believe there is another woman or doesn't want to believe it — "My husband and I are not statistics," she declares, "we're individuals." Arnie responds: "For your husband, divorce is a fiscal inconvenience. But for you, this can be the most important financial decision that you make in your life."

At the conclusion of their meeting, Lydia is wavering. Citing "friendship to Julia" and "admiration for your principles," Arnie offers to review the proposed settlement agreement and tell Lydia his conclusions over lunch at a fancy restaurant that following Thursday. Meanwhile, without Lydia's knowledge, Arnie has his private detective surveil the husband. She succeeds in getting several eight by ten glossy photographs of Lydia's husband and the inevitable other woman in very compromising positions, all of which are meticulously described.

Arnie takes the glossies to the fancy lunch, where Lydia informs him that she has decided to accept the settlement offer. "In the long run, there are more important things than money," she insists. Tapping the envelope containing the glossies, Arnie muses that he will just put the "investigation" of her "husband's affairs, financial, otherwise" on hold. Predictably curious, Lydia asks if it will obligate her financially to look in the envelope. "In no way," Arnie assures, but then in a rare burst of compassion, he warns Lydia that "it may be painful." Of course she looks, then quickly escapes to the lady's room to give up her lunch, as nonchalant Arnie had previously told the investigator she would. Arnie summons the waiter for dessert.

In the next scene, a retributive Lydia, in a sit-down with her husband and counsel, can hardly contain her anger as she hurls insults and her pocketbook across the conference table. Arnie uses other, financial information the investigator obtained to force the husband to increase his offer considerably. The not-so-veiled threat is that otherwise the information will get the husband in trouble with the law. . . .

Afterwards, Arnie is pleased with himself ("we really socked it to them"), but Lydia is crying uncontrollably. She tells Arnie: "I think what you did was despicable. I'll never be able to look at him again with any kind of respect or affection." For Arnie, she says, it was "all so easy. . . . Just sock it to him and get the money. I lost my life, my children lost a family. And there's no amount of money that would compensate for that." Arnie asks Lydia if she wants to return the money. She does not. Having thereby proved his point to his own satisfaction, Arnie predicts that in two weeks Lydia will be recommending him to a friend. In two months, she will be inviting him to dinner. . . .

Client autonomy is an ethical issue. It is the analogue in law to informed consent in medicine. It is difficult to define and harder to teach. The episode I have just described (and my summary does not do it justice) is nearly perfect in presenting the autonomy issue in equipoise. Without his client's permission, Arnie Becker used an investigator to obtain a legally irrelevant but inflammatory fact — opposing counsel points out that in California the husband's affair has no bearing on the grant of a divorce or support obligations. Arnie then used that fact to get his client angry enough to fight for a larger settlement, employing weapons that would inevitably destroy the modicum of civility the couple still enjoyed and which Lydia had declared at the outset she wanted to retain.

Did Arnie exceed his authority when he connived to override his client's stated wishes in order to secure the money he truly (perhaps correctly) believed she would later regret not having? Should he have requested Lydia's authorization before hiring a detective to follow her husband? Did he give insufficient respect to Lydia's declaration that "there are more important things than money"? Did Arnie manipulate Lydia? Or did he save her? Whichever he did, did he act properly? . . .

NOTES & QUESTIONS

1. In addition to using questionable techniques and tactics in his divorce practice, Arnie Becker flirts with and takes advantage of his attractive female clients. In the episode discussed by Professor Gillers, Arnie also mentioned to Lydia that she would "look great in or out of a bikini." There is evidence to suggest that some actual divorce lawyers behave in similarly troubling ways. A survey revealed that of 508 responding divorce lawyers one in five had had sex with a client or knew another lawyer who had. Stephen Labaton, *Are Divorce Lawyers Really the Sleaziest?* New York Times, 5 Sept. 1993, E5.

2. Charles B. Rosenberg, a Los Angeles attorney, served as the legal advisor to *L.A. Law*. His assignment was to make the laws and legal proceedings in the series as accurate as they could be given the demands of creating engaging television drama. Rosenberg recognized that one of the keys to the series' popularity was the interesting characters. Viewers could feel sympathy, empathy, and antipathy for them. Arnie Becker and Douglas Brackman, Jr., McKenzie, Brackman, Chaney & Kuzak's penny-pinching managing partner, "are good examples of characters in whom the initial interest was generated by antipathy." Charles B. Rosenberg, *Inside* L.A. Law, ABA Journal, Nov. 1988, at 57.

D.   CHILD CUSTODY

Not only the husband and wife but also the couple's children experience the pain, anger, and confusion associated with divorce. Each year over two million children are required to cope with their parents' divorces, a figure that has tripled since 1960. Experts now project that more than half of all the children in the United States will experience the divorce of their parents before their eighteenth birthdays. Michael Asimow, *Divorce in the Movies: From the Hays Code to "Kramer vs. Kramer,"* 24 Legal Studies Forum 221, 257 (2000).

The great majority of divorcing parents are able to agree on the post-divorce custodial arrangements for their children, but popular culture, not surprisingly, delights in the drama of custody fights. Indeed, popular culture sometimes bends and misportrays legal standards in order to enhance the drama of a custody fight.

PEACE BETWEEN THE SEXES: LAW AND GENDER IN *KRAMER vs. KRAMER*
David Ray Papke
30 University of San Francisco Law Review 1199 (1996)

When scholars contemplate law and legal proceedings in popular culture, there is perhaps an inevitable tendency to turn to considerations of accuracy. Edward Bennett Williams, the famous trial lawyer, complained before his death that Perry Mason and a bevy of other fictional lawyers from prime-time television in the 1950s and 1960s created unrealistic expectations. With Mason always dramatically exonerating his innocent client and identifying the true perpetrator, clients, jurors, and others were invariably disappointed when real-life criminal defense lawyers proved much less resourceful. Even the very best of criminal defense lawyers, Williams noted, are lucky to win acquittals in the majority of their cases. More specifically, Charles and Mariann Pezella Winick have added that, although cross-examination is important to criminal trials, actual witnesses rarely break down on the stand and confess the way they often do in fictional television trials. Taking this variety of cultural criticism even one step further, Jon L. Breen argues explicitly that the "accuracy" of a trial in popular culture is a crucial issue in critical evaluation. Breen lists and thereby denigrates three especially inaccurate courtroom novels: William Ard's *Hell is a City*, Harold R. Daniels' *The Accused*, and Barbara Frost's *Innocent Bystander*.

Both at the time of its release and more recently, *Kramer vs. Kramer* has itself prompted this type of criticism. After previously reviewing the movie and reporting on the popular hubbub it generated, *Time* doubled back to explore the child custody questions the movie addresses. Much of *Kramer vs. Kramer*, *Time* concluded, was "legally out dated.". . .

Criticism of this sort does no harm, and there is indeed something to be gained from alerting the citizenry to differences between the law and legal proceedings in popular culture and what might be understood as "real life." However, those who are determined to apply a legal truth test to popular culture, or to *Kramer vs. Kramer* in particular, should also realize that the "legal inaccuracies" are not mistakes, much less attempts to dupe the lay public. Critics with a bent for noting "legal inaccuracies" should dismount the high horse of expertise and recognize that cultural conventions and prescriptions, much more than faithfulness to the law, shape works of popular culture.

In *Kramer vs. Kramer*, as previously suggested, law provides the movie's gender battlefield, and in particular, the producers employ a resurrected and misrepresented maternal preference standard. If one reviews the history of American child custody standards, one is struck by the amazing shifts with regard to gender. In the early Republic, when divorce was rare by modern standards and sometimes granted by legislatures rather than courts, child custody almost always went to the father. This paternal preference began to disappear in the mid-nineteenth century, and in the decades after the Civil War the "tender years" approach settled into place. Reflecting a Victorian sense that the mother was the true nurturer and care giver for children, the "tender years" doctrine resulted in custody awards to the mother whenever there was a contest over young children. Then, in still another striking shift in the second half of the twentieth century, this doctrine also gave way. Due to legal arguments couched with reference to state and federal equal protection standards, and more generally to shifting gender norms, courts moved to a gender-neutral standard and attempted to determine which custodial option would be in the "best interests of the child." A few states seemed stalled in the Victorian Age, but Justice Brennan's stern words in an opinion invalidating an Alabama statute that made only husbands and not wives susceptible to alimony, should have provided pause:

> Legislative classifications that distribute benefits and burdens on the basis of gender carry the inherent risk of reinforcing the stereotypes about the "proper place" of women and their need for special protection. . . . Thus, even statutes purportedly designed to compensate for and ameliorate the effects of past discrimination must be carefully tailored. Where, as here, the State's compensatory and ameliorative purposes are as well served by a gender-neutral classification as one that gender-classifies and therefore carries with it the baggage of sexual stereotypes, the State cannot be permitted to classify on the basis of sex.

By 1979, the year in which *Kramer vs. Kramer* was released, New York (the state where the movie is set) had abandoned maternal preference and moved to a "best interests" test, but you would never guess it from the movie. Attorney Shaughnessy, played by veteran actor Howard Duff, warns Ted Kramer that courts favor mothers in custody battles over young children. The task, Shaughnessy is certain, is to prove Joanna is an unfit mother. Shaughnessy also apparently overlooks the fact that the parties had already divorced (admittedly off-screen), and Ted had custody, so the issue was not custody per se but rather custody modification. Even assuming a maternal preference rule, modification hearings place great weight on maintaining child care continuity. Real law notwithstanding, fictional Judge Atkins sees things the way attorney Shaughnessy does. Atkins' award of custody to Joanna Kramer relies almost completely on the "tender years" approach. Atkins, in Shaughnessy's words, "went for motherhood right down the line.". . . .

NOTES & QUESTIONS

1. When *Kramer vs. Kramer* was released, members of the divorce bar pointed out the film's misleading characterizations of child custody law. *See Custody: Kramer vs. Reality*, Time, 4 Feb. 1980, 77.

2. With good reason, Ted Kramer asks his attorney if the trial court decision might be appealed, but Shaughnessy discourages him by warning that on appeal he will have to put Billy on the stand. Parties, of course, do not testify in appellate proceedings, and the film in this sense continues to proffer legal inaccuracies. What themes might the legal inaccuracies in *Kramer vs. Kramer* enhance? Why might the producers have chosen to present the law as they did?

3. The modern standard in custody disputes in almost all jurisdictions is the best interests of the child. The following excerpt attempts to explain why the standard has continued to control even though many have underscored its weaknesses.

WHY HAS THE BEST-INTEREST STANDARD SURVIVED? THE HISTORIC AND SOCIAL CONTEXT
Janet L. Dolgin
16 Children's Legal Rights Journal 2 (1996)

For almost two centuries, American family law has asserted that it places children and their welfare at the heart of custody and parentage determinations. That statement, institutionalized in the United States as the "best-interest" standard (or principle), has become almost impossible to attack. However, the best-interest standard is widely criticized for providing little concrete guidance to courts asked to settle disputes involving children's custody. The standard, as applied, grants courts remarkable flexibility. As a result, reliance on the standard ensures widely discrepant, even contradictory, results in custody cases, depending on the presiding judge. The standard, presumed to determine and protect the interests of children, more often seems to encourage courts to focus on and to protect the interests of the disputing adults.

The consistency with which state legislatures have historically required courts to apply the best-interest standard, or with which courts themselves have depended upon judicial precedent for applying the standard, is puzzling in light of the steady flow of criticism that has been applied to the standard since its inception. From time to time, negative appraisals of the standard have resulted in statutory adjustments, but not in a definitive replacement of the standard with an essentially different approach to custody determinations.

The continued vitality of the best-interest standard as the central principle in custody cases seems puzzling. However, its success can be explained. That explanation, which depends on an examination of the historic context within which the standard developed and within which it has been applied, suggests that the survival of the best-interest principle is essentially unrelated to actual children and the protection of their interests. . . .

The principle has been used to assimilate and justify a shifting array of assumptions and conclusions about custody, and sometimes about parentage. The principle can be, and has been, used to prefer mothers; to prefer fathers; to prefer joint custody; and to prefer "psychological," over biological parents; or biological over psychological parents. In every case to which it is applied, the best-interest principle asserts that children constitute the primary concern of the law. In so asserting, the principle associates itself, and the results to which it leads, with old-fashioned, decent, proper families. And thus the principle always sides with tradition. But, equally, the best-interest principle sides with modernity. It can justify both tradition and the changes that undermine tradition. It affirms the continuing value of traditional family life despite widespread social upheaval and at the same time, masks, and thus helps to ensure, departures from tradition. The best-interest principle has served modernity and transformation in the name of social continuity and tradition. Thus, it has survived and remained central to the law's regulation of family matters during a long period of astonishing transformation in the form and meaning of family.

NOTES & QUESTIONS

1. The survival of the standard does not mean that "gender wars" in the area of child custody have ended. Women and men both sometimes feel that the standard allows the "other side" to prevail unfairly. One scholar has attempted to capture the contradictions for a female feminist seeking child custody:

> Motherhood is the central dilemma in feminist thinking. Some feminists argue that the family contributes as much to women's subordination in society as discrimination in the workplace. The stereotype of women as "natural" mothers, they claim, has shackled women to the family and prevented their rise in the outside world. Other feminists, however, point out that mothers still perform the great bulk of child-raising duties both within marriage and increasingly outside of it,

and they need support in that effort. To deny their motherhood, these feminists believe, is to disadvantage them and their children.

Nowhere is this more evident than in cases involving child custody. As a result of the rejection of the maternal law, mothers have lost the special protection of the law afforded them in their "natural" role as custodians of young children. Many feminists are reluctant to challenge this new direction in the law; they fear that fighting such a trend would encourage the stereotyping of women as "natural mothers," which could be used against them by men in the home and in the workplace.

Mary Ann Mason, *The Custody Wars: Why Children Are Losing the Legal Battle, and What We Can Do About It* 12 (1999).

2. Some fathers, meanwhile, have argued that behind the façade of the child's best interests many family law judges continue to favor mothers in contested child custody cases. This perception, in turn, is a major impetus for the contemporary fathers' rights movement. The leaders of the movement also point to what they take to be an anti-father bias in support awards, the denigration of so-called "deadbeat dads," the toleration of visitation-blocking mothers, and the refusal to respect DNA evidence of nonpaternity. *See* William C. Smith, *Dads Want Their Day*, ABA Journal, Feb. 2003, at 38.

3. The relationship of gender and child custody decisions has proven to be a gold mine for popular culture. Filmmakers and other producers of popular culture have used child custody battles to explore a wide range of issues regarding gender in contemporary society. In *The Good Mother* (1988) a divorced mother played by Diane Keaton loses custody of her daughter to her ex-husband after her lover innocently allows the daughter to touch his genitals. In *Striptease* (1996) a Florida stripper played by Demi Moore tries to enlist an infatuated Congressman in her struggle to regain custody of her daughter from her ex-husband. In *When Innocence is Lost* (1997) a single mother returning to school loses custody when at trial her husband argues the child is better off in the care of his own mother than in day care.

4. Custody battles and their ramifications can also be the basis of comedy. In *Mrs. Doubtfire* (1993) a noncustodial father played by Robin Williams so desperately misses his children that he disguises himself as a nanny, one Mrs. Euphegenia Doubtfire. Distaining drag comedy, the remake of *The Parent Trap* (1998) revolves around twin girls, both played by Lindsey Lohan, and their successful efforts to reunite their divorced parents. The original custody decree for the girls — one to the father, the other to the mother — is an example of "split custody," that is, the awarding of the children to the parents almost as if they were assets to be divided.

5. Prime-time television series have not only portrayed child custody fights but also found ways to combine serious drama and lighthearted comedy in the portrayals. Short-lived series such as *Civil Wars* (1991–93) and *Family Law* (1999–2000) featured small law firms specializing in family law and composed of lawyers with their own, sometimes quirky problems. In the first episode of the latter, one of the plot lines concerned the sad story of a recovering alcoholic who falls off the wagon and therefore abandons a custody fight. A second plot line, meanwhile, involved a silly couple battling over their deceased dog's ashes. In *Judging Amy* (CBS; 1999–2005) a recently divorced lawyer played by Amy Brenneman leaves corporate practice in New York City and, in an unbelievably short period of time, becomes a family court judge in Connecticut. Her court seems to have jurisdiction over everything from sobering juvenile justice matters to child custody disputes. The judge sometimes receives advice from her own mother, a know-it-all social worker played by Tyne Daley. The latter has three tips on how to be a good family court judge: (1) Pee before going on the bench, (2) Do not wear perfume, and (3) Make sure there is no food in your teeth.

E. ADOPTION AND SURROGACY

While some spouses struggle over which one might have custody of the children after divorce, others struggle mightily to have children in the first place. Heartbreaking tales of men with low sperm counts or women unable to conceive are common, and many disappointed couples turn out their lights praying for a pregnancy. Adoption, technology-assisted reproduction, and surrogacy are ways couples might have the child they desperately want, and law and legal institutions are part of each process. Actual or imagined cases in which the process is complicated or doomed provide material for the culture industry.

1. Adoption

Modern adoption law in the United States began in 1851, with the enactment in Massachusetts of the nation's first comprehensive adoption statute. It required that living biological parents of the child give formal permission for adoption and that the adopter and his spouse (if any) formally petition to adopt. Under the statute a judge was then to consider the adoption, asking in the process if the adoption petitioner or petitioners were able to raise the child in a proper fashion. During subsequent decades other states enacted comparable laws, and by the turn of the century modern adoption procedures were available in virtually every state.

None of this is to say, meanwhile, that the socio-legal characteristics of American adoption have remained fixed during the last century and a half. In the final decades of the nineteenth century many expressed concern and litigated cases over the comparative inheritance rights of biological and adopted children. In the early twentieth century self-styled "child savers" launched programs through which established families would adopt the presumably neglected children of working-class, immigrant families. In the mid-twentieth century the number of adoptions skyrocketed, and the most sought-after adoptee ceased to be a young boy who might perform farm labor and instead became a healthy, helpless infant. How might one explain the most recent changes?

PONDERING PAST PURPOSES: A CRITICAL HISTORY OF AMERICAN ADOPTION LAW

David Ray Papke

102 West Virginia Law Review 459 (1999)

No single factor explains these changes, but it is possible to place twentieth-century adoption into the context of consumption and acquisition. Private consumption of goods, of course, dates back to the beginning of the Republic, but historians have pointed to the 1920s as the decade in which the range of consumer goods and the magnitude of consumer demands became truly noteworthy. Advertising contributed to the demand by calling attention to products and by extolling their attributes. More profoundly, advertising promoted "consumption as a way of life."

What could be obtained through consumer purchases? Goods and services are only the obvious answers. Advertising also suggested that through purchase and acquisition "the age-old discontents of loneliness, sickness, weaknesses, lack of sexual satisfaction" could be made to disappear. Advertising suggested as well that new needs and doubts could be addressed, and, indeed, advertising seeks "to generate new anxieties instead of allaying old ones."

In an historical period in which occupations, ethnic origins, and religious affiliations have declined in importance, consumption could indeed become central in self-image and identity. Many are inclined to define themselves through the goods they purchase and the presumed ways those goods respond to traditional or newly constructed needs.

What's more, advertising and the consumption it promotes spill over from the literal consumer marketplace to other sectors not normally associated with the purchase of goods, services and alleviation of personal problems. Print and television "news," for example, is a commercial product, and its producers either sell the product directly to consumers or rely on advertising sales related to the product. Ronald Reagan was notorious for promoting his candidacies and presidency with the well crafted "sound-bite," but almost thirty years earlier Dwight Eisenhower raised eyebrows when he hired an advertising firm to promote his political proposals and programs. Students in universities often approach their courses and degrees as "consumer goods," and many professors speak openly of the need to "market" the courses they are offering.

Certain childless adults or couples wanting children beyond the number biology has provided fit into this large picture. In addition to purchasing their share of conventional consumer goods, many also seek to obtain the child held out by advertising and general cultural imagery as central to a good, successful life. "Family" in contemporary America is taken to include children or at least a single child. Adoption is a way to accomplish this goal. . . .

Before long the traditional pattern of potentially adoptable children outnumbering adopters was reversed, and a striking change also took place with regard to adoption preferences. In earlier periods adoptive children might have been young adults able to provide help on the farm or juvenile delinquents who needed to be "rescued" from their ethnic families and lives of crime. But in the midst of the twentieth-century adoption boom, infants became the most wanted adoptive children. Would-be parents were willing to spend large amounts of money for babies, especially healthy, white babies. These babies constituted an economic drain on their parents' assets; the babies had no economic value. But still, in the context of what sociologist Viviana Zelizer calls the "sentimentalization of adoption," would-be adoptive parents became willing to expend large amounts of time and money on an infant, on "[t]he priceless child." . . .

NOTES & QUESTIONS

1. The palpable need of many would-be adoptive parents to acquire a child and thereby achieve a sense of familial completeness does not mean they will be distant or uncaring parents. Adoption usually proves to be a warm and genuinely affectionate development for adoptees and adoptive parents.

2. The perceived "shortage" of healthy white newborns for adoption led, among other things, to an abandonment of efforts to achieve an ethnic or racial "match" between the child and the adoptive parents. The number of international adoptions grew, with Americans constituting the great majority of adopters, and in many cases American Caucasians adopted Filipino, Korean, and — most recently — Chinese children "across race." In the United States Caucasians also showed a new interest in adopting Native Americans and African Americans. This, in turn, prompted expressions of concern from some leaders of minority communities.

3. Twila L. Perry argues that the popular film *Losing Isaiah* (1995) plays off a bias against African American mothers. In their heart of hearts, do most Caucasians believe that African American children would be better off with Caucasian parents?

TRANSRACIAL AND INTERNATIONAL ADOPTION: MOTHERS, HIERARCHY, RACE, AND FEMINIST LEGAL THEORY
Twila L. Perry
l0 Yale Journal of Law & Feminism 101 (1998)

The idea that Black parents must teach Black children how to survive in a racist society was not invented in response to the controversy over transracial adoption. Instead, this view represents the acknowledgment by many Black people of a long history of struggle to ensure that Black children are able to survive physically and emotionally in a racially hostile world. Many Blacks would agree that Black parents face unique challenges in raising Black children, and they celebrate the fact that generations of Black children have been successfully raised against the odds.

However, white society's view of Black women mothering Black children is often at odds with this perspective. A number of scholars have written exclusively about society's devaluation of Black mothers, noting the widespread stereotypes of the emasculating matriarch, the lazy welfare mother, and the licentious Jezebel. In recent conservative discourse, Black mothers are portrayed as raising a future generation of welfare cheats, violent criminals, and absent fathers.

I have argued elsewhere that the mothering of Black children by Black women has been devalued in both the public and the legal discourse surrounding transracial adoption. The media frequently presents the public with scenarios in which screaming, crying Black children are ripped from the arms of loving white foster parents who want to adopt them only to be returned to out of control, drug-addicted Black mothers destined to abuse them, or even kill them. Some legal scholarship advocating transracial adoption incorporates and reifies this approach to promote the argument that the use of race as a factor in adoption is harmful to Black children.

Films, in particular, have a long tradition of objectifying and misrepresenting the experiences of Black people and they have, through both narrative and imagery, replicated and reinforced a negative portrayal of Black mothers. Films can tell a story about race and about the intersection of race and the law that can exert a powerful influence on society's view of what the law on a particular issue should be.

A recent movie, entitled *Losing Isaiah*, provides a potent example of the way in which the portrayal of Black mothers in film can be used to support the argument that the law should be structured to favor the adoption of Black children by whites.

The plot of *Losing Isaiah* involves a Black birth mother's attempt to reclaim her three-year-old son from a white middle class family with whom the child was placed for foster care shortly after birth. The white family is in the process of adopting Isaiah when his mother initiates the case for his return.

The movie opens with Isaiah's birth mother in a crack-induced daze. A voice from another room in a shabby tenement yells out, "Get that cryin' baby outta here!" Isaiah's mother staggers with her newborn son out into the street, where she places him in a garbage can while she goes in search of drugs. The next morning Isaiah is rescued by a sanitation worker seconds before he is crushed by the trash compactor of a garbage truck. A few hours later, Isaiah's mother wakes up from her drug-induced haze, remembers where she has left her baby and goes to retrieve him. Seeing that the garbage has been picked up, she assumes, without investigation, that Isaiah is dead and simply goes on with her life. Meanwhile, Isaiah has been placed with a warm, loving, white family with whom he thrives. They grow to love Isaiah and want to adopt him. Eventually Isaiah's birth mother learns that her son is alive. She enrolls in a drug rehab program, kicks her crack habit, and retains a lawyer to seek her child's return.

The movie abounds with negative images of Black mothers. In addition to Isaiah's mother, who left him in a garbage can, there is another young Black mother in the movie who treats her young son with coldness and crudeness. The only exception is in one scene in which the child is breakdancing. In that scene, and in that scene only, the mother beams with warmth and pride.

The central courtroom scene in the movie promotes numerous negative images of Black women and Black families. Isaiah's mother admits on the witness stand that her son was conceived by accident during an anonymous drugs-for-sex encounter. When asked by the judge whether she has anyone to assist her in the care of her son should he be returned back to her, Isaiah's mother replies that the only people she can rely on are also recovering crack addicts. The implication is that there is no family that is in contact with or cares about this young girl, no family that is thrilled that she has overcome her drug habit and is on the road to rehabilitating her life. The movie depicts no concerned and caring sisters, brothers, aunts, or uncles — no loving Black grandmother waiting to shower attention and affection on her newly discovered grandson.

In the end, the court returns Isaiah to his birth mother who can only offer him a life of squalor and chaos. Her frustrations bring her to the brink of child abuse. Finally, in an ambiguous ending, she calls the white adoptive mother for help, and possibly to return Isaiah, to her. In this way, Isaiah's mother confirms her own inadequacy and confirms that the white adoptive mother was the better mother after all.

Although Black women may often see themselves as successfully mothering against the odds, this is often not the perception of the larger society. The legal discourse on both foster care and transracial adoption, and the media images represented in a film such as *Losing Isaiah*, are examples of a widespread negative view of the competence of Black mothers in raising Black children. . . .

NOTES & QUESTIONS

1. In the final scene of *Losing Isaiah* the Caucasian adoptive mother and the African American biological mother sit on the rug at a day care facility and play together with little Isaiah. Above and beyond the racial tensions of the film, could there be room under the law for a child to have two mothers? American adoption law has traditionally employed an "either/or approach," that is, after an adoption the adoptive parents fully supplant the biological parents. The so-called "open adoption" movement, by contrast, has argued that in many cases an adopted child would benefit from ongoing contact with his or her biological parents. Some states have statutes that formally anticipate this arrangement. See, as an example, Indiana Code 31-19-16: Postadoption Contact Privileges.

2. Imagine a film in which an "open adoption" arrangement pulls apart. Would your film implicitly take a stand either for or against "open adoption"?

2. Surrogacy

For some couples seeking a child, adoption is unappealing. They want instead to have a child with biological connections to one or, if possible, both members of the couple. Fertility clinics and other institutions often provide assistance by facilitating artificial insemination, in vitro fertilization, and — in very recent years — egg donation. The processes strike some as "tampering with nature," but many defend the processes as the only ways they can have their "own" children.

Beginning in the 1980s, growing numbers of couples turned to surrogacy arrangements. In most situations the male member of the couple was able to provide sperm, but the female member of the couple was either unable to conceive or completely infertile. The couple then turned to a second woman, who either (1) had implanted in her womb the fertilized eggs from the couple, or (2) allowed herself to be artificially inseminated with sperm from the male member of the couple. Both the surrogate mother and, sometimes, those who arranged the surrogacy charged fees, and the entire arrangement was contractual.

The most discussed surrogacy contract involved a childless New Jersey couple, William and Elizabeth Stern, and a would-be surrogate mother, Mary Beth Whitehead. The parties signed the contract in 1985, and its major provisions are reprinted below.

SURROGATE PARENTING AGREEMENT
Matter of Baby M
537 A.2d 1227 (1988) (Appendix)

THIS AGREEMENT is made with reference to the following facts:

(1) WILLIAM STERN, Natural Father, is an individual over the age of eighteen (18) years and is desirous of entering into this Agreement.

(2) The sole purpose of this Agreement is to enable WILLIAM STERN and his infertile wife to have a child which is biologically related to WILLIAM STERN.

(3) MARY BETH WHITEHEAD, Surrogate, and RICHARD WHITEHEAD, her husband, are over the age of eighteen (18) years and desirous of entering into this Agreement.

NOW THEREFORE, in consideration of the mutual promises contained herein and the intentions of being legally bound hereby, the parties agree as follows:

1. MARY BETH WHITEHEAD, Surrogate, represents that she is capable of conceiving children. MARY BETH WHITEHEAD understands and agrees that in the best interest of the child, she will not form or attempt to form a parent-child relationship with any child or children she may conceive, carry to term and give birth to, pursuant to the provisions of this Agreement, and shall freely surrender custody to WILLIAM STERN, Natural Father, immediately upon birth of the child; and terminate all parental rights to said child pursuant to this Agreement.

2. MARY BETH WHITEHEAD, Surrogate, and RICHARD WHITEHEAD, her husband, have been married since 12/2/73, and RICHARD WHITEHEAD is in agreement with the purposes, intents and provisions of this Agreement and acknowledges that his wife, MARY BETH WHITEHEAD, Surrogate, shall be artificially inseminated pursuant to the provisions of this Agreement. RICHARD WHITEHEAD agrees that in the best interest of the child, he will

not form or attempt to form a parent-child relationship with any child or children MARY BETH WHITEHEAD, Surrogate, may conceive by artificial insemination as described herein, and agrees to freely and readily surrender immediate custody of the child to WILLIAM STERN, Natural Father; and terminate his parental rights; RICHARD WHITEHEAD further acknowledges that he will do all acts necessary to rebut the presumption of paternity of any offspring conceived and born pursuant to aforementioned agreement as provided by law, including blood testing and/or HLA testing.

3. WILLIAM STERN, Natural Father, does hereby enter into this written contractual Agreement with MARY BETH WHITEHEAD, Surrogate, where MARY BETH WHITEHEAD shall be artificially inseminated with the semen of WILLIAM STERN by a physician. MARY BETH WHITEHEAD, Surrogate, upon becoming pregnant, acknowledges that she will carry said embryo/fetus(s) until delivery. MARY BETH WHITEHEAD, Surrogate, and RICHARD WHITEHEAD, her husband, agree that they will cooperate with any background investigation into the Surrogate's medical, family, and personal history and warrants the information to be accurate to the best of their knowledge. MARY BETH WHITEHEAD, Surrogate, and RICHARD WHITEHEAD, her husband, agree to surrender custody of the child to WILLIAM STERN, Natural Father, immediately upon birth, acknowledging that it is the intent of this Agreement in the best interests of the child to do so; as well as institute and cooperate in proceedings to terminate their respective parental rights to said child, and sign any and all necessary affidavits, documents, and the like, in order to further the intent and purposes of this Agreement. It is understood by MARY BETH WHITEHEAD, and RICHARD WHITEHEAD, that the child to be conceived is being done so for the sole purpose of giving said child to WILLIAM STERN, its natural and biological father. MARY BETH WHITEHEAD and RICHARD WHITEHEAD agree to sign all necessary affidavits prior to and after the birth of the child and voluntarily participate in any paternity proceedings necessary to have WILLIAM STERN'S name entered on said child's birth certificate as the natural or biological father.

4. That the consideration for this Agreement, which is compensation for services and expenses, and in no way is to be construed as a fee for termination of parental rights or a payment in exchange for a consent to surrender the child for adoption, in addition to other provisions contained herein, shall be as follows:

(A) $10,000 shall be paid to MARY BETH WHITEHEAD, Surrogate, upon surrender of custody to WILLIAM STERN, the natural and biological father of the child born pursuant to the provisions of this Agreement for surrogate services and expenses in carrying out her obligations under this Agreement:

(B) The consideration to be paid to MARY BETH WHITEHEAD, Surrogate, shall be deposited with the Infertility Center of New York (hereinafter ICNY), the representative of WILLIAM STERN, at the time of the signing of this Agreement, and held in escrow until completion of the duties and obligations of MARY BETH WHITEHEAD, Surrogate, as herein described.

(C) WILLIAM STERN, Natural Father, shall pay the expenses incurred by MARY BETH WHITEHEAD, Surrogate, pursuant to her pregnancy, more specifically defined as follows:

(1) All medical, hospitalization, and pharmaceutical, laboratory and therapy expenses incurred as a result of MARY BETH WHITEHEAD's pregnancy, not covered or allowed by her present health and major medical insurance, including all extraordinary medical expenses and all reasonable expenses for treatment of any emotional or mental conditions or problems related to said pregnancy, but in no case shall any such expenses be paid or reimbursed after a period of six (6) months have elapsed since the date of the termination of the pregnancy, and this Agreement specifically precludes any expenses for lost wages or other non-itemized incidentals (see Exhibit "B") related to said pregnancy.

(2) WILLIAM STERN, Natural Father, shall not be responsible for any latent medical expenses occurring six (6) weeks subsequent to the birth of the child, unless the medical problem or abnormality incident thereto was known and treated by a physician prior to the expiration of said six (6) week period and in written notice of the same sent to ICNY, as representative of WILLIAM STERN by certified mail, return receipt requested, advising of this treatment.

(3) WILLIAM STERN, Natural Father, shall be responsible for the total costs of all paternity testing. Such paternity testing may, at the option of WILLIAM STERN, Natural Father, be required prior to release of the surrogate fee from escrow. In the event WILLIAM STERN, Natural Father, is conclusively determined not to be the biological father of the child as a result of an HLA test, this Agreement will be deemed breached and MARY BETH WHITEHEAD, Surrogate, shall not be entitled to any fee. WILLIAM STERN, Natural Father, shall be entitled to reimbursement of all medical and related expenses from MARY BETH WHITEHEAD, Surrogate, and RICHARD WHITEHEAD, her husband.

(4) MARY BETH WHITEHEAD'S reasonable travel expenses incurred at the request of WILLIAM STERN, pursuant to this Agreement.

5. MARY BETH WHITEHEAD, Surrogate, and RICHARD WHITEHEAD, her husband, understand and agree to assume all risks, including the risk of death, which are incidental to conception, pregnancy, childbirth, including but not limited to, postpartum complications.

6. MARY BETH WHITEHEAD, Surrogate, and RICHARD WHITEHEAD, her husband, hereby agree to undergo psychiatric

evaluation by JOAN EINWOHNER, a psychiatrist as designated by WILLIAM STERN or an agent thereof. WILLIAM STERN shall pay for the cost of said psychiatric evaluation. MARY BETH WHITEHEAD and RICHARD WHITEHEAD shall sign, prior to their evaluations, a medical release permitting dissemination of the report prepared as a result of said psychiatric evaluations to ICNY or WILLIAM STERN and his wife.

7. MARY BETH WHITEHEAD, Surrogate, and RICHARD WHITEHEAD, her husband, hereby agree that it is the exclusive and sole right of WILLIAM STERN, Natural Father, to name said child.

8. "CHILD" as referred to in this Agreement shall include all children born simultaneously pursuant to the inseminations contemplated herein.

9. In the event of the death of WILLIAM STERN, prior or subsequent to the birth of said child, it is hereby understood and agreed by MARY BETH WHITEHEAD, Surrogate, and RICHARD WHITEHEAD, her husband, that the child will be placed in the custody of WILLIAM STERN'S wife.

10. In the event that the child is miscarried prior to the fifth (5th) month of pregnancy, no compensation, as enumerated in paragraph 4(A), shall be paid to MARY BETH WHITEHEAD, Surrogate. However, the expenses enumerated in paragraph 4(C) shall be paid or reimbursed to MARY BETH WHITEHEAD, Surrogate. In the event the child is miscarried, dies, or is stillborn subsequent to the fourth (4th) month of pregnancy and said child does not survive, the Surrogate shall receive $1,000.00 in lieu of the compensation enumerated in paragraph 4(A). In the event of a miscarriage or stillbirth as described above, this Agreement shall terminate and neither MARY BETH WHITEHEAD, Surrogate, nor WILLIAM STERN, Natural Father, shall be under any further obligation under this Agreement.

11. MARY BETH WHITEHEAD, Surrogate, and WILLIAM STERN, Natural Father, shall have undergone complete and genetic evaluation, under the direction and supervision of a licensed physician, to determine whether the physical health and well-being of each is satisfactory. Said physical examination shall include testing for venereal diseases, specifically including but not limited to, syphilis, herpes, and gonorrhea. Said venereal disease testing shall be done prior to, but not limited to, each series of inseminations.

12. In the event that pregnancy has not occurred within a reasonable time, in the opinion of WILLIAM STERN, Natural Father, this Agreement shall terminate by written notice to MARY BETH WHITEHEAD, Surrogate, at the residence provided to the ICNY by the Surrogate, from ICNY, as representative of WILLIAM STERN, Natural Father.

13. MARY BETH WHITEHEAD, Surrogate, agrees that she will not abort the child once conceived except, if in the professional medical

opinion of the inseminating physician, such action is necessary for the physical health of MARY BETH WHITEHEAD or the child has been determined by said physician to be physiologically abnormal. MARY BETH WHITEHEAD further agrees, upon the request of said physician to undergo amniocentesis or similar tests to detect genetic and congenital defects. In the event said test reveals that the fetus is genetically or congenitally abnormal, MARY BETH WHITEHEAD, Surrogate, agrees to abort the fetus upon demand of WILLIAM STERN, Natural Father, in which event the fee paid to the Surrogate will be in accordance to Paragraph 10. If MARY BETH WHITEHEAD refuses to abort the fetus upon demand of WILLIAM STERN, his obligations as stated in this Agreement shall cease forthwith, except as to obligations of paternity imposed by statute.

14. Despite the provisions of Paragraph 13, WILLIAM STERN, Natural Father, recognizes that some genetic and congenital abnormalities may not be detected by amniocentesis or other tests, and therefore, if proven to be the biological father of the child, assumes the legal responsibility for any child who may possess genetic or congenital abnormalities.

15. MARY BETH WHITEHEAD, Surrogate, further agrees to adhere to all medical instructions given to her by the inseminating physician as well as her independent obstetrician. MARY BETH WHITEHEAD also agrees not to smoke cigarettes, drink alcoholic beverages, use illegal drugs, or take non-prescription medications or prescribed medications without written consent from her physician. MARY BETH WHITEHEAD agrees to follow a prenatal medical examination schedule to consist of no fewer visits than: one visit per month during the first seven (7) months of pregnancy, two visits (each to occur at two-week intervals) during the eighth and ninth month of pregnancy.

16. MARY BETH WHITEHEAD, Surrogate, agrees to cause RICHARD WHITEHEAD, her husband, to execute a refusal of consent form.

17. Each party acknowledges that he or she fully understands this Agreement and its legal effect, and that they are signing the same freely and voluntarily and that neither party has any reason to believe that the other(s) did not freely and voluntarily execute said Agreement.

18. In the event any of the provisions of this Agreement are deemed to be invalid or unenforceable, the same shall be deemed severable from the remainder of this Agreement and shall not cause the invalidity or unenforceability of the remainder of this Agreement. If such provision shall be deemed invalid due to its scope or breadth, then said provision shall be deemed valid to the extent of the scope or breadth permitted by law. . . .

NOTES & QUESTIONS

1. After the child was born, Mary Beth Whitehead briefly relinquished her to the Sterns, but Whitehead then realized she could not bear to part with the child. Whitehead recalled her feelings in her book regarding the case:

> The Sterns and the Infertility Center had told me I was doing a beautiful thing, but I wasn't. All the way through my pregnancy, I had tried to believe it. I had suppressed the reality; I had denied my feelings. I had not allowed myself to deal with it. But now I couldn't pretend anymore.

> I began to feel angry and defensive. My body, my soul, my heart, my breathing, my everything had gone into making this baby. What had Bill Stern done? Put some sperm in a cup. What had Betsy Stern done? Bought some clothes, a box of diapers, and a case of formula.

> All I did was sob and cry. I just couldn't stop crying. It just kept coming, and the emptiness I felt was something I never want to feel again.

> Eventually I fell asleep. Suddenly I opened my eyes. The room was dark, and I was lying in a pool of milk. The sheets were full of milk. I knew it was time to feed my baby. I knew she was hungry, but I could not hear her crying. The room was quiet as I sat up in the bed, alone in the darkness with the milk running down my chest and soaking my nightgown. I held out my empty arms and screamed at the top of my lungs, "Oh, God, what have I done — I want my baby!"

Mary Beth Whitehead (with Loretta Schwartz-Nobel), *A Mother's Story: The Truth About the* Baby M *Case* 25-27 (1989).

2. Whitehead and her attorney argued, among other things, that Elizabeth Stern was not infertile as recited in the agreement and, as a result, the contract was void. Does the savings clause in paragraph 18 of the agreement destroy this argument? Should surrogacy arrangements be available under the law only when the would-be mother is infertile?

3. Whitehead refused to abide by paragraph 7 of the agreement, which gave William Stern the exclusive right to name the child. He and his wife chose the name Melissa, but Whitehead preferred the name Sarah and used that name when obtaining a birth certificate for the child. Why would naming rights be an important provision in a surrogacy agreement?

4. Ultimately, Whitehead fled to Florida with the child. When law enforcement officials found her, they seized the child and returned her to the custody of the Sterns. A lower court ruled that the surrogacy agreement was enforceable and formally awarded the child to the Sterns, but Whitehead appealed. In the following opinion the New Jersey Supreme Court ruled on the enforceability of surrogacy agreements.

MATTER OF BABY M
537 A.2d 1227 (N.J. 1988)

Wilentz, C.J.

We have concluded that this surrogacy contract is invalid. Our conclusion has two bases: direct conflict with existing statutes and conflict with the public policies of this State, as expressed in its statutory and decisional law.

One of the surrogacy contract's basic purposes, to achieve the adoption of a child through private placement, though permitted in New Jersey "is very much disfavored." *Sees v. Baber*, 74 N.J. 201, 217, 377 A.2d 628 (1977). Its use of money for this purpose — and we have no doubt whatsoever that the money is being paid to obtain an adoption and not, as the Sterns argue, for the personal services of Mary Beth Whitehead — is illegal and perhaps criminal. N.J.S.A. 9:3-54. In addition to the inducement of money, there is the coercion of contract: the natural mother's irrevocable agreement, prior to birth, even prior to conception, to surrender the child to the adoptive couple. Such an agreement is totally unenforceable in private placement adoption. *See*, 74 N.J. at 212-14, 377 A.2d 628. Even where the adoption is through an approved agency, the formal agreement to surrender occurs only *after* birth (as we read N.J.S.A. 9:2-16 and -17, and similar statutes), and then by regulation, only after the birth mother has been offered counseling. N.J.A.C. 10:121A-5.4(c). Integral to these invalid provisions of the surrogacy contract is the related agreement, equally invalid, on the part of the natural mother to cooperate with, and not to contest, proceedings to terminate her parental rights, as well as her contractual concession, in aid of the adoption, that the child's best interests would be served by awarding custody to the natural father and his wife — all of this before she has even conceived, and, in some cases, before she has the slightest idea of what the natural father and adoptive mother are like.

The foregoing provisions not only directly conflict with New Jersey statutes, but also offend long-established State policies. . . .

[The contract] guarantees the separation of a child from its mother; it totally ignores the child; it takes the child from the mother regardless of her wishes and her maternal fitness; and it does all of this, it accomplishes all of its goals, through the use of money.

Beyond that is the potential degradation of some women that may result from this arrangement. In many cases, of course, surrogacy may bring satisfaction, not only to the infertile couple, but to the surrogate mother herself. The fact, however, that many women may not perceive surrogacy negatively but rather see it as an opportunity does not diminish its potential for devastation to other women.

In sum, the harmful consequences of this surrogacy arrangement appear to us all too palpable. In New Jersey the surrogate mother's agreement to sell her child is void. Its irrevocability infects the entire contract, as does the money that purports to buy it. . . .

NOTES & QUESTIONS

1. After the New Jersey Supreme Court found the surrogacy contract unenforceable, it went on to decide who should have custody of the child, William Stern or Mary Beth Whitehead. The applicable standard for this determination is the best-interests-of-the-child standard, which was discussed earlier in this chapter. Citing to the testimony of experts who had testified at trial, the Court granted custody to Stern. It also remanded the case to the lower court for a determination of the visitation rights, if any, for Whitehead. The decision of the New Jersey Supreme Court was unanimous in granting Whitehead visitation rights.

2. Not surprisingly, the culture industry recognized the dramatic possibilities in the case. ABC Circle Films produced the three-hour *Baby M* in 1996. JoBeth Williams starred as Mary Beth Whitehead and received both an Emmy nomination for Outstanding Lead Actress in a Mini-Series or a Special and a Golden Globe nomination for Best Performance by an Actress in a Mini-Series or Motion Picture Made for Television.

3. *Baby M* captures many of the most important developments involving Whitehead and the Sterns. The film conveys nicely Whitehead's pronounced eagerness to serve as a surrogate and her unsuccessful efforts to serve as a surrogate for another childless couple before contracting with the Sterns. The film portrays Whitehead's flight to Florida with the baby she insisted on calling "Sarah." And, most powerfully, the film recreates Whitehead's frightening calls to the Sterns during which she accused Bill Stern of molesting her daughter Tuesday and threatened to kill herself and the baby. Overall, Whitehead emerges as an irrational and duplicitous person, and most viewers will find themselves hoping the Sterns prevail. Would it have been possible to portray Whitehead sympathetically?

4. *Baby M* is cognizant of the class dimensions of the case and folds them into the drama. William Stern, a biochemist, and Elizabeth Stern, a pediatrician, lead structured, dignified, and interpersonally sensitive lives. By contrast, Rick Whitehead, a garbage man, drinks too much, and Mary Beth Whitehead eats in bed. Whenever the child returns to the Stern home after a supervised visit to the Whiteheads, the Sterns find the child dressed in a tacky, garish outfit. In surrogacy arrangements in general, women from the working class serve as surrogates for couples from the middle and upper classes. Whitehead's lawyer in *Baby M* may be figuratively correct when he suggests that in surrogacy arrangements it will always be sanitation workers delivering babies for doctors.

5. The actual ruling of the New Jersey Supreme Court in *Matter of Baby M* receives only minor attention in the film *Baby M*. At the end of the film, shortly before the final credits, a summary of the decision is scrolled on the screen. Beyond the general difficulties inherent in dramatizing appellate decisions, producers of the film may have wondered if viewers would understand that it might be legal to enter into a contract which is unenforceable. In the following excerpt Martha A. Field argues this is the ideal approach.

SURROGACY CONTRACTS — GESTATIONAL AND TRADITIONAL: THE ARGUMENT FOR NONENFORCEMENT
Martha A. Field
31 Washburn Law Journal 1 (1991)

"Surrogacy" is the word we use for the practice of a woman contracting to bear a child for another family to raise. The law is just beginning to take notice of and regulate this practice. Accordingly, a great deal of debate is taking place concerning what should be done about surrogacy, both in the United States and in other countries. In this country, the issue is being handled at a state rather than a national level, so potentially many different systems could evolve.

One issue often discussed is whether paid surrogacy should be criminalized, or indeed, whether it is already criminal as a form of babyselling, which every state punishes. While I argue against the option of criminalization, I do not favor enforcing surrogacy contracts, the way one would enforce a contract to buy land or chattels. Instead, I will argue surrogacy should be legal but the contract unenforceable. Thus, surrogacy contracts become "voidable contracts," a familiar category in contract law. The best position for a state or national government to take, for the time being at least, is to tolerate surrogacy but not to endorse or encourage it. . . .

It is not to women's advantage to give up control of the reproductive function or to facilitate men having babies without voluntary cooperation of any woman. We are in a society where men have wealth, power, and physical strength. What advantages do women have? At least equal intelligence, I would submit, and also a little more control over the reproductive function. Admittedly, what seems a reproductive advantage to many women is a reproductive burden to others. But whichever side of that line a woman is on, and even if she does not consider herself a feminist or identify primarily as a woman, it is to her advantage to keep control over her own reproductive functions. The surrogacy debate is part of the range of hard-fought issues over who is going to make the greater part of the decision in this important facet of life.

NOTES & QUESTIONS

1. Other states have not necessarily accepted the New Jersey approach to surrogacy. The California Supreme Court, in a 6-1 decision, held that surrogacy contracts were enforceable and, thus, the surrogate mother's rights gave way to the intended parents' rights. *Johnson v. Calvert*, 851 P.2d 776 (Cal. 1993). In its analysis the majority said the intent of the parties should determine whom the law recognizes as a surrogate child's parent. The lone dissenter said the courts should recognize two valid claims to parenthood and then award custody based on the best interests of the child. *See* Mark Hansen, *Surrogacy Contract Upheld — California Supreme Court Says Such Agreements Don't Violate Public Policy*, ABA Journal, Aug. 1993, at 34.

2. Professor Lisa Ikemoto has noted that the media accounts of the California case stressed its racial features. To wit, the would-be parents Mark and Crispina Calvert are, respectively, Caucasian and Filipino, while Anna Johnson, the surrogate mother, is African American. These racial identities, Ikemoto argues, should not be overlooked. "White father, Asian mother and Black non-mother. The legal result parallels the racial hierarchy in society." Lisa Ikemoto, *Destabilizing Thoughts in Surrogacy Legislation*, 28 University of San Francisco Law Review 633, 644 (1994).

Chapter 12

BUSINESS LAW

A. FILMOGRAPHY

Boiler Room (2000)

The Corporation (2003)

Enron — The Smartest Guys in the Room (2005)

Other People's Money (1991)

Wall Street (1987)

B. BUSINESS PARTICIPANTS

1. Corporations, Stockholders, and Other Stakeholders

Popular depictions of businesses understandably focus on corporations because corporations have become a ubiquitous part of modern daily life and society. As you consider the corporations portrayed in the films discussed in this chapter and other portrayals of corporations in popular culture with which you are familiar, think about whether the story being told about each corporation reflects the way in which you and others view corporations. Should law allow corporations to be run solely to maximize their corporate profits for their stockholders? Should corporate boards of directors, executives, managers, and stockholders be legally required to be socially responsible and look after their employees' well-being and community interests?

FRAMING THE MARKET: REPRESENTATIONS OF MEANING AND VALUE IN LAW, MARKETS, AND CULTURE
Robin Paul Malloy
51 Buffalo Law Review 1 (2003)

Two films, *Wall Street* and *Other People's Money*, contain significant scenes involving corporate stockholder meetings, and raise interesting issues about the nature of market values and the purpose of exchange. They also raise questions about the nature of the firm, the characteristics of ownership, and the community obligations of business. Both films involve a takeover bid by an investor seeking to break up a company as a way of enhancing stockholder value. The lead characters in each film make appeals to the stockholders, urging the stockholders to vote in favor of the takeover, and for liquidation of the firm in an effort to maximize stockholder value.

In *Wall Street*, Gordon Gekko, played by Michael Douglas, takes the center stage at a stockholder meeting held in the surroundings of a well-appointed convention center. In the room, there are plenty of well-dressed stockholders who are seated on chairs at the floor level, looking up to a platform stage upon which sits the president and his thirty-three corporate vice presidents. After the corporate president warns stockholders that Gekko is a destroyer of companies, and that they should reject any takeover offer from him, Gekko takes up the microphone, from the floor, and declares, "I am not a destroyer of companies, I am a liberator of them." Gekko goes on to tell stockholders to vote in favor of his takeover bid because he will make them rich. He tells them "greed is good, greed simplifies, greed clarifies, greed in all of its forms makes the marketplace work." He tells them to ignore the concerns of the inefficient management of the company, and to pursue their own self-interest, to follow their greed in the pursuit of wealth. The clarity of the self-interested pursuit of greed will bring them to a freedom that only Gekko can deliver.

Similarly, in *Other People's Money*, Danny DeVito, playing Larry the Liquidator, makes an appeal to stockholders to vote in favor of his takeover bid because he will make them money. He tells them that the company, while profitable, is worth more dead (liquidated) than alive. He tells stockholders to vote for making the best return on their money, and that they have no obligation to the employees of the company or to the community where its factory is located. Their only obligation is to make the best profit for themselves.

In contrast to these views, Gregory Peck, playing the role of the eighty-one-year-old founder and president of the New England Wire and Cable Company in *Other People's Money*, argues that a company is worth more than the value of its stock. He says that a business is about people. It is about people who work together pursuing a common purpose, and who share the same friendships and live in the same community. He cautions the stockholders to avoid selfish and greedy actions and instead asks them to vote with their feelings. He asks them to vote for the continuation of a profitable business. He asserts that a business is more than a collection of capital goods. He tells them that a business is a community.

In contrast to the scene from *Wall Street*, the stockholder meeting in *Other People's Money* occurs at the factory, and the film's director presents us with images of the "blue collar" town and workers who are present both inside and outside of the meeting. The meeting is not set in some sterile convention hall as in *Wall Street*, but is held in the very town that will be affected by closing the plant. The dispute is not about an inefficient management team; it is about a company that is no longer as productive as other investments because new technologies are cutting into its market. The common theme between these films is the same, however. Each involves the takeover of a company by a rational, but "heartless," Wall Street "money-man" declaring that the only obligation people owe one another is to maximize wealth in the pursuit of self-interest.

In both *Wall Street* and *Other People's Money*, the takeover advocates address the legal owners of the company, the stockholders, and tell them to maximize their wealth by voting to liquidate the companies while they are still valuable. In contrast, Peck's character frames the appeal differently. He basically asserts that a company has obligations to its "stakeholders," and not just to its legal owners. He positions the proper market analysis as including the community, the schools, residents, workers, and others that have contributed to the company over the years. The company is not simply a detached and impersonal capital good; it is more than a physical object; it is a web of interconnected interests and values. He argues that resource determinations should account for a broader set of interests than those reflected by legal owners simply pursuing self-interest. In part, therefore, Peck's character questions the value frame and the interpretive reference set by the wealth maximizing character, Larry the Liquidator. By changing the value frame and the interpretive reference, Peck's character can logically promote a different economic calculus.

In viewing these scenes, one gets a close-up look at the real tension between two different visions of the market. It becomes clear that the disagreements are as much, or more, about values as they are about facts. It is not just a debate about the profitability of the various companies in question, for instance, but about the values to be promoted and endorsed by a market economy.

These two film clips also deal with tensions surrounding the meaning of property. Both involve corporate takeovers, and, in a similar way, each raises fundamental questions about ownership and the corporate form. Each asks us to consider who owns a company — the stockholders, the management, the workers, the community? How does ownership relate to having a "stakeholder" interest? Are claims by the community in this type of situation any different than the ones made by fans when their favorite major league football or baseball team threatens to pull out and move to a new city? Do corporations exist simply to maximize profit for the stockholders? Is there such a thing as good corporate citizenship? What is the basic nature and role of the firm in law and society, and how do alternative conceptions of the firm, and of the market, relate to matters of information costs, risk assessment and management, production costs, market price, firm valuation, and labor relations? These considerations set up an examination of the exchange relationships within the firm, and between the firm, its constituent parts, and the community. Understanding the relationships helps us establish a map or plan for a more detailed investigation of factors to address in legal reasoning and public policy making. . . .

NOTES & QUESTIONS

1. How realistic are these alternative visions of corporations in *Wall Street* and *Other People's Money*? If Professor Malloy is correct about stockholders having to choose between pursuing their self-interested greed versus fulfilling their community-interested obligations, what roles do and should corporate boards of directors, executives, employees, and managers play? Do these other corporate stakeholders or constituencies merely serve as faithful or unfaithful agents of stockholders? Compare both of these movies' scenes, focusing on corporate stockholder meetings, to probable apathy by most individual stockholders. In reality, will it be worthwhile for most individuals to spend enough of their scarce attention, effort, and time to become informed voting stockholders?

2. Should those corporate stockholders who choose to vote guard against being too myopic and greedy or too long-sighted and caring? Think realistically about what actually would happen if you let every corporation whose stock you own influence your ethics and life so fundamentally. Alternatively, are you really better off by remaining unmoved by suffering of employees in corporations whose stock you own?

3. Both *Other People's Money* and *Wall Street* focus on how disruptive hostile takeovers can be to interests other than those of the stockholders'. Professor Barbara White describes a number of similar popular portrayals of hostile takeovers:

> During the 80s, in the heyday of the hostile takeovers in the U.S., news organizations and show business media spotlighted attention on the community fallouts from the waves of mergers and acquisitions. Acquirers were often portrayed as voracious greedy vultures picking on firms in a manner that destroyed a valuable company and/or valued ways of community life and doing so solely for the purpose of making money. One merely needs to think of popular movies on the subject produced at the time to have a sense of public perception: *Big Business* (1988, Comedy, Lily Tomlin, Bette Midler — a corporate struggle over whether to close down a factory that will also destroy a southern town's way of life); *Other People's Money* (1991, Comedy, Danny DeVito — corporate raider's efforts to acquire a local company that is the lifeblood of a New England community); and the most notorious, *Wall Street* (1987, Drama, Michael Douglas, Charlie Sheen, Martin Sheen — young ambitious stock broker learns that his idol, a major corporate raider, is really and can only be greedy and unscrupulous in order to be successful.) Even in *Pretty Woman* (1990, Julia Roberts, Richard Gere), the hero, a successful, albeit ethically questionable, corporate raider, is psychologically redeemed when he decides to keep one corporate acquisition intact and build it up further instead of selling off its component parts for profit. These movies and others like them mirrored the sentiments held by the United States public at large regarding the disruption to corporations' and people's lives that the waves of corporate acquisitions and mergers had caused. News media gave similarly heart-rendering stories of families' and communities' lives in upheaval as a result of shifts in corporate winds.

Barbara White, *Conflicts in the Regulation of Hostile Business Takeovers in the United States and the European Union*, 9 Ius Gentium 161, 176 (2003). Consider other films discussed in this chapter, as well as any other popular business narratives with which you are familiar. How many of them for purposes of more dramatic storytelling focus on how corporate (mis)behavior causes misfortunes and negative consequences for identified and sympathetic victims' lives?

4. Is the separation of control and ownership that is typical of large modern publicly traded corporations a desirable governance structure for stockholders? Consider this perspective based upon stockholder happiness:

> However, once we frame "best interests" in terms of shareholders' psychological needs, it is clear that the separation of ownership and control, and in particular the situation of shareholder passivity, acts as a barrier to — rather than facilitator of — shareholder happiness.

James McConvill, *The Separation of Ownership and Control Under a Happiness-Based Theory of the Corporation*, The Company Lawyer, 26(2) (2005), 35. How persuasive is framing stockholders "best interests" in psychological as opposed to financial terms likely to be? Should business law be designed to maximize stockholders' happiness? How should business law balance stockholders' happiness with other corporate stakeholders' happiness? Is it realistic at present for us to expect lawyers, policy makers, and the public at large to care more about how corporations impact people's happiness than merely their monetary wealth? *See* Rafael Di Tella & Robert MacCulloch, *Some Uses of Happiness Data in Economics*, 20 Journal of Economic Perspectives 25 (2006); Ed Diener, *Subjective Well-Being: The Science of Happiness and a Proposal for a National Index*, 55 American Psychologist 34 (2000); Ed Diener & Martin E. P. Seligman, *Beyond Money: Toward an Economy of Well-Being,* 5 Psychological Science in the Public Interest 1 (2004); Daniel Kahneman et al., *Toward National Well-Being Accounts*, 94 American Economic Review 429 (2003); and Daniel Kahneman & Alan B. Krueger, *Developments in the Measurement of Subjective Well-Being*, 20 Journal of Economic Perpsectives 3 (2006). How do you feel about basing other areas of law upon considerations of happiness? *See* Thomas D. Griffith, *Progressive Taxation and Happiness*, 45 Boston College Law Review 1363 (2004); and Diane M. Ring, *Why Happiness?: A Commentary on Griffith's Progressive Taxation and Happiness*, 45 Boston College Law Review 1413 (2004). How do you feel about law firm reforms based upon considerations of happiness? *See* Martin E. P. Seligman et al., *Why Lawyers Are Unhappy*, 23 Cardozo Law Review 33 (2001).

5. While people could actually value their personal happiness over their financial wealth, do they mistakenly believe that increased financial wealth leads to increased personal subjective happiness? If people incorrectly forecast how increased financial wealth should lead to increased personal subjective happiness, then why is there no disconfirming feedback evidence to cause people to learn the error of their ways? Do people have different private versus public views about how their personal subjective happiness depends on their financial wealth?

6. Corporations are often depicted in popular culture as very resourceful and powerful, but nefarious and up to no good. An example is the secretive and sinister Umbrella Corporation in the science fiction and horror thriller *Resident Evil* (2002). Why do most American movies focus on portraying most corporations as being evil? Do corporations make good villains because they represent big and impersonal forces that are beyond any single individual's control? Is there a sense in popular culture of corporations being modern-day Goliaths and of those who do battle against corporations in popular culture being modern-day Davids? Do pop cultural portrayals of corporations as evil, faceless, and soulless entities merely satisfy people's existing suspicions about possible abuse of massive concentrations of power and wealth?

7. Debra Schleef describes a face-to-face interview of a male, second-year business student at a prestigious private university in the Midwest, in which the student lionizes corporate raiders like Gordon Gekko, the fictional character played by Michael Douglas in *Wall Street*. According to the student:

> You're supposed to hate those guys. Those guys are really good guys. They are helping people, consumer Americans. If a company gets broken up, and all the workers get fired, it's probably 'cause they're not producing as efficiently as they could. . . . The manager is responsible for maximizing shareholder return, getting as much money as possible. Where does he get off, taking a half percent off the bottom line and giving it to Meals on Wheels or something? [That] is theft.

Debra Schleef, *Empty Ethics and Reasonable Responsibility: Vocabularies of Motive among Law and Business Students*, 22 Law & Social Inquiry 619, 626 (1997). Do students become socialized in business and law schools to hold pro-business or pro-corporate views? How do business and law schools differ in terms of their entering and graduating students' beliefs and perspectives about business? Does taking business law courses makes law students more sympathetic to corporate interests?

8. Consider this explanation of differences between owning stocks and owning call options written on those stocks:

> From a legal perspective, a stockholder is entitled to any financial gains or losses from selling the stock in the future, to any periodic dividend payments, and to vote at annual shareholder meetings or special meetings. In contrast, a stock option holder is entitled only to any financial gains or losses from exercising or selling the stock option in the future. The stock option holder is not entitled to receive any periodic dividend payments, nor to exercise voting rights at shareholder meetings.

Peter H. Huang, *Teaching Corporate Law from an Option Perspective*, 34 Georgia Law Review 571, 576–79 (2000). Do you believe that most individual stockholders buy stocks in order to secure rights to dividends, get potential capital gains, or vote at stockholder meetings? Do you feel there should be a legal prohibition against explicitly trading in corporate voting rights? What do you think about corporate voting swaps, in which a "deal splits up stock ownership rights into corporate voting rights and financial rights, and then swaps those corporate voting rights for cash"? *Id.* at 578.

9. Consider how the actions of Gordon Gekko in *Wall Street* and others engaged in corporate takeovers are described:

> The 1987 film *Wall Street* chronicled the pursuits of a corrupt and greed-driven raider who ruthlessly manipulated stocks, conducted insider trading, and contributed to the destruction of major corporations. Virtually all books on the subject chronicled the alleged abuses and arrogance of financial entrepreneurs engaged in both hostile and friendly deals.

John Pound, *The Rise of the Political Model of Corporate Governance and Corporate Control*, 68 New York University Law Review 1003, 1037 (1993). Does this portrayal of those who engage in corporate takeovers appear to be fair and unbiased? Could threats of hostile corporate takeovers discipline corporate management from indulging in managerial bonuses, salaries, perks, laziness, and self-dealing? Can, does, and should law and popular culture differentiate between socially desirable and undesirable corporate takeovers?

10. Consider this fact: many individual stockholders who have been victims of corporate misbehavior or securities fraud are not familiar with the intricacies of accounting, business, corporate finance, economics, and statistics. Similarly, most jurors are not familiar with the intricacies of accounting, business, corporate finance, economics, and statistics. Corporate directors and executives are of course more likely to be familiar with the intricacies of accounting, business, corporate finance, economics, and statistics. Does this difference have any impact on how most corporate wrongdoing or securities lawsuits ultimately get resolved? Is any such disparity reflected in popular culture regarding business lawsuits?

2.   Corporate Boards of Directors, Executives, and Managers

ON THE PROPER MOTIVES OF CORPORATE DIRECTORS (OR, WHY YOU DON'T WANT TO INVITE HOMO ECONOMICUS TO JOIN YOUR BOARD)
Lynn A. Stout
28 Delaware Journal of Corporate Law 1 (2003)

For those who do not see the humor in the suggestion that directors might be driven by fear of personal liability, a short primer on the nature and enforcement of directors' fiduciary duties may be instructive.

In brief, directors' fiduciary duties come in two basic flavors: the duty of care and the duty of loyalty. These two flavors reflect the fact that when people misbehave, they tend to do so in one of two common ways. First, they may misbehave by acting like fools (acting carelessly). Second, they may misbehave by acting like knaves (acting dishonestly).

The duty of loyalty is designed, in theory, to address the knavishness problem. Put more bluntly, the duty of loyalty addresses the possibility that directors might try to steal from their firms. The duty of loyalty discourages such theft by imposing liability on directors who enter unfair "interested transactions," meaning transactions between the firm and the director (or between the firm and some individual or entity in which the director has a personal interest) under terms that are unfavorable to the firm. It also penalizes directors who steal from their firms by "taking corporate opportunities" — business opportunities that, for a variety of reasons, ought to have gone to the firm.

A problem arises, however, when we look to the remedy that is normally granted when a court finds that a director has violated the duty of loyalty.

When a director has participated in an unfair transaction with the firm, the usual remedy is to make the director pay a fair price. If the director has violated the duty of loyalty by taking a corporate opportunity, she must return to the firm any profits made from that opportunity. In sum, the remedy for a breach of the duty of loyalty is to make the director give back whatever she has stolen from the firm.

This is not the kind of threat to strike terror into a larcenous heart. As any parent can tell you, if the only punishment a child receives for stealing from the cookie jar is that she has to give back the cookies if caught, you can expect a lot of stolen cookies. For similar reasons, it is easy to suspect that the threat of being held liable for breach of the duty of loyalty is not the sole, or even the principal, reason most corporate directors do not steal from their firms. Although the duty of loyalty on first inspection deters corporate directors from stealing, closer analysis suggests that as a practical matter the rule does not have much bite.

This toothlessness is even more obvious in the case of the director's duty of care. In theory, corporate directors owe their firms a duty to manage those tens of trillions of dollars of corporate assets with the care of a reasonably prudent person. In practice (as any law student who has taken a class in corporations knows) the duty of care is ameliorated — some might say eviscerated — by a doctrine known as the business judgment rule. The business judgment rule is a legal presumption that a director has, in fact, met the standards of the duty of care. This presumption can only be overcome if a plaintiff can show that the director did not act "on an informed basis," "in good faith," or "in the honest belief that the action taken was in the best interests of the company." The last two elements (good faith and honest belief) usually go unchallenged in any case that does not involve the sort of conflict of interest that gives rise to a loyalty question. As a result, whether the business judgment rule applies to a particular director usually turns solely on whether that director bothered to "inform" herself before acting. Furthermore, the test for whether a director is uninformed is not mere negligence, but gross negligence.

The business judgment rule accordingly allows a director who makes even a minimal effort to become "informed" to make foolhardy decisions all day long, without fear of liability. And what about the rare case of the director who is found to have been uninformed? Even then, other barriers protect directors from personal liability. For example, Delaware corporation law allows corporations to adopt charter provisions that eliminate director liability for breach of the duty of care. A number of large corporations have taken advantage of this provision. In firms that have not, if a lawsuit claiming breach of director care is brought, the odds are that it will be settled, and either an insurance company will foot the bill (under a director's liability policy) or the corporation itself will pay (under an indemnity provision).

Taking these factors together, it is only a slight exaggeration to suggest that a corporate director is statistically more likely to be attacked by killer bees than she is to have to ever pay damages for breach of the duty of care. This reality of business life is well-recognized among corporate scholars. In response, several have suggested in recent articles that corporate directors exercise care not because they fear legal sanctions, but because they fear what might be called "social sanctions" — because they do not want to lose face, acquire a bad reputation, or become the object of disapproving glances and cutting remarks.

This is an intriguing argument. There are several reasons, however, to suspect that the fear of social sanctions may provide only a weak incentive for exercising care for most directors in most circumstances. While directors involved in more-spectacular corporate crimes (for example, a massive accounting fraud) can suffer unpleasant notoriety, allegations of garden-variety negligence or conflict of interest are far less likely to attract media attention. In most cases neither the general public, nor a director's immediate social circle, would know (much less care) whether she was doing a good job as a fiduciary. Similarly, it can be difficult for others to judge whether an allegation of breach of fiduciary duty has merit, or is simply an attempt to extract money from the director's liability insurer through the threat of a "strike suit." For these and other reasons, external sanctions — including not only legal sanctions, but also social sanctions — are inadequate to explain why a purely self-interested director would take her fiduciary duties seriously. . . .

NOTES & QUESTIONS

1. How do popular culture and media coverage depict corporate directors? How do you feel toward Enron's board of corporate directors? What factors do you believe motivate desirable and undesirable behavior of corporate directors? Do you think corporate directors are more afraid of punishment in the form of financial and legal sanctions or loss of personal and social reputation? Do you believe that large monetary fines or even small jail sentences are more likely to deter malfeasance by corporate directors?

2. Some corporate law scholars think that the business judgment rule safeguards against corporate directors, who acted competently even though corporate outcomes turned out badly, being mistaken to have acted negligently by judges, juries, and shareholders, all of whom typically have less business expertise and may also exhibit hindsight bias. This cognitive bias occurs when people are prone to exaggerate in hindsight what one knew in foresight. In other words, hindsight vision is 20/20. Do you find this explanation for having a business judgment rule convincing? Why does there not exist a similar type of rule for medical doctors and malpractice because legal fact finders, judges, and shareholders, all of whom also lack medical and surgical expertise, may exhibit hindsight bias?

3. Consider Professor Lynn A. Stout's conclusions:

> Most important, if we want the social institution of the board of directors to be effective, we should do our best to accomplish three things. First, we should try to ensure that directors receive social signals that will encourage them to adopt an other-regarding, rather than a purely self-interested, perspective — that will convince them that they ought to "do the right thing." Second, we should make sure that doing the right thing is not too personally costly for directors. Third, we should

make sure that we pick the sort of people who want to do the right thing in the first place.

Lynn A. Stout, *On the Proper Motives of Corporate Directors (Or, Why You Don't Want to Invite Homo Economicus to Join Your Board)*, 28 Delaware Journal of Corporate Law 1, 24-25 (2003). Can members of corporate boards of directors benefit from such continuing education programs as Stanford Law School's directors' college or directors' consortium, detailed at http://www.law. stanford.edu/programs/execed/programs.html? Would you like to be a member of a corporate board of directors someday? Can a single member of a corporate board of directors have a good or corrupting influence upon other members of a corporate board of directors?

4. How appropriate, helpful, and insightful was it for the movie *The Corporation* to apply a tool for psychiatrists and psychologists to make diagnoses of human psychiatric illnesses, the Diagnostic and Statistical Manual of Mental Disorders, Fourth Edition (DSM-IV), to corporations, and find that according to the DSM-IV, corporations display highly anti-social psychopathic "personalities"? Does a corporation have a personality and, if so, is that personality its corporate culture? Would it surprise you if most corporations and organizations in general had multiple personalities? Should lawmakers require that directors, executives, and managers of corporations undergo mandatory psychological counseling and therapy?

5. Does the public take today's managerial chief executive officers to be more or less powerful business figures than their financial, deal-making counterparts? Are corporate managers or investment bankers more sympathetic as business figures? According to Professor William W. Bratton, Jr., "Today's popular conception of the powerful business figure is not the managerialist chief executive officer but the capitalist deal maker — the financial entrepreneur or the investment banker. Characterized in the vocabulary of the new economic theory, these figures acquire power as transaction cost engineers. They conceive and initiate transactions, depriving the managerial beneficiaries of the more costly existing contracts of power and wealth." William W. Bratton, Jr., *The New Economic Theory of the Firm: Critical Perspectives from History*, 41 Stanford Law Review 1471, 1523 (1989). Do managers fit more comfortably within the public's conceptions of business than financial engineers of corporate transactions? Are most people more likely to identify with a corporate executive officer, such as Martha Stewart, or a financial entrepreneur, such as Ivan Boesky?

6. In the movie *Working Girl* (1988), Katherine Parker (played by Sigourney Weaver), an associate partner in mergers and acquisitions at Petty, Marsh, & Company, steals an idea for a merger deal from her assistant Tess McGill (played by Melanie Griffith). Do you feel that the gender of these characters made any difference, dramatically or in some other manner? Compare them with Caroline Butler (played by Teri Garr) in *Mr. Mom* (1983). She is a successful advertising executive who must overcome a lecherous boss, Ron Richardson (played by Martin Mull), and a sexist client. Another fictional businesswoman is J.C. Wiatt (played by Diane Keaton) in *Baby Boom* (1987). She is a management consulting executive who is forced to give up her career when she becomes a single mom and intolerant executives at Sloane Curtis & Co.

demote her, but she ultimately triumphs upon founding her own gourmet baby food company. Do you feel that portrayals of businesswomen are typically less or more sympathetic than portrayals of businessmen? Are they portrayed as equally competent in popular culture?

7. Professor Manuel A. Utset suggests:

> [T]ime-inconsistent preferences can lead managers to engage in nibbling opportunism and gatekeepers to repeatedly procrastinate monitoring and disciplining managers, notwithstanding the fact that doing so defeats their long-term preferences. This time-inconsistent explanation of misbehavior helps explain, at least in part, the puzzling behavior of mid-level managers, accountants, and lawyers in the recent corporate scandals; in misbehaving, these actors appear to have risked far too much compared to the benefits that (even in the most optimistic scenarios) they could have expected to receive.

Manuel A. Utset, *Time-Inconsistent Management & the Sarbanes-Oxley Act*, 31 Ohio Northern University Law Review 417, 444 (2005).

Are you someone who repeatedly plans to start a new diet in a few days in order to lose some weight and become healthier? Do you know a smoker who had a life-long preference to quit smoking cigarettes, but who nevertheless ended up smoking a couple of packs daily for his entire life until finally developing lung cancer? Are you familiar with people who really would like to live comfortably in their senior years, but find that nonetheless they are constantly spending over their monthly budgets prior to retirement? If people have self-control problems in their personal and private lives, could those same people display self-control problems in their business and corporate lives?

8. Besides Gordon Gekko in *Wall Street* and Larry the Liquidator in *Other People's Money*, there are many examples of business executives being portrayed as evil characters in popular culture. For example, Dick Jones, the senior vice president of Omni Consumer Products, murders another vice president, Bob Morton, when Morton threatens Jones' tenure in the science fiction movie *Robocop* (1987). Why do you believe that most American movies choose to portray most business executives as being at least unsympathetic, if not downright evil?

9. Consider Professor Nancy B. Rapoport's analysis of whether *Titanic* (1997) or *The Perfect Storm* (2000) provides a more accurate metaphor for Enron:

> The metaphor most used to describe Enron's quick descent into chapter 11 has been "the perfect storm." That "perfect storm" metaphor irks me to no end. I maintain, and this essay is designed to illustrate, that what brought Enron down — at least as far as we know — wasn't a once-in-a-lifetime alignment of elements beyond its control. Rather, Enron's demise was a synergistic combination of human errors and hubris: a "Titanic" miscalculation, rather than a "perfect storm."

Nancy B. Rapoport, *Enron, Titanic, and the Perfect Storm*, 71 Fordham Law Review 1373, 1374–75. Before you started law school, how much did you know about what happened at Enron? After seeing *Enron — The Smartest Guys in the Room*, do you feel that you understand much better than before about what happened at Enron? If you had been an employee working at Enron, do you feel that you would have wanted to believe that Enron stock was a good investment?

10. In Professor Lynn A. Stout's analysis of why stockholders of publicly traded corporations permit boards of directors to control their corporation's assets, she makes the analogy that "as the legendary Ulysses served his own interests by binding himself to the mast of his ship, investors may be serving their own interests by binding themselves to boards." Lynn A. Stout, *The Shareholder as Ulysses: Some Empirical Evidence on Why Investors in Public Corporations Tolerate Board Governance*, 152 University of Pennsylvania Law Review 667, 669 (2003). Is Professor Stout's analogy convincing and helpful? Besides ceding their authority to boards of directors, are there other legal and non-legal mechanisms for stockholders to bind themselves from temptations? Assume that Professor Stout's analogy correctly describes a role played by corporate boards of directors. How can you explain the dominance and popularity of a model that focuses on corporate boards of directors as monitors who police against potential misbehavior by other corporate executives?

3. Individual Investors, Institutional Investors, and Securities Regulators

THE MECHANISMS OF MARKET INEFFICIENCY: AN INTRODUCTION TO THE NEW FINANCE
Lynn A. Stout
28 Journal of Corporation Law 635 (2003)

Real people, of course, are not always rational. Sometimes we are misled by our emotions, and sometimes we make foolish mistakes. The fundamental insight of behavioral finance is that human emotion and error can influence investment choices just as they influence choices to play lotteries or wear seatbelts. The trick, of course, is to figure out in advance just how this influence operates. To do this, behavioral finance theorists rely on the psychological literature, and especially on empirical studies of human behavior in experimental games, to identify predictable forms of "cognitive bias" that lead people consistently to make mistakes. They then examine whether these systematic biases can help explain or predict empirically-observed market anomalies that cannot be explained or predicted by rational-actor-based traditional finance.

It is difficult to overstate just how rapidly the behavioral finance literature has grown over the past decade. Over one hundred papers and a number of books have been produced on the topic, which has also inspired specialty journals. Indeed, the number of behavioral finance papers being produced now rivals scholarly production in traditional finance.

At the same time, many of the behavioral finance studies that have captured public attention are not the sort that would convince a skeptic that the field necessarily has much to offer in terms of developing our structural understanding of securities markets. For example, one recent study reports that stock prices are significantly influenced by the lunar cycle, while another concludes that seasonal affective disorder (SAD) leads stock returns to rise and fall with the seasonal lengthening and shortening of daylight hours. A third "behavioral finance" theory that has been discussed in the national media — if not in a peer-edited journal — explains the late-1990s stock market bubble as a consequence of the increased use of antidepressants such as Prozac and Zoloft, with an attendant collective surge in investor optimism. (Sadly, this entertaining theory suffers from a number of flaws, most obviously its inability to explain the Crash of 2000 absent evidence the investing public suddenly and collectively "went off its meds.")

These sorts of studies have raised the profile of behavioral finance in the popular media. Unfortunately, they have also contributed to a perception among many theorists that behavioral finance is more suitable for dinner party conversation than for serious research. This perception has been reinforced by the rather large number of cognitive biases that have been argued to influence securities prices, some of them quirky, some of them short-lived, and some of them apparently contradictory. The net result has been the widespread impression that while behavioral finance sometimes may be useful to arbitrageurs, it has little to offer theorists other than a prediction that securities prices sometimes depart from informed estimates of value in arbitrary and capricious ways.

This impression is unjustified. More careful review of the behavioral finance literature quickly reveals that, in addition to offering insights into the effects of seasonal and lunar cycles, behavioral finance can also help explain market phenomena that are far more enduring and consequential. . . .

NOTES & QUESTIONS

1. How convinced are you that most small retail investors are prone to rely on cognitive biases, emotions, and heuristics in making investment decisions? Why do you think small retail investors do not learn from their investing errors? Do you believe that securities markets will eventually weed out small retail investors who do not make their stock picks rationally? Are large institutional investors, such as hedge funds, mutual funds, and pension funds, likely to have their own set of cognitive biases, heuristics, and emotional motivations for investment decisions?

2. Professor Lynn A. Stout elsewhere states:

American investors take it as a matter of faith that the brokers and mutual fund managers to whom they entrust their savings will use those funds to actually purchase securities on their behalf. They take it as a matter of faith that the corporations that issue securities really exist, have real assets, and make real profits. Because they have faith, American investors buy trillions of dollars of corporate equities each year, even when they are not quite sure what it is that they are buying. . . . This is not to say that American investors necessarily believe that corporate insiders and securities professionals are honest and dependable individuals. . . . At a minimum, however, American investors must believe that somehow the legal system constrains these individuals sufficiently that the benefits of investing outweigh the risks. They must believe that the regulators are regulating, and the watchdogs are watching. . . . [T]hey must at least trust the system.

Lynn A. Stout, *The Investor Confidence Game*, 68 Brooklyn Law Review 407, 419-20 (2002). If she is correct, then erosion of investor confidence and trust in securities markets by corporate scandals is a serious economic, legal, and social problem. Do you believe that faith by small retail investors in American securities regulation can be and has been restored? Is there possibly a problem of small retail investors being overconfident in U.S. securities markets and securities regulation?

3. Professor David A. Hoffman observes:

[C]ourts hold purchasers of securities to something similar to a duty of care. Courts require investors to investigate their purchases, to coldly process risk, to disregard oral statements of optimism, and in general to be economically rational. If investors fail to meet these expectations, judges deny them the protection of the securities laws. In this way, courts impose on public securities investors a special kind of legal duty, novel in scope and, I will argue, ungrounded in principle.

David A. Hoffman, *The "Duty" to Be a Rational Shareholder*, 90 Minnesota Law Review 537, 538 (2006). Do you feel that most small retail investors are likely to behave as rational shareholders? Do you believe that courts treating small retail investors as if they were rational shareholders can lead small retail investors to become rational shareholders?

4. Consider this analysis of why irrational anxiety and exuberance of investors may persist over time for both small retail investors and institutional investors:

As with Bill Murray's character, Phil, in the movie *Groundhog Day*, noiseless feedback and stationary environments promote learning effects. But investing yields very noisy feedback because people can quite naturally (and perhaps even subconsciously) confuse their investment successes with financial insight and confuse their investment failures with bad luck. In addition, empirical evidence suggests that securities markets are highly nonstationary environments. . . .

Although securities markets are highly competitive, valuation in securities markets is an extremely subjective process. Emotional factors often influence the assessment of securities values across investors, just as emotions often affect subjective appraisals of the value of residential properties across home buyers and home owners. In fact, because securities, unlike consumer durables and real estate, are never consumed, securities markets, even more than other durable goods markets, involve subjective, often ephemeral and potentially very emotional anticipations of the future. Whereas reasonable people may agree on the past and the present (although there is reason to be skeptical of even these propositions as evidenced by the well-known fallibility of eyewitness testimony and memory), reasonable people often disagree on the future, both in terms of the set of contemplated outcomes and their various relative likelihoods. People are repeatedly caught off guard upon the realization of previously subjectively unforeseen contingencies.

Peter H. Huang, *Regulating Irrational Exuberance and Anxiety in Securities Markets*, in *The Law and Economics of Irrational Behavior* 506–07 (Francesco Paresi & Vernon Smith, eds., 2005). Can learning by investors be problematic? Does investing most resemble a video game that you can learn how to play optimally after many repeated iterations or a game of chance such as a slot machine or blackjack at which you can improve but can never learn to master completely? Can you think of reasons why investors would be unable to learn how to invest better over time?

5. Do you feel that most investors are motivated to believe they are smart when they make a lot of money investing and to believe they are unlucky when they lose a lot of money investing? Do you think that these are other personal contexts in which most people have motivated beliefs: "my spouse and kids love me"; "my colleagues and neighbors like me"; and "God is looking out for me, my family, and friends"? Can and should legal policy do anything to correct people's motivated beliefs?

6. Do such movies as *Boiler Room* (1992) and *Rogue Trader* (1999) depict environmental and situational contexts that foster an individualistic type of a lone gun-slinger frame of reference and mentality? Do you find it surprising that sexual harassment lawsuits alleging hostile workplace environments have been filed and settled against male-dominated stock brokerages? What do you make of empirical data finding that: (a) men are more overconfident compared to women; (b) individual male stock investors trade more frequently than individual women stock investors; and (c) individual male stock investors do worse financially than individual women stock investors?

7. Are securities brokers and professionals more or less likely than average people to be overly competitive, exploitive, opportunistic, and self-regarding? Do securities employers look to hire employees who enjoy taking risks, are indifferent toward risk-taking, or averse toward risk-taking? What sort of personality types do you think are more likely to enter and stay in securities professions?

8. Consider this account of moody investing:

There is experimental evidence of systematic differences between two psychological processes that people utilize to construct their preferences, namely valuation by calculation and valuation by feelings. Recent research in psychology and the neurosciences reveals that humans comprehend and face risk utilizing two fundamental systems, one analytic and the other experiential. Of course, in practice, "reason and emotion are intertwined as the threads in an oriental carpet." But, moody investing refers to investing that is (at least, partially) non-cognitive. . . . Affect and images crucially shape people's attitudes towards securities and their judgments concerning securities. On the positive affect side, in 2000 and 2001, a $3 million advertising campaign in European and Asian magazines and newspapers introduced

a series of global mutual funds alongside fashion supermodels. . . . On
the negative affect side, perceived dangers of genetically manipulated
organisms can stigmatize biotechnological stocks. . . . Finally, a recent
event study documented that positive abnormal returns and increased
trading volume followed a company's Super Bowl television commercials.

Peter H. Huang, *Moody Investing and the Supreme Court: Rethinking
Materiality of Information and Reasonableness of Investors*, 13 Supreme Court
Economic Review 102–05 (2005). Do you believe that cognitive or moody
investing more accurately describes how most retail small investors actually
behave? Do securities issuers and other professionals intend for their communications with investors to affect investors' cognitions or moods? If investors
are less aware of how securities advertisements, communications, and disclosures affect their moods than their cognitions, then can and should securities
regulators be more worried about cognitive or moody investing?

9. Professors Steven J. Choi & Adam C. Pritchard argue that:

If cognitive defects are pervasive, will intervention help? Even well-
intentioned and fully rational regulators may find it difficult to solve
the problem of cognitive illusions among investors. Disclosure, the prevailing regulatory strategy in the securities markets, may not protect
investors if cognitive biases prevent them from rationally incorporating the information disclosed into their investment decisions. More
fundamentally, if everyone suffers from cognitive defects, doesn't that
also include the commissioners and staff of the SEC?

Steven J. Choi & Adam C. Pritchard, *Behavioral Economics and the SEC*,
56 Stanford Law Review 1, 5–6 (2003). How can, does, and should law and
regulatory policy balance concerns over the relative decision-making and judgment competencies of investors as opposed to securities regulators? *See also*
Stephen J. Choi, *Behavioral Economics and the Regulation of Public Offerings*,
10 Lewis & Clark Law Review 85 (2006).

10. Consider this analysis of some online brokerage ads:

Television commercials by online securities brokerages not only
emphasized the personal control, ease, and profitability of such trading, but also were rich in emotional imagery. . . .

A Discover Brokerage Direct television commercial about online trading depicted a conversation between a passenger and a stock-trading
tow-truck driver, who states, "That's my home. Looks more like an
island. Technically, it's a country." Another television commercial
included a stock-trading teenager, who owned his own helicopter.
A series of Schwab commercials featured such celebrities as former
teenage Russian tennis star Anna Kournikova. An E*TRADE advertisement claimed "that on-line investing is 'A cinch. A snap. A piece of
cake'"). . . .

Peter H. Huang, *Regulating Irrational Exuberance and Anxiety in Securities
Markets*, in *The Law and Economics of Irrational Behavior, supra*, 511–13
(2005). What is one's likely reaction upon seeing these sorts of television

commercials depicting individuals being able to "get rich very quickly" via online investing? Were you amused, placed in a good mood, and more likely to look into how to be an online stock investor? How would you have reacted if you had also seen sad, vivid, and visceral depictions of unlucky online investors or day traders losing their shirts, life savings, retirement nest eggs, or kids' college education funds?

C. BUSINESS ENVIRONMENTS

1. Capital Markets and Initial Public Offerings

Much of the dotcom stock market boom involved unprecedented first-day stock price spikes of Initial Public Offerings (IPOs). In this next section, Professor Christine Hurt analyzes IPOs.

MORAL HAZARD AND THE INITIAL PUBLIC OFFERING
Christine Hurt
26 Cardozo Law Review 711 (2005)

Rising skepticism among the public has created a backlash against corporations, underwriters, analysts, and mutual funds that has resulted in numerous investigations, civil and criminal, into various trading practices, some of which have been around in various forms for years. At the same time, the number of individual investors participating in the capital markets has grown substantially, highlighting the discrepancies in investing opportunities between Wall Street regulars and retail investors.

One of the first trading practices to come under regulatory and shareholder fire was the initial public offering (IPO) process, which has revealed itself to be undemocratic at best and manipulative at worst. During the late 1990s and early 2000s (the "1999–2000 Boom"), a growing number of companies "went public," making the transition from being privately owned to having shares traded and owned by public investors. During the 1999–2000 Boom, IPOs generated $65 billion each year, compared with $8 billion per year in the 1980s. Among those companies going public were an increasing number of companies without a significant history of positive earnings. However, the prices of shares of these companies were skyrocketing in value during the first hours or days of the offering. Although large first-day returns of IPO shares have been reported for decades, the first-day returns during this period were unprecedented. However, most individual investors were never buyers of original IPO shares. In the presence of very high demand for shares in almost any IPO, underwriters allocated the majority of original IPO shares to regular customers, mostly institutional investors, and few retail investors are able to buy these shares until they were resold by an original buyer. Because of the high demand for IPO shares, any investor who was offered the opportunity to buy original IPO shares at the offering price was buying an almost guaranteed first-day profit.

Unfortunately, the majority of the shares issued in IPOs in the last few years did not retain that initial profit, and the share price eventually plummeted, resulting in a loss for the retail investor who purchased in the aftermarket. For every person inside the IPO loop who sold high, a retail investor bought high. What at first seems to be a very respectable process, managed by the most elite investment banks, analysts, and venture capitalists substantially conforming to existing securities laws, turns out to be a Wall Street-sponsored "pump-and-dump" scheme.

Historically, taking a company public was the equivalent of receiving the Good Housekeeping Seal of Approval; not only was the company a success story, but Wall Street was vouching for its potential for all the investing public to see. However, after the end of the most recent IPO boom, investors are beginning to realize that Wall Street was very willing to sell its stamp of approval for the opportunity to use a company's IPO for personal gain. In the 1999–2000 Boom the investing public fell victim to the oldest trick in the IPO order book: The Pump-and-Dump. Together, existing securities laws and industry customs have worked together to create a system that not only routinely excludes the small investor from seizing the opportunity to be an original buyer of IPO shares but also cleverly attracts the same investor to purchase these same shares in the aftermarket, locking in a profit for the fortunate original buyers. . . .

Securities laws universally condemn "pump-and-dump" schemes whereby insiders and underwriters hype a company's stock and create an illusion of high demand, then sell their shares once the public has accepted the hype and bought the stock. Wall Street generally derides these activities, assigning them to "microcap companies," internet scams and telemarketing ventures. Disturbingly, the movie *Boiler Room* juxtaposes a fly-by-night investment banking firm staffed with loud, aggressive men of varying ethnic backgrounds without Ivy League educations against Wall Street investment banking firms staffed with sophisticated, WASP-ish MBAs. Of course, the former firm engages almost exclusively in illegal pump-and-dump schemes. Divorcing these stereotypes from the actual behavior, imagine a scenario in which any group of underwriters and company insiders tout the value of a stock, create arrangements whereby other industry insiders create demand in the stock in return for cheap stock, and then sell their shares shortly after a successful IPO. This scenario, which describes the U.S. IPO process, is a pump-and-dump scheme.

Each step in the IPO process, when performed by industry players acting in their self-interest, creates an ingenious method to extract wealth from the retail investor. Because industry custom and legal practices combine together to restrict supply and generate demand, IPO share prices may increase substantially, allowing both issuer and industry insiders to sell early and realize profit. However, the average IPO stock will then see a dramatic decrease, leaving the retail investors with built-in losses. . . .

NOTES & QUESTIONS

1. Do small retail investors actually understand the above types of details about how the IPO process worked? Should greed and irrational exuberance by investors be considered in regulating IPOs?

2. You can find a transcript of the PBS *Frontline* television program *Dot Con*, which aired on January 24, 2002 at http://www.pbs.org/wgbh/pages/frontline/shows/dotcon/etc/script.html. There is a website for that program at http://www.pbs.org/wgbh/pages/frontline/shows/dotcon/ that provides additional online resource materials about IPOs. Explore some of the hyperlinks on these websites. After doing so, what do you think of the legality and morality of how investment banks conducted IPOs in 1999–2000?

3. Does disclosing potential conflicts of interest by securities analysts who also work at investment banks actually lead to investors being more trusting and securities analysts feeling more justified in engaging in hyperbole? In other words, do you think a danger exists that upon disclosure about potential conflicts of interest, audience members feel that speakers are less prone to exaggerate, but speakers feel they can exaggerate more than previously because their audience has been duly warned of their potential conflicts of interest. *See Conflicts of Interest: Challenges and Solutions in Business, Law, Medicine, and Public Policy* (Don A. Moore et al., eds., 2005). Is investor confidence and trust in IPO markets only a cognitive decision?

4. How easy will it be for corporate America to restore investor confidence and trust in IPO markets? Do people who get rich in IPO markets do so because of their superior abilities, hard work, or personal and social connections?

5. Have you ever watched any of these financial news programs: *The Wall Street Journal Report with Maria Bartiromo*, in national syndication; *Closing Bell* with Maria Bartiromo, on CNBC; James Cramer's *Mad Money*, on CNBC; *The Suze Orman Show*, on CNBC; *Squawk Box*, on CNBC; and *Market Wrap* with Ron Insana, on MSNBC? Is it easy to distinguish between entertainment and information on these shows? While watching these programs, are you less or more likely to buy or sell corporate stocks? Do some commentators on these shows appear to be unbiased cheerleaders for corporate America? Is it likely that stock analysts who appeared on such programs and recommended buying particular stocks during the last bull market contributed to irrational exuberance? Do you trust anchors of these shows to be knowledgeable and unbiased? What do you think about financial news hosts becoming celebrities, media darlings, and popular icons?

6. You can view the PBS *Frontline* television show *Secret History of the Credit Card* (Nov. 23, 2004) at http://www.pbs.org/wgbh/pages/frontline/shows/credit/view/. There is a companion website for that program at http://www.pbs.org/wgbh/pages/frontline/shows/credit/more/ that provides additional online resource material about derivatives markets. Explore some of the hyperlinks on that website. Also explore and peruse these websites about financial education or planning: The Decision Education Foundation, at http://www.decisioneducation.org/; Visa's Practical Money Skills for Life, at http://www.practicalmoneyskills.com/english/index.php; Financial Engines, at http://www.financialengines.com/FeContent?act=welcome; The Saint Paul Foundation, What's My Score, at http://www.whatsmyscore.org/; and the University of Minnesota, Freshman Survival Skills, at http://www.collegelife. umn.edu/fsoscourse.shtem. Do you find these websites to be amusing, confusing, educational, or informative?

2. Securities Markets and Fraud

According to Professors Jennifer H. Arlen and William J. Carney, "Fraud on the Market usually occurs when agents fear themselves to be in their last period of employment." Jennifer H. Arlen & William J. Carney, *Vicarious Liability for Fraud on Securities Markets: Theory and Evidence*, 1992 University of Illinois Law Review 691, 693. As you read the following excerpt, consider whether you agree that securities markets fail to discipline corporate and securities fraud when corporate directors and managers are in their last period of employment.

DEAL PROTECTION PROVISIONS IN THE LAST PERIOD OF PLAY
Sean J. Griffith
71 Fordham Law Review 1899 (2003)

Another negative net present value project that managers in their last period of play may consider is securities fraud. Professors Arlen and Carney have shown that last period incentives may drive "fraud on the market" schemes. In securities law, "fraud on the market" consists of issuing false statements to increase or maintain the firm's stock price. A manager's midstream incentives generally do not favor committing fraud on the market because at some point the statements are likely to be revealed as false, causing the paper gains in stock price to vanish. Moreover, when the statements are revealed as false, the manager is likely to be fired. Yet fraud on the market occurs, Professors Arlen and Carney argue, as a result of the last period problem:

> [A]n agent generally will not commit Fraud on the Market so long as his future employment seems assured. When the firm is ailing, however, an agent's expectations of future employment no longer serve as a constraint on behavior. In this situation a manager may view securities fraud as a positive net present value project. Aside from criminal liability, in a last period the expected costs of fraud (civil liability and job loss) are minimal, while the expected benefits of fraud may have increased. As remote as the prospects for success may seem, these benefits include possible preservation of employment as well as the value of the manager's assets related to the firm's stock, if by committing fraud he is able to buy sufficient time to turn the ailing firm around.

Managers facing the failure of their business may thus prefer to risk lying to the market, potentially incurring legal liability, than to suffer the immediate and certain consequences of the market's reaction to the truth — that is, the further decline of their share price and creditworthiness and the further degradation of their business prospects.

Far from academic abstraction, these concerns can be seen to motivate several of the recent accounting scandals, including Enron and WorldCom. Putting aside the apparent self-interest of Enron's chief financial officer, the use of off-balance sheet financing activities seems to have been directed towards the end of keeping news of Enron's increasing losses from the market until a turnaround in the company's fortunes occurred. The turnaround never came, the financing activities revealed management as dishonest, and the company failed. Similarly, the dishonest financial reporting of WorldCom may be seen as management's attempt to conceal the truth about a fast-failing company long enough for a market turnaround (or an extension of credit) to save their jobs. Again, they failed.

Another corporate law last period problem occurs when a company is sold, as in a "bust up" acquisition. In the film *Wall Street*, for example, Michael Douglas portrayed a prototypically loathsome raider, proposing to buy Blue Star Airlines, auction its fleet of airplanes, fire its employees, and use its pension fund to finance the acquisition, thus plunging the fictional company into a paradigmatic last period scenario. In such situations, ordinary mid-stream constraints will not operate with their usual force and may not operate at all. Blue Star managers and directors will be indifferent to product market constraints because the firm, ceasing to operate as a going concern, will no longer take products to market, indifferent to capital market constraints because the firm will no longer need to raise capital, indifferent to labor market constraints because there will be no more hirings or promotions, indifferent to the market for corporate control because control has already been wrested from them, and indifferent to intra-firm norms because the firm will soon be extinct. Faced with the destruction of the firm and, perhaps, the end of their careers, directors and managers are freed from the concerns that ordinarily constrain their decision-making and may therefore be more apt to behave foolishly or selfishly. . . .

NOTES & QUESTIONS

1. How do the requirements of apartment complexes that renters pay their monthly rents on the first of each month or that renters pay one month's rent in addition to a cleaning deposit upon moving into their apartments affect renters' incentives regarding paying their last month's rent? Can you see why corporate directors and managers can have perverse incentives for engaging in corporate malfeasance or securities fraud if their employment or their corporation is near its end?

2. You can find "detailed information relating to the prosecution, defense, and settlement of federal class action securities fraud litigation" at http://securities.stanford.edu/, a public database provided by Stanford Law School. This website also contains articles, reports, and research studies about how federal class action securities fraud litigation changed after passage in 1995 of the Private Securities Litigation Reform Act (PSLRA). Explore some of these resources. After doing so, do you think that this public database succeeds at correcting some misimpressions that people are likely to have about federal class action securities fraud litigation based upon sensationalist documentaries or media coverage and fictional accounts in popular culture?

3. Are an individual's political beliefs likely to be highly correlated with that individual's sympathy for securities plaintiffs or defendants? Do you think a focus on apocryphal widows and orphans as defrauded securities plaintiffs by journalists, politicians, and regulators is more than just merely a theatrical device? Do you find talk of wanting securities markets to be a level playing field to be mere rhetoric? Could a level playing field drain itself?

4. Do securities markets reward hard work, pure chance, or private information? Is the movie *Wall Street* representative of popular culture in the way it depicts insider securities trading as being evil and immoral?

5. What did you think about Martha Stewart being prosecuted for insider securities trading? Did Martha Stewart declare her innocence of being engaged in insider securities trading in order to commit securities fraud against her stockholders?

6. In the last scene of the movie *Wall Street*, we see Bud Fox (played by Charlie Sheen) ascending the steps of the New York state court building instead of the United States federal court building. In the United States, it is the responsibility of the federal government, and not any individual state government, to oversee the regulation of securities markets; any securities fraud that Gordon Gekko and Bud Fox would have committed in the movie *Wall Street* would have been a federal, not state, offense. This means that Fox is entering an incorrect building, assuming that he is on his way to help the Securities and Exchange Commission or the Justice Department convict his former mentor. This minor inaccuracy relates to the issue of whether legal accuracy matters in popular culture. Did you notice this mistake? Do you believe that most viewers of the movie knew of this error? Would they be less inclined to believe the business and legal accuracy of the rest of the story told in the movie if they were informed of these mix-ups?

3. Derivatives Markets and Debacles

DERIVATIVES ON TV: A TALE OF TWO DERIVATIVES DEBACLES IN PRIME-TIME
Peter H. Huang, Kimberly D. Kraviec & Frank Partnoy
4 Green Bag 2d 257 (2001)

On March 5, 1995, the CBS newsmagazine *60 Minutes* broadcast a story about derivatives, focusing on Orange County. Reporter Steve Kroft introduced derivatives as "too complicated to explain, but too important to ignore," and described derivatives as "highly exotic, little understood, and virtually unregulated." *60 Minutes* concluded its introduction to derivatives by noting that "some people believe they're [derivatives] so unpredictable they could bring down the world banking system." The show opened with aerial images of picturesque Orange County: birds flying over the blue Pacific, palm tree-lined homes with pools, yachts, a plush golf course, and sandy beaches, under the sun.

Throughout the program, Kroft and his guests likened derivatives to gambling, repeatedly emphasizing that derivatives are essentially bets. This analogy is misleading because buying certain derivatives is like buying insurance against an accident, while not buying those derivatives is essentially betting on the accident not happening. The interviewees (primarily private and public fund managers) also emphasized the complexity of derivatives. Kroft claimed that, no matter who they interviewed and no matter how hard they tried, viewers and investors were unlikely to understand derivatives. A Painesville, Ohio councilman and two female treasurers from Ohio school districts corroborated this point by claiming that they had purchased derivatives without realizing that they had done so and without understanding the risks involved. To emphasize this point, Kroft exhibited the coupon rate formula for one Orange County derivative contract, a formula that obviously would appear impossibly complex to a viewer unfamiliar with derivatives (but could have been explained step-by-step).

The program continued to liken derivatives investing to complex science by stating that Wall Street hired "rocket scientists" with mathematics or physics Ph.D.s, but no finance background, neglecting to note that Wall Street also hired many finance Ph.D.s (or even salesmen with little technical training). Kroft compared rocket scientists to genetic engineers and derivatives to Frankenstein's monsters.

60 Minutes concluded by suggesting ominously that viewers may already own derivatives in mutual funds or pension plans without realizing it. In the parting shot, Kroft queried the Ohio councilman as to where the money that his city treasury had lost in derivatives went. After several moments of embarrassed silence, the councilman was forced to admit that he had no idea. Unfortunately, neither did *60 Minutes'* producers.

On February 8, 2000, the PBS show *NOVA: Trillion Dollar Bet* described the discovery of the Black-Scholes option pricing formula and its use by LTCM [Long-Term Capital Management]. The show opened with aerial images of Chicago and trading in the pits of the Chicago Mercantile Exchange, while stating the golden rule of capitalism: "if you want to make money, you have to take risks."

NOVA explored the tension between much modern financial theory, exemplified by economist Merton Miller's explanation of the random walk theory of stock prices and the efficient markets hypothesis, and the views held by many professional traders that it is possible to predict market prices and thus "beat the market." This view was stressed by one trader's explanation of the importance of fear, human judgment, intuition, and psychology. Financial economist Zvi Bodie articulated the view that traders may succeed due more to luck than skill.

NOVA provided a good overview of the history of options pricing and the development of modern options pricing models. Paul Samuelson, for example, discussed early attempts to price options, referring to a precise option pricing formula as the "Holy Grail." The *NOVA* commentators described the shortcomings of early financial models, which attempted to capture mathematically a typical investor's risk preferences, emotions, and guesses about other investors' expectations. The problem with such models, as Bodie explained, is that they required unobservable inputs.

Scholes described the great contribution to the field made by Fisher Black and Scholes: eliminating all unobservable variables from the model except one: the riskiness of the underlying stock. By depicting synchronized moving colored graphs, the show clearly explained and illustrated the crucial ideas of dynamic hedging and portfolio replication.

Robert Merton then explained his continuous-time version of the Black-Scholes model. *NOVA* successfully countered the fearful reactions television viewers often have to mathematical formulae by devoting significant time to the formula itself. The show depicted Merton writing the stock call option pricing formula, while Samuelson and Miller explained the formula's importance. To illustrate the formula's impact on financial markets, *NOVA* depicted traders using the formula to price options and hedge risks. The program concluded its historical overview of options pricing by describing how Scholes and Merton won the Nobel Prize in economics for their option pricing models.

NOVA, unlike *60 Minutes*, emphasized the use of options for hedging purposes, rather than painting derivatives as risky vehicles used only for speculation. The commentators described options as a form of insurance that effectively controls risk and explained the risk transfer and risk allocation effects of derivatives.

NOVA then detailed the circumstances surrounding the creation of LTCM, emphasizing the role that the founders' reputations played in attracting investors to the fund. For example, *Wall Street Journal* reporter Roger Lowenstein described the awe LTCM's founding members inspired on Wall Street, and other commentators explained that the most prestigious investors, banks, and institutions competed to invest in LTCM. Lowenstein noted that many institutional managers felt honored to meet and invest with Merton and Scholes, modern finance's high priests, whose models they had studied in business school.

NOVA succinctly and clearly educated viewers about both LTCM's investment strategy and the secrecy it employed in its operations. The program described LTCM's search for deviations from historical pricing relationships across global markets and emphasized LTCM's phenomenal early returns (while showing Scholes golfing on lush courses). The show then described the Asian crisis while explaining that LTCM's many bets diverged instead of converging, causing large losses.

NOVA introduced the issue of systemic risk by having Lowenstein explain the great fear that markets would seize up if LTCM attempted to dump or unwind its huge positions. The show then revisited the financial models versus human judgment debate by describing the Federal Reserve-brokered private bailout of LTCM. A question posed by Fed Chairman Alan Greenspan — "How much dependence should be placed on financial modeling, which for all its sophistication, can get too far ahead of human judgment?" — and statements by Peter Fisher, Greenspan's deputy, indicated that models do not always work. In contrast, Scholes asserted that many things, including bad luck, could be responsible for LTCM's difficulties and that the models themselves were not necessarily to blame.

NOVA concluded that the Black-Scholes model continues to be used in complex financial markets as a powerful tool for managing risk, but that the model assumes functioning markets and is not a crystal ball. The piece ended with Samuelson observing that there always is room for judgment. . . .

Overall, coverage of LTCM was more accurate than coverage of Orange County. There are several possible reasons for this difference. First, *60 Minutes* and *NOVA* have different target audiences. Because *60 Minutes* is a popular show that reaches a wide audience with divergent backgrounds and educations, its producers necessarily strive for non-technical stories appealing to most viewers. Alarmist stories painting derivatives as dangerous, incomprehensible, and capable of mass destruction are more likely to attract viewers' attention (and win ratings) than are more balanced stories accurately educating the public about derivatives. *NOVA*, on the other hand, is a PBS program aimed at more sophisticated viewers with an interest in the sciences.

The intervening five years between the two shows may also account for the differential coverage. Both the size of derivative markets and media coverage of derivatives increased substantially during that period. Consequently, derivatives were less foreign to most people in 2000 than they were in 1995, and the general public may have had the interest and the ability to understand more sophisticated coverage by 2000.

It is important to emphasize the dangers of one-sided, inaccurate television reporting like that in the *60 Minutes* show on derivatives. A *60 Minutes* viewer without prior knowledge of derivatives would necessarily view derivatives as risky gambles capable of wreaking havoc on both individual investors and the financial system as a whole, while providing few or no social benefits. Because these viewers can also be voters, jurors, shareholders, legislators, or judges, their inaccurate, negative opinions can greatly impact derivatives use and regulation. A simple description on television of a derivative in a context familiar to most consumers (for example, a homeowner's option to prepay her mortgage without penalty and thus reduce her total borrowing costs) would be far more educational, though certainly less entertaining.

60 Minutes focused exclusively on speculation and failed to mention the many beneficial uses of derivatives, including hedging for improved risk management. Nor did it discuss "regulatory arbitrage," the use of derivatives to avoid taxes or other regulations.

In addition, by failing to distinguish OTC (Over-the-Counter) derivatives which are not traded on exchanges from exchange-traded derivatives, *60 Minutes* implied that the dangers highlighted in the show applied equally to all derivatives, a patently false conclusion. These two markets differ in ways that are difficult to overemphasize. In fact, nearly all of the derivatives characteristics discussed in the show apply only to OTC derivatives, and not to exchange-traded derivatives. OTC derivatives represent a relatively new market that is largely unregulated. Because there is often no active market for a particular OTC derivative, there is less liquidity and less transparency in that market. Consequently, OTC derivatives end-users must perform their own pricing and marking-to-market, a fairly costly function that requires relatively sophisticated programming and investment skills. Additionally, OTC derivatives present credit-risk problems that exchange-traded derivatives do not, because the exchange clearinghouse acts as the counterparty in all exchange trades. Many OTC derivatives end-users, however, feel that the many benefits of custom-tailored derivatives outweigh these costs.

60 Minutes' closing segment suggesting that money lost in derivatives transactions had somehow mysteriously disappeared revealed that the show's producers failed to understand that derivatives investment is a zero-sum game. Every dollar one party loses trading derivatives is gained by the counterparty. The wealth lost by the Ohio municipality did not disappear; it was redistributed to a smarter or luckier counterparty.

In contrast to *60 Minutes*, *NOVA's* derivatives coverage was educational and raised many controversial issues. First, it raised the issue of whether LTCM had unwisely accepted too much risk, ensuring a disaster if markets did not behave as predicted, or whether the market behavior was so unforeseeable that none of the carefully constructed market risk models could anticipate its occurrence. An analysis of this issue has implications reaching far beyond the problems LTCM faced. The capital-at-risk model most market participants use to evaluate their positions' riskiness does not account for very low probability events that might disrupt capital markets, a criticism often raised by those who argue for greater regulation of derivative markets.

NOVA also raised the issue of whether derivatives implicate systemic risk concerns. The Federal Reserve's involvement in LTCM's "bail-out" was precipitated by fears that attempts to unwind LTCM's positions in an already illiquid market would cause or contribute to an illiquidity driven crash. Although no federal funds were used in LTCM's private bailout, a taxpayer bailout, like that of the U.S. Savings and Loan industry, implicates difficult policy questions. The whole economy may suffer if the government doesn't prevent a systemic crisis. A government bailout, however, presents a definite moral hazard problem because the benefits of more risk-seeking accrue only to private parties, while the costs are shared by society generally.

Finally, *NOVA* raised important questions about professional investors' increasing reliance on mathematical models to predict market prices. If market prices reflect unpredictable human behaviors and attitudes far more than they reflect any evidence of intrinsic value, then computer-generated trading may ignore some of the most important determinants of market prices. *NOVA* thus concluded by raising a debate with important implications regarding the roles of specialists, market makers, floor traders, and physical exchanges generally — a debate further intensified by major technological innovations changing how capital markets operate. . . .

NOTES & QUESTIONS

1. You can find a transcript of the *NOVA* television show *Trillion Dollar Bet* at http://www.pbs.org/wgbh/nova/transcripts/2704stockmarket.html. There is a companion website for that program at http://www.pbs.org/wgbh/nova/stockmarket/ that provides additional online resource materials about derivatives markets. Explore some of the hyperlinks on these websites. After doing so, what do you think about derivatives markets?

2. What, when, and where had you heard about derivatives before today? Did you realize that examples of straightforward derivatives in the movies include the orange juice futures in *Trading Places* (1983) and the stock options that the villain in *Mission Impossible II* (2000) wanted instead of cash from the CEO of a biotech company?

3. Did you believe that derivatives markets have some connection to mathematical derivatives from calculus? Do you find mathematical discussions, references, or subjects confusing? Do you feel that mathematical and quantitative analysis improves, obfuscates, or is divorced from legal and policy discourse?

4. Do American people, politicians, and regulators have a love-hate relationship with numbers and quantification? On the one hand, numbers are seductive because they imply some degree of measurability, order, predictability, and precision in our lives. On the other hand, numbers are often seen to be and criticized for being arbitrary, inhuman, rigid, and subjective. Can and should legal and public policy combat innumeracy? Does popular culture feed a common public desire to believe in a fundamental tension between art, humanities, and literature versus mathematics, science, and technology?

5. Do depictions of business law, economics, and finance in popular culture have a special responsibility to be at least not misleading, if not accurate? How do reactions to popular culture related to business law, economics, and finance compare to reactions to popular culture related to medicine or science? Might non-physicians and non-scientists realize that they lack medical and scientific expertise and training, while people who are not experts in, nor even trained in business law, economics, and finance believe they are nonetheless knowledgeable about business law, economics, and finance?

6. Do you feel that disclosure about CEO compensation, including stock options, will help investors make better-informed choices about which corporate stocks to buy or sell? Do you think disclosure about CEO compensation, including stock options, will cause CEO compensation to decrease? Do you think shame or guilt among CEOs over their compensation, including stock options, is likely to last for a shorter period of time than envy or jealousy by employers, shareholders, and the public over CEO compensation, including stock options?

4. Markets, Monetary Commensurability, and Capitalism

DANGERS OF MONETARY COMMENSURABILITY: A PSYCHOLOGICAL GAME MODEL OF CONTAGION

Peter H. Huang

146 University of Pennsylvania Law Review 1701 (1998)

Incommensurability claims have been in vogue of late in the legal academy. But, as with many instances of legal scholarship drawing on other academic disciplines, something often gets lost in the translation or (mis)application of ideas from other fields of inquiry. In this case, the idea of incommensurability comes from the philosophical literature, in particular, discussions of practical reasoning. There is much intuitive appeal to incommensurability claims, as vividly illustrated by the reader's or audience's reactions to such choice situations as those forcibly contemplated in *Sophie's Choice* or made in *Indecent Proposal*. Yet, perhaps because of the strong emotional resonance or moral outrage these "desperate exchanges" or "double binds" evoke in us, they may be mere fanciful, atypical hypotheticals and not real-life decisions faced every day by individuals, legal decisionmakers, or policy analysts who are engaged in so-called "cool" rational deliberation. . . .

The idea that any particular language constrains both a communicator and her audience should not be surprising, especially to multilingual individuals. Thus, the notion that people who have been exposed to the discourse of monetary commensurability might think and behave differently from those who have not is certainly plausible and a real possibility. Furthermore, there is evidence that students of economics act differently in experimental situations than students not exposed to economics. For example, a well-known study revealed that first-year economics graduate students are more apt to free-ride in experiments requiring private contributions to public goods. First-year economics graduate students also had difficulty with the meaning of "fairness" and basing their decisions on considerations of "fairness." This study has been criticized, however, for not controlling for age and gender differences between the "noneconomic" control groups (undergraduates and high school students with equal numbers of males and females) and the economics graduate students (predominantly older males). Another study, not subject to this particular criticism, investigated the effect of enrolling in an introductory microeconomics course at Cornell University on the answers to questions about a pair of hypothetical ethical dilemmas. The control group was an introductory astronomy class. There were two subject groups, one taught by an economist who specialized in the field of industrial organization and taught some rudimentary game theory, and one taught by a development economist who did not include any instruction on game theory. Students completed a survey during the first and last weeks of class. This survey consisted of four questions: two questions about losing or finding an envelope containing $100 and an individual's name and phone number, and two questions about receiving delivery of ten personal computers but only being billed for nine. Students indicated the probability that they would be honest, as well as their perceived probability that others would be honest. Because the above study design has a potential drawback of students understating the "undesirable" effects of their education to themselves and others, another complementary study design involved actual choices in experimental games with monetary payoffs. Students played a game involving cooperativeness, namely, the well-known prisoner's dilemma. The prisoner's dilemma is a two-person, one-shot game in which each player chooses to cooperate or defect.

The key feature of the prisoner's dilemma is that defecting is a dominant strategy for each player in that it yields higher payoffs to either player than does cooperating regardless of how the other player behaves. Both players defecting, however, results in the lowest total monetary payoff of all of the four possible outcomes. Thus, the prisoner's dilemma provides a setting to investigate the conflict between individual and social or group rationality (assuming the game is one-shot and there is common knowledge of players' rationality and preferences). Frank et al. found that the probability of an economics major defecting is about 0.17 higher than that of a non-economics major defecting when the subjects were not allowed to make promises about what they would do. When such promises, which were unenforceable due to their anonymity, were allowed, there were virtually no differences in defection rates. An exit questionnaire revealed that while 31% of the economics students explained their behavior solely with respect to features of the game, only 17% of the non-economics students did so. Finally, the study revealed that: (1) expectations about the other player's choice strongly influence a player's behavior; and (2) even holding expectations constant, economics students defect at a significantly higher rate than do non-economics students.

Other studies have found that economics majors behave significantly more like the neoclassical economics model predicts than do non-economics majors in ultimatum bargaining games. These are two-person games in which the first player (the allocator) has to propose how to divide a sum of money (ten dollars in the experiments) between that player and another player (the receiver), who can accept the proposed split, or refuse, in which case both players get nothing. The fact that these games are one-shot should rule out reputation and repetition effects. Standard economic theory predicts a division of $9.99 to player one and only $0.01 to the other player. But, experimental research found that fifty-fifty splits are the most commonly made proposal by allocators, while receivers will reject very one-sided proposals as being unfair. In both the role of allocator and receiver, economics (or commerce) majors acted more like standard economic theory predicts than non-economics majors (or psychology students). This experimental design assigned allocator and receiver roles through a preliminary word game, which might have led allocators to feel they deserved a bigger split than receivers did because they "earned" their position. This issue has been addressed in two well-known related studies, which replaced the word game with a coin flip game. Further, the above findings are robust with respect to the size of the monetary payoffs involved and the nationality of the subjects involved.

What do all of these findings mean? They certainly provide support for two propositions: (1) Economics is a language that affects the behavior and expectations of speaker and listener; and (2) there is a tendency for economics models to become self-fulfilling, although this is not always the case.

The issue of whether or not exposure to monetary commensurability by itself, as opposed to more generally the language of economics, affects behavior is not resolved by the above findings, however, because all of the above experiments investigating the impact of economics instruction are joint tests of not only the behavioral impacts of learning about monetary commensurability, but also the behavioral impacts of learning about other aspects of the language of economics, such as the assumption of rationality in the sense of the pursuit of self-interest. . . .

What is perhaps most disturbing about commensurability to incommensurabilists is commensurability with money because it is argued that money is a one-dimensional cardinal scale which flattens out and impoverishes the multidimensional contours and richness of life. But such a one-dimensional view of money is by no means universal, as evidenced by the findings of economic sociology and behavioral economics. Of course, the same criticism of projection of multiple dimensions of reality into a single dimension of analysis already applies to utilitarianism in general, even when utility functions are not expressed in wealth, but only are reducible to abstract "utils.". . .

NOTES & QUESTIONS

1. Are some people troubled by explicit monetary commensurability being different from implicit monetary commensurability because the former leaves no "wiggle room" while the latter preserves possibilities for being deliberately ignorant, imprecise, or vague about monetary commensurability and trade-offs? Do you view your experience with American legal education as fostering a belief in explicit and universal monetary commensurability? Why do some people find monetary commensurability morally disturbing, while others do not?

2. Professor Holly Doremus is concerned about whether our consumer society is compatible with environmental values that respect nature:

> Frugality strikes me as perhaps the most difficult of the indirect environmental values to develop in today's America. Indeed, I wonder whether today it is properly considered "conventional" at all, in the wake of the "greed is good" 1980s, with conspicuous consumption considered nearly patriotic and the Vice-President arguing publicly that while energy conservation may be a "personal virtue" it is not one the government should encourage. Nonetheless, frugality is not an entirely forgotten value. A movement has developed to celebrate and encourage "voluntary simplicity," and prominent commentators have argued that endless consumption, far from proving satisfying, is a barrier to a happy, fulfilling life. For those who adopt it, frugality can apparently provide considerable personal satisfaction and can encourage environmentally responsible behavior.

Holly Doremus, *Shaping the Future: The Dialectic of Law and Environmental Values*, 37 U.C. Davis Law Review 233, 252 (2003). Do you share her concerns? What roles do and can portrayals of business and consumption in popular culture have in shaping our environmental values?

3. Consider this observation about our attitudes toward wealth maximization:

> We find evidence of manipulation of the belief set in our popular culture toward wealth maximization; examples include . . . the notion that "greed is good" from the famous line in the Hollywood movie *Wall Street*, and the adage, "If you are so smart, why aren't you rich?" Advertisements consist of nothing but attempts to modify belief sets, by everything from providing simple information to more active influence through suggestion of counterfactual rules (e.g., if you owned this car, the opposite sex would love you). The consumer society is fueled by the notion that one should acquire ever fancier and more sophisticated physical possessions. The consumer society "works" even if consumers do not actually consume or enjoy the objects that they buy, so long as consumers purchase.

William H. Widen, *Spectres of Law & Economics*, 102 Michigan Law Review 1423, 1439 (2004). Are corporations likely to last in a competitive market system if they only sell products that consumers are induced to purchase via commercial advertising, peer pressure, social conformity, and sophisticated marketing, but do not actually consume or enjoy? Do you really enjoy or even actually consume all that you purchase? *See* Tim Kasser, *The High Price of Materialism* (2002). Does a market society require that its consumers perpetually want products they will not like? *See* Juliet B. Schor, *The Overspent American: Why We Want What We Don't Need* (1999). Do people living in modern societies face overwhelmingly too many choices in their lives? *See* Barry Schwartz, *The Pardox of Choice: Why More Is Less* (2004). Should a government enact legal and public policy to strive for higher social well-being, even if that sacrifices its gross domestic product? *See* Lynn Sherr, *Gross National Happiness: Himalayan Kingdom of Bhutan Favors Contentment over Commerce*, at http://www.abcnews.go.com/2020/Intenational/story?id=1296605.

4. In the movie *Star Trek: First Contact* (1996), Captain Jean-Luc Picard (played by Patrick Stewart) explains how economics in the twenty-fourth century differs from that of the twenty-first century. In the future people are no longer motivated by the pursuit of money, but rather by the good of mankind. Dr. Zefram Cochrane (played by James Cromwell), who is the twenty-first-century inventor of the warp drive, bristles at being called heroic, stating instead that his motivation for inventing warp drive was merely to make money. Consider this viewpoint on the relationship between greed and capitalism offered by a scholar in law and economics, Professor Eric Posner:

> Shylock is a threat to capitalism. Capitalism needs moderation, not excess; far-sightedness, not cunning; self-interest, not greed. *The Merchant of Venice* posed the question of how the creatures of the market can be kept from undermining it, for recall that Shylock's remedy would spell the end of the merchant of Venice. The answer, for dramatic purposes anyway, lay in the law, albeit in the bizarre legal formalism of Portia. This formalism, though a satire, foreshadowed the practices of modern judges, who must draw on legal resources to produce just or preferred outcomes. The use of emotional language in

addition to formalistic language is an overlooked aspect of this tradition, and the tensions it produces are condensed in the concept of
greed, which is both the basis of and threatening to the institutions
that judges are supposed to defend.

Eric A. Posner, *The Jurisprudence of Greed*, 151 University of Pennsylvania
Law Review 1097, 1132 (2003). If there is a fundamental tension between
greed and commerce, how should judges, juries, and lawmakers navigate this
underlying opposition? Can judges, juries, and lawmakers affect people's characters? Should judges, juries, and lawmakers affect people's characters?

Consider this passage about market values in scenes from two very different
movies:

> One scene from the film *Class Action* [1991] involves a discussion of
> cost and benefit analysis related to the question of repairing a defect
> in an automobile that a company has on the market. This scene is
> reminiscent of the Ford Pinto litigation, and is reflective of the more
> recent rash of lawsuits involving allegedly defective Firestone tires. In
> the film, the automobile in question has a defective turn signal switch
> that causes sparks to ignite the vehicle in certain types of collisions.
> The sparks cause the vehicle to explode, and a number of plaintiffs are
> suing the company for burns and deaths. In this particular scene, the
> company president explains to the corporate lawyers that statistical
> studies were done by the company indicating that it would be cheaper
> to deal with potential lawsuits than to recall and fix all of the cars.
> "It's a simple cost and benefit analysis." Thus, the company knowingly
> chose to leave the defective cars on the market and allow people to be
> injured and killed. . . .

> Disney's *Pocahontas* [1995] presents the contrast of two competing
> frames of reference for market analysis. One view, put forward by the
> character of John Smith, is based on a belief in science, technology,
> and the separation of man from the natural world. The other view,
> represented in the character of Pocahontas, is grounded in a con-
> nection to nature, and based on an emotive sense of belonging and a
> non-monetary sense of value. The scene, therefore, positions tension
> between two competing value frames and different sets of interpretive
> references.

> In one particular scene, Captain Smith is alone with Pocahontas in the
> woods. He is telling her about his home in London, and explaining the
> way in which the English will show Pocahontas and her people how "to
> make the most of their land." He explains how England has civilized
> "savages" all over the world and showed them how to industrialize and
> make progress. Smith sees the land and its resources in terms of the
> ability to commodify them for purposes of economic gain and wealth
> maximization. Pocahontas responds that her people already know
> how to make good use of the land, and that they are not savages just
> because they are different from the English. She explains the connec-
> tion between nature and her people, and wonders if Smith can ever

understand the value of the land without calculating its monetary worth.

In a sense Pocahontas reiterates the theme of each of the other films. Each reflects a deeply contested public discourse regarding the nature of market life. Each contests assertions of ownership and of the pursuit of self-interest as a sustainable and worthy criterion for social organization. Each raises questions of valuation and of participation in the decision-making process. Each offers competing frames and references and challenges us to develop supportable and persuasive justifications for invoking one frame rather than another. Similarly, each provides us with an understanding of the way in which alternative cultural-interpretive frames promote different potential distributions, as well as competing meanings and values.

Collectively, these scenes from selective contemporary film illustrate, at a popular culture level, the highly contested interpretive conflicts represented in modern legal and economic discourse. Debates concerning these same issues fill law reviews, law school curriculums, courthouses, and legislative hearings. Gaining a better understanding of these discursive tensions, and their implications for law and market economy, requires an interpretive approach to law and economics. Furthermore, once we understand the framing and referencing conflicts that ground these interpretive conflicts, we can employ a variety of social science tools to assist us in clarifying and enlightening the process of pragmatic legal decision-making.

Robin Paul Malloy, *Framing the Market: Representations of Meaning and Value in Law, Markets, and Culture*, 51 Buffalo Law Review 1, 40–43 (2003). Do you find some forms of cost-benefit analysis to be disturbing or unavoidable? Do you engage in cost-benefit analysis in your own personal decisions, such as whom to date, marry, and have children with; or which job offer to accept; or how and where to live? Do you believe that often cost-benefit analysis is more a form of rationalization undertaken after the fact in order to justify a decision that has already been made, as opposed to a form of rational analysis undertaken before the fact in order to come to a decision that still remains to be made?

6. Do you believe that people are capable of unbiased cost-benefit analysis? Are what counts as costs and benefits fixed and immutable over time or culturally and socially constructed for a particular time? Can otherwise reasonable people differ in their assessments over what should count as costs and benefits, as well as what sorts of techniques are best for estimating or measuring costs and benefits? Do you find judicial opinions and regulatory decisions more or less trustworthy if they engage in cost-benefit analysis? *See* Jonathan Baron & Andrea D. Gurmankin, *Cost-Benefit Analysis Can Increase Trust in Decision Makers*, *available at* http://www.sas.upenn.edu/~baron/cba.html.

7. Consider this familiar type of exchange between a child and parent:

"Nicholas, time for bed."

"Daddy, let's make a deal."

"I'm listening."

"If I'm quiet, can I play Batman for ten minutes?"

"Okay, but only for five minutes."

"It's a deal, Daddy."

Actually, it is a contract. Nicholas offers peace and quiet in exchange for ten minutes of play time. His father counter-offers with five minutes. Nicholas accepts. There is ample consideration: Nicholas gets to kill Mr. Freeze a few more times, and his father can perhaps use the time to catch up on something. Even though Nicholas is only a child, he is a skilled negotiator. He is well versed in the basics of contract law. To think, all he did to gain this wealth of knowledge was watch Disney videos. *See* Michael A. Baldassare, *Cruella de Vil, Hades, and Ursula the Sea-Witch: How Disney Films Teach Our Children the Basics of Contract Law*, 48 Drake Law Review 333, 334-35 (2000). Do children really learn contract law basics from watching Disney videos? If so, then is this a good thing for children, parents, and society? Do children learn about not only contracts law but also ethics, morality, and relationships?

Baldassare goes on to conclude: "Disney does not deserve all the credit. The myths upon which many of these films are based already contained the contracts examined in this Essay. However, the presentation of these lessons in Disney films is significant for two reasons. First, the lessons are accessible to children long before they can read. This enables them to begin learning the basics of contract law much earlier than they would otherwise. Second, even when children learn to read, they are not likely to read the same story as often as younger children watch the same video." *Id. at* 357. How convincing do you find the above two reasons for the power of Disney films? Does it make a difference that when little children read books or listen to oral stories adults are involved? Is it troubling that children who watch Disney videos are also likely to want Disney merchandise and toys associated with the videos? *See generally* Daniel Acuff & Robert Reiher, *Kidnpped: How Irresponsible Marketers Are Stealing the Minds of Your Children* (2005); Susan Linn, *Consumng Kids: Protecting Our Children from the Onslaught of Marketing and Advertising* (2005); Juliet B. Schor, *Born to Buy: The Commercialized Child and the New Consumer Culture* (2004); and Betsy Taylor, *What Kids Really Want That Money Can't Buy* (2003).

Chapter 13

INTERNATIONAL LAW

A. FILMOGRAPHY

Death and the Maiden (1994)

In the Name of the Father (1993)

Judgment in Berlin (1988)

Music Box (1989)

Red Corner (1997)

B. CHARACTERISTICS

In everyday speech, international law is the law that governs the relationships existing between and among countries. Its rules originated in Roman and canon law but coalesced with the rise of the Renaissance states. In order of importance, the sources of international law are treaties (which can be either bilateral or multilateral and may or may not be "self-executing"), customary law, learned works, and case law (which has persuasive but not precedential value). Because of its deep respect for and regular reliance on scholarly writings, international law is particularly suitable for academic study.

An entity claiming nationhood must prove that it has a defined territory, a stable population, a functioning government, and the ability to engage in foreign relations. These four elements are the sine qua non of sovereignty and, in bifurcated political systems like those of Australia, Canada, and the United States, help to define and distinguish the roles of the states (or provinces) and the federal government.

Because only nations can assert rights and take on duties under international law, individuals, partnerships, corporations, and others are barred from the field. Nevertheless, their claims and concerns can and often have been asserted in international tribunals by countries acting on their behalf (usually in the aftermath of a war). Since 1945, such interests also have been championed by an ever-growing number of INGOs, or international non-governmental organizations. Specifically recognized by Article 71 of the United Nations Charter, INGOs have become particularly important advocates of human rights.

Although a lawyer appearing on behalf of a government in an international court is called an "agent" rather than an "attorney," he or she has the same duties as the government lawyer who appears in a domestic court. Unlike domestic courts, however, international courts cannot hear a case unless both parties agree. Likewise, international courts lack the enforcement powers possessed by domestic courts. These are obvious and serious weaknesses, and have severely limited the utility of international courts. They also explain why governments often resort to such extra-judicial processes as conciliation, mediation, and arbitration and sometimes opt to take their arguments directly to the "court of international public opinion."

C. FREEDOM

What rights do parties (particularly the criminally accused) have under international law? In the film *Red Corner,* Chinese officials operate in a manner that runs afoul of the United States Constitution, but do their acts violate international law? Consider, in this regard, the following treaty, which has been signed by both the People's Republic of China and the United States.

INTERNATIONAL COVENANT ON CIVIL AND POLITICAL RIGHTS
Opened for signature Dec. 16, 1966
Entered into force Mar. 23, 1976
999 U.N.T.S. 171, 6 I.L.M. 368

Article 9

1. Everyone has the right to liberty and security of person. No one shall be subjected to arbitrary arrest or detention. No one shall be deprived of his liberty except on such grounds and in accordance with such procedure as are established by law.

2. Anyone who is arrested shall be informed, at the time of arrest, of the reasons for his arrest and shall be promptly informed of any charges against him.

3. Anyone arrested or detained on a criminal charge shall be brought promptly before a judge or other officer authorized by law to exercise judicial power and shall be entitled to trial within a reasonable time or to release. It shall not be the general rule that persons awaiting trial shall be detained in custody, but release may be subject to guarantees to appear for trial, at any other stage of the judicial proceedings, and, should occasion arise, for execution of the judgement.

4. Anyone who is deprived of his liberty by arrest or detention shall be entitled to take proceedings before a court, in order that that court may decide without delay on the lawfulness of his detention and order his release if the detention is not lawful.

5. Anyone who has been the victim of unlawful arrest or detention shall have an enforceable right to compensation.

Article 10

1. All persons deprived of their liberty shall be treated with humanity and with respect for the inherent dignity of the human person.

2. (a) Accused persons shall, save in exceptional circumstances, be segregated from convicted persons and shall be subject to separate treatment appropriate to their status as unconvicted persons;

   (b) Accused juvenile persons shall be separated from adults and brought as speedily as possible for adjudication.

3. The penitentiary system shall comprise treatment of prisoners, the essential aim of which shall be their reformation and social rehabilitation. Juvenile offenders shall be segregated from adults and be accorded treatment appropriate to their age and legal status.

Article 14

1. All persons shall be equal before the courts and tribunals. In the determination of any criminal charge against him, or of his rights and obligations in a suit at law, everyone shall be entitled to a fair and public hearing by a competent, independent and impartial tribunal established by law. The press and the public may be excluded from all or part of a trial for reasons of morals, public order (ordre public) or national security in a democratic society, or when the interest of the private lives of the parties so requires, or to the extent strictly necessary in the opinion of the court in special circumstances where publicity would prejudice the interests of justice; but any judgement rendered in a criminal case or in a suit at law shall be made public except where the interest of juvenile persons otherwise requires or the proceedings concern matrimonial disputes or the guardianship of children.

2. Everyone charged with a criminal offence shall have the right to be presumed innocent until proved guilty according to law.

3. In the determination of any criminal charge against him, everyone shall be entitled to the following minimum guarantees, in full equality:

   (a) To be informed promptly and in detail in a language which he understands of the nature and cause of the charge against him;

   (b) To have adequate time and facilities for the preparation of his defence and to communicate with counsel of his own choosing;

   (c) To be tried without undue delay;

   (d) To be tried in his presence, and to defend himself in person or through legal assistance of his own choosing; to be informed, if he does not have legal assistance, of this right; and to have legal assistance assigned to him, in any case where the interests of justice so require, and without payment by him in any such case if he does not have sufficient means to pay for it;

(e) To examine, or to have examined, the witnesses against him and to obtain the attendance and examination of witnesses on his behalf under the same condition as witnesses against him;

(f) To have the free assistance of an interpreter if he cannot understand or speak the language used in court;

(g) Not to be compelled to testify against himself or to confess guilt.

4. In the case of juvenile persons, the procedure shall be such as will take account of their age and the desirability of promoting their rehabilitation.

5. Everyone convicted of a crime shall have the right to his conviction and sentence being reviewed by a higher tribunal according to law.

6. When a person has by a final decision been convicted of a criminal offence and when subsequently his conviction has been reversed or he has been pardoned on the ground that a new or newly discovered fact shows conclusively that there has been a miscarriage of justice, the person who has suffered punishment as a result of such conviction shall be compensated according to law, unless it is proved that the non-disclosure of the unknown fact in time is wholly or partly attributable to him.

7. No one shall be liable to be tried or punished again for an offence for which he has already been finally convicted or acquitted in accordance with the law and penal procedure of each country.

NOTES & QUESTIONS

1. In *Red Corner,* United States citizen Jack Moore (played by Richard Gere) finds himself wrongly accused of murder. While the American embassy in Beijing monitors the situation, its options for intervening directly are limited. In addition, political reasons cause it to tread warily. As a result, Moore finds himself at the mercy of his hosts.

A country that does not treat foreigners well, however, runs the risk that other countries will do likewise to its citizens. Thus, the principle of reciprocity often helps to mitigate extreme conduct. In addition, where a country has formally granted rights to foreign nationals (either by treaty or under its own law), embassies have much greater leverage.

Ironically, the United States has consistently failed to live up to its obligations under the 1963 Vienna Convention on Consular Relations, 21 U.S.T. 77, 596 U.N.T.S. 261, which requires foreign officials to be notified whenever one of their citizens is arrested. Although the International Court of Justice has ordered the United States to abide by the treaty, *see Case Concerning Avena and Other Mexican Nationals (Mexico v. United States of America)*, 2004 I.C.J.

12, 43 I.L.M. 581, the United States Supreme Court has declined (at least for the moment) to give effect to this judgment. *See Medellin v. Dretke,* 544 U.S. 660 (2005). For a further discussion, compare Vicki S. Jackson, *World Habeas Corpus,* 91 Cornell Law Review 303 (2006) (applauding the ICJ's decision) with Julian G. Ku, *International Delegations and the New World Court Order,* 81 Washington Law Review 1 (2006) (criticizing the ICJ's decision).

2. While meeting with Moore, defense attorney Shen Yuelin (Ling Bai) tells him that if he pleads innocent, he will undoubtedly be found guilty, sentenced to die, and executed within a week (with his family billed for the cost of the bullet used to kill him). Thus, his only hope is to plead guilty, admit his crime, and humbly accept his punishment. Does this mean that there is no presumption of innocence in the Chinese legal system, or merely that the Chinese legal system only tries those who are guilty?

3. Criminal justice systems typically are designed to serve four specific functions: truth-finding, punishment, restitution, and rehabilitation. In movies about American courts, truth-finding normally is deemed the most important, while in *Red Corner* the filmmakers suggest that the Chinese legal system places a premium on rehabilitation. How accurate is either of these views?

4. Suppose the situation in *Red Corner* was reversed, and Moore was a Chinese defendant in a United States courtroom. In what ways would the story have changed?

D. EXTRATERRITORIALITY

In the film *Judgment in Berlin,* Martin Sheen plays Herbert J. Stern, the New Jersey federal district judge who presided over the trial of Hans Tiede and Ingrid Ruske. In August 1978, the two East Germans had escaped to West Berlin by diverting a Polish airliner. Incensed, the Soviet Union demanded that the pair be severely punished as hijackers, and the United States hoped that Stern would conduct a quick trial, hand down a suitably harsh verdict, and thereby put the incident to rest. But Stern refused to be rushed and in time concluded that American law guaranteed Tiede and Ruske a trial by a jury of their peers.

UNITED STATES v. TIEDE
86 F.R.D. 227 (U.S. Ct. Berlin 1979)

Stern, Judge.

The Prosecution's basic position is that the United States Constitution does not apply to these proceedings because Berlin is a territory governed by military conquest. The Prosecution maintains that the question whether constitutional rights must be afforded in territories governed by United States authorities outside the United States depends on the nature and degree of association between such territories and the United States, and that the relationship between the United States and Berlin is such that the Constitution does not apply in proceedings in Berlin.

As a corollary to this position, the Prosecution contends that everything which concerns the conduct of an occupation is a "political question" not subject to court review. Thus, it states in its brief: "Berlin is an occupied city. It is not United States territory. The United States presence there grows out of conquest, not the consent of the governed. The United States and the other Western Allies have, over time, made political judgments to turn over to the Berliners control of important institutions and functions of governance. But these decisions reflect political judgments, not legal necessity."

The Prosecution further argues that this Court is not an independent tribunal established to adjudicate the rights of the defendants and lacks the power to make a ruling contrary to the foreign policy interests of the United States. This, it contends, follows from the fact that "United States occupation courts in Germany have been instruments of the United States occupation policy."

It was not until 1951 that the state of war was formally ended. It was not until 1955 that sovereignty was returned to the German people everywhere in the Western zones of occupation excepting, of course, Berlin. It is against this background that we must evaluate the claim of the Prosecution that the civilian German population in Berlin in 1979 may be governed by the United States Department of State without any constitutional limitation.

The Prosecution maintains that any rights to which the defendants are entitled must be granted by Secretary of State [Cyrus] Vance, or they do not exist at all: "The basic point is this: a defendant tried in the United States Court for Berlin is afforded certain rights found in the Constitution, but he receives these rights not by force of the Constitution itself . . . , but because the Secretary of State has made the determination that these certain rights should be provided." Further, the Prosecution argues, such rights would be granted not because of constitutional dictates, but because they would be in accord with our longstanding foreign policy.

Pursuing its thesis that this Court is nothing more than an implementing arm of the United States' foreign policy, the Prosecution instructs the Court that the Secretary of State has determined, as a matter of foreign policy, that the right to a jury trial should not be afforded to the defendants. The Prosecution's brief asserts: "The conduct of occupation is fundamentally different from the exercise of civil government in the United States. The actions of an occupying power, from necessity, may be inconsistent with the wishes or attitudes of the occupied population. In short, the assumptions and values which underlie the great common law conception of trial by jury do not necessarily have a place in the conduct of an occupation. Whether it does in a particular situation is quintessentially a political question, to be determined by the officers responsible for the United States conduct of this occupation, and not by this Court."

The Court finds the Prosecution's argument to be entirely without merit. First, there has never been a time when United States authorities exercised governmental powers in any geographical area — whether at war or in times of peace — without regard for their own Constitution. *Ex parte Milligan*, 71 U.S. (4 Wall.) 2, 18 L. Ed. 281 (1866). Nor has there ever been a case in which constitutional officers, such as the Secretary of State, have exercised the powers of their office without constitutional limitations. Even in the long-discredited case of *In re Ross*, 140 U.S. 453, 11 S. Ct. 897, 35 L. Ed. 581 (1891), in which American consular officers were permitted to try United States citizens in certain "non-Christian" countries, the Court made its decision under the Constitution — not in total disregard of it. The distinction is subtle but real: the applicability of any provision of the Constitution is itself a point of constitutional law, to be decided in the last instance by the judiciary, not by the Executive Branch.

This fundamental principle was forcefully and clearly announced by the Supreme Court more than a century ago in *Ex parte Milligan*, 71 U.S. (4 Wall.) 2, 120–21, 18 L. Ed. 281 (1866):

> [The Framers of the American Constitution] foresaw that troublous times would arise, when rulers and people would become restive under restraint, and seek by sharp and decisive measures to accomplish ends deemed just and proper; and that the principles of constitutional liberty would be in peril, unless established by irrepealable law. The history of the world had taught them that what was done in the past might be attempted in the future. The Constitution of the United States is a law for rulers and people, equally in war and in peace, and covers with the shield of its protection all classes of men, at all times, and under all circumstances. No doctrine, involving more pernicious consequences, was ever invented by the wit of man than that any of its provisions can be suspended during any of the great exigencies of government. Such a doctrine leads directly to anarchy or despotism, but the theory of necessity on which it is based is false; for the government, within the Constitution, has all the powers granted to it, which are necessary to preserve its existence; as has been happily proved by the result of the great effort to throw off its just authority.

Although the Supreme Court was reviewing the power of military commissions organized by military authorities in the United States during the Civil War, the wisdom of the principle set forth above is nowhere better demonstrated than in this city, during this occupation, and before this Court.

The Prosecution's position, if accepted by this Court, would have dramatic consequences not only for the two defendants whom the United States has chosen to arraign before the Court, but for every person within the territorial limits of the United States Sector of Berlin. If the occupation authorities are not governed by the Constitution in this Court, they are not governed by the Constitution at all. And, if the occupation authorities may act free of all constitutional restraints, no one in the American Sector of Berlin has any protection from their untrammeled discretion. If there are no constitutional protections, there is no First Amendment, no Fifth Amendment or Sixth Amendment; even the Thirteenth Amendment's prohibition of involuntary servitude would be inapplicable. The American authorities, if the Secretary of State so decreed, would have the power, in time of peace and with respect to German and American citizens alike, to arrest any person without cause, to hold a person incommunicado, to deny an accused the benefit of counsel, to try a person summarily and to impose sentence — all as a part of the unreviewable exercise of foreign policy.

This Court does not suggest that the American occupation authorities intend to carry the Prosecution's thesis to its logical conclusion. Nonetheless, people have been deceived before in their assessment of the intentions of their own leaders and their own government; and those who have left the untrammeled, unchecked power in the hands of their leaders have not had a happy experience. It is a first principle of American life — not only life at home but life abroad — that everything American public officials do is governed by, measured against, and must be authorized by the United States Constitution.

As the Supreme Court made clear in *Ex parte Milligan*, the Constitution is a living document to be applied under changing circumstances, in changing conditions and even in different places. This Court finds devoid of merit the suggestion that the Prosecution has no constitutional obligations or that this Court lacks the competence to inquire into those obligations. The Constitution of the United States manifestly applies to these proceedings.

Second, the Court rejects the Prosecution's contention that, even if the Constitution applies to these proceedings, it is the State Department rather than the Court which interprets the Constitution.

It is clear, because the Constitution applies to these proceedings, that the defendants have the right to due process of law. Due process requires that if the United States convenes this Court, it must come before the Court as a litigant and not as a commander. The Secretary of State, in establishing a court, appointing a judge, and then electing to appear before it as a litigant, delegates his powers to the Court. Thereafter, the United States may, and indeed it should, press strongly for its views. It may argue them and, if it is so authorized, may appeal from an adverse decision. It may not, however, compel that its views be victorious. Thus, the responsibility falls solely upon the Court to declare the requirements of the Constitution in this proceeding.

The sole but novel question before the Court is whether friendly aliens, charged with civil offenses in a United States court in Berlin, under the unique circumstances of the continuing United States occupation of Berlin, have a right to a jury trial. This Court is not concerned with the procedures to be used by a United States military commission trying a case in wartime or during the belligerent occupation of enemy territory before the termination of war. This case does not involve the theft or destruction of military property. Nor does it involve spying, an offense against Allied military authority or a violation of the laws of war. Further, this Court does not sit as an international tribunal, but only as an American court.

The defendants are German citizens. It is of no moment whether they be deemed citizens of the Federal Republic or of the German Democratic Republic because the United States is at peace with, and maintains diplomatic relations with, both states. Thus, in law, the defendants are friendly aliens. They are not enemy nationals, enemy belligerents, or prisoners of war. The defendants are charged with non-military offenses under German law which would have been fully cognizable in the open and functioning German courts in West Berlin, but for the withdrawal of the German courts' jurisdiction by the United States Commandant.

The Court takes judicial notice that the occupation regime in existence in Greater Berlin in 1979 is unique in the annals of international relations. Berlin has played, and is destined to play in the future, a special role in the preservation of the free world. The genesis of the occupation is to be found in belligerent occupation, but the relationship between the "occupiers" and the "occupied" in Greater Berlin has undergone fundamental changes since Berlin was initially occupied in 1945 by force of arms. The Court therefore rejects the Prosecution's suggestion that the obligations of the American occupation authorities to the people of Berlin are to be determined solely by rules of law applicable to belligerent occupation of enemy territories.

The parties have extensively briefed and argued whether, in the setting of this case, the Constitution requires a jury trial. The Court finds that none of the precedents cited are dispositive of the issue and that the Constitution requires that these defendants be afforded a trial by jury.

The Prosecution seeks to distinguish most prior decisions dealing with the rights of an accused in occupation courts from the instant proceeding on the ground that the prior adjudications concerned the rights to be afforded to American citizens, whereas the defendants here are aliens. Although it is true that most of the cases discussed concerned prosecutions of American citizens abroad, the Court finds the purported distinction unpersuasive in the context of a trial of friendly aliens, accused of non-military offenses, in Berlin in 1979. The Prosecution conceded in oral argument that in its view aliens, as well as citizens, enjoyed the same "non-rights" in this Court; that is, neither need be afforded a trial by jury. More importantly, whatever distinction may still be permissible between citizens and friendly aliens in civil cases, the Fifth Amendment to the Constitution requires, in terms admitting of no ambiguity, that "no person" shall be deprived of life or liberty without due process of law; similarly, the Sixth Amendment protects all who are "accused," without qualification. Finally, it appears to the Court that the United States is precluded from treating these defendants less favorably than United States citizens, not only by its own Constitution, but also by [the 1963 Tokyo Convention], an international agreement [on aerial hijacking] to which the United States is a party.

Therefore, this Court believes that these defendants should be afforded the same constitutional rights that the United States would have to afford its own nationals when brought before this Court. In sum, this Court does not hold that jury trials must be afforded in occupation courts everywhere and under all circumstances; the Court holds only that if the United States convenes a United States court in Berlin, under the present circumstances, and charges civilians with non-military offenses, the United States must provide the defendants with the same constitutional safeguards that it must provide to civilian defendants in any other United States court.

NOTES & QUESTIONS

1. Did Judge Stern reach the right conclusion, i.e., the United States Constitution was applicable to the citizens of West Berlin? Or should he have deferred to the executive branch, as the prosecution urged? If he had, what would have been the practical consequences for the defendants? And to what extent would his decision have been binding on future American courts?

2. After reading Judge Stern's opinion and viewing the film, do you get the sense that he was engaging in "result-oriented" judging? If so, is this a basis for criticizing him and invalidating the decision?

E.   REPARATIONS OR TRUTH COMMISSIONS?

In recent years, countries emerging from civil wars, dictatorships, and the like have often convened so-called "truth commissions" or "reconciliation commissions" to achieve national closure. To encourage abusers to come forward and tell their stories, such entities normally are empowered to grant witnesses amnesty or immunity. When victims learn what happened to them, they obtain this information at the expense of their right to reparations. Critics of the commissions sometimes suggest this sacrifice is too great and that the commissions provide cheap justice.

The play *Death and the Maiden* by Chilean writer Ariel Dorfman provocatively explores truth commissions and those affected by them. It contemplates the extent to which a reconstituted democracy might and should turn its back on the victims of the regime it replaced. In the film adaptation of the play, the lawyer Gerardo Escobar, played by Stuart Wilson, agrees to serve as a member of the commission in an unnamed third-world country. While doing so will presumably help his nation to heal, it leaves his wife Paulina, played by Sigourney Weaver, with no ready means of avenging her rape at the hands of Dr. Roberto Miranda, played by Ben Kingsley — a former government official who may or may not be guilty of the crime.

ON DORFMAN'S *DEATH AND THE MAIDEN*
David Luban
10 Yale Journal of Law & the Humanities. 115 (1998)

Of course the Investigating Commission isn't going to do it [bring Paulina's torturer to justice], because political realities make that impossible. The fledgling democracy dangles from a chain of compromises and constraints. Democracy in return for amnesty. A truth commission in return for confidential findings. The army in its barracks, but still armed and watchful and menacing. An investigation, but only for victims who are dead, because living victims may still be dangerous to their tormentors, and their tormentors are still dangerous to the democracy. Paulina knows these realities but rejects them; Gerardo accepts them. Perhaps he even approves of them. As he tells Paulina, "A member of the president's Commission . . . should be showing exemplary signs of moderation and equanimity. . . ."

In his image of his mission, Gerardo ironically is not very far from Roberto Miranda, who lectures him when Paulina is out of the room: "She isn't the voice of civilization, you are. She isn't a member of the president's Commission, you are." Later, the doctor insists that "the country is reaching reconciliation and peace."

Gerardo, it seems, has an optimistic view of his mission and of the nation's future. During the dictatorship, he took deadly risks as an activist, but he was lucky: Paulina never revealed his identity under torture. If she had, she tells the doctor, someone would be investigating Gerardo's murder rather than the other way around. Because he was lucky, Gerardo never had a personal reason to abandon his belief in happy endings. If the truth be known, he has avoided unpleasant knowledge that might shake his optimism.

For example, after Paulina's release, Gerardo never asked her exactly what they did to her. He told himself that it would be better for her that way, just as he told himself a few hours ago that lying to Paulina about whether he had accepted the President's invitation would be better for her. Both times, actually, Gerardo did what was better for him. To Paulina, "human rights violations" means rape and having her face shoved into a bucket of her own shit and electric current burning her genitals so that she can never have a baby. To Gerardo, much as he loves her, "human rights violations" remains a deeply emotional, but essentially abstract, legal category. He has vowed to devote his career to justice, but to do that he needs to believe in happy endings. He needs to believe that the living can put the past behind them. He is a lawyer, and law itself, implicitly promising to lift us out of the state of nature, rests on those beliefs. Otherwise, law can never end the chain of violence. As Doctor Miranda tells Paulina, "someone did terrible things to you and now you're doing something terrible to me and tomorrow somebody else is going to — on and on and on."

When Gerardo explains to Paulina which cases his Commission is entitled to investigate, he can't bring himself to use the ugly and impolitic word "murder." Instinctively, he finds a euphemism: He speaks of "cases that are beyond — let's say, repair." Only murder, he seems to think, is beyond repair; only death is irreversible. Paulina bitterly echoes, "Beyond repair. Irreparable, huh?" And he replies, "I don't like to talk about this, Paulina."

Of course he doesn't. How can he harbor any hopes for their marriage if the damage his wife sustained, which was less than murder, turns out to be irreparable? And how can he harbor any hopes for a democratic society if the damage to all the dictatorship's other living victims is irreparable? Gerardo cannot cope with Jean Amery's observation, based on his own experiences at the hands of the Gestapo: "Anyone who has suffered torture never again will be able to be at ease in the world. . . . Faith in humanity, already cracked by the first slap in the face, then demolished by torture, is never acquired again." Jacobo Timerman, tortured for thirty months by the Argentine police during the Dirty War, confesses: "I cannot prevent the memories of the tortures from spreading themselves over my daily life — like a jigsaw puzzle that a neat and careful child spreads piece by piece over the floor of his room." To go on, Gerardo needs to hold the concrete physical reality of torture and humiliation, the jigsaw puzzle, at arm's length.

Perhaps that is why Gerardo is so shocked at the sight of Roberto Miranda, bleeding from a head wound, helplessly bound to a chair in Gerardo's own living room, gagging on Paulina's underpants stuffed in his mouth. When Gerardo has collected himself, he says: "Paulina, I want you to know that what you are doing is going to have serious consequences." To which she replies ironically: "Serious, huh? Irreparable, huh?"

What is irreparable, and what is not? Can a society be repaired unless its killers, rapists, and torturers are named and exposed? Can it be repaired if its killers, rapists, and torturers are named and exposed? That is the overarching question of transitional justice; it may even be the overarching question of life in human society. Just as no relationship can survive in the complete absence of truth, no relationship can survive in the complete absence of lies, nor in the complete absence of forgiveness. . . .

Gerardo wants to heal his nation by doing justice. What did Paulina want when she took Doctor Miranda captive? At first, she tells Gerardo, she wanted to torture him in every way that they tortured her. Then she wanted to rape him, perhaps with a broom handle. But finally, she says:

> I began to realize that wasn't what I really wanted — something that physical. And you know what conclusion I came to, the only thing I really want? I want him to confess. I want him to sit in front of that cassette recorder and tell me what he did — not just to me, everything, to everybody — and then have him write it out in his own handwriting and sign it and I would keep a copy forever — with all the information, the names and data, all the details. That's what I want.

Now, at last, we know what the trial is about. Paulina wants to do the legal justice work of the Investigating Commission — the work that politics prevents it from doing.

Well, Paulina is hardly the first vigilante with that idea. As Felix Frankfurter once warned, "There can be no free society without law administered through an independent judiciary. If one man can be allowed to determine for himself what is law, every man can. That means first chaos, then tyranny." Taking justice into your own hands is dangerous; even Paulina admits at one point that she "still had a doubt" that Miranda is the right man. Gerardo, a lawyer to the core, entirely agrees with Frankfurter:

> *Gerardo:* You know that I have spent a good part of my life defending the law. If there was one thing that revolted me in the past regime it was that they accused so many men and women and did not give the accused any chance of defending themselves, so even if this man committed genocide on a daily basis, he has the right to defend himself.

Paulina does not bother to point out that Gerardo is admitting that the previous regime's denial of due process revolted him more than what they did to his wife. Instead, she drops a bombshell:

> *Paulina:* But I have no intention of denying him that right, Gerardo. I'll give you all the time you need to speak to your client, in private.

If we wanted to treat Dorfman's characters allegorically, Paulina would be named "Memory" and Gerardo "Due Process." Gerardo must be the doctor's defense lawyer, because only due process stands between the doctor and the accusing, possibly inaccurate, power of memory.

But Dorfman's characters are not mere allegories, and Gerardo, a man of compassion as well as a lawyer, worries that due process alone may yield the wrong outcome:

> *Gerardo*: There's a problem, of course, you may not have thought of, Paulina. What if he has nothing to confess?
>
> *Paulina*: Tell him if he doesn't confess, I'll kill him.
>
> *Gerardo*: Paulina, you're not listening to me. What can he confess if he's innocent?
>
> *Paulina*: If he's innocent? Then he's really screwed.

Paulina may sound heartless, but she is merely stating a straightforward fact about every system of criminal justice in the world. Due process is entirely consistent with wrong verdicts, in which case, if you're innocent, you're really screwed. As Robert Cover has reminded us, the rule of law is not merely due process, impartially administered rights, or textual interpretation. The rule of law is channeled violence, and even when it works punctiliously, innocent people are occasionally screwed. Paulina may understand the meaning of due process better than Gerardo. Due process will not stop her from blowing a hole in Roberto Miranda's head if he refuses to confess to crimes he may never have committed. To Gerardo's credit, he wants something more than due process.

To achieve that something more, he makes unauthorized use of the testimony he has just elicited from Paulina. The truth commissioner metamorphoses into the defense lawyer, and Gerardo supplies Miranda with details from Paulina's tape to include in his confession. After all, the doctor pleads, "I need to know what it is I did, you've got to understand that I don't know what I have to confess. . . . I'll need your help, you'd have to tell me." Truth can always be coopted to ulterior purposes; as every lawyer knows, ulterior uses of truth are the only uses adjudicatory systems recognize. Adjudication's aim is closure. Factfinding is only an instrument of closure; and to the extent that institutional truth-seeking obstructs closure, all legal systems avoid it. . . .

Actually, Paulina doesn't want truth and justice purely for their own sakes either. Three times during the play she explains what else she wants: She wants Schubert back — her favorite composer, unbearable to her for the past fifteen years. What does Schubert represent to Paulina?

"There is no way of describing what it means to hear that wonderful music in the darkness," she tells Gerardo, "when you haven't eaten for the last three days, when your body is falling apart. . . ." Schubert, with what she calls his "sad, noble sense of life," represents the civilization outside the torturers' basement — the entire world of art and science and philosophy, of beauty and meaning, of humanity. When the doctor first played the music, and talked to her about music, science, and philosophy, she wildly supposed that he was different from the others, that the two of them shared civilization and were in that way different from the vile and foulmouthed soldiers who tortured and mocked her.

But then he betrayed her. In Polanski's film version, she describes her horror the first time she heard the doctor, her healer, slowly taking his pants off to rape her. The civilized doctor, it turns out, was just another savage, and when he raped her and talked filth to her, he took civilization away. Now she means to get it back. . . .

Polanski's film version of *Death and the Maiden* ingeniously dramatizes the morbid connection between sexuality and violence by reversing roles: When Paulina takes Roberto prisoner, she bends very close to him, she straddles him, she presses her face to his ankles to bite off the electrical tape she is using to bind his legs. As he gapes at her, she lifts her skirt, removes her underpants, and crams them into his mouth to stifle his yells.

What I am suggesting is that Dorfman meant his title, *Death and the Maiden*, to serve double duty: first, as a metaphor for the torture doctor and Paulina; second, as an emblem of both the noble and the base sides of the civilization that Paulina wants to recover. The torture doctor, Dorfman seems to suggest, raped Paulina because of his civilization rather than in spite of it. It is, after all, a civilization that enshrines pornographic images of Death raping the Maiden in the world's great museums, in the Uffizi and the Prado. The implicit question, then, is whether Paulina should want civilization back.

I don't mean to suggest that the answer is obviously no, and I certainly don't mean to suggest that Schubert's quartet is tainted by connections between a title Schubert never gave it and pictures he never saw. To the degree that civilization includes works as unambiguously beautiful as Schubert's D minor quartet, Paulina is right to want it back. Nevertheless, the question is a legitimate one because of the ambiguously beautiful, morally problematic, images that emerge from masculine civilization's id — what Roberto calls "the swamp." Few artists transcribe that id as faithfully as Hans Baldung Grien, and few images represent the swamp as purely as the *Death and the Maiden* motif. Like Schubert, Paulina may have never seen pictorial versions of *Death and the Maiden*, just as she never laid eyes on her rapist [because he had blindfolded her]. Significantly, music, the most immediate and least representational of the arts, becomes Paulina's emblem for civilization; she entertains no doubts about its worth and beauty, just as she entertains no doubts about the entirely aural evidence that Roberto Miranda is the man who raped her. Dorfman invites us to question her certitude on both counts — of Miranda's guilt and of civilization's innocence.

To some it will seem mistaken to focus on specifically sexual human rights abuses, and to infer connections between political rape and culture. Like Dorfman, I disagree. In their book on the Argentine dirty war, John Simpson and Jana Bennett report that junior officers placed bets on who could bring back the prettiest girls to torture and rape. This, I think, is not simply one random horror story out of many that might be told. The Serbian "rape motels" in Bosnia have focused attention on the systematic infliction of rape and forced impregnation as specifically political crimes. The Statute of the International Criminal Tribunal for former Yugoslavia added rape to the standard list of crimes against humanity, and includes "causing serious bodily or mental harm to members of the group," an offense that includes rape, in the definition of genocide.

Of course, soldiers raping civilians is nothing new, nor is the political use of rape to terrorize civilian populations. Shakespeare's *Henry V* brings the French town of Harfleur to its knees by threatening to let his men rape at will if he has to take the town by force. What seems genocidal in the Bosnian Serb strategy is the calculated effort to make the Muslim women outcasts in their own culture by despoiling them and impregnating them with unwanted babies.

Political rape exploits a constellation of traditional values and shadowy fantasies in patriarchal societies. First among these is the value placed on chastity and a woman's yielding of her sexuality exclusively to her husband or proper mate; ineluctably, the rape victim has been shamed as well as tortured because her rapist has made her sexuality common. She is sullied goods. At every moment of her ordeal she expects death, but she also anticipates that if she survives she will never be entirely her own woman, nor even her husband's. For that matter, nothing she says or does can completely dispel the menfolk's lingering suspicion that she liked it at least a little bit. (Do the pictures not illustrate what men guess but seldom say — that maidens enjoy their trysts with Death?) Rape drives its victims to the margin of a patriarchal community, and in that way it weakens the community as a whole. In Bosnia, shunning has been the terrible fate of too many rape victims and their bastard children. Gerardo has never admitted to himself that Paulina was raped as well as tortured fifteen years ago. The reasons are as obvious to Paulina as they are to us.

When, like Paulina, the victim is a political activist, her rapists humiliate her further by demonstrating that she is only a body to be used at their pleasure, not a citizen with political rights and ideals and will. Of course, all political torture aims to teach its victims, men as well as women, that they are nothing but passive bodies in pain, not the active shapers of destiny they had fancied themselves. That is how torture works as an instrument of state. But when the victim is a woman and the torture is rape, her humiliation becomes triply political. Like a male victim, she is passive rather than active and subjugated rather than victorious. But, in addition, her rapists expel her from the recent and still-fragile world of women's political emancipation into a history-nightmare — a nightmare of traditionalist society in which, or so the rapists want to teach her, she was never anything more than [a] cunt. Political rape humiliates her male comrades as well. The same cultural habits that make chastity valuable and rape shameful to its victims obligate men to protect their women's honor. The man who fails stands exposed and impotent. Again, Gerardo has never admitted to himself that Paulina was raped as well as tortured fifteen years ago. The reasons — all the reasons, not only her shame, but his as well — are as obvious to Paulina as they are to us. And that returns us to the question of whether Paulina should want civilization back, contaminated as it is with swampland fantasies of Death and the Maiden.

Well, Paulina at least gets her Schubert back; in Polanski's film version she compromises her demand for justice and spares Doctor Miranda. In the final scene, Gerardo and Paulina attend a concert performance of the Death and the Maiden quartet, and Doctor Miranda is there, too. As they sit down, Paulina's eyes briefly meet the doctor's. "Then she turns her head and faces the stage."

Just as she accepts the bad in civilization along with the good, she accepts the compromises of transitional justice. Dorfman seems to suggest that in the end they may be one and the same compromise: an agreement to leave the fascists untouched in return for democratizing a civilization of which they too can approve. (The play is more ambiguous than the film, for there Dorfman ends the penultimate scene with Paulina still undecided about whether to spare the doctor. And in the final concert scene we don't know whether the doctor is present in the flesh or only in Paulina's fantasy.)

In the play, Dorfman's directions for the final scene require "a giant mirror which descends, forcing the members of the audience to look at themselves. Selected slowly moving spots flicker over the audience, picking out two or three at a time, up and down rows." The mirror is an interesting and powerful device. For one thing, it reminds us, the audience, that we are akin to a jury: Judgment of Miranda, but also of Paulina and Gerardo, is a task Dorfman charges to us.

More importantly, however, the mirrors and spotlights force us to confront our own complicity. Dorfman presumably had in mind a Chilean performance in which the spotlights may well have picked out actual torturers in the audience — torturers in the best circles of society, torturers who by agreement of their peers will never be brought to justice.

It once seemed to me that this sensational idea would be merely melodramatic in a British or American theater. Although I haven't seen the stage version, I now think differently. A North Atlantic audience may not include rapists, torturers, murderers, or beneficiaries and accomplices of dirty war. But a North Atlantic audience contains many — perhaps everyone, certainly me — who can't decide whether sparing the doctor would represent a happy ending or not. That seems embarrassing enough.

NOTES & QUESTIONS

1. Why does Paulina let Dr. Miranda go rather than kill him? Is it because her need for vengeance has been satisfied, or because at the moment when she must act she cannot overcome her own doubts as to his culpability? One commentator has suggested that the answer lies somewhere in the middle:

> After a long dark night of the soul, she lets her suspect go. Was he guilty? We don't know, but we suspect so. Has she gotten what she needed from the episode, that is, some kind of emotional satisfaction? We think so. Should she have done what she did? She explains that she does not trust the government, including her husband, who is part of the administration, to do justice for her and her fellow victims. She prefers to put her faith into her own personal truth commission. But can she trust that what comes out of her prisoner's mouth is truth? Perhaps all she really needed was to exert some kind of control over her own life and over her prisoner's. The power of life and death is, after all, the ultimate power — the power we give to our judicial system. Can the South African government trust that what those brought before it confess is true? The truth commissions had safeguards; they

had ways to test the veracity of those brought before them. But could their safeguards have failed? Possibly. Does it matter?

Christine Alice Corcos, *Prosecutors, Prejudices and Justice: Observations on Presuming Innocence in Popular Culture and Law,* 34 University of Toledo Law Review 793, 811–12 (2003).

2. Professor Teresa Godwin Phelps frequently invokes the themes of Dorfman's play in her treatment of truth commissions in Argentina, Chile, El Salvador, and South Africa. She suggests, "History shows us that revenge cycles end when the victims cede the right to take revenge to the state and the state properly fulfills this duty." Teresa Godwin Phelps, *Shattered Voices: Language, Violence, and the Work of Truth Commissions* 5 (2004).

F.   TERRORISM

Since 9/11, the United States has been engaged in a war on terrorism that has forced a national debate over how to balance civil rights and public safety. Yet in other countries this discussion had been going on for many years. In England, for example, the "Northern Ireland question" had often led officials to take shortcuts that were later justified on the grounds of national security.

In the following excerpt the authors summarize the problems in the hasty prosecutions and convictions of the Guildford Four and Maguire Seven.

MISCARRIAGES OF JUSTICE IN THE WAR AGAINST TERROR
Kent Roach & Gary Trotter
109 Penn State Law Review 967 (2005)

The Guildford Four were convicted of murder in 1975 for pub bombings by the IRA in 1974 that killed seven people. An appeal taken in 1977 failed on the basis that alibi evidence, including claims by others that they had committed the bombings, was not convincing given the confessions. In 1989, the Home Secretary referred the case back to the Court of Appeal after new scientific evidence was discovered indicating that police reports were not taken contemporaneously with the alleged confessions. New evidence also emerged about an alibi witness and other exculpatory evidence that was not disclosed. In 1989, the convictions were quashed after the Director of Prosecutions decided not to contest the convictions of the four: Paul Hill, Carole Richardson, Gerald Conlon, and Patrick Armstrong. A public inquiry also was made into the case, and the case was subsequently dramatized into a movie, *In the Name of the Father.*

The Guildford case was also related to that of the Maguire Seven, who were convicted in 1976 of possessing explosives. The convictions rested on the basis of forensic tests that showed traces of nitroglycerine, even though no explosives were found. The Maguire Seven included Gerald Conlon's aunt, Anne Maguire, and his father, Giuseppe Conlon, who died in prison in 1980. Gerald Conlon, part of the Guildford Four, allegedly confessed to the police that his aunt had taught him how to make bombs. Most of the Maguire Seven were

sentenced to terms of imprisonment of fourteen years. In 1987, the Home
Secretary refused to refer the Maguires' case to the Court of Appeal on the
basis that he had no doubts about the scientific evidence linking them with
explosives. Subsequent tests carried out at the behest of the public inquiry,
however, revealed the possibility of innocent contamination, as well as the fact
that not all of the scientists' notes had been disclosed to the defense at the
original trial. In 1991, the Home Secretary referred the case back to the Court
of Appeal with the Director of Public Prosecutions conceding that the convictions were unsafe. The Court of Appeal quashed the convictions on the basis
"that the possibility of innocent contamination cannot be excluded and on this
ground alone, we think that the convictions of all the appellants are unsafe
and unsatisfactory. . . ." The Maguires insisted that no explosives had been
found in the house and complained that the Court of Appeal's innocent contamination theory did not constitute a full exoneration.

The May public inquiry sided with the Maguires over the Court of Appeal by
endorsing statements by the Maguires' counsel that the "Crown's case, as presented at trial was so improbable as to be frankly incredible." Lord May
explained the wrongful conviction as following from frequent references in the
Guildford Four trial to the Maguires' residence as a "bomb factory." He concluded:

> [T]he "bomb factory" assumption pervaded the entire case and was
> allowed to obscure the improbability of what was alleged against the
> Maguire Seven. I do not criticize the jury: the context of the prevailing
> bombing campaign and the atmosphere of the trial are likely to have
> made it impossible for them to make a wholly objective and dispassion-
> ate appraisal of the admissible evidence alone.

In less diplomatic terms, the jury was influenced by tunnel vision, fear, and
stereotypes. The connection between the Guildford and Maguire cases illustrates how the cell nature of modern terrorism, when combined with unreliable interrogations and forensic evidence, can lead to multiple and related
miscarriages of justice. . . .

NOTES & QUESTIONS

1. What is it about effective terrorism in and of itself that might contribute
to the likelihood of flawed and biased police investigations and prosecutions?

2. Are Irish terrorists who plagued Great Britain in the 1970s and 1980s
comparable to Muslim terrorists in the contemporary United States? President
George Bush and members of his administration have for the most part
described the current struggle in the United States and elsewhere as a "war
on terror." However, some have questioned the appropriateness of this characterization, noting that it indicts a methodology rather than the social composition or ideological program of those on whom we are warring.

3. As the preceding excerpt by Professors Roach and Trotter suggests, the
story of the Guildford Four was dramatized for the big screen. The film starred
Daniel Day-Lewis as defendant Gerald Conlon and Emma Thompson as

determined defense lawyer Gareth Pierce. The following excerpt from an article by Professors Steve Greenfield and Guy Osborn considers the argument that the filmmakers were reckless in the way they made the actual case into a film.

PULPED FICTION? CINEMATIC PARABLES OF (IN)JUSTICE
Steve Greenfield & Guy Osborn
30 University of San Francisco Law Review 1181 (1996)

Some of the criticisms were fairly mundane or semantic — for instance the issue of whether or not Gerry Conlon did in fact bring some sausages to his Auntie Annie is not particularly material or interesting. Other points have included the "false" depiction of Gerry and Giuseppe Conlon sharing a cell at times during their sentence. In fact, current practice dictates that persons convicted of such offenses do not share cells with anyone, let alone members of their own family, and the two were only in the same prison at the same on a very limited number of occasions. The film also lacks substantial portions of Gerry Conlon's visit to England — noticeably the amount of time he spent in Southhampton before moving to London. However, as Robert Kee notes:

> Some inaccuracies about the Belfast life and family of the Daniel Day-Lewis/Jerry Conlon character are reasonably acceptable as part of that artistic license with which the producers seek to justify their treatment of the whole story. These instances are no more important than the inevitable physical differences in having an actor portray a real person. Robert Kee, *In the Name of the Father,* The Times (London), 6 Feb. 1994, 6-3.

Another problematic area is the portrayal of Gareth Pierce and, in particular, her role in discovering the evidence that effectively leads to the freeing of the Four. Early in the film she is introduced and identified by the camera moving from the wig on the passenger seat in the car to her face — instantly showing her legal credentials. However, not only was the use of the barristerial wig factually incorrect in that Pierce was in fact a solicitor, her heartfelt plea at the end of the film to the court of appeal in fact could not have happened, as she did not have a right of audience to appear in such a court. The evidence she is said to have discovered that forms the basis of her plea was unearthed by the Avon and Somerset police, and not — as the film depicts — by Pierce.

Some of the more fundamental criticism relating to *In the Name of the Father* was based on a claim that the film exacerbated the persistent feeling in some quarters that the Four were in fact guilty. *The Daily Telegraph* emphasized this point when reporting on the acquittal of the three police officers charged with conspiracy to pervert the course of justice:

> Until now the received view of the Guildford Four, at least since they were released by the Court of Appeal in 1989, is that they were all innocent victims of a scandalous miscarriage of justice who spent many years in prison for crimes they did not commit. The acquittal of the three ex-policemen, and some of the new evidence heard in the course of their Old Bailey trial, suggests there are

reasonable grounds for suspecting that two of the Guildford Four, Mr. Patrick Armstrong and Mr. Gerry Conlon, might have been guilty after all. This raises the disturbing possibility that the real miscarriage of justice in their case occurred when they walked free. Iris Bennett, quoting the Daily Telegraph, in *Let Him Have It* 67 (1996).

This notion that the Four were after all responsible lies at the heart of much of the film's criticism. There is no doubt that a persistent theme running throughout the Irish miscarriage of justice cases is not that the police had caught the wrong people but had merely been overeager in the investigation and collection of the evidence. This theme neatly ignores the central arguments concerning the reliability of confession evidence and the methods employed by the police to obtain them. By permitting appeals on the basis of unreliable scientific evidence, or corrupt police notes, the dispute concerning police behavior is never addressed. While police brutality was never admitted in court, oppressive police actions are shown in the film as being part of the interrogation process.

The interrogation scene involves several police officers who are surrounding Conlon in an interrogation room. The scene starts with the senior officer talking to another police officer, who has already observed Conlon, outside of the room where Conlon is being questioned. The following exchange takes place:

Senior Officer: "Is he leading us up the garden path?"

Other Officer: "I dunno . . . I can make him confess."

Senior Officer: "Well why don't you have a word in his ear? You live in the same town; he'll understand you."

Other Officer: "Will you have the bomber?"

Senior Officer: "Our job is to stop the bombing."

As both officers enter the cell, there is an atmosphere of brooding menace. While the other officers talk quietly in background, the junior one circles Conlon, and whispers in his ear softly:

Police Officer: "I'm gonna shoot your da."

Conlon: "What did you say to me?"

Police Officer: "Little Bridie will have no daddy. I'm gonna shoot Giuseppe."

Conlon then becomes hysterical and has to be restrained by the other officers, including the Senior Officer, who reassures him that no one will harm his father. Meanwhile, the officer who has made the threats leaves the cell, dementedly pointing a gun at his own head. Conlon breaks down completely and says: "Give me the [expletive] statement, for [expletive] sake give me the statement, give me a pen. Right there's my [expletive] name there, you can write what you like."

The film also acknowledges the position of the police when the members of the Balcombe Street gang are arrested and confess to the Guildford and

Woolwich bombings. The hard-natured, cynical, IRA terrorist McAndrew is used to contrast with a more sympathetic portrayal of Conlon; Sheridan makes his Gerry Conlon the archetypal loveable Irish rogue, while McAndrew is the murderous Republican psychopath that we read about in the tabloid press.

By laying the blame for the bombings firmly with others, Conlon and Hill's alibi is accepted, and they are shown to be in London at the time of the bombing. The film asserts their innocence and has no difficulty with the notion that while the Balcombe Street gang may have been primarily responsible, the Guildford Four may also have been involved. . . .

In the Name of the Father lays the blame squarely at the door of the police officers, who both bully the evidence from the Four and lie in court. An important point that the film does draw out is the extent to which the confession evidence is used to drag others into the frame:

> Frighteningly, the effect of duress does not stop with the person who is subjected to it and in the case of Gerry Conlon and the others of the Guildford Four, things they said were used to enmesh Gerry's father, his Aunt Annie Maguire and five other relatives and friends who collectively became known as the Maguire Seven. Michael Mansfield & Tony Wardle, *Presumed Guilty* 82 (1994).

The police corruption is compounded when they find the "real" bombers. . . .

It is the existence of the jury that deflects much of the potential criticism, for it is a group of the accused's peers who have determined their guilt, not the police officers or politicians. The process is potentially pure, but it has been corrupted from within at both ends [and] actually enhanced. . . . After all, the Guildford Four are freed at an appeal hearing, indicating the ability of the system to correct original mistakes. The implication is that if the defense had been shown a copy of the alibi evidence, the Four would not have been convicted in the first instance. Fault lies clearly with those conducting the prosecution, not with the process itself. . . .

In the Name of the Father portrays the police in a . . . brutal light: eager to obtain a conviction through applying undue pressure. The desirability of admitting unsupported confessional evidence is not raised as an issue — rather, the emphasis is on the Four being able to demonstrate their innocence through the introduction of alibi evidence. The overriding view is of a system, basically sound, but subject to corruption by the infamous "few bad apples." Eventually the process can defeat this attempt to pervert the system, and the innocent, in the case of the Four, are freed. . . .

The superhero lawyer Gareth Pierce played by Emma Thompson makes an interesting addition to the genre. Like Cher [in the movie *Suspect*] she is female, but more importantly, she is shown to single-handedly save the Four through her quick-wittedness in deliberately asking for the "wrong" file. This information was actually discovered by the investigating police force, and this final portrayal is interesting. As Simon Jenkins notes, it is in many ways the pivotal point of the film — the instant when the Four finally obtain justice. Pierce, ostensibly a quiet and unassuming person, is portrayed by Emma Thompson, as Jenkins writes

Hair aflame with anger, she screams at the Old Bailey judge whose own words . . . are taken from the court report. Thompson's words are pure fiction. Conlon's alibi was actually supplied to the defence during the appeal by police investigators. Solicitors (sadly) do not yet appear in the Old Bailey. They certainly do not appear wigless and screaming. Much else in the film, as Robert Kee has pointed out, is a "farrago of rubbish." Simon Jenkins, *Stories that Get in the Way of Facts*, The Times (London), 12 March 1994, 16. . . .

Conclusion

The issue of using films in such a way to depict real events is undoubtedly contentious. Some commentators have argued that filmic portrayal is actually damaging if it is not accurate:

> The fictional presentation of the Guildford case in the feature film *In the Name of the Father* suggested the appeal rested on the discovery by defence lawyers of an alibi statement which had never been seen before, marked "Not to be seen by the defence." In this and in other respects too numerous to mention, the film was a travesty of the facts, which manages to weaken the drama of what really happened. David Rose, *In the Name of the Law* 339 (1996).

It may however be the case that by going beyond the minutiae of detail, film may in fact be immensely important in terms of raising the consciousness of the general public . . . A major strength of *In the Name of the Father* is its gloves-off account of the events that led to the dreadful miscarriage of justice perpetrated against the Guildford Four. While some have claimed that the only authentic way to portray such events is by means of the documentary, with no subjectivity to cloud the "truth," as [Alexander] Kluge notes this also is not a guarantor of accuracy or authenticity of representation:

> A documentary film is shot with three cameras: (1) the camera in the technical sense; (2) the filmmaker's mind; and (3) the generic patterns of the documentary film, which are founded on the expectations of the audience that patronizes it. For this reason one cannot simply say that the documentary film portrays facts. It photographs isolated facts and assembles from them a coherent set of facts according to three divergent schemata. All remaining possible facts and factual contexts are excluded. The naive treatment of documentation therefore provides a unique opportunity to concoct fables. In and of itself, the documentary is no more realistic than the feature film. Alexander Kluge, *A Perspective* 4 (1988).

What makes the [film] important is not found in a semantic debate about minutiae of detail, but rather through a wider view of [its] worth in terms of raising consciousness or awareness of the issues that pervade [it].

NOTES & QUESTIONS

1. Professors Greenfield and Osborn compare the portrayal of Gareth Pierce by Emma Thompson in *In the Name of the Father* to that of attorney Kathleen Riley by Cher in *Suspect* (1987). Is the comparison a good one? While the former film is a fictional version of an actual case, the latter is fiction pure and simple. Furthermore, attorney Riley is hardly portrayed as an independent, resourceful lawyer. She would never have succeeded as a public defender in a murder case without the help of a sympathetic juror who leaves the courtroom to undertake detective work and ultimately becomes her lover.

2. More generally, Greenfield and Osborn seem willing to grant the filmmakers substantial "artistic license" in adapting the story of the Guildford Four for the screen. Judging whether a film dramatizing real-life events plays too fast and loose with what really happened is a difficult task. The definition of a "documentary" is hardly fixed and seems largely to stand for any film that is not totally fictional. *See* James Monaco, *How to Read a Film: The Art, Technology, Language, History, and Theory of Film and Media* 429 1981). Some use the term "docudrama" to suggest pop cultural works that wander too recklessly from the facts. "Of course, the godfather of the docudrama was Orson Welles's historic radio program *The War of the Worlds* (1938), whose documentary techniques were so lifelike that hundreds of thousands of listeners thought we really were being invaded by Martians." *Id.* at 398. In more recent years, hundreds of made-for television movies have been "docudramas." For a fine treatment of the actual facts in the Guildford Four case, see Kent Roach and Gary Trotter, *Miscarriages of Justice in the War Against Terrorism*, *supra*, 177–79.

3. Does *In the Name of the Father* suggest that a defendant caught up in a trial like the one depicted in the film cannot get justice because of the nature of the times? Does the public really want security at the expense of liberty? Does the film suggest how the English legal system can redress the balance, or does it merely serve as an indictment while failing to provide any alternatives?

4. The court depicted in the film is a "Diplock court," a type of tribunal in which the ordinary protections afforded a British citizen are not available to the defendants (who are residents of Northern Ireland). The Diplock courts were named after the report that recommended their adoption, which in turn took the name of its chairman, Lord Diplock. *See* Matthew S. Podell, *Removing Blinders from the Judiciary:* In re Artt, Brennan, Kirby *as an Evolutionary Step in the United States-United Kingdom Extradition Scheme, 23* Boston College International and Comparative Law Review 263, 267–68 (2000).

Such courts, of course, are difficult to square with at least two international treaties to which the United Kingdom is a party: the International Covenant on Civil and Political Rights (Article 14, § 3(g) of which guarantees that criminal defendants shall not be compelled to testify against themselves or confess guilt), and the 1950 European Convention on Human Rights and Fundamental Freedoms, 213 U.N.T.S. 222, which in Article 6 provides:

> In the determination of his civil rights and obligations or of any criminal charge against him, everyone is entitled to a fair and public hearing within a reasonable time by an independent and impartial tribunal established by law. Judgment shall be pronounced publicly, but the press and public may be excluded from all or part of the trial in the interests of morals, public order or national security in a democratic society, where the interests of juveniles or the protection of the private life of the parties so require, or to the extent strictly necessary in the opinion of the court in special circumstances where publicity would prejudice the interests of justice.

1. Everyone charged with a criminal offence shall be presumed innocent until proved guilty according to law.

2. Everyone charged with a criminal offence has the following minimum rights:

   a) to be informed promptly, in a language which he understands and in detail, of the nature and cause of the accusation against him;

   b) to have adequate time and facilities for the preparation of his defence;

   c) to defend himself in person or through legal assistance of his own choosing or, if he has not sufficient means to pay for legal assistance, to be given it free when the interests of justice so require;

   d) to examine or have examined witnesses against him and to obtain the attendance and examination of witnesses on his behalf under the same conditions as witnesses against him;

   e) to have the free assistance of an interpreter if he cannot understand or speak the language used in court.

The British Parliament enacted the Human Rights Act 1998 in order to give effect to the European Convention. Its Article 6, entitled "Right to a fair trial," reads as follows:

1. In the determination of his civil rights and obligations or of any criminal charge against him, everyone is entitled to a fair and public hearing within a reasonable time by an independent and impartial tribunal established by law. Judgment shall be pronounced publicly but the press and public may be excluded from all or part of the trial in the interest of morals, public order, or national security in a democratic society, where the interests of juveniles or the protection of the private life of the parties so require, or to the extent strictly necessary in the opinion of the court in special circumstances where publicity would prejudice the interests of justice.

2. Everyone charged with a criminal offence shall be presumed innocent until proved guilty according to law.

3. Everyone charged with a criminal offence has the following minimum rights:

(a) to be informed promptly, in a language which he understands and in detail, of the nature and cause of the accusation against him;

(b) to have adequate time and facilities for the preparation of his defence;

(c) to defend himself in person or through legal assistance of his own choosing or, if he has not sufficient means to pay for legal assistance, to be given it free when the interests of justice so require;

(d) to examine or have examined witnesses against him and to obtain the attendance and examination of witnesses on his behalf under the same conditions as witnesses against him;

(e) to have the free assistance of an interpreter if he cannot understand or speak the language used in court.

Notice that neither the Convention nor the Act specifically discusses whether it is impermissible to draw adverse inferences from a defendant's silence. Why is this, and what are the consequences of the omission? *See* Mark Berger, *Reforming Confession Law British Style: A Decade of Experience with Adverse Inferences from Silence,* 31 Columbia Human Rights Law Review 243 (2000).

5. Despite the lessons taught by the Guildford Four case, the United Kingdom continues to struggle in balancing the rights of the accused with the need for security. In the wake of the July 2005 London train bombings, jittery police officers mistakenly shot and killed a Brazilian electrician because they thought he was a terrorist, leading to yet another public examination of the subject. *See* Tod Robberson, *Britons Question Anti-Terror Agenda: Proposals Seen as Unnecessarily Restrictive,* St. Paul Pioneer Press, 9 Oct. 2005, at 5A.

G. EXTRADITION

In the film *Music Box,* lawyer Ann Talbot, played by Jessica Lange, jumps to her father's defense (Mike Laszlo, played by Armin Mueller-Stahl) after he is accused by the United States of being a Nazi war criminal. Yet as the evidence of Laszlo's guilt keeps growing, Talbot finds it increasingly difficult to remain convinced of his innocence. That her client is also her father only compounds her confusion over what is demanded of her as a lawyer, daughter, and human being. As noted in previous chapters of this text, Hollywood films tend to be character-driven narratives. Major characters are psychologically defined early in the film, and then they struggle with events, other characters, *and* themselves in the course of the film.

THE CONFLICTS OF LAW AND THE CHARACTER OF MEN: WRITING *REVERSAL OF FORTUNE* AND *JUDGMENT AT NUREMBERG*

Suzanne Shale
30 University of San Francisco Law Review 991 (1996)

Although not all movies terminate their story according to the same principles, in Hollywood, by and large, they do. The conventional Hollywood story form adopts the narrative mode of the classical tradition, in which the story firmly concludes with a sense of satisfying completeness. What makes us feel that sense of satisfaction, of desirable closure? The answer lies in the play of the main components of Hollywood narrative we have already identified: character, action, conflict, and change. The protagonist's struggle to achieve her goal, and the transformative effects of this odyssey, must have reached some resolution before we feel that matters have been brought to a close. Part of the pleasure of watching a movie is to learn what the protagonist's goal may be and then look forward to finding out how or, indeed, whether she achieves it.

Courtroom dramas rarely end immediately when the trial ends. There is almost always more to be resolved, a scramble of loose ends, a belated epiphany, a final twist or unanticipated denouement. While some trial movies merely require a brief epilogue, a dotting of i's and crossing of t's, the majority still have some story distance to go. *A Few Good Men* closes, unusually, as the lawyer walks from the courtroom. *In the Name of the Father* ends soon after the trial comes to a close, but cannot resist an epilogue referring to the lives of the characters as they continued beyond the confines of the film narrative. In *Judgment at Nuremberg*, Judge Haywood has still to have important discussions with Hans Rolfe and Ernst Janning, and Madame Bertholt has still to retreat from him, before his story ends. In *Let Him Have It*, we have still to witness Derrick Bentley's execution before the film closes. In *Reversal of Fortune*, Claus has a meeting with Dershowitz and one last bad joke to go. In *Music Box* and, famously, in *Witness for the Prosecution*, the story has still to turn a crucial twist before the meaning of the film's trial events is made clear. Indeed, the ending in *Witness for the Prosecution* subverts the meaning of the entire preceding narrative.

Each film closes at that point in the narrative when all of the key elements of the protagonist's story have reached a resolution. The ending of the trial will coincide with the ending of the movie only where the trial itself has resolved the last of the major dramatic conflicts the story has set in motion. *In the Name of the Father* can finish shortly after Gerry Conlon's appeal hearing secures his release from custody because we have already seen how the miscarriage of justice and his experiences in prison transform the innocent Conlon from a callow youth to a man of judgment and determination. Judge Haywood's story continues beyond his tribunal verdict because *Judgment at Nuremberg* is about Judge Haywood and his attitude toward justice. His verdict is only the beginning of a sequence in which we come to see and understand the spirit of the man and the full import of his decision. *Music Box*, the tale of a woman lawyer defending her father who is accused of concealing his fascist past, does not close its story at the end of the trial because the film is about the age-old conflicts between love and duty, and loyalty and truth. In *Music Box*, the trial is not supposed to resolve the underlying dramatic conflict. It is in the story to provide the most strenuous and symbolically significant test of the daughter's loyalty, as she wavers between her desire to believe that her father is innocent and her fear that he is not. *Witness for the Prosecution* is as much a story about the testing of a great advocate as a story about the trial of the defendant. At the end of the criminal trial, Charles Laughton's advocate's greatest challenge — the unfamiliar humiliation of having been deceived — is yet to come. . . .

NOTES & QUESTIONS

1. By calling into question the memories of the government's witnesses and challenging the authenticity of its evidence, Talbot is able to keep her father out of the hands of his pursuers. Yet after she does so, she discovers that he is, in fact, guilty. Does this make her a villain, a hero, or simply a lawyer who has done her job? *Compare* Jonathan R. Cohen, *The Culture of Legal Denial,* 84 Nebraska Law Review 247 (2005) (criticizing lawyers for failing to take their clients to task) *with* Abbe Smith, *Defending Defending: The Case for Unmitigated Zeal on Behalf of People Who Do Terrible Things,* 28 Hofstra Law Review 925 (2000) (suggesting that defense attorneys must do everything in their power to help their clients).

2. Consider as well the relevance of Rule 3.3 of the ABA Model Rules of Professional Conduct. It requires a lawyer to take reasonable remedial measures when she has misled (or allowed others to mislead) a tribunal. Should Talbot be subject to discipline under this rule? Might the narrative imperatives preclude any such discipline *in the film*, given the emphasis on the daughter's blind love for her father?

3. Assuming that Talbot turns over the evidence that proves her father's guilt, is it too late for the United States to bring a new proceeding against Laszlo? If it is too late, might another country initiate a proceeding against Laszlo? Could it bring its own action and demand his extradition? Beyond considerations of viable national jurisdiction, consider the relatively new jurisdiction of the International Criminal Court, which was created in 1998 and sits at The Hague. Could the International Criminal Court try Laszlo? *Cf.* Steven Feldstein, Comment, *Applying the Rome Statute of the International Criminal Court: A Case Study of Henry Kissinger,* 92 California Law Review 1663, 1666, 1727 (2004) (noting that the court has jurisdiction only over events occurring after July 1, 2002 and, in any event, "is not meant to serve as a common court of judgment for even medium-level perpetrators. Its governing statute and historical legacy both point to the same conclusion: that the court's objective is to try the highest-level perpetrators of the most heinous crimes.")

Chapter 14

MILITARY LAW

A. FILMOGRAPHY

Breaker Morant (1979)

The Court-Martial of Billy Mitchell (1955)

A Few Good Men (1992)

Soldier's Girl (2002)

Starship Troopers (1997)

B. CONSTITUTIONAL CONTROL OF THE MILITARY

The relationship of the military to civilian authority and civilian society is fundamentally a question of constitutional law. Popular representations of military law in popular culture often build on the constitutional tension that arises from the military's unique system of governance, which balances the rights of individuals against the responsibility to raise and maintain an effective fighting force.

1. Sources of Military Law

THE CONSTITUTION OF THE UNITED STATES
Article I, Section 8, Clauses 12–14

The Congress shall have power to raise and support armies, but no appropriation of money to that use shall be for a longer term than two years; to provide and maintain a navy; [and] to make rules for the government and regulation of the land and naval forces.

PREAMBLE TO THE MANUAL FOR COURTS-MARTIAL

Military law consists of the statutes governing the military establishment and regulations issued thereunder, the constitutional powers of the President and regulations issued thereunder, and the inherent authority of military commanders. Military law includes jurisdiction exercised by courts-martial and the jurisdiction exercised by commanders with respect to non-judicial punishment. The purpose of military law is to promote justice, to assist in maintaining good order and discipline in the armed forces, to promote efficiency and effectiveness in the military establishment, and thereby to strengthen the national security of the United States.

NOTES & QUESTIONS

1. Following the Vietnam War, the U.S. Supreme Court adopted a doctrine of deference to policy judgments made by the military itself or by Congress when legislating on military subjects. This doctrine, known as "military deference" or "judicial deference to the military" was applied in *Rostker v. Goldberg*, 453 U.S. 57 (1981), an equal-protection challenge to selective service laws that required men, but not women, to register for the draft. Justice Rehnquist wrote for the Court, "This is not, however, merely a case involving the customary deference accorded congressional decisions. The case arises in the context of Congress' authority over national defense and military affairs, and perhaps in no other area has the Court accorded Congress greater deference." *Id.* at 64–65.

2. On what basis are military-related decisions deserving of special deference in the face of constitutional challenge? *Rostker* grounded its justification in textual analysis. In concluding that "the Constitution itself requires such deference to congressional choice," *id.* at 67, the Court cited the following finding contained in the Report of the Senate Armed Services Committee:

> Article I, section 8 of the Constitution commits exclusively to the Congress the power to raise and support armies, provide and maintain a Navy, and make rules for Government and regulation of the land and naval forces, and pursuant to these powers it lies within the discretion of the Congress to determine the occasions for expansion of our Armed Forces, and the means best suited to such expansion should it prove necessary.

Id. at 65. Therefore, because Congress acted "under an explicit constitutional grant of authority," *id.* at 70, the usual heightened level of judicial scrutiny applicable to sex-based legal classifications under the Fifth Amendment did not control the decision.

3. Why would Justice Rehnquist propose special deference when Congress acts "under an explicit constitutional grant of authority"? Under Article I of the Constitution, does not Congress *always* act under an explicit constitutional grant of authority? In any event, is it within the power of Congress to issue "findings" of constitutional interpretation? In a later case, Justice Scalia crafted an alternate textual justification for judicial deference to the military that relied on tallying the number of clauses within Article I, Section 8 that reference the military. Under this analysis, the decision of the drafters of the Constitution to separate the military powers into five different clauses [Article I, Section 8, Clauses 12–16], rather than consolidate them into fewer clauses, counsels greater judicial deference to legislative choice: "What is distinctive here is . . . the insistence (evident from the number of Clauses devoted to the subject) with which the Constitution confers authority over the Army, Navy, and militia upon the political branches." *United States v. Stanley*, 483 U.S. 669, 682 (1987). Is Scalia's textual analysis any more persuasive?

4. *Rostker* also grounded its deference to military-related judgment in claims of judicial incompetence: "Not only is the scope of Congress' constitutional power in this area broad, but the lack of competence on the part of the courts is marked." *Id.* at 65. Quoting *Gilligan v. Morgan*, 413 U.S. 1 (1973), the Kent State shootings case in which the Court declined a continuing supervisory role over the activities of the Ohio National Guard, Rehnquist wrote:

> [I]t is difficult to conceive of an area of governmental activity in which the courts have less competence. The complex, subtle, and professional decisions as to the composition, training, equipping, and control of a military force are essentially professional military judgments, subject *always* to civilian control of the Legislative and Executive Branches.

Rostker, supra, 65–66. Is it fair to state that military issues are beyond the competence of the civilian judiciary? Are questions of military good order and discipline more difficult for courts to handle than, for example, questions of cutting-edge science? *Cf. Daubert v. Merrell Dow Pharms, Inc.*, 509 U.S. 579 (1993) (establishing judicial standards for assessing the reliability of scientific expert testimony). Is it significant that Article III of the Constitution makes no mention of the military?

2.   Court-Martial Procedure

Court-martial movies illustrate the true procedural fault lines in military justice, even if exaggerated for dramatic effect. In such common film themes as the rush to trial, the denial of the right to call witnesses, inexperienced defense counsel, and unlawful command influence over the proceedings, we see the fears that arise — in heightened visual shorthand, to be sure — from real procedural choices the military justice system has made in the service of two masters, military justice and the maintenance of good order and discipline.

Professor Jonathan Turley's article and the film *A Few Good Men* provide scholarly and visual primers, respectively, on basic court-martial procedure. On the whole, Article I military courts-martial and Article III civilian criminal trials are more similar than dissimilar in procedural rhythm and style. The differences are, or at least are supposed to be, justified by the need to maintain good order and discipline within military units.

TRIBUNALS AND TRIBULATIONS: THE ANTITHETICAL ELEMENTS OF MILITARY GOVERNANCE IN A MADISONIAN DEMOCRACY
Jonathan Turley
70 George Washington Law Review 649 (2002)

1.   The Military Judge

One of the most central guarantees for criminal defendants in the federal system is the guarantee of an Article III judge with lifetime tenure. Although this same guarantee is not imposed on the states as an essential constitutional right, it offers protection in the federal system for defendants against the desire of elected or appointed judges to appease popular or political interests. The "independence" of judges with lifetime tenure can be overstated, but there should be no honest debate that such protection from termination or retaliation fosters independent thought and action. In the military, judges operate in an environment that could not be more inimical to such independence. These judges often rotate from their judicial roles into non-judicial roles. Any given judge can thus expect to serve in a different capacity in a matter of years. The promotion and reputation of such officers can be significantly affected by their rulings in criminal cases, particularly high-profile cases. Moreover, these judges are officers who have considerable dependence and identification with the military system and the COC [chain of command] system. In any given case, these judges are expected at times to differ sharply with convening authorities and other high-ranking officers. They are also expected to impose sanctions against other officers in the trial counsel and defense offices. Although many judges perform their functions admirably, there is a lack of structural independence for judges and much of the system depends on the belief that individual judges will resist obvious conflicts or pressures in the performance of their roles.

The role of judges in military prosecutions is also different in the extent to which judges are not used in critical stages. As noted below, the convening authority performs a number of roles associated with judges in the civilian system despite the close association of the convening authority (and staff judge advocate) with the prosecution. In a [civilian] preliminary hearing, a judge determines whether there is sufficient cause to charge a defendant and may issue a binding order releasing the defendant. In the military system, this decision (and the grand jury function) is folded into the role of the investigating officer at the Article 32 proceeding who need not be a judge and whose recommendation may be ignored by the convening authority. It is only after the Article 32 investigation that a military judge is assigned who may independently dismiss the charges.

2. The Convening Authority

One of the most curious elements in the military system is the role of the convening authority. While various high ranking officials like the President or Secretary of Defense can convene a general courts-martial, the vast majority of such cases are convened upon the order of the convening authority. Generally the highest ranking member in command, the convening authority is often a general staff officer in charge of a large force or fleet. As such, this commander may have ultimate command authority over the defendant, the trial counsel, witnesses, and members of the jury. Moreover, while judges are not taken from the command of a convening authority, a given military judge cannot be certain that a later transfer will not place him or her under the command of a given convening authority. . . .

The convening authority clearly plays a prosecutorial role as well as a judicial role. It is the convening authority who makes the initial judgment that a servicemember should stand trial. If the convening authority decides to bring charges, he will "prefer" those charges and both the charges and a charge sheet are given to the accused. This will trigger the Article 32 proceeding, where an investigating officer will conduct an investigation to determine the basis for the charges. During the Article 32 proceeding, however, the convening authority continues to exercise a significant level of control or discretion over the investigation, including serving as the final decision maker on many requests for resources or motions regarding experts or witnesses. The convening authority is not obligated to accept the recommendations of the investigating officer on either motions or the final conclusion as to the basis for the charges. If an investigating officer can find no basis for the charges, then, his recommendation for dismissal of charges can simply be rejected by the convening authority. Because it was the convening authority who preferred the charges, such contrary determinations of the merits of the preferral are not always welcomed or accepted. The result is a system that allows some independent investigation but the decision to proceed to trial ultimately rests with the same party who made the initial charging decision. . . .

3. The Prosecutor and Defense Counsel

In the military system, the prosecutor ("trial counsel") holds a level of authority that is largely unknown in the civilian system. Where the civilian system struggles to maintain a relative balance of power between the prosecutor and the defense attorney, the military system gives a trial counsel a degree of practical control over the development of a defense case. This power derives from the convening authority. Although the convening authority holds considerable power over the bringing, maintenance, and prosecution of a case, the true day-to-day authority is exercised by his subordinate, the staff judge advocate. The staff judge advocate recommends rulings and decisions on issues raised by counsel in the early development of a case before the assignment of the military judge (and later in any plea negotiations). The staff judge advocate also plays a critical role in securing "nominations" for who will serve on a given panel of members. The staff judge advocate normally works closely with the trial counsel and is closely aligned with the prosecution. The trial counsel and staff judge advocate thus largely determine the resources and schedule for a case through the Article 32 investigation. Trial counsel exercises a critical role throughout the trial that would be viewed as unacceptable in a civilian system, including a requirement that requests for defense witnesses be submitted to the trial counsel with a statement of the expected testimony from the witness. It is then determined whether this request is reasonable in terms of relevance and necessity.

Some aspects of military representation are more favorable than the civilian system. Like the civilian system, a military defendant is guaranteed defense counsel, but unlike the civilian system, such detailed counsel is afforded regardless of financial ability to pay private counsel. Moreover, military defendants may request a particular detailed defense counsel, and such "individual military counsel" is supplied if "reasonably" available. In a number of important respects, however, the military system affords substantially less representational protection than the civilian system. For example, in the civilian system, a defendant is allowed a private attorney at public expense, albeit at a standardized pay scale that is lower than standard private fees. In the military, a defendant is forced to either accept military counsel or pay for his own civilian attorney. The difference in quality of defense could not be more extreme for indigent defendants in the civilian and military systems. Most detailed military counsel are relatively young and inexperienced lawyers. For example, in the Navy, defense counsel in capital cases may be recent law graduates with little trial, let alone capital case, experience. Once these young attorneys have a year or so of experience, they are generally transferred out of the defense trial office in a rotation system that virtually guarantees inexperienced counsel for military defendants. These attorneys would be categorically excluded from many federal cases as incompetent due to their inexperience. . . .

4. The Military Jury

The military jury system also contains elements inversive to the civilian system. A military jury is composed of individuals ("members") who would be routinely stricken for cause in the civilian system. The simple selection of people from the same branch and command would be viewed as inherently incompatible with jury service in the civilian system. Such jurors on the whole are likely to have greater bias and be more inclined to view the prosecution as "protecting" their service and their command. While biased members are barred from serving, such bias does not include the inherent risk of prejudice in selecting from the immediate command.

A military jury has a closer affinity to state juries than federal juries, despite the federal status of the court and personnel. Federal juries are required to have twelve members, though fewer than twelve jurors may ultimately vote on a verdict. Like some state juries, military juries can number less than twelve. In fact, there is considerable variation in the actual number of members for given forms of courts-martial, and these rules set a minimum, not a uniform, number of members. In a general court-martial, there must be a minimum of at least five members, unless the accused opts for a bench trial. After December 2002, however, a death penalty case will have twelve members. . . .

The other significant difference between military and civilian juries is the absence of random selection. One of the most essential and most protected elements of a fair trial under the Sixth Amendment is the random selection of a jury pool and the process of voir dire. In the military, it is the convening authority who selects members to sit in a given case. This selection is made according to the convening authority's judgment as to the "best qualified" individuals on the basis for their "age, education, training, experience, length of service, and judicial temperament." There is no requirement of random selection or that the selected members represent a cross-section of either the military community or the local civilian community. To the contrary, unless there is an objection from an accused enlisted servicemember, the jury may be composed entirely of officers. Even with an objection, the military rules only guarantee a third of the panel will be enlisted personnel. Although the military does apply the constitutional rules barring the discriminatory use of challenges on the basis of race and gender, the entire thrust of the jury selection process is one of perceived competence by the convening authority rather than the more representative function of civilian juries. . . .

Once selected and seated for the duration of the trial, the members are not required to reach a unanimous decision in criminal matters. Rather, a conviction for any crime other than a capital offense can be secured on a two-thirds vote of the members. Although the Supreme Court has recognized that unanimity is not constitutionally required in state courts, the military still runs afoul of the minimal standard established for the state systems. Unanimity is not required if the state jury is a twelve-member panel, but if the state employs a six-member panel, unanimity is required. Not only does the military allow panels below the constitutional standard of a six-member panel, but it allows for non-unanimous verdicts in direct conflict with these rulings.

5. The Witnesses

For defense counsel, pre-trial preparation and witness selection can be a much more abbreviated process because cases go to trial in less than half the time of civilian cases. The danger of unlawful command influence is also greatest for witnesses than any other party to a court-martial. Although the judge and defense counsel are not under the command of the convening authority, a witness may be subject to that authority and, particularly in a high-profile case, may feel that testimony will reflect upon his or her career. The appearance of these witnesses is further controlled by the convening authority in the early stages of a case, a level of control condemned as inimical to due process. . . .

NOTES & QUESTIONS

1. The Uniform Code of Military Justice (UCMJ), 10 U.S.C. §§ 801-946, sets out rules of procedure and a substantive criminal code for the military's separate system of criminal justice. The UCMJ represents the principal exercise of congressional power to make rules for the government and regulation of the military.

2. *A Few Good Men* is the story of two young marines charged with the murder of a fellow marine at the United States Naval Station, Guantanamo Bay, Cuba. The defendants told Lt. Junior Grade Daniel Kaffee, a military defense lawyer played by Tom Cruise, that a superior officer ordered them to give the victim a "Code Red," an informal, off-the-books disciplinary measure in which marines administer minor physical hazing to a colleague whose performance has fallen short of standard. The defense argued the victim's death was accidental, precipitated by an underlying medical condition that made him unusually susceptible when defendants bound and gagged him. The theme of the prosecution's case was that no such order was ever given. The military trial counsel, or prosecutor, argued the defendants intended to kill the victim in retaliation for reporting earlier misconduct to civilian authorities. *A Few Good Men* is best known for Kaffee's dramatic cross-examination of Col. Nathan Jessup, the commanding officer at Guantanamo Bay played by Jack Nicholson.

Kaffee challenges Jessup's ability to control the conduct of his men and goads him into boasting that, yes, he did give the order for the Code Red. Famously, Lt. Kaffee shouts, "I want the truth!" and Col. Jessup roars back, "You can't handle the truth!"

3. While the battle between Lt. Kaffee and Col. Jessup is fascinating to aficionados of effective cross-examination, the intellectual center of *A Few Good Men* is found in its nuanced treatment of military orders and the legal obligation of subordinate personnel to obey them. Article 90 (10 U.S.C. § 890) of the UCMJ directs as follows:

> Any person subject to this chapter who willfully disobeys a lawful command of his superior commissioned officer shall be punished, if the offense is committed in time of war, by death or such other punishment as a court-martial may direct, and if the offense is committed at any other time, by such punishment, other than death, as a court-martial may direct.

Clearly, the decision to disobey an order is a serious one. Indeed, military regulations elaborate on this Article by cautioning junior personnel that, when reasonably in doubt, they should assume the order is lawful and comply:

> An order requiring the performance of a military duty or act may be inferred to be lawful and it is disobeyed at the peril of the subordinate. This inference does not apply to a patently illegal order, such as one that directs the commission of a crime.

> The order must relate to military duty, which includes all activities reasonably necessary to accomplish a military mission, or safeguard or promote the morale, discipline, and usefulness of members of a command and directly connected with the maintenance of good order in the service. However, the dictates of a person's conscience, religion, or personal philosophy cannot justify or excuse the disobedience of an otherwise lawful order.

Manual for Courts-Martial, pt. IV, ¶ 14.c (2)(a).

4. Even among members of the defense team in *A Few Good Men* there is disagreement and discomfort in their attempt to prove a superior officer gave an order to administer a Code Red. Lurking behind the defense of obedience to orders is the proviso that the defense is inapplicable if the accused "knew the orders to be unlawful or a person of ordinary sense and understanding would have known the orders to be unlawful." Rules for Courts-Martial 916(d), *in* Manual for Courts-Martial, pt. II, at 109. Lt. Kaffee's co-counsel hears echoes of Nuremberg and My Lai in the protest of "I was just following orders," but Kaffee argues from the perspective of the marine who is asked to make the judgment call on the legality of an order: "Do you really think that's the same as two teenage marines executing a routine order they never believed would result in harm?" Is it reasonable to expect that military personnel can make a determination "on the ground" whether an order relates to activities "reasonably necessary" to promote discipline and "directly connected" to the maintenance of good order? What if your superior, a vastly more experienced servicemember such as Col. Jessup, tells you that a Code Red is "an invaluable part of close-infantry training"? Under what circumstances should you be expected to know that it is not?

5. How do the events depicted in *A Few Good Men* compare to the instances of detainee abuse committed at the Abu Ghraib prison in Iraq and symbolized by the iconic photograph of a grinning Pfc. Lynddie England, a 22-year-old Army clerk, smoking a cigarette, signaling "thumbs up," and pointing at the genitalia of naked prisoners? England initially took the position, consistent with the defense raised in *A Few Good Men*, that she obeyed orders to treat prisoners in the manner her superiors told her was necessary for successful interrogations. When she changed course, for purposes of a plea agreement, and testified that she knew her conduct was wrong, the court rejected her guilty plea as inconsistent with other evidence introduced by the defense. At court-martial, England was convicted and sentenced to three years in prison and a dishonorable discharge.

6. In the end, against all odds, Lt. Kaffee obtains an acquittal for his clients on the charges of murder and conspiracy to commit murder. He is shocked, however, when the military jury finds the defendants guilty of conduct unbecoming a marine, a charge that appears to be based on Article 134 of the UCMJ (10 U.S.C. § 934), which prohibits conduct "to the prejudice of good order and discipline" and "conduct of a nature to bring discredit upon the armed forces." The more senior of the two enlisted defendants, however, understands the verdict immediately. He realizes that good order and discipline actually required him to resist the order, because someone had to step forward to protect the victim, Willie, against the misconduct of superiors. "We were supposed to fight for people who couldn't fight for themselves. We were supposed to fight for Willie."

7. "Good order and discipline" and the actions necessary to maintain it seem to be moving targets defined by experience within the military. It is easy — often too easy — to justify a broad range of conduct by insisting it is simply part and parcel of good order and discipline, shielded from review by civilians who could not understand military necessity. In *A Few Good Men*, Col. Jessup takes advantage of the malleability of good order and discipline by lecturing Lt. Kaffee, a junior lawyer far removed from the "business end" of the military: "I have neither the time nor the inclination to explain myself to a man who rises and sleeps under the blanket of the very freedom that I provide and then questions the manner in which I provide it." Jessup's statement could be seen as a very crude statement of the doctrine of judicial deference to the military. Given the difficulty of evaluating either the strength of good order and discipline within the military or efforts to maintain or improve it, do courts have any choice other than to defer to military or congressional judgment on this issue?

C.   UNLAWFUL COMMAND INFLUENCE IN COURTS-MARTIAL

Imagine a system of justice in which a single authority acts as your employer, your landlord, and your mayor. Should you find yourself accused of criminal conduct, that same authority will supervise the initial investigation, decide whether and how seriously you will be charged, appoint the members of the jury to hear your case, and review the findings and sentence. Furthermore, it is likely that everyone on the jury and all the witnesses who testify in your trial also work for the same authority. This is the comprehensive authority that rests in military command. Military commanders are simultaneously responsible for the quality of military justice and the quality of good order and discipline within their units, a potential conflict that requires careful management.

UNIFORM CODE OF MILITARY JUSTICE
(UNLAWFULLY INFLUENCING ACTION OF COURT)
10 U.S.C. § 837

(a) No authority convening a general, special, or summary court-martial, nor any other commanding officer, may censure, reprimand, or admonish the court or any member, military judge, or counsel thereof, with respect to the findings or sentence adjudged by the court, or with respect to any other exercise of its or his functions in the conduct of the proceeding. No person subject to this chapter may attempt to coerce or, by any unauthorized means, influence the action of a court-martial or any other military tribunal or any member thereof, in reaching the findings or sentence in any case, or the action of any convening, approving, or reviewing authority with respect to his judicial acts.

(b) In the preparation of an effectiveness, fitness, or efficiency report, or any other report or document used in whole or in part for the purpose of determining whether a member of the armed forces is qualified to be advanced, in grade, or in determining the assignment or transfer of a member of the armed forces or in determining whether a member of the armed forces should be retained on active duty, no person subject to this chapter may, in preparing any such report (1) consider or evaluate the performance of duty of any such member as a member of a court-martial, or (2) give a less favorable rating or evaluation of any member of the armed forces because of the zeal with which such member, as counsel, represented any accused before a court-martial.

---

1. The Structure of Unlawful Command Influence

Lest you believe that court-martial movies always over-dramatize unlawful command influence, consider the following case heard by the highest court in the military justice system, the Court of Appeals for the Armed Forces. In *United States v. Gore*, the court found unlawful command influence in the direct intimidation of a witness.

UNITED STATES v. GORE
Court of Appeals for the Armed Forces
60 M.J. 178 (2004)

Anticipating Appellant's guilty plea pursuant to the signed pretrial agreement, defense counsel [Lieutenant Maye, equivalent in rank to an Army Captain] worked to prepare a sentencing case for Appellant. On November 18, three days before the trial was scheduled to resume, Lt. Maye went to Appellant's unit to obtain possible defense witnesses. Lt. Maye testified that he wanted to identify individuals who would fill out questionnaires detailing support of Appellant. Lt. Maye sought out Equipment Operator Chief E-7 (Chief) Metheny in particular, as Appellant "wanted Chief Metheny to assist in our defense."

Chief Metheny "immediately said, 'Well, I'll testify. Do you need me to testify? I'll testify.'" Accepting this offer, they discussed travel plans for the Chief to be a witness at the court-martial and the general substance of Chief Metheny's expected testimony on behalf of Appellant. Lt. Maye testified that Chief Metheny told him that "he thought [Appellant] was a really nice guy. And he said he thinks that [Appellant] should be retained." Lt. Maye also testified that Chief Metheny agreed to distribute questionnaires to other senior enlisted personnel that he believed would also testify in support of Appellant.

On the afternoon of November 20, the day before trial, defense counsel returned to Appellant's command because he "was surprised that Chief Metheny hadn't contacted me, hadn't come over and dropped off the questionnaires." Lt. Maye testified that as he walked onto the command quarterdeck, Chief Metheny met him and informed him, "I can't help you, Lieutenant . . . I'm not testifying. . . . My skipper said no way. He said that I can't help Constructionman Gore." When asked about the questionnaires, defense counsel testified that Chief Metheny said, "Lieutenant, my CO [Commanding Officer] said we cannot help Constructionman Gore. End of story." As the two parted, Chief Metheny yelled out, "Hey Lieutenant, this is between me and you."

Lt. Maye left the command but shortly returned, accompanied by his officer-in-charge, Lt. Weber. Lt. Maye sought to arrange a second meeting with Chief Metheny and to have Chief Metheny repeat his statements in the presence of Lt. Weber. Defense counsel and Lt. Weber discussed with Chief Metheny his basis for refusing to testify. Chief Metheny stated that neither he, nor anyone else in his command, would testify on behalf of Appellant in light of the order by the commanding officer, Commander Morton. Chief Metheny "alluded to negative ramifications that would stem from testifying and terminated the meeting." He reinforced this point when he grabbed his collar device and stated that he attained his present grade of chief in 11 years when he was expected to make it in 16 years and that one gets ahead by not bucking the system.

[On the morning of trial. Lt. Maye again met with Chief Metheny.] Defense counsel testified that Chief Metheny said, "Lieutenant, I'm here. The CO told me to be here, but I'm not going to be any help to you. The CO told me to to[e] the line and that's what I'm doing. I'm not testifying." Chief Metheny further stated that the accused was going to be released within 30 days and the accused was not worth risking his career. Finally, Lt. Maye testified that Chief Metheny stated that the commanding officer had called him on the telephone the night before trial and told him "You're going to Pensacola and you know what the . . . command's position is on this matter."

Since original detailed defense counsel, Lt. Maye, was now a witness for Appellant, substitute defense counsel argued the motion at the special court-martial. Initially Lt. Maye provided all of the previously detailed testimony as to his prior contacts with Chief Metheny both at the command in Gulfport and the morning of trial in Pensacola.

Following the testimony of the original defense counsel, the defense called Chief Metheny as a witness. He testified that he had minimum contact with the Appellant who served in his platoon for less than two weeks prior to his alleged unauthorized absence. Chief Metheny denied telling Lt. Maye that he would be willing to testify at the court-martial as a character witness on behalf of Appellant. Chief Metheny stated his personal view that he had seen a lot worse stay in the Navy, but he reaffirmed that he had nothing positive to say as a professional opinion about Appellant. Chief Metheny did confirm that he agreed to distribute the defense questionnaires to others in the command who may be able to fill them out, but explained that he "hadn't gotten around to it." Regarding his conversation with Lt. Maye the morning of trial, Chief Metheny made repeated denials that contradicted the testimony of Lt. Maye.

Next, Lt. Weber testified as a defense witness. Lt. Weber testified that he sat in on the second meeting with Lt. Maye and Chief Metheny, and that they discussed whether Chief Metheny was going to be a witness for Appellant during sentencing. He corroborated the testimony of Lt. Maye. Lt. Weber stated that he was "in shock basically as to what was going on." Lt. Weber testified, "And I said, 'Chief, are you serious? Is this going to have a consequence on your promotion?' And his response to me was, 'How long have you been in the Navy?'"

Contrary to Lt. Weber's testimony, Cmdr. Morton [Commander, two ranks higher than a Navy Lieutenant and equivalent to an Army Lieutenant Colonel] testified that he did not try to influence Chief Metheny's testimony. Cmdr. Morton stated, "I was really offended I guess, above all else, that somebody could come in and take one of my people away without my knowledge. So I told the Chief, 'You're not going to go.'" Cmdr. Morton explained that the conversation with Chief Metheny arose because the Chief was advising him that he would be absent from work. Cmdr. Morton testified that his was an "operational unit, ready to deploy" and he and other command members were missing "a very important meeting with our superior discussing our combat readiness to be here." He explained that it "bothered" him that the "request directing to my subordinate was made without any knowledge of the impact to my command."

Cmdr. Morton testified that he was confused and unaware that Appellant would need to have witnesses speak on his behalf at sentencing. He testified that he had briefly discussed with Chief Metheny the facts of Appellant's offenses and the terms of the pretrial agreement. He testified that he told

Chief Metheny the case was a "done deal." Cmdr. Morton explained that he had "never been in this position to see what a special court actually does. And I thought it was a foregone conclusion that once the [pretrial] agreement was signed [that the case was settled.]" Cmdr. Morton denied that he had any motivation to prevent Appellant from getting witnesses to speak on his behalf. He asserted that he did not understand that Chief Metheny was going to be a defense witness because he asserted Chief Metheny barely knew Appellant and he did not see how Chief Metheny's testimony was germane. He then explained, "Chief Metheny is one to really talk on. He is a Seabee's Seabee. He will do anything for any troop, anytime. I know he can talk and talk. I said, 'Stick to the facts, the facts that you know.' That's all I told him."

Cmdr. Morton explained that he reconsidered his decision not to permit Chief Metheny to testify when he got a telephone call from the legalman chief, in the base staff judge advocate's office, informing him "that the defense counsel had claimed some foul play on my part, that I was limiting Chief Metheny's ability to get there." Cmdr. Morton said that he met with the chief and told him to "go down to Pensacola and answer all questions that you're asked."

We now consider whether the military judge erred in fashioning the remedy for the unlawful command influence that tainted the proceedings. The military judge rejected Chief Metheny's testimony finding, "His demeanor continued to betray dishonesty, both in the ashen tone of his skin, which varied as his testimony continued, and his constant movement in the witness box." Also, "his face was red and head bowed when answering the question," he appeared to be "acutely uncomfortable," and "his eyes were averted from the direction of the Court." Chief Metheny appeared to the court as being under "considerable duress." He was a man desperate to please his commanding officer.

The military judge found Lt. Weber to be a credible witness that corroborated the scope, degree, and impact of the unlawful command influence on Chief Metheny. Ultimately, the military judge concluded that "in order to determine that no unlawful command influence had been exerted it would have to defy logic, disbelieve two officers of the court and adopt the testimony of Chief Metheny whose erratic, nervous and deceptive deportment and questionable substantive contribution are documented in [my] findings of fact."

In summary, both parties and the lower court agree that the military judge correctly found that unlawful command influence existed. The military judge's findings of fact were not clearly erroneous and support this conclusion. Because Appellant had not yet entered pleas, the CA's [Convening Authority's] interference with potential witnesses affected both Appellant's ability to contest the charges and to present a sentencing case. It was within the military judge's discretion to determine that dismissal with prejudice was the appropriate remedy in light of the egregious conduct of the CA that prejudiced Appellant's court-martial.

NOTES & QUESTIONS

1. Unlawful command influence can take a variety of forms, from subtle to egregious. All stem, however, from the unavoidable reality that military justice is carried out within the context of an underlying military chain of command that is responsible for the maintenance of good order and discipline. Issues of unlawful command influence can arise when senior military officials comment on pending criminal prosecutions and implicitly suggest an expected outcome to the subordinates who will prosecute, defend, and sit in judgment as jury members. Consider, for example, the high-profile prosecution of 1st Lt. Kelly Flinn, the Air Force's first female B-52 pilot. She was charged with failure to obey an order, false statements, adultery, fraternization, and conduct unbecoming an officer, offenses arising out of her affair with the civilian spouse of another servicemember. The Flinn controversy became the symbol of the military's struggle during the 1990s to enforce rules governing sexual morality on an even-handed basis as women gained numbers and influence within the institution. While Sheila Widnall, the civilian Secretary of the Air Force, was weighing whether to accept Flinn's resignation and grant an honorable discharge instead of proceeding to court-martial, Gen. Ronald Fogleman, Chief of Staff of the U.S. Air Force, made the following statement in testimony before Congress:

> We are very interested in a thing called improper relationships that end up undermining the morale and discipline of an organization. I would really like to see people not comment so much on it until they have all the facts, and we cannot get the facts out until you either have a court-martial or you have a resolution of the affair so that you can put the facts out. And the facts have not come out. Some of them are starting to come out. And I think that in the end, this is not an issue of adultery. This is an issue about an officer who was entrusted to fly nuclear weapons, who disobeyed an order, who lied. That's what this is about.

FY98 Defense Appropriations: Hearing Before the Subcommittee on Defense of the Senate Committee on Armed Services, 105th Cong. (1997). Should Gen. Fogleman's statement constitute a violation of Article 37 (10 U.S.C. § 837) of the UCMJ, the provision prohibiting unlawful command influence? Where do you draw the line between the maintenance of good order and discipline and unlawful command influence? *Cf. Davis v. United States*, 58 M.J. 100 (2003) (reversing the decision of a convening authority who told subordinates that those convicted of using drugs "should not come crying to him about their situations or their families"). Ultimately, Lt. Flinn was permitted to resign and avoid court-martial, but she received a general rather than an honorable discharge.

2. *Breaker Morant*, a film based on the true story of a 1902 court-martial, painted a picture of unlawful command influence in its most brutal and unadorned form. Lt. Harry "Breaker" Morant was an Australian serving in a special forces unit of the British Army in South Africa during the Boer War. Along with two other Australian officers, he was tried by court-martial for the murder of Boer prisoners and a German missionary, although the film suggests the British Army expected Lt. Morant's unit, the Bushveldt Carbineers, to operate outside the standard rules of armed conflict and more in line with the tactics of the Boer commandos. As the film's title character noted, "It's a new kind of war. It's a new war for a new century." With respect to the enemy, he explained, "They're farmers. They're people from small towns. They shoot at us from houses and from paddocks. Some of them are women, some of them are children, and some of them are missionaries."

The defendants contended that superiors sent informal orders down the chain of command to shoot prisoners instead of taking them into custody. However, Field General Lord Kitchener, the senior commander of British and Colonial forces, had political reasons for ensuring convictions:

> Viewing the movie with this perspective, we see the court-martial as a sham — a legal process in form only because the higher-ups of Whitehall, Australia, and Pretoria have already predetermined the outcome. Whitehall needs convictions and executions to foreclose Germany from entering the war under the guise of protecting South African civilian populations from the unorthodox military tactics and civilian internment programs of the British forces. With the outcome set in the councils of power, the British Army court subverts the legal process itself. Kitchener orders the court-martial in the field, Pietersburg, to distance it from his headquarters, Pretoria. Command influence for conviction permeates the court-martial. The experienced prosecutor has six weeks to prepare; the inexperienced defense counsel gets two days. The presiding officer consistently rules for the prosecution and against defense on motions and objections. Prosecution witnesses swear to tell the truth but testify falsely. Higher authorities conveniently and fortuitously transfer defense witnesses to new posts in India. Rigged procedures give predictable results: guilty as charged on all counts.

Drew L. Kershen, *Breaker Morant*, 22 Oklahoma City University Law Review 107 (1997). One of the co-defendants in *Breaker Morant*, Lt. Peter Handcock, remarked, "Jesus, they're playing with a double-headed penny, aren't they?"

3. The military justice system relies more on the exercise of professional judgment and good faith by individual commanders, and less on procedural checks and balances, in comparison to the civilian system of criminal justice. When individual judgment fails, however, the system fails, as it did in *Breaker Morant*. No military officer has ever been prosecuted for exerting the unlawful command influence prohibited by Article 37. Proposals to limit the potential for unlawful command influence often seek to add additional procedural safeguards and remove discretionary choices of commanders. One option often advanced is for members of military juries to be chosen randomly from a pool of eligible persons instead of being selected individually by the convening authority. Opponents argue that any improvement in military justice would come at the expense of military discipline and readiness.

2. Recommendations for UCMJ Reform

REPORT OF THE COMMISSION ON THE 50TH ANNIVERSARY OF THE UNIFORM CODE OF MILITARY JUSTICE
(2001)

Sponsored by the National Institute of Military Justice, a private nonprofit organization dedicated to the fair administration of military justice, this Commission was formed on the occasion of the 50th anniversary of the Uniform Code of Military Justice, the greatest reform in the history of United States military law. The UCMJ was drafted in the aftermath of World War II, at a time when protecting the rights of military personnel was foremost in the minds of lawmakers. The outcry of veterans' organizations and bar associations made legislators aware of the arbitrary and summary nature of many of the two million courts-martial held during the war. By setting a higher standard of due process for servicemembers accused of crimes, the UCMJ, augmented by significant revisions in 1968 and 1983, became a model for criminal justice. It protected accused servicemembers against self-incrimination fifteen years before *Miranda v. Arizona*, provided for extensive pretrial screening investigations, permitted relatively broad access to free counsel, and incorporated many of the best features of federal and state criminal justice systems.

This landmark legislation created the fairest and most just system of courts-martial in any country in 1951. But the UCMJ has failed to keep pace with the standards of procedural justice adhered to not only in the United States, but in a growing number of countries around the world, in 2001. The UCMJ governs a criminal justice system with jurisdiction over millions of United States citizens, including members of the National Guard, reserves, retired military personnel, and the active-duty force, yet the Code has not been subjected to thorough or external scrutiny for thirty years. The last comprehensive study of courts-martial took place in 1971, when Secretary of Defense Melvin Laird, troubled by allegations of racism at courts-martial, appointed a task force to study the administration of military justice. This legislative and executive inattention is a new phenomenon; between 1951 and 1972, military justice was the focus of dozens of congressional hearings and the subject of countless official reports from government agencies.

Based on the response to the Commission's request for comments on the current military justice system, a "bottom-up" review of military justice is long overdue. In recent years, countries around the world have modernized their military justice systems, moving well beyond the framework created by the UCMJ fifty years ago. In contrast, military justice in the United States has stagnated, remaining insulated from external review and largely unchanged despite dramatic shifts in armed forces demographics, military missions, and disciplinary strategies. Since the Tailhook episode in 1991, the armed forces have faced a near-constant parade of high-profile criminal investigations and courts-martial, many involving allegations of sexual misconduct, each a threat to morale and a public relations disaster.

As many witnesses before the Commission pointed out, the far-reaching role of commanding officers in the court-martial process remains the greatest barrier to operating a fair system of criminal justice within the armed forces. Fifty years into the legal regime implemented by the UCMJ, commanding officers still loom over courts-martial, able to intervene and affect the outcomes of trials in a variety of ways. The Commission recognizes that, in order to maintain a disciplinary system as well as a justice system, commanders must have a significant role in the prosecution of crime at courts-martial. But this role must not be permitted to undermine the standard of due process to which servicemembers are entitled.

The question of what role such authorities should play in the disciplinary and criminal structure of the modern armed forces warrants further study. But based on the Commission's experience, and on the input received in submissions and testimony, there is one action that should be taken immediately: Convening authorities must not be permitted to select the members of courts-martial.

There is no aspect of military criminal procedures that diverges further from civilian practice, or creates a greater impression of improper influence, than the antiquated process of panel selection. The current practice is an invitation to mischief. It permits — indeed, requires — a convening authority to choose the persons responsible for determining the guilt or innocence of a servicemember who has been investigated and prosecuted at the order of that same authority. The Commission trusts the judgment of convening authorities as well as the officers and enlisted members who are appointed to serve on courts-martial. But there is no reason to preserve a practice that creates such a strong impression of, and opportunity for, corruption of the trial process by commanders and staff judge advocates. Members of courts-martial should be chosen at random from a list of eligible servicemembers prepared by the convening authority, taking into account operational needs as well as the limitations on rank, enlisted or officer status, and same-unit considerations currently followed in the selection of members. Article 25 of the UCMJ should be amended to require this improvement in the fundamental fairness of court-martial procedure.

While the selection of panel members is clearly the focal point for the perception of improper command influence, the present Code entrusts to the convening authority numerous other pretrial decisions that also contribute to a perception of unfairness. For example, the travel of witnesses to Article 32 hearings, pretrial scientific testing of evidence, and investigative assistance for both the government and the defense are just a few of the common instances in which the convening authority controls the pretrial process and can withhold or grant approval based on personal preference rather than a legal standard. This issue goes to the core of a serviceperson's rights to due process and equal protection under the law. Pretrial decisions involve legal judgments that can — and often do — affect the outcome of trials. For that reason, like the selection of panel members, decisions on pretrial matters should be removed from the purview of the convening authority and placed within the authority of a military judge.

The combined power of the convening authority to determine which charges shall be preferred, the level of court-martial, and the venue where the charges will be tried, coupled with the idea that this same convening authority selects the members of the court-martial to try the cases, is unacceptable in a society that deems due process of law to be the bulwark of a fair justice system.

DON'T TUG ON SUPERMAN'S CAPE: IN DEFENSE OF CONVENING AUTHORITY SELECTION AND APPOINTMENT OF COURT-MARTIAL PANEL MEMBERS
Christopher W. Behan
176 Military Law Review 190 (2003)

Responsibility and authority must go hand in hand. Civil society recognizes the responsibility of commanders and holds them accountable even for the criminal actions of their subordinates. Careers, lives, and international relations between nations can all be affected by the discipline or indiscipline of individual service members. To hold a commander responsible for good order and discipline, without a corresponding grant of authority over the system or the disposition of his personnel involved in it, places him and the system itself in an untenable position.

Through his role in sending cases to courts-martial and selecting panel members, the commander is able to exert lawful control over the military justice system. The cases he refers to courts-martial communicate his sense of acceptable and unacceptable conduct. In appointing subordinates to courts-martial, he fulfills several goals. He reinforces his priorities through the personnel he appoints to the court. If the courts-martial process is meaningful to him, he appoints his most trusted subordinates, using criteria similar to what he would employ in matching personnel with other missions; if the process means little to him, he sends the lazy and the expendable to judge his soldiers. Either way, he sends a message. In addition, he fulfills a training function through the operation of the military justice system, ensuring that the next generation of leaders is prepared to administer the system.

It is important to emphasize the difference between lawful influence over the military justice system, which involves carefully selecting the cases that go to trial and the members that sit in judgment of them, and unlawful command influence, which consists of attempting to exercise coercion or unauthorized influence over the action of a court-martial or its members as to findings and sentence. Lawful influence is a function of command, closely related to the core responsibilities of a commander to care for and discipline his troops. Unlawful influence is not only a crime, it is a poor management and command practice. The best commanders will avoid arbitrary and reckless meddling with the military justice system, as they would in any other aspect of command. Service members are, after all, their human capital . . . .

Honor, integrity, and trustworthiness define the character of American military commanders, just as discipline and adherence to the rule of law form the backbone of the most effective military the world has ever known.

Divesting convening authorities of the power to appoint panel members to attain a more idealistically pure system of justice exalts form over substance and the military justice system over the military. In the words of Generals William Westmoreland and George Prugh, "There is a fundamental anomaly that vests a commander with life-or-death authority over his troops in combat but does not trust that same commander to make a sound decision with respect to justice and fairness to the individual."

NOTES & QUESTIONS

1. Is it a coincidence that the last comprehensive congressional review of military justice took place in 1971, just before the end of the military draft? Does Congress lack incentive to monitor the quality of military justice when servicemembers are all volunteers?

2. Who makes the stronger argument with respect to the disadvantages or advantages of allowing commanders to individually select members of military juries? Article 25 of the UCMJ (10 U.S.C. § 825) requires convening authorities to select members of the military jury on a basis far different from the empanelment of civilian juries: "When convening a court-martial, the convening authority shall detail as members thereof such members of the armed forces as, in his opinion, are best qualified for the duty by reason of age, education, training, experience, length of service, and judicial temperament." In what ways are defendants in the military justice system advantaged or disadvantaged by juries comprised of members considered "best qualified" to serve? Does the requirement that a member be evaluated for "judicial temperament" create the potential for mischief? What does the civilian criminal justice system hope to achieve by random selection of jury panels from lists of licensed drivers or registered voters?

3. The potential for unlawful command influence can emerge in extraordinarily subtle, almost imperceptible ways. Even if military officials scrupulously avoid interfering with or influencing the military justice system and its participants, a certain bias may still be present in the desire of judges, lawyers, and jury members to please their respective chains of command. The command-centered nature of military justice may also give rise to an inherent structural weakness in its operation. For example, in a system that has no independent prosecutorial authority and depends on the judgment of senior commanders to make appropriate charging decisions, is it inevitable that more junior servicemembers will disproportionately bear the consequences of the command's misconduct or mistakes? Is it reasonable to expect that senior commanders will exercise judgment to police their own conduct? In *Breaker Morant*, defense counsel requested that Lord Kitchener be called as a witness to confirm or deny an order to shoot prisoners, but the court-martial's presiding officer denied the request.

4. Consider the final argument of the defense lawyer in *Breaker Morant's* court-martial, which evokes a contemporary concern, more than a century later, that the military justice system may be focusing its attention on the malfeasance of junior servicemembers to the neglect of poor leadership by their superiors: "Now, I don't ask for proclamations condoning distasteful methods of war. But I do say that we must take for granted that it does happen. Let's not give our officers hazy, vague instructions about what they may and may not do." Even more prescient, in the context of the continuing controversy over detainee abuse in the Iraq War and the applicability of international conventions against torture, is Lt. Morant's wry observation that "I suppose this is the first time the enemy hasn't been in uniform." Do you think the command-centered structure of the military justice system contributed to the Army's decision to court-martial very junior personnel such as Pfc. Lynndie England and Spc. Charles Graner for abuses committed at Abu Ghraib prison in Iraq? *See* Douglas Jehl & Eric Schmitt, *In Abuse, a Portrayal of Ill-Prepared, Overwhelmed G.I.'s*, N.Y. Times, 9 May 2004, § 1, 11.

5. In *The Court-Martial of Billy Mitchell*, command influence reached all the way to the Commander-in-Chief of the armed forces, the President of the United States. One scene shows President Calvin Coolidge complaining privately to the military prosecutor in mid-trial, that "this Mitchell business is getting out of hand" and reminding him "the sooner this is over with, the better it will be for the whole country." Would this have been unlawful command influence as defined by the UCMJ? Review Article 37 (10 U.S.C. § 837), quoted at the beginning of this sub-chapter, particularly the language describing who is barred from unlawfully influencing a proceeding. Under Article 2 of the UCMJ (10 U.S.C. § 802), persons subject to prosecution under the UCMJ generally include members in active service, cadets and midshipmen, and retired members of the military. Does the influence of civilians present the same danger to the military justice system?

D.   THE FIRST AMENDMENT AND THE MILITARY

In *The Court-Martial of Billy Mitchell*, a film fairly faithful to actual events, Col. Mitchell made the following statement to the press:

> Flying is a very dangerous business, and a normal amount of accidents are to be expected. But these recent disasters of the Shenandoah and the planes of the Army of the Mexican flight are outside the range of normal accidents. I would not be keeping faith with my dead comrades if I kept quiet any longer. These accidents are the direct result of incompetence, criminal negligence, and the almost treasonable administration of our national defense by the Navy and the War Department.

Col. Mitchell was convicted by court-martial in 1925. Members of the military jury found the statement, which was intended to highlight what Col. Mitchell believed was a dangerous inattention to both pilot safety and the importance of air power in military defense, was prejudicial to good order and discipline and of a nature to bring discredit upon the armed forces.

1. The Speech Rights of Servicemembers

UNIFORM CODE OF MILITARY JUSTICE
(GENERAL ARTICLE)
10 U.S.C. § 934

Though not specifically mentioned in this chapter, all disorders and neglects to the prejudice of good order and discipline in the armed forces, all conduct of a nature to bring discredit upon the armed forces, and crimes and offenses not capital, of which persons subject to this chapter may be guilty, shall be taken cognizance of by a general, special, or summary court-martial, according to the nature and degree of the offense, and shall be punished at the discretion of that court.

NOTES & QUESTIONS

1. Article 134 of the UCMJ, known as the General Article, was upheld in *Parker v. Levy*, 417 U.S. 733 (1973), against a challenge that the statute was unconstitutionally vague under the Due Process Clause of the Fifth Amendment and unconstitutionally broad under the First Amendment. Captain Levy was a drafted Army physician who refused an order to conduct dermatology training for Special Forces personnel and personally encouraged Black enlisted personnel to resist combat duty in Vietnam. The Court easily could have affirmed Captain Levy's court-martial conviction by relying on the military's authority to control breaches of internal discipline, a category which certainly would have included Levy's own failure to obey orders and his encouragement of disobedience in soldiers of lower rank. Instead, the Court used *Parker v. Levy* to establish the modern doctrine of broad judicial deference to military judgment.

2. Consider the application of *Parker v. Levy* in the contemporary context of servicemembers who object to the use of torture against detainees held in Iraq and Afghanistan.

LETTER FROM CAPTAIN IAN FISHBACK TO
SENATOR JOHN MCCAIN
151 Cong. Rec. S12433 (Nov. 7, 2005)

Dear Senator McCain:

I am a graduate of West Point currently serving as a Captain in the U.S. Army Infantry. I have served two combat tours with the 82nd Airborne Division, one each in Afghanistan and Iraq. While I served in the Global War on Terror, the actions and statements of my leadership led me to believe that United States policy did not require application of the Geneva Conventions in Afghanistan or Iraq. On 7 May 2004, Secretary of Defense Rumsfeld's testimony that the United States followed the Geneva Conventions in Iraq and the "spirit" of the Geneva Conventions in Afghanistan prompted me to begin an approach for clarification. For 17 months, I tried to determine what specific standards governed the treatment of detainees by consulting my chain of command through battalion commander, multiple JAG lawyers, multiple Democrat and Republican Congressmen and their aides, the Ft. Bragg Inspector General's office, multiple government reports, the Secretary of the Army and multiple general officers, a professional interrogator at Guantanamo Bay, the deputy head of the department at West Point responsible for teaching Just War Theory and Law of Land Warfare, and numerous peers who I regard as honorable and intelligent men.

Instead of resolving my concerns, the approach for clarification process leaves me deeply troubled. Despite my efforts, I have been unable to get clear, consistent answers from my leadership about what constitutes lawful and humane treatment of detainees. I am certain that this confusion contributed to a wide range of abuses including death threats, beatings, broken bones, murder, exposure to elements, extreme forced physical exertion, hostage-taking, stripping, sleep deprivation, and degrading treatment. I and troops under my command witnessed some of these abuses in both Afghanistan and Iraq.

This is a tragedy. I can remember, as a cadet at West Point, resolving to ensure that my men would never commit a dishonorable act; that I would protect them from that type of burden. It absolutely breaks my heart that I have failed some of them in this regard.

That is in the past and there is nothing we can do about it now. But, we can learn from our mistakes and ensure that this does not happen again. Take a major step in that direction; eliminate the confusion. My approach for clarification provides clear evidence that confusion over standards was a major contributor to the prisoner abuse. We owe our soldiers better than this. Give them a clear standard that is in accordance with the bedrock principles of our nation.

Some do not see the need for this work. Some argue that since our actions are not as horrifying as al Qaeda's, we should not be concerned. When did al Qaeda become any type of standard by which we measure the morality of the United States? We are America, and our actions should be held to a higher standard, the ideals expressed in documents such as the Declaration of Independence and the Constitution.

Others argue that clear standards will limit the President's ability to wage the War on Terror. Since clear standards only limit interrogation techniques, it is reasonable for me to assume that supporters of this argument desire to use coercion to acquire information from detainees. This is morally inconsistent with the Constitution and justice in war. It is unacceptable.

Both of these arguments stem from the larger question, the most important question that this generation will answer. Do we sacrifice our ideals in order to preserve security? Terrorism inspires fear and suppresses ideals like freedom and individual rights. Overcoming the fear posed by terrorist threats is a tremendous test of our courage. Will we confront danger and adversity in order to preserve our ideals, or will our courage and commitment to individual rights wither at the prospect of sacrifice? My response is simple. If we abandon our ideals in the face of adversity and aggression, then those ideals were never really in our possession. I would rather die fighting than give up even the smallest part of the idea that is "America."

Once again, I strongly urge you to do justice to your men and women in uniform. Give them clear standards of conduct that reflect the ideals they risk their lives for.

With the Utmost Respect,

Capt. Ian Fishback

1st Battalion, 504th Parachute Infantry Regiment, 82nd Airborne Division, Fort Bragg, North Carolina

NOTES & QUESTIONS

1. Col. Billy Mitchell attempted repeatedly, without success, to convince his superiors that the military should not abandon the fledgling Army Air Corps after World War I. He believed his pilots were risking their lives flying obsolete and deteriorating aircraft while other nations were gaining a military advantage over the United States through the projection of air power. He eventually decided he had no choice but to "go public" with his concerns, and he invited the platform of his own court-martial. He was prosecuted because the military — and President Coolidge — believed the public airing of his dissent diminished the prestige of the armed forces, disrupted discipline, and weakened national security. Very similar objections were raised when Capt. Fishback publicized his frustrations with the military chain of command and its lack of responsiveness to reports of prisoner abuse and inconsistent guidelines for treatment of detainees. Should Capt. Fishback be subject to court-martial for his disclosures, which were first made to the organization Human Rights Watch? *See* Eric Schmitt, *Officer Criticizes Detainee Abuse Inquiry*, N.Y. Times, 28 Sept. 2005, A10 (reporting Fishback's belief that "Army investigators seemed more concerned about tracking down young soldiers who reported misconduct than in following up the accusations and investigating whether higher-ranking officers knew of the abuses"). What if the military asserted that Fishback's revelations inflamed the enemy and put American servicemembers at risk? To what extent, if at all, should servicemembers have the right to speak out, either among themselves or to civilians, on matters related to their military service? Under what circumstances should dissenting speech by servicemembers be punishable as a breach of good order and discipline or protected as an exercise of First Amendment rights?

2. Many people assume that servicemembers enjoy a distinctly lesser First Amendment right to free speech than employees in the civilian world, but the difference is more one of degree. When the government is acting as an employer and not as a regulator of speech in general, it can restrict employee speech if it disrupts the efficient provision of public services. *See Pickering v. Board of Education*, 391 U.S. 563, 570 (1968) (finding the statements at issue did not detract from "either discipline by immediate superiors or harmony among coworkers"; apparently the annoyance of school district officials at a teacher's dissent did not count). Of course, the nature of the government's enforcement in civilian and military contexts is different. In the military, disruptive dissent is potentially subject to criminal sanction; in civilian public schools, for example, a teacher is subject to firing or demotion.

3. One of the effects of a broad doctrine of judicial deference to military judgment may be that we no longer expect the military to articulate specifically why dissenting speech by a servicemember in a particular situation disrupts good order and discipline. Can good order and discipline be maintained within the military only in the absence of dissent? It is reasonable to assume that servicemembers will not follow orders if they have been exposed to differing viewpoints on matters related to military duty?

4. The UCMJ itself may offer some guidance in determining when dissenting speech by servicemembers affects good order and discipline, but the nuances of the military's criminal code have been blurred over time in a regime of judicial deference. Regulatory guidance requires that "disloyal statements" punishable under the General Article, Article 134, be "made with the intent to promote disloyalty or disaffection toward the United States," such as "praising the enemy, attacking the war aims of the United States, or denouncing our form of government" with the requisite intent. Manual for Courts-Martial, pt. IV, ¶ 72, at 104. Article 88 of the UCMJ (10 U.S.C. § 888) prohibits commissioned officers from using "contemptuous words" against the President, the Vice-President, Congress, and civilian military leaders. However, dissent alone, even if vehement, is not contemptuous: "If not personally contemptuous, adverse criticism of one of the officials or legislatures named in the article in the course of a political discussion, even though emphatically expressed, may not be charged as a violation of this article." Manual for Courts-Martial, pt. IV, ¶ 12, at 16–17. Does the plain language of the UCMJ and its accompanying regulations suggest the military must protect the expression of dissent within the ranks unless the speaker intends to promote disloyalty or uses speech, as did Capt. Levy, to encourage others to breach good order and discipline? Does a comparison of Articles 134 and 88 suggest that enlisted personnel can even be contemptuous in their dissent?

5. Speech by servicemembers can be distributed immediately and worldwide when those serving in Iraq are able to blog about their experiences in almost real time. Hundreds of servicemembers share stories with Internet readers interested in unfiltered, first-person accounts of war. *See* Jonathan Finer, *The New Ernie Pyles: Sgtlizzie and 67cshdocs: On Internet Blogs, Soldiers in Iraq Serve Up Inside Story on the War*, Washington Post, 12 Aug. 2005, A1. The military has adapted to the shifting electronic landscape by issuing regulations governing blog postings from Iraq. Servicemembers must register their blogs with the military in advance and military officials must periodically review their content. *See* Memorandum from Headquarters, Multi-National Corps Iraq, *Unit and Soldier Owned and Maintained Websites* (Apr. 6, 2005). Consistent with *Pickering v. Board of Education*, the policy attempts to balance the needs of operational security ("loose lips sink ships") with tolerance for the expressive activities of servicemembers: "Risks of the release of information must be weighed against the benefits of publishing to the Internet." Specifically prohibited is the posting of information that is classified; reports casualties before notification of next of kin; is subject to the Privacy Act;

concerns ongoing investigations; or which would not be released under the Freedom of Information Act. (Query whether many soldiers, or even many Judge Advocates, would know the limits of FOIA.) So then why, as reported by the *Washington Post* in the above article, did the military order an Army doctor to discontinue his blog after he posted an entry describing the devastating injuries he treated following an attack on a mess hall? Is it inevitable that the military will make viewpoint-based decisions in editing the speech of servicemembers, prohibiting depictions of the war in words and pictures that are unfavorable to the military while permitting military-friendly stories, under circumstances in which neither would harm operational security? Are there any reasonable means of limiting the natural bias of self-protectiveness when the military censors stories from a war zone?

6. Effective civilian control of the military under the Constitution depends on an adequate flow of information to civilians. The military may, in many instances, be the only source of information necessary to congressional and executive decisions in governing and regulating the military and in conducting war. Does Congress have a constitutional obligation to err on the side of protecting servicemembers' speech in order to ensure relevant information is disclosed? Consider the testimony of Col. Billy Mitchell in his 1925 court-martial, which revealed his professional opinion — mocked grandly by the military trial counsel — that one day soldiers would invade by leaping in parachutes from airplanes, that airships would travel a thousand miles per hour, and that the Japanese would mount a crippling air attack on the islands of Hawaii.

2.   Pentagon Endorsement of Films

Military stories can be shaped by means other than the control of information from those closest to military activities. The Pentagon also controls a powerful financial and creative incentive for filmmakers to produce stories that support the military's viewpoint and enhance its ability to recruit.

DOD ASSISTANCE TO NON-GOVERNMENT, ENTERTAINMENT-ORIENTED MOTION PICTURE, TELEVISION, AND VIDEO PRODUCTIONS
Department of Defense Instruction 5410.16 (1988)

It is Department of Defense policy that:

3.1. Government assistance may be provided to an entertainment-oriented motion picture, television, or video production when cooperation of the producers with the Government results in benefiting the Department of Defense or when this would be in the best national interest, based on consideration of the following factors:

3.1.1. The production must be authentic in its portrayal of actual persons, places, military operations, and historical events. Fictional portrayals must depict a feasible interpretation of military life, operations, and policies.

3.1.2. The production is of informational value and considered to be in the best interest of public understanding of the U.S. Armed Forces and the Department of Defense.

3.1.3. The production may provide services to the general public relating to, or enhancing, the U.S. Armed Forces recruiting and retention programs.

3.1.4. The production should not appear to condone or endorse activities by private citizens or organizations when such activities are contrary to U.S. Government policy.

NOTES & QUESTIONS

1. In his 2004 book, *Operation Hollywood: How the Pentagon Shapes and Censors the Movies*, David L. Robb argued that *The Court-Martial of Billy Mitchell* was "a classic case of self-censorship" by a film studio. *Id.* at 345. The Pentagon was unhappy with the screenplay's reference to a Navy cover-up of the cause of the *Shenandoah* incident. Reluctant to offend the Pentagon and risk losing its assistance in the making of popular war-themed films — and hoping it would release the still-sealed trial transcript — Warner Brothers offered to change the screenplay to downplay any suggestion the Navy had attempted to influence the testimony of Mrs. Lansdowne, the widow of the ill-fated aviator. *Billy Mitchell's* writer and producer, Milton Sperling, took these notes from his meeting with the Army:

> We will alter the circumstances surrounding Mrs. Lansdowne's appearance on the witness stand. Over [her] protests, we eliminated her actual testimony because we did not wish to say that the Navy was capable of attempting to induce a witness to perjure herself. We restricted her to a re-statement of the events, as she told us, surrounding the fatal flight of her husband.

Id. at 349. Compare Mrs. Lansdowne's actual testimony, which clearly stated that the Navy attempted to influence her to testify falsely. *See* Douglas Waller, *A Question of Loyalty: Gen. Billy Mitchell and the Court-Martial that Gripped the Nation* 195–202 (2004). Despite Warner Brothers' cooperation, the Pentagon never released the trial transcript.

2. Kirk T. Schroder points out that the four factors in the Department of Defense's instructions are subjective and can be interpreted in curious ways. In 1986, military officials viewed *Top Gun*, starring Tom Cruise, as a valuable recruitment vehicle, but the times have changed:

> [T]his film probably could not get the approval necessary for such grand U.S. Navy assistance in today's social climate. At the time the film was produced, the U.S. Navy was not concerned with the portrayal of its aviators as swashbuckling womanizers, hell-bent on drinking, fighting and sexual conquest. However, since the advent of the Tailhook scandal and other similar publicized sex scandals related to the U.S. armed forces, the willingness to assist this kind of production might be, understandably, lessened.

Kirk T. Schroder, *Getting the Pentagon Into the Picture*, Entertainment and Sports Lawyer 15:2 (Summer 1997), 18.

3. In an interview prompted by the popularity of Iraq War themes in television and film, David Robb described Hollywood as "embedded with the military." He believes that the lure of Pentagon endorsement "is blinding Hollywood into white-washing the Iraq conflict." On the other hand, Phil Strub, head of the Pentagon's film liaison office, explains the issue this way: "These days, there is an unwillingness to criticize individual servicemen and women, which was quite common in the Vietnam era. Americans are very disinclined to do that now, and we're very glad this attitude tends to pervade all entertainment." *See* César G. Soriano & Ann Oldenburg, *With America at War, Hollywood Follows*, USA Today, 8 Feb. 2005, A1. Is the Vietnam experience a valid explanation? If so, do we glorify today's servicemembers in film and television out of guilt for anti-war protest 35 years ago or out of guilt for not serving in the all-volunteer military ourselves?

4. Does the government engage in prohibited viewpoint discrimination when it assists in the making of films that carry a message favorable to the military, but declines to assist when the message is unfavorable? *Operation Hollywood* quotes Professor Jonathan Turley's argument that the military's influence on filmmaking borders on the unconstitutional:

> This work thrives in the shadow of the First Amendment. Though the Constitution generally bars the government from preventing or punishing free speech, it is less clear about the degree to which the government may assist speech that it favors. To that end, the military uses access to military units, bases, and even stock military footage and open areas such as the Presidio to force prepublication review and script changes.

Operation Hollywood, 17, 115. Another prominent scholar of constitutional law, Erwin Chemerinsky, takes the argument further:

> The Supreme Court has said that above all, the First Amendment means that the government cannot participate in viewpoint discrimination. The government cannot favor some speech due to its viewpoint and disfavor others because of its viewpoint. The Court has said that when the government is giving financial benefits, it can't decide who to give to, or not give to, based on the viewpoint expressed.

Id. at 47–48. Asked why the Pentagon has been permitted to make viewpoint-based choices for decades, Professor Chemerinsky responded: "Nobody has sued."

5. Are Professors Turley and Chemerinsky correct? Does it depend on whether you view the Pentagon as acting as a regulator of the speech of others, as a facilitator of the speech of others, or as a speaker itself? *Compare Legal Services Corp. v. Velazquez*, 531 U.S. 533 (2001) (invalidating government restrictions on claims and arguments that federally-funded legal services lawyers could raise) with *Rosenberger v. Rector of the University of Virginia*, 515 U.S. 819 (1995) (invalidating university restrictions on the religious content of publications issued by university-funded student groups) and *Rust v. Sullivan*, 500 U.S. 173 (1991) (upholding regulation prohibiting recipients of federal funding for family planning services from providing abortion counseling or referrals). In *Velazquez*, Justice Kennedy attempted to reconcile the three cases by focusing on the government's role with respect to limitations on speech:

> We have said that viewpoint-based funding decisions can be sustained in instances in which the government is itself the speaker, or instances, like *Rust*, in which the government used private speakers to transmit specific information pertaining to its own program. As we said in *Rosenberger*, when the government disburses public funds to private entities to convey a governmental message, it may take legitimate and appropriate steps to ensure that its message is neither garbled nor distorted by the grantee.

Velazquez, supra, 541. When the Pentagon provides assistance to films with a message expected to enhance military recruiting and denies it to films considered military-unfriendly, is it acting as a regulator of dissenting viewpoints or as a speaker in its own right?

E.   DON'T ASK, DON'T TELL

The legislative codification of the policy excluding gay men and lesbians from military service, euphemistically called "Don't Ask, Don't Tell," was the product of a long summer of congressional hearings in 1993.

POLICY CONCERNING HOMOSEXUALITY IN THE ARMED FORCES: HEARINGS BEFORE THE SENATE ARMED SERVICES COMMITTEE
103rd Cong. 601–02 (1993)

Testimony of Colonel Frederick C. Peck, U.S. Marine Corps: And then later in my career I went to Los Angeles, where I was in charge of the Marine Corps Public Affairs Office, which is often called our Hollywood Liaison Office, and I worked with the entertainment industry out there. And let me tell you, I probably do not need to say this, but I worked with a lot of people in Hollywood whose sexual orientations and a lot of other things about their personal lifestyles were much, much different than my own. I think I was successful there. I think I have been successful in the civilian educational environment. And I am saying this to tell you that I am not a homophobe. I am not the kind of person who has led some cloistered, sheltered military life, who has never had to deal with the homosexuals before. I worked with them all the time. I can work with homosexuals, shoulder to shoulder.

But I do not think I can live with them and coexist with them in a military environment. It is one thing to share an office with someone; it is quite another thing to share a lifestyle; and that is what the military is: It is a way of life.

My oldest son, Scott, is a student at the University of Maryland; he is just about to graduate. If he were to walk into a recruiter's office, it would be the recruiter's dream come true. He is 6 foot 1, blue-eyed, blonde hair, great student. But if he were to go and seriously consider joining the military, I would have to, number 1, personally counsel against it, and number 2, actively fight it.

Because my son, Scott, is a homosexual; and I do not think there is any place for him in the military. I love him as much as I do any of my sons. I respect him; I think he is a fine person; but he should not serve in the military.

I spent 27 years of my life in the military, and I know what it would be like for him if he went in. And it would be hell. And if we went into combat, he would be at grave risk if he were to follow in my footsteps as an infantry platoon leader or a company commander. I would be very fearful that his life would be in jeopardy from his own troops.

And I am not saying that that is right, or wrong, or whatever. I am telling you that is the way it is. And fraggings, let me tell you, did not begin or end in Vietnam. Fratricide is something that exists out there, and there are people who would put my son's life at risk in our own Armed Forces.

NOTES & QUESTIONS

1. *Soldier's Girl* is the dramatization of the short and tragic military service of Private First Class Barry Winchell, a young man suspected of being gay who was brutally murdered, asleep in the barracks, by a fellow soldier. The film, however, is primarily a military love story. It portrays the romantic relationship between Private Winchell and an ambiguously transgendered military veteran, Calpernia Addams.

2. During the "Don't, Ask, Don't Tell" congressional hearings held during the summer of 1993, military witnesses were nonchalant about the prospect of violence against gay servicemembers. A retired Marine Corps Colonel, for example, testified blandly to instances in which gay sailors were thrown overboard:

> I can think on a number of occasions, once en route to the Med, aboard ship, when a man didn't show up for morning quarters. It was determined that he was a well-known homosexual, and he went over the side. Of course, we conducted an investigation. We do all the proper things. But the fact is, the man is gone. The same thing is true in combat. Cowards in combat, the response is immediate. It is final. Your own men take care of that. They do it with brutal efficiency, and they do it with utterly no fear of retribution.

Policy Implications of Lifting the Ban on Homosexuals in the Military: Hearings Before the House Armed Services Committee, 103rd Cong. 171 (1993). The Chair of the House Armed Services Committee, Marine Corps veteran Ronald V. Dellums of California, was so disturbed by the tone of the hearing that he stopped the questioning in order to establish on the record that the military was not advocating the murder of gay servicemembers. *Id.* at 172–73.

3. The Senate Armed Services Committee was especially enamored with the small sleeping berths on aircraft carriers and submarines, taking camera crews through living quarters as part of the congressional hearings on gay men and women in the military. The tours were designed to trigger squeamishness about lack of privacy with images of shipboard life in which "bunks smaller than phone booths were stacked three deep, sometimes by the dozens, in rows slightly more than two feet apart." *See* 1993 Cong. Q. Wkly. Rep. 1241. Is this concern for privacy valid? In *Vernonia School District 47J v. Acton*, 515 U.S. 646 (1995), Justice Scalia minimized the privacy interests of high school athletes, noting that they undressed in front of one another, took group showers, and used toilet stalls without doors. "School sports," he concluded, "are not for the bashful." *Id.* at 657. Do members of the military have a greater expectation of privacy than high school football players?

4. Those who oppose military service by gay people often raise issues related to showering and other personal activities. If military men and women do not shower or bunk together in shared quarters, they ask, why should straight servicemembers be asked to shower and bunk in the company of colleagues who take a sexual interest in persons of the same sex? Is this comparison valid? Can the military make the case that it is the one place in our society in which it is not feasible for gay and straight people of the same sex to manage shared personal intimacies in the same way they did as civilians? Consider the following observations about civilian norms of privacy in same- and opposite-sex contexts:

> Despite the military's efforts to maintain separate facilities for the sexes, however, the analogy fails to capture that heterosexuals showering with open gays is much less of a departure from the norms of civilian society than men showering with women. If men and women showered together in prisons, gyms, summer camps, university dorms, high school and college locker rooms, and professional changing areas in hospitals, courthouses, and fire and police stations, then perhaps it would seem reasonable for men and women to shower together in the military. Men and women do not, however, shower together in any of these civilian settings. Open gays and heterosexuals, by contrast, shower together in all of these settings. In addition, the analogy is premised on the flawed assumption that communal showers typify military practice. As noted above, by the end of the decade [the 1990s] most junior enlisted personnel will be housed in private bedrooms with a bathroom to share with one other individual.

Aaron Belkin & Melissa Sheridan Embser-Herbert, *A Modest Proposal: Privacy as a Flawed Rationale for the Exclusion of Gays and Lesbians from the U.S. Military*, at http://www.gaymilitary.ucsb.edu (the website of the University of California, Santa Barbara's Center for the Study of Sexual Minorities in the Military, the leading research institution for the study of "Don't Ask, Don't Tell"). Even in Iraq, fixed U.S. military installations house enlisted soldiers in small trailers that provide accommodations similar to the college-dormitory-style rooms featured in the barracks scenes in *Soldier's Girl. See* Kirk Semple, *G.I.'s Deployed in Iraq Desert with Lots of American Stuff*, N.Y. Times, 13 Aug. 2005, A1.

5. Does "Don't Ask, Don't Tell" accurately describe the policy codified by Congress and implemented by Department of Defense regulation?

10 U.S.C. § 654
Policy Concerning Homosexuality in the Armed Forces

(a) Findings. Congress makes the following findings:

(1) Section 8 of article I of the Constitution of the United States commits exclusively to the Congress the powers to raise and support armies, provide and maintain a Navy, and make rules for the government and regulation of the land and naval forces.

(2) There is no constitutional right to serve in the armed forces.

(3) Pursuant to the powers conferred by section 8 of article I of the Constitution of the United States, it lies within the discretion of the Congress to establish qualifications for and conditions of service in the armed forces.

(4) The primary purpose of the armed forces is to prepare for and to prevail in combat should the need arise.

(5) The conduct of military operations requires members of the armed forces to make extraordinary sacrifices, including the ultimate sacrifice, in order to provide for the common defense.

(6) Success in combat requires military units that are characterized by high morale, good order and discipline, and unit cohesion.

(7) One of the most critical elements in combat capability is unit cohesion, that is, the bonds of trust among individual service members that make the combat effectiveness of a military unit greater than the sum of the combat effectiveness of the individual unit members.

(8) Military life is fundamentally different from civilian life in that (A) the extraordinary responsibilities of the armed forces, the unique conditions of military service, and the critical role of unit cohesion, require that the military community, while subject to civilian control, exist as a specialized society; and (B) the military society is characterized by its own laws, rules, customs, and traditions, including numerous restrictions on personal behavior, that would not be acceptable in civilian society.

(9) The standards of conduct for members of the armed forces regulate a member's life for 24 hours each day beginning at the moment the member enters military status and not ending until that person is discharged or otherwise separated from the armed forces.

(10) Those standards of conduct, including the Uniform Code of Military Justice, apply to a member of the armed forces at all times that the member has a military status, whether the member is on base or off base, and whether the member is on duty or off duty.

(11) The pervasive application of the standards of conduct is necessary because members of the armed forces must be ready at all times for worldwide deployment to a combat environment.

(12) The worldwide deployment of United States military forces, the international responsibilities of the United States, and the potential for involvement of the armed forces in actual combat routinely make it necessary for members of the armed forces involuntarily to accept living conditions and working conditions that are often spartan, primitive, and characterized by forced intimacy with little or no privacy.

(13) The prohibition against homosexual conduct is a longstanding element of military law that continues to be necessary in the unique circumstances of military service.

(14) The armed forces must maintain personnel policies that exclude persons whose presence in the armed forces would create an unacceptable risk to the armed forces' high standards of morale, good order and discipline, and unit cohesion that are the essence of military capability.

(15) The presence in the armed forces of persons who demonstrate a propensity or intent to engage in homosexual acts would create an unacceptable risk to the high standards of morale, good order and discipline, and unit cohesion that are the essence of military capability.

(b) Policy. A member of the armed forces shall be separated from the armed forces under regulations prescribed by the Secretary of Defense if one or more of the following findings is made and approved in accordance with procedures set forth in such regulations:

(1) That the member has engaged in, attempted to engage in, or solicited another to engage in a homosexual act or acts unless there are further findings, made and approved in accordance with procedures set forth in such regulations, that the member has demonstrated that (A) such conduct is a departure from the member's usual and customary behavior; (B) such conduct, under all the circumstances, is unlikely to recur; (C) such conduct was not accomplished by use of force, coercion, or intimidation; (D) under the particular circumstances of the case, the member's continued presence in the armed forces is consistent with the interests of the armed forces in proper discipline, good order, and morale; and (E) the member does not have a propensity or intent to engage in homosexual acts.

(2) That the member has stated that he or she is a homosexual or bisexual, or words to that effect, unless there is a further finding, made and approved in accordance with procedures set forth in the regulations, that the member has demonstrated that he or she is not a person who engages in, attempts to engage in, has a propensity to engage in, or intends to engage in homosexual acts.

(3) That the member has married or attempted to marry a person known to be of the same biological sex. . . .

(e) Rule of Construction. Nothing in subsection (b) shall be construed to require that a member of the armed forces be processed for separation from the armed forces when a determination is made in accordance with regulations prescribed by the Secretary of Defense that (1) the member engaged in conduct or made statements for the purpose of avoiding or terminating military service; and (2) separation of the member would not be in the best interest of the armed forces.

(f) Definitions. In this section:

(1) The term "homosexual" means a person, regardless of sex, who engages in, attempts to engage in, has a propensity to engage in, or intends to engage in homosexual acts, and includes the terms "gay" and "lesbian."

(2) The term "bisexual" means a person who engages in, attempts to engage in, has a propensity to engage in, or intends to engage in homosexual and heterosexual acts.

(3) The term "homosexual act" means (A) any bodily contact, actively undertaken or passively permitted, between members of the same sex for the purpose of satisfying sexual desires; and (B) any bodily contact which a reasonable person would understand to demonstrate a propensity or intent to engage in an act described in subparagraph (A).

GUIDELINES FOR FACT-FINDING INQUIRIES INTO HOMOSEXUAL CONDUCT
Department of Defense Directive 1332.14 (1993)

E3.A4.2. DEFINITIONS

2.4. Homosexual Conduct. "Homosexual conduct" is a homosexual act, a statement by the member that demonstrates a propensity or intent to engage in homosexual acts, or a homosexual marriage or attempted marriage.

2.4.1. A "homosexual act" means any bodily contact, actively undertaken or passively permitted, between members of the same sex for the purpose of satisfying sexual desires and any bodily contact (for example, hand-holding or kissing, in most circumstances) that a reasonable person would understand to demonstrate a propensity or intent to engage in such an act.

2.4.2. A "statement that a member is a homosexual or bisexual, or words to that effect," means language or behavior that a reasonable person would believe was intended to convey the statement that a person engages in, attempts to engage in, or has a propensity or intent to engage in homosexual acts. This may include statements such as "I am a homosexual," "I am gay," "I am a lesbian," "I have a homosexual orientation," and the like.

2.4.4. "Propensity to engage in homosexual acts" means more than an abstract preference or desire to engage in homosexual acts; it indicates a likelihood that a person engages in or will engage in homosexual acts.

2.5. Sexual Orientation. An abstract sexual preference for persons of a particular sex, as distinct from a propensity or intent to engage in sexual acts.

E3.A4.3. BASES FOR CONDUCTING INQUIRIES

3.1. A commander will initiate an inquiry only if he or she has credible information that there is a basis for discharge. Credible information exists when the information, considering its source and the surrounding circumstances, supports a reasonable belief that there is a basis for discharge. It requires a determination based on articulable facts, not just a belief or suspicion.

3.2. A basis for discharge exists if (1) the member has engaged in a homosexual act; (2) the member has said that he or she is a homosexual or bisexual, or made some other statement that indicates a propensity or intent to engage in homosexual acts; or (3) the member has married or attempted to marry a person of the same sex.

3.3. Credible information does not exist, for example, when (1) the individual is suspected of engaging in homosexual conduct, but there is no credible information, as described, to support that suspicion; or (2) the only information is the opinions of others that a member is homosexual; or (3) the inquiry would be based on rumor, suspicion, or capricious claims concerning a member's sexual orientation; or (4) the only information known is an associational activity such as going to a gay bar, possessing or reading homosexual publications, associating with known homosexuals, or marching in a gay rights rally in civilian clothes. Such activity, in and of itself, does not provide evidence of homosexual conduct.

3.4. Credible information exists, for example, when (1) a reliable person states that he or she observed or heard a Service member engaging in homosexual acts, or saying that he or she is a homosexual or bisexual or is married to a member of the same sex; or (2) a reliable person states that he or she heard, observed, or discovered a member make a spoken or written statement that a reasonable person would believe was intended to convey the fact that he or she engages in, attempts to engage in, or has a propensity or intent to engage in homosexual acts; or (3) a reliable person states that he or she observed behavior that amounts to a non-verbal statement by a member that he or she is a homosexual or bisexual; i.e., behavior that a reasonable person would believe was intended to convey the statement that the member engages in, attempts to engage in, or has a propensity or intent to engage in homosexual acts.

E3.A4.4. PROCEDURES

4.2. Commanders shall exercise sound discretion regarding when credible information exists. They shall examine the information and decide whether an inquiry is warranted or whether no action should be taken.

4.3. Commanders or appointed inquiry officials shall not ask, and members shall not be required to reveal, whether a member is a heterosexual, a homosexual, or a bisexual. However, upon receipt of credible information of homosexual conduct (as described in section E3.A4.3., above) commanders or appointed inquiry officials may ask members if they engaged in such conduct.

4.5. A statement by a Service member that he or she is a homosexual or bisexual creates a rebuttable presumption that the Service member engages in, attempts to engage in, has a propensity to engage in, or intends to engage in homosexual acts.

4.6. The Service member bears the burden of proving, by a preponderance of the evidence, that he or she is not a person who engages in, attempts to engage in, has a propensity to engage in, or intends to engage in homosexual acts.

E3.A4.5. LEGAL EFFECT

The procedures in this enclosure create no substantive or procedural rights.

NOTES & QUESTIONS

1. The shorthand reference of "Don't Ask, Don't Tell" is a starkly oversimplified description of a policy that, in application, is complex and sometimes disingenuous. The statutory codification of the policy, which sets out the conduct or statements that constitute a basis for discharge, is very broad. A servicemember can be discharged if, at any time or in any place, even when off-duty or on leave, she engages in a homosexual act or states that she is a homosexual. The statutory definition of "homosexual act" is more comprehensive than the usual meaning of the phrase. It includes not only bodily contact for the purpose of satisfying sexual desires but also bodily contact *which a reasonable person would understand to demonstrate a propensity or intent to engage* in the former — the standard example being hand-holding. Prohibited statements ("I'm gay," or any words to that effect) include those made to other servicemembers, civilians, relatives, or medical and legal professionals. In short, it is impossible in practical terms to actually *be* gay and not live in violation of the policy.

2. The "Don't Ask, Don't Tell" compromise, if there was one, can be found in implementing regulations of the Department of Defense and their limitations on the ability of the military to investigate servicemembers for the purpose of discovering a violation of § 654. It should be obvious that if the investigative arm of the military is brought to bear on a servicemember's life, particularly if she is partnered, the military will undoubtedly uncover evidence of a statutory basis for discharge. Under DOD Directive 1332.14 excerpted above, however, the military can begin an investigation only if a commander first has a reasonable belief, based on credible information, that there is a basis for discharge under the statute. Credible information must be based on articulable facts and not mere belief, opinion, suspicion, or rumor.

3. Imagine how difficult it is for young servicemembers to understand the disingenuous dance around reality that comprises "Don't Ask, Don't Tell" and its implementing regulations. If you were the judge advocate responsible for advising a commander whether she had a legal basis for initiating an investigation of Barry Winchell in *Soldier's Girl*, what would you advise? Could the commander form a reasonable belief, based on credible information, that a basis for discharge exists? Do you need to make a factual determination whether Winchell knows or understands the sex of his apparent girlfriend, Calpernia Addams? To add to the factual complexity, *Soldier's Girl* strongly suggests that Winchell's primary tormentor was conflicted about his own sexual orientation and may have been motivated by jealousy as much as irrational hatred.

4. *Cook v. Rumsfeld,* 429 F. Supp. 2d 385 (D. Mass. 2006) is the most recent federal court decision upholding "Don't Ask, Don't Tell." Plaintiffs, twelve recently discharged gay servicemembers, raised claims grounded in due process, equal protection, and the First Amendment. In briefs filed in opposition to the government's motion to dismiss, lawyers for the plaintiffs (Wilmer Cutler Pickering Hale and Dorr LLP, providing pro bono services, and the Servicemembers Legal Defense Network, the premier organization defending servicemembers targeted under the policy) pressed for the first serious examination of the doctrine of judicial deference to the military in any "Don't Ask, Don't Tell" challenge. One of the key issues in the case was whether the court was obligated to defer to congressional fact-finding during the summer 1993 "Don't Ask, Don't Tell" debate.

5. Review the findings of Congress codified in 10 U.S.C. § 654(a) in support of banning gay people from military service. Are these statements proper congressional findings? Does Congress have the power to make findings on what the Constitution means, as when it states in § 654(a)(1) that the Constitution "commits exclusively to the Congress" (and not to courts) the power to govern and regulate the armed forces? *Cf. City of Boerne v. Flores,* 521 U.S. 507 (1997) (holding that the Religious Freedom Restoration Act exceeded Congress's constitutional authority; Congress could not "define its own powers by altering the Fourteenth Amendment's meaning"). To what extent should the court defer to factual findings that may not square with available evidence? Where do you draw the line between a congressional finding and a congressional opinion? For example, Congress found in § 654(a)(15) that a person's propensity or intent to engage in homosexual acts posed an unacceptable risk to military unit cohesion, yet the military often reduces enforcement of the policy in time of war, presumably when unit cohesion would be most important. The *Cook v. Rumsfeld* complaint argued as follows:

> Section 654(a) purports to list "findings" made by Congress. Many of those "findings" are not findings of fact but assertions about constitutional law. Those assertions include declarations of what powers and discretion the Constitution grants the Congress, and assertions about what "rights" the Constitution does not protect. The remaining "findings" are merely opinions unsupported by the evidence before Congress. As a result, the "findings" are not entitled to any special deference by this Court.

Complaint, *Cook v. Rumsfeld,* No. CV 04-12546 GAO, ¶ 43, at 10 (D. Mass. filed Dec. 6, 2004). The court recognized the unusual nature of these congressional "findings," characterizing them as "a mix of propositions of constitutional law, observations about the requirements of military service, and policy judgments." *Cook,* 429 F. Supp. 2d at 389. Nevertheless, these findings were held sufficient under rational-basis review (and a healthy dose of judicial deference) to uphold "Don't Ask, Don't Tell."

6. One of the drawbacks of facial (as opposed to as-applied) constitutional challenges in a rational-basis context is that individual stories — the rich building blocks of film and other varieties of popular culture — will largely be erased in favor of broad assertions and assumptions. The following excerpt from the pleadings in *Cook v. Rumsfeld* describes the lives and experiences of gay servicemembers and the reality of how two gay servicemembers come to the military's attention in a supposedly "Don't Ask, Don't Tell" world.

COOK v. RUMSFELD (D. MASS. 2004)
Complaint

1. Plaintiffs are twelve citizens who served our country honorably in the United States Army, Navy, Air Force, or Coast Guard. All served at some point during the global war on terrorism; many served much longer, devoting their adult lives to the service of our nation. Several were decorated, awarded medals or ribbons, or received commendations for outstanding service to our country. Each plaintiff also is either gay or lesbian. Each was forced to leave the military prematurely, and despite valuable contributions, solely because of his or her sexual orientation. Those discharges violated plaintiffs' constitutional rights.

Monica Hill

100. Plaintiff Monica Hill joined the United States Air Force on December 21, 1994, having won an Air Force scholarship to medical school.

101. For her residency, Dr. Hill worked at a civilian hospital in Columbus, Ohio. While in Columbus, she lived in the community with her partner of fourteen years, Terri Cason, who was a nurse at the hospital.

102. In the summer of 2001, Dr. Hill was scheduled to report to Andrews Air Force Base for her permanent active duty assignment. Dr. Hill arranged for an apartment in Northern Virginia, not far from the base, and arranged to have her possessions moved on July 18, 2001.

103. Cason's health deteriorated dramatically in July 2001. In two weeks, Cason went from working at the hospital to being unable even to do household chores. Cason's doctors first thought she had an infectious disease, and treated her with antibiotics. On July 14, 2001, Cason's doctors changed their diagnosis. Cason had lung cancer, with additional metastatic brain lesions. This diagnosis meant that Cason had between two months and two years to live.

104. Desperate to remain with her dying partner, and feeling it was irresponsible to move her partner from her treating physician, Dr. Hill decided to seek permission to delay reporting to Andrews Air Force Base. In explaining her situation, she revealed the nature of her relationship with Cason. Dr. Hill requested a two-year deferment on July 22, 2001. In response, the Air Force canceled Dr. Hill's orders to report to Andrews Air Force Base.

105. Cason died in September 2001.

106. Several months after her orders were cancelled, the Air Force informed Dr. Hill that discharge proceedings were pending against her based on her statement in her request for deferment that she is a lesbian. The Air Force began an investigation into Dr. Hill's sexual orientation. During the investigation, the investigating officer suggested in hostile and accusatory tones that Dr. Hill had invented the story of Cason's illness, and that Dr. Hill had revealed her sexual orientation solely to escape going on active duty. Dr. Hill was required to provide Cason's death certificate as proof that she had not invented the story. Additionally, the investigating officer repeatedly asked Dr. Hill about her sexual orientation and for details of her sexual history.

107. The investigation concluded that Dr. Hill had made a "homosexual admission" requiring discharge under "Don't Ask, Don't Tell," and that she had made the statement for the purpose of being separated from the military. The Air Force began discharge proceedings. Dr. Hill was honorably discharged on October 2, 2002, because of 10 U.S.C. § 654 and the applicable regulations issued under it.

108. Following her discharge, the Air Force began recoupment proceedings against Dr. Hill, seeking to recover the cost of her medical education.

109. At the time of her discharge, Dr. Hill had served in the Air Force Reserve for nearly eight years. She had attained the rank of Captain (0-3) and was a physician specializing in internal medicine.

Justin Peacock

124. Justin Peacock entered the Coast Guard on September 17, 2001. Following basic training, Peacock reported for duty to Cape Disappointment, Washington. Although Peacock kept the fact that he is gay secret, rumors circulated about his sexual orientation. Peacock endured repeated jokes and taunts about his perceived sexual orientation.

125. The jokes and teasing became progressively worse in the spring of 2002. During one night of watch duty, several other Cost Guardsmen repeatedly teased Peacock about what they perceived to be his sexual orientation. In response, Peacock asked, "So what if I am gay?," or words to that effect. Many of the Coast Guardsmen present when this incident occurred later testified that they did not believe Peacock was making a statement about his sexual orientation. Rather, they interpreted his remark as an attempt to sarcastically rebuff the harassment he was enduring.

126. Later that spring, Peacock's civilian roommate, a man, visited the local military exchange with Peacock. The two were not romantically involved. However, another Coast Guardsman falsely alleged that Peacock was seen holding hands at the exchange with his roommate for approximately two seconds.

127. During this time, a fellow seaman began harassing Peacock repeatedly, calling him "a stupid faggot" among other things. Peacock reported this harassment to his Executive Officer. Peacock's executive officer admonished

the seaman who made that remark, but also inappropriately began an investigation into whether Peacock is gay. The Executive Officer asked the seaman who had harassed Peacock if he had any evidence that Peacock is gay. Peacock's Executive Officer then expanded his investigation, asking other seamen if they had evidence that Peacock is gay.

128. On August 26, 2002, someone reported the alleged handholding incident at the military exchange to Peacock's command. Based on this report, an officially sanctioned investigation of Peacock began on September 4, 2002. The Coast Guard then moved to discharge Peacock for homosexual acts, including the allegation he held hands with another man. Peacock presented evidence to the board that he had been investigated in violation of Defense Department, Department of Homeland Security, and United States Coast Guard regulations that, among other things, forbade investigations based on rumors.

129. Despite testimony contradicting much of the alleged conduct, Peacock lost his case. Peacock was honorably discharged from the Cost Guard on July 31, 2003, because of 10 U.S.C. § 654 and the applicable regulations issued under it.

130. At the time of his discharge, Peacock had served in the Coast Guard for almost two years. He was promoted from E-3 to E-4 during the investigation into his alleged homosexual conduct, and earned a Boatswain's Mate specialty and several awards and commendations, including the Coast Guard Unit Commendation Medal, Coast Guard Meritorious Unit Commendation, and the National Defense Service Ribbon.

NOTES & QUESTIONS

1. *Lawrence v. Texas*, 539 U.S. 558 (2003), has changed the landscape of challenges to the constitutionality of "Don't Ask, Don't Tell." *Lawrence* overruled *Bowers v. Hardwick*, 478 U.S. 186 (1986), and held that substantive guarantees of liberty found in the Due Process Clause of the Fourteenth Amendment include the right to engage in consensual sexual intimacy without interference from the government. *Hardwick* had been the constitutional linchpin underlying "Don't Ask, Don't Tell," offering the easy justification that if same-sex intimacy could be criminalized, then it certainly could be considered disqualifying for military service. Prior to *Lawrence*, however, constitutional challenges to the policy struggled with how to present the lives of servicemembers without conceding the commission of disqualifying conduct, a litigation dead end under *Hardwick*.

2. Earlier challenges to the military's ban on gay servicemembers attempted to shield themselves from *Hardwick* by drawing a distinction between status and conduct. These "pure statement" cases argued that mere acknowledgment of sexual orientation, or the "status" of being gay, did not necessarily suggest any propensity or intent to engage in the same-sex intimacy that seemed clearly unprotected under *Hardwick*. The strained attempt to distinguish sexual orientation and sexual conduct led to some absurd stances in litigation, including testimony by expert witnesses on behalf of Col. Margarethe Cammermeyer, a decorated Vietnam veteran, that "a person's public identification of his or her sexual orientation does not necessarily imply sexual conduct, past or present, or a future desire for sexual behavior" and "there is almost no relationship between an individual's orientation and his or her sexual conduct." *Cammermeyer v. Aspin*, 850 F. Supp. 910 (D. Wash. 1994), *dismissed as moot*, 97 F.3d 1235 (1996) (holding, surprisingly, the exclusionary policy unconstitutional on the basis of the status/conduct distinction).

3. The military sought to discharge Col. Cammermeyer for saying "yes" when asked (before "Don't Ask") in a security clearance interview if she was a lesbian, which made it possible to frame her challenge as a "pure statement" claim. However, because films have no choice but to dramatize the lives of featured characters, the status/conduct distinction her lawyers so carefully maintained for purposes of litigation evaporated in the 1995 made-for-television movie *Serving in Silence: The Margarethe Cammermeyer Story*. Glenn Close's Emmy-award-winning performance as Col. Cammermeyer juxtaposed her legal challenge to the U.S. Army with her developing intimate relationship with another woman, a relationship that, of course, violated the exclusionary policy. Is it ethical for lawyers to present the lives of their clients in ways they know are inaccurate or misleading?

4. Contemporary challenges to "Don't Ask, Don't Tell" have abandoned the status/conduct distinction and now present the intimate lives of gay servicemembers in an open and realistic manner. The stories behind the discharges of Monica Hill and Justin Peacock serve to show the inaccuracy of conventional wisdom about "Don't Ask, Don't Tell." Contrary to common belief, the policy does not permit military service by gay people as long as they remain discreet. It permits military service by gay people only as long as they are able to keep their intimate lives a secret, even under circumstances of personal tragedy or harassment by others. Did the military comply with "Don't Ask, Don't Tell" and its implementing regulations in discharging Justin Peacock?

5. The stories told about the lives of gay servicemembers today in litigation are infinitely richer than the stories told a generation ago. Lucian K. Truscott IV's 1978 novel *Dress Gray*, set at the U.S. Military Academy at West Point, is still the most well known work of fiction involving gay people in military service. The gay cadet in *Dress Gray*, unfortunately, begins the story as the victim of a murder on page one. Truscott is a third-generation graduate of West Point, the son of a retired colonel who testified before Congress in favor of lifting the ban on gay servicemembers, and the grandson of a four-star general in World War II.

F. MILITARY CONSCRIPTION AND THE OBLIGATION FOR NATIONAL SERVICE

Making the Corps (1997) was the path-breaking account of Marine Corps basic training written by Thomas E. Ricks, a senior defense reporter for the Wall Street Journal and now the Washington Post. His book was noteworthy for its description of the widening political and ideological distance between the military and civilian society in the all-volunteer era, and it ushered in a new area of research in political science and sociology examining the "civil-military gap" and its consequences for effective civilian control of the military under the Constitution. In a fascinating blend of expertise in journalism, popular culture, and military culture, Ricks also penned *A Soldier's Duty* (2001), a fictional thriller based on the breakdown of civilian control in a military that had grown alienated from civilian society. When evaluating the costs and benefits of the transition from a draft military to an all-volunteer force, we have rarely considered the constitutional costs of a military that is less politically and ideologically representative of American society.

1. The Constitutional Consequences of an All-Volunteer Force

WHY PROGRESSIVES LOST THE WAR WHEN THEY LOST THE DRAFT
Diane H. Mazur
32 Hofstra Law Review 553 (2003)

It is no coincidence that the Court's encouragement of a constitutional distance between military and civilian spheres has overlapped perfectly, almost to the year, with the establishment of the all-volunteer force. A constitutional distance is more difficult to enforce in a draft-based military that continually rotates a representative cross-section of civilians through military service. In a volunteer or recruited military, by contrast, forces of self-selection operate to shape the composition and nature of the armed services. During the last five years, a significant body of research in sociology and political science has examined what has been termed the "civil-military gap," or the distance of knowledge, experience, attitude, and culture between military and civilian societies in the United States. The issue has become one of central concern in the academic study of the military, but it has its most important application in measuring the health of the constitutional and legal relationship between the military institution and the society it protects. Study of the civil-military gap was prompted by the intuitive, anecdotal perception of academics that the military was changing in a very fundamental way, and in a way that threatened traditional notions of military professionalism and civilian control. This intuitive perception was significant because it was shared by people with close connections to the military as veterans, academic researchers, or specialized reporters — people not normally predisposed to express criticism or concern about the direction taken by the military. They were people, and I include myself with them, who spoke from loyalty to the military institution and an uneasiness about the state of civil-military relations under the Constitution . . . .

The civil-military gap as it exists today, after a generation of an all-volunteer force, is a gap based in ideological and political partisanship, at odds with the constitutional assumption of a politically neutral military. By definition, a draft that imposes shared obligation for military service ensures a military that is more representative of the society from which it draws its members, and the kind of representativeness that contemporary opponents of the draft fear most is an ideological representativeness. Today we have a military that is built instead on a foundation of ideological self-selection, which is conveniently consistent with, and is abetted by, the Court's view of the military as an institution necessarily separate from the society around it. How does this recruited military sell itself? It sells itself as a place where constitutional separatism is reinforced; it sells itself as a place where constitutional resistance is a necessity for military effectiveness. Unfortunately, an offer of constitutional immunity can be a dangerous intoxicant, particularly in a time of popular and partisan disagreement over constitutional interpretation and evolution.

The civil-military gap has consequences for civilian control of the military in the operational sense of whether the military will follow the direction of its civilian leaders in using military force. Most political science research in civil-military relations has focused on relative decisionmaking authority between civilian and military leaders in specific contexts. However, this is not the only consequence of the civil-military gap. Thirty years after the advent of the all-volunteer force, a confluence of trends threatens civil-military relations more comprehensively. The gap of knowledge and experience between military and civilian societies is increasing as the military draws its members from an increasingly narrow and self-selected slice of America. The gap of constitutional values between military and civilian societies is increasing as the Court continues to reinforce the notion that constitutional values are inconsistent with military effectiveness. No one is questioning the Court's conclusions about constitutional values and military effectiveness because civilian society has lost its base of experience with which to do so. As a result, the military is increasingly selling itself, consciously or unconsciously, as a haven of constitutional immunity, drawing disproportionate numbers of recruits who enlist for ideological reasons. And the circle continues.

We live in a time in which the military is portrayed as an institution that not only protects the values of this country, but is often asked to define them. It was no coincidence, for example, that *Grutter v. Bollinger*, 539 U.S. 306 (2003), grounded its recent approval of affirmative action in higher education in large part on the existence of similar admissions policies at West Point, Annapolis, and the Air Force Academy. Military judgment was applied, without objection by the dissenters, to corroborate a judicial finding of compelling purpose under the Equal Protection Clause, an absolutely extraordinary use of military policy in deciding a constitutional question. Justice O'Connor's unspoken assumption seemed to be that if the military believed it was appropriate and beneficial to admit students to its academies on a race-conscious basis, then by definition the practice could not be constitutionally invidious. Perhaps the step taken in *Grutter* was not surprising. Military perspectives on law, morality, order, and discipline are now frequently viewed, by all three branches of government, as models to which the rest of us should aspire, and the development raises no particular notice or concern. Research suggests, however, that the most constitutionally corrosive aspect of the civil-military gap may be the temptation it creates for government to use the military not for its professional expertise in the skills of war, but for politically partisan purposes within the domestic sphere. The most effective weapon against misuse of a large standing army for politically partisan purposes always has been, perhaps counter-intuitively, a requirement for universal military service, or at least universal eligibility for military service. This is why progressives lost the war when they lost the draft . . . .

NOTES & QUESTIONS

1. The film *Starship Troopers* was adapted from one of the classic novels of science fiction, Robert A. Heinlein's *Starship Troopers*, which was originally published in 1959 and is still in print. It is remarkable how relevant the book's themes of civil-military relations and civilian control of the military continue to be almost a half-century later. In both versions, the principal military offensive takes place in response to a devastating surprise attack by extra-terrestrials on Buenos Aires, and the scenes of destruction in the 1997 film are eerily reminiscent of the September 11, 2001 attack in New York.

2. In 1976, shortly after the transition to an all-volunteer force, the U.S. Supreme Court held that the military had a constitutional responsibility to avoid "both the reality and the appearance of acting as a handmaiden for partisan political causes," a responsibility that was "wholly consistent with the American constitutional tradition of a politically neutral military establishment under civilian control." *Greer v. Spock*, 424 U.S. 828, 839 (1976). Research by a Duke University political scientist, however, found that military officers in the all-volunteer era have largely abandoned this ethic of political neutrality. They were much more likely than draft-era officers to indicate a partisan allegiance to the Republican Party and identify their ideology as conservative. Ole R. Holsti, *A Widening Gap Between the U.S. Military and Civilian Society? Some Evidence, 1976-1996*, 23 International Security 5 (1998). Why did *Spock* assume that a politically neutral military was necessary for effective civilian control? Was political neutrality a function of the draft's leavening effect, which tended to make the military more politically and ideologically representative of civilian society? Does it matter whether the military is politically and ideologically representative? Is representativeness more important in an era in which courts have withdrawn from an active role in monitoring military judgment?

3. Throughout American history, an obligation for military service has been linked to expansion of the right to vote, most recently illustrated in the ratification of the Twenty-Sixth Amendment in 1971. If young men were old enough to fight in Vietnam, proponents argued, then they were old enough to vote. *See* Pamela S. Karlan, *Ballots and Bullets: The Exceptional History of the Right to Vote*, 71 University of Cincinnati Law Review 1345 (2003). Sometimes military service is associated with preferential voting rights. In the 2000 presidential election, Florida officials disregarded rules governing overseas absentee ballots in order to count what should have been invalid ballots presumably sent by servicemembers. *See* Diane H. Mazur, *The Bullying of America: A Cautionary Tale About Military Voting and Civil-Military Relations*, 4 Election Law Journal 105 (2005).

4. *Starship Troopers* turns that history on its head by presenting a society in which *only* veterans of military service are entitled to the voting franchise. In this society, there is no military draft, and no one is forced to serve in the military. However, the choice not to serve means never having the voting voice of a full citizen. Advertisements encouraging young people to join the military trumpet the promise that "Service Guarantees Citizenship." Is the "no military service, no vote" rule of *Starship Troopers* just a difference in degree from the contemporary assumption that citizens who have served in the military have the strongest moral authority to criticize government defense policy? Is it just a difference in degree from the 2004 presidential campaign, in which military service became a measure of each candidate's prowess in foreign policy? In *The Court-Martial of Billy Mitchell*, Col. Mitchell viewed his criticism of the Army as entirely apolitical. Can you imagine similar criticism of the Defense Department today being viewed as apolitical?

5. *Starship Troopers* provides tongue-in-cheek commentary on the militarization of society that finds an analog in contemporary civil-military relations. The film describes its militaristic society as "a world that works," one in which servicemembers and military veterans are the most effective antidote for civilian chaos and failure. It defines civic virtue within the citizenry as military virtue, and measures political authority by the capacity to apply military force. Were these same themes present in the aftermath of Hurricane Katrina in 2005 when both state and federal authorities were often eager to cede local civic control in New Orleans to the military? General Charles L. Dunlap, a military lawyer serving in the Air Force's Judge Advocate General Corps, has written of the danger inherent in a society that views the military as the answer to domestic problems:

> The transfer of public confidence from the elected leaders to the military challenges civilian control of the armed forces. Specifically, Finer [Samuel E. Finer, author of a classic in civil-military relations, *The Man on Horseback*] argued that, as confidence in politicians and the civil process weakens, an intervening military is deemed a "deliverer." That appears to be the case today. James Fallows captured the sentiment of many Americans when, after contrasting the military's efficiency with the failures of civilian government, he declared, "I am beginning to think that the only way the national government can do anything worthwhile is to invent a security threat and turn the job over to the military."

Charles J. Dunlap, Jr., *Welcome to the Junta: The Erosion of Civilian Control of the U.S. Military*, 29 Wake Forest Law Review 341, 357 (1994).

6. Are proposals to reinstitute some form of mandatory national service in this country — civilian, military, or a combination of the two — realistic? Why or why not? It is much more difficult to argue today that a military draft would disproportionately impact the poor or uneducated, because current draft law, if activated, no longer provides the broad exemptions for college attendance in effect during the Vietnam War. *See* 50 U.S.C. app. § 456(i)(2) (offering postponement of military induction only until the end of a college semester already in progress or, for seniors, the end of the academic year).

2. Women in the Military

ROSTKER v. GOLDBERG
453 U.S. 57 (1981)

The question presented is whether the Military Selective Service Act violates the Fifth Amendment to the United States Constitution in authorizing the President to require the registration of males and not females.

In light of the floor debate and the Report of the Senate Armed Services Committee hereinafter discussed, it is apparent that Congress was fully aware not merely of the many facts and figures presented to it by witnesses who testified before its Committees, but of the current thinking as to the place of women in the Armed Services. In such a case, we cannot ignore Congress' broad authority conferred by the Constitution to raise and support armies when we are urged to declare unconstitutional its studied choice of one alternative in preference to another for furthering that goal.

This case is quite different from several of the gender-based discrimination cases we have considered in that, despite appellees' assertions, Congress did not act "unthinkingly" or "reflexively and not for any considered reason." The question of registering women for the draft not only received considerable national attention and was the subject of wide-ranging public debate, but also was extensively considered by Congress in hearings, floor debate, and in committee. The foregoing clearly establishes that the decision to exempt women from registration was not the "accidental by-product of a traditional way of thinking about females." The issue was considered at great length, and Congress clearly expressed its purpose and intent.

Women as a group, however, unlike men as a group, are not eligible for combat. The restrictions on the participation of women in combat in the Navy and Air Force are statutory. Under 10 U.S.C. § 6015 [repealed in 1993], "women may not be assigned to duty on vessels or in aircraft that are engaged in combat missions," and under 10 U.S.C. § 8549 [repealed in 1991] female members of the Air Force "may not be assigned to duty in aircraft engaged in combat missions." The Army and Marine Corps preclude the use of women in combat as a matter of established policy. Congress specifically recognized and endorsed the exclusion of women from combat in exempting women from registration. In the words of the Senate Report: "The principle that women should not intentionally and routinely engage in combat is fundamental, and enjoys wide support among our people."

The existence of the combat restrictions clearly indicates the basis for Congress' decision to exempt women from registration. The purpose of registration was to prepare for a draft of combat troops. Since women are excluded from combat, Congress concluded that they would not be needed in the event of a draft, and therefore decided not to register them.

Justice White, with whom Justice Brennan joins, dissenting:

On the contrary, the record as I understand it, supports the District Court's finding that the services would have to conscript at least 80,000 persons to fill positions for which combat-ready men would not be required. The consistent position of the Defense Department representatives was that their best estimate of the number of women draftees who could be used productively by the services in the event of a major mobilization would be *approximately 80,000 over the first six months.* (Emphasis added.) This number took into account the estimated number of women volunteers.

Justice Marshall, with whom Justice Brennan joins, dissenting:

The Court today places its imprimatur on one of the most potent remaining public expressions of "ancient canards about the proper role of women." It upholds a statute that requires males but not females to register for the draft, and which thereby categorically excludes women from a fundamental civic obligation. Because I believe the Court's decision is inconsistent with the Constitution's guarantee of equal protection of the laws, I dissent.

NOTES & QUESTIONS

1. If Congress were to reinstitute the draft, must *Rostker v. Goldberg* be disregarded or overruled? Consider the following commentary on combat duties performed by women in the Iraq War:

Many commanders in Iraq say they see a widening gap between war-zone realities and policies designed to limit women's exposure to combat. Although the Army is barred from assigning women to ground combat battalions, in Iraq it skirts the ban with a twist in terminology. Instead of being "assigned," women are "attached in direct support of" the battalions, according to Army officers familiar with the policy. As a result, the Army avoids having to seek Pentagon and congressional approval to change the policy, officers said. "What has changed? Nothing," said Lt. Col. Bob Roth of the 3rd Infantry Division. "You just want someone to feel better by saying we don't allow women in dangerous situations."

Ann Scott Tyson, *For Female GIs, Combat Is a Fact: Many Duties in Iraq Put Women at Risk Despite Restrictive Policy*, Washington Post, 13 May 2005, A1.

2. What factors should a court consider in deciding whether precedent no longer controls or must be overruled? In *Planned Parenthood of Southeastern Pennsylvania v. Casey*, 505 U.S. 833, 854–55 (1992), Justice O'Connor's plurality opinion considered whether an earlier rule had become unworkable in practice and whether underlying facts had changed so significantly as to remove the rule's original justification. How would application of those factors affect a reconsideration of *Rostker v. Goldberg*? Could the government likely still meet a standard of intermediate scrutiny and demonstrate that exclusion of women from the draft was substantially related to military effectiveness, concededly an important government purpose? Should a court be able to look behind any asserted justifications and question whether women were being excluded from a fundamental civic obligation primarily for the purpose of making a statement that involuntary military service is not appropriate for women? *See United States v. Virginia,* 518 U.S. 515, 541 (1996) (holding that government "may not exclude qualified individuals based on fixed notions concerning the roles and abilities of males and females").

3. The following excerpts suggest our ability to ensure equal protection of the law may be affected by our decision whether to raise a military by an involuntary draft or by the recruitment of volunteers.

WHY PROGRESSIVES LOST THE WAR WHEN THEY LOST THE DRAFT
Diane H. Mazur
32 Hofstra Law Review 553 (2003)

Perhaps the greatest misunderstanding that civilians have with respect to women in military service is the false assumption that gender controversy is inherent in the nature of the military institution. The reality is that the transition to the all-volunteer force, not military culture in and of itself, has had the greater effect on the constitutional equality of women serving in the military. At the same time that the Court has strengthened its commitment to equality for civilian women, it has developed a doctrine of deference to military judgment that can only erode those constitutional protections for military women. Similarly, at the same time civilian society has increasingly accepted values of constitutional equality as unremarkable, the all-volunteer military has increasingly drawn self-selected constituencies on the basis of resistance to values of constitutional equality. The military has become a venue where tradition — real and imaginary — trumps the Constitution and where the clock can be turned back with the approval of the government and many of its citizens. It is difficult to overestimate the detrimental effect that ideological self-selection grounded in both social conservatism and Republican political partisanship has had on the constitutional relationship of women to military service. To be blunt, the military increasingly sells itself as the home for the disaffected white male and, unfortunately, as a home for women who are comfortable with the disaffected white male. We are enlisting a greater number of young men, and young women as well, who are accustomed to relationships of disparate power and respect between men and women, and we are seeing the results of that dysfunctional evolution in repeated scandals of sexual harassment and assault. The military has become a quiet battleground for notions of equality and citizenship, obscured by our uncritical support for and lack of meaningful interaction with the institution . . . .

REHNQUIST'S VIETNAM: CONSTITUTIONAL SEPARATISM AND THE STEALTH ADVANCE OF MARTIAL LAW
Diane H. Mazur
77 Indiana Law Journal 701 (2002)

Two examples of the less-direct ways in which Rehnquist's influence has found expression in gendered aspects of military culture involve haircuts and uniforms. Styles of military haircuts for men have evolved as a means of expressing "separateness" from civilian society. A generation ago, most military men would have cut their hair in a way that minimized any distinction from civilian peers. Today, the typical male servicemember shaves or "buzzes" his head in an extreme style that, if not perceived immediately as military, could be mistaken only for a haircut sported by some of the most culturally extreme members of civilian society. That transformation has had consequences for women as well. When both military men and military women wore their hair in a more androgynous style, the difference in their appearance was fairly small. Today, the cultural expectation is that military women will wear their hair long but "put up" while on duty, a style that during the Vietnam generation would have been considered oddly formal. These changes in the outward appearance of servicemembers might seem superficial and insignificant, but they are not. What is critically important about this otherwise frivolous discourse is the reality that polarization in haircuts between men and women can be used as a way of enforcing "difference" and as a way of perpetuating the assumption that women cannot fit the standard template of a servicemember.

Uniforms have become more ostentatiously masculine or "combat-identified" as well. A generation ago, for example, Air Force personnel who performed field duties, such as aircraft maintenance, wore simple, green utility uniforms called fatigues. Today, however, dignified fatigues have been replaced by a camouflage-printed "Battle Dress Uniform" designed to look more like the uniforms worn by personnel in the Army and the Marine Corps. The only possible reason for substituting a new utility uniform would be its "combat-identified" flair, because there would be little need for camouflaged stealth on a gray concrete flightline. Evolution in military uniforms, however, just like evolution in military hairstyles, can be a symptom of a larger trend. In an effort to accentuate the "difference" from civilian society that the Court has endorsed, we see stereotypical attempts to make the military seem more "military." In an effort to accentuate the "difference" between male and female servicemembers that the Court has endorsed, we see an evolution in cultural style that polarizes the gendered appearance of servicemembers. Those same gendered differences are then employed to justify why the presence of women is so destabilizing to the status quo, although the status quo itself is an artificial construction . . . .

NOTES & QUESTIONS

1. Opposition to expansion of roles for women in military service often relies on framing the debate as one of "political correctness" or of using the military for "social experimentation." To the extent that service of women in non-traditional military career fields was an experiment, the experiment took place thirty years ago when the military began assigning women to a wide range of non-clerical and non-medical duties. Nonetheless, the use of language as a framing device remains powerful today:

> The role of women in the Services changed and expanded to meet the needs of the Services. For the all-volunteer force to succeed, the Services needed high-quality personnel, and women were a relatively

untapped source of intellect, discipline, dedication, and leadership. The expansion of women's roles was a carefully crafted strategy based on operational requirements, not on equal opportunity or political correctness. Unfortunately, many cadets and midshipmen today often misunderstand this point. This lack of understanding can contribute to a culture that diminishes the regard given to women and leads to questioning their presence at the Academies. In turn, this diminished regard leaves open the possibility of harassment.

Report of the Defense Task Force on Sexual Harassment and Violence at the Military Service Academies (2005).

2. *Starship Troopers* opens a window into a society in which both men and women are obligated as citizens to perform military service. Probably not without coincidence, *Starship Troopers* also portrays a society in which military service by women is entirely unremarkable and in which sexual harassment and discrimination on the basis of sex is almost non-existent. The film offers all the powerful imagery that often animates military policy on women and gay people — women serving in infantry duty, men and women showering together, and men and women bunking together in the barracks — and none of the characters takes particular notice.

3. *Starship Troopers* also disaggregates the traditional trinity of military warfare, sporting contests, and men. General George C. Marshall is said to have ordered: "I want an officer for a secret and dangerous mission. I want a West Point football player." The high school that produces the latest crop of military enlistees in *Starship Troopers* fields a football team with a female quarterback who is quick, wily, and able to throw a football on a clothesline to her receivers. The style of football is more "Arena League" football than traditional, with an emphasis on intelligence and quickness rather than brute strength, perhaps an analogy to the changing nature of military warfare.

INDEX

[References are to pages.]

C

CHILD CUSTODY

CLIENTS

CONSTITUTIONAL LAW

CONSTITUTIONAL LAW—Cont.

CORPORATIONS (See BUSINESS LAW)

CRIMINAL LAW

[References are to pages.]

[References are to pages.]

[References are to pages.]

[References are to pages.]

[References are to pages.]

W